W9-BXC-821

SAXON® MATH
Intermediate 4

Student Edition

Stephen Hake

SAXON™

A Harcourt Achieve Imprint

www.SaxonPublishers.com

1-800-284-7019

ACKNOWLEDGEMENTS

This book was made possible by the significant contributions of many individuals and the dedicated efforts of talented teams at Harcourt Achieve.

Special thanks to Chris Braun for conscientious work on Power Up exercises, Problem Solving scripts, and student assessments. The long hours and technical assistance of John and James Hake were invaluable in meeting publishing deadlines. As always, the patience and support of Mary is most appreciated.

– Stephen Hake

Staff Credits

Editorial: Joel Riemer, Hirva Raj, Paula Zamarra, Smith Richardson, Gayle Lowery, Robin Adams, David Baceski, Brooke Butner, Cecilia Colome, Pamela Cox, James Daniels, Leslie Bateman, Michael Ota, Stephanie Rieper, Ann Sissac, Chad Barrett, Heather Jernt

Design: Alison Klassen, Joan Cunningham, Alan Klemp, Julie Hubbard, Lorelei Supapo, Andy Hendrix, Rhonda Holcomb

Production: Mychael Ferris-Pacheco, Jennifer Cohorn, Greg Gaspard, Donna Brawley, John-Paxton Gremillion

Manufacturing: Cathy Voltaggio, Kathleen Stewart

Marketing: Marilyn Trow, Kimberly Sadler

E-Learning: Layne Hedrick

ISBN 13: 978-1-6003-2540-3
ISBN 10: 1-6003-2540-8

© 2008 Houghton Mifflin Harcourt Publihsers, Inc. and Stephen Hake

All rights reserved. No part of the material protected by this copyright may be reproduced or utilized in any form or by any means, in whole or in part, without permission in writing from the copyright owner. Requests for permission should be mailed to: Paralegal Department, 6277 Sea Harbor Drive, Orlando, FL 32887.

Saxon is a registered trademark of Houghton Mifflin Harcourt Publihsers, Inc.

6 7 8 0868 14 13 12 11 10 9

ABOUT THE AUTHOR

Stephen Hake has authored six books in the **Saxon Math** series. He writes from 17 years of classroom experience as a teacher in grades 5 through 12 and as a math specialist in El Monte, California. As a math coach, his students won honors and recognition in local, regional, and statewide competitions.

Stephen has been writing math curriculum since 1975 and for Saxon since 1985. He has also authored several math contests including Los Angeles County's first Math Field Day contest. Stephen contributed to the 1999 National Academy of Science publication on the Nature and Teaching of Algebra in the Middle Grades.

Stephen is a member of the National Council of Teachers of Mathematics and the California Mathematics Council. He earned his BA from United States International University and his MA from Chapman College.

CONTENTS OVERVIEW

TABLE OF CONTENTS

Integrated and Distributed Units of Instruction

Strands Key:
NO = Number and Operations
A = Algebra
G = Geometry

M = Measurement
DAP = Data Analysis and Probability
PS = Problem Solving
CM = Communication

RP = Reasoning and Proof
C = Connections
R = Representation

Strands Key:
NO = Number and Operations
A = Algebra
G = Geometry

M = Measurement
DAP = Data Analysis and Probability
PS = Problem Solving
CM = Communication

RP = Reasoning and Proof
C = Connections
R = Representation

TABLE OF CONTENTS

Strands Key:
NO = Number and Operations
A = Algebra
G = Geometry

M = Measurement
DAP = Data Analysis and Probability
PS = Problem Solving
CM = Communication

RP = Reasoning and Proof
C = Connections
R = Representation

TABLE OF CONTENTS

Strands Key:
NO = Number and Operations
A = Algebra
G = Geometry

M = Measurement
DAP = Data Analysis and Probability
PS = Problem Solving
CM = Communication

RP = Reasoning and Proof
C = Connections
R = Representation

TABLE OF CONTENTS

Strands Key:
NO = Number and Operations
A = Algebra
G = Geometry

M = Measurement
DAP = Data Analysis and Probability
PS = Problem Solving
CM = Communication

RP = Reasoning and Proof
C = Connections
R = Representation

TABLE OF CONTENTS

Section 11 Lessons 101–110, Investigation 11

Strands Key:
NO = Number and Operations
A = Algebra
G = Geometry
M = Measurement
DAP = Data Analysis and Probability
PS = Problem Solving
CM = Communication
RP = Reasoning and Proof
C = Connections
R = Representation

TABLE OF CONTENTS

Dear Student,

We study mathematics because it plays a very important role in our lives. Our school schedule, our trip to the store, the preparation of our meals, and many of the games we play involve mathematics. The word problems in this book are often drawn from everyday experiences.

When you become an adult, mathematics will become even more important. In fact, your future may depend on the mathematics you are learning now. This book will help you to learn mathematics and to learn it well. As you complete each lesson, you will see that similar problems are presented again and again. *Solving each problem day after day is the secret to success.*

Your book includes daily lessons and investigations. Each lesson has three parts.

1. The first part is a Power Up that includes practice of basic facts and mental math. These exercises improve your speed, accuracy, and ability to do math *in your head.* The Power Up also includes a problem-solving exercise to help you learn the strategies for solving complicated problems.

2. The second part of the lesson is the New Concept. This section introduces a new mathematical concept and presents examples that use the concept. The Lesson Practice provides a chance for you to solve problems using the new concept. The problems are lettered a, b, c, and so on.

3. The final part of the lesson is the Written Practice. This section reviews previously taught concepts and prepares you for concepts that will be taught in later lessons. Solving these problems will help you practice your skills and remember concepts you have learned.

Investigations are variations of the daily lesson. The investigations in this book often involve activities that fill an entire class period. Investigations contain their own set of questions but do not include Lesson Practice or Written Practice.

Remember to solve every problem in each Lesson Practice, Written Practice, and Investigation. Do your best work, and you will experience success and true learning that will stay with you and serve you well in the future.

Temple City, California

HOW TO USE YOUR TEXTBOOK

Saxon Math Intermediate 4 is unlike any math book you have used! It doesn't have colorful photos to distract you from learning. The Saxon approach lets you see the beauty and structure within math itself. You will understand more mathematics, become more confident in doing math, and will be well prepared when you take high school math classes.

Power Yourself Up

Start off each lesson by practicing your basic skills and concepts, mental math, and problem solving. Make your math brain stronger by exercising it every day. Soon you'll know these facts by memory!

Learn Something New!

Each day brings you a new concept, but you'll only have to learn a small part of it now. You'll be building on this concept throughout the year so that you understand and remember it by test time.

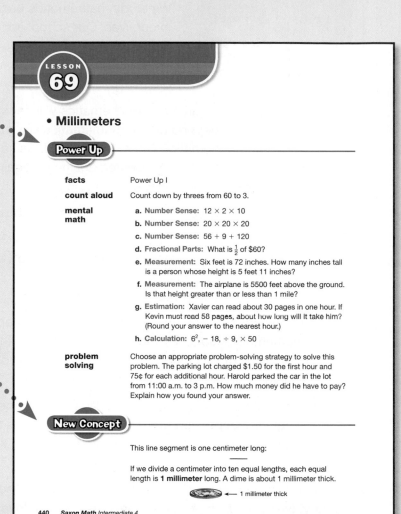

LESSON
69

• **Millimeters**

Power Up

facts	Power Up I
count aloud	Count down by threes from 60 to 3.
mental math	**a. Number Sense:** $12 \times 2 \times 10$
	b. Number Sense: $20 \times 20 \times 20$
	c. Number Sense: $56 + 9 + 120$
	d. Fractional Parts: What is $\frac{1}{2}$ of $60?
	e. Measurement: Six feet is 72 inches. How many inches tall is a person whose height is 5 feet 11 inches?
	f. Measurement: The airplane is 5500 feet above the ground. Is that height greater than or less than 1 mile?
	g. Estimation: Xavier can read about 30 pages in one hour. If Kevin must read 58 pages, about how long will it take him? (Round your answer to the nearest hour.)
	h. Calculation: $6^2, -18, \div 9, \times 50$
problem solving	Choose an appropriate problem-solving strategy to solve this problem. The parking lot charged $1.50 for the first hour and 75¢ for each additional hour. Harold parked the car in the lot from 11:00 a.m. to 3 p.m. How much money did he have to pay? Explain how you found your answer.

New Concept

This line segment is one centimeter long:

If we divide a centimeter into ten equal lengths, each equal length is **1 millimeter** long. A dime is about 1 millimeter thick.

← 1 millimeter thick

Activity

Transformations and Congruent Triangles

Material needed:
• Lesson Activity 31

(Formulate) For this activity, you will develop a plan to predict the movement of a triangle to determine **congruence**.

a. Cut out the two right triangles from **Lesson Activity 31**, or use triangle manipulatives.

b. (Predict) Place the two triangles in the positions shown below. Plan a way to move one triangle using a translation and a rotation to show that the triangles are congruent. Remember that one triangle must be on top of the other in the final position. Write your conclusion. Include direction and degrees in your answer.

c. (Predict) Place the two triangles in the positions shown below. Plan a way to move one triangle to show that the triangles are congruent. Remember that one triangle must be on top of the other in the final position. Write your conclusion. Include direction and degrees in your answer.

(Lesson Practice)

a. (Conclude) Can a right triangle have two right angles? Why or why not?

b. What is the name for a triangle that has at least two sides equal in length?

c. (Model) Use a color tile to model a translation, reflection, and rotation.

498   *Saxon Math Intermediate 4*

Get Active!

Dig into math with a hands-on activity. Explore a math concept with your friends as you work together and use manipulatives to see new connections in mathematics.

Check It Out!

The Lesson Practice lets you check to see if you understand today's new concept.

(Written Practice)   *Distributed and Integrated*

1. One hundred fifty feet equals how many yards?
(Inv. 2, 71)

2. Tammy gave the clerk $6 to pay for a book. She received 64¢ in change. Tax was 38¢. What was the price of the book?
(83)

3. DaJuan is 2 years older than Rebecca. Rebecca is twice as old as Dillon. DaJuan is 12 years old. How old is Dillon? (*Hint:* First find Rebecca's age.)
(94)

4. Write each decimal as a mixed number:
(84)
   a. 3.295   b. 32.9   c. 3.09

*5. a. (Represent) Three fourths of the 84 contestants guessed incorrectly. How many contestants guessed incorrectly? Draw a picture to illustrate the problem.
(Inv. 5, 95)

   b. What percent of the contestants guessed incorrectly?

6. These thermometers show the average daily minimum and maximum temperatures in North Little Rock, Arkansas, during the month of January. What is the range of the temperatures?
(18, 97)

7. a. What is the diameter of this circle?
(21)
   b. What is the radius of this circle?

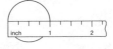

Lesson 100   633

Exercise Your Mind!

When you work the Written Practice exercises, you will review both today's new concept and also math you learned in earlier lessons. Each exercise will be on a different concept — you never know what you're going to get! It's like a mystery game — unpredictable and challenging.

As you review concepts from earlier in the book, you'll be asked to use higher-order thinking skills to show what you know and why the math works.

The mixed set of Written Practice is just like the mixed format of your state test. You'll be practicing for the "big" test every day!

HOW TO USE YOUR TEXTBOOK

Become an Investigator!

Dive into math concepts and explore the depths of math connections in the Investigations.

Continue to develop your mathematical thinking through applications, activities, and extensions.

INVESTIGATION 11

Focus on
• Volume

Shapes such as cubes, pyramids, and cones take up space. The amount of space a shape occupies is called its **volume**. We measure volume with **cubic units** like cubic centimeters, cubic inches, cubic feet, and cubic meters.

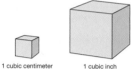

1 cubic centimeter   1 cubic inch

The model of the cube we constructed in Lesson 99 has a volume of one cubic inch.

Here is a model of a rectangular solid built with cubes that each have a volume of 1 cubic centimeter. To find the volume of the rectangular solid, we can count the number of cubic centimeters used to build it.

One way to count the small cubes is to count the cubes in one layer and then multiply that number by the number of layers. There are six cubes on the top layer, and there are two layers. The volume of the rectangular solid is 12 cubic centimeters.

Count cubes to find the volume of each rectangular solid below. Notice the units used in each figure.

Investigation 11   **699**

Focus on

• Problem Solving

We study mathematics to learn how to use tools that help us solve problems. We face mathematical problems in our daily lives. We can become powerful problem solvers by using the tools we store in our minds. In this book we will practice solving problems every day.

This lesson has three parts:

Problem-Solving Process The four steps we follow when solving problems.

Problem-Solving Strategies Some strategies that can help us solve problems.

Writing and Problem Solving Describing how we solved a problem.

Four-Step Problem-Solving Process

Solving a problem is like arriving at a new location, so the process of solving a problem is similar to the process of taking a trip. Suppose we are on the mainland and want to reach a nearby island.

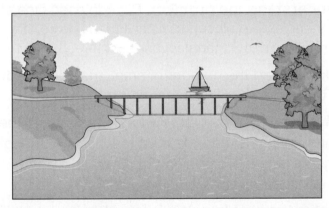

Step	Problem-Solving Process	Taking a Trip
1	**Understand** Know where you are and where you want to go.	We are on the mainland and want to go to the island.
2	**Plan** Plan your route.	We might use the bridge, the boat, or swim.
3	**Solve** Follow the plan.	Take the journey to the island.
4	**Check** Check that you have reached the right place.	Verify that we have reached our new location.

When we solve a problem, it helps to ask ourselves some questions along the way.

Step	Follow the Process	Ask Yourself Questions
1	Understand	What information am I given? What am I asked to find or do?
2	Plan	How can I use the given information to solve the problem? What strategy can I use to solve the problem?
3	Solve	Am I following the plan? Is my math correct?
4	Check	Does my solution answer the question that was asked? Is my answer reasonable?

Below we show how we follow these steps to solve a word problem.

Example 1

Ricardo arranged nine small congruent triangles in rows to make one large triangle.

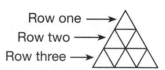

Row one ⟶
 Row two ⟶
 Row three ⟶

If Ricardo extended the triangle to 5 rows, how many small triangles will there be in row four and row five?

Step 1: Understand the problem. Ricardo used nine small congruent triangles. He placed the small triangles so that row one has 1 triangle, row two has 3 triangles, and row three has 5 triangles.

We are asked to find the number of small triangles in row four and row five if the large triangle is extended to 5 rows.

Step 2: Make a plan. The first row has one triangle, the second row has three triangles, and the third row has five triangles. We see that there is a pattern. We can make a table and continue the pattern to extend the large triangle to five rows.

Step 3: Solve the problem. We follow our plan by making a table that shows the number of triangles used in each row if the large triangle is extended to 5 rows.

Row	one	two	three	four	five
Number of Triangles	1	3	5	7	9

+2   +2   +2   +2

We see that the number of small triangles in each row increases by 2 when a new row is added.

$$5 + 2 = 7 \qquad 7 + 2 = 9$$

This means row four has **7 triangles** and row five has **9 triangles**.

Step 4: Check the answer. We look back at the problem to see if we have used the correct information and have answered the question. We made a table to show the number of small triangles that were in each row. We found a pattern and extended the triangle to 5 rows. We know that row four has 7 small triangles and that row five has 9 small triangles.

We can check our answer by drawing a diagram and counting the number of triangles in each row.

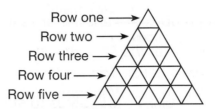

Our answer is reasonable and correct.

Example 2

Mr. Jones built a fence around his square-shaped garden. He put 5 fence posts on each side of the garden, including one post in each corner. How many fence posts did Mr. Jones use?

Step 1: Understand the problem. Mr. Jones built a square fence around his garden. He put 5 fence posts on each side of the garden. There is one fence post in each corner.

Step 2: Make a plan. We can make a model of the fence using paper clips to represent each fence post.

Step 3: Solve the problem. We follow our plan by creating a model. First we will show one fence post in each corner.

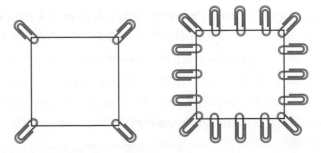

We know each side has five fence posts. We see that each side of our model already has two fence posts. We add three fence posts to each side to show five posts per side.

Each side of the fence now has five posts, including the one in each corner. We find that Mr. Jones used **16 fence posts** to build the fence.

> **Step 4: Check the answer.** We look back at the problem to see if we used the correct information and answered the question. We know that our answer is reasonable because each side of the square has 5 posts, including the one in each corner. We also see that there are four corner posts and 3 posts on each of the four sides. Mr. Jones used 16 posts to build the fence.

1. List in order the four steps of the problem-solving process.

2. What two questions do we answer to understand a problem?

Refer to the following problem to answer questions **3–8**.

> *Katie left her house at the time shown on the clock. She arrived at Monica's house 15 minutes later. Then they spent 30 minutes eating lunch. What time did they finish lunch?*

3. (**Connect**) What information are we given?

4. (**Verify**) What are you asked to find?

5. Which step of the four-step problem-solving process did you complete when you answered questions 3 and 4?

6. Describe your plan for solving the problem.

7. (**Explain**) Solve the problem by following your plan. Show your work. Write your solution to the problem in a way someone else will understand.

8. Check your work and your answer. Look back to the problem. Be sure you use the information correctly. Be sure you found what you were asked to find. Is your answer reasonable?

Problem-Solving Strategies

As we consider how to solve a problem, we choose one or more strategies that seem to be helpful. Referring to the picture at the beginning of this lesson, we might choose to swim, to take the boat, or to cross the bridge to travel from the mainland to the island. Other strategies might not be as effective for the illustrated problem. For example, choosing to walk or bike across the water are strategies that are not reasonable for this situation.

When solving mathematical problems we also select strategies that are appropriate for the problem. **Problem-solving strategies** are types of plans we can use to solve problems. Listed below are ten strategies we will practice in this book. You may refer to these descriptions as you solve problems throughout the year.

Act it out or make a model. Moving objects or people can help us visualize the problem and lead us to the solution.

Use logical reasoning. All problems require reasoning, but for some problems we use given information to eliminate choices so that we can close in on the solution. Usually a chart, diagram, or picture can be used to organize the given information and to make the solution more apparent.

Draw a picture or diagram. Sketching a picture or a diagram can help us understand and solve problems, especially problems about graphs or maps or shapes.

Write a number sentence or equation. We can solve many word problems by fitting the given numbers into equations or number sentences and then finding the unknown numbers.

Make it simpler. We can make some complicated problems easier by using smaller numbers or fewer items. Solving the simpler problem might help us see a pattern or method that can help us solve the complex problem.

Find/Extend a pattern. Identifying a pattern that helps you to predict what will come next as the pattern continues might lead to the solution.

Make an organized list. Making a list can help us organize our thinking about a problem.

Guess and check. Guessing the answer and trying the guess in the problem might start a process that leads to the answer. If the guess is not correct, use the information from the guess to make a better guess. Continue to improve your guesses until you find the answer.

Make or use a table, chart, or graph. Arranging information in a table, chart, or graph can help us organize and keep track of data. This might reveal patterns or relationships that can help us solve the problem.

Work backwards. Finding a route through a maze is often easier by beginning at the end and tracing a path back to the start. Likewise, some problems are easier to solve by working back from information that is given toward the end of the problem to information that is unknown near the beginning of the problem.

9. Name some strategies used in this lesson.

The chart below shows where each strategy is first introduced in this textbook.

Strategy	Lesson
Act It Out or Make a Model	1
Use Logical Reasoning	13
Draw a Picture or Diagram	9
Write a Number Sentence or Equation	28
Make It Simpler	20
Find/Extend a Pattern	8
Make an Organized List	46
Guess and Check	15
Make or Use a Table, Chart, or Graph	3
Work Backwards	57

Writing and Problem Solving

Sometimes, a problem will ask us to explain our thinking. This helps us measure our understanding of math and it is easy to do.

- Explain how you solved the problem.
- Explain how you know your answer is correct.
- Explain why your answer is reasonable.

For these situations, we can describe the way we followed our plan. This is a description of the way we solved Example 1.

> *We made a table and continued a pattern to extend the large triangle to five rows. We found that row four had 7 small triangles and row five had 9 small triangles.*

10. Write a description of how we solved the problem in Example 2.

Other times, we will be asked to write a problem for a given equation. Be sure to include the correct numbers and operations to represent the equation.

11. Write a word problem for $9 + 5 = 14$.

• Review of Addition

Power Up

facts   Power Up A[1]

count aloud   Count by twos from 2 to 20.

mental math   Add ten to a number in **a–f.**

    a. Number Sense: $20 + 10$

    b. Number Sense: $34 + 10$

    c. Number Sense: $10 + 53$

    d. Number Sense: $5 + 10$

    e. Number Sense: $25 + 10$

    f. Number Sense: $10 + 8$

    g. What number is one less than 36?

problem solving   Six students are planning to ride the roller coaster at the amusement park. Three students can sit in each row of the roller coaster. How many rows will six students fill?

Focus Strategy: Act It Out

(**Understand**) We are told that six students will ride the roller coaster. Three students can sit in each row. We are asked to find the number of rows six students will fill.

(**Plan**) Six student volunteers can *act out* the situation in the problem.

(**Solve**) Your teacher will call six students to the front of the classroom and line them up in rows of three. Three students will fill one row of the roller coaster, and three more students will fill a second row of the roller coaster. Since there are no students left over, we know that six students will fill **two rows** of the roller coaster.

---

[1] For instructions on how to use the Power Up activities, please consult the preface.

Check We know our answer is reasonable because by acting out the problem, we see that six students divide into two equal groups of three. Each group of three students fills one row.

How many rows would six students fill if only two students can sit in each row?

New Concept

Reading Math

We can write an addition number sentence both horizontally and vertically. Write an addition number sentence in horizontal form. Write an addition number sentence in vertical form.

Addition is the combining of two groups into one group. For example, when we count the dots on the top faces of a pair of dot cubes, we are adding.

$$4 + 3 = 7$$

four   plus   three   equals   seven

The numbers that are added are called **addends.** The answer is called the **sum.** The addition $4 + 3 = 7$ is a **number sentence.** A number sentence is a complete sentence that uses numbers and symbols instead of words. Here we show two ways to add 4 and 3:

4	addend		3	addend
+ 3	addend		+ 4	addend
7	sum		7	sum

Notice that if the order of the addends is changed, the sum remains the same. This is true for any two numbers and is called the **Commutative Property of Addition. When we add two numbers, either number may be first.**

$$4 + 3 = 7 \qquad\qquad 3 + 4 = 7$$

When we add zero to a number, the number is not changed. This property of addition is called the **Identity Property of Addition.** If we start with a number and add zero, the sum is identical to the starting number.

$$4 + 0 = 4 \qquad 9 + 0 = 9 \qquad 0 + 7 = 7$$

Example 1

Write a number sentence for this picture:

A number sentence for the picture is
4 + 5 = 9. The number sentence **5 + 4 = 9**
is also correct.

When adding three numbers, the numbers may be added in any order. Here we show six ways to add 4, 3, and 5. Each way the answer is 12.

$$
\begin{array}{cccccc}
4 & 4 & 3 & 3 & 5 & 5 \\
3 & 5 & 4 & 5 & 4 & 3 \\
+\,5 & +\,3 & +\,5 & +\,4 & +\,3 & +\,4 \\
\hline
12 & 12 & 12 & 12 & 12 & 12
\end{array}
$$

Example 2

Show six ways to add 1, 2, and 3.

We can form two number sentences that begin with the addend 1.

$$1 + 2 + 3 = 6 \qquad 1 + 3 + 2 = 6$$

We can form two number sentences that begin with the addend 2.

$$2 + 1 + 3 = 6 \qquad 2 + 3 + 1 = 6$$

We can form two number sentences that begin with the addend 3.

$$3 + 1 + 2 = 6 \qquad 3 + 2 + 1 = 6$$

Many word problems tell a story. Some stories are about **putting things together.** Read this story:

D'Jon had 5 marbles. He bought 7 more marbles.
Then D'Jon had 12 marbles.

There is a plot to this story. D'Jon had **some** marbles. Then he bought **some more** marbles. When he put the marbles together, he found the **total** number of marbles. Problems with a **"some and some more"** plot can be expressed with an addition **formula.** A formula is a method for solving a certain type of problem. Below is a formula for solving problems with a "some and some more" plot:

Reading Math

We translate the problem using an addition formula.

D'Jon had:
5 marbles

He bought some more: 7 marbles

Total: 12 marbles

Formula	Problem
Some	5 marbles
+ Some more	+ 7 marbles
Total	12 marbles

Here we show the formula written horizontally:

Formula: Some + Some more = Total

Problem: 5 marbles + 7 marbles = 12 marbles

A story can become a word problem if one or more of the numbers is missing. Here are three word problems:

D'Jon had 5 marbles. He bought 7 more marbles. Then how many marbles did D'Jon have?

D'Jon had 5 marbles. He bought some more marbles. Then D'Jon had 12 marbles. How many marbles did D'Jon buy?

D'Jon had some marbles. He bought 7 more marbles. Then D'Jon had 12 marbles. How many marbles did D'Jon have before he bought the 7 marbles?

To solve a word problem, we can follow the four-step problem-solving process.

Step 1: Read and translate the problem.

Step 2: Make a plan to solve the problem.

Step 3: Follow the plan and solve the problem.

Step 4: Check your answer for reasonableness.

A plan that can help us solve word problems is to *write a number sentence.* We write the numbers we know into a formula.

Example 3

Matias saw 8 ducks. Then he saw 7 more ducks. How many ducks did Matias see in all?

This problem has a "some and some more" plot. We write the numbers we know into the formula.

Formula: Some + Some more = Total

Problem: 8 ducks + 7 ducks = Total

We may shorten the number sentence to $8 + 7 = t$.

We find the total by adding 8 and 7.

Matias saw **15 ducks** in all.

One way to check the answer is to see if it correctly completes the problem.

Matias saw 8 ducks. Then he saw 7 more ducks. Matias saw **15 ducks** *in all.*

Math Symbols

Any uppercase or lowercase letter may be used to represent a number. For example, we can use T or t to represent a total.

Example 4

Samantha saw 5 trees in the east field, 3 trees in the west field, and 4 trees in the north field. How many trees did Samantha see in all?

In this story there are three addends.

Formula	Problem
Some	5 trees
Some more	3 trees
+ Some more	+ 4 trees
Total	Total

Using addition, we find that Samantha saw **12 trees** in all.

We check the answer to see if it is reasonable.

> There are three addends: 5 trees, 3 trees, and 4 trees. When we put all the trees together, we add $5 + 3 + 4$. The number of trees is **12.**

Some of the problems in this book will have an addend missing. When one addend is missing and the sum is given, the problem is to find the missing addend. What is the missing addend in this number sentence?

2	+	?	=	7
two	plus	?	equals	seven

Since we know that $2 + 5 = 7$, the missing addend is 5. A letter can be used to represent a missing number, as we see in the example below.

Example 5

Find each missing addend:

a.
$$\begin{array}{r} 4 \\ + n \\ \hline 7 \end{array}$$

b. $b + 6 = 10$

a. The letter n stands for a missing addend. Since $4 + 3 = 7$, the letter n stands for the number **3** in this number sentence.

b. In this problem, the letter b is used to stand for the missing addend. Since $4 + 6 = 10$, the letter b stands for the number **4.**

Add:

a. $5 + 6$ **b.** $6 + 5$ **c.** $8 + 0$

d. $4 + 8 + 6$ **e.** $4 + 5 + 6$

f. D'Anya ran 5 laps in the morning. She ran 8 laps in the afternoon. How many laps did she run in all? Write a number sentence for this problem.

g. (**Formulate**) Write two number sentences for this picture to show the Commutative Property.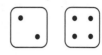

h. (**List**) Show six ways to add 1, 3, and 5.

Find each missing addend:

i. $7 + n = 10$ **j.** $a + 8 = 12$

k. (**Connect**) Copy these two patterns on a piece of paper. In each of the six boxes, write either "addend" or "sum."

$$\boxed{} + \boxed{} = \boxed{} \qquad \begin{array}{r} \boxed{} \\ + \boxed{} \\ \hline \boxed{} \end{array}$$

Written Practice   *Distributed and Integrated*

(**Formulate**) Write a number sentence for problems **1** and **2**. Then solve each problem.

*1. There were 5 students in the first row and 7 students in the second row. How many students were in the first two rows?

*2. Ling had 6 coins in her left pocket and 3 coins in her right pocket. How many coins did Ling have in both pockets?

Find each sum or missing addend:

3. $9 + 4$ **4.** $8 + 2$

$$\textbf{*5.} \quad \begin{array}{r} 4 \\ + n \\ \hline 9 \end{array} \qquad \textbf{*6.} \quad \begin{array}{r} w \\ + 5 \\ \hline 8 \end{array} \qquad \textbf{*7.} \quad \begin{array}{r} 6 \\ + p \\ \hline 8 \end{array} \qquad \textbf{*8.} \quad \begin{array}{r} q \\ + 8 \\ \hline 8 \end{array}$$

Beginning in this lesson, we star the exercises that cover challenging or recently presented content. We encourage students to work first on the starred exercises with which they might want help, saving the easier exercises for last.

9. 3 + 4 + 5

10. 4 + 4 + 4

11. 6 + r = 10

12. x + 5 = 6

13.   5
      5
  + 5

14.   8
      0
  + 7

15.   6
      5
  + 4

16.   9
      9
  + 9

17.   m
  + 9
   10

18.   9
  + f
   12

19.   z
  + 5
   10

20.   0
  + n
    3

21. 3 + 2 + 5 + 4 + 6

22. 2 + 2 + 2 + 2 + 2 + 2 + 2

(**Represent**) Write a number sentence for each picture:

*23.

*24.

*25. (**List**) Show six ways to add 2, 3, and 4.

*26. Multiple Choice Sometimes a missing number is shown by a shape instead of a letter. Choose the correct number for △ in the following number sentence:

$$\triangle + 3 = 10$$

A 3   **B** 7   **C** 10   **D** 13

*27. (**Represent**) Draw a dot cube picture to show 5 + 6.

*28. (**Connect**) Write a horizontal number sentence that has a sum of 17.

*29. (**Connect**) Write a vertical number sentence that has a sum of 15.

*30. (**Formulate**) Write and solve an addition word problem using the numbers 10 and 8.

• Missing Addends

Power Up

facts   Power Up A

count aloud   Count by fives from 5 to 50.

mental math   For **a–f,** add ten to a number.

    a. Number Sense: 40 + 10

    b. Number Sense: 26 + 10

    c. Number Sense: 39 + 10

    d. Number Sense: 7 + 10

    e. Number Sense: 10 + 9

    f. Number Sense: 10 + 63

    g. What number is one less than 49?

problem solving   Choose an appropriate problem-solving strategy to solve this problem. Maria, Sh'Meika, and Kimber are on a picnic. They want to draw sketches of the clouds in the sky. Sh'Meika brought 15 sheets of paper and 6 pencils to share with the other two girls. How many sheets of paper and how many pencils can each girl have if they share equally?

New Concept

Thinking Skill

Discuss

What is another way you can find the number of the third roll?

Represent Derek rolled a dot cube three times. The picture below shows the number of dots on the top face of the cube for each of the first two rolls.

First roll   Second roll

The total number of dots on all three rolls was 12.

Math Language

An **equation** is a number sentence that uses the symbol = to show that two quantities are equal. Here are two examples:

$5 + 2 = 7$
$6 + n = 8$

These are not equations:

$5 + 2$
$4 > 6$

Let's draw a picture to show the number of dots on the top face of the cube for Derek's third roll.

We will write a number sentence, or an *equation,* for this problem. The first two numbers are 5 and 3. We do not know the number of the third roll, so we will use a letter. We know that the total is 12.

$$5 + 3 + t = 12$$

To find the missing addend, we first add 5 and 3, which makes 8. Then we think, "Eight plus what number equals twelve?" Since 8 plus 4 equals 12, the third roll was ⬚.

Example

Visit www. SaxonMath.com/ Int4Activities for a calculator activity.

Find each missing addend:

a. $\begin{array}{r} 6 \\ n \\ + 5 \\ \hline 17 \end{array}$

b. $4 + 3 + 2 + b + 6 = 20$

a. We add 6 and 5, which makes 11. We think, "Eleven plus what number equals seventeen?" Since 11 plus 6 equals 17, the missing addend is **6.**

b. First we add 4, 3, 2, and 6, which equals 15. Since 15 plus 5 is 20, the missing addend is **5.**

Lesson Practice

Find each missing addend:

a. $8 + a + 2 = 17$ **b.** $b + 6 + 5 = 12$

c. $4 + c + 2 + 3 + 5 = 20$

Written Practice   *Distributed and Integrated*

(Formulate) Write a number sentence for problems **1** and **2.** Then solve each problem.

[1]* **1.** Jordan's rabbit, Hoppy, ate 5 carrots in the morning and 6 carrots in the
(1)   afternoon. How many carrots did Hoppy eat in all?

---

[1] The italicized numbers within parentheses underneath each problem number are called *lesson reference numbers.* These numbers refer to the lesson(s) in which the major concept of that particular problem is introduced. If additional assistance is needed, refer to the discussion, examples, or practice problems of that lesson.

*2. Five friends rode their bikes from the school to the lake. They rode
(1) 7 miles and then rested. They still had 4 miles to go. How many miles
was it from the school to the lake?

Find each sum or missing addend:

3. $9 + n = 13$
(1)

4. $7 + 8$
(1)

5. p
(1) $\underline{+\ 6}$
     13

*6. 5
(2) 2
     $\underline{+\ w}$
       12

7. 4
(1) 8
     $\underline{+\ 5}$

8. 9
(1) 3
     $\underline{+\ 7}$

*9. 8
(2) b
     $\underline{+\ 3}$
       16

10. 9
(1) 7
     $\underline{+\ 3}$

11. 2
(1) 9
     $\underline{+\ 6}$

12. 3
(1) 8
     $\underline{+\ 2}$

13. 9
(1) 5
     $\underline{+\ 3}$

14. 2
(2) m
     $\underline{+\ 4}$
       9

15. 5
(2) 3
     $\underline{+\ q}$
       9

16. 2
(2) 3
     $\underline{+\ r}$
       7

17. 5
(2) 3
     $\underline{+\ t}$
       10

18. 8
(1) 4
     $\underline{+\ 6}$

19. 2
(2) x
     $\underline{+\ 7}$
       11

20. 5
(1) 2
     $\underline{+\ 6}$

*21. $5 + 5 + 6 + 4 + x = 23$
(2)

*22. (List) Show six ways to add 4, 5, and 6.
(1)

(Represent) Write a number sentence for each picture:

*23.
(1)

24.
(1)

25. (**Verify**) What is the name of the answer when we add?
(1)

*26. **Multiple Choice** Which number is ☐ in the following number
(1) sentence?

$$6 + \square = 10$$

A 4 **B** 6 **C** 10 **D** 16

*27. (**Represent**) Draw a picture to show $6 + 3 + 5$.
(2)

*28. (**Connect**) Write a horizontal number sentence that has a sum of 20.
(1)

29. (**Connect**) Write a vertical number sentence that has a sum of 24.
(1)

*30. (**Formulate**) Write and solve an addition word problem using the
(1) numbers 7, 3, and 10.

Early Finishers

Real-World Connection

There were 35 pictures at the art exhibit. The pictures were made using oils, pastels, or watercolors. Thirteen of the pictures were made using watercolors. An equal number of pictures were made using oils as were made using pastels. How many pictures were made using pastels? Explain how you found the answer.

• Sequences
• Digits

facts	Power Up A
count aloud	Count by twos from 2 to 40.
mental math	**Number Sense:** Add ten, twenty, or thirty to a number in **a–f.**

a. 20
   + 20

b. 23
   + 20

c. 43
   + 10

d. 24
   + 30

e. 50
   + 30

f. 10
   + 65

g. What number is one less than 28?

problem solving

Kazi has nine coins to put in his left and right pockets. Find the ways Kazi could place the coins in his left and right pockets.

Focus Strategy: Make a Table

(**Understand**) We are told that Kazi has nine coins that he can put in his left and right pockets. We are asked to find the ways Kazi could place the coins in his left and right pockets.

If Kazi puts all nine coins in his left pocket, he would have zero coins for his right pocket. This means "9 left, 0 right" is a possibility.

If Kazi moves one coin from the left pocket to his right pocket, eight coins would remain in his left pocket ($9 - 1 = 8$). This possibility would be "8 left, 1 right." We begin to see that there are multiple ways Kazi can put the coins into his left and right pockets.

(**Plan**) We can *make a table* to organize the ways Kazi could place the coins.

Solve We make a table with one column labeled "left" and the other labeled "right." We start by writing the combinations we have already found. Then we fill in new rows until we finish the table.

Notice that the sum of the numbers in each row is 9. Also notice that there are ten rows, which means there are ten different ways Kazi could put the coins into his left and right pockets.

Check We know our answer is reasonable because Kazi can put from 0 to 9 coins in one pocket and the rest in the other pocket, which is ten ways. We made a table to help us find all the ways.

Number of Coins

Left	Right
9	0
8	1
7	2
6	3
5	4
4	5
3	6
2	7
1	8
0	9

What is another problem-solving strategy that we could use to solve the problem?

New Concepts

Sequences

Reading Math

The three dots written after a sequence such as 1, 2, 3, 4, 5, … mean that the sequence continues without end even though the numbers are not written.

Counting is a math skill we learn early in life. Counting by ones we say, "one, two, three, four, five, …."

$$1, 2, 3, 4, 5, \ldots$$

These numbers are called **counting numbers.** The counting numbers continue without end. We may also count by numbers other than one.

Counting by twos: 2, 4, 6, 8, 10, …

Counting by fives: 5, 10, 15, 20, 25, …

These are examples of counting patterns. A counting pattern is a **sequence.** A counting sequence may count up or count down. We can study a counting sequence to discover a rule for the sequence. Then we can find more numbers in the sequence.

Example 1

Find the rule and the next three numbers of this counting sequence:

10, 20, 30, 40, ____ , ____ , ____ , …

The rule is **count up by tens.** Counting this way, we find that the next three numbers are **50, 60,** and **70.**

Example 2

Find the rule of this counting sequence. Then find the missing number in the sequence.

$$30, 27, 24, 21, \underline{\hspace{1cm}}, 15, \dots$$

The rule is **count down by threes.** If we count down three from 21, we find that the missing number in the sequence is **18.** We see that 15 is three less than 18, which follows the rule.

Digits

To write numbers, we use **digits. Digits are the numerals 0, 1, 2, 3, 4, 5, 6, 7, 8, and 9.** The number 356 has three digits, and the last digit is 6. The number 67,896,094 has eight digits, and the last digit is 4.

Example 3

The number 64,000 has how many digits?

The number 64,000 has **five digits.**

Example 4

What is the last digit of 2001?

The last digit of 2001 is **1.**

Example 5

(Model) **How many different three-digit numbers can you write using the digits 1, 2, and 3? Each digit may be used only once in every number you write.**

We can act out the problem by writing each digit on a separate slip of paper. Then we vary the arrangement of the slips until all of the possibilities have been discovered. We can avoid repeating arrangements by writing the smallest number first and then writing the rest of the numbers in counting order until we write the largest number.

$$123, 132, 213, 231, 312, 321$$

We find we can make **six different numbers.**

Lesson Practice

(Generalize) Write the rule and the next three numbers of each counting sequence:

a. 10, 9, 8, 7, _____, _____, _____, ...

b. 3, 6, 9, 12, _____, _____, _____, ...

Connect Find the missing number in each counting sequence:

    c. 80, 70, ____, 50, ...   **d.** 8, ____, 16, 20, 24, ...

How many digits are in each number?

    e. 18   **f.** 5280   **g.** 8,403,227,189

What is the last digit of each number?

    h. 19   **i.** 5281   **j.** 8,403,190

    k. How many different three-digit numbers can you write using the digits 7, 8, and 9? Each digit may be used only once in every number you write. List the numbers in counting order.

Written Practice

Distributed and Integrated

Formulate Write a number sentence for problems **1** and **2**. Then solve each problem.

*1. Diana has 5 dollars, Sumaya has 6 dollars, and Britt has 7 dollars.
(1) Altogether, how much money do the three girls have?

*2. On Taye's favorite CD there are 9 songs. On his second-favorite CD
(1) there are 8 songs. Altogether, how many songs are on Taye's two favorite CDs?

*3. How many digits are in each number?
(3)
    a. 593   **b.** 180   **c.** 186,527,394

*4. What is the last digit of each number?
(3)
    a. 3427   **b.** 460   **c.** 437,269

Find each missing addend:

5. $5 + m + 4 = 12$ ***6.** $8 + 2 + w = 16$
(2)   (2)

Conclude Write the next number in each counting sequence:

*7. 10, 20, 30, ____, ...   ***8.** 22, 21, 20, ____, ...
(3)   (3)

*9. 40, 35, 30, 25, ____, ...   ***10.** 70, 80, 90, ____, ...
(3)   (3)

Generalize Write the rule and the next three numbers of each counting sequence:

*11. 6, 12, 18, ____, ____, ____, …
(3)

12. 3, 6, 9, ____, ____, ____, …
(3)

13. 4, 8, 12, ____, ____, ____, …
(3)

*14. 45, 36, 27, ____, ____, ____, …
(3)

Connect Find the missing number in each counting sequence:

*15. 8, 12, ____, 20, …
(3)

*16. 12, 18, ____, 30, …
(3)

17. 30, 25, ____, 15, …
(3)

18. 6, 9, ____, 15, …
(3)

19. How many small rectangles are shown? Count by twos.
(3)

20. How many X s are shown? Count by fours.
(3)

```
X X   X X   X X
X X   X X   X X

X X   X X   X X
X X   X X   X X
```

*21. **Represent** Write a number sentence for the picture below.
(1)

22.	4	**23.**	9	**24.**	8	**25.**	2
(1)	8	(1)	5	(1)	4	(1)	9
	7		7		7		7
	+ 5		+ 8		+ 2		+ 5

*26. **Multiple Choice** If △ = 3 and □ = 4, then △ + □ equals which of
(1) the following?

  A 3   **B** 4   **C** 5   **D** 7

*27. How many different arrangements of three letters can you write using
(3) the letters a, b, and c? The different arrangements you write do not
need to form words.

*28. (**Connect**) Write a horizontal number sentence that has a sum of 9.
(1)

*29. (**Connect**) Write a vertical number sentence that has a sum of 11.
(1)

*30. (**Formulate**) Write and solve an addition word problem that has a
(1) sum of 12.

*Real-World
Connection*

Ivan noticed that the first three house numbers on the right side of a
street were 2305, 2315, and 2325.

a. What pattern do you see in this list of numbers?

b. If this pattern continues, what will the next three house numbers
be?

c. The houses on the left side of the street have corresponding
numbers that end in 0. What are the house numbers for the first
6 houses on the left side of the street?

d. What pattern is used for the house numbers on the left side of the
street?

• Place Value

Power Up

facts	Power Up A
count aloud	Count by fives from 5 to 100.
mental math	Add ten, twenty, or thirty to a number in **a–f.**

    a. Number Sense: 66 + 10

    b. Number Sense: 29 + 20

    c. Number Sense: 10 + 76

    d. Number Sense: 38 + 30

    e. Number Sense: 20 + 6

    f. Number Sense: 40 + 30

    g. Add 10 to 77 and then subtract 1. What is the final answer?

problem solving
Choose an appropriate problem-solving strategy to solve this problem. Lorelei has a total of nine coins in her left and right pockets. She has some coins (at least two) in each pocket. Make a table that shows the possible number of coins in each pocket.

New Concept

Model To learn **place value,** we will use money manipulatives and pictures to show different amounts of money. We will use $100 bills, $10 bills, and $1 bills.

Example 1

Write the amount of money that is shown in the picture below.

Since there are 2 hundreds, 4 tens, and 3 ones, the amount of money shown is **$243.**

Example 2

(Model) **Use money manipulatives or draw a diagram to show $324 using $100 bills, $10 bills, and $1 bills.**

To show $324, we use 3 hundreds, 2 tens, and 4 ones.

3 hundreds   2 tens   4 ones

The value of each place is determined by its position. Three-digit numbers like 324 occupy three different places.

Math Language

We can use money to show place value because our number system and our money system are both base-ten systems.

ones place ⎯⎯⎯⎯⎯⎯⎯
tens place ⎯⎯⎯⎯⎯⎯
hundreds place ⎯⎯

<u>3</u> <u>2</u> <u>4</u>

Thinking Skill

(Connect)

What does the zero in $203 represent? What does the zero in $230 represent?

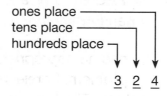

Activity

Comparing Money Amounts

Materials needed:
• money manipulatives from **Lesson Activities 2, 3,** and **4**

(Model) Use money manipulatives to show both $203 and $230. Write the amount that is the greater amount of money.

Example 3

The digit 7 is in what place in 753?

The 7 is in the third place from the right, which shows the number of hundreds. This means the 7 is in the **hundreds place.**

Lesson Practice

a. **Model** Use money manipulatives or draw a diagram to show $231 using $100 bills, $10 bills, and $1 bills.

b. **Model** Use money manipulatives or draw a diagram to show $213. Which is less, $231 or $213?

The digit 6 is in what place in each of these numbers?

c. 16   **d.** 65   **e.** 623

f. Use three digits to write a number equal to 5 hundreds, 2 tens, and 3 ones.

Written Practice

Distributed and Integrated

1. When Roho looked at the group of color tiles, he saw 3 red, 4 blue, 5 green, and 1 yellow. How many color tiles were there in all? Write the number sentence to find the answer.
(1)

***2.** **Represent** Write a number sentence for this picture:
(1)

3. How many cents are in 4 nickels? Count by fives.
(3)

5¢   5¢   5¢   5¢

Find each sum or missing addend:

4. $\begin{array}{r} 4 \\ + n \\ \hline 12 \end{array}$
(1)

5. $\begin{array}{r} 4 \\ 5 \\ + 3 \\ \hline \end{array}$
(1)

6. $\begin{array}{r} 13 \\ + y \\ \hline 19 \end{array}$
(1)

7. $\begin{array}{r} 7 \\ + s \\ \hline 14 \end{array}$
(1)

***8.** $4 + n + 5 = 12$
(2)

9. $n + 2 + 3 = 8$
(2)

Generalize Write the rule and the next three numbers of each counting sequence:

*10. 9, 12, 15, ____, ____, ____, ...
(3)

*11. 30, 24, 18, ____, ____, ____, ...
(3)

*12. 12, 16, 20, ____, ____, ____, ...
(3)

*13. 35, 28, 21, ____, ____, ____, ...
(3)

14. How many digits are in each number?
(3)
    a. 37,432   **b.** 5,934,286   **c.** 453,000

*15. What is the last digit of each number?
(3)
    a. 734   **b.** 347   **c.** 473

*16. **Represent** Draw a diagram to show $342 in $100 bills, $10 bills,
(4)   and $1 bills.

17. How much money does this picture show?
(4)

Connect Find the missing number in each counting sequence:

18. 24, ____, 36, 42, ...   ***19.** 36, 32, ____, 24, ...
(3)   (3)

*20. How many ears do 10 rabbits have? Count by twos.
(3)

*21. The digit 6 is in what place in 365?
(4)

*22. **Represent** Write a number sentence for this picture:
(1)

23. Find the missing addend:
(2)
$$2 + 5 + 3 + 2 + 3 + 1 + n = 20$$

*24. **(Explain)** How do you find the missing addend in problem **23?**
(2)

25. Show six ways to add 6, 7, and 8.
(1)

*26. **Multiple Choice** In the number 123, which digit shows the number of
(4) hundreds?

   A 1   **B** 2   **C** 3   **D** 4

*27. **(Predict)** What is the tenth number in the counting sequence below?
(3)

$$1, 2, 3, 4, 5, \ldots$$

*28. How many different three-digit numbers can you write using the digits
(3) 2, 5, and 8? Each digit may be used only once in every number you
write. List the numbers in counting order.

*29. **(Connect)** Write a number sentence that has addends of 6 and 7.
(1)

*30. **(Formulate)** Write and solve an addition word problem using the
(1) numbers 2, 3, and 5.

*Real-World
Connection*

Andres was asked to solve this riddle:

> *What number am I? I have three digits. There is a 4 in the
> tens place, a 7 in the ones place, and a 6 in the hundreds place.*

Andres said the answer was 467. Did Andres give the correct answer?
Use money manipulatives to explain your answer.

• Ordinal Numbers
• Months of the Year

facts	Power Up A
count aloud	Count by fours from 4 to 40.
mental math	**Number Sense:** Add a number ending in zero to another number in **a–e.**

a.	24	**b.**	36	**c.**	50	
	+ 60		+ 10		+ 42	

d.	33	**e.**	40	
	+ 30		+ 50	

f. Add 10 to 44 and then subtract 1. What is the final answer?

g. Add 10 to 73 and then subtract 1. What is the final answer?

problem solving

Choose an appropriate problem-solving strategy to solve this problem. Farica has a total of nine coins in her left and right pockets. She has some coins (at least two) in each pocket. She has more coins in her right pocket than in her left pocket. Make a table that shows the possible number of coins in each pocket.

New Concepts

Ordinal Numbers

If we want to count the number of children in a line, we say, "one, two, three, four, ..." These numbers tell us how many children we have counted. To describe a child's position in a line, we use words like *first, second, third,* and *fourth.* Numbers that tell position or order are called **ordinal numbers.**

Example 1

There are ten children in the lunch line. Pedro is fourth in line.

    a. How many children are in front of Pedro?

    b. How many children are behind him?

A diagram may help us understand the problem. We draw and label a diagram using the information given to us.

Math Language

Ordinal numbers tell which one.

Which one is Pedro? *He is the fourth person.*

Cardinal numbers tell how many.

How many people are in front of Pedro? *There are 3 people in front of Pedro.*

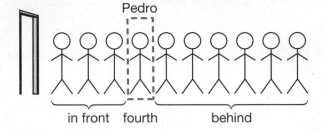

in front   fourth   behind

    a. Since Pedro is fourth in line, we see that there are **three children** in front of him.

    b. The rest of the children are behind Pedro. From the diagram, we see that there are **six children** behind him.

Ordinal numbers can be abbreviated. The abbreviation consists of a counting number and the letters *st, nd, rd,* or *th.* Here we show some abbreviations:

first 1st	sixth 6th	eleventh 11th
second 2nd	seventh... 7th	twelfth.......... 12th
third 3rd	eighth 8th	thirteenth 13th
fourth 4th	ninth 9th	twentieth...... 20th
fifth 5th	tenth 10th	twenty-first .. 21st

Example 2

Andy is 13th in line. Kwame is 3rd in line. How many students are between Kwame and Andy?

We begin by drawing a diagram.

third   thirteenth

From the diagram we see that there are **nine students** between Kwame and Andy.

Months of the Year

We use ordinal numbers to describe the months of the year and the days of each month. The table below lists the twelve months of the year in order. A common year is 365 days long. A leap year is 366 days long. The extra day in a leap year is added to February every four years.

Month	Order	Days
January	first	31
February	second	28 or 29
March	third	31
April	fourth	30
May	fifth	31
June	sixth	30
July	seventh	31
August	eighth	31
September	ninth	30
October	tenth	31
November	eleventh	30
December	twelfth	31

> **Math Language**
>
> Thirty days have September, April, June, and November. All the rest have 31, except February, which has 28.

When writing dates, we can use numbers to represent the month, day, and year. For example, if Adolfo was born on the twenty-sixth day of February in 1998, then he could write his birth date this way:

2/26/98

The form for this date is **"month/day/year."** The 2 stands for the second month, which is February, and the 26 stands for the twenty-sixth day of the month.

Example 3

J'Nae wrote her birth date as 7/8/99.

  a. In what month was J'Nae born?

  b. In what year was she born?

  a. In the United States, we usually write the number of the month first. The first number J'Nae wrote was 7. She was born in the seventh month, which is **July.**

  b. We often abbreviate years by using only the last two digits of the year. We assume that J'Nae was born in **1999.**

Example 4

Mr. Chitsey's driver's license expired on 4/29/06. Write that date using the name of the month and all four digits of the year.

The fourth month is April, and "06" represents the year 2006. Mr. Chitsey's license expired on **April 29, 2006.**

Lesson Practice

a. Jayne was third in line, and Zahina was eighth in line. How many people were between them? Draw a picture to show the people in the line.

b. Write your birth date in month/day/year form.

c. In month/day/year form, write the date that Independence Day will next be celebrated.

Written Practice *Distributed and Integrated*

*1. **Formulate** At the grocery store there were 5 people in the first line,
(1) 6 people in the second line, and 4 people in the third line. Altogether, how many people were in the three lines? Write a number sentence to find the answer.

Find each missing addend:

2. 2
(2) 6
 + x
 ——
 15

3. 1
(2) y
 + 7
 ——
 14

4. 3
(2) z
 + 5
 ——
 12

5. 1
(2) n
 + 6
 ——
 13

6. 2
(2) 5
 + w
 ——
 10

7. 2
(1) + a
 ——
 7

8. r
(1) + 5
 ——
 11

9. 3
(1) + t
 ——
 5

*10. Tadeo was born on 8/15/93. Write Tadeo's birth date using the name of
(5) the month and all four digits of the year.

Conclude Write the rule and the next three numbers of each counting sequence:

11. 12, 15, 18, ——, ——, ——, ...
(3)

12. 16, 20, 24, _____, _____, _____, ...
(3)

*13. 28, 35, 42, _____, _____, _____, ...
(3)

*14. Find the missing number: 30, _____, 42, 48
(3)

*15. Explain How did you find the missing number in problem **14?**
(3)

*16. Represent Draw a diagram to show $432 in $100 bills, $10 bills,
(4) and $1 bills.

*17. Represent Write a number sentence for the picture below.
(1)

18. The digit 8 is in what place in 845?
(4)

*19. Represent Use three digits to write the number that equals
(4) 2 hundreds plus 3 tens plus 5 ones.

*20. Predict If the pattern is continued, what will be the next circled
(3) number?

1, 2,③, 4, 5,⑥, 7, 8,⑨, 10, …

21. Seven boys each have two pets. How many pets do the boys have?
(3) Count by twos.

22.	**23.**	**24.**	**25.**
(1)	(1)	(1)	(1)
5	5	9	8
8	7	7	7
4	3	6	3
7	8	5	5
4	4	4	4
+ 3	+ 2	+ 2	+ 9

*26. Multiple Choice Jenny was third in line. Jessica was seventh in line.
(5) How many people were between Jenny and Jessica?

    A 3   **B** 4   **C** 5   **D** 6

27. **(Predict)** What is the tenth number in this counting sequence?
(3)

$$2, 4, 6, 8, 10, \ldots$$

*28. How many different arrangements of three letters can you write using
(3) the letters r, s, and t? The different arrangements you write do not need to form words.

*29. **(Connect)** Write a number sentence that has addends of 5 and 4.
(1)

*30. **(Formulate)** Write and solve an addition word problem using the
(1) numbers 1, 9, and 10.

Real-World Connection

During the fourth month of every year, Stone Mountain Park near Atlanta, Georgia, hosts Feria Latina, one of the largest Hispanic cultural events in the state. What is the name of the month in which Feria Latina is held? If Amy and Carlos attend the festival next year on the 21st of the month, how would you write that date in month/date/year form?

• Review of Subtraction

facts	Power Up A
count aloud	Count by threes from 3 to 30.
mental math	**Number Sense:** Nine is one less than ten. When adding 9 to a number, we may mentally add 10 and then think of the number that is one less than the sum. For 23 + 9 we may think, "23 + 10 is 33, and one less than 33 is 32."

a.   33
    + 10
  ———

b.   33
    + 9
  ———

c.   46
    + 10
  ———

d.   46
    + 9
  ———

e.   65
    + 10
  ———

f.   65
    + 9
  ———

problem solving

Choose an appropriate problem-solving strategy to solve this problem. At the arcade, Bao won 8 prize tickets and Sergio won 4 prize tickets. They decide to share the tickets equally. How many tickets should Bao give Sergio so that they have an equal number of prize tickets? How many tickets will each boy have? Explain how you arrived at your answer.

Remember that when we add, we combine two groups into one group.

$$4 + 2 = 6$$

four   plus   two   equals   six

When we **subtract,** we separate one group into two groups. To take away two from six, we subtract.

$$6 \quad - \quad 2 \quad = \quad 4$$

six   minus   two   equals   four

When we subtract one number from another number, the answer is called the **difference.** If we subtract two from six, the difference is four.

$$
\begin{array}{r}
6 \\
-\,2 \\
\hline
4
\end{array} \text{ difference}
$$

Here we write "two subtracted from six" horizontally:

$$6 - 2 = 4$$

We can check a subtraction answer by adding the difference to the number subtracted. This is like doing the problem "in reverse." The sum of the addition should equal the starting number.

Subtract Down		**Add Up**
Six minus two equals four.	$\begin{array}{r} 6 \\ -\,2 \\ \hline 4 \end{array}$	Four plus two equals six.

Subtract
$$6 \quad 2 = 4$$
Add

The order of numbers matters in subtraction. The expression $6 - 2$ means "take two from six." This is not the same as $2 - 6$, which means "take six from two."

(**Discuss**) Since addition and subtraction are opposite operations, we can use addition to check subtraction and use subtraction to check addition. When operations are opposite, one operation undoes the other. How could we use subtraction to check the addition $6 + 8 = 14$?

A **fact family** is a group of three numbers that can be arranged to form four facts. The three numbers 2, 4, and 6 form an addition and subtraction fact family.

$$
\begin{array}{cccc}
\begin{array}{r} 2 \\ +\,4 \\ \hline 6 \end{array} &
\begin{array}{r} 4 \\ +\,2 \\ \hline 6 \end{array} &
\begin{array}{r} 6 \\ -\,2 \\ \hline 4 \end{array} &
\begin{array}{r} 6 \\ -\,4 \\ \hline 2 \end{array}
\end{array}
$$

Recognizing addition and subtraction fact families can help us learn the facts.

Math Language

An **expression** is a number, a letter, or a combination of numbers and letters. Expressions usually contain one or more operation symbols.

3   *a*   4*n*   6 + *t*

An *equation* is a number sentence that states that two expressions are equal. An equation always includes an equal sign.

$$\underbrace{3 + 5}_{} = \underbrace{8}_{}$$

expressions

The numbers 3, 5, and 8 form an addition and subtraction fact family. Write two addition facts and two subtraction facts using these three numbers.

$$\begin{array}{r} 3 \\ + 5 \\ \hline 8 \end{array} \qquad \begin{array}{r} 5 \\ + 3 \\ \hline 8 \end{array} \qquad \begin{array}{r} 8 \\ - 3 \\ \hline 5 \end{array} \qquad \begin{array}{r} 8 \\ - 5 \\ \hline 3 \end{array}$$

(**Connect**) We can write a fact family using three numbers because addition and subtraction are related operations. How would you write a fact family for 9, 9, and 18?

Lesson Practice

Subtract. Then check your answers by adding.

a. $\begin{array}{r} 14 \\ - 8 \\ \hline \end{array}$ **b.** $\begin{array}{r} 9 \\ - 3 \\ \hline \end{array}$ **c.** $\begin{array}{r} 15 \\ - 7 \\ \hline \end{array}$ **d.** $\begin{array}{r} 11 \\ - 4 \\ \hline \end{array}$ **e.** $\begin{array}{r} 12 \\ - 5 \\ \hline \end{array}$

f. (**Connect**) The numbers 5, 6, and 11 form a fact family. Write two addition facts and two subtraction facts using these three numbers.

g. (**Explain**) How can you check a subtraction answer? Give an example.

Written Practice

Distributed and Integrated

*1. (6) $\begin{array}{r} 14 \\ - 5 \\ \hline \end{array}$ ***2.** (6) $\begin{array}{r} 15 \\ - 8 \\ \hline \end{array}$ **3.** (6) $\begin{array}{r} 9 \\ - 4 \\ \hline \end{array}$ **4.** (6) $\begin{array}{r} 11 \\ - 7 \\ \hline \end{array}$

5. (6) $\begin{array}{r} 12 \\ - 8 \\ \hline \end{array}$ **6.** (6) $\begin{array}{r} 11 \\ - 6 \\ \hline \end{array}$ **7.** (6) $\begin{array}{r} 15 \\ - 7 \\ \hline \end{array}$ **8.** (6) $\begin{array}{r} 9 \\ - 6 \\ \hline \end{array}$

9. (6) $\begin{array}{r} 13 \\ - 5 \\ \hline \end{array}$ **10.** (6) $\begin{array}{r} 12 \\ - 6 \\ \hline \end{array}$ **11.** (1) $\begin{array}{r} 8 \\ + n \\ \hline 17 \end{array}$ **12.** (1) $\begin{array}{r} a \\ + 8 \\ \hline 14 \end{array}$

13. (1) $3 + w = 11$ **14.** (2) $1 + 4 + m = 13$

*15. (6) (**Connect**) The numbers 4, 6, and 10 form a fact family. Write two addition facts and two subtraction facts using these three numbers.

Generalize Write the rule and the next three numbers of each counting sequence:

*16. 16, 18, 20, ____, ____, ____, ...
(3)

*17. 21, 28, 35, ____, ____, ____, ...
(3)

*18. 20, 24, 28, ____, ____, ____, ...
(3)

*19. How many days are in the tenth month of the year?
(5)

20. **Represent** Draw a diagram to show $326.
(4)

21. The digit 6 is in what place in 456?
(4)

Find each missing addend:

22. $2 + n + 4 = 13$ **23.** $a + 3 + 5 = 16$
(2)   (2)

*24. What is the name for the answer when we subtract?
(6)

*25. **List** Show six ways to add 3, 4, and 5.
(1)

*26. **Multiple Choice** The ages of the children in Tyrese's family are 7
(1)   and 9. The ages of the children in Mary's family are 3, 5, and 9. Which
        number sentence shows how many children are in both families?

    A $3 + 7 = 10$ **B** $7 + 9 = 16$

    C $2 + 3 = 5$ **D** $3 + 5 + 9 = 17$

27. How many different three-digit numbers can you write using the
(3)   digits 6, 3, and 9? Each digit may be used only once in every number
        you write. List the numbers in counting order.

*28. Write a horizontal number sentence that has a sum of 23.
(1)

*29. Write a horizontal number sentence that has a difference of 9.
(6)

*30. **Formulate** Write and solve an addition word problem using the
(1)   numbers 6, 5, and 11.

LESSON 7

• Writing Numbers Through 999

facts	Power Up A
count aloud	Count by tens from 10 to 200.
mental math	Add one less than ten to a number in **a–c.**

    a. Number Sense: 28 + 9

    b. Number Sense: 44 + 9

    c. Number Sense: 87 + 9

    d. Review: 63 + 20

    e. Review: 46 + 50

    f. Review: 38 + 30

problem solving

Choose an appropriate problem-solving strategy to solve this problem. Steve has 5 pencils. Perry has 3 pencils. Chad has only 1 pencil. How can one boy give one other boy some pencils so that they each have the same number of pencils? Explain your answer.

New Concept

Whole numbers are the counting numbers and the number zero.

0, 1, 2, 3, 4, 5, …

Reading Math

The names of two-digit numbers greater than twenty that do not end in zero are written with a hyphen.

Examples:
twenty-three
fifty-one
eighty-seven

To write the names of whole numbers through 999 (nine hundred ninety-nine), we need to know the following words and how to put them together:

0....zero	10....ten	20....twenty
1....one	11....eleven	30....thirty
2....two	12....twelve	40....forty
3....three	13....thirteen	50....fifty
4....four	14....fourteen	60....sixty
5....five	15....fifteen	70....seventy
6....six	16....sixteen	80....eighty
7....seven	17....seventeen	90....ninety
8....eight	18....eighteen	100....one hundred
9....nine	19....nineteen	

You may refer to this chart when you are asked to write the names of numbers in the problem sets.

Example 1

Use words to write the number 44.

We use a hyphen and write **"forty-four."** Notice that "forty" is spelled without a "u."

To write three-digit numbers, we first write the number of hundreds and then we write the rest of the number. **We do not use the word _and_ when writing whole numbers.**

Example 2

Use words to write the number 313.

First we write the number of hundreds. Then we write the rest of the number to get **three hundred thirteen.** (We do not write "three hundred _and_ thirteen.")

Example 3

Use words to write the number 705.

First we write the number of hundreds. Then we write the rest of the number to get **seven hundred five.**

Example 4

Use digits to write the number six hundred eight.

Six hundred eight means "six hundreds plus eight ones." There are no tens, so we write a zero in the tens place and get **608.**

In Lesson 4 we used $100 bills, $10 bills, and $1 bills to demonstrate place value. Here we show another model for place value. Small squares represent ones. The long, ten-square rectangles represent tens. The large, hundred-square blocks represent hundreds.

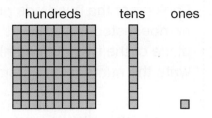

hundreds   tens   ones

Example 5

Use words to write the number shown by this model:

Two hundreds, one ten, and eight ones is 218, which we write as **two hundred eighteen.**

Example 6

Which of these two numbers is greater: 546 or 564?

We compare whole numbers by considering the place value of the digits. Both numbers have the same digits, so the position of the digits determines which number is greater.

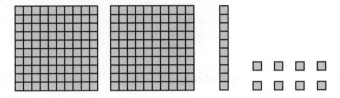

hundreds ⌐   ⌐ tens

5 4 6
5 6 4

Both numbers have 5 hundreds. However, 564 has 6 tens while 546 has only 4 tens. This means **564 is greater,** and 546 is less no matter what digit is in the ones place.

Example 7

Arrange these numbers in order from least to greatest:

36 254 105 90

Arranging whole numbers vertically with last digits aligned also aligns other digits with the same place value.

$$36$$
$$254$$
$$105$$
$$90$$

Looking at the hundreds place, we see that 254 is the greatest number listed and 105 is the next greatest. By comparing the tens place of the two-digit numbers, we see that 36 is less than 90. We write the numbers in order:

36, 90, 105, 254

Lesson Practice

Represent Use words to write each number:

a. 0   **b.** 81

c. 99   **d.** 515

e. 444   **f.** 909

Represent Use digits to write each number:

g. nineteen   **h.** ninety-one

i. five hundred twenty-four

j. eight hundred sixty

k. Use words to write the number shown by this model:

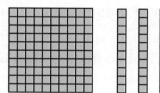

l. **Compare** Which of these two numbers is less: 381 or 359?

m. Write these numbers in order from least to greatest:

154   205   61   180

Written Practice   *Distributed and Integrated*

Formulate Write and solve equations for problems **1** and **2**.

* 1. Anitra has 8 dollars. She needs 6 dollars more to buy the radio. How
 (1) much does the radio cost?

* 2. Peyton poured 8 ounces of water into a pitcher containing 8 ounces of
(1) lemon juice. How many ounces of liquid were in the mixture?

Find the missing addend:

3. $5 + n + 2 = 11$
(2)

4. $2 + 6 + n = 15$
(2)

Subtract. Check by adding.

* 5.   13
(6) $-\ 5$

6.   16
(6) $-\ 8$

7.   13
(6) $-\ 7$

8.   12
(6) $-\ 8$

Represent Use digits to write each number:

* 9. two hundred fourteen
(7)

* 10. five hundred thirty-two
(7)

Represent Use words to write each number:

* 11. 301
(7)

* 12. 320
(7)

* 13. **Represent** Use words to write the number shown by this model:
(7)

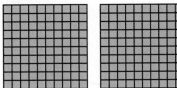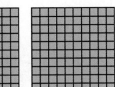

14. **Represent** Write a number sentence for this picture:
(1)

Generalize Write the rule and the next three numbers of each counting sequence:

15. 12, 18, 24, _____, _____, _____, . . .
(3)

* 16. 15, 18, 21, _____, _____, _____, . . .
(3)

Connect Find the missing number in each counting sequence:

* 17. 35, 42, _____, 56, . . .
(3)

* 18. 40, _____, 56, 64, . . .
(3)

19. **Connect** How much money is shown by this picture?
(4)

*20. **Connect** The numbers 7, 8, and 15 form a fact family. Write two
(6) addition facts and two subtraction facts using these three numbers.

*21. **Explain** Brad was twelfth in line. His sister was sixth in line. How
(5) many people were between Brad and his sister? Explain how you can
use the four-step problem-solving process to solve this problem.

22. Which month is five months after October?
(5)

23. Six nickels equals how many cents? Count by fives.
(3)

24. 4 + 7 + 8 + 5 + 4   **25.** 2 + 3 + 5 + 8 + 5
(1)   (1)

26. 5 + 8 + 6 + 4 + 3 + 7 + 2
(1)

*27. **Multiple Choice** Which addition equation is related to 12 − 5 = 7?
(6)
   A 7 + 5 = 12   **B** 12 + 5 = 17
   C 12 + 7 = 19   **D** 12 − 7 = 5

*28. How many different three-digit numbers can you write using the
(3) digits 4, 1, and 6? Each digit may be used only once in every number
you write. List the numbers in order from least to greatest.

*29. Compare 126 and 162. Which number is less?
(7)

*30. The table shows the lengths of three rivers in
(7) North America.

List the rivers in order from longest to shortest.

**The Lengths of Rivers
(in miles)**

River	Length
Alabama	729
Green	730
Kuskokwim	724

• Adding Money

facts	Power Up B
count aloud	Count by fives from 5 to 100.
mental math	Add one less than ten to a number in problems **a–c**.

    a. Number Sense: 56 + 9

    b. Number Sense: 63 + 9

    c. Number Sense: 48 + 9

    d. Review: 74 + 20

    e. Review: 60 + 30

    f. Review: 49 + 40

problem solving

Copy this design of ten circles on a piece of paper. In each circle, write a number from 1 to 10 that continues the pattern of "1, skip, skip, 2, skip, skip, 3, ..."

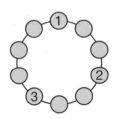

Focus Strategy: Extend a Pattern

(**Understand**) We are asked to copy the design of ten circles and to write a number in each circle. Three circles in the design are already filled with numbers. We are asked to continue the pattern of "1, skip, skip, 2, skip, skip, 3, ..."

(**Plan**) We will draw the design on our paper and *extend the pattern.*

(**Solve**) Copy the design of ten circles on your paper and write "1" in the top circle, as shown. Moving down and to the right (clockwise), skip two circles (skip, skip) and then write "2" in the next circle.

Then skip two more circles and write "3" in the next circle. Then skip two more circles and write "4." Continue skipping two circles and then writing the next counting number. Your completed design should look like the picture at right.

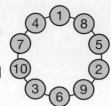

Check We completed the task by extending the pattern of "1, skip, skip, 2, skip, skip, 3, …" in the circle design until we filled all ten circles. We know our answer is reasonable because the pattern is still valid if we start at the end and work forward.

New Concept

Money manipulatives can be used to model or act out the addition of money amounts.

Sakura had $24. Then she was given $15 on her birthday. How much money does Sakura now have?

We can use and to add $15 to $24.

Sakura had $24.

    2   4

She was given $15.

+
    1   5

Now she has …

    3   9

The total is 3 tens and 9 ones, which is $39.

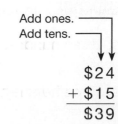

Thinking Skill

Verify

Explain why 3 tens + 9 ones equals 39.

We can also add $24 and $15 with pencil and paper. When we use pencil and paper, we first add the digits in the ones place. Then we add the digits in the tens place. (Remember to include the dollar sign in the answer.)

Add ones. ⌐
Add tens. ⌐

$$
\begin{array}{r}
\$24 \\
+\ \$15 \\
\hline
\$39
\end{array}
$$

Example

Sh'Tania had $32. She earned $7 babysitting. Then how much money did Sh'Tania have?

We add $32 and $7. To add with pencil and paper, we write the numbers so that the digits in the ones place are lined up.

$$\begin{array}{r} \$32 \\ + \$\ 7 \\ \hline \$39 \end{array}$$

After babysitting Sh'Tania had **$39.**

Adding Money Amounts

Materials needed:
- money manipulatives from Lesson 4 (from **Lesson Activities 2, 3,** and **4**)

Use money manipulatives to act out these word problems:

1. Nelson paid $36 to enter the amusement park and spent $22 on food and souvenirs. Altogether, how much money did Nelson spend at the amusement park?

2. The plumber charged $63 for parts and $225 for labor. Altogether, how much did the plumber charge?

Lesson Practice Add:

a. $53 + $6

b. $14 + $75

c. $36 + $42

d. $27 + $51

e. $15 + $21

f. $32 + $6

Written Practice *Distributed and Integrated*

Represent In problems **1** and **2**, use digits to write each number.

*1. three hundred forty-three
(7)

*2. three hundred seven
(7)

*3. Use words to write the number 592.
(7)

Find each missing addend:

4.
(2)
```
  2
  4
+ n
────
 12
```

5.
(2)
```
  1
  r
+ 6
────
 10
```

6.
(2)
```
  1
  t
+ 7
────
 14
```

7.
(2)
```
  2
  6
+ n
────
 13
```

*8.
(8)
```
  $25
+ $14
```

9.
(8)
```
  $85
+ $14
```

10.
(8)
```
  $22
+ $ 6
```

*11.
(8)
```
  $40
+ $38
```

*12.
(6)
```
 13
- 9
```

13.
(6)
```
 17
- 5
```

14.
(6)
```
 17
- 8
```

15.
(6)
```
 14
- 6
```

*16. (**Formulate**) D'Jeran has $23. Beckie has $42. Together, D'Jeran and
(1, 8) Beckie have how much money? Write an equation to solve this problem.

*17. (**Represent**) Use words to write the number shown by this model:
(7)

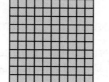

*18. Salma was born on the fifth day of August in 1994. Write her birth date
(5) in month/day/year form.

(**Generalize**) Write the rule and the next three numbers of each counting
sequence:

*19. 12, 15, 18, ____, ____, ____, ...
(3)

*20. 28, 35, 42, ____, ____, ____, ...
(3)

21.
(1)
```
  5
  8
  7
  6
  4
+ 3
```

22.
(1)
```
  9
  7
  6
  4
  8
+ 7
```

23.
(1)
```
  2
  5
  7
  3
  5
+ 4
```

*24. **List** Show six ways to add 5, 6, and 7.
(1)

*25. **Connect** Write two addition facts and two subtraction facts using 7,
(6)   8, and 15.

*26. Multiple Choice If 7 + ◆ = 15, then which of the following is *not*
(6)   true?

    A ◆ − 7 = 15   **B** 15 − 7 = ◆

    C 15 − ◆ = 7   **D** ◆ + 7 = 15

*27. How many different three-digit numbers can you write using the digits
(3, 7)   7, 6, and 5? Each digit may be used only once in every number you
    write. List the numbers in order from least to greatest.

28. Compare 630 and 603. Which is greater?
(7)

*29. The table shows the number of skyscrapers
(7)   in three cities.

    Write the names of the cities in order from
    the least number of skyscrapers to the
    greatest number of skyscrapers.

Skyscrapers

City	Number
Boston	16
Hong Kong	30
Singapore	14

*30. ✏️ **Formulate** Write and solve an addition word problem that has a
(1)   sum of 16.

Real-World Connection

Mel works at the Cumberland Island National Seashore. He began the day with $13 in the cash register. A family of four visiting the seashore gives Mel $4 each for their entrance fees. What is the total amount Mel collects from the family? How much money is in the cash register now?

• Adding with Regrouping

Power Up

facts	Power Up B
count aloud	Count by threes from 3 to 30.
mental math	**Number Sense:** Nineteen is one less than 20. When adding 19 to a number, we may mentally add 20 and then think of the number that is one less than the sum.

a. $\begin{array}{r} 36 \\ + 20 \\ \hline \end{array}$	**b.** $\begin{array}{r} 36 \\ + 19 \\ \hline \end{array}$	**c.** $\begin{array}{r} 47 \\ + 20 \\ \hline \end{array}$
d. $\begin{array}{r} 47 \\ + 19 \\ \hline \end{array}$	**e.** $\begin{array}{r} 24 \\ + 20 \\ \hline \end{array}$	**f.** $\begin{array}{r} 24 \\ + 19 \\ \hline \end{array}$

problem solving

Twenty students are going on a field trip. Each car can hold 4 students. How many cars are needed for all the students?

Focus Strategy: Draw a Picture

(**Understand**) We are told that 20 students are going on a field trip. We are also told that each car can hold 4 students. We are asked to find the number of students each car can hold.

(**Plan**) We could act out this problem, but we can find the answer more quickly if we *draw a picture.* We could draw dots or other symbols to stand for the 20 students and then circle groups of 4 students.

(**Solve**) We draw 20 dots on our paper to show 20 students. Then we circle groups of 4 dots. Each circle with 4 dots inside it stands for one car.

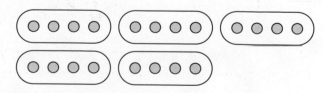

We drew 5 circles, which means that **5 cars** are needed for the field trip. Remember, each dot stands for one student, and each circle stands for one car.

(Check) We know our answer is reasonable because drawing a picture helped us to see how the students divide evenly into 5 equal groups of 4 students each.

We might wonder how many cars would be needed for a different number of students, such as 18. For 18 students, we can erase two dots in the picture, but we see that five cars (represented by the circles) are still needed to carry all 18 students.

New Concept

When we add, we sometimes have to regroup because we cannot have a number larger than 9 as the sum of any place value.

Example 1

Karyn had $39. She earned $14 more by raking leaves. How much money does Karyn have altogether?

(Model) We may use $10 bills and $1 bills to add $14 to $39.

Karyn had $39.

3

9

She earned $14.   +

1

4

Altogether she has . . .

4

13

Thinking Skill

(Verify)

Why is 4 tens + 13 ones equal to 5 tens + 3 ones?

Since there are more than ten $1 bills in the right-hand column, we exchange ten of the $1 bills for one $10 bill.

5

3

Now we have 5 tens and 3 ones, which equals **$53.**

Thinking Skill

Discuss

How do we know when to regroup?

We use a similar method when we add numbers with pencil and paper. To add 14 to 39, we add the digits in the ones place and get 13.

Add ones.

$$
\begin{array}{r}
3\,9 \\
+\ 1\,4 \\
\hline
\textcircled{13}
\end{array}
$$

← 1 ten and 3 ones

Thirteen ones is the same as 1 ten and 3 ones. We write the 3 in the ones place and add the 1 ten to the other tens. We show this by writing a 1 either above the column of tens or below it. Then we add the tens.

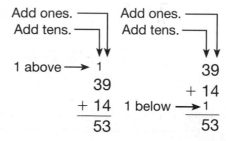

Add ones. — Add tens. —

1 above →

$$
\begin{array}{r}
1 \\
39 \\
+\ 14 \\
\hline
53
\end{array}
$$

Add ones. — Add tens. —

$$
\begin{array}{r}
39 \\
+\ 14 \\
\hline
1 \\
53
\end{array}
$$

1 below →

Example 2

One of the largest carrots ever grown weighed 18 pounds. One of the largest zucchinis ever grown weighed 64 pounds. Together, how many pounds did those two vegetables weigh?

We combine the weights of the two vegetables by adding:

$$
\begin{array}{r}
1 \\
18 \\
+\ 64 \\
\hline
82
\end{array}
$$

Together the vegetables weighed **82 pounds.**

Lesson Practice

Model Demonstrate each problem using money manipulatives. Then add using pencil and paper.

a. $\begin{array}{r} \$36 \\ +\ \$29 \\ \hline \end{array}$ b. $\begin{array}{r} \$47 \\ +\ \$\ 8 \\ \hline \end{array}$ c. $\begin{array}{r} \$57 \\ +\ \$13 \\ \hline \end{array}$

Use pencil and paper to add:

d. $68 + 24$ e. $\$59 + \$8$ f. $46 + 25$

Represent In problems **1** and **2**, use digits to write each number:

*1. six hundred thirteen
(7)

*2. nine hundred one
(7)

3. Use words to write 941.
(7)

Find each missing addend for problems **4–7.**

4.
(2)
```
  2
  4
+ f
───
 11
```

5.
(2)
```
  5
  g
+ 2
───
 13
```

6.
(2)
```
  h
  4
+ 7
───
 15
```

7.
(2)
```
  2
  7
+ n
───
 16
```

*8.
(9)
```
 33
+ 8
```

*9.
(9)
```
 $47
+ $18
```

*10.
(9)
```
 27
+ 69
```

*11.
(9)
```
 $49
+ $25
```

*12.
(6)
```
 17
− 8
```

13.
(6)
```
 12
− 6
```

14.
(6)
```
  9
− 7
```

15.
(6)
```
 13
− 6
```

16. What is the name for the answer when we add?
(1)

17. What is the name for the answer when we subtract?
(6)

*18. Which month is two months after the twelfth month?
(5)

Generalize Write the rule and the next three numbers of each counting sequence:

*19. 30, 36, 42, ____, ____, ____, …
(3)

*20. 28, 35, 42, ____, ____, ____, …
(3)

21. Which digit is in the hundreds place in 843?
(4)

22. 28 + 6
(9)

*23. $47 + $28
(9)

24. 35 + 27
(9)

* 25. (Formulate) Mio bought pants for $28 and a shirt for $17. Altogether,
(1, 9) how much did the pants and shirt cost? Write an equation for this
problem.

* 26. Multiple Choice What number is shown by this
(7) model?

    A 31   **B** 13

    C 103   **D** 130

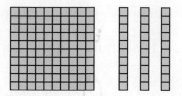

* 27. How many different arrangements of three letters can you write
(3) using the letters l, m, and n? Each letter may be used only once,
and the different arrangements you write do not need to form
words.

28. Compare 89 and 98. Which is less?
(7)

* 29. The table shows the maximum speed that some
(7) animals can run for a short distance.

Write the names of the animals in order from the
fastest to the slowest.

Speeds of Animals

Animal	Speed (miles per hour)
White-tailed deer	30
Mule deer	35
Reindeer	32

* 30. (Formulate) Write and solve an addition word problem that has
(1) a sum of 7.

Early Finishers

Real-World Connection

Terri's basketball team has played four games this season. In the first
game, the team scored 26 points. If the team scored 14 points in the first
half, how many points did the team score in the second half?

In the first four games of the season, Terri's team scored 26, 34, 35,
and 29 points. What is the total number of points the team has scored
this season?

LESSON
10

• Even and Odd Numbers

Power Up

multiples	Power Up K
	A hundred number chart lists the whole numbers from 1 to 100. On your hundred number chart, shade the numbers we say when we count by 2s. What do we call these numbers? What are the last digits of these numbers?
count aloud	Count by fours from 4 to 40.

mental math

a. **Number Sense:** 28 + 9

b. **Number Sense:** 36 + 19

c. **Number Sense:** 43 + 9

d. **Number Sense:** 25 + 19

e. **Number Sense:** 56 + 9

f. **Number Sense:** 45 + 19

problem solving

Choose an appropriate problem-solving strategy to solve this problem. In his backyard garden, Randall planted three rows of carrots. He planted eight carrots in each row. Altogether, how many carrots did Randall plant? Explain how you arrived at your answer.

New Concept

The numbers we say when we start with 2 and then count up by twos are **even numbers.** Notice that every even number ends in either 2, 4, 6, 8, or 0.

2, 4, 6, 8, 10, 12, 14, 16, 18, 20, 22, 24, 26, ...

The list of even numbers goes on and on. We do not begin with zero when we count by twos. However, the number 0 is an even number.

Example 1

Thinking Skill

Generalize

Think about any two even numbers. Will the sum of two even numbers always be an even number, or will the sum of two even numbers always be an odd number? Use examples to support your answer.

Which one of these numbers is an even number?

463   285   456

We can tell whether a number is even by looking at the last digit. **A number is an even number if the last digit is even.** The last digits of these numbers are 3, 5, and 6. Of these, the only even digit is 6, so the even number is **456.**

If a whole number is not an even number, then it is an **odd number.** We can make a list of odd numbers by beginning with the number 1. Then we add two to get the next odd number, add two more to get the next odd number, and so on. The sequence of odd numbers is

1, 3, 5, 7, 9, 11, 13, 15, 17, 19, 21, 23, 25, …

Example 2

Use the digits 2, 7, and 6 to write a three-digit odd number greater than 500. Use each digit only once.

Since 2 and 6 are even, the number must end in 7. To be greater than 500, the first digit must be 6. The answer is **627.**

Example 3

Model **How many different three-digit numbers can you write using the digits 0, 1, and 2? Each digit may be used only once, and the digit 0 may not be used in the hundreds place. List the numbers from least to greatest, and label the numbers you write as even or odd.**

We list the numbers and identify each number as even or odd. **Four** numbers are possible:

102 even

120 even

201 odd

210 even

Thinking Skill

Generalize

Will the sum of any two odd numbers be an odd number or an even number? Explain how you know.

An even number of objects can be separated into two equal groups. Six is an even number. Here we show six dots separated into two equal groups:

If we try to separate an odd number of objects into two equal groups, there will be one extra object. Five is an odd number. One dot is left over because five dots will not separate into two equal groups.

• ← one dot left over

Example 4

The same number of boys and girls were in the classroom. Which of the following numbers could be the total number of students in the classroom?

$$25 \quad 26 \quad 27$$

An even number of students can be divided into two equal groups. Since there are an equal number of boys and girls, there must be an even number of students in the classroom. The only even number listed is **26.**

Lesson Practice

(**Classify**) Write "even" or "odd" for each number:

a. 563   **b.** 328   **c.** 99   **d.** 0

e. Use the digits 3, 4, and 6 to write an even number greater than 500. Use each digit only once.

f. (**Explain**) How can you tell whether a number is even?

g. How many different three-digit numbers can you write using the digits 4, 0, and 5? Each digit may be used only once, and the digit 0 may not be used in the hundreds place. List the numbers in order and label each number as even or odd.

Written Practice

Distributed and Integrated

(**Represent**) In problems **1** and **2,** use digits to write each number.

* 1. five hundred forty-two
(7)

* 2. six hundred nineteen
(7)

* 3. The numbers 4, 7, and 11 form a fact family. Write two addition facts and
(6) two subtraction facts using those three numbers.

Represent In problems **4** and **5,** use words to write each number.

*4. 903
(7)

*5. 746
(7)

*6. Which three-digit odd number greater than 600 has the digits
(10) 4, 6, and 7?

Find each missing addend in problems **7–10.**

7.   4
(2)   *n*
     + 3
    ——
     14

8.   *p*
(2)   4
     + 2
    ——
     13

9.   5
(2)   *q*
     + 7
    ——
     14

10.   *r*
(2)   3
     + 2
    ——
     11

11.   15
(6)   – 7
    ——

12.   14
(6)   – 7
    ——

13.   17
(6)   – 8
    ——

14.   11
(6)   – 6
    ——

*15. $25
(9)   + $38
    ——

16. $19
(9)   + $34
    ——

*17.   42
(9)   + 8
    ——

18.   17
(9)   + 49
    ——

*19. **Generalize** Write the rule and the next three numbers of this counting sequence:
(3)

18, 21, 24, ——, ——, ——, …

*20. **Predict** What is the eighth number in this counting sequence?
(3, 5)

6, 12, 18, 24, …

*21. **Formulate** If Jabari has $6 in a piggy bank, $12 in his wallet, and $20
(1, 8) in his drawer, how much money does Jabari have in all three places?
Write an equation for this problem.

22. 2 + 3 + 5 + 7 + 8 + 4 + 5
(1)

*23. Write today's date in month/day/year form.
(5)

*24. **Represent** Use words to write the number shown by this model:
(7)

58   *Saxon Math* Intermediate 4

* 25. What number is the largest two-digit even number?
(10)

* 26. **Multiple Choice** If $\triangle + 4 = 12$, then which of these is *not* true?
(6)

    A $4 + \triangle = 12$ **B** $12 - \triangle = 4$

    C $12 + 4 = \triangle$ **D** $12 - 4 = \triangle$

* 27. List in order from least to greatest all the three-digit numbers you can
(10) write using the digits 8, 3, and 0 in each number. The digit 0 may not be
used in the hundreds place.

* 28. Write "odd" or "even" for each number:
(10)

    a. 73   **b.** 54   **c.** 330   **d.** 209

* 29. (**Connect**) Write a horizontal subtraction number sentence.
(6)

* 30. (**Formulate**) Write and solve an addition word problem. Then explain
(1) why your answer is reasonable.

Early Finishers

Real-World Connection

Janine noticed that the top lockers at school were odd numbers and the bottom locker numbers were even. Below is a list of the first five numbers on the bottom lockers:

    300   302   304   306   308

    a. Are these numbers even or odd? How do you know?

    b. If this pattern continues, what will the next bottom locker number be?

Focus on

• Number Lines

When we "draw a line" with a pencil, we are actually drawing a **line segment.** A line segment is part of a line.

```
_____
```

Line segment

A **line** continues in opposite directions without end. To illustrate a line, we draw an arrowhead at each end of a line segment. The arrowheads show that the line continues.

Line

To make a **number line,** we begin by drawing a line. Next, we put **tick marks** on the line, keeping an equal distance between the marks.

Then we label the marks with numbers. On some number lines every mark is labeled. On other number lines only some of the marks are labeled. The labels on a number line tell us how far the marks are from zero.

Example 1

To what number is the arrow pointing?

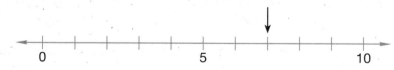

If we count by ones from zero, we see that our count matches the numbers labeled on the number line. We know that the distance from one tick mark to the next is 1.

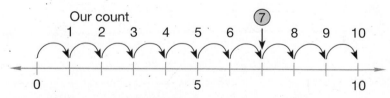

We find that the arrow points to the number **7.**

On some number lines the distance from one tick mark to the next is not 1. We may need to count by twos, by fives, by tens, or by some other number to find the distance between tick marks.

Example 2

To what number is the arrow pointing?

If we count by ones from tick mark to tick mark, our count does not match the numbers labeled on the number line. We try counting by twos and find that our count does match the number line. The distance from one tick mark to the next tick mark on this number line is 2. The arrow points to a mark that is one mark to the right of 4 and one mark to the left of 8. The number that is two more than 4 and two less than 8 is **6.**

Example 3

To what number is the arrow pointing?

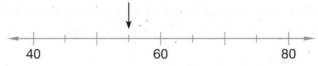

Zero is not shown on this number line, so we will start our count at 40. Counting by ones does not fit the pattern. Neither does counting by twos. Counting by fives does fit the pattern.

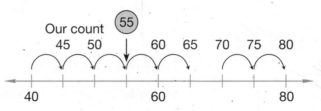

We find that the arrow points to the number **55.**

To what number is each arrow pointing in problems **1** and **2**?

1.

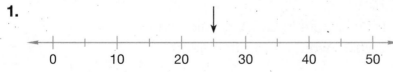

2.

Drawing Number Lines

a. Carefully copy the two number lines below onto your paper. Then write the number represented by each tick mark below the tick marks on your paper.

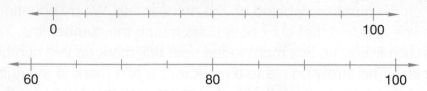

b. Draw a number line from 0 to 10 labeling 0 and 10. Then draw tick marks for 2, 4, 6, and 8, but do not label the tick marks.

Numbers greater than zero are called **positive numbers.** A number line may also show numbers less than zero. Numbers less than zero are called **negative numbers.** Zero is neither positive nor negative. To write a negative number using digits, we place a negative sign (minus sign) to the left of the digit.

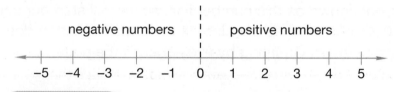

Example 4

a. Use words to write −10.

b. Use digits to write negative twelve.

a. negative ten

b. −12

We use negative numbers to describe very cold temperatures. For example, on a cold winter day, the temperature in Lansing, Michigan, might be "five degrees below zero", which would be written as −5 degrees.

Negative numbers are also used in other ways. One way is to show a debt. For example, if Tom has $3 and needs to pay Richard $5, he can pay Richard $3, but Tom will still owe Richard $2. We can write −$2 to describe how much debt Tom has.

Example 5

At noon the temperature was 4 degrees. By nightfall the temperature had decreased 7 degrees. What was the temperature at nightfall?

We can use a number line to solve this problem. We start at 4 and count down 7.

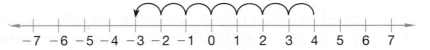

The temperature at nightfall was **−3 degrees.**

Example 6

Write the next four numbers in each counting sequence:

    a. ..., 10, 8, 6, 4, ____, ____, ____, ____, ...

    b. ..., 9, 7, 5, 3, ____, ____, ____, ____, ...

Even and odd numbers may be negative or positive.

    a. This is a sequence of even numbers. We count down by twos and write the next four even numbers. Notice that zero is even.

        ..., 10, 8, 6, 4, __**2**__, __**0**__, __**−2**__, __**−4**__, ...

    b. This is a sequence of odd numbers. We count down by twos and write the next four odd numbers.

        ..., 9, 7, 5, 3, __**1**__, __**−1**__, __**−3**__, __**−5**__, ...

Example 7

To what number is the arrow pointing?

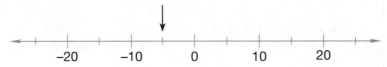

Counting by fives fits the pattern. The arrow points to a number that is five less than zero, which is **−5.**

3. **Represent** At 3 p.m. the temperature was 2 degrees. At 5 p.m. the temperature was 6 degrees colder. What was the temperature at 5 p.m.?

4. **Represent** Amy had $2, but she needed to pay Molly $5. Amy paid Molly $2 and owes her the rest. What negative number describes how much debt Amy has?

5. Write the number that is fifteen less than zero

    a. using digits.

    b. using words.

6. **Conclude** Write the next four numbers in this counting sequence:

$$\ldots, 20, 15, 10, 5, \rule{1cm}{0.4pt}, \rule{1cm}{0.4pt}, \rule{1cm}{0.4pt}, \rule{1cm}{0.4pt}, \ldots$$

To what number is each arrow pointing in problems **7** and **8**?

7.

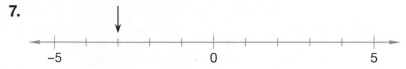

8.

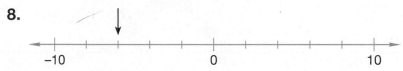

A number line can help us **compare** two numbers. When we compare two numbers, we decide whether one of the numbers is **greater than, equal to,** or **less than** the other number.

To show the comparison for two numbers that are not equal, we may use the greater than/less than symbols:

$$> \qquad <$$

The comparison symbol points to the smaller number. We read from left to right. If the pointed end comes first, we say "is less than."

$$3 < 4 \qquad \text{"Three is less than four."}$$

If the open end comes first, we say "is greater than."

$$4 > 3 \qquad \text{"Four is greater than three."}$$

A number line is usually drawn so that the numbers become greater as we move to the right. When comparing two numbers, we might think about their positions on the number line. To compare 2 and −3, for example, we see that 2 is to the right of −3. This means that 2 is greater than −3.

$$2 > -3$$

Generalize As we move to the right on a number line, the numbers become greater in value. What related statement can we say about moving to the left on a number line?

Example 8

Compare: 2 ◯ −2

The numbers 2 and −2 are not equal. On a number line we see that 2 is greater than −2.

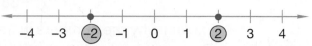

We replace the circle with the proper comparison symbol:

2 > −2

Connect Is −2 greater than zero or less than zero? Explain why.

Example 9

a. Use words to write the comparison 5 > −10.

b. Use digits and a comparison sign to write "negative three is less than negative two."

a. Five is greater than negative ten.

b. −3 < −2

Compare:

9. −3 ◯ 1

10. 3 ◯ 2

11. 2 + 3 ◯ 3 + 2

12. −4 ◯ −5

13. **Represent** Use words to write the comparison −1 < 0.

14. **Represent** Use digits and a comparison symbol to write "negative two is greater than negative three."

Example 10

Arrange these numbers in order from least to greatest:

2, −1, 0

Numbers appear on a number line in order, so using a number line can help us write numbers in order.

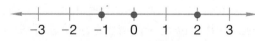

We see the numbers arranged from least to greatest are **−1, 0, 2.**

Arrange the numbers from least to greatest:

15. 0, −2, −3

16. 10, −1, 0

Investigate Further

One common attribute was used to group the following numbers:

245   27   −61   149

These numbers do not belong in the group:

44   − 38   720   150

Explain why the numbers were sorted into these two groups. Then write a negative number that belongs in the first group, and explain why your number belongs.

• Addition Word Problems with Missing Addends

facts	Power Up A
count aloud	Count by twos from 2 to 50 and then back down to 2.
mental math	**Number Sense:** Add a number ending in 0 or 9 to another number.

a.	28 + 30	**b.**	28 + 29	**c.**	37 + 50
d.	37 + 49	**e.**	56 + 40	**f.**	56 + 39

problem solving

Choose an appropriate problem-solving strategy to solve this problem. Copy this design of ten circles on your paper, following the same pattern as described in Lesson 8. Then, outside each circle, write the sum of the numbers in that circle and the two circles on either side. For example, the number outside of circle 1 should be 13.

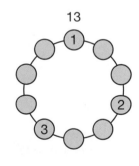

New Concept

In the "some and some more" problems we have solved so far, both the "some" number and the "some more" number were given in the problem. We added the numbers to find the total.

In this lesson we will practice solving word problems in which the total is given and an addend is missing. We can solve these problems just like arithmetic problems that have a missing addend—we subtract to find the missing number.

Example 1

Walter had 8 marbles. Then Lamont gave him some more marbles. Walter has 17 marbles now. How many marbles did Lamont give him?

If we can recognize the plot, we can write a number sentence to solve the problem. Walter had some marbles. Then he received some more marbles. This problem has a "some and some more" plot so it can be represented with an addition formula. We know the "some" number. We know the total number. We put these numbers into the formula.

Math Symbols

We can use *M* or *m* to represent the missing addend.

Formula: Some + Some more = Total

Problem: 8 marbles + *m* marbles = 17 marbles

We see that one of the addends is missing. One way to find the missing number is to ask an addition question.

"Eight plus what number equals seventeen?"

$$8 + m = 17$$

Since $8 + 9 = 17$, we know that Lamont gave Walter **9 marbles.**

One way to check the answer is to see if it correctly completes the problem.

Walter had 8 marbles. Then Lamont gave him 9 marbles. Walter now has 17 marbles.

Example 2

Jamie picked some apples. Then she picked 5 more apples. Now Jamie has 12 apples. How many apples did Jamie pick at first?

This is a "some and some more" word problem. We fill in the formula.

$$
\begin{array}{ll}
\text{Some} & n \text{ apples} \\
+ \text{ Some more} & + 5 \text{ apples} \\
\hline
\text{Total} & 12 \text{ apples}
\end{array}
$$

We can find the missing number by asking an addition question or by asking a subtraction question.

"Five added to what number equals twelve?"

"Twelve minus five equals what number?"

Seven is the answer to both questions. First Jamie picked **7 apples.**

Some addition problems are about parts adding up to a whole.

Formula: Some + Some more = Total

Formula: Part + Part = Whole

The problem in Example 3 is about a whole class divided into two parts.

Example 3

> There are 24 students in the whole class. If there are 14 boys in the class, how many girls are there?
>
> One part of the class is boys and the other part is girls.
>
> **Formula:** Part + Part = Whole
>
> **Problem:** 14 boys + girls = 24 students
>
> We can write the number sentence $14 + g = 24$.
>
> Since $14 + 10 = 24$, we know that there are **10 girls** in the class.
>
> **Justify** Is the answer reasonable? How do you know?

Reading Math

We translate the problem using an addition formula.

One part: 14 boys
Other part: girls
Whole class: 24 students

Lesson Practice

Formulate Write and solve equations for problems **a–c.**

a. Lucille had 4 marigolds. Lola gave her some more marigolds. Now Lucille has 12 marigolds. How many marigolds did Lola give Lucille?

b. Twelve of the 25 students in the class were girls. How many boys were in the class?

c. At 7:00 a.m. the air was cool, but by noon the temperature had increased 25 degrees to 68°F. What was the temperature at 7:00 a.m.?

Written Practice *Distributed and Integrated*

Formulate Write and solve equations for problems **1** and **2.**

* **1.** If a winter day has 10 hours of daylight, then the day has how
(1)   many hours of darkness? (*Hint:* A whole day has 24 hours.)

*2. Tamira read 6 pages before lunch. After lunch she read some more.
(11) If Tamira read 13 pages in all, how many pages did she read after lunch?

3. (**Represent**) Use digits to write the number six hundred forty-two.
(7)

*4. (**Represent**) Use digits and symbols to write this comparison:
(Inv. 1) "Negative twelve is less than zero."

*5. Compare: −2 ◯ 2
(Inv. 1)

*6. Use the digits 5, 6, and 7 to write an even number between 560 and
(10) 650.

*7. (**Represent**) To what number is each arrow pointing?
(Inv. 1)

a.

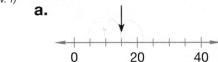

b.

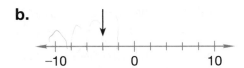

*8. (**Analyze**) The books were put into two stacks so that an equal
(10) number of books was in each stack. Was the total number of
books an odd number or an even number? Explain your thinking.

9. 5
(2) *b*
+ 7
─────
18

10. *n*
(2) 5
+ 3
─────
15

11. 7
(2) *a*
+ 4
─────
12

12. *m*
(2) 2
+ 8
─────
14

13. 12
(6) − 3
─────

14. 14
(6) − 7
─────

15. 12
(6) − 8
─────

16. 13
(6) − 6
─────

*17. 74
(9) + 18
─────

*18. 93
(9) + 39
─────

19. 28
(9) + 45
─────

20. 28
(9) + 47
─────

Conclude Write the next three numbers in each counting sequence:

*21. ..., 12, 9, 6, ____, ____, ____, ...
(Inv. 3)

22. ..., 30, 36, 42, ____, ____, ____, ...
(3)

*23. **Connect** The numbers 5, 9, and 14 form a fact family. Write two
(6) addition facts and two subtraction facts using these three numbers.

24. 4 + 3 + 5 + 8 + 7 + 6 + 2
(1)

25. **List** Show six ways to add 7, 8, and 9.
(1)

*26. **Multiple Choice** If 3 + ▲ = 7 and if ■ = 5, then ▲ + ■ equals which
(1) of the following?

    A 4   **B** 5   **C** 8   **D** 9

*27. How many different odd three-digit numbers can you write using the
(10) digits 5, 0, and 9? Each digit may be used only once, and the digit 0
may not be used in the hundreds place.

*28. Compare. Write >, <, or =.
(Inv. 1)
    a. 89 ◯ 94   **b.** 409 ◯ 177   **c.** 61 ◯ 26

*29. The land areas of three counties are
(7) shown in the table.

Write the names of the counties in
order from smallest area to largest area.

Land Area by County

County	State	Area (sq mi)
Cass	Iowa	564
Hood River	Oregon	522
Weber	Utah	576

*30. **Formulate** Write and solve an addition word problem. Then explain
(1) why your answer is reasonable.

• Missing Numbers in Subtraction

facts   Power Up A

**mental
math**   Add a number ending in 9 to another number in **a–f.**

  a. Number Sense: 52 + 29

  b. Number Sense: 63 + 9

  c. Number Sense: 14 + 39

  d. Number Sense: 26 + 49

  e. Number Sense: 57 + 19

  f. Number Sense: 32 + 59

  g. Money: $12 + $10

  h. Money: $12 + $9

**problem
solving**   Choose an appropriate problem-solving strategy
to solve this problem. Make a design of numbered
circles like those in Lessons 10 and 11, but use
seven circles instead of ten. Use the pattern
"1, skip, skip, 2, skip, skip, 3, ..." to number
the circles, starting with the circle at top. Outside each circle,
write the sum of the number in the circle and the two circles
on either side. Describe the pattern to a classmate or write a
description of the pattern.

New Concept

Since Lesson 1 we have practiced finding missing numbers in
addition problems. In this lesson we will practice finding missing
numbers in subtraction problems.

Thinking Skill

Discuss

Why can we add to find a missing number in a subtraction problem?

Remember that we "subtract down" to find the bottom number and "add up" to find the top number.

Subtract Down		**Add Up**
Nine minus six equals three.	$\begin{array}{r} 9 \\ -\ 6 \\ \hline 3 \end{array}$	Three plus six equals nine.

We may use either "subtracting down" or "adding up" to find the missing number in a subtraction problem.

Example 1

Find the missing number: $\begin{array}{r} 14 \\ -\ n \\ \hline 6 \end{array}$

We may either "subtract down" or "add up." Which way seems easier?

Subtract Down		**Add Up**
Fourteen minus what number equals six?	$\begin{array}{r} 14 \\ -\ n \\ \hline 6 \end{array}$	Six plus what number equals fourteen?

Often it is easier to find a missing number in a subtraction problem by "adding up." If we add 8 to 6 we get 14, so the missing number is **8.** We can check our answer by replacing n with 8 in the original problem.

$$\begin{array}{r} 14 \\ -\ 8 \\ \hline 6 \end{array} \quad \text{check}$$

Since $14 - 8 = 6$, we know our answer is correct.

Example 2

Find the missing number: $\begin{array}{r} b \\ -\ 5 \\ \hline 7 \end{array}$

Try both "subtracting down" and "adding up."

Subtract Down		**Add Up**
What number minus five equals seven?	$\begin{array}{r} b \\ -\ 5 \\ \hline 7 \end{array}$	Seven plus five equals what number?

Since 7 plus 5 is 12, the missing number must be **12.** We replace b with 12 in the original problem to check our answer.

$$\begin{array}{r} 12 \\ -\ 5 \\ \hline 7 \end{array} \quad \text{check}$$

Lesson Practice   Find each missing number. Check your answers.

a. $\begin{array}{r} 14 \\ -\ n \\ \hline 6 \end{array}$ b. $\begin{array}{r} n \\ -\ 5 \\ \hline 2 \end{array}$ c. $\begin{array}{r} 9 \\ -\ n \\ \hline 2 \end{array}$ d. $\begin{array}{r} n \\ -\ 7 \\ \hline 5 \end{array}$

Written Practice   *Distributed and Integrated*

Formulate   Write and solve equations for problems **1–3.**

*1. Laura found nine acorns in the park. Then she found some more acorns
(11)   in her backyard. If Laura found seventeen acorns in all, how many
acorns did she find in the backyard?

*2. Caterpillars change into butterflies every day at the butterfly center.
(1, 9)   In one week 35 caterpillars changed into butterflies. The next week
27 more caterpillars changed into butterflies. Altogether, how many
caterpillars changed to butterflies?

*3. Demetrius used a 12-inch ruler to stir the paint in the can. When he
(11)   removed the ruler, 5 inches of it were not coated with paint. How many
inches of the ruler were coated with paint?

*4. **Represent**   Use words and digits to write the number
(7)   shown by this model:

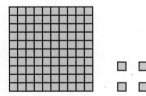

5. Nathan's little sister was born on the seventh day of June in 2002. Write
(5)   her birth date in month/day/year form.

*6. Write a three-digit odd number less than 500 using the digits 9, 4, and
(4)   6. Which digit is in the tens place?

*7. **Connect**   To what number is the arrow pointing?
(Inv. 1)

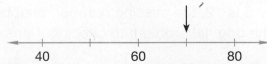

8. (2)
$$\begin{array}{r} 5 \\ n \\ +\ 6 \\ \hline 15 \end{array}$$

9. (2)
$$\begin{array}{r} a \\ 2 \\ +\ 5 \\ \hline 15 \end{array}$$

10. (2)
$$\begin{array}{r} 7 \\ 2 \\ +\ n \\ \hline 15 \end{array}$$

11. (2)
$$\begin{array}{r} 4 \\ a \\ +\ 2 \\ \hline 15 \end{array}$$

*12. (12)
$$\begin{array}{r} n \\ -\ 6 \\ \hline 8 \end{array}$$

13. (6)
$$\begin{array}{r} 16 \\ -\ 8 \\ \hline \end{array}$$

14. (6)
$$\begin{array}{r} 14 \\ -\ 7 \\ \hline \end{array}$$

*15. (12)
$$\begin{array}{r} 12 \\ -\ a \\ \hline 7 \end{array}$$

*16. (12)
$$\begin{array}{r} b \\ -\ 6 \\ \hline 6 \end{array}$$

*17. (12)
$$\begin{array}{r} 13 \\ -\ c \\ \hline 8 \end{array}$$

*18. (9)
$$\begin{array}{r} \$48 \\ +\ \$16 \\ \hline \end{array}$$

19. (9)
$$\begin{array}{r} \$37 \\ +\ \$14 \\ \hline \end{array}$$

(**Conclude**) Write the next three numbers in each counting sequence:

*20. (3) ..., 28, 35, 42, ____, ____, ____, ...

*21. (3) ..., 18, 21, 24, ____, ____, ____, ...

22. (3) How many cents is nine nickels? Count by fives.

*23. (Inv. 1) (**Explain**) Write the following comparison using words and explain why the comparison is correct.

$$-3 > -5$$

*24. (Inv. 1) Arrange these numbers from least to greatest: 0, −2, 4

25. (1) 7 + 3 + 8 + 5 + 4 + 3 + 2

*26. (6) **Multiple Choice** "Five subtracted from n" can be written as which of the following?

   A $5 - n$ **B** $n - 5$ **C** $5 + n$ **D** $n + 5$

*27. (10) How many different three-digit numbers can you write using the digits 4, 2, and 0? Each digit may be used only once, and the digit 0 may not be used in the hundreds place.

*28. (Inv. 1) Compare. Write >, <, or =.

   a. 310 ◯ 295   **b.** 56 ◯ 63   **c.** 104 ◯ 89

29. The table shows the typical weight of three animals.
(7)

Write the names of the animals in order from greatest weight to the least weight.

Typical Weight of Animals

Animal	Weight (pounds)
Fox	14
Badger	17
Otter	13

30. **Formulate** Write and solve an addition word problem. Then explain
(1) why your answer is reasonable.

Early Finishers

Real-World Connection

Brianna earned $15 walking her neighbor's dog in the afternoons. She used part of the money she earned to buy a CD. After buying the CD, Brianna has $6 left. Write and solve an equation to find how much Brianna paid for the CD.

With the money she has left, Brianna wants to purchase a book that costs $10. Write and solve an equation to find how much Brianna needs. Explain how you found your answer.

• Adding Three-Digit Numbers

multiples

Power Up K

On your hundred number chart, circle all the numbers on the chart that we say when we count by 3s from 3 to 99. Do you see a pattern of even and odd numbers? Explain.

mental math

a. **Number Sense:** $30 + 60$

b. **Number Sense:** $74 + 19$

c. **Number Sense:** $46 + 9$

d. **Number Sense:** $63 + 29$

e. **Number Sense:** $42 + 50$

f. **Number Sense:** $16 + 39$

g. **Money:** $\$20 + \$20$

h. **Money:** $\$19 + \$20$

problem solving

The months of the year repeat. Twelve months after January is January of the next year. Twenty-four months after January is January again. What month is twenty-five months after January?

Focus Strategy: Use Logical Reasoning

(**Understand**) We are given this information:

1. The months of the year repeat.
2. Twelve months after January is January of the next year.
3. Twenty-four months after January is January again.

We already know the months of the year (January, February, March, and so on). We are asked to find the month that is twenty-five months after January.

Plan We will *use logical reasoning.* We will combine our knowledge of the months of the year with the given information to answer the question.

Solve We are told that twenty-four months after January is January. Twenty-five months is one month more than twenty-four months (24 + 1 = 25). We know that one month after January is February. So **February** is twenty-five months after January.

Check We know our answer is reasonable because the months of the year repeat. Twenty-four months after January is January, so by using logical reasoning, we know that twenty-five months after January is February.

New Concept

Esmerelda and Denise were playing a game. Esmerelda had $675. Denise landed on Esmerelda's property, so she paid Esmerelda $175 for rent. How much money does Esmerelda have now?

Thinking Skill

Justify

Why can we use $100 bills, $10 bills, and $1 bills to represent an addition problem?

We can use money manipulatives to add $175 to $675. The sum is 7 hundreds, 14 tens, and 10 ones.

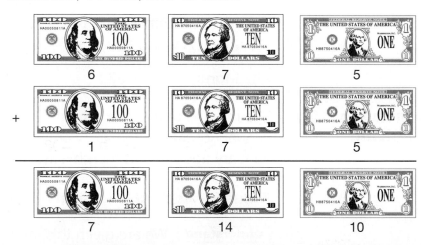

Thinking Skill

Verify

Why did we exchange ten $1 bills for one $10 bill?

We can exchange 10 ones for 1 ten and 10 tens for 1 hundred, giving us 8 hundreds, 5 tens, and no ones. Esmerelda has $850.

We can also use pencil and paper to solve this problem. First we add the ones and regroup. Then we add the tens and regroup. As a final step, we add the hundreds.

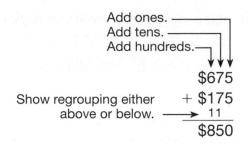

Add ones.
Add tens.
Add hundreds.

$675
+ $175
  11
$850

Show regrouping either above or below. ⟶

Example

Rayetta bought a used car to drive to college. She paid $456 to have it repainted and paid $374 for new tires. Altogether, how much did Rayetta spend for the paint work and tires?

We begin by adding the digits in the ones column, and we move one column at a time to the left. We write the first digit of two-digit answers either above or below the next place's column. We find that Rayetta spent **$830.**

11
$456
+ $374
$830

Thinking Skill

Discuss

In which place did we need to regroup? Explain why.

Activity

Adding Money

Materials needed:

• money manipulatives from Lesson 4 (from **Lesson Activities 2, 3,** and **4**)

Use money manipulatives to act out the problem in the example. Then describe in writing how you can regroup the bills so that you use the fewest number of bills.

Lesson Practice Add:

a. $579
     + $186

b.   408
     + 243

c. $498
     + $ 89

d. $458 + $336

e. 56 + 569

Written Practice *Distributed and Integrated*

* **1.** For recess, 77 students chose to play outside and 19 students chose to
(1, 9) play in the gym. How many students were playing at recess altogether?

* **2.** Five of the twelve students had no homework to take home on Friday.
(11) How many students had homework to take home?

*3. **(Represent)** Use words to write the number 913.
(7)

*4. **(Represent)** Use digits to write the number seven hundred
(7)
forty-three.

*5. **(Represent)** Use digits and symbols to write this comparison:
(Inv. 1)
"Seventy-five is greater than negative eighty."

*6. Compare:
(7,
Inv. 1) **a.** 413 ◯ 314   **b.** −4 ◯ 3

7. **(Connect)** The numbers 7, 9, and 16 form a fact family. Write two
(6)
addition facts and two subtraction facts using these three numbers.

*8. **(Represent)** To what number is each arrow pointing?
(Inv. 1)

a.

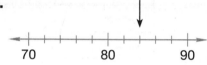

b.

| ***9.** (13) | $475
 + $332 | ***10.** (13) | $714
 + $226 | ***11.** (13) | 743
 + 187 | ***12.** (13) | 576
 + 228 |

| **13.** (2) | 8
 5
 + k
 17 | **14.** (2) | 4 <br> n
 + 6
 15 | **15.** (2) | 9 <br> a
 + 6
 17 | **16.** (2) | n
 3
 + 7
 16 |

| ***17.** (12) | 8
 − n
 2 | **18.** (6) | 17
 − 8 | **19.** (6) | 13
 − 7 | ***20.** (12) | n
 − 8
 7 |

| ***21.** (12) | 14
 − n
 6 | ***22.** (12) | 16
 − a
 9 | **23.** (12) | n
 − 9
 7 | **24.** (9) | $49
 + $76 |

*25. **(Conclude)** Write the next three numbers in each counting sequence:
(3,
Inv. 1)

 a. ..., 28, 35, 42, _____, _____, _____, ...

 b. ..., 15, 10, 5, _____, _____, _____, ...

*26. **Multiple Choice** Which number shows the sum of the sets
(7) below?

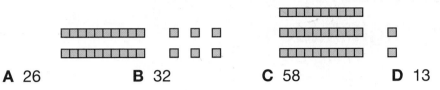

 A 26   **B** 32   **C** 58   **D** 13

*27. What temperature is 5 degrees less than 1 degree?
(Inv. 1)

*28. Brothers and sisters are siblings. The table shows
(7) the names and ages of Jeremy and his siblings.

 Write the names in order from youngest
 to oldest.

Jeremy and his Siblings

Name	Age (in years)
Jeremy	10
Jack	8
Jackie	13

*29. **(Justify)** Will the sum of three even numbers be odd or even?
(10) Explain and give several examples to support your answer.

*30. How many different three-digit numbers can you write using the digits
(10) 0, 6, and 7? Each digit may be used only once, and the digit 0 may not
 be used in the hundreds place. Label your numbers as even or odd.

- # Subtracting Two-Digit and Three-Digit Numbers
- # Missing Two-Digit Addends

Power Up

multiples	Power Up K

The multiples of 4 are the numbers we say when we count by fours: 4, 8, 12, 16, and so on. On your hundred number chart, circle the multiples of 4. Which of the circled numbers are even numbers? Are all the even numbers on the chart circled?

mental math

Add a number ending in two zeros to another number in **a–c.**

a. Number Sense: 300 + 400

b. Number Sense: 600 + 300

c. Number Sense: 250 + 300

d. Number Sense: 63 + 29

e. Number Sense: 28 + 49

f. Money: Two dimes and one nickel have the same value as what coin?

g. Money: How many quarters equal one dollar?

h. Money: If one pencil costs 20¢, how much do two pencils cost?

problem solving

Choose an appropriate problem-solving strategy to solve this problem. Twelve months after February is February. Twenty-four months after February is February again. On February 14, Paloma's sister was 22 months old. In what month was Paloma's sister born?

Subtracting Two-Digit and Three-Digit Numbers

KimRee had $37. She spent $23 to buy a game. How much money did KimRee have then?

We will use bills to illustrate this problem.

KimRee had $37.

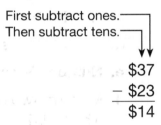

3   7

She spent $23.

2   3

_____

Then she had …

1   4

The picture shows that KimRee had 3 tens and 7 ones and that she took away 2 tens and 3 ones. We see that she had 1 ten and 4 ones left over, which is $14.

The problem is a subtraction problem. With pencil and paper, we solve the problem this way:

First subtract ones.
Then subtract tens.

$$\begin{array}{r} \$37 \\ -\ \$23 \\ \hline \$14 \end{array}$$

Example 1

Subtract: 85 − 32

We read this problem as "eighty-five minus thirty-two." This means that 32 is subtracted from 85. We can write the problem and its answer like this:

$$\begin{array}{r} 85 \\ -\ 32 \\ \hline \mathbf{53} \end{array}$$

Verify Explain why the answer is reasonable.

Example 2

Subtract 123 from 365.

The numbers in a subtraction problem follow a specific order. This problem means "start with 365 and subtract 123." We write the problem and its answer like this:

$$\begin{array}{r} 365 \\ -\ 123 \\ \hline \mathbf{242} \end{array}$$

Verify Explain why the answer is reasonable.

Missing Two-Digit Addends

The missing addend in the problem below has two digits. We can find the missing addend one digit at a time.

ones column
tens column

$$\begin{array}{r} 56 \\ +\ \_\_ \\ \hline 98 \end{array}$$ Six plus what number is eight? (2)
Five plus what number is nine? (4)

The missing digits are 4 and 2, so the missing addend is 42.

Example 3

Find the missing addend:
$$\begin{array}{r} 36 \\ +\ w \\ \hline 87 \end{array}$$

The letter w stands for a two-digit number. We first find the missing digit in the ones place. Then we find the missing digit in the tens place.

$$\begin{array}{r} 36 \\ +\ w \\ \hline 87 \end{array}$$ Six plus what number is seven? (1)
Three plus what number is eight? (5)

The missing addend is **51.**

We check our answer by replacing w with 51 in the original problem.

$$\begin{array}{rr} 36 & 36 \\ +\ w & +\ 51 \\ \hline 87 & 87 \end{array}$$ check

Example 4

Find the missing addend: $m + 17 = 49$

We want to find the number that combines with 17 to total 49. The missing addend contains two digits. We will find the digits one at a time.

$$\begin{array}{r} m \\ +\ 17 \\ \hline 49 \end{array}$$ What number plus seven is nine? (2)
What number plus one is four? (3)

We find that the missing addend is **32.** We check our answer.

$$m + 17 = 49$$
$$32 + 17 = 49 \quad \text{check}$$

Lesson Practice

Model Solve problems **a** and **b** using money manipulatives. Then subtract using pencil and paper.

a. $485 - $242

b. $56 - $33

c. Subtract 53 from 97.

d. Subtract twenty-three from fifty-four.

Find the missing addend in each problem:

e.
$$\begin{array}{r} 24 \\ +\ q \\ \hline 65 \end{array}$$

f.
$$\begin{array}{r} m \\ +\ 31 \\ \hline 67 \end{array}$$

g. $36 + w = 99$

h. $y + 45 = 99$

Written Practice *Distributed and Integrated*

Formulate Write and solve equations for problems **1** and **2**.

*1. The surf shop had forty-two surfboards. The shop received a shipment
(1) with seventeen more surfboards. How many surfboards were at the surf shop?

*2. Machiko saw four grasshoppers in her backyard on Monday. On
(11) Tuesday she saw some more grasshoppers. She saw a total of eleven grasshoppers on those two days. How many grasshoppers did she see on Tuesday?

*3. Use the digits 1, 2, and 3 to write an even number less than 200. Use
(10) each digit only once.

*4. (**Connect**) Use the numbers 9, 7, and 2 to write two addition facts and
(6) two subtraction facts.

*5. Subtract seven hundred thirteen from eight hundred twenty-four.
(14)

*6. Compare:
(Inv. 1)
    a. 704 ◯ 407   **b.** −3 ◯ −5

7. What is the total number of days in the first two months of a common
(5) year?

*8. (**Represent**) To what number is the arrow pointing?
(Inv. 1)

*9. (13)	$346 + $298	***10.** (13)	499 + 275	***11.** (13)	$421 + $389	***12.** (13)	$506 + $210
*13. (14)	$438 − $206	**14.** (12)	17 − a 9	**15.** (1)	7 + b 14	**16.** (12)	5 − c 2
17. (1)	8 + d 15	***18.** (12)	15 − k 9	**19.** (2)	3 n + 2 13	***20.** (14)	476 − 252
21. (14)	47 − 16	***22.** (14)	28 − 13	***23.** (14)	75 + t 87	***24.** (14)	24 + e 67

*25. (**Conclude**) Write the next three numbers in each counting sequence:
(3,
Inv. 1)
    a. ... , 81, 72, 63, _____, _____, _____, ...

    b. ... , 12, 8, 4, _____, _____, _____, ...

*26. Multiple Choice If $\square - 7 = 2$, then which of these is *not* true?
(12)

A $7 - \square = 2$ **B** $\square - 2 = 7$

C $2 + 7 = \square$ **D** $\square = 7 + 2$

*27. **Verify** When you add four even numbers, will the sum be
(10) even or odd? Explain why, and give several examples to support your answer.

28. A piano has 36 black keys and 52 white keys. Does a piano have
(1, 7) more black keys or white keys? How many keys does a piano have altogether?

*29. **Verify** Will the sum of three odd numbers be odd or even? Explain
. (10) why, and give several examples to support your answer.

30. How many different three-digit numbers can you write using the digits
(10) 9, 1, and 0? Each digit may be used only once, and the digit 0 may not be used in the hundreds place. Label the numbers you write as even or odd.

Real-World Connection

The Helman family took a 745-mile car trip to visit relatives. The trip took three days because they made stops to sightsee each day. On the first day, they traveled 320 miles, and on the third day, they traveled 220 miles. How many miles did they travel on the second day? Explain why your answer is reasonable.

• Subtracting Two-Digit Numbers with Regrouping

Power Up

facts	Power Up A
count aloud	Count by fours from 4 to 60.
mental math	Add a number ending in two zeros to another number in **a–c**.

    a. Number Sense: 400 + 500

    b. Number Sense: 600 + 320

    c. Number Sense: 254 + 100

    d. Number Sense: 39 + 25

    e. Number Sense: 19 + 27

    f. Money: What is the value of 3 nickels and 2 pennies?

    g. Money: What is the value of 3 quarters?

    h. Money: The price of a baseball glove is $19. The price of a baseball is $3. What is the total cost of one glove and one ball?

problem solving

Talmai has a total of 10 coins in his left and right pockets. He has four more coins in his right pocket than in his left pocket. How many coins does Talmai have in each pocket?

Focus Strategy: Guess and Check

(**Understand**) We are told the total number of coins (10). We are told Talmai's right pocket contains four more coins than his left pocket. We are asked to find the number of coins in each pocket.

(**Plan**) We can try *guessing* the numbers of coins and then *checking* whether the numbers fit the problem.

Solve We will use fact families to only guess pairs of numbers that have a sum of 10. We try to make a *reasonable* guess. We can eliminate the guess of 5 coins in each pocket because we know Talmai has different numbers of coins in his two pockets.

We might try guessing 6 coins for the right pocket and 4 coins for the left pocket. This guess would be wrong because it would mean Talmai has 2 more coins in one pocket than in the other pocket (6 − 4 = 2). If we make a wrong guess, we revise our guess and check again.

For a different guess, we might try 7 coins and 3 coins. Seven coins is four more than three coins (7 − 3 = 4), which fits the problem. This means Talmai has **7 coins in his right pocket and 3 coins in his left pocket.**

Check We know our answer is reasonable because 7 coins plus 3 coins totals 10 coins, and 7 coins is 4 more than 3 coins. We used fact families and the strategy of *guess and check* to solve the problem.

New Concept

Roberto had $53. He spent $24 to buy a jacket. Then how much money did Roberto have?

We will use pictures of bills and our money manipulatives to help us understand this problem.

Roberto had $53.

5   3

He spent $24.

−   2   4

Then he had ...

?   ?

Thinking Skill

Discuss

Explain why 5 tens and 3 ones equals the same number as 4 tens and 13 ones.

The picture shows that Roberto had 5 tens and 3 ones and that he took away 2 tens and 4 ones. We see that Roberto had enough tens but not enough ones. To get more ones, Roberto traded 1 ten for 10 ones.

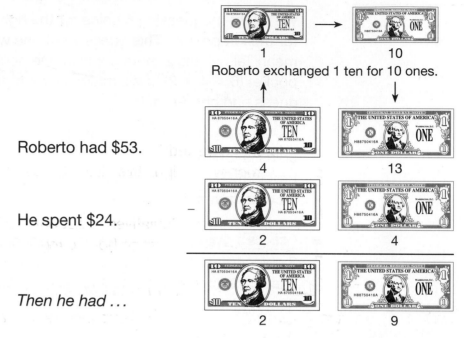

Roberto exchanged 1 ten for 10 ones.

Roberto had $53.

He spent $24.

Then he had ...

After trading 1 ten for 10 ones, Roberto had 4 tens and 13 ones. Then he was able to take 2 tens and 4 ones from his money to pay for the jacket. The purchase left him with 2 tens and 9 ones, which is $29.

Trading 1 ten for 10 ones is an example of **regrouping,** or **exchanging.** (In subtraction, this process may also be called **borrowing.**) We often need to regroup when we subtract.

Example

Santino had $56. He spent $29 to repair his bike. Then how much money did Santino have?

We subtract $29 from $56, writing $56 on top.

$$\begin{array}{r} \$56 \\ -\ \$29 \\ \hline ? \end{array}$$

We understand that $56 means 5 tens and 6 ones and that $29 means 2 tens and 9 ones. Since $6 is less than $9, we need to regroup before we can subtract. We take $10 from $50 and add it to the $6. From 5 tens and 6 ones we get 4 tens and 16 ones, which is still equal to $56.

We subtract and get 2 tens and 7 ones, which is **$27.** We usually show the regrouping this way:

$$\begin{array}{r} \overset{4}{\$\cancel{5}}\,{}^{1}6 \\ -\ \$2\ 9 \\ \hline \$2\ 7 \end{array}$$

Activity

Subtracting Money

Materials needed:

• money manipulatives from Lesson 4 (from **Lesson Activities 2, 3,** and **4**)

Use money manipulatives to act out the problem in the example. Then describe in writing how to regroup the bills so that you can subtract.

Lesson Practice   (Model) Use money manipulatives or draw pictures to show each subtraction:

a.	$53	**b.**	$56	**c.**	$42	**d.**	$60
	− $29		− $27		− $24		− $27

Use pencil and paper to find each difference:

e. 63 − 36   **f.** 40 − 13

g. 72 − 24   **h.** 24 − 18

Written Practice   *Distributed and Integrated*

(Formulate) Write and solve equations for problems **1** and **2.**

* 1. Jimmy found six hundred eighteen acorns under one tree. He found
(1, 13)   one hundred seventeen acorns under another tree. How many acorns did Jimmy find in all?

* 2. On the first day Rueben collected sixteen leaves. On the second day
(11, 14)   Rueben collected some more leaves, giving him a total of seventy-six leaves. How many leaves did he collect on the second day?

3. Use the digits 3, 6, and 7 to write an even number less than 400. Use each digit only once.
(10)

*4. (**Represent**) Use words to write the number 605.
(7)

5. The smallest two-digit odd number is 11. What is the smallest two-digit even number?
(10)

6. Compare:
(Inv. 1)

    a. 75 ◯ 57   **b.** 5 + 7 ◯ 4 + 8

*7. Subtract 245 from 375.
(14)

*8. To what number is the arrow pointing?
(Inv. 1)

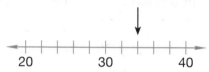

| ***9.** | $426 | **10.** | $278 | **11.** | 721 | ***12.** | 409 |
| (13) | + $298 | (13) | + $456 | (13) | + 189 | (13) | + 198 |

13.	d	**14.**	18	***15.**	38	**16.**	c
(1)	+ 7	(12)	− a	(14)	+ b	(12)	− 4
	12		9		59		1

| **17.** | $456 | ***18.** | $54 | ***19.** | 46 | ***20.** | 35 |
| (14) | − $120 | (15) | − $27 | (15) | − 28 | (15) | − 16 |

*21. (**Analyze**) What is the total number of days in the last two months of the year?
(5)

*22. (**Connect**) The numbers 5, 6, and 11 form a fact family. Write two addition and two subtraction facts using these three numbers.
(6)

*23. 3 + 6 + 7 + 5 + 4 + 8
(1)

(**Conclude**) Write the next three numbers in each counting sequence:

24. ... , 72, 63, 54, _____, _____, _____, ...
(3)

*25. ... , −7, −14, −21, _____, _____, _____, ...
(Inv. 1)

*26. **Multiple Choice** If □ = 6 and if □ + △ = 10, then △ equals which
(1)   of the following?

   A 3   **B** 4   **C** 5   **D** 6

*27. **Verify** Will the sum of an odd number and an even number be
(10)   odd or even? Explain why, and give several examples to support your
        answer.

28. The numbers of students who attend three different elementary schools
(7)   are shown in this table:

Enrollment

School	Number of Students
Washington	370
Lincoln	312
Roosevelt	402

Write the names of the schools in order from the least number of
students to greatest.

*29. A chimpanzee weighs about 150 pounds. A gorilla weighs about
(6, 7) 450 pounds. Which animal weighs more? About how much more does
        it weigh?

30. How many different three-digit numbers can you write using the digits
(10)   4, 0, and 8? Each digit may be used only once, and the digit 0 may not
        be used in the hundreds place.

Early Finishers

Real-World Connection

The zookeeper keeps a chart showing how much food the giant panda
at the zoo eats each day. The chart shows that the panda ate 61 pounds
of food on Monday and 55 pounds of food on Tuesday. How much more
food did the panda eat on Monday than on Tuesday? Use base ten
blocks to solve the problem. Then check your answer using pencil and
paper.

- # Expanded Form
- # More on Missing Numbers in Subtraction

multiples

Power Up K

The multiples of five are the numbers we say when we count by fives. On your hundred number chart, circle the multiples of 5. Which digits are in the ones place in all the circled numbers? Which of the circled numbers are even numbers?

mental math

Add three numbers in **a–c.**

   a. Number Sense: $30 + 40 + 20$

   b. Number Sense: $300 + 400 + 200$

   c. Number Sense: $3 + 4 + 2$

   d. Review: $36 + 19$

   e. Review: $39 + 27$

   f. Money: What is the value of 3 dimes and 1 nickel?

   g. Money: What is the value of 1 quarter and 1 nickel?

   h. Money: What is the total cost of a movie ticket for $8 and a drink for $3?

problem solving

Choose an appropriate problem-solving strategy to solve this problem. Sally has four coins in her pocket totaling 25¢. What coins does Sally have in her pocket?

New Concepts

Expanded Form

The number 365 means "3 hundreds and 6 tens and 5 ones."
We can write this as

$$300 + 60 + 5$$

This is the **expanded form** of 365.

Example 1

Write 275 in expanded form.

The expanded form of 275 is **200 + 70 + 5.**

Example 2

Write 407 in expanded form.

Since there are no tens, we write the following:

400 + 7

More on Missing Numbers in Subtraction

We have found missing numbers in subtraction problems by "subtracting down" or "adding up." We can use these methods when subtracting numbers with one or more digits.

Subtract Down

$$\begin{array}{r} 56 \\ -\ w \\ \hline 14 \end{array}$$
Six minus what number is four? (2)
Five minus what number is one? (4)

We find that the missing number is 42.

Add Up

$$\begin{array}{r} n \\ -\ 36 \\ \hline 43 \end{array}$$
Three plus six is what number? (9)
Four plus three is what number? (7)

We find that the missing number is 79.

Example 3

Find the missing number:
$$\begin{array}{r} 64 \\ -\ w \\ \hline 31 \end{array}$$

We write the first number on top and find the missing number one digit at a time by "subtracting down" or "adding up."

Thinking Skill

Verify

Why can we use addition to solve a subtraction problem?

$$\begin{array}{r} 64 \\ -\ w \\ \hline 31 \end{array} \Bigg\downarrow$$ Four minus what number is one? (3)
Six minus what number is three? (3)

or

$$\begin{array}{r} 64 \\ -\ w \\ \hline 31 \end{array} \Bigg\uparrow$$ One plus what number is four? (3)
Three plus what number is six? (3)

We find that the missing number is **33**. We check our work by using 33 in place of w in the original problem.

$$\begin{array}{r} 64 \\ -\ w \\ \hline 31 \end{array} \qquad \begin{array}{r} 64 \\ -\ 33 \\ \hline 31 \end{array} \text{ check}$$

Lesson Practice Write each number in expanded form:

a. 86 **b.** 325 **c.** 507

Find each missing number:

d. $\begin{array}{r} 36 \\ -\ p \\ \hline 21 \end{array}$ **e.** $\begin{array}{r} 47 \\ -\ q \\ \hline 24 \end{array}$ **f.** $\begin{array}{r} m \\ -\ 22 \\ \hline 16 \end{array}$

g. $w - 32 = 43$ **h.** $43 - x = 32$

Written Practice *Distributed and Integrated*

Formulate Write and solve equations for problems **1** and **2**.

* 1. Twenty-three horses grazed in the pasture. The rest of the horses were
(11, 14) in the corral. If there were eighty-nine horses in all, how many horses were in the corral?

* 2. Three hundred seventy-five students were standing in the auditorium.
(1, 13) The other one hundred seven students in the auditorium were sitting down. Altogether, how many students were in the auditorium?

3. Use the numbers 22, 33, and 55 to write two addition facts and two
(6) subtraction facts.

* 4. **Represent** Write 782 in expanded form.
(16)

5. The largest three-digit odd number is 999. What is the smallest
(10) three-digit even number?

6. Compare:
(Inv. 1)
   a. 918 ◯ 819   **b.** −7 ◯ −5

7. Six weeks is how many days? Count by sevens.
(3)

*8. (Represent) To what number is the arrow pointing?
(Inv. 1)

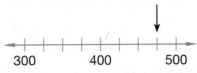

9. $576   **10.** $243   **11.**   186   **12.**   329
(13) + $128   (13) + $578   (13) + 285   (13) + 186

13. d **14.**   17   **15.**   8   **16.** c
(14) + 12   (12) − a (1) + b (12) − 7
     17   9   14   2

*17. 25   ***18.** 42   ***19.** 46   ***20.** 42
(15) − 19   (15) − 28   (15) − 18   (15) − 16

*21. 68   ***22.** b ***23.** 62   ***24.** m
(16) − d (16) − 34   (16) − h (16) − 46
    34   15   21   32

*25. (Conclude) Write the next three numbers in each counting sequence:
(3)
   a. ..., 16, 20, 24, _____, _____, _____, ...

   b. ..., 16, 12, 8, _____, _____, _____, ...

*26. Multiple Choice If $n − 3 = 6$, then which of these number sentences
(12, 16) is *not* true?
   A $6 + 3 = n$ **B** $3 + 6 = n$
   C $6 − 3 = n$ **D** $n − 6 = 3$

27. Elevation is a measure of distance above sea level. The elevations of
(7) three cities are shown in the table:

Elevations of Cities

City	State	Elevation (in feet above sea level)
Augusta	ME	45
Troy	NY	35
Hilo	HI	38

Write the names of the cities in order from the greatest elevation to least.

* 28. Draw a number line and mark the locations of the numbers 23, 26, and
(Inv. 1) 30 by placing dots on the number line.

* 29. **Explain** Malika's age is an odd number. The sum of Malika's age
(10) and Elena's age is an even number. Is Elena's age an odd number or an
even number? Explain how you know.

* 30. **Explain** Write an addition word problem for the equation
(11) 33 + *m* = 51. Solve the problem for *m* and explain why your answer
is reasonable.

Real-World Connection

Trisha rolled a dot cube three times. She rolled 3, 5, and 4. Write all
the three-digit numbers Trisha can make using these digits one time in
each number. Then write the greatest and least number in expanded
form.

• Adding Columns of Numbers with Regrouping

facts	Power Up B
count aloud	Count by fives from 5 to 50 and then back down to 5.
mental math	**a. Number Sense:** 200 + 300 + 400
	b. Number Sense: 240 + 200 + 100
	c. Number Sense: 36 + 20 + 9
	d. Number Sense: 45 + 10 + 29
	e. Number Sense: 56 + 20 + 19
	f. Number Sense: 24 + 39 + 10
	g. Money: What is the value of 2 dimes, 2 nickels, and 2 pennies?
	h. Money: What is the total cost of a $4 sandwich, a $1 bag of pretzels, and a $1 drink?
problem solving	Choose an appropriate problem-solving strategy to solve this problem. There were more than 20 but fewer than 30 math books on the shelf. Austin arranged the books into two equal stacks, and then he rearranged the books into three equal stacks. Use these clues to find how many math books were on the shelf. Explain how you found your answer.

We have practiced solving addition problems in which we regrouped 10 ones as 1 ten, but sometimes the sum of the digits in the ones column is 20 or more. When this happens, we move a group of two or more tens to the tens column.

Example 1

The number of students in four classrooms is 28, 26, 29, and 29. How many students are there in all four classrooms?

Thinking Skill

Connect

How would the answer change if we were adding dollars?

We arrange the numbers vertically and then add the ones. The sum is 32, which is 3 tens plus 2 ones. We record the 2 in the ones place and write the 3 either above or below the tens column. Then we finish adding.

$$
\begin{array}{r}
3 \text{ above} \rightarrow 3 \\
28 \\
26 \\
29 \\
+ 29 \\
\hline
112
\end{array}
\qquad
\begin{array}{r}
28 \\
26 \\
29 \\
+ 29 \\
3 \text{ below} \rightarrow 3 \\
\hline
112
\end{array}
$$

Altogether, there are **112 students.**

Example 2

Add: 227 + 88 + 6

Thinking Skill

Conclude

To add whole numbers, why do we line up the rightmost digits instead of the leftmost digits?

We line up the last digits of the numbers. Then we add the digits in the ones column and get 21.

$$
\begin{array}{r}
227 \\
88 \\
+ \quad 6 \\
\hline
\text{㉑}
\end{array}
$$

The number 21 is 2 tens plus 1 one. We record the 1 in the ones place and write the 2 in the tens column. Then we add the tens and get 12 tens.

$$
\begin{array}{r}
\overset{2}{2}27 \\
88 \\
+ \quad 6 \\
\hline
\text{⑫}1
\end{array}
$$

We record the 2 in the tens place and write the 1, which is 1 hundred, in the hundreds column. Then we finish adding.

$$
\begin{array}{r}
\overset{1\ 2}{227} \\
88 \\
+\quad 6 \\
\hline
\mathbf{321}
\end{array}
$$

Lesson Practice   Add:

a.
$$
\begin{array}{r}
47 \\
29 \\
46 \\
+\ 95 \\
\hline
\end{array}
$$

b.
$$
\begin{array}{r}
28 \\
47 \\
+\ 65 \\
\hline
\end{array}
$$

c.
$$
\begin{array}{r}
38 \\
22 \\
31 \\
+\ 46 \\
\hline
\end{array}
$$

d.
$$
\begin{array}{r}
438 \\
76 \\
+\ 5 \\
\hline
\end{array}
$$

e. 15 + 24 + 11 + 25 + 36

Written Practice   *Distributed and Integrated*

Write and solve equations for problems **1** and **2**.

*1. Twenty-four children visited the school science fair. The remainder of
(11) the visitors were adults. There were seventy-five visitors in all. How many visitors were adults?

*2. Four hundred seven fans sat on one side of the field at a soccer play-off
(1, 13) game. Three hundred sixty-two fans sat on the other side of the field. Altogether, how many fans saw the game?

*3. Use the digits 9, 2, and 8 to write an even number less than 300. You
(10) may use each digit only once. Which digit is in the tens place?

*4. (**Represent**) Write 813 in expanded form. Then use words to write the
(7, 16) number.

5. The largest two-digit even number is 98. What is the smallest
(10) two-digit odd number?

* 6. (Represent) To what number is the arrow pointing?
(Inv. 1)

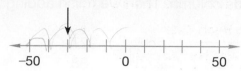

* 7. 294
(17)   312
   +   5

8. $189
(13) + $298

9. $378
(13) + $496

10. 109
(13) + 486

* 11. 14 + 28 + 35 + 16 + 227
(17)

12. 14 − a = 7
(12)

13. 8 + b = 14
(1)

* 14. c − 13 = 5
(16)

15. 11
(12) − d
   9

16. e
(12) − 5
  8

* 17. 38
(15) − 29

* 18. 57
(15) − 38

19. 34
(14) + b
  86

* 20. 48
(16) − c
  25

21. d
(16) − 46
  12

22. y
(16) − 15
  24

(Conclude) Write the next three numbers in each counting sequence:

* 23. ..., 48, 44, 40, ____, ____, ____, ...
(3)

* 24. ..., 12, 15, 18, ____, ____, ____, ...
(3)

* 25. (Connect) The numbers 6, 9, and 15 form a fact family. Write four
(6) addition and four subtraction facts using these three numbers.

* 26. Multiple Choice Nancy is thinking of two numbers whose sum is
(1, 6) 10 and whose difference is 2. What are the two numbers?

    A 2 and 8   **B** 3 and 7

    C 6 and 4   **D** 2 and 10

27. Four friends measured their resting heart rates by counting their pulses
(7) for a minute. The results shown are in the table below:

Resting Heart Rate

Name	Beats per Minute
Miguel	72
Victoria	68
Simon	64
Megan	76

Write the names of the friends in order from the lowest resting heart rate
to the highest.

*28. Draw a number line and make dots to show the locations of the
(Inv. 1) numbers 13, 10, and 9.

*29. **Explain** Darrius's age is an even number. The sum of Darrius's age
(10) and Keb's age is an even number. Is Keb's age an odd number or an
even number? Explain how you know.

*30. **Explain** Write an addition word problem for the equation
(11) $n + 10 = 25$. Solve the problem for n, and explain why your answer is
reasonable.

Early Finishers

Real-World Connection

Mr. Sanchez adds fresh fruit to a special display in the grocery store
several times a day. One day he added 102 oranges, 115 apples,
53 pears, 87 peaches, and 44 grapefruit to the display. How many
pieces of fruit did he add to the display that day?

LESSON 18

• **Temperature**

multiples

Power Up K

On your hundred number chart, circle the multiples of three. Draw an "X" on the multiples of four. Shade the boxes that have numbers with both a circle and an X. What do you notice about the number 12?

mental math

a. **Number Sense:** 250 + 300 + 100

b. **Number Sense:** 20 + 36 + 19

c. **Number Sense:** 76 + 9 + 9

d. **Number Sense:** 64 + 9 + 10

e. **Number Sense:** 27 + 19 + 20

f. **Number Sense:** 427 + 200

g. **Money:** What is the value of 1 quarter, 2 dimes, and 1 nickel?

h. **Money:** Each package of soccer shin guards is $9. What is the cost of two packages of shin guards?

problem solving

Choose an appropriate problem-solving strategy to solve this problem. Name the date that is eleven months after August 15, 2008.

New Concept

A **scale** is a type of number line often used for measuring. Scales are found on rulers, gauges, thermometers, speedometers, and many other instruments. To read a scale, we must first determine the distance between the marks on the scale. Then we can find the values of all the marks on the scale.

We use a thermometer to measure temperature. Temperature is usually measured in degrees **Fahrenheit** (°F) or in degrees **Celsius** (°C). On many thermometers, the distance between the tick marks is two **degrees.**

Example 1

Math Language

A *degree* is a unit for measuring temperature and is shown using the degree symbol (°).

What temperature is shown on this Fahrenheit thermometer?

There are five spaces between 30° and 40° on this scale, so each space cannot equal one degree. If we try counting by twos, we find that our count matches the scale. We count up by twos from 30° and find that the temperature is **32°F.** Water freezes at 32°F.

Example 2

What temperature is shown on this Celsius thermometer?

Most of the world uses the Celsius scale to measure temperature. On this thermometer we see that the tick marks are also two degrees apart. If we count down by twos from zero, we find that the temperature shown is four degrees below zero, which we write as **−4°C.** Water freezes at 0°C, so −4°C is below freezing.

Example 3

Corina looked at the thermometer outside her window at 7:00 a.m. and again when she returned from school at 3:00 p.m. How many degrees warmer was the temperature at 3:00 p.m. than at 7:00 a.m.?

The 7:00 a.m. temperature was 54°F. The 3:00 p.m. temperature was 68°F. We may solve an equation or count up from 54° to 68° to find that the temperature was **14° warmer** at 3:00 p.m.

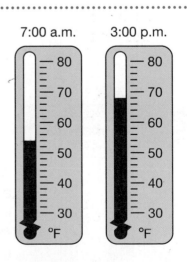

7:00 a.m.   3:00 p.m.

Activity

Measuring Temperature

Materials needed:
- **Lesson Activity 14**
- outside thermometer (Fahrenheit or Celsius)

Use a thermometer to measure the temperature outside your classroom for a week. Measure a morning temperature at the same time each day and an afternoon temperature at the same time each day.

Record the temperatures each day on **Lesson Activity 14.** Record the difference between the morning and afternoon temperature each day as well.

At the end of the week, write two conclusions about the data you collected.

Lesson Practice What temperature is shown on each of these thermometers? Include correct units.

a.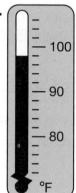

b.

c. These thermometers show the average daily minimum and maximum temperatures in Duluth, Minnesota, during the month of January. What are those temperatures? What is the difference between the two temperatures shown?

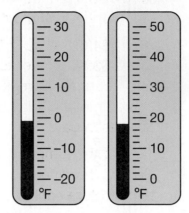

d. Using the temperatures from problem **c,** find the difference between the average daily minimum temperature and the average daily maximum temperature in Duluth during January.

Written Practice

Distributed and Integrated

(**Formulate**) Write and solve equations for problems **1** and **2.**

* 1. Tomas ran to the fence and back in 58 seconds. If it took Tomas
(11, 14) 21 seconds to run to the fence, how many seconds did it take him to run back from the fence?

2. Two hundred ninety-seven boys and three hundred fifteen girls attend
(1, 13) Madison School. How many children attend Madison School?

* 3. (**Connect**) Use the numbers 8, 17, and 9 to write two addition facts and
(6) two subtraction facts.

* 4. The tens digit is 4. The ones digit is 9. The number is between 200 and
(4) 300. What is the number?

* 5. (**Predict**) What is the eighth number in the following counting
(3, 5) sequence? Describe the pattern you observe.

4, 8, 12, 16, ...

*6. **(Represent)** To what number is the arrow pointing?
(Inv. 1)

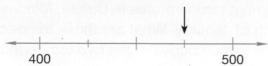

$$400 \qquad 500$$

7. $392
(13) + $278

8. $439
(13) + $339

9. 774
(13) + 174

10. 389
(13) + 398

*11. 13
(17) 25
46
25
+ 29

12. 18
(16) − a
12

13. 8
(1) + b
16

14. c
(12) − 5
3

*15. 62
(15) − 48

*16. 82
(15) − 58

17. 28
(17) 36
57
+ 47

18. 35
(16) − y
14

19. 45
(14) + p
55

*20. 75
(16) − l
42

*21. c
(16) − 47
31

22. e
(14) + 15
37

*23. **(Represent)** Write 498 in expanded form.
(16)

24. Compare:
(Inv. 1)
   a. 423 ◯ 432
                    b. 3 ◯ −3

*25. These thermometers show the highest Fahrenheit temperature and the
(18) lowest Celsius temperature recorded at a school last year. What were
those temperatures?

a.

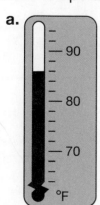

b.

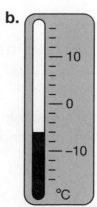

*26. Multiple Choice Which of these numbers is an odd number that
(10) is greater than 750?

    A 846   **B** 864   **C** 903   **D** 309

27. Write these numbers in order from greatest to least:
(7)

                    166   48   207   81

*28. (Formulate) Lexington, Kentucky, receives an average of 46 inches of
(15) precipitation each year. Huron, South Dakota, receives an average of
25 fewer inches. Write and solve an equation to find the average amount
of precipitation Huron receives each year.

29. Write a subtraction number sentence using the numbers 15 and 10.
(12)

*30. How many odd numbers are greater than 1 and less than 20?
(10)

Real-World Connection

If the Celsius temperature is known, we can estimate the Fahrenheit
temperature by doubling the Celsius temperature and adding 30.

  a. Using this method, estimate the Fahrenheit temperature at which
water freezes, if we know that water freezes at 0°C. Explain how
you know your estimate is reasonable.

  b. The average temperature in Austin, Texas, for the month of
November is 20°C. Explain how you can find the estimated
average Fahrenheit temperature in Austin, Texas, for that same
month. Then use the method to find the estimated Fahrenheit
temperature.

LESSON 19

• Elapsed-Time Problems

Power Up

multiples

Power Up K

The multiples of six are 6, 12, 18, and so on. On your hundred number chart, circle the numbers that are multiples of six. Which of the circled numbers are also multiples of five?

mental math

a. **Number Sense:** 27 + 100

b. **Number Sense:** 63 + 200

c. **Number Sense:** 28 + 20 + 300

d. **Number Sense:** 36 + 9 + 200

e. **Number Sense:** 48 + 29 + 300

f. **Number Sense:** What number should be added to 2 to get a total of 10?

g. **Money:** What is the value of 1 dime, 1 nickel, and 3 pennies?

h. **Money:** What is the total cost of a 55¢ apple and a 40¢ milk?

problem solving

Choose an appropriate problem-solving strategy to solve this problem. Matsu has eight coins in his pocket totaling 16¢. What coins does Matsu have in his pocket?

New Concept

The scale on a clock is actually two scales in one. One scale marks hours and is usually numbered. The other scale marks minutes and seconds and is usually not numbered. On the next page, we have numbered the scale for minutes and seconds outside the clock. Notice that on this scale we count by fives to go from one big mark to the next. Counting by fives can help us find the number of minutes before or after the hour.

To tell time, we read the position of the short hand on the hour scale and the position of the long hand on the minute scale. If the clock also has a hand for seconds, we can read its position on the minute scale, which is also the second scale.

To write the time of day, we write the hour followed by a colon. Then we write two digits to show the number of minutes after the hour. We use the abbreviations **a.m.** for the 12 hours before noon and **p.m.** for the 12 hours after noon. This form is referred to as **digital form.** We write **noon** as 12:00 p.m., and **midnight** is written as 12:00 a.m.

Example 1

If it is evening, what time is shown by the clock?

Since the short hand is between the 9 and the 10, we know it is after 9 p.m. and before 10 p.m. For the long hand, we count 5, 10, 15, 20 minutes after 9:00 p.m. The clock shows **9:20 p.m.**

Sixty minutes is one hour, 30 minutes is half an hour, and 15 minutes is a quarter of an hour. If the time is 7:30, we might say that the time is "half past seven." At 6:15 we might say that the time is a "quarter after six."

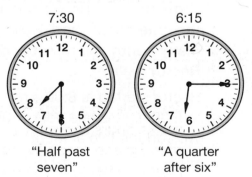

7:30   6:15

"Half past seven"   "A quarter after six"

Sometimes, when it is getting close to the next hour, we say how many minutes it is until the next hour. When the time is 5:50, we might say, "It is ten minutes to six." When it is 3:45, we might say, "It is a quarter to four."

3:45

"A quarter to four"

Represent Sketch a clock that shows 11:15.

Example 2

Use digital form to show what time it is at a quarter to nine in the evening.

A quarter to nine is 15 minutes before nine. In the evening, this time is **8:45 p.m.**

Represent Draw a picture of a clock that shows the time as a quarter to nine in the evening.

Suppose Yolis's soccer practice starts at 4:00 p.m. and ends at 5:00 p.m. The amount of time from the beginning to the end of her practice is called the elapsed time. **Elapsed time** is the difference between two points in time.

Example 3

Hector participated in a walk-a-thon fundraiser on Saturday morning. The clocks show the time he started and the time he finished. How many hours and minutes did Hector walk?

Start

Finish

Hector started at 8:00 a.m. and finished at 9:45 a.m. From 8:00 a.m. to 9:00 a.m. is one hour. From 9:00 a.m. to 9:45 a.m. is 45 minutes. We add the two amounts of time together and find that Hector walked for **1 hour 45 minutes.**

 **Activity**

Finding Elapsed Time

Material needed:
- **Lesson Activity 17**

Use **Lesson Activity 17** to label the hours and draw hands on two clocks, one showing the time your school starts and the other showing the time your school ends. Then calculate the number of hours and minutes from the start to the end of school.

Lesson Practice   If it is morning, what time is shown by each clock?

a.

b.

c.

d. Use digital form to show what time it is at ten minutes to nine in the evening.

e. How many hours equal a whole day?

f. How many minutes equal an hour?

g. How many seconds equal a minute?

h. Latoya's school day begins at the time shown on the left and ends at the time shown on the right. How long is a school day at Latoya's school? You may use your student clock to solve.

Start   Finish

Write and solve equations for problems **1** and **2**.

*1. (11) **Formulate** On the first day, Shaquana read fifty-one pages. She read some more pages on the second day. She read seventy-six pages in all. How many pages did she read on the second day?

*2. (11, 14) Twelve of the twenty-seven children in Room 9 are boys. How many girls are in Room 9?

*3. (6) If $a + b = 9$, then what is the other addition fact for a, b, and 9? What are the two subtraction facts for a, b, and 9?

*4. (7, 16) **Represent** Write 905 in expanded form. Then use words to write the number.

5. (Inv. 1) Use digits and symbols to write this comparison: "One hundred twenty is greater than one hundred twelve."

*6. (19) After school on Wednesday, Jana began her homework at the time shown on the clock. She finished her homework at 5:20 p.m. How much time did it take Jana to finish her homework?

*7. (18) Water freezes at 32° on the Fahrenheit scale. At what temperature on the Celsius scale does water freeze?

8. (13)
$$\begin{array}{r} \$468 \\ + \$293 \\ \hline \end{array}$$

9. (13)
$$\begin{array}{r} 468 \\ + 185 \\ \hline \end{array}$$

10. (13)
$$\begin{array}{r} \$187 \\ + \$698 \\ \hline \end{array}$$

11. (12)
$$\begin{array}{r} 14 \\ - a \\ \hline 7 \end{array}$$

12. (1)
$$\begin{array}{r} 8 \\ + b \\ \hline 16 \end{array}$$

13. (12)
$$\begin{array}{r} c \\ - 8 \\ \hline 7 \end{array}$$

14. (12)
$$\begin{array}{r} 14 \\ - d \\ \hline 9 \end{array}$$

*15. (15)
$$\begin{array}{r} 74 \\ - 58 \\ \hline \end{array}$$

*16. (15)
$$\begin{array}{r} \$44 \\ - \$28 \\ \hline \end{array}$$

*17. (15)
$$\begin{array}{r} 23 \\ - 18 \\ \hline \end{array}$$

*18. (15)
$$\begin{array}{r} \$62 \\ - \$43 \\ \hline \end{array}$$

*19.
(17)
```
  25
  28
  46
+ 88
```

20.
(16)
```
  45
-  p
 ───
  21
```

21.
(14)
```
  13
+  b
 ───
  37
```

*22.
(16)
```
   f
- 45
 ───
  32
```

23. Four dollars equals how many quarters? Count by fours.
(3)

*24. (**Connect**) Write a number sentence for this picture:
(1)

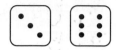

*25. (**Conclude**) Write the next three numbers in each counting sequence
(3,
Inv. 1) and explain the patterns you see.

   a. ..., 8, 16, 24, _____, _____, _____, ...

   b. ..., 8, 6, 4, _____, _____, _____, ...

*26. Multiple Choice If $9 - \triangle = 4$, then which of these is *not* true?
(7)
    A $9 - 4 = \triangle$ **B** $\triangle - 4 = 9$
    C $4 + \triangle = 9$ **D** $\triangle + 4 = 9$

*27. The thermometer shows the low temperature on a cold
(18) winter day in Fargo, North Dakota. What was the low
temperature that day?

*28. (**Represent**) Write the expanded form of 709.
(16)

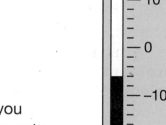

29. How many different arrangements of three letters can you
(3) write using the letters e, i, and o? The different arrangements
you write do not need to form words.

30. The numbers of goals three hockey players scored during their
(7) professional careers are shown in the table:

Career Goals Scored

Player	Number of Goals
Phil Esposito	717
Wayne Gretzky	894
Marcel Dionne	731

Write the number of goals scored from least to greatest.

LESSON 20

• Rounding

facts Power Up B

count aloud Count by threes from 3 to 30 and then back down to 3.

mental math
a. **Number Sense:** 56 + 400
b. **Number Sense:** 154 + 200
c. **Number Sense:** 54 + 29
d. **Number Sense:** 35 + 9 + 200
e. **Number Sense:** 48 + 19 + 200
f. **Number Sense:** What number should be added to 3 to get a total of 10?
g. **Money:** What is the value of one quarter and 4 dimes?
h. **Money:** What is the total cost of a 39¢ stamp and a 20¢ envelope?

problem solving
The class's math books were placed neatly on the shelf in two stacks. D'Karla saw the stacks and knew without counting that there was an even number of books. How did she know?

Focus Strategy: Make It Simpler

(**Understand**) We are told D'Karla knew there was an even number of books in two stacks without counting. We are asked to explain how she knew.

(**Plan**) We will begin with a simpler problem to make observations about even numbers of objects. We will explain how D'Karla knew there was an even number of books without counting.

Solve We might think, "Two books can be placed side by side (1 + 1). Three books can make unequal stacks of 2 books and 1 book (2 + 1). Four books can make equal stacks of 2 books each (2 + 2). Five books can only make unequal stacks (3 + 2 or 4 + 1). Six books can make two equal stacks of 3 books each (3 + 3)."

| 1 + 1 = 2 | 2 + 1 = 3 | 2 + 2 = 4 | 3 + 2 = 5 | 3 + 3 = 6 |

We notice that 2, 4, and 6 books can be placed into equal stacks. If all the books are the same thickness (like a class's math books), we expect that the stacks would be equally tall.

We wonder, "Can any even number of books be placed into two equal stacks?" The answer is yes—8 books can make two stacks of 4 books each, 10 books can make two stacks of 5 books each, and 12 books can make two stacks of 6 books each. We have *made a generalization* that even numbers of objects can be divided into two equal groups.

D'Karla knew that two stacks of equal height meant there was an even number of books.

Check We know our answer is reasonable because we made observations to find that an even number of objects can be divided into two equal groups. Our strategy can be described as making it simpler. We applied our observations about even numbers of objects to the problem.

New Concept

Math Language

We often use rounded amounts instead of exact amounts because they are easier to work with and to understand.

One of the sentences below uses an *exact amount*. The other sentence uses a *rounded number.* Which sentence below uses the rounded amount?

The radio costs about $70.

The radio costs $68.47.

The first sentence uses the rounded amount. Sometimes we choose to round an amount to the nearest multiple of ten. The **multiples** of ten are the numbers we say when we count by tens. Here we show some multiples of ten:

10, 20, 30, 40, 50, 60, 70, 80, 90, 100, 110, 120, ...

To **round** a number to the nearest ten, we choose the closest number that ends in zero. A number line can help us understand rounding. We will use the number line below to help us round 67 to the nearest ten.

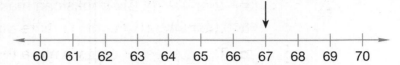

We see that 67 is between 60 and 70. Since 67 is closer to 70 than it is to 60, we say that 67 is "about 70." When we say this, we have rounded 67 to the nearest ten.

Example 1

Eighty-two people attended the matinee at the movie theater. About how many people attended the matinee?

Rounding to the nearest ten means rounding to a number we would say when counting by tens (10, 20, 30, 40, and so on). We will use a number line marked off in tens to picture this problem.

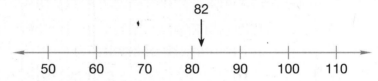

We see that 82 is between 80 and 90. Since 82 is closer to 80 than it is to 90, we round 82 to 80. About **80 people** attended the matinee.

Example 2

Thinking Skill

Summarize

Using your own words, explain how to round to the nearest ten.

Round 75 to the nearest ten.

Seventy-five is halfway between 70 and 80.

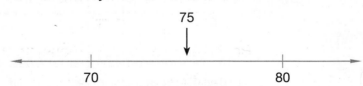

Although the number we are rounding is halfway between 70 and 80, the rule is to round up. This means 75 rounds to **80.**

Sometimes we want to round dollars and cents to the nearest dollar. To find the nearest dollar, we look closely at the number of cents. To determine whether $7.89 is closer to $7 or to $8, we ask ourselves whether 89 cents is more than or less than half a dollar. Half a dollar is 50 cents. Since 89 cents is more than half a dollar, $7.89 is closer to $8 than $7. To round money amounts to the nearest dollar, we round up if the number of cents is 50 or more. We round down if the number of cents is less than 50.

Example 3

Round each amount of money to the nearest dollar:

a. $6.49   b. $12.95   c. $19.75

a. The number of cents is less than 50. We round down to **$6.**

b. The number of cents is more than 50. We round up to **$13.**

c. The number of cents is more than 50. We round up to the next dollar, which is **$20.**

Sometimes we want to round money to amounts other than to the nearest dollar. For example, we might choose to round $6.49 to $6.50 since $6.50 is very close to $6.49 and is fairly easy to add and subtract.

Example 4

Round each amount of money to the nearest 25 cents:

a. $3.77   b. $7.48   c. $5.98

Let's imagine that we have only dollar bills and quarters, and that we want to make the amount of money closest to each given amount.

a. The closest we can get to $3.77 is **$3.75.**

b. The closest we can get to $7.48 is **$7.50.**

c. The closest we can get to $5.98 is **$6.00.**

Lesson Practice

Represent Round each number to the nearest ten. For each problem, draw a number line to show your work.

a. 78   b. 43   c. 61   d. 45

Round each amount of money to the nearest dollar:

e. $14.29   f. $8.95   g. $21.45   h. $29.89

Round each amount of money to the nearest 25 cents:

i. $12.29   j. $6.95   k. $5.45   l. $11.81

Written Practice   *Distributed and Integrated*

Write and solve equations for problems **1** and **2**.

*1. **Formulate** A bakery employee baked seventy-two raisin muffins in
(11, 14) two batches. Twenty-four muffins were baked in the first batch. How many muffins were baked in the second batch?

*2. Four hundred seventy-six people attended the Friday evening
(1, 13) performance of a school play. Three hundred ninety-seven people
attended the Saturday evening performance. Altogether, how many
people attended those performances?

3. The ones digit is 5. The tens digit is 6. The number is between 600 and
(4) 700. What is the number?

4. **(Represent)** Write 509 in expanded form. Then use words to write the
(7, 16) number.

*5. **(Represent)** Use digits and symbols to write this comparison:
(Inv. 1)
Negative twenty is less than ten.

*6. The temperature one winter day in Iron Mountain, Michigan,
(18) is shown on the thermometer. Write the temperature in
degrees Fahrenheit and in degrees Celsius.

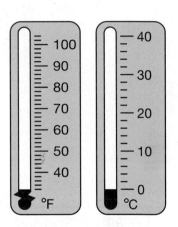

*7. **(Connect)** On Wednesday afternoons in September, flag
(19) football practice begins at the time shown on the clock and
ends at 5:40 p.m. How long is practice on those days?

*8. **(Explain)** Round each number to the nearest ten and explain how
(20) you rounded each number.

  a. 47   **b.** 74

9. $\begin{array}{r} \$476 \\ + \$285 \end{array}$ (13)   **10.** $\begin{array}{r} \$185 \\ + \$499 \end{array}$ (13)   **11.** $\begin{array}{r} 568 \\ + 397 \end{array}$ (13)   **12.** $\begin{array}{r} 478 \\ + 196 \end{array}$ (13)

13. $\begin{array}{r} 17 \\ - a \\ \hline 9 \end{array}$ (12)   **14.** $\begin{array}{r} 14 \\ - b \\ \hline 14 \end{array}$ (12)   **15.** $\begin{array}{r} 13 \\ - c \\ \hline 6 \end{array}$ (12)   ***16.** $\begin{array}{r} \$35 \\ - \$28 \end{array}$ (15)

*17. (15)
```
  23
- 15
```

*18. (15)
```
  63
- 36
```

*19. (15)
```
  74
- 59
```

20. (14)
```
    m
+  22
   45
```

*21. (16)
```
   k
- 15
  32
```

*22. (16)
```
  47
-  k
  34
```

23. (17)
```
   28
   36
   44
+ 58
```

24. (17)
```
   49
   28
   32
+ 55
```

*25. (20) Round each amount of money to the nearest dollar:

    a. $25.67   **b.** $14.42

*26. (7, 9) **Multiple Choice** Which number sentence describes this model?

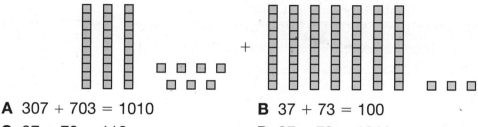

    A 307 + 703 = 1010   **B** 37 + 73 = 100

    C 37 + 73 = 110   **D** 37 + 73 = 1010

27. (3) How many different arrangements of three letters can you write using the letters b, r, and z? Each letter may be used only once, and the different arrangements you write do not need to form words.

*28. (20) Round each amount of money to the nearest 25 cents:

    a. $7.28   **b.** $4.48

29. (7) This table shows the land areas in square miles of four islands:

Islands of the World

Name	Location	Area (sq mi)
Micronesia	Pacific Ocean	271
Isle of Youth	Caribbean Sea	926
Isle of Man	Atlantic Ocean	227
Reunion	Indian Ocean	970

Write the names of the islands in order from greatest to least land area.

*30. (1) **Formulate** Write and solve an addition word problem that has a sum of 18.

Focus on

• Units of Length and Perimeter

A ruler is a tool used to measure length. In your desk you might have an *inch* ruler. Many inch rulers are one *foot* long. Twelve inches equals one foot. You might also have a yardstick in your classroom. A **yard** is three feet, which is 36 inches. A *mile* is a much larger unit of length. One mile is 5280 feet. Inches, feet, yards, and miles are units of length in the **U.S. Customary System.**

U.S. Customary Units of Length

Abbreviations	Equivalents
inch.... in.	12 in. = 1 ft
foot.... ft	3 ft = 1 yd
yard.... yd	36 in. = 1 yd
mile.... mi	5280 ft = 1 mi

Visit www. SaxonMath.com/ Int4Activities for an online activity.

1. A big step is about one yard. Tony walked the length of the room in 5 big steps. The room was about how many yards long? About how many feet long?

2. The electrician placed the light switch 4 feet above the floor. How many inches is four feet?

3. A mile is 5280 feet. How many feet is 2 miles?

The **metric system** is the system of measurement used by most of the world and is especially important in science. The basic unit of length in the metric system is the **meter.** You might have a meterstick in your classroom.

4. Use a yardstick and a meterstick to compare a yard and a meter. Which is longer?

5. Howie ran 100 yards. Jonah ran 100 meters. Who ran farther?

Model If you take a BIG step, you move about one meter. Place a meterstick on the floor, and practice taking a step that is one meter long.

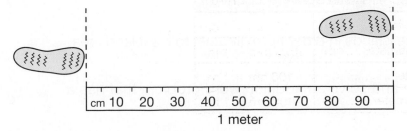

1 meter

6. **Estimate** What is the length of your classroom in meters? Make an estimate by taking one-meter steps along the length of the classroom.

In your desk you may have a **centimeter** ruler. A centimeter is a small part of a meter. One hundred centimeters equals one meter (just as 100 *cents* equals one dollar).

7. How many centimeters equal one meter?

8. Use an inch ruler and a centimeter ruler to compare an inch and a centimeter. Which is longer?

9. **Estimate** A ruler that is one foot long is about how many centimeters long?

10. **Estimate** Use an inch ruler to measure the length of a sheet of paper. About how many inches long is it?

11. Use a centimeter ruler to measure the length of your paper. About how many centimeters long is it?

12. **Estimate** Use inch and centimeter rulers to measure this picture of a pencil. The pencil is about

   a. how many inches long?

   b. how many centimeters long?

13. **Estimate** Use your rulers to measure a dollar bill. A dollar bill is about

   a. how many inches long?

   b. how many centimeters long?

Centimeter rulers and metersticks sometimes have small marks between the centimeter marks. The small marks are one **millimeter** apart. A dime is about one millimeter thick. Ten millimeters equals one centimeter, and 1000 millimeters equals a meter. We will learn more about millimeters in a later lesson.

To measure long distances, we can use **kilometers.** A kilometer is 1000 meters, which is a little more than half a mile.

Metric Units of Length

Abbreviations	Equivalents
millimeter......mm	10 mm = 1 cm
centimeter ....cm	1000 mm = 1 m
meter ....m	100 cm = 1 m
kilometer.......km	1000 m = 1 km

14. **Estimate** About how many BIG steps would a person take to walk a kilometer?

15. A mile is about 1609 meters. Which is longer, a mile or a kilometer?

16. How many millimeters equal one meter?

17. **Estimate** This key is about

    a. how many inches long?

    b. how many centimeters long?

    c. how many millimeters long?

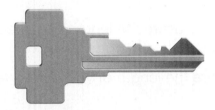

18. **Estimate** This rectangle is

    a. how many centimeters long?

    b. how many centimeters wide?

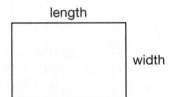

19. If an ant started at one corner of the rectangle above and crawled along all four sides back to the starting point, how many centimeters would it crawl?

The distance around a shape is its **perimeter.** To find the perimeter of a shape, we add the lengths of all of its sides.

In problem **18,** we found the perimeter of the rectangle by adding the length, the width, the length, and the width. Here we show a formula for the perimeter of a rectangle:

Perimeter of rectangle = length + width + length + width

If we use the letter *P* for perimeter, *l* for length, and *w* for width, the formula becomes:

$$P = l + w + l + w$$

Since there are two lengths and two widths, we often write the formula this way:

$$P = 2l + 2w$$

20. Keisha ran the perimeter of the block below. How far did Keisha run?

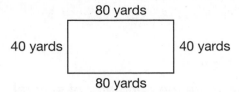

80 yards

40 yards   40 yards

80 yards

21. What is the perimeter of this square?

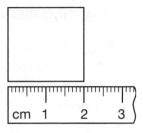

cm   1   2   3

22. What is the perimeter of a square with sides 10 in. long?

23. Find the perimeter of the triangle at right:

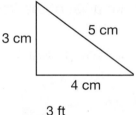

3 cm   5 cm

4 cm

24. a. What is the length of the rectangle at right?

b. What is the width of the rectangle?

c. What is the perimeter of the rectangle?

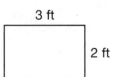

3 ft

2 ft

25. (**Analyze**) Uncle Beau's cows graze in a grassy field surrounded by a wire fence. Which represents the perimeter of the field: the grassy field or the wire fence?

26. (**Analyze**) A glass mirror on Amanda's wall is surrounded by a wooden frame. Which represents the perimeter of the mirror: the glass mirror or the wooden frame?

27. (**Estimate**) What is the perimeter of your classroom in meters? Make an estimate by taking one-meter steps along the edges of the classroom.

28. (**Explain**) What is the meaning of this formula?

$$P = 2l + 2w$$

Activity

Estimating the Perimeter

Material needed:
- ruler or yardstick

Use an inch ruler or a yardstick to estimate the perimeter of several items in your classroom.

Items might include:

- your desktop
- your teacher's desktop
- a door
- a book cover
- the classroom board

Make a list of the items you choose and the estimated perimeter for each item.

Investigate Further

Describe the relationship between the two sets of data in this table:

Perimeters of Squares

Perimeter (in inches)	4	8	12	16	20	24
Side length (in inches)	1	2	3	4	5	6

(**Predict**) What is the perimeter of a square with a side length of 10 inches? How do you know?

(**Generalize**) Write a formula that could be used to find the perimeter of any square.

• Triangles, Rectangles, Squares, and Circles

multiples

Power Up K

The multiples of 7 are 7, 14, 21, and so on. On your hundred number chart, circle the numbers that are multiples of seven. Which of the circled numbers is an even number as well as a multiple of five?

mental math

a. **Number Sense:** $44 + 32$

b. **Number Sense:** $57 + 19$

c. **Number Sense:** $32 + 43 + 100$

d. **Number Sense:** What number should be added to 6 to get a total of 9?

e. **Money:** What is the total value of 2 quarters, 3 dimes, and 1 nickel?

f. **Money:** What is the total cost of a $200 bicycle and a $24 helmet?

g. **Estimation:** Round $13.89 to the nearest dollar.

h. **Estimation:** Round 73 yards to the nearest ten yards.

problem solving

Choose an appropriate problem-solving strategy to solve this problem. The P.E. instructor divided the 21 students into four teams. If the P.E. instructor divided the class as evenly as possible, how many students were on each of the four teams?

New Concept

In this lesson we will practice drawing triangles, rectangles, squares, and circles.

Example 1

Represent Draw a triangle whose sides all have the same length.

Math Language

A triangle whose sides are all equal in length is called an **equilateral triangle.**

You may need to practice on a separate sheet of paper to understand how to draw this triangle. A triangle has three sides, but those sides can be positioned many different ways. If you start with a "square corner," the third side will be too long.

square corner

This side is longer than the other two sides.

A triangle whose sides are the same length looks like this:

Example 2

Represent Draw a rectangle whose sides all have the same length.

A rectangle has four sides and square corners. It does not have to be longer than it is wide. A rectangle whose sides are the same length looks like this:

This figure looks like a square. We know that it is a square because it has 4 sides with the same length. It is also a rectangle. **A square is a special kind of rectangle.**

Example 3

Thinking Skill

Analyze

What is the perimeter of this rectangle?

Represent Draw a rectangle that is 3 cm long and 2 cm wide.

We use a centimeter ruler to help us make the drawing.

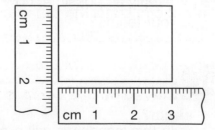

A **circle** is a closed, curved shape in which all points on the shape are the same distance from the center. To draw circles, we can use a tool called a **compass.** Below we show two types of compasses:

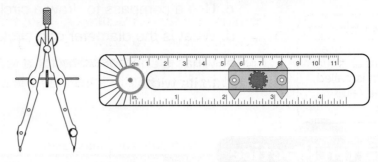

Math Language

When we talk about one radius, we say "radius." When we talk about more than one radius, we say "radii." The plural of radius is **radii.**

There are two points on a compass: a pivot point and a pencil point. We swing the pencil point around the pivot point to draw a circle. The distance between the two points is the **radius** of the circle.

The radius of a circle is the distance from the **center** of the circle to the edge of the circle. The **diameter** of a circle is the distance across the circle through the center. As the diagram below illustrates, the diameter of a circle equals two radii.

Math Language

The **circumference** of a circle is the distance around— or the perimeter of—a circle.

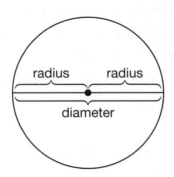

radius   radius

diameter

Drawing a Circle

Material needed:
- compass

Represent Use a compass to draw a circle with a radius of 2 cm. Label the diameter and the radius.

Example 4

If the radius of a circle is 2 cm, then what is the diameter of the circle?

Since the diameter of a circle equals two radii, the diameter of a circle with a 2-cm radius is **4 cm.**

a. Draw a triangle with two sides that are the same length.

b. Draw a rectangle that is about twice as long as it is wide.

c. Use a compass to draw a circle with a radius of 1 inch.

d. What is the diameter of a circle that has a 3-cm radius?

e. What is another name for a rectangle whose length is equal to its width?

Written Practice   *Distributed and Integrated*

Write and solve equations for problems **1** and **2**.

1. Hiroshi had four hundred seventeen marbles. Harry had two hundred
(1, 13) twenty-two marbles. How many marbles did Hiroshi and Harry have
in all?

*2. Tisha put forty pennies into a pile. After Jane added all of her pennies,
(11, 14) there were seventy-two pennies in the pile. How many pennies did
Jane add to the pile?

3. The ones digit is 5. The number is greater than 640 and less than 650.
(4) What is the number?

*4. (Represent) Write seven hundred fifty-three in expanded form.
(16)

*5. (Connect) If x + y = 10, then what is the other addition fact for x, y,
(6) and 10? What are the two subtraction facts for x, y, and 10?

*6. These thermometers show the average daily low and high
(18) temperatures in San Juan, Puerto Rico, during the month
of January. What are those temperatures?

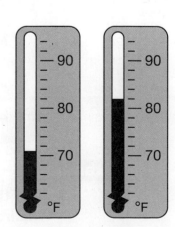

*7. **Model** Use a centimeter ruler to measure the rectangle below.
(Inv. 2)

    a. What is the length?

    b. What is the width?

    c. What is the perimeter?

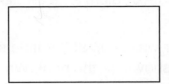

8.   493
(13) **+ 278**

9. $486
(13) **+ $378**

10. $524
(13) **+ $109**

*11. **Represent** Draw a triangle. Make each side 2 cm long. What is the
(Inv. 2, 21) perimeter of the triangle?

*12. **Represent** Draw a square with sides 2 inches long. What is the
(Inv. 2, 21) perimeter of the square?

13.   17
(12) $- a$
    9

14.   45
(15) $- 29$

15.   15
(12) $- b$
    6

16.   62
(15) $- 45$

17.   24
(14) $+ d$
   45

18.   14
(16) $- b$
    2

*19. y
(16) $- 36$
   53

*20.   75
(16) $- p$
   45

21.   46
(17)   35
    27
  + 39

22.   14
(17)   28
    77
  + 23

23.   14
(17)   23
    38
  + 64

24.   15
(17)   24
    36
  + 99

*25. **Conclude** Write the next three numbers in each counting sequence:
(3, Inv. 1)

    a. ..., 28, 35, 42, _____, _____, _____, ...

    b. ..., 40, 30, 20, _____, _____, _____, ...

*26. **(Explain)** If you know the length and the width of a rectangle, how
(Inv. 2) can you find its perimeter?

*27. **Multiple Choice** Alba drew a circle with a radius of 4 cm. What was
(21) the diameter of the circle?

A 8 in. **B** 2 in. **C** 8 cm **D** 2 cm

*28. Each school morning, Christopher wakes up at the time shown on the left
(19) and leaves for school at the time shown on the right. What amount of time
does Christopher spend each morning getting ready for school?

*29. Round each number to the nearest ten. You may draw a number line.
(20)
a. 76 **b.** 73 **c.** 75

*30. Round each amount of money to the nearest 25 cents.
(20)
a. $6.77 **b.** $7.97

*Real-World
Connection*

Erin and Bethany both drew circles on their paper. The radius of
Erin's circle is 14 cm. The diameter of Bethany's circle is 26 cm.
Bethany said that her circle is bigger. Was Bethany correct? Explain
your answer.

LESSON 22

- # Naming Fractions
- # Adding Dollars and Cents

Power Up

facts	Power Up A
count aloud	As a class, count by sevens from 7 to 35.

mental math

a. **Number Sense:** $63 + 21$

b. **Number Sense:** $36 + 29 + 30$

c. **Number Sense:** $130 + 200 + 300$

d. **Geometry:** If a triangle measures 1 centimeter on each side, what is the perimeter?

e. **Time:** What time is 2 hours after 1:00 p.m.?

f. **Money:** What is the total cost of two pens that are $1 each and one pair of scissors that is $4?

g. **Estimation:** Round $2.22 to the nearest 25 cents.

h. **Measurement:** How many centimeters are equal to 1 meter?

problem solving

Seven days after Tuesday is Tuesday. Fourteen days after Tuesday is Tuesday. Twenty-one days after Tuesday is Tuesday. What day of the week is 70 days after Tuesday?

Focus Strategy: Find/Extend a Pattern

Understand We are asked to find which day of the week is 70 days after Tuesday. We are told that 7, 14, and 21 days after Tuesday are all Tuesdays. These numbers form a pattern.

Plan We will *find the pattern* that describes how the days of the week repeat. We can *extend the pattern* to help us answer the question.

Solve We look for a pattern in the numbers given to us: 7, 14, 21. We say these numbers when we count up by sevens. Counting up by sevens is a pattern that can be extended:

7, 14, 21, 28, 35, 42, 49, 56, 63, 70

Seven days is one week, 14 days is two weeks, 21 days is 3 weeks, and so on. Seventy days equals the number of days in 10 weeks. Ten weeks after Tuesday is Tuesday, which means that **70 days after Tuesday is Tuesday.**

Check We know our answer is reasonable because 70 days is the same as 10 weeks, and 10 weeks after a certain day of the week will be that day of the week again.

New Concepts

Naming Fractions

Part of a whole can be named with a **fraction.** A fraction is written with two numbers. The bottom number of a fraction is called the **denominator.** The denominator tells how many equal parts are in the whole. The top number of a fraction is called the **numerator.** The numerator tells how many of the parts are being counted. When naming a fraction, we name the numerator first; then we name the denominator using its ordinal number. Some fractions and their names are shown below:

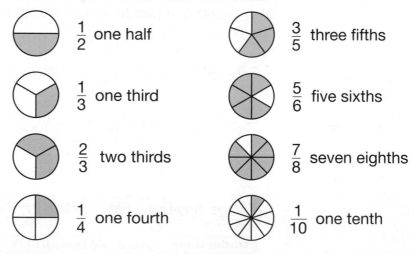

$\frac{1}{2}$ one half $\frac{3}{5}$ three fifths

$\frac{1}{3}$ one third $\frac{5}{6}$ five sixths

$\frac{2}{3}$ two thirds $\frac{7}{8}$ seven eighths

$\frac{1}{4}$ one fourth $\frac{1}{10}$ one tenth

> **Math Language**
>
> There are exceptions when we use ordinals to name denominators. For example, we use the word **half** instead of *second* to name a denominator of 2. Also, we sometimes use the word **quarter,** as well as fourth, to name a denominator of 4.

Analyze Use the pictures to write these fractions in order from greatest to least.

Example 1

What fraction of the circle is shaded?

There are four equal parts and three are shaded.
Therefore, the fraction of the circle that is shaded is
three fourths, which we write as

$$\dfrac{3}{4}$$

Justify Which is greater, $\dfrac{3}{4}$ or $\dfrac{3}{5}$? Explain how you know.

Example 2

A dime is what fraction of a dollar?

Ten dimes equal one dollar, so one dime is $\dfrac{1}{10}$ of a dollar.

Example 3

Three quarters are what fraction of a dollar?

Four quarters equal a dollar, so each quarter is $\dfrac{1}{4}$ of a dollar. Three
quarters are $\dfrac{3}{4}$ of a dollar.

Adding Dollars and Cents

We add dollars and cents the same way we add whole numbers.
The dot, called a **decimal point,** separates dollars from cents.
To add dollars to dollars and cents to cents, we align the decimal
points. We remember to write the dollar sign and the decimal
point in the sum.

Visit www.
SaxonMath.com/
Int4Activities
for a calculator
activity.

Activity

Counting Money

Materials needed:
- money manipulatives (from **Lesson Activity 2**)
- money manipulatives (from **Lesson Activites 7, 8,** and **9**)

Use money manipulatives to perform the following tasks:

1. Place $1.43 in one stack and $1.34 in another stack. Which amount is greater? Explain why.

2. Make three stacks of money: $1.32, $2.13, and $1.23. Then arrange the stacks in order of value from least to greatest.

3. (Model) Act out the following problem: At a yard sale, J'Nessa bought a skateboard for $3.50 and a basketball for $2.75. How much did she spend on the two items?

Example 4

At the school book fair, Syaoran bought two books, one for $3.75 and the other for $2.75. How much did Syaoran pay for both books?

First we add the pennies, then we add the dimes, and then we add the dollars. Since ten pennies equals a dime and ten dimes equals a dollar, we regroup when the total in any column is ten or more.

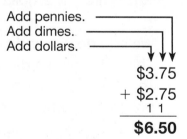

Add pennies.
Add dimes.
Add dollars.

$$\begin{array}{r} \$3.75 \\ + \$2.75 \\ \hline {\scriptstyle 1\ 1} \\ \hline \$6.50 \end{array}$$

Syaoran paid **$6.50** for both books.

Compatible numbers are two or more numbers that are relatively easy to work with. Money amounts that end in 25¢, 50¢, and 75¢ are compatible with each other because we can add and subtract with these numbers mentally. In Example 5, we use compatible numbers to estimate a sum. When we **estimate**, we are finding an approximate value.

Example 5

For her garden, Imelda purchased some packets of vegetable seeds for $3.27 and some tomato plants for $4.49. What is a reasonable estimate for the total cost of her purchase?

To estimate, we can use the compatible numbers $3.25 and $4.50, which are close to $3.27 and $4.49. We mentally add the compatible numbers and find that the total cost is about **$7.75.**

Lesson Practice What fraction of each shape is shaded?

a.

b.

Use the models below to order the fractions from least to greatest.

c. $\frac{1}{3}, \frac{2}{10}, \frac{1}{4}$

d. $\frac{2}{5}, \frac{3}{8}, \frac{1}{2}$

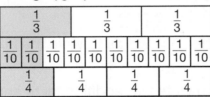

Use your fraction manipulatives to order the fractions below from greatest to least.

e. $\frac{3}{4}, \frac{1}{5}, \frac{2}{3}$

f. $\frac{6}{10}, \frac{4}{5}, \frac{1}{2}$

g. Three dimes are what fraction of a dollar?

You may use money manipulatives to add.

h. $2.75
   + $2.75

i. $3.65
   + $4.28

j. A notebook at the school bookstore costs $1.49. What is a reasonable estimate of the cost of two notebooks? Explain why your estimate is reasonable.

Written Practice *Distributed and Integrated*

Write and solve equations for problems **1** and **2**.

*1. A carpenter has two boards. The sum of the lengths of the boards is
(11, 14) 96 inches. The length of one board is 48 inches. What is the length of the other board?

2. Jafari was 49 inches tall at the beginning of summer. He grew 2 inches
(1, 9) over the summer. How tall was Jafari at the end of summer?

3. Use the digits 1, 2, and 3 to write an odd number less than 200. Each
(10) digit may be used only once.

Conclude Write the next three numbers in each counting sequence:

* **4.** ... , 80, 72, 64, _____, _____, _____, ...   * **5.** ... , 60, 54, 48, _____, _____, _____, ...
(3)   (3)

* **6.** **Represent** Draw a square with sides 3 cm long. What is the perimeter
(Inv. 2, of the square?
21)

* **7.** A yard is how many feet long?
(Inv. 2)

8. What is the place value of the 9 in 891?
(4)

* **9.** Write 106 in expanded form. Then use words to write the number.
(7, 16)

10. Use the numbers 6, 9, and 15 to write two addition facts and two
(6) subtraction facts.

11. Use digits and symbols to write that eighteen is greater than negative
(Inv. 1) twenty.

* **12. a.** Round 28 to the nearest ten.   **b.** Round $5.95 to the nearest dollar.
(20)

* **13.** A desk is about how many meters high?
(Inv. 2)

* **14.** The first four odd numbers are 1, 3, 5, and 7. What is their sum?
(1)

* **15.** Draw a circle that has a diameter of 2 cm. What is the radius of the circle?
(21)

* **16.** What fraction of this rectangle is shaded?
(22)

* 17. The door was two meters tall. Two meters is how many centimeters?
(Inv. 2)

18. $51 - 43$
(15)

19. $70 - 44$
(15)

20. $37 - 9$
(15)

21. $\$8.79 + \$0.64$
(22)

22. $\$5.75 + \$2.75$
(22)

23. $\begin{array}{r} n \\ +13 \\ \hline 17 \end{array}$
(14)

* 24. $\begin{array}{r} x \\ -42 \\ \hline 27 \end{array}$
(16)

* 25. $\begin{array}{r} 37 \\ -p \\ \hline 14 \end{array}$
(16)

* 26. Sketch a circle. Draw two diameters to divide the circle into four
(22) equal parts. Shade one of the parts. What fraction of the circle is
shaded?

* 27. Multiple Choice If the equation $20 + n = 60$ is true, then
(6) which of the following equations is *not* true?

    A $60 - 20 = n$
    B $60 - n = 20$

    C $n - 20 = 60$
    D $n + 20 = 60$

* 28. **Explain** One item in a supermarket is marked $1.26. Another
(22) item is marked $3.73. What is a reasonable estimate for the cost of
both items? Explain why your estimate is reasonable.

29. This table shows the heights of four waterfalls:
(7)

Waterfalls

Name	Location	Height (ft)
Multnomah	Oregon	620
Maletsunyane	Lesotho, Africa	630
Wentworth	Australia	614
Reichenbach	Switzerland	656

Write the names of the waterfalls in order from least height to greatest
height.

* 30. **Predict** What is the tenth number in this counting sequence?
(3)

$$4, 8, 12, 16, 20, \ldots$$

• Lines, Segments, Rays, and Angles

multiples

Power Up K

On your hundred number chart, circle the multiples of 9. Write the circled numbers from least to greatest in a column. What patterns can you find in the column of numbers?

mental math

Number Sense: Add hundreds, then tens, and then ones.

a. 320
    + 256

b. 645
    + 32

c. 145
    + 250

d. **Geometry:** If each side of a square is 1 inch, what is the perimeter?

e. **Time:** What time is 5 hours after 3:00 p.m.?

f. **Money:** What is the total cost of three pieces of gum that are 8¢ each?

g. **Estimation:** The lawn is 62 feet across. Round that length to the nearest ten feet.

h. **Measurement:** How many millimeters are equal to 1 centimeter?

problem solving

Choose an appropriate problem-solving strategy to solve this problem. The days of the week repeat. Seven days before Saturday was Saturday, and seven days after Saturday is Saturday again. What day is ten days after Saturday? What day was ten days before Saturday?

New Concept

Thinking Skill

Connect

Is this figure a ray? Explain why or why not.

A line goes on and on. When we draw a line, we draw two arrowheads to show that the line continues in both directions.

Line

Part of a line is a line segment, or just *segment.* When we draw a segment, we do not include arrowheads. We can, however, use dots to show the **endpoints** of the segment.

Segment

A **ray** is sometimes called a *half-line.* A ray begins at a point and continues in one direction without end. When we draw a ray, we include one arrowhead to show that the ray continues in one direction.

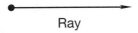

Ray

Example 1

Write "line," "segment," or "ray" to describe each of these physical models:

    a. a beam of starlight

    b. a ruler

    a. A beam of starlight begins at a "point," the star, and continues across space. This is an example of a **ray.**

    b. A ruler has two endpoints, so it is best described as an example of a **segment.**

Lines and segments that go in the same direction and stay the same distance apart are **parallel.**

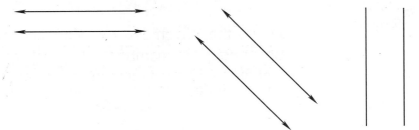

Pairs of parallel lines and segments

When lines or segments cross, we call them **intersecting lines.**

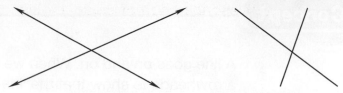

Pairs of intersecting lines and segments

Intersecting lines or segments that form "square corners" are **perpendicular.**

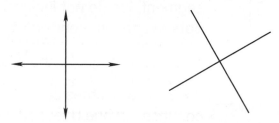

Pairs of perpendicular lines and segments

Angles are formed where lines or segments intersect or where at least two rays begin. An angle has a **vertex** and two sides. The vertex is the point where the two sides meet (the "corner").

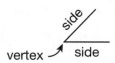

An angle is named by how "open" it is. An angle like the corner of a square is called a **right angle.**

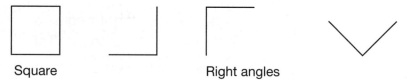

Square   Right angles

To show that an angle is a right angle, we can draw a small square in the corner of the right angle.

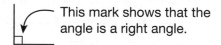

This mark shows that the angle is a right angle.

Angles that are smaller than right angles are called **acute angles.** Some people remember this by saying, "a cute little angle." Angles that are larger than right angles are **obtuse angles.**

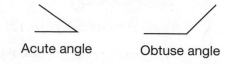

Acute angle   Obtuse angle

Thinking Skill

Model

Look for objects in your classroom that have parallel, perpendicular, or intersecting line segments. Describe how each segment is different.

Example 2

Describe each of these angles:

a. b. c.

a. The angle is smaller than a right angle, so it is an **acute angle.**

b. The angle makes a square corner, so it is a **right angle.**

c. The angle is larger than a right angle, so it is an **obtuse angle.**

The figure in the following example has four angles. We can name each angle by the letter at the vertex of the angle. The four angles in the figure are angle *Q*, angle *R*, angle *S*, and angle *T*.

Example 3

Identify each of the four angles in this figure as acute, right, or obtuse.

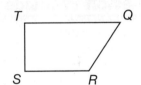

Angle *Q* is smaller than a right angle, so **angle *Q* is acute.** Angle *R* is larger than a right angle, so **angle *R* is obtuse.** Angles *S* and *T* both form square corners, so **angles *S* and *T* are right.**

Example 4

Draw a triangle that has one right angle.

We begin by drawing two line segments that form a right angle. Then we draw the third side.

Notice that the other two angles are acute angles.

Represent Draw and describe the characteristics of a triangle that has an obtuse angle.

Activity

Real-World Segments and Angles

1. Look for examples of the following figures in your classroom. Describe and classify each example.

   a. parallel segments

   b. perpendicular segments

c. intersecting segments

d. right angles

e. acute angles

f. obtuse angles

2. Bend your arm so that the angle at the elbow is an acute angle, then a right angle, and then an obtuse angle. Bend your leg so that the angle behind your knee is an acute angle, then a right angle, and then an obtuse angle.

3. Using your own words:

   a. describe acute, right, and obtuse angles.

   b. describe parallel, perpendicular, and intersecting lines.

Lesson Practice

a. Draw two segments that intersect but are *not* perpendicular.

b. Draw two lines that are perpendicular.

c. Draw a ray.

d. Are the rails of a train track parallel or perpendicular? How do you know? Locate and describe the angles of items in or around your classroom.

e. A triangle has how many angles?

f. Multiple Choice Which of these angles does *not* look like a right angle?

A   B   C   D

Written Practice   *Distributed and Integrated*

Write and solve equations for problems **1** and **2**.

1. Twenty-eight children were in the first line. Forty-two children were in
   (1, 9)   the second line. Altogether, how many children were in both lines?

*2. Tina knew that there were 28 books in the two stacks. Tina counted
(11, 14)   12 books in the first stack. Then she figured out how many books were
   in the second stack. How many books were in the second stack?

3. Use the digits 1, 2, and 3 to write an odd number greater than 300.
(10) Each digit may be used only once.

*4. **Conclude** Write the next three numbers in each counting sequence:
(3)

a. ... , 40, 36, 32, ____, ____, ____, ...

b. ... , 30, 27, 24, ____, ____, ____, ...

*5. **Connect** Use the numbers 15, 16, and 31 to write two addition facts
(6) and two subtraction facts.

6. Use digits and a comparison symbol to show that six hundred
(Inv. 1) thirty-eight is less than six hundred eighty-three.

*7. a. Round 92 to the nearest ten.
(20)

b. Round $19.67 to the nearest dollar.

*8. **Explain** The radius of a nickel is 1 centimeter. If 10 nickels are placed
(21) in a row, how long will the row be? Describe how you found your answer.

*9. Use a centimeter ruler to measure this rectangle:
(Inv. 2)

a. What is the length?

b. What is the width?

c. What is the perimeter?

*10. Multiple Choice Which of these shapes has four right angles?
(23)

A   B   C   D

*11. What fraction of this triangle is shaded?
(22)

*12. The clock shows the time that Reginald's last class of
(19) the day begins. The class ends at 2:55 p.m. How long is
Reginald's last class of the day?

* 13. $83
(15)   − $27

* 14. 42
(15)   − 27

* 15. 72
(15)   − 36

16. $4.28
(22)   + $1.96

17. $4.36
(22)   + $2.95

18. 57
(14)   + k
         88

* 19. 67
(16)   − b
         16

* 20. k
(16)   − 22
         22

21. 42 − 7
(15)

* 22. 55 − 48
(15)

23. 31 − 20
(14)

24. 25 + 25 + 25 + 25
(17)

25. **a.** How many nickels equal one dollar?
(22)

b. One nickel is what fraction of a dollar?

c. Seven nickels are what fraction of a dollar?

* 26. **Multiple Choice** If $26 + m = 63$, then which of these equations is
(6)   *not* true?

A $m + 26 = 63$ **B** $m − 63 = 26$

C $63 − m = 26$ **D** $63 − 26 = m$

* 27. **Multiple Choice** Which of these figures illustrates a ray?
(23)

A    **B**

C    **D**

* 28. **Explain** A music store is having a sale. Single CDs cost $11.99 each.
(22)   Double CDs cost $22.99 each. What is a reasonable estimate of the cost
        of 3 single CDs? Explain why your answer is reasonable.

29. Compare. Write >, <, or =.
(Inv. 1)
a. 68 ◯ 71   **b.** 501 ◯ 267   **c.** 706 ◯ 709

* 30. In the student council elections, 1300 votes were cast for the two
(11, 14)   candidates. One candidate received 935 votes. Write and solve an
            equation to find the number of votes the other candidate received.

• Inverse Operations

facts	Power Up B
count aloud	Count by sevens from 7 to 42.

mental math

a. **Number Sense:** 365 + 321 (Add hundreds, then tens, and then ones.)

b. **Number Sense:** 40 + 300 + 25

c. **Number Sense:** 300 + 50 + 12

d. **Number Sense:** Seven can be split into 3 + 4. If 7 is split into 2 + ☐, what number is represented by ☐?

e. **Time:** What time is 4 hours after 6:15 p.m.?

f. **Money:** What is the total value of 8 dimes and 12 pennies?

g. **Estimation:** One wall of the classroom is 28 feet long. Round that length to the nearest ten feet.

h. **Measurement:** How many meters are equal to 1 kilometer?

problem solving

Choose an appropriate problem-solving strategy to solve this problem. The two-digit numbers 18 and 81 are written with digits whose sum is nine. On your paper, list in order the two-digit numbers from 18 to 81 whose digits have a sum of nine.

18, ____, ____, ____, ____, ____, ____, 81

What do you notice about the sequence of numbers?

Math Language

We can write related equations using the same numbers because addition and subtraction are **inverse operations**. One operation undoes the other.

We have seen that the three numbers in an addition or subtraction fact form three other facts as well. If we know that $n + 3 = 5$, then we know these four facts:

$$
\begin{array}{cccc}
n & 3 & 5 & 5 \\
+\,3 & +\,n & -\,n & -\,3 \\
\hline
5 & 5 & 3 & n
\end{array}
$$

Notice that the last of these facts, $5 - 3 = n$, shows us how to find n. We subtract 3 from 5 to find that n equals 2.

Example 1

Write another addition fact and two subtraction facts using the numbers in this equation:

$$36 + m = 54$$

Which fact shows how to find m?

We arrange the numbers to write three facts. Notice that the sum, 54, becomes the first number of both subtraction facts.

$$m + 36 = 54 \qquad 54 - m = 36 \qquad 54 - 36 = \tilde{m}$$

The fact that shows how to find m is

$$54 - 36 = m$$

Example 2

Write another subtraction fact and two addition facts using the numbers in this equation:

$$72 - w = 47$$

Which fact shows how to find w?

Notice that the first number of a subtraction fact remains the first number of the second subtraction fact.

$$72 - 47 = w$$

Also notice that the first number of a subtraction fact is the sum when the numbers are arranged to form an addition fact.

$$47 + w = 72 \qquad w + 47 = 72$$

The fact that shows how to find w is

$$72 - 47 = w$$

Example 3

Find the missing number: $r + 36 = 54$

We can form another addition fact and two subtraction facts using these numbers.

$$36 + r = 54 \qquad 54 - r = 36 \qquad 54 - 36 = r$$

The last fact, $54 - 36 = r$, shows us how to find r. We subtract 36 from 54 and get **18**.

Example 4

Find the missing number: $t - 29 = 57$

We can write the first number of a subtraction equation as the sum of an addition equation.

$$57 + 29 = t$$

Thus, t equals **86**.

Lesson Practice   Find each missing number:

a. $23 + m = 42$ **b.** $q + 17 = 45$

c. $53 - w = 28$ **d.** $n - 26 = 68$

e. $36 + y = 63$ **f.** $62 - a = 26$

Written Practice   *Distributed and Integrated*

*1. Rafael placed two 1-foot rulers end to end. What was the total length of
(Inv. 2) the two rulers in inches?

*2. During the one-hour television show, there were 12 minutes of
(11, 24) commercials. How many minutes of the hour were not commercials?
Write an equation.

*3. Multiple Choice All the students lined up in two equal rows. Which
(10) could *not* be the total number of students?

   A 36   **B** 45   **C** 60   **D** 24

*4. **Connect** Find the missing numbers in this counting sequence:
(3)

$$\ldots, 9, 18, \underline{\qquad}, \underline{\qquad}, 45, \underline{\qquad}, \ldots$$

* 5. **(Predict)** Find the sixth number in this counting sequence:
(3, 5)

$$7, 14, 21, \ldots$$

6. Compare: $15 - 9 \bigcirc 13 - 8$
(Inv. 1)

7. **a.** Round 77 to the nearest ten.
(20)

b. Round $29.39 to the nearest dollar.

c. Round $9.19 to the nearest 25 cents.

* 8. **(Estimate)** A professional basketball player might be about how many
(Inv. 2) meters tall?

* 9. Jeong and her friends attended an evening movie that
(19) began at the time shown on the clock. The movie ended
at 9:05 p.m. How long was the movie?

* 10. **(Conclude)** Which street is parallel to Elm?
(23)

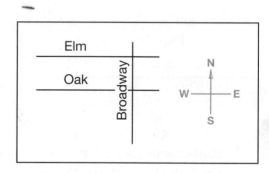

* 11. **a.** How many dimes equal one dollar?
(22)

b. One dime is what fraction of a dollar?

c. Nine dimes are what fraction of a dollar?

* 12. **(Represent)** Draw a rectangle that is 5 centimeters long and
(Inv. 2, 2 centimeters wide. What is the perimeter?
21)

* 13. Describe each type of angle shown below:
(23)

a.   **b.** **c.**

14. $31
(15) − $14

15. $468
(13) + $247

16. 57
(14) − 37

17. $4.97
(22) + $2.58

* 18. $36 - c = 19$
(24)

19. $b + 65 = 82$
(24)

* 20. $87 + d = 93$
(24)

* 21. $n - 32 = 19$
(24)

22. $48 - 28$
(14)

23. $41 - 32$
(15)

24. $76 - 58$
(15)

25. $416 + 35 + 27 + 43 + 5$
(17)

* 26. Multiple Choice Which point on this number line could represent −3?
(Inv. 1)

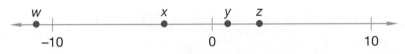

A point *w*　　**B** point *x*　　**C** point *y*　　**D** point *z*

* 27. **Explain** How is a segment different from a line?
(23)

* 28. **Estimate** Concert tickets cost $18 each, not including a $4.25
(22) transaction fee for each ticket. What is a reasonable estimate of the
cost to purchase two concert tickets? Explain why your estimate is
reasonable.

29. The thermometer shows the high temperature on an
(18) April day in Nashville, Tennessee. What was the high
temperature that day?

* 30. **Formulate** Write and solve an addition word problem
(1) that has a sum of 43.

LESSON 25

• Subtraction Word Problems

facts   Power Up B

count aloud   Count down by tens from 250 to 10.

mental math

    a. Number Sense: $35 + 60 + 100$

    b. Number Sense: $200 + 50 + 432$

    c. Number Sense: $56 + 19 + 200$

    d. Geometry: What is the diameter of a circle that has a 1-centimeter radius?

    e. Time: What time is 4 hours after 11:20 a.m.?

    f. Money: What is the total cost of a $19 hammer and a $3 box of nails?

    g. Estimation: The lunch cost $5.47. Round $5.47 to the nearest 25 cents.

    h. Measurement: How many feet are equal to one mile?

problem solving

Choose an appropriate problem-solving strategy to solve this problem. In some sequences, the count from one number to the next increases. In the sequence below, from 1 to 4 is 3, from 4 to 9 is 5, and from 9 to 16 is 7. Continue this sequence to the tenth term, which is 100.

$$1, 4, 9, 16, \ldots$$

What do you notice about the increase from one number to the next?

New Concept

We have practiced solving word problems with a "some and some more" plot. Recall that "some and some more" problems use an addition formula.

In this lesson, we will begin to practice solving word problems that have a subtraction plot. One type of problem with a subtraction plot is a "some went away" problem. Read this "some went away" problem:

> *Jannik had 7 marbles. Then he lost 3 marbles. He has 4 marbles left.*

We can write the information from this word problem in a subtraction formula like this:

Reading Math

We translate the problem using a subtraction formula.

Jannik had:
7 marbles
He lost: 3 marbles
Marbles left: 4

Formula	Problem
Some	7 marbles
− Some went away	− 3 marbles
What is left	4 marbles

We can also write the formula horizontally.

Formula: Some − Some went away = What is left

Problem: 7 marbles − 3 marbles = 4 marbles

In a "some went away" problem there are three numbers. Any one of the numbers may be missing. We use the subtraction formula and write the numbers we know in a subtraction problem and then find the missing number.

Recall that we solve a word problem using the four-step problem-solving process.

Step 1: Read and translate the problem.

Step 2: Make a plan to solve the problem.

Step 3: Follow the plan and solve the problem.

Step 4: Check your answer for reasonableness.

A plan that can help us solve word problems is to *write an equation.* We do this by writing the numbers we know in an equation using the subtraction formula.

Example 1

Jaxon had some pencils. Then he gave away 15 pencils. Now he has 22 pencils left. How many pencils did Jaxon have in the beginning?

Jaxon gave away some pencils. This word problem has a "some went away" plot. We are told how many pencils "went away" and how many pencils are left. To find how many pencils Jaxon had in the beginning, we use the subtraction formula to write an equation. We fill in the numbers given and use a letter for the missing number.

	Formula	Problem
	Some	p pencils
	− Some went away	− 15 pencils
	What is left	22 pencils

We can solve for the missing number in this subtraction problem by adding.

$$
\begin{array}{r}
22 \text{ pencils} \\
+ 15 \text{ pencils} \\
\hline
37 \text{ pencils}
\end{array}
$$

Jaxon had **37 pencils** in the beginning. Now we check the answer in the original problem.

$$
\begin{array}{r}
37 \text{ pencils} \\
- 15 \text{ pencils} \\
\hline
22 \text{ pencils}
\end{array}
$$

Example 2

Celia had 42 seashells. She sent some seashells to her aunt. She has 29 seashells left. How many seashells did Celia send to her aunt?

Celia sent some seashells to her aunt. This problem has a "some went away" plot. We are asked to find the number that went away. We know how many seashells she had before and after she sent some to her aunt. We write the numbers we know in the formula.

Formula	Problem
Some	42 seashells
− Some went away	− s seashells
What is left	29 seashells

To solve for the missing number, we subtract.

$$
\begin{array}{r}
42 \\
- 29 \\
\hline
13
\end{array}
$$

We find that Celia sent **13 seashells** to her aunt. Now we check to see whether 13 seashells makes the problem correct.

$$
\begin{array}{r}
42 \text{ seashells} \\
- 13 \text{ seashells} \\
\hline
29 \text{ seashells}
\end{array}
$$

Example 3

LuAnn had 65 beads. Then she used 13 beads to make a necklace. How many beads does LuAnn have left to use?

This problem also has a "some went away" plot. We write the numbers in an equation using the subtraction formula and then find the missing number. This time, we practice writing the formula horizontally.

Formula: Some − Some went away = What is left

Problem: 65 beads − 13 beads = b beads

To find the missing number, we simply subtract.

65 beads − 13 beads = 52 beads

We find that LuAnn has **52 beads** left.

Justify Is the answer reasonable? Explain why or why not.

Lesson Practice

Formulate Write and solve subtraction equations for problems **a–c.**

a. Marko had 42 cards. Then he mailed some cards. Now he has 26 cards. How many cards did Marko mail?

b. Tamika donated 42 books. Now she has 26 books. How many books did Tamika have in the beginning?

c. Barbara had 75 cents. Then she spent 27 cents. How many cents does Barbara have now?

Written Practice

Distributed and Integrated

Formulate Write and solve equations for problems **1–3.**

*1. Barke had 75 stamps. Then he gave some stamps to Joey. Now he
(25) has 27 stamps. How many stamps did Barke give away?

*2. Rafiki had sixty-three baseball cards. He gave fourteen baseball cards
(25) to Amie. How many baseball cards does Rafiki have left?

*3. Mrs. Rushing had a package of lined cards. She used seventy-five
(25) cards in class last week. She has forty-seven cards left. How many
cards were in the package before last week?

4. There are 12 months in a whole year. How many months are in half of a
(5) year?

* 5. **(Connect)** Find the missing numbers in each counting sequence:
_(3, Inv. 1)

    a. ..., 5, 10, ____, ____, 25, ____, ...

    b. ..., 5, 0, ____, ____, −15, ____, ...

* 6. **(Represent)** Use digits and a comparison symbol to write that seven
_(Inv. 1) hundred sixty-two is less than eight hundred twenty-six.

* 7. a. Round 78 to the nearest ten.
₍₂₀₎

    b. Round $7.80 to the nearest dollar.

    c. Round $7.80 to the nearest 25 cents.

* 8. If the diameter of a wheel on Joshua's bike is 20 inches, then what is
₍₂₁₎ the radius of the wheel?

* 9. The last recess of the afternoon at Taft Elementary School
₍₁₉₎ begins at the time shown on the clock. The recess ends
at 1:35 p.m. How long is the last recess of the afternoon?

* 10. **(Conclude)** Which street is perpendicular
₍₂₃₎ to Elm?

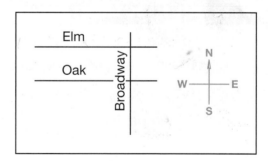

* 11. What fraction of this shape is shaded?
₍₂₂₎

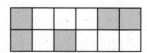

* 12. Draw a square whose sides are 4 cm long. What is the perimeter of the
_(Inv. 2, 21) square?

* 13. **(Represent)** To what number is the arrow pointing?
_(Inv. 1)

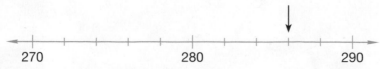

14. $52
(15)   − $14

15. 476
(13)   + 177

16. 62
(15)   − 38

17. $4.97
(22)   + $2.03

*18. 36
(24)   − g
        18

*19. 55
(24)   + b
        87

*20. d
(24)   − 23
        58

*21. y
(24)   + 14
        32

22. 42 37
(15)

23. 52 22
(14)

24. 73 − 59
(15)

25. 900 + 90 + 9
(17)

*26. Multiple Choice Which of these measurements is *not* equivalent to
(Inv. 2) one meter?

   A 1000 mm   **B** 100 cm   **C** 1000 km   **D** 1 m

*27. ⟨ Explain ⟩ How is a ray different from a segment?
(23)

28. The Illinois River and the Potomac River have a combined length of
(11, 14) 803 miles. The Illinois River is 420 miles long. Write and solve an
         equation to find the length of the Potomac River.

29. At a school supply store, pencil erasers cost 59¢ each. A drawing pad
(22)   costs $3.39. What is a reasonable estimate of the total cost of a drawing
        pad and an eraser? Explain why your estimate is reasonable.

30. In Bismarck, North Dakota, the average high temperature in January is
(18)   21°F. The average low temperature is −1°F. How many degrees warmer
        is a temperature of 21°F than a temperature of −1°F?

Real-World Connection

There were 119 third grade students, 121 fourth grade students and
135 fifth grade students in the auditorium. One hundred eighty-seven of
the students returned to class. Which number is greater, the number of
students still in the auditorium, or the number of students who returned
to class? How do you know?

• Drawing Pictures of Fractions

facts	Power Up B
count aloud	Count by sevens from 7 to 49.
mental math	**Number Sense:** Add from the left and then regroup ones. For example, 35 + 26 is 50 plus 11, which is 61.

a. 55
$+ 25$

b. 36
$+ 26$

c. 48
$+ 22$

d. 37
$+ 45$

e. 235
$+ 145$

f. 156
$+ 326$

g. Money: What is the total cost of a $110 desk and a $45 chair?

h. Estimation: The length of the whiteboard was 244 cm. Round this length to the nearest ten centimeters.

problem solving

Choose an appropriate problem-solving strategy to solve this problem. Jennifer has three coins in her left pocket that total 65¢. Which coins does Jennifer have in her left pocket?

New Concept

We can understand fractions better if we learn to draw pictures that represent fractions.

Example 1

Draw a rectangle and shade two thirds of it.

We draw a rectangle. Then we divide the rectangle into three equal parts. As a final step, we shade any two of the equal parts.

Thinking Skill

Verify

Is $\frac{1}{3}$ of this figure shaded? Explain why or why not.

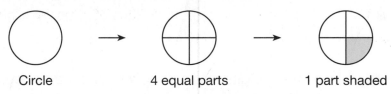

Rectangle → 3 equal parts → 2 parts shaded

There are other ways to divide the rectangle into three equal parts. Here is another way we could shade two thirds of the rectangle:

Rectangle → 3 equal parts → 2 parts shaded

Example 2

Draw a circle and shade one fourth of it.

First we draw a circle. Then we divide the circle into four equal parts. Then we shade any one of the parts.

Circle → 4 equal parts → 1 part shaded

Lesson Practice　**Represent** Draw and shade each shape:

a. Draw a square and shade one half of it.

b. Draw a rectangle and shade one third of it.

c. Draw a circle and shade three fourths of it.

d. Draw a circle and shade two thirds of it.

e. Is one half of this circle shaded? Why or why not?

Written Practice　*Distributed and Integrated*

Formulate Write and solve equations for problems **1–3.**

* **1.** Mandisa had 42 pebbles. She threw some into the lake. Then she had
(25)　27 pebbles left. How many pebbles did Mandisa throw into the lake?

*2. Dennis had a bag of pebbles. He put 17 pebbles on the ground.
(25) Then there were 46 pebbles left in the bag. How many pebbles were in the bag before Dennis took some out?

*3. Salvador saw one hundred twelve stars. Eleanor looked the other way
(11, 13) and saw some more stars. If they saw three hundred seventeen stars in all, how many did Eleanor see?

4. Use the digits 4, 5, and 6 to write an even number less than 500. Each
(4, 10) digit may be used only once. Which digit is in the tens place?

*5. (Represent) Draw a square and shade three fourths of it.
(26)

6. What is the perimeter of this triangle?
(Inv. 2)

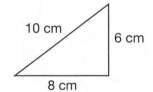
10 cm 6 cm 8 cm

*7. (Represent) Use digits and symbols to show that negative twenty is
(Inv. 1) less than negative twelve.

8. a. Round 19 to the nearest ten.
(20)

   b. Round $10.90 to the nearest dollar.

9. One meter equals how many centimeters?
(Inv. 2)

10. This clock represents a time during a school day.
(19) Write the time.

*11. (Conclude) Which street makes a right angle with Oak?
(23)

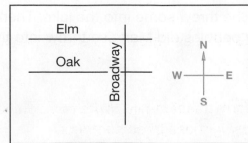

* 12. What fraction of this figure is shaded?
(22)

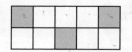

* 13. The thermometer at right shows the average temperature during
(18) February in Galveston, Texas. What is that temperature?

* 14. (24)	**15.** (13)	**16.** (15)	**17.** (22)
y $+\ 63$ $\overline{\hspace{1em}81}$	$\$486$ $+\ \$277$	$\$68$ $-\ \$39$	$\$5.97$ $+\ \$2.38$

* 18. $n + 42 = 71$
(24)

* 19. $87 - n = 65$
(24)

* 20. $27 + c = 48$
(24)

* 21. $e - 14 = 28$
(24)

22. $42 - 29$
(15)

23. $77 - 37$
(14)

24. $41 - 19$
(15)

25. $4 + 7 + 15 + 21 + 5 + 4 + 3$
(17)

* 26. Multiple Choice In which figure is $\frac{1}{2}$ *not* shaded?
(26)

A   **B**   **C**   **D**

* 27. (Conclude) Is the largest angle of this triangle acute, right, or
(23) obtuse?

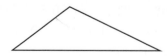

28. How many different three-digit numbers can you write using the digits
(10) 0, 7, and 3? Each digit may be used only once, and the digit 0 may
not be used in the hundreds place. Label the numbers you write as
even or odd.

* 29. (Estimate) Is $14 a reasonable estimate for the sum of $5.45 and
(22) $8.59? Explain why or why not.

30. The numbers 8, 9, and 17 form a fact family. Write two addition facts
(6) and two subtraction facts using these three numbers.

LESSON 27

- **Multiplication as Repeated Addition**
- **More Elapsed-Time Problems**

Power Up

facts	Power Up B
count aloud	Count by fours from 4 to 40 and then back down to 4.
mental math	In **a–c,** add ones, then tens, and then hundreds. Remember to regroup the ones.

    a. Number Sense: 147 + 225

    b. Number Sense: 356 + 126

    c. Number Sense: 239 + 144

    d. Number Sense: 9 = 4 + ☐

    e. Geometry: What is the radius of a circle that has a diameter of 2 inches?

    f. Money: Hala had $7. Then she spent $2 on a toothbrush. How much money did Hala have left?

    g. Estimation: The large dog weighed 88 pounds. Round that weight to the nearest ten pounds.

    h. Measurement: Dan took two steps that were each 61 centimeters long. Altogether, how many centimeters did he move?

problem solving
Choose an appropriate problem-solving strategy to solve this problem. At 12:00 the hands of the clock point in the same direction. At 6:00 the hands point in opposite directions. Draw pictures of clocks to show the hours that the hands of a clock form right angles.

Multiplication as Repeated Addition

Suppose we want to find the total number of dots shown on these four dot cubes:

One way we can find the total number of dots is to count the dots one by one. Another way is to recognize that there are 5 dots in each group and that there are four groups. We can find the answer by adding four 5s.

$$5 + 5 + 5 + 5 = 20$$

We can also use **multiplication** to show that we want to add 5 four times.

$$4 \quad \times \quad 5 \quad = \quad 20 \qquad \text{or} \qquad \begin{array}{r} 5 \\ \times\ 4 \\ \hline 20 \end{array}$$

Four groups of five equals twenty

If we find the answer this way, we are multiplying. We call the × a **multiplication sign.** We read 4 × 5 as "four times five."

Thinking Skill

Discuss

How do we decide which number to multiply times 5?

Example 1

Change this addition problem to a multiplication problem:

$$6 + 6 + 6 + 6 + 6$$

We see five 6s. We can change this addition problem to a multiplication problem by writing either

$$5 \times 6 \qquad \text{or} \qquad \begin{array}{r} 6 \\ \times\ 5 \\ \hline \end{array}$$

Elapsed Time

Recall that the amount of time between two different points in time is called elapsed time. We can count forward or backward on a clock to solve some elapsed-time problems.

Activity

Finding Time

Material needed:
- **Lesson Activity 17**

Use **Lesson Activity 17** to complete these problems. You may use your student clock to solve.

1. Sketch a clock showing the time on the classroom clock. Then sketch a clock showing the time 2 hours ago. Write the time under both clocks.

2. Sketch a clock showing the time lunch begins. Then sketch a clock showing the time lunch ends. Write the time under both clocks. How many minutes long is lunch?

Example 2

In the afternoon, Siew-Ai arrives home from school 1 hour 50 minutes later than the time shown on the clock. What time does Siew-Ai arrive home from school?

The time on the clock is 1:45 p.m.

We will describe two ways to find the time that is 1 hour 50 minutes later.

Method 1: Count forward 1 hour 50 minutes.

   Step 1: Count forward 1 hour from 1:45 p.m. to 2:45 p.m.

   Step 2: Count forward 50 minutes from 2:45 p.m. to **3:35 p.m.**

Method 2: Count forward 2 hours and then count back 10 minutes.

   Step 1: Count forward 2 hours from 1:45 p.m. to 3:45 p.m.

   Step 2: Count back 10 minutes from 3:45 p.m. to **3:35 p.m.**

Discuss Describe where the hands of the clock will be when it is 3:35 p.m.

Example 3

On Monday morning, an elementary school had a fire drill 4 hours 25 minutes before the time shown on the clock. When was the fire drill?

The time shown on the clock is 1:15 p.m. We count back 4 hours 25 minutes.

- Count back 4 hours from 1:15 p.m. to 9:15 a.m.
- Count back 25 minutes from 9:15 a.m. to **8:50 a.m.**

(Discuss) How do we know that the time shown on the clock is p.m. and not a.m.?

(Verify) Describe where the hands of the clock will be when it is 8:50 a.m.

(**Lesson Practice**) Change each addition problem to a multiplication problem:

a. 3 + 3 + 3 + 3

b. 9 + 9 + 9

c. 7 + 7 + 7 + 7 + 7 + 7

d. 5 + 5 + 5 + 5 + 5 + 5 + 5 + 5

Use a student clock to answer problems **e** and **f.** Show 10:35 a.m. on your student clock.

e. If it is morning, what time will it be in 2 hours 25 minutes?

f. If it is morning, what time was it 6 hours 30 minutes ago?

(**Written Practice**) *Distributed and Integrated*

*1. (25) (Formulate) Just before noon Adriana saw seventy-eight people watching the game. At noon she saw only forty-two watching the game. How many people had left the game by noon? Write an equation and solve the problem.

*2. (Inv. 2, 21) If each side of a square floor tile is one foot long, then

a. each side is how many inches long?

b. the perimeter of the tile is how many inches?

*3. (10) (List) Write the even numbers between 31 and 39.

(Conclude) Find the next three numbers in each counting sequence:

*4. (3) ..., 12, 15, 18, _____, _____, _____, ...

*5. (3) ..., 12, 24, 36, _____, _____, _____, ...

*6. **Represent** Write 265 in expanded form.
(16)

*7. **Represent** Use words to write −19.
(Inv. 1)

*8. a. Round 63 to the nearest ten.
(20)

    b. Round $6.30 to the nearest dollar.

    c. Round $6.30 to the nearest 25 cents.

9. Compare:
(Inv. 1)

    a. 392 ◯ 329   **b.** − 15 ◯ − 20

10. To what number is the arrow pointing?
(Inv. 1)

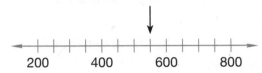

*11. Draw a square with sides 2 centimeters long. Then shade one fourth of
(21, 26) the square.

*12. **Explain** What fraction of this figure is shaded? Describe
(22) how you found your answer.

*13. Aric plays percussion instruments in the school band. Band
(27) practice ends 3 hours after the time shown on the clock. What
time does band practice end?

14. $67   **15.**   483   **16.**   71   **17.** $5.88
(15)   − $29   (13) + 378   (15) − 39   (22) + $2.39

*18.   *d*   ***19.** 66   ***20.** 87   ***21.**   *b*
(24)   + 19   (24) + *f*   (24) − *r*   (24) − 14
      36   87   67   27

22. 400 − 300   **23.** 663 − 363
(14)   (14)

*24. Change this addition problem to a multiplication problem:
$$9 + 9 + 9 + 9$$
(27)

*25. **a.** One dollar equals how many pennies?
(22)

b. A penny is what fraction of a dollar?

c. Eleven pennies are what fraction of a dollar?

*26. **Multiple Choice** If ☐ = 3 and △ = 4, then what does ☐ + △ + ☐
(1) equal?

    A 343   **B** 7   **C** 10   **D** 11

*27. (**Represent**) Draw a dot on your paper to represent a point. Then, from
(23) that point, draw two perpendicular rays.

*28. (**Formulate**) Ronald Reagan was elected president in 1980 and again in
(11, 14) 1984. During those elections, he won a total of 1014 electoral votes. In
1984, he won 525 electoral votes. Write and solve an equation to find
the number of electoral votes Ronald Reagan won in 1980.

*29. (**Estimate**) The cost of a new T-shirt is $15.95. Wendy would like
(22) to purchase two T-shirts. Is $40 a reasonable estimate for the cost of
her purchase? Explain why or why not.

30. Show six different ways to add 2, 4, and 6.
(1)

Real-World Connection

Mr. Perez left work at 4:59 p.m. He stopped at the store for 15 minutes.
Then he drove for 24 minutes to get home.

  a. What time did Mr. Perez arrive at his house?

  b. How much time elapsed from the time Mr. Perez left work and the
time he arrived home?

  c. Describe where the hands on the clock will be when Mr. Perez
gets home.

• Multiplication Table

facts	Power Up A
count aloud	Count by sevens from 7 to 56.
mental math	**a. Number Sense:** 54 + 120
	b. Number Sense: 210 + 25 + 35
	c. Number Sense: 350 + 30 + 200
	d. Number Sense: 5 = 3 + ☐
	e. Time: What time will it be 3 hours after 4:40 a.m.?
	f. Money: Ebony had $14. Then she spent $5 on colored pencils. How much money did Ebony have left?
	g. Measurement: One yard is 3 feet. The tree is 7 yards tall. How many feet tall is the tree?
	h. Estimation: Mia has $4.78 in her wallet. Round $4.78 to the nearest 25 cents.
problem solving	The hour hand moves around the face of a clock once in 12 hours. How many times does the hour hand move around the face of the clock in a week?

Focus Strategy: Write a Number Sentence

(**Understand**) We collect the information from the problem and combine it with information we already know:

1. The hour hand moves around the face of a clock once in 12 hours.

2. There are 24 hours in a day.

3. One week is 7 days.

We are asked to find how many times the hour hand moves around the face of a clock in one week.

(**Plan**) We take the information we know and *write a number sentence* to solve the problem.

(**Solve**) The hour hand moves once around the clock in 12 hours. This means it moves 2 times around in 24 hours (1 day).

If the hour hand moves 2 times around in 1 day, then it moves 2 + 2 times around in 2 days. To find how many times the hour hand moves around in 7 days, we can add the number 2 seven times: 2 + 2 + 2 + 2 + 2 + 2 + 2. We can also multiply:

2 times around × 7 = 14 times around

We find that the hour hand moves **14 times around the clock** in a week.

(**Check**) We know our answer is reasonable because there are 7 days in a week. We double the number 7 because the hour hand moves around the clock twice each day.

We wrote a number sentence to solve this problem. As a class, discuss other strategies that can be used to solve the problem.

New Concept

Here we show sequences for counting by ones and twos:

Ones:	1	2	3	4	5	6	7	8	9	10	11	12
Twos:	2	4	6	8	10	12	14	16	18	20	22	24

These sequences—and those for threes, fours, and so on through twelves—appear in the following **multiplication table.**

Multiplication Table

	0	1	2	3	4	5	6	7	8	9	10	11	12
0	0	0	0	0	0	0	0	0	0	0	0	0	0
1	0	1	2	3	4	5	6	7	8	9	10	11	12
2	0	2	4	6	8	10	12	14	16	18	20	22	24
3	0	3	6	9	12	15	18	21	24	27	30	33	36
4	0	4	8	12	16	20	24	28	32	36	40	44	48
5	0	5	10	15	20	25	30	35	40	45	50	55	60
6	0	6	12	18	24	30	36	42	48	54	60	66	72
7	0	7	14	21	28	35	42	49	56	63	70	77	84
8	0	8	16	24	32	40	48	56	64	72	80	88	96
9	0	9	18	27	36	45	54	63	72	81	90	99	108
10	0	10	20	30	40	50	60	70	80	90	100	110	120
11	0	11	22	33	44	55	66	77	88	99	110	121	132
12	0	12	24	36	48	60	72	84	96	108	120	132	144

Thinking Skill

Analyze

Each term in the sequence for 4s is double the corresponding term in the sequence for 2s. Name other sequences where the terms are doubled.

We can use a multiplication table to find the answer to problems such as 3 × 4 by using rows and columns. Rows run left to right, and columns run top to bottom. We start by finding the row that begins with 3 and the column that begins with 4. Then we look for the number where the row and column meet.

Column

Row →

	0	1	2	3	4	5	6	7	8	9	10	11	12
0	0	0	0	0	0	0	0	0	0	0	0	0	0
1	0	1	2	3	4	5	6	7	8	9	10	11	12
2	0	2	4	6	8	10	12	14	16	18	20	22	24
3	0	3	6	9	(12)	15	18	21	24	27	30	33	36
4	0	4	8	12	16	20	24	28	32	36	40	44	48
5	0	5	10	15	20	25	30	35	40	45	50	55	60
6	0	6	12	18	24	30	36	42	48	54	60	66	72
7	0	7	14	21	28	35	42	49	56	63	70	77	84
8	0	8	16	24	32	40	48	56	64	72	80	88	96
9	0	9	18	27	36	45	54	63	72	81	90	99	108
10	0	10	20	30	40	50	60	70	80	90	100	110	120
11	0	11	22	33	44	55	66	77	88	99	110	121	132
12	0	12	24	36	48	60	72	84	96	108	120	132	144

Each of the two numbers multiplied is called a **factor.** The answer to a multiplication problem is called a **product.** In this problem, 3 and 4 are factors, and 12 is the product. Now look at the row that begins with 4 and the column that begins with 3. We see that the product of 4 and 3 is also 12. Changing the order of factors does not change the product. This is true for any two numbers that are multiplied and is called the **Commutative Property of Multiplication.**

Here are two more properties of multiplication we can see in the multiplication table. Notice that the product of zero and any number is zero. This is called the **Property of Zero for Multiplication.** Also notice that the product of 1 and any other factor is the other factor. This is called the **Identity Property of Multiplication.**

Thinking Skill

Conclude

How are the Identity Property of Addition and the Identity Property of Multiplication alike? How are they different?

The three properties we have looked at are summarized in this table. The letters m and n can be any two numbers. Later, we will learn about two other properties of multiplication.

Properties of Multiplication

Commutative Property	$m \times n = n \times m$
Identity Property	$1 \times n = n$
Zero Property	$0 \times n = 0$

Lesson Practice Use the multiplication table to find each product:

a. 9
  $\times 3$

b. 3
  $\times 9$

c. 6
  $\times 4$

d. 4
  $\times 6$

e. 7
  $\times 8$

f. 8
  $\times 7$

g. 5
  $\times 8$

h. 8
  $\times 5$

i. 10
  $\times 10$

j. 10
  $\times 8$

k. 11
  $\times 9$

l. 12
  $\times 12$

m. Which property of multiplication is shown below?

$$12 \times 11 = 11 \times 12$$

n. Use the Zero Property of Multiplication to find the product:

$$0 \times 25$$

o. Use the Identity Property of Multiplication to find the product:

$$1 \times 25$$

Formulate Write and solve equations for problems **1** and **2**.

* 1. Seventy-two children attend the morning session at a preschool.
(1)   Forty-two children attend the afternoon session. How many children
attend those sessions altogether?

* 2. Sherri needs $35 to buy a baseball glove. She has saved $18. How
(11, 24)   much more does she need?

* 3. **Represent** Draw a rectangle that is 4 cm long and 3 cm wide.
(Inv. 2, 21)   What is the perimeter of the rectangle?

Connect Find the missing numbers in each counting sequence:

* 4. ..., 12, ____, ____, 30, 36, ____, ...
(3)

* 5. ..., 36, ____, ____, 24, 20, ____, ...
(3)

* 6. **Connect** Change this addition problem to a multiplication problem.
(27, 28)   Then find the product on the multiplication table shown in this lesson.

$$6 + 6 + 6 + 6 + 6 + 6 + 6$$

7. a. Round 28 to the nearest ten.
(20)

   b. Round $12.29 to the nearest dollar.

   c. Round $12.29 to the nearest 25 cents.

* 8. **Represent** A *right triangle* has one right angle. Draw a right triangle.
(Inv. 2, 23)   Draw the two perpendicular sides 3 cm long and 4 cm long.

* 9. On Saturday morning, Mason went to the public library
(27)   at the time shown on the clock. He arrived home
90 minutes later. What time did Mason arrive home from
the library?

*10. What fraction of this group is shaded?
(22)

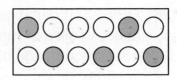

*11. **(Represent)** Write 417 in expanded form. Then use words to write the
(7, 16) number.

*12. **a.** What temperature is shown on this thermometer?
(18)

    b. If the temperature increases by ten degrees, what will the
    temperature be?

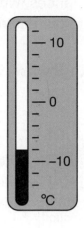

13.   76
(15)   − 29

14. $286
(13)   + $388

15. $73
(15)   − $39

16. $5.87
(22)   + $2.43

*17. $46 - c = 19$
(24)

*18. $n + 48 = 87$
(24)

*19. $29 + y = 57$
(24)

*20. $d - 14 = 37$
(24)

21. $78 - 43$
(14)

22. $77 - 17$
(14)

23. $53 - 19$
(15)

*24. **(Interpret)** Use the multiplication table to find each product:
(28)
    a. 8×11 **b.** 7×10 **c.** 5×12

25. Compare: 1 yard ◯ 1 meter
(Inv. 1,
Inv. 2)

*26. **Multiple Choice** Which of the following shows 3 ones and
(4)   4 hundreds?
    A 304   **B** 403   **C** 4003   **D** 3400

*27. **(Analyze)** The product of 9 and 3 is 27. How many times does this
(28)   product appear in this lesson's multiplication table? What property
    of multiplication does this show?

* 28. For a short distance, a cheetah can run at a speed of 70 miles per
(25) hour. An elk can run at a speed of 45 miles per hour. Write and solve
a subtraction equation to find the difference between the two animals'
speeds.

* 29. **Estimate** During an online auction, D'Wayne bid $37 for one item
(20) and $54 for another item. If D'Wayne purchases both items at those
prices, what is a reasonable estimate of his total cost? Explain why
your estimate is reasonable.

30. **Predict** What is the tenth number in this counting sequence?
(3)

90, 80, 70, 60, 50, ...

Early Finishers

Real-World Connection

Rebecca and her friend were placing pictures on pages of a scrapbook.
Rebecca put 6 pictures on five pages, and her friend put 5 pictures on
six pages. Did the girls have the same number of pictures? Explain how
you know.

• Multiplication Facts:
0s, 1s, 2s, 5s

facts	Power Up B
count aloud	Count by threes from 3 to 45 and then back down to 3.
mental math	We can split numbers to help us add. Adding 35 and 8, we may notice that 35 needs 5 more to make 40 and that 8 splits into 5 + 3. To add 35 and 8, we could add 35 + 5 + 3.

  a. **Number Sense:** 35 + 7

  b. **Number Sense:** 68 + 7

  c. **Number Sense:** 38 + 5

  d. **Measurement:** The width of a large paper clip is 1 centimeter. How many millimeters wide is the paper clip?

  e. **Measurement:** The high temperature for the day was 84°F. Then the temperature dropped 14 degrees. What was the new temperature?

  f. **Time:** What time was it 2 hours before 1:00 a.m.?

  g. **Money:** Anne bought a notebook for $2, a compass for $4, and a ruler for $1. What was the total cost of the items?

  h. **Number Sense:** 8 = 3 + ☐

problem solving	Choose an appropriate problem-solving strategy to solve this problem. Hope has seven coins in her right pocket. None of the coins are dollar or half-dollar coins. What is the lowest possible value of all seven coins? What is the highest possible value of all seven coins?

We will begin memorizing the basic multiplication facts. Eighty-eight of the facts in the multiplication table shown in Lesson 28 have 0, 1, 2, or 5 as one of the factors.

Zero times any number equals zero.

$$0 \times 5 = 0 \qquad 5 \times 0 = 0 \qquad 7 \times 0 = 0 \qquad 0 \times 7 = 0$$

One times any number equals the number.

$$1 \times 5 = 5 \qquad 5 \times 1 = 5 \qquad 7 \times 1 = 7 \qquad 1 \times 7 = 7$$

Two times any number doubles the number.

$$2 \times 5 = 10 \qquad 2 \times 7 = 14 \qquad 2 \times 6 = 12 \qquad 2 \times 8 = 16$$

Five times any number equals a number that ends in zero or in five.

$$5 \times 1 = 5 \qquad 5 \times 3 = 15 \qquad 5 \times 7 = 35 \qquad 5 \times 8 = 40$$

We say the multiples of 5 when counting by fives. The sixth number we say when counting by fives is 30, so $6 \times 5 = 30$. **However, counting is not a substitute for memorizing the facts.**

Thinking Skill

Generalize

How can we decide if a number is divisible by 2? By 5?

Lesson Practice Complete Power Up C.

Written Practice *Distributed and Integrated*

Formulate Write and solve equations for problems **1** and **2**.

*1. Jasmine made ninety-two mums to sell at the school fundraiser. At the
(25) end of the fundraiser, twenty-four mums remained. How many mums did Jasmine sell?

*2. Rochelle collected 42 seashells. Then Zuri collected some seashells.
(11, 24) They collected 83 seashells in all. How many seashells did Zuri collect?

*3. Conner estimated that the radius of one of the circles on the
$_{(Inv.\ 2,\ 21)}$ playground was 2 yards. If Conner was correct, then

   a. the radius was how many feet?

   b. the diameter was how many feet?

(**Connect**) Find the missing numbers in each counting sequence:

4. ..., 8, _____, _____, 32, 40, _____, ...
$_{(3)}$

5. ..., 14, _____, _____, 35, 42, ...
$_{(3)}$

6. Use the digits 4, 5, and 6 to write a three-digit odd number less than
$_{(10)}$ 640. Each number may be used only once.

*7. (**Represent**) Use digits and a comparison symbol to write that
$_{(Inv.\ 1)}$ two hundred nine is greater than one hundred ninety.

*8. Fernando arrived home from school at the time shown
$_{(27)}$ on the clock. He snacked for 5 minutes, and then he
spent 35 minutes completing his homework. What time
did Fernando complete his homework?

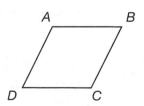

*9. (**Represent**) Draw a rectangle 3 cm long and 1 cm wide. Then shade
$_{(21,\ 26)}$ two thirds of it.

*10. Find each product:
$_{(28,\ 29)}$
   a. 2×8 **b.** 5×7 **c.** 2×7 **d.** 5×8

*11. (**Conclude**) In this figure, what type of angle is angle A?
$_{(23)}$ Explain how you know.

*12. (**Connect**) To what number is the arrow pointing?
$_{(Inv.\ 1)}$

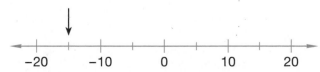

13. At what temperature does water freeze
   (18)
   a. on the Fahrenheit scale?

   b. on the Celsius scale?

14. $83
(15) $- \$19$

15. $286
(13) $+ \$387$

16. 72
(15) $- 38$

17. $5.87
(22) $+ \$2.79$

*18. 19
(24) $+ q$
       ——
       46

*19. 88
(24) $- n$
       ——
       37

*20. 88
(24) $- m$
       ——
       47

*21. g
(24) $+ 14$
       ——
       47

22. $870 - 470$
(14)

23. $525 - 521$
(14)

*24. (**Connect**) Change this addition problem to a multiplication problem.
(27, 28) Then find the product on the multiplication table.

$$8 + 8 + 8$$

25. $1 + 9 + 2 + 8 + 3 + 7 + 4 + 6 + 5 + 10$
(1)

*26. Multiple Choice Which of these does *not* equal 24?
(28)
   A 3×8 **B** 4×6 **C** 2×12 **D** 8×4

*27. Name the property of multiplication shown by each of these examples:
(28)
   a. $0 \times 50 = 0$

   b. $9 \times 6 = 6 \times 9$

   c. $1 \times 75 = 75$

28. a. Round $3.49 to the nearest dollar.
(20)
   b. Round $3.49 to the nearest 25 cents.

*29. (**Connect**) Write a multiplication equation that has a product of 18.
(28)

*30. Suppose $x + y = z$. Write one more addition and two subtraction
(24) equations using x, y, and z.

LESSON
30

• Subtracting Three-Digit Numbers with Regrouping

Power Up

facts	Power Up B
count aloud	Count by fives from 5 to 100 and then back down to 5.
mental math	Practice splitting the second number to add in **a–c**.

a. **Number Sense:** 36 + 8

b. **Number Sense:** 48 + 6

c. **Number Sense:** 47 + 9

d. **Measurement:** One of the two identical chairs weighed 13 pounds. How much did the two chairs weigh?

e. **Measurement:** How many inches equal 1 yard?

f. **Time:** What time was it 4 hours before 6:25 a.m.?

g. **Money:** Scott received his allowance of $20. If he puts $5 into his savings account, how much will Scott have left over to spend?

h. **Estimation:** The ceiling was 274 cm above the floor. Round that measurement to the nearest ten centimeters.

problem solving	Choose an appropriate problem-solving strategy to solve this problem. How many times does the minute hand move around the face of a clock in 300 minutes?

New Concept

We have already learned how to subtract three-digit numbers without regrouping. In this lesson we will subtract three-digit numbers with regrouping.

Example 1

Find the difference: $365 − $187

Thinking Skill

Discuss

How do we know when we need to regroup?

We write the first number on top. We line up the last digits. We cannot subtract 7 ones from 5 ones.

$$\begin{array}{r} \$365 \\ -\ \$187 \\ \hline ? \end{array}$$

We exchange 1 ten for 10 ones. Now there are 5 tens and 15 ones. We can subtract 7 ones from 15 ones to get 8 ones.

$$\begin{array}{r} \overset{5}{\cancel{\$3}}\overset{1}{\cancel{6}}5 \\ -\ \$1\,8\,7 \\ \hline 8 \end{array}$$

We cannot subtract 8 tens from 5 tens, so we exchange 1 hundred for 10 tens. Now there are 2 hundreds and 15 tens, and we can continue subtracting.

$$\begin{array}{r} \overset{2}{\cancel{\$3}}\overset{5}{\cancel{6}}\overset{1}{5} \\ -\ \$1\,8\,7 \\ \hline 7\,8 \end{array}$$

We subtract 1 hundred from 2 hundreds to finish. The difference is **$178.**

$$\begin{array}{r} \overset{2}{\cancel{\$3}}\overset{5}{\cancel{6}}\overset{1}{5} \\ -\ \$1\,8\,7 \\ \hline \$1\,7\,8 \end{array}$$

Example 2

Visit www. SaxonMath.com/ Int4Activities for a calculator activity.

Before she spent $1.12, Olivia had $4.10. What amount of money does Olivia have now?

We subtract pennies, then dimes, and then dollars. We remember to align the decimal points.

$$\begin{array}{r} \overset{0}{\cancel{\$4.1}}\overset{1}{0} \\ -\ \$1.1\,2 \\ \hline 8 \end{array} \rightarrow \begin{array}{r} \overset{3}{\cancel{\$4}}.\overset{0}{\cancel{1}}\overset{1}{0} \\ -\ \$1.1\,2 \\ \hline .9\,8 \end{array} \rightarrow \begin{array}{r} \overset{3}{\cancel{\$4}}.\overset{0}{\cancel{1}}\overset{1}{0} \\ -\ \$1.1\,2 \\ \hline \$2.9\,8 \end{array}$$

 **Activity**

Subtracting Money

Materials needed:
- money manipulatives from Lesson 22 (or **Lesson Activities 2, 8,** and **9**)

Use your money manipulatives to complete the following tasks:

1. Model $4.31 and $3.42 using your manipulatives. Which amount is greater? Explain why.

2. Arrange $2.31, $3.21, and $1.32 in order from least to greatest.

3. Using your manipulatives subtract $5.46 from $1.24. How much money is left?

4. **Model** Act out this problem:

   Carla went to the store with $7.54. She bought a container of juice for $2.12. How much money did Carla have left?

Example 3

> **During a special 15%-off sale at a sporting goods store, the price of a $9.49 baseball cap will be reduced by $1.42. What is a reasonable estimate of the sale price of the cap?**
>
> We can use compatible numbers to estimate. The regular price of the cap is close to $9.50 and the price is reduced by about $1.50. Subtracting $1.50 from $9.50, we find that a reasonable estimate of the sale price is **$8.00.**

Lesson Practice   Subtract:

a. $365
− $287

b. $4.30
− $1.18

c. 563
− 356

d. 240 − 65

e. 459 − 176

f. 157 − 98

g. L'Rae entered the store with $8.24 and bought a gallon of milk for $2.27. What is a reasonable estimate of how much money L'Rae has now? Explain.

Formulate Write and solve equations for problems **1** and **2**.

*1. The room was full of students when the bell rang. Then forty-seven
(25) students left the room. Twenty-two students remained. How many
students were there when the bell rang? Use the subtraction formula
to write an equation and solve the problem.

*2. On Friday, 56 fourth grade students wore black shoes to school.
(11, 24) There are 73 fourth grade students in all. How many fourth grade
students did not wear black shoes to school on Friday?

*3. **Multiple Choice** A nickel is worth 5¢. Gilbert has an even number of
(10) nickels in his pocket. Which of the following could *not* be the value of
his nickels?

    A 45¢   **B** 70¢   **C** 20¢   **D** 40¢

*4. Jillian's social studies class ends 15 minutes later than
(27) the time shown on the clock. What time does Jillian's
class end?

*5. **Predict** What is the sixth number in this counting sequence?
(3)

$$6, 12, 18, \ldots$$

*6. **Represent** To what number is the arrow pointing?
(Inv. 1)

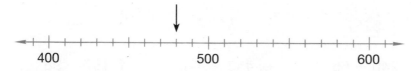

*7. **Model** Use a compass to draw a circle with a radius of 1 inch. Then
(21, 26) shade one fourth of the circle.

8. **Represent** Write 843 in expanded form. Then use words to write the
(7, 16) number.

*9. Multiply:
(28, 29)

    a. 6 × 8   **b.** 4 × 2   **c.** 4 × 5   **d.** 6 × 10

*10. (**Connect**) Write two addition facts and two subtraction facts using the
(6) numbers 10, 20, and 30.

*11. (**Model**) Use a centimeter ruler to measure the rectangle below.
(Inv. 2)
    a. How long is the rectangle?

    b. How wide is the rectangle?

    c. What is the perimeter of the rectangle?

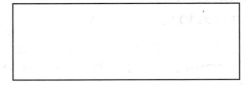

*12. (**Conclude**) What type of angle is each angle of a rectangle?
(23)

| ***13.** | **14.** | **15.** | ***16.** |
| (30) | (22) | (24) | (30) |

*13. $\begin{array}{r} 746 \\ -\ 295 \\ \hline \end{array}$ **14.** $\begin{array}{r} \$3.86 \\ +\ \$2.78 \\ \hline \end{array}$ **15.** $\begin{array}{r} 61 \\ -\ 48 \\ \hline \end{array}$ ***16.** $\begin{array}{r} \$4.86 \\ -\ \$2.75 \\ \hline \end{array}$

17. $51 + m = 70$ **18.** $86 - a = 43$
(24)   (24)

19. $25 + y = 36$ **20.** $q - 24 = 37$
(24)   (24)

21. ✏ (**Explain**) How can you round 89 to the nearest ten? Explain.
(20)

22. 25¢ + 25¢ + 25¢ + 25¢
(17)

23. There are 100 cents in a dollar. How many cents are in half of a
(22) dollar?

*24. (**Represent**) Change this addition problem to a multiplication problem.
(27, 28) Then find the product on the multiplication table.

                $7 + 7 + 7 + 7 + 7 + 7 + 7$

25. 4 + 3 + 8 + 4 + 2 + 5 + 7
(1)

*26. Multiple Choice Which of these sets of numbers is not an
(6)
addition/subtraction fact family?

  A 1, 2, 3   **B** 2, 3, 5   **C** 2, 4, 6   **D** 3, 4, 5

*27. Find each product on the multiplication table:
(28)
  a. 10×10 **b.** 11×11 **c.** 12×12

*28. (**Formulate**) Write a subtraction word problem using the numbers
(2)
8, 10, and 18.

29. (**Justify**) Is $500 a reasonable estimate for the difference
(30)
$749 − $259? Explain why or why not.

30. Suppose $a + b = c$. Write one more addition and two subtraction
(24)
equations using a, b, and c.

Early Finishers

Real-World Connection

Paolo had $12.70. Then his mother paid him $3.25 for mopping. He
bought a paperback book that costs $4.99.

  a. Use compatible numbers to estimate how much money Paolo
  has now.

  b. Then find the actual amount of money Paolo has now.

  c. Was your estimate reasonable? Explain why or why not.

Focus on

• Multiplication Patterns

• Area

• Squares and Square Roots

One model of multiplication is a rectangular **array.** An array is a rectangular arrangement of numbers or symbols in columns and rows. Here we see an array of 15 stars arranged in five columns and three rows. This array shows that 5 times 3 equals 15. This array also shows that 5 and 3 are both factors of 15.

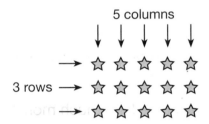

Refer to this array of Xs to answer problems **1–4** below.

```
x   x   x   x
x   x   x   x
x   x   x   x
```

1. How many rows are in the array?

2. How many columns are in the array?

3. How many Xs are in the array?

4. (**Connect**) What multiplication fact is illustrated by the array?

Some numbers of objects can be arranged in more than one array. In problems **5–7** we will work with an array of 12 Xs that is different from the array we discussed above.

5. (**Represent**) Draw an array of 12 Xs arranged in two rows.

6. How many columns of Xs are in the array you drew?

7. (**Connect**) What multiplication fact is illustrated by the array you drew?

Below we show an array of 10 Xs:

```
x   x   x   x   x
x   x   x   x   x
```

8. Which two factors of 10 are shown by this array?

9. **Verify** Can you draw a rectangular array of ten Xs with three rows?

10. **Verify** Can you draw a rectangular array of ten Xs with four rows?

11. **Verify** Can you draw a rectangular array of ten Xs with five rows?

12. **Represent** Draw an array of Xs arranged in six columns and three rows. Then write the multiplication fact illustrated by the array.

13. **Represent** The chairs in a room were arranged in six rows with four chairs in each row. Draw an array that shows this arrangement, and write the multiplication fact illustrated by the array.

Area

Another model of multiplication is the **area** model. The area model is like an array of connected squares. The model below shows that $6 \times 4 = 24$.

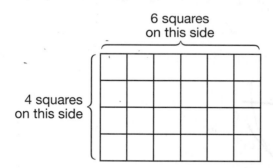

6 squares on this side

4 squares on this side

Represent Use **Lesson Activity 20** (1-cm grid paper) to work problems **14–16, 20,** and **23–25.**

14. Outline a 6 cm by 4 cm rectangle like the one shown above. How many small squares are in the rectangle?

15. Outline a 8 cm by 3 cm rectangle. How many small squares are in the rectangle? What multiplication fact is illustrated by the rectangle?

16. Outline another rectangle that is made up of 24 squares. Make this rectangle 2 cm wide. How long is the rectangle? What multiplication fact is illustrated by the rectangle?

Model With your finger, trace the edges of a sheet of paper. As your finger moves around the paper, it traces the perimeter of the paper. Now use the palm of your hand to rub over the surface of the paper. As you do this, your hand sweeps over the *area* of the paper. The area is the amount of surface within the perimeter (boundary) of a flat figure.

17. Use your finger to trace the perimeter of your desktop.

18. Use the palm of your hand to sweep over the area of your desktop.

We measure the area of a shape by counting the number of squares of a certain size that are needed to cover its surface. Here is a **square centimeter:**

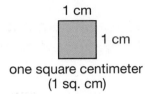

1 cm

1 cm

one square centimeter
(1 sq. cm)

19. How many square centimeters cover the area of this rectangle?

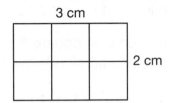

3 cm

2 cm

20. ⬭ **Represent** Use 1-cm grid paper or a centimeter ruler to outline a 4 cm by 3 cm rectangle. What is the area of the rectangle? What is the perimeter?

Here is a **square inch:**

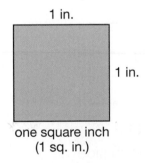

1 in.

1 in.

one square inch
(1 sq. in.)

21. How many square inches are needed to cover the rectangle below?

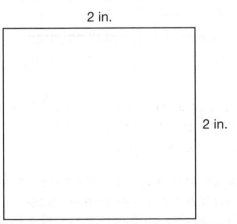

2 in.

2 in.

22. (**Represent**) Use your inch ruler to draw a rectangle 3 in. long and 3 in. wide. What is the area of the rectangle? What is the perimeter?

The floors of buildings such as classrooms are often measured in square feet. A square tile with sides one foot long can be a model of a square foot.

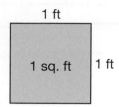

1 ft

1 sq. ft   1 ft

We tile an area by completely covering the area with shapes so that there are no gaps or overlaps.

23. Jarrod began tiling the floor of the kitchen with square tiles that were one foot on each side. The first tiles he placed are shown below.

a. What is the total number of tiles Jarrod will use to cover the floor?

b. What is the area of the room?

Activity 1

Finding Perimeter and Area

Materials needed:

- construction paper squares (1 foot on each side)

Use a one-foot square to estimate the perimeter and area of these objects. Record the approximate length, width, perimeter, and area of each object in a table like the one shown at the end of this activity.

a. your desktop

b. the front cover of your math book

c. a rectangular surface of your choice

Sample Table

Object	Length	Width	Perimeter	Area
Desktop				
Book cover				
Bulletin board				

Activity 2

Estimating Perimeter and Area

Material needed:

- ruler

Use an inch ruler or a centimeter ruler to estimate the perimeter and area of some smaller rectangular items in your classroom. Make a list of the items you chose. Record your estimate of the perimeter and area of each item.

Squares and Square Roots

Some rectangles are squares. A square is a rectangle whose length and width are equal.

24. **(Represent)** On 1-cm grid paper, outline four squares, one each with the following unit measurements: 1 by 1, 2 by 2, 3 by 3, and 4 by 4. Write the multiplication fact for each square.

We say that we "square a number" when we multiply a number by itself. If we square 3, we get 9 because $3 \times 3 = 9$. Likewise, 4 squared is 16 because 4×4 is 16.

25. What number do we get if we square 6? Outline a square on grid paper to show the result.

26. What number equals 7 squared? Outline a square on grid paper to illustrate the answer.

The numbers 1, 4, 9, 16, 25, and so on form a sequence of **square numbers,** or **perfect squares.** Notice that the increase from one term to the next term forms a sequence of odd numbers.

$$\overset{+3}{\overset{\frown}{1,}} \quad \overset{+5}{\overset{\frown}{4,}} \quad \overset{+7}{\overset{\frown}{9,}} \quad \overset{+9}{\overset{\frown}{16,}} \quad 25, \ldots$$

27. (**Conclude**) Find the next five terms in this sequence of square numbers.

28. Look back at the multiplication table in Lesson 28. What pattern do the square numbers make in the table?

To find the **square root** of a number, we find a number that, when multiplied by itself, equals the original number. The square root of 25 is 5 because $5 \times 5 = 25$. The square root of 36 is 6. A square drawn on grid paper can help us understand the idea of square roots. When searching for a square root, we know the number of small squares in all, and we are looking for the length of a side.

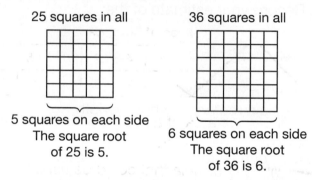

25 squares in all   36 squares in all

5 squares on each side
The square root
of 25 is 5.

6 squares on each side
The square root
of 36 is 6.

We indicate the square root of a number by using a square root symbol.

$$\sqrt{}$$

Square root symbol

We read the symbol as "the square root of." To read $\sqrt{25} = 5$, we say, "The square root of twenty-five equals five."

29. a. What number equals 9 squared?

    b. What is the square root of 9?

30. Find each square root:

    a. $\sqrt{4}$ **b.** $\sqrt{16}$ **c.** $\sqrt{64}$

31. (**Analyze**) If the area of a square is 49 square centimeters, how long is each side of the square?

a. One common attribute was used to group these figures:

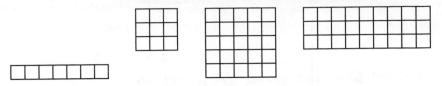

These figures do not belong in the group:

Find the area of each figure, and explain why the figures were sorted in this way. Draw another figure that belongs in the first group, and explain why that figure belongs.

b. Describe the relationship between the two sets of data in this table:

Area of Squares

Area (sq. in.)	1	4	9	16	25	36
Side Length (in.)	1	2	3	4	5	6

(**Predict**) What is the area of a square with a side length of 10 inches? How do you know?

(**Generalize**) Write a formula that could be used to find the perimeter of any square.

• Word Problems About Comparing

Power Up

facts	Power Up B
count aloud	Count by fours from 4 to 60 and then back down to 4.
mental math	In problems **a–c,** practice splitting the second number to add.

    a. Number Sense: 57 + 8

    b. Number Sense: 78 + 6

    c. Number Sense: 49 + 4

    d. Number Sense: 63 + 19 + 200

    e. Time: The Johnsons are driving to Yosemite National Park. They expect that the drive will take 6 hours. If the Johnsons left their house at 6:50 a.m., at what time would they expect to arrive at the park?

    f. Measurement: Many adults are about 2 yards tall. Two yards is how many feet?

    g. Geometry: True or False: Parallel lines intersect.

    h. Estimation: Madison has $18.47. Round this amount to the nearest 25 cents.

problem solving

Choose an appropriate problem-solving strategy to solve this problem. Here we show four squares. The first is made up of 1 small square. The second, third, and fourth squares are made up of 4, 9, and 16 small squares. Describe the pattern that you see. How many small squares would make up the sixth square of the pattern? Explain how you arrived at your answer.

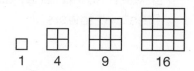

There are 43 apples in the large basket. There are 19 apples in the small basket.

The difference tells us "how many more" and "how many fewer." There are 24 *more* apples in the large basket than in the small basket. There are 24 *fewer* apples in the small basket than in the large basket.

When we compare the number of apples in the two baskets, we see that 43 is **greater than** 19. To find **how much greater** 43 is than 19, we subtract.

Larger amount	43
− Smaller amount	− 19
Difference	24

As we think about this story, we realize that it is not a "some went away" story because nothing went away. This is a different kind of story. In this story we are comparing two numbers. One way to compare two numbers is to subtract to find their difference. We subtract the smaller number from the larger number. Here we show two ways to write the formula:

$$\begin{array}{r} \text{Larger} \\ - \text{ Smaller} \\ \hline \text{Difference} \end{array}$$

Larger − Smaller = Difference

A diagram can help us understand a larger-smaller-difference plot. In the following diagram, we have used the numbers from the apple problem. There are two towers, a "larger" tower and a "smaller" tower. The "difference" is the difference in the heights of the two towers.

Reading Math

We translate the problem using a *larger-smaller-difference* formula.

Larger: 43 apples
Smaller: 19 apples
Difference: 24 apples

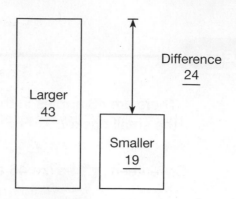

Recall that we solve a word problem using the four-step problem-solving process:

Step 1: Read and translate the problem.

Step 2: Make a plan to solve the problem.

Step 3: Follow the plan and solve the problem.

Step 4: Check your answer for reasonableness.

A plan that can help us solve word problems is to *write an equation.*

We do this by using a formula and writing the numbers we know in an equation that we can solve to find the answer.

Example 1

Andrea picked 42 apples at the apple orchard. Her younger brother picked 13 apples. How many more apples did Andrea pick than her brother?

To find "how many more," we use a subtraction formula. Here we are comparing the two numbers 42 and 13.

Formula	Problem
Larger	42 apples
− Smaller	− 13 apples
Difference	d

Andrea picked **29 more apples** than her brother picked.

To check the answer, we see if it correctly completes the problem.

Forty-two apples are 29 apples more than 13 apples.

Example 2

There were 17 apples in a basket and 63 apples in a barrel. How many fewer apples were in the basket than were in the barrel?

We are asked to find "how many fewer." The formula is the same as the formula for finding "how many more." We use a subtraction formula to compare the numbers.

Formula	Problem
Larger	63 apples
− Smaller	− 17 apples
Difference	d

There were **46 fewer apples** in the basket than were in the barrel.

We check the answer.

Seventeen apples are 46 apples fewer than 63 apples.

Example 3

The number represented by point *B* is how much greater than the number represented by point *A*?

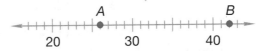

We see that point *A* represents 26 and point *B* represents 42. We use these numbers in the larger-smaller-difference formula.

$$\text{Larger} - \text{Smaller} = \text{Difference}$$
$$42 - 26 = d$$

We find that 42 is **16 greater** than 26.

We can check our answer by counting the number of units from point *A* to point *B*.

Lesson Practice

Formulate Write and solve an equation for each problem.

a. Forty-three is how much greater than twenty-seven?

b. Maricela has 42 CDs. Frank has 22 CDs. How many fewer CDs does Frank have?

c. Cesar had 53 shells. Juanita had 95 shells. How many more shells did Juanita have?

Written Practice *Distributed and Integrated*

Formulate Write and solve equations for problems 1–3.

* **1.** There were 43 parrots in the flock. Some flew away. Then there were
(25) 27 parrots in the flock. How many parrots flew away?

*2. One hundred fifty is how much greater than twenty-three?
(31)

*3. Twenty-three apples is how many fewer than seventy-five apples?
(31)

*4. On Saturday morning, Brady awoke at the time
(27) shown on the clock. Three hours later, he left home
to go to softball practice. What time did Brady leave
home?

*5. (Represent) Write 412 in expanded form. Then use words to write the
(7, 16) number.

6. What fraction of this figure is shaded?
(22)

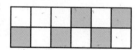

*7. The rectangle shown at right is 4 cm long and 2 cm
(Inv. 2, wide.
Inv. 3)

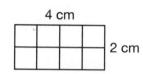

4 cm

2 cm

   a. What is the perimeter?

   b. What is the area?

8. Multiply:
(28, 29)

   a. 2 × 5   **b.** 5 × 7   **c.** 2 × 7   **d.** 4 × 11

*9. (Connect) Write two addition facts and two subtraction facts using the
(6) numbers 20, 30, and 50.

10. At 8 p.m. the temperature was 3°C. By 8 a.m. the next morning, the
(18) temperature had fallen 8 degrees. What was the temperature at
8 a.m.?

*11. The number represented by point *A* is how much less than the number
(31) represented by point *B*?

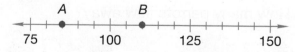

12. Multiply:
(28, 29)

    a. 5 × 8   **b.** 2 × 8   **c.** 5 × 9

13. a. How many quarters equal one dollar?
(22)

    b. A quarter is what fraction of a dollar?

    c. Three quarters are what fraction of a dollar?

*14. （**Represent**）Use digits and symbols to write this comparison:
(Inv. 1)

    Three hundred nine is less than three hundred ninety.

*15. Three hundred nine is how much less than 390?
(31)

*16. $4.22   ***17.**   909   ***18.** $422   ***19.**   703
(30)   − $2.95   (30)   − 27   (30)   − $144   (30)   − 471

20. $4.86   **21.**   370   **22.**   22   **23.**   76
(22)   + $2.95   (30)   − 209   (24)   + *n*   (24)   − *c*
                                     37   28

*24. （**Connect**）What multiplication fact is illustrated by this
(Inv. 3)   square?

*25. Find each square root:
(Inv. 3)

    a. $\sqrt{9}$ **b.** $\sqrt{25}$

*26. Multiple Choice Which of these does *not* equal 9?
(Inv. 3)
    A 3 squared   **B** $\sqrt{81}$
    C $\sqrt{18}$ **D** $\sqrt{25} + \sqrt{16}$

27. Multiply:
(28,
Inv. 3)
    a. 1 × 1   **b.** 5 × 5   **c.** 8 × 8   **d.** 9 × 9

28. Compare. Write >, <, or =.
(Inv. 1)
    a. 510 ◯ 501   **b.** 722 ◯ 976   **c.** 234 ◯ 238

* 29. 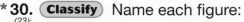 **Estimate** The land area of Aztec Ruins National Monument in New
(13, 22) Mexico is 318 acres. The land area of Casa Grande Ruins National
Monument in Arizona is 473 acres. What is a reasonable estimate of
the total acreage of these two national monuments? Explain why your
estimate is reasonable.

* 30. **Classify** Name each figure:
(23)

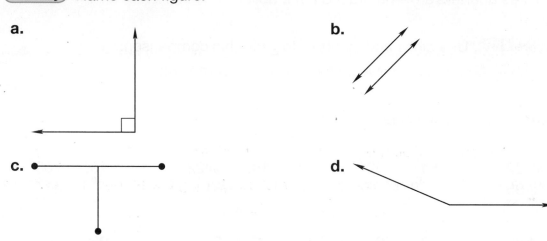

a.

b.

c.

d.

Early Finishers

*Real-World
Connection*

Tricia outlined two rectangles on her paper. Rectangle *A* measured
4 cm by 6 cm, and rectangle *B* measured 5 cm by 5 cm. Use 1-cm
grid paper or a centimeter ruler to draw both rectangles. Then find the
area of each rectangle. Which rectangle has the larger area? Use the
larger − smaller = difference formula.

• Multiplication Facts:
9s, 10s, 11s, 12s

facts	Power Up B
count aloud	Count down by fours from 40 to 4.
mental math	In problems **a–c,** practice splitting the second number to add.

    a. Number Sense: 49 + 6

    b. Number Sense: 65 + 8

    c. Number Sense: 38 + 8

    d. Number Sense: 920 + 38 + 7

    e. Time: Simone goes to bed each night at 9:15 p.m. She wants to watch a movie that lasts 2 hours. At what time must Simone begin the movie to finish it by her bedtime?

    f. Measurement: There are 8 squares along each edge of a checkerboard. If each square has 1-inch sides, what is the perimeter of the checkerboard?

    g. Money: The bicycle was $240, and the lock was $35. What was the total cost for the two items?

    h. Estimation: The length of the car is 176 inches. Round this length to the nearest ten inches.

problem solving

Choose an appropriate problem-solving strategy to solve this problem. TJ has seven coins in his right pocket. He does not have any dollar or half-dollar coins. TJ has at least one penny, one nickel, one dime, and one quarter, but he has no more than two coins of any type. What are the possible values of all seven coins? (There are four possibilities.)

Some 9s multiplication facts are listed below. Look for patterns in the facts. Notice that the first digit of each product is one less than the number that is multiplied by nine. Also notice that the two digits of each product add up to nine.

$$9 \times 2 = 18 \quad (1 + 8 = 9)$$
$$9 \times 3 = 27 \quad (2 + 7 = 9)$$
$$9 \times 4 = 36 \quad (3 + 6 = 9)$$
$$9 \times 5 = 45 \quad (4 + 5 = 9)$$
$$9 \times 6 = 54 \quad (5 + 4 = 9)$$
$$9 \times 7 = 63 \quad (6 + 3 = 9)$$
$$9 \times 8 = 72 \quad (7 + 2 = 9)$$
$$9 \times 9 = 81 \quad (8 + 1 = 9)$$
$$9 \times 10 = 90 \quad (9 + 0 = 9)$$

These two patterns can help us quickly multiply by nine.

Example 1

What is the first digit of each product?

a.	b.	c.	d.	e.
9	3	9	4	9
× 6	× 9	× 7	× 9	× 8
?_	?_	?_	?_	?_

The first digit is one less than the number multiplied by nine.

a.	b.	c.	d.	e.
9	3	9	4	9
× 6	× 9	× 7	× 9	× 8
5_	2_	6_	3_	7_

Example 2

What is the second digit of each product?

a.	b.	c.	d.	e.
9	3	9	4	9
× 6	× 9	× 7	× 9	× 8
5?	2?	6?	3?	7?

Complete each two-digit product so that the sum of the digits is nine.

a.	b.	c.	d.	e.
9	3	9	4	9
× 6	× 9	× 7	× 9	× 8
54	27	63	36	72

In Examples 3, 4, and 5, look for patterns that appear when whole numbers are multiplied by 10, 11, and 12.

Example 3

Thinking Skill

Generalize

What strategy could you use to remember the 10s multiplication facts?

Find the number of millimeters that equal the given length in centimeters.

Centimeters	1	2	3	4	5	6	7	8	9	10	11	12
Millimeters	10	20	30	40	?	?	?	?	?	?	?	?

Notice that one centimeter equals 10 millimeters. We will use our 10s multiplication facts to complete the table.

Centimeters	1	2	3	4	5	6	7	8	9	10	11	12
Millimeters	10	20	30	40	50	60	70	80	90	100	110	120

Example 4

A sheet of notebook paper is 11 inches long. Find the length in inches of 12 sheets laid end to end by completing this table.

Sheets	1	2	3	4	5	6	7	8	9	10	11	12
Inches	11	22	33	44	?	?	?	?	?	?	?	?

We are told that notebook paper is 11 inches long. We will use our 11s multiplication facts to complete the table.

Sheets	1	2	3	4	5	6	7	8	9	10	11	12
Inches	11	22	33	44	55	66	77	88	99	110	121	132

Example 5

Find the number of inches in 12 feet by completing this table:

Feet	1	2	3	4	5	6	7	8	9	10	11	12
Inches	12	24	36	48	?	?	?	?	?	?	?	?

Notice that one foot equals 12 inches. We will use our 12s multiplication facts to complete the table.

Feet	1	2	3	4	5	6	7	8	9	10	11	12
Inches	12	24	36	48	60	72	84	96	108	120	132	144

Lesson Practice   Find the product for each multiplication fact:

a.	9 × 3	b.	5 × 9	c.	8 × 9	d.	6 × 9
e.	9 × 4	f.	7 × 9	g.	9 × 2	h.	9 × 9
i.	10 × 5	j.	10 × 7	k.	10 × 3	l.	10 × 9
m.	11 × 6	n.	11 × 4	o.	11 × 7	p.	11 × 9
q.	12 × 3	r.	12 × 5	s.	12 × 2	t.	12 × 4

Written Practice   *Distributed and Integrated*

*1. **Formulate** There are two hundred fifteen pages in the book. Kande
(25) has read eighty-six pages. How many more pages are left to read?
Write and solve an equation.

2. Use the digits 7, 8, and 9 to make an even number greater than 800.
(10) Use each digit only once.

3. **Compare** Use digits and a comparison symbol to show that four
(Inv. 1) hundred eighty-five is less than six hundred ninety.

*4. **Conclude** This is a sequence of square numbers. What are the
(3, next three numbers in the sequence? How do you know?
Inv. 3)

$$1, 4, 9, 16, \_\_\_, \_\_\_, \_\_\_, \dots$$

5. One evening Jermaine finished washing the dishes at the
(19) time shown on the clock. What time did Jermaine finish
washing the dishes?

*6. **Represent** Write 729 in expanded form and use words to write the number.
(7, 16)

*7. **(Connect)** Change this addition problem to a multiplication problem.
(27, 28) Then find the product on the multiplication table.

$$6 + 6 + 6 + 6 + 6 + 6 + 6$$

8. Is the value of three nickels and two dimes an even number of cents or
(10) an odd number of cents?

9. a. Round 66 to the nearest ten.
(20)

  b. Round $6.60 to the nearest dollar.

  c. Round $6.60 to the nearest 25 cents.

10. a. Use a metric ruler to measure the length of each side of
(Inv. 2) this square in centimeters.

  b. What is the perimeter of the square?

*11. **(Analyze)** Which two uppercase letters are formed with only
(23) two perpendicular line segments?

12. If $62 - w = 48$, then what is the value of w?
(24)

13. What fraction of this rectangle is shaded?
(22)

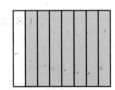

*14. **(Represent)** Draw an array of Xs to show the multiplication 5×5.
(Inv. 3)

*15. **(Represent)** The number represented by point B is how much greater
(31) than the number represented by point A?

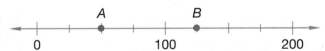

Multiply:

*16. a. 9×6 **b.** 9×8 **c.** 9×4 **d.** 9×10
(32)

*17. a. 6×6 **b.** 4×4 **c.** 7×7 **d.** 10×10
(Inv. 3)

*18. **a.** 2×11 **b.** 8×11 **c.** 5×11 **d.** 3×11
(32)

*19. **(Represent)** **a.** What multiplication fact is illustrated
(Inv. 3)   by this square?

     b. Find $\sqrt{25}$.

*20. $\sqrt{81}$ ***21.** $\$3.60 - \$1.37$ ***22.** $413 - 380$
(Inv. 3)   (30)   (30)

*23. $875 - 218$ **24.** Compare: $24 + 36 \bigcirc 12 + 48$
(30)   (Inv. 1)

*25. What number equals 8 squared?
(Inv. 3)

*26. **Multiple Choice** Jacob saw an array of freshly baked rolls on a pan.
(25,   There were four rows of rolls with four rolls in each row. How many rolls
Inv. 3)   will be left on the pan if he eats one roll?

     A 3   **B** 7   **C** 12   **D** 15

*27. Which property of multiplication does this story illustrate?
(28,   *Twenty-four desks were arranged in 4 rows with 6 desks*
Inv. 3)   *in each row. Then they were moved into 6 rows with 4 desks in*
        each row.

*28. **(Formulate)** In 2000, a professional baseball pitcher struck out
(13)   347 batters and another professional pitcher struck out 284 batters.
   Write and solve an equation to find the total number of batters the
   two pitchers struck out.

*29. **(Estimate)** The average depth of the East China Sea is 620 feet. The
(30)   average depth of the Yellow Sea is 121 feet. Estimate the difference
   between the two average depths. Explain why your estimate is
   reasonable.

*30. **(Predict)** Write the sixth term of each pattern:
(32)   **a.** 11, 22, 33, 44, 55, ...   **b.** 12, 24, 36, 48, 60, ...

• Writing Numbers Through Hundred Thousands

Power Up

facts	Power Up C
count aloud	As a class, count by threes from 30 to 60 and then back down to 30.
mental math	**a. Number Sense:** $60 - 40$
	b. Number Sense: $80 - 30$
	c. Number Sense: $800 - 300$
	d. Number Sense: $340 + 35 + 115$
	e. Geometry: The square table was 3 feet along each edge. What was the perimeter of the table?
	f. Time: Carole records her favorite television show. Each episode is 1 hour long. If Carole watches two episodes in a row starting at 6:20 p.m., what time will she finish?
	g. Measurement: The high temperature on the hot day was 36° Celsius. The low temperature was 27° Celsius. The difference between the high and low temperatures for the day was how many degrees?
	h. Estimation: Layne's pen was 128 millimeters long. Round this length to the nearest ten millimeters.
problem solving	Choose an appropriate problem-solving strategy to solve this problem. A checkerboard has 64 small squares. There are 8 squares along each side. If a square checkerboard had only 36 small squares, then how many squares would there be along each side?

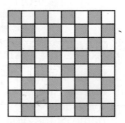

Recall that the places in a three-digit number are the ones place, the tens place, and the hundreds place. The three places to the left of the hundreds place are the thousands place, the ten-thousands place, and the hundred-thousands place.

hundred thousands
ten thousands
thousands
hundreds
tens
ones

— — — , — — —

Analyze How is the value of each place related to the value of the place to its right?

In order to make the numbers easier to read, we can use commas when writing numbers equal to or greater than one thousand. To read a whole number with four, five, or six digits, we read the number to the left of the comma, say "thousand" at the comma, and then read the number after the comma. When we write a number in words, we place a comma after the word *thousand.*

4,507	is read	four **thousand,** five hundred seven
34,507	is read	thirty-four **thousand,** five hundred seven
234,507	is read	two hundred thirty-four **thousand,** five hundred seven

Four-digit whole numbers are often written without a comma, like when we write the year. In this book we will typically not use a comma when writing a four-digit whole number. However, we will use commas to express any whole number with more than four digits.

Example 1

Reading Math

When we see a comma, we write the place-value name of the digit to the left of the comma. This comma represents the thousands place.

Use words to write 23456.

To make the number easier to read, we insert a comma three places from the right-hand end of the number.

23,456

Then we write the number that is to the left of the comma.

twenty-three

Next we write "thousand" followed by a comma.

twenty-three thousand,

Finally, we write the number that is to the right of the comma.

twenty-three thousand, four hundred fifty-six

Example 2

In the 2000 Census, Fort Worth had a population of 534,694. Use words to write the population.

First we name the part of the number to the left of the comma and then write "thousand."

five hundred thirty-four thousand

Then we name the rest of the number, remembering to write a comma after the word thousand.

five hundred thirty-four thousand, six hundred ninety-four

Example 3

Write 75,634 in expanded form.

The 7 is in the ten-thousands place. It has a value of 70,000. So we write

70,000 + 5000 + 600 + 30 + 4

Example 4

Which digit in 345,678 is in the hundred-thousands place?

The digit **3** is in the hundred-thousands place.

Example 5

Compare: 510,000 $\bigcirc$ 501,000

We compare the numbers place by place, beginning with the greatest place value (hundred thousands).

510,000 > 501,000

Example 6

Write these numbers in order from least to greatest:

23,000   230,000   78,000   870,000   500,000

First we compare the numbers place by place, beginning with the greatest place value (hundred thousands). Then we order the numbers from least to greatest.

23,000   78,000   230,000   500,000   870,000

Example 7

Use digits to write eight hundred ninety-five thousand, two hundred seventy.

It is a good idea to read the entire number before we begin writing it. We see the word *thousand,* so we know to place a thousands comma after the digits that tell how many thousands.

___ ___ ___, ___ ___ ___

We read the part of the number before the word *thousand* and write this number in front of the comma. For "eight hundred ninety-five thousand" we write

<u> 8 </u> <u> 9 </u> <u> 5 </u>, ___ ___ ___

Now, to the right of the comma, we write the last part of the number: "two hundred seventy."

895,270

Lesson Practice As a class, read the following numbers aloud:

a. 125,000   **b.** 435,000

c. 12,500   **d.** 25,375

e. 4875   **f.** 250,625

Represent Use words to write the numbers in problems **g–i.**

g. 2750   **h.** 14,518

i. 500,000

Use digits to write the numbers in problems **j–l.**

j. twenty thousand

k. twelve thousand, three hundred fifty

l. one hundred twenty thousand, five hundred

m. Write 5280 in expanded form.

n. Write 2040 in expanded form.

o. Which digit in 284,359 is in the ten-thousands place?

p. Compare: 760,000 ◯ 670,000

q. The dates in the table below are important to aerospace history. Arrange the dates in order from earliest to latest.

Event in Aerospace History	Date
First human lands on the moon	1969
Wright brothers invent the first successful airplane	1903
Russians launch Sputnik, the first artificial satellite	1957
Charles Lindbergh completes the first nonstop, solo flight across the Atlantic Ocean	1927

Written Practice   *Distributed and Integrated*

*1. Marcos is reading a book with 211 pages. K'Neesha is reading a
(31) book with 272 pages. How many more pages will K'Neesha read than Marcos? Write and solve an equation.

*2. **Represent** Write the number 3425 in expanded form. Then use words
(16, 33) to write the number.

*3. **Represent** Draw two parallel lines. Then draw a perpendicular line that
(23) makes right angles where it intersects the parallel lines.

*4. The square root of 49 is how much less than four squared?
(Inv. 3, 31)

*5. **Represent** On 1-cm grid paper, draw a 6 cm by 2 cm rectangle.
(Inv. 2, Inv. 3)

    a. What is the perimeter of the rectangle?

    b. What is the area of the rectangle?

*6. Place commas in 250000. Then use words to write the number.
(33)

*7. **Conclude** What are the next four numbers in this counting sequence?
(3)

    . . . , 230, 240, 250, 260, ____, ____, ____, ____, . . .

*8. Which digit in 123,456 is in the ten-thousands place?
(33)

9. Compare: $9 \times 4 \bigcirc \sqrt{36}$
(Inv. 1, Inv. 3)

*10. After school yesterday, Luis began playing outside at the
(27) time shown on the clock. He played for 2 hours 25 minutes.
What time did Luis finish playing outside?

*11. **Represent** To what number is the arrow pointing?
(Inv. 1)

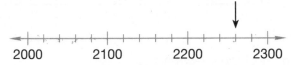

Multiply:

*12. **a.** 5×8 **b.** 4×4 **c.** 8×8 **d.** 12×12
(29, Inv. 3)

*13. **a.** 9×3 **b.** 9×4 **c.** 9×5 **d.** 9×10
(29, 32)

*14. **Connect** Write two addition facts and two subtraction facts using the
(6) numbers 40, 60, and 100.

15. **Connect** Change this addition problem to a multiplication problem:
(27)

$$20 + 20 + 20 + 20 + 20$$

*16. $\$7.37$
(30) $- \$2.68$

*17. 921
(30) $- 58$

18. 464
(13) $+ 247$

*19. 329
(24, 30) $+ z$
    547

20. $\$4.88$
(22) $+ \$2.69$

*21. 555
(24) $- c$
    222

22. Judy's birth date is 5/27/98. In which month was she born?
(5)

23. ₍₂₁₎ **Represent** Draw a circle with a radius of 1 inch. What is the diameter of the circle? Explain how you know.

24. ₍₁₇₎
```
   4
   8
  12
  16
  14
  28
+ 37
```

25. ₍₁₇₎
```
   5
   8
   7
  14
   6
  21
+ 15
```

*26. ₍₃₃₎ Compare: 25,000 ◯ 250,000

*27. _(Inv. 3) **Multiple Choice** Look at the sequence below. Which of the following numbers is *not* in the sequence?

$$1, 4, 9, 16, 25, 36, \ldots$$

A 64   **B** 49

C 80   **D** 100

*28. ₍₁₃₎ **Formulate** The state of Kentucky had 189 public libraries in 2006. The state of Maryland had 176 public libraries. Write and solve an equation to find the number of public libraries Kentucky and Maryland had altogether.

*29. _(Inv. 2, 32) Eight feet is how many inches? Count by 12s.

*30. _(Inv. 2, 32) Nine centimeters is how many millimeters? Count by 10s.

• Writing Numbers Through Hundred Millions

Power Up

facts	Power Up A
count aloud	Count by sevens from 7 to 63.
mental math	**a. Number Sense:** $65 - 30$
	b. Number Sense: $650 - 300$
	c. Number Sense: $58 + 4 + 100$
	d. Number Sense: $36 + 29 + 200$
	e. Number Sense: $520 + 36 + 126$
	f. Measurement: Compare: 14 in. $\bigcirc$ 1 ft
	g. Time: If the time is 7:45, how many minutes is it until 8:00?
	h. Estimation: The tabletop was 73 centimeters above the floor. Round that height to the nearest ten centimeters.
problem solving	Choose an appropriate problem-solving strategy to solve this problem. Ramone has seven coins in his right pocket. He does not have any dollar or half-dollar coins. Ramone has at least one penny, one nickel, one dime, and one quarter, but he has no more than two coins of any type. Although Ramone has an odd number of coins, their total value is an even number of cents. What is the total value of the coins?

New Concept

In Lesson 33 we wrote numbers through hundred thousands. In this lesson we will write numbers through hundred millions.

To write a whole number with seven, eight, or nine digits, we use another comma to indicate millions.

Whole-Number Place Values

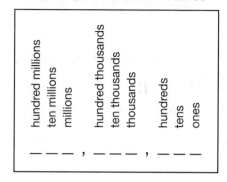

To read a whole number with seven, eight, or nine digits, we first read the digits to the left of the millions comma and say "million" at the comma. Then we read the next three digits and say "thousand" at the next comma. We finish by reading the remaining digits.

15,000,000	is read	fifteen **million**
2,500,000	is read	two **million,** five hundred thousand
1,258,300	is read	one **million,** two hundred fifty-eight thousand, three hundred

Generalize How many hundred thousands equal one million? Explain why.

Example 1

Use words to write 12345678.

Counting from the right, we place a comma every three digits.

12,345,678

Next we write the part of the number to the left of the millions comma.

twelve million

Since there are more digits to read, we place a comma after the word *million.* Then we write the part of the number up to the thousands comma.

twelve million, three hundred forty-five thousand

Since there are still more digits to read, we place a comma after the word *thousand* and write the rest of the number.

twelve million, three hundred forty-five thousand, six hundred seventy-eight

When writing numbers, every comma is followed by at least three digits. Sometimes it is necessary to use one or more zeros in order to get the correct number of digits after a comma.

Example 2

Use digits to write two million, three hundred thousand.

We see the word *million,* so we use this form:

_____ _____ _____, _____ _____ _____, _____ _____ _____

In front of the word *million,* we read "two," so we write

__2__, _____ _____, _____ _____ _____ _____

Next we read "three hundred thousand," so we write

__2__, __3__ __0__ __0__, _____ _____ _____

Now we fill the three places after the thousands comma with zeros.

2,300,000

In newspapers we often see large numbers written in short word form.

2 million people gathered for the Rose Parade.
95 thousand fans filled the stadium.

Connect Use digits to write the numbers 2 million and 95 thousand.

Example 3

Compare: 113 million ◯ 311 million

We compare the digits place by place, beginning with the greatest place value (millions).

113 million < 311 million

Example 4

Write these numbers in order from least to greatest:

7 million   250 thousand   12 million

First we compare the digits place by place, beginning with the greatest place value (millions). Then we order the numbers from least to greatest.

250 thousand, 7 million, 12 million

Lesson Practice   **Represent** Use words to write each number:

a. 121,340,000

b. 12,507,000

c. 5,075,000

Use digits to write each number:

   d. twenty-five million

   e. twelve million, five hundred thousand

   f. two hundred eighty million

   g. Compare: 34 million ◯ 43 million

   h. Arrange these numbers in order from least to greatest:

      5 million   25 thousand   750 thousand

   i. Arrange these numbers in order from least to greatest:

      12,375   1,000,000   987,000

Written Practice — Distributed and Integrated

Formulate Write and solve equations for problems **1** and **2**.

*1. Four hundred sixty-five is how much greater than twenty-four?
(31)

*2. Marcie had four hundred twenty marbles. Kareem had one hundred twenty-three marbles. How many fewer marbles did Kareem have?
(31)

*3. **Represent** On 1-cm grid paper, draw a square that is 4 cm on each side.
(Inv. 2, Inv. 3)

   a. What is the perimeter of the square?

   b. What is the area of the square?

*4. **Represent** Write the number 25,463 in expanded form.
(16, 33)

5. **Represent** Draw a circle that has a diameter of 4 centimeters. What is the radius of the circle?
(21)

6. Jharma arrived home from school at the time shown on the clock and finished her homework 1 hour 35 minutes later. What time did Jharma finish her homework?
(27)

7. **Explain** What fraction of the circles is shaded? Describe
(22) how you found your answer.

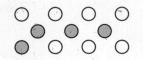

8. **Connect** Change this addition problem to a multiplication problem.
(27, 29) Then find the product.

$$12 + 12 + 12 + 12 + 12$$

9. **Estimate** Round 76 to the nearest ten. Round 59 to the nearest ten.
(20) Then add the rounded numbers.

10. Compare:
(Inv. 1,
34) **a.** 3 ◯ −4   **b.** two million ◯ 200,000

11. The number represented by point A is how much less than the number
(31) represented by point B?

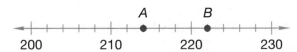

$$A \qquad B$$
$$200 \qquad 210 \qquad 220 \qquad 230$$

Multiply:

12. **a.** 5×7 **b.** 6×6 **c.** 9×9 **d.** 10×10
(29,
Inv. 3)

13. **a.** 3×9 **b.** 9×7 **c.** 8×9 **d.** 9×1
(29, 32)

14. **a.** 11×11 **b.** 6×12 **c.** 8×11 **d.** 10×12
(32)

15. **a.** **Represent** Use words to write 3,500,000.
(34, 33)

b. **Represent** Use digits to write seven hundred fifty thousand.

16.   535   ***17.***   908   ***18.*** $471
(30)   − 268   (30)   − 43   (30)   − $346

19. $c + 329 = 715$ **20.** $c − 127 = 398$
(24, 30)   (24)

21. If the radius of a circle is 12 inches, then the diameter of the circle is
(Inv. 2,
21) how many feet?

*22. Five squared is how much more than $5 + 5$?
(Inv. 3, 31)

*23. (Connect) Select two odd numbers and one even number that form
(6, 10) an addition/subtraction fact family. Then use the numbers to write two
addition facts and two subtraction facts.

*24. $\sqrt{9} + \sqrt{16}$
(Inv. 3)

25. (Represent) Draw a triangle that has one obtuse angle.
(23)

*26. **Multiple Choice** Which digit in 3,756,289 is in the thousands
(34) place?

    A 3   **B** 7   **C** 5   **D** 6

*27. In the year 2000, the four most populous U.S. states and their
(34) populations were:

California	33,871,648
Florida	15,982,378
New York	18,976,457
Texas	20,851,820

These states are listed in alphabetical order. List the names of the states
in order of population, beginning with the greatest population.

*28. (Predict) What is the twelfth term in this counting sequence?
(3, 32)

$$11, 22, 33, 44, \ldots$$

*29. (Predict) What is the eighth term in this counting sequence?
(3, 32)

$$12, 24, 36, 48, \ldots$$

*30. (Estimate) M'Lisa would like to purchase about 100 balloons for
(20, 22) her birthday party. One bag of 25 balloons costs $2.49. What is a
reasonable estimate of M'Lisa's cost to purchase about 100 balloons?
Explain why your estimate is reasonable.

• Naming Mixed Numbers and Money

Power Up

facts   Power Up C

count aloud   Count by fours from 40 to 80.

mental math

   a. Number Sense: 750 − 200

   b. Number Sense: 86 − 50

   c. Number Sense: 43 + 9 + 110

   d. Measurement: The needle is pointing to what number on this scale?

   e. Measurement: It took Paul only two minutes to finish the quiz. How many seconds is that?

   f. Money: Kalea had $45. She bought a pair of slacks for $25. How much money does she have left?

   g. Estimation: Each paperback at the used bookstore costs $1.93. About how much would 5 paperbacks cost?

   h. Calculation: 4 × 5, − 10, + 2, + 3

problem solving

Choose an appropriate problem-solving strategy to solve this problem. The pattern of the sequence below is 1 × 1, 2 × 2, 3 × 3, and so on. Use a multiplication table to help you continue this sequence of square numbers up to 100.

1, 4, 9, 16, _____, _____, _____, _____, _____, 100

New Concept

A **mixed number** is a whole number combined with a fraction. The mixed number $3\frac{1}{2}$ is read "three and one half."

Example 1

Thinking Skill

Analyze

How many fourths are equal to $2\frac{1}{4}$? Explain why.

How many circles are shaded?

Two whole circles are shaded, and one fourth of another circle is shaded. The total number of shaded circles is two and one fourth, which we write as

$$2\frac{1}{4}$$

Example 2

Use words to write $3\frac{1}{2}$.

We use the word *and* when naming mixed numbers.

three and one half

Example 3

Use words to write $4\frac{2}{3}$.

four and two thirds

Math Symbols

We do not use a decimal point with a cent sign. The notation 0.50¢ is incorrect because it does not represent fifty cents. Instead, it represents 50 hundredths (or $\frac{1}{2}$) of one cent.

We can show amounts of money by using a number and a cent sign (¢). We put a cent sign after a number to tell how many cents there are.

324¢   20¢   4¢

We can also use a dollar sign ($) to show amounts of money. We put the dollar sign in front of the money amount, and we use a decimal point and two places to the right of the decimal point to show the number of cents. The money amounts below are the same as the previous amounts, but they are expressed with a dollar sign and decimal point rather than a cent sign.

$3.24 $0.20 $0.04

Sometimes we use mixed numbers to name an amount of money. For example, we might say "seven and one-half dollars" to name $7.50 because 50 cents is one half-dollar. When writing a check, we can write the number of dollars in words and the cents as a fraction on the "dollars" line.

Example 4

Anita is writing a check for her water bill. Show how she would write fifteen dollars and twenty-five cents using a dollar sign.

When we use a dollar sign and need to show cents, we put a decimal point between dollars and cents.

$15.25

Example 5

Anita needs to pay her cable bill. Show how to write $30.76 using words.

We write the number of dollars in words, write "and," and then write the number of cents.

thirty dollars and seventy-six cents

Example 6

Show how to write the "dollars" line on this check.

Jan Jones
567 8th Street

2032

DATE *July 3, 2007*

PAY TO THE ORDER OF *Water Company* $ | *$37.80* |

_____ DOLLARS

✳ **MY**BANK

Memo *Water Bill*   *Jan Jones*

We write the number of dollars in words, write "and," and then the cents as a fraction. Since 100 cents equals a dollar, the denominator is 100.

thirty-seven and $\frac{80}{100}$

Example 7

Kasim has one quarter, one dime, and one nickel. Write how much money she has using a cent sign. Then write the same amount using a dollar sign and decimal point.

First we find how many cents Kasim has. A quarter is twenty-five cents, a dime is ten cents, and a nickel is five cents.

25¢ + 10¢ + 5¢ = **40¢**

Now we write forty cents using a dollar sign and decimal point.

$0.40

Example 8

Which of the following does not represent the value of a quarter?

25¢ $0.25   0.25¢   25 cents

The third choice, **0.25¢,** does not represent the value of a quarter. Instead, it represents a quarter (or $\frac{1}{4}$) of one cent.

What mixed numbers are illustrated by the shaded pictures?

a.

b.

Represent Draw and shade circles to illustrate these mixed numbers:

c. $1\frac{1}{4}$

d. $2\frac{3}{4}$

Represent Use words to write each mixed number.

e. $12\frac{3}{4}$

f. $2\frac{7}{10}$

g. $6\frac{9}{100}$

Connect Write each amount with a cent sign instead of a dollar sign.

h. $0.17

i. $0.05

Connect Write each amount with a dollar sign instead of a cent sign.

j. 8¢

k. 30¢

l. **Analyze** Write the value of two quarters, two dimes, and one nickel with a dollar sign. Then use a cent sign to write this amount again.

m. Use words to write $20.05.

n. **Represent** Show how to write the dollars line on a check for $12.25.

Written Practice   *Distributed and Integrated*

Write and solve equations for problems **1–3.**

*1.
(31)
Thirty-seven nations sent athletes to the 1968 Winter Olympics in Grenoble, France. Thirty years later, seventy-two nations sent athletes to the 1998 Winter Olympics in Nagano, Japan. How many more nations sent athletes in 1998 than in 1968?

*2.
(Inv. 2)
Explain Every morning Mario runs around the block. The block is 300 yards long and 100 yards wide. How many yards does Mario run when he runs around the block? Did you find the perimeter or area of the block? Explain your answer.

3. Ninety-seven oranges were in the first bunch, fifty-seven oranges were in
(1, 17)   the second bunch, and forty-eight oranges were in the third bunch. How
many oranges were in all three bunches?

*4. What mixed number is pictured in this figure?
(35)

5. Armena had four dollars and sixty-five cents. Use a dollar sign and a
(35)   decimal point to write this amount.

6. The thermometer shows the high temperature for
(18)   one winter day in Fairlawn, Ohio. What was the high
temperature that day?

7. **Multiple Choice** Which of these angles does *not* look like a right
(23)   angle?

A   **B**   **C**   **D**

*8. The square root of 81 is how much less than seven squared?
(Inv. 3,
31)

*9. On Saturday night, ShayZee fell asleep at the time shown
(27)   on the clock. Two hours twenty minutes later, ShayZee
woke up. What time did ShayZee wake up?

*10. ⬤**Represent** Use words to write $2\frac{3}{10}$.
(35)

*11. Find the numbers represented by point *A* and point *B*. Then find the
(31)   difference.

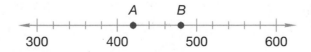

*12. **Represent** Use words to write $1.43.
₍₃₅₎

Multiply:

13. **a.** 6×9 **b.** 4×9 **c.** 3×9 **d.** 10×9
₍₃₂₎

14. **a.** 6×6 **b.** 7×7 **c.** 8×8 **d.** 11×11
_(Inv. 3)

15. $\sqrt{25} - \sqrt{16}$
_(Inv. 3)

*16. **Represent** Draw a rectangle that is 3 cm long and 3 cm wide. Divide
_(21, 26) the rectangle into thirds and shade $\frac{2}{3}$ of it.

*17. $6.05   ***18.**   489   **19.** $5.32
₍₃₀₎ $- \$2.53$ _(24, 30) $+ \quad z$ ₍₂₂₎ $+ \$3.44$
                                 766

*20. c ***21.**   423   **22.**   670
_(24, 30) $+ \; 294$ ₍₃₀₎ $- \; 245$ _(24, 30) $- \quad z$
      870   352

*23. **Represent** Use digits to write two hundred fifty million.
₍₃₄₎

*24. **Conclude** What are the next three numbers in this counting sequence?
₍₃₎

         ..., 3400, 3500, 3600, 3700, ____, ____, ____, ...

25. **a.** Round 77 to the nearest ten.
₍₂₀₎

     b. Round $6.82 to the nearest dollar.

*26. **Multiple Choice** If $7 + \square = 10$, then which of the following numbers
_(1, 6) equals $7 - \square$?

     A 3   **B** 4   **C** 7   **D** 10

*27. Compare:
_(33, 35)

     a. thirty thousand $\bigcirc$ 13,000

     b. 74¢ $\bigcirc$ $0.74

*28. Write these numbers in order from greatest to least:
(33, 34)

        125 thousand   125 million   12,500,000

*29. **Predict** Write the twelfth term of each pattern below:
(32)

    a. 11, 22, 33, 44, …

    b. 12, 24, 36, 48, …

*30. Name a real-world example of
(23)

    a. parallel lines.

    b. perpendicular lines.

Real-World Connection

The school choir is having a car wash to raise money to buy new songbooks. Each car wash will cost 350¢.

    a. Write this money amount using a dollar sign and a decimal point.

    b. Draw and shade circles to represent $3\frac{1}{2}$ as a mixed number.

    c. Use words to write $3\frac{50}{100}$.

• Fractions of a Dollar

facts	Power Up C
count aloud	Count by fours from 40 to 80.
mental math	**a. Number Sense:** $630 + 45 + 210$
	b. Number Sense: $78 + 7 + 10$
	c. Number Sense: $67 + 19 + 100$
	d. Money: Jason has three bank accounts. His account balances are $120, $85, and $37. Altogether, how much money does Jason have in his bank accounts?
	e. Measurement: Isaac ran 5 kilometers. How many meters did Isaac run?
	f. Time: Chase went to bed at 9:00 p.m. He woke up 9 hours later. At what time did Chase wake up?
	g. Estimation: Carina has $1.87 in her left pocket and $2.35 in her right pocket. Round each amount to the nearest 25 cents.
	h. Calculation: $6 \times 3, + 8, + 8, - 4$

problem solving

Tom has a penny, a nickel, a dime, and a quarter. Two of the coins are in his left pocket and two are in his right pocket. What combinations of coins could be in his left pocket?

Focus Strategies: Make an Organized List; Draw a Picture

(**Understand**) We are told that two of Tom's four coins are in his left pocket and that two are in his right pocket. We are asked to find the combinations of coins that could be in his left pocket.

Plan We can *make an organized list* or *draw a picture* of each pair of coins that Tom could have in his left pocket. To be sure we do not skip any possible pairs, we will consider each coin separately and list the other coins that could be paired with it.

Solve We can start with the least valuable coin, the penny. If one of the coins in Tom's left pocket is a penny, then these are the possible pairs:

If Tom does not have a penny in his left pocket, but he does have a nickel, then these are the possible pairs:

If Tom does not have a penny or a nickel in his left pocket, then only one possible pair remains:

We found that there are 6 different pairs of coins Tom could have put into his left pocket:

      1. penny and nickel

      2. penny and dime

      3. penny and quarter

      4. nickel and dime

      5. nickel and quarter

      6. dime and quarter

Check We know that our answer is reasonable because we organized our work to consider every possible pair of coins Tom could have in his left pocket, and we made sure not to repeat pairs of coins.

Each of the 6 coin pairs is called a **combination.** In this problem, we found all the combinations of 2 coins that can be made from the set that includes one penny, one nickel, one dime, and one quarter. When describing a combination, the order in which we list the parts of the combination does not matter. Thus, and is the same combination as and .

New Concept

Thinking Skill

Verify

Explain why a dime is $\frac{1}{10}$ of a dollar.

Since Lesson 22 we have used coins as fractions of a dollar. Because 100 pennies equals one dollar, each penny is $\frac{1}{100}$ of a dollar. Likewise, since 20 nickels equals a dollar, each nickel is $\frac{1}{20}$ of a dollar. We may describe part of a dollar by using a fraction or by using a dollar sign and decimal point.

Example 1

a. **Three pennies are what fraction of a dollar?**

b. **Write the value of three pennies using a dollar sign and a decimal point.**

a. One penny is $\frac{1}{100}$ of a dollar, so three pennies are $\frac{3}{100}$ of a dollar.

b. The value of three pennies can also be written as **$0.03.**

Example 2

a. **Which coin equals one fourth of a dollar?**

b. **Write $\frac{1}{4}$ of a dollar using a dollar sign and a decimal point.**

a. Since four quarters equals a dollar, a **quarter** is one fourth of a dollar. (The term *one quarter* means "one fourth.")

b. A quarter of a dollar is **$0.25.**

Example 3

a. **Three dimes are what fraction of a dollar?**

b. **Write the value of three dimes using a dollar sign and a decimal point.**

a. Each dime is $\frac{1}{10}$ of a dollar, so three dimes are $\frac{3}{10}$ of a dollar.

b. The value of three dimes is 30 cents, which we can write as **$0.30.** So $\frac{3}{10}$ of a dollar is $0.30.

Example 4

Compare: $\frac{1}{20}$ of a dollar $\bigcirc$ $\frac{1}{2}$ of a dollar

A nickel is $\frac{1}{20}$ of a dollar and is less than $\frac{1}{2}$ of a dollar.

$$\frac{1}{20} \text{ of a dollar} < \frac{1}{2} \text{ of a dollar}$$

Example 5

Look at these coins. How many different ways can we group three coins?

Use money manipulatives to find how many different ways we can group three coins. If the three coins include a penny, then the possible combinations are

penny, nickel, dime

penny, nickel, quarter

penny, dime, quarter

If a penny is not included, then the only combination is

nickel, dime, quarter

We have found **four combinations.**

(Verify) Describe another way to find that there are four possible combinations.

Lesson Practice

a. (Analyze) Write the value of three quarters using a dollar sign and a decimal point. Then write three quarters as a fraction of a dollar.

b. What fraction of a dollar is three nickels? Write the value of three nickels using a dollar sign and a decimal point.

c. Fifty pennies are what fraction of a dollar? Write the value of 50 pennies using a dollar sign and a decimal point.

d. Compare: $\frac{1}{10}$ of a dollar $\bigcirc$ $\frac{1}{4}$ of a dollar

e. Compare: $\frac{1}{2}$ of a dollar $\bigcirc$ $\$0.25$

f. Look at these coins:

List all of the different ways to pair two coins. You may use money manipulatives to solve.

Written Practice

Distributed and Integrated

Formulate Write and solve equations for problems **1–3.**

*1. Quinh is 49 inches tall. His dad is 70 inches tall. Quinh is how many
(31) inches shorter than his dad?

*2. Smith went into the store with $36.49. He bought a book and left
(25) the store with $11.80. How much money did Smith spend in the store?

*3. Beth answered eleven of the twenty-five questions at school. She
(24) answered the rest of the questions as homework. How many questions did Beth answer as homework?

*4. Write the number of shaded rectangles shown as a mixed
(35) number.

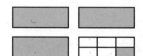

*5. **Verify** Which letter below appears to have no right angles?
(23)

T   H   E   N

*6. **Represent** Use words to write 2,700,000.
(34)

*7. **Represent** Use digits to write eighty-two thousand, five hundred.
(33)

8. Each day, classes at Kennedy Elementary School end
(27) 4 hours 20 minutes later than the time shown on the clock.
What time do classes end each day?

9. **Connect** Change this addition problem to a multiplication problem:
(27)

$$4 + 4 + 4 + 4 + 4 + 4 + 4 + 4$$

10. a. Round 176 to the nearest ten.
(20)

b. Round $17.60 to the nearest dollar.

*11. **Represent** The number represented by point *X* is how much less than
(31) the number represented by point *Y*?

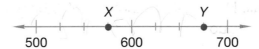

Multiply:

12. a. 2×8 **b.** 5×6 **c.** 4×5 **d.** 5×8
(29)

13. a. 3×3 **b.** 5×5 **c.** 9×9 **d.** 10×10
(Inv. 3)

14. a. 9×7 **b.** 9×4 **c.** 9×8 **d.** 9×12
(32)

15. $\sqrt{36} + \sqrt{49}$
(Inv. 3)

*16. $7.32   **17.** $4.89   ***18.** 464
(30) $- $3.45   (22) $+ $2.57   (30) $- 238

19. 548   ***20.** 487   ***21.** 250
(13) $+ 999   (24, 30) $+ \quad z$ (24, 30) $- \quad c$
                721   122

22. $c - 338 = 238$ **23.** $87 - b = 54$
(24)   (24)

*24. Which digit in 8,367,254 is in the ten-thousands place?
(34)

*25. Multiple Choice Which of the money amounts below does *not* equal
 (36) one half of a dollar?

   A 2 quarters   **B** 0.50¢   **C** $0.50   **D** 50¢

*26. Multiple Choice If a rectangle is 5 in. long and 4 in. wide, then its
 (Inv. 3) area is _____.

   A 9 in.   **B** 18 in.   **C** 20 sq. in.   **D** 18 sq. in.

27. Compare:
 (Inv. 1,
   36)   **a.** −12 ◯ −21   **b.** $\frac{1}{4}$ of a dollar ◯ $0.25

28. (**Predict**) Write the tenth term of each pattern below:
 (32)

   a. 12, 24, 36, 48, 60, …

   b. 11, 22, 33, 44, 55, …

*29. Look at these bills:
 (36)

   List all of the different ways to pair two bills.

30. ✏ **Estimate**) The state of Louisiana has 397 miles of coastline. The state
 (20) of Oregon has 296 miles of coastline. What is a reasonable estimate of
   the combined length of those coastlines? Explain why your estimate is
   reasonable.

*Real-World
Connection*

Maria had a quarter, a dime, and a nickel in her pocket. How much
money did Maria have in her pocket?

   a. Write the amount as a fraction of a dollar.

   b. Write the value of the coins using a dollar sign and a decimal
      point.

   c. Compare the amount to $\frac{1}{2}$ of a dollar.

• Reading Fractions and Mixed Numbers from a Number Line

Power Up

facts	Power Up D
count aloud	Count down by fives from 150 to 50.
mental math	**a. Number Sense:** $780 - 200$
	b. Number Sense: $870 - 230$
	c. Number Sense: $157 + 19$
	d. Number Sense: $58 + 6$

e. Measurement: The needle is pointing to what number on this scale?

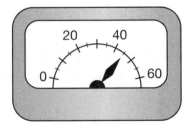

f. Geometry: Altogether, how many sides do four triangles have?

g. Estimation: Choose the more reasonable estimate for the diameter of a music CD: 12 cm or 12 m.

h. Calculation: $3 \times 3 \times 3 + 3$

problem solving

Choose an appropriate problem-solving strategy to solve this problem. The rectangle shown represents how a plot of land will be divided among four different owners. Area *C* is the same size as area *D*. Areas *C* and *D* together are the same size as area *B*. Areas *B*, *C*, and *D* together are the same size as area *A*. What fraction of the whole rectangle is each area?

	A	B	
		C	D

New Concept

To name mixed numbers on a number line, we first count the number of segments between consecutive whole numbers. If there are four segments between the whole numbers, each segment equals $\frac{1}{4}$. If there are six segments between the whole numbers, each segment equals $\frac{1}{6}$.

Thinking Skill

Verify

How many fourths are between 5 and 6? Between 6 and 7? On this number line?

Example 1

To what number is the arrow pointing?

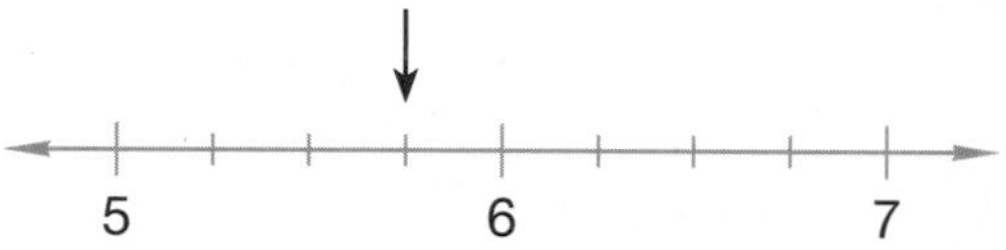

There are four segments between 5 and 6. Each segment equals $\frac{1}{4}$. The arrow points to $\mathbf{5\frac{3}{4}}$.

Example 2

To what number is each arrow pointing?

a.

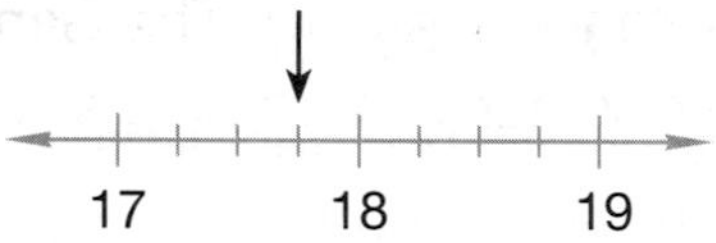

b.

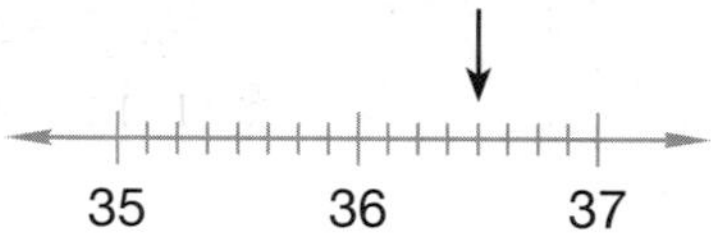

c. Copy and show $23\frac{1}{2}$ on the number line.

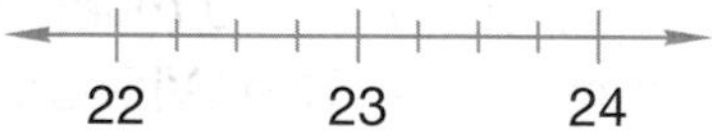

d. Copy and show $9\frac{1}{4}$ on the number line.

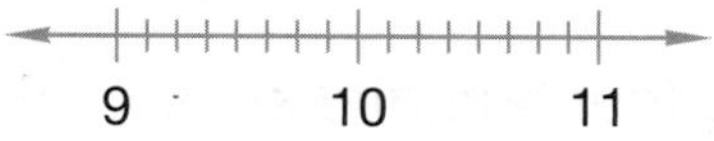

a. There are four segments between 17 and 18. Each segment equals $\frac{1}{4}$. The arrow points to $\mathbf{17\frac{3}{4}}$.

b. There are eight segments between 36 and 37. Each segment equals $\frac{1}{8}$. The arrow points to $\mathbf{36\frac{4}{8}}$**, or** $\mathbf{36\frac{1}{2}}$.

c.

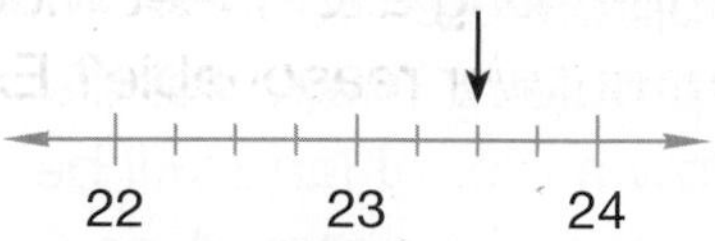

d.

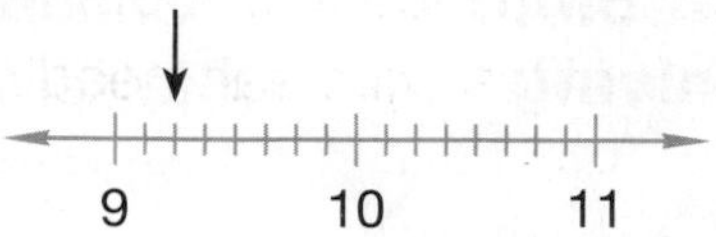

Lesson Practice **Represent** Name each fraction or mixed number marked by the arrows below:

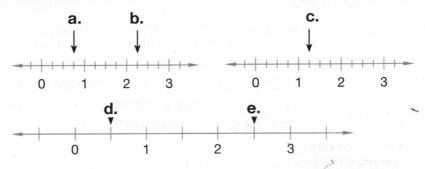

f. Copy and locate $25\frac{3}{4}$, $26\frac{1}{2}$, and $27\frac{1}{4}$ on the number line.

Written Practice *Distributed and Integrated*

Formulate Write and solve equations for problems **1** and **2**.

* 1. The Pearl River in Mississippi is 411 miles long. The San Juan River
(31) in Colorado is 360 miles long. How many miles longer is the Pearl River?

* 2. If the length of the Sabine River in Texas were 50 miles longer, it would
(11, 24) be the same length as the Wisconsin River. The Wisconsin River is 430 miles long. How long is the Sabine River?

* 3. **Represent** Use digits to write four hundred seventy-five thousand,
(33) three hundred forty-two. Then circle the digit in the ten-thousands place.

4. **Explain** Leah wants to put square floor tiles that measure one foot
(Inv. 3) on each side in a room that is 9 feet long and 9 feet wide. How many floor tiles will Leah need? Is your answer reasonable? Explain why.

* 5. **Represent** To what mixed number is the arrow pointing?
(37)

*6. **(Represent)** Draw a rectangle whose length is 5 cm and whose width
(Inv. 2, 21) is 3 cm. What is the perimeter of the rectangle?

*7. What mixed number is shown by the shaded rectangles?
(35)

*8. **(Represent)** Use words to write $12\frac{3}{10}$.
(35)

*9. **(Represent)** Write 7026 in expanded form. Then use words to write the
(16, 33) number.

10. On the morning of an important game, Gail woke up at the
(27) time shown on the clock. She wanted to wake up 2 hours
35 minutes later. What time did Gail want to wake up?

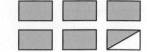

*11. **a.** Three quarters are what fraction of a dollar?
(36)

b. Write the value of three quarters using a dollar sign and a
decimal point.

12. **(Connect)** What multiplication fact is illustrated by this
(Inv. 3) rectangle?

Multiply for problems **13–15.**

13. **a.** 9×6 **b.** 9×5 **c.** 9×0
(29, 32)

14. **a.** 10×10 **b.** 7×7 **c.** 8×8
(Inv. 3)

15. **a.** 5×7 **b.** 6×5 **c.** 2×8
(29)

16. $\sqrt{81} + \sqrt{49}$ ***17.** $\$6.63 - \$3.55$
(Inv. 3)   (30)

18. $\$4.99 + \$2.88$ **19.** $a - 247 = 321$
(22)   (24)

*20. $z + 296 = 531$ ***21.** $523 - z = 145$
(24, 30)   (24, 30)

22. $28 + 46 + 48 + 64 + 32 + 344$
(17)

***23. a.** **Conclude** What are the next three numbers in this counting
(3) sequence?

$$\ldots, 450, 460, 470, 480, \underline{\quad}, \underline{\quad}, \underline{\quad}, \ldots$$

   b. **Generalize** What is one rule for this sequence?

24. If the diameter of a circle is one foot, then the radius of the circle is how
(Inv. 2, 21) many inches?

***25.** Compare:
(33, 36)

   a. $\frac{1}{4}$ of a dollar $\bigcirc$ $\frac{1}{2}$ of a dollar

   b. $101{,}010$ $\bigcirc$ $110{,}000$

***26.** **Multiple Choice** One yard does *not* equal which of the following?
(Inv. 2)

   A 36 in.   **B** 3 ft

   C 1 m   **D** 2 ft + 12 in.

***27.** In the year 2000, the four least populous U.S. states and their
(33) populations were as follows:

Alaska	626,932
North Dakota	642,200
Vermont	608,827
Wyoming	493,782

   List these states in order of population size, beginning with the
   smallest population.

***28.** **Justify** An adult cheetah weighs about 130 pounds. An adult
(13) mountain lion weighs about 170 pounds. A student estimates that
   a mountain lion weighs about twice as much as a cheetah. Is the
   estimate reasonable? Explain why or why not.

29. For a very short distance, a world-class sprinter can run at a speed of
(20) about 23 miles per hour. Round that speed to the nearest ten miles per
   hour.

***30.** In Barrow, Alaska, the average maximum temperature in July is 47°F. The
(18) average minimum temperature is 34°F. How many degrees cooler is a
   temperature of 34°F compared to a temperature of 47°F?

LESSON

38

- ## Multiplication Facts (Memory Group)

Power Up

facts	Power Up D
count aloud	Count by sevens from 7 to 63.
mental math	**a. Number Sense:** $365 - 120$
	b. Number Sense: $45 + 8 + 120$
	c. Number Sense: $56 + 19 + 200$
	d. Money: $\$3.45 + \$1.00$
	e. Money: $\$5.75 + \$2.00$
	f. Money: $\$0.85 + \$2.00$
	g. Estimation: Choose the more reasonable estimate for the high temperature on a cold, winter day: 30°F or 30°C.
	h. Calculation: $5 \times 2 + 3 + 42 - 5$
problem solving	Choose an appropriate problem-solving strategy to solve this problem. Hamid has a penny, a nickel, a dime, and a quarter. Two of the coins are in his left pocket and two are in his right pocket. What could be the total value of the two coins in his right pocket?

New Concept

There are only ten multiplication facts from 0×0 through 9×9 that we have not practiced. We call these facts the **memory group.**

$$3 \times 4 = 12 \qquad 4 \times 7 = 28$$
$$3 \times 6 = 18 \qquad 4 \times 8 = 32$$
$$3 \times 7 = 21 \qquad 6 \times 7 = 42$$
$$3 \times 8 = 24 \qquad 6 \times 8 = 48$$
$$4 \times 6 = 24 \qquad 7 \times 8 = 56$$

Multiplication facts can be practiced by doing timed, written tests on a daily basis. You should continue to practice often in order to memorize the facts.

Besides the facts from 0×0 to 9×9, it is helpful to memorize the 10s, 11s, and 12s. Recall that the multiples of 10 and 11 follow patterns that help us remember them.

Tens 10, 20, 30, 40, 50, 60, 70, 80, 90, 100, 120

Elevens 11, 22, 33, 44, 55, 66, 77, 88, 99, 110, **121, 132**

The multiples of 12 also have patterns that help us to remember them.

Twelves 12, 24, 36, 48, **60, 72, 84, 96, 108, 120, 132, 144**

Example

The school orders pencils in boxes of 12 pencils. Complete this table showing the number of pencils in the given number of boxes.

Boxes	1	2	3	4	5	6	7	8	9	10	11	12
Pencils	12	24	36	48								

To find the number of pencils, we multiply the number of boxes by 12.

Boxes	1	2	3	4	5	6	7	8	9	10	11	12
Pencils	12	24	36	48	60	72	84	96	108	120	132	144

Lesson Practice

a. Brainstorm ways to recall the ten memory-group facts. Then complete Power Up F.

Find each product:

b. $\begin{array}{r} 11 \\ \times\ 11 \\ \hline \end{array}$

c. $\begin{array}{r} 12 \\ \times\ 12 \\ \hline \end{array}$

d. $\begin{array}{r} 12 \\ \times\ 9 \\ \hline \end{array}$

e. $\begin{array}{r} 12 \\ \times\ 6 \\ \hline \end{array}$

f. $\begin{array}{r} 12 \\ \times\ 8 \\ \hline \end{array}$

g. $\begin{array}{r} 12 \\ \times\ 7 \\ \hline \end{array}$

h. $\begin{array}{r} 12 \\ \times\ 5 \\ \hline \end{array}$

i. $\begin{array}{r} 12 \\ \times\ 11 \\ \hline \end{array}$

Written Practice   *Distributed and Integrated*

1. **Formulate** There were two hundred twenty boats on the river. There
(31) were four hundred five boats in the harbor. How many more boats were in the harbor? Write and solve an equation.

*2. **Represent** Five hundred seventy-five thousand, five hundred forty-
(33) two people lived in the city. Use digits to write that number of people.

*3. **Represent** Write 2503 in expanded form. Then use words to write the
(16, 33) number.

*4. **Model** On 1-cm grid paper, draw a rectangle 6 cm long and
(Inv. 2, 4 cm wide.
Inv. 3)

    a. What is the perimeter of the rectangle?

    b. What is the area of the rectangle?

*5. **Represent** To what mixed number is the arrow pointing?
(37)

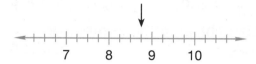

6. **Conclude** Which street is parallel to Broad
(23) Street?

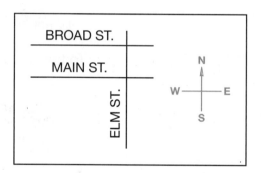

*7. What mixed number is shown by the shaded circles?
(35)

8. a. Round 624 to the nearest ten.
(20)

    b. Round $6.24 to the nearest dollar.

    c. Round $6.24 to the nearest 25 cents.

9. On a school day, Alberto finishes eating breakfast
(19) every morning at the time shown on the clock. He
starts eating lunch at 12:30 p.m. How long after Alberto
finishes eating breakfast does he start eating lunch?

*10. a. **(Connect)** Fifty cents is what fraction of a dollar?
(36)

b. Write the value of fifty cents using a dollar sign and a decimal point.

11. **(Represent)** Use words to write $2\frac{11}{100}$.
(35)

*12. **(Connect)** This square illustrates six squared. What
(Inv. 3) multiplication fact is illustrated by the square?

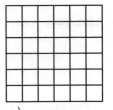

Multiply:

*13. a. 3×4 **b.** 3×6 **c.** 3×8
(38)

*14. a. 4×6 **b.** 4×7 **c.** 4×8
(38)

*15. a. 6×7 **b.** 6×8 **c.** 7×8
(38)

*16. Compare: $\frac{1}{10}$ of a dollar $\bigcirc$ $\frac{1}{2}$ of a dollar
(36)

17. $\$7.23$ **18.** $\$5.42$ **19.** 943
(30) $- \$2.54$ (22) $+ \$2.69$ (30) $- 276$

20. $z - 581 = 222$ **21.** $c + 843 = 960$
(24)   (24)

22. If the radius of a circle is 100 cm, then the diameter of the circle is how
(Inv. 2, many meters?
21)

23. $28 \div 36 + 78 + \sqrt{49}$ ***24.** $\sqrt{144} - \sqrt{121}$
(17,   (Inv. 3,
Inv. 3)   32)

*25. Multiple Choice Which of the following is *not* $\frac{1}{10}$ of a dollar?
(36)
     A dime   **B** 0.10¢   **C** $0.10   **D** 10¢

*26. Multiple Choice Which digit in 457,326,180 is in the hundred-
(34) thousands place?
     A 1   **B** 6   **C** 4   **D** 3

27. **Conclude** Name and describe each angle below.
(23)

a.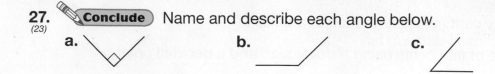

b.

c.

*28. Consider the sequence 12, 24, 36, 48, ...
(3)

a. **Generalize** Write a rule that describes how to find the next term of the sequence.

b. **Predict** What is the eleventh term of the sequence?

29. **Estimate** Mrs. Rojas would like to purchase a CD that costs
(20) $14.99 and a DVD that costs $18.95 for the school library. What is a reasonable estimate of the amount of money she will spend? Explain why your estimate is reasonable.

*30. The table below shows the cost of tickets to a game. Use the table to
(38) help find the cost of tickets for a family of six.

Number of Tickets	1	2	3	4
Cost	$11	$22	$33	$44

Real-World Connection

Yolanda planted eleven flowers in each of 12 rows. How many flowers did she plant? Draw a table and complete it to show the number of flowers in 12 rows.

• Reading an Inch Scale to the Nearest Fourth

facts	Power Up E
count aloud	Count by threes from 30 to 60 and back down to 30.
mental math	To add 99¢, 98¢, or 95¢ to another amount of money, add one dollar and then subtract 1¢, 2¢, or 5¢.

    a. Money: $3.45 + $0.99

    b. Money: $5.75 + $0.98

    c. Money: $0.85 + $0.95

    d. Measurement: Brian threw the baseball 30 yards. How many feet did he throw the ball?

    e. Geometry: If a square is 2 inches on each side, what is the square's perimeter?

    f. Time: It is 10:20 a.m. Carmelita must leave for her appointment at 11:00 a.m. How many minutes is it until Carmelita must leave?

    g. Estimation: Ramesh wants to buy a board game for $9.55 and a deck of cards for $1.43. What are two dollar amounts he could use to estimate the total cost of both items?

    h. Calculation: $4 \times 8 + 68 + 92 + 9$

problem solving

Choose an appropriate problem-solving strategy to solve this problem, Cantara's mom cut an orange in half. Then she cut each half in half. Cantara ate three of the orange pieces. What fraction of the orange did Cantara eat?

To measure lengths in inches, we use an inch scale. Inch scales are found on rulers and on tape measures. An inch scale often has tick marks between the inch marks. These tick marks let us read the inch scale to the nearest half inch, quarter inch, or eighth inch. In this lesson we will practice reading to the nearest quarter inch. Remember that one quarter inch is the same as one fourth inch.

When reading inch scales, keep in mind that $\frac{2}{4}$ equals $\frac{1}{2}$. The two circles below show these equivalent fractions. You can recall this relationship by remembering that two quarters equal half of a dollar.

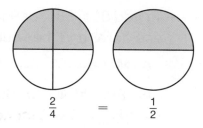

$$\frac{2}{4} \quad = \quad \frac{1}{2}$$

Example 1

How long is the toothpick to the nearest quarter inch?

The toothpick is 2 inches plus a fraction. It is closest to $2\frac{2}{4}$ inches. Instead of writing $\frac{2}{4}$, we write $\frac{1}{2}$. So the toothpick is $2\frac{1}{2}$ inches long. We abbreviate this length as **$2\frac{1}{2}$ in.**

Activity

Make a Ruler and Measure

Materials needed:
- inch ruler
- strip of tagboard (6 inches long by 1 inch wide)

Model With a ruler, mark and label the inch marks on the tagboard strip.

inch	1	2	3	4	5	6

Set the ruler aside and visually find the midpoint between the inch marks. Draw the half-inch marks and label them.

| inch | $\frac{1}{2}$ | 1 | $\frac{1}{2}$ | 2 | $\frac{1}{2}$ | 3 | $\frac{1}{2}$ | 4 | $\frac{1}{2}$ | 5 | $\frac{1}{2}$ | 6 |

Then visually find the midpoint between the inch and the half-inch marks. Draw and label the quarter-inch tick marks as $\frac{1}{4}, \frac{2}{4}, \frac{3}{4}$ as shown below.

| inch | $\frac{1}{4}$ $\frac{1}{2}$ $\frac{2}{4}$ $\frac{3}{4}$ | 1 | $\frac{1}{4}$ $\frac{1}{2}$ $\frac{2}{4}$ $\frac{3}{4}$ | 2 | $\frac{1}{4}$ $\frac{1}{2}$ $\frac{2}{4}$ $\frac{3}{4}$ | 3 | $\frac{1}{4}$ $\frac{1}{2}$ $\frac{2}{4}$ $\frac{3}{4}$ | 4 | $\frac{1}{4}$ $\frac{1}{2}$ $\frac{2}{4}$ $\frac{3}{4}$ | 5 | $\frac{1}{4}$ $\frac{1}{2}$ $\frac{2}{4}$ $\frac{3}{4}$ | 6 |

Use your tagboard ruler to measure the segments below. Then keep the tagboard ruler to use for the measurement problems in this book.

a. _____

b. _____

c. _____

Example 2

Hajari has three boards. One board is $1\frac{1}{2}$ inches thick, the second board is 2 inches thick, and the third board is $2\frac{1}{2}$ inches thick. If Hajari selects two of the boards and stacks one on top of the other, then the two boards could have a combined thickness of how many inches?

We can sketch a picture of the possible combinations and calculate the combined thickness.

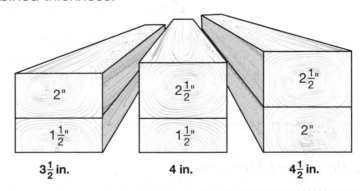

$3\frac{1}{2}$ in.   4 in. $4\frac{1}{2}$ in.

Lesson Practice

a. **Represent** Draw a picture that shows that $\frac{2}{4}$ equals $\frac{1}{2}$.

Name each point marked by an arrow on this inch scale:

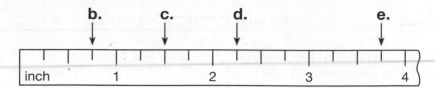

f. **Estimate** Measure the length and width of your notebook paper to the nearest half inch.

g. Use your pencil and ruler to draw points *A, B,* and *C* in order on a straight line so that the distance from *A* to *B* is $1\frac{1}{2}$ inches, and the distance from *B* to *C* is $\frac{3}{4}$ inch. Then find the distance from *A* to *C.*

h. Pam selected three different sizes of blocks from a set. She has a 1-inch block, a $1\frac{1}{2}$-inch block, and a 2-inch block. If she stacks two blocks together, what are all the possible combined heights she could make? You may use strips of paper to solve.

Written Practice *Distributed and Integrated*

1. **Explain** Trinity is twelve years old. Trinity's mother is thirty-five years
(31) old. Trinity's mother is how many years older than Trinity? Describe this type of word problem.

* 2. Four hundred sixty-eight thousand, five hundred two boxes were in the
(33) warehouse. Use digits to write that number of boxes.

* 3. **Represent** Write the number 3905 in expanded form. Then use words
(16, 33) to write the number.

4. **Verify** J'Maresh collected two hundred forty-three aluminum cans
(10, 13) while volunteering at the recycling center. Leilani collected three hundred sixty-four aluminum cans. Was the total number of cans collected an even number or an odd number?

* 5. **Represent** Use words to write $100\frac{1}{100}$.
(35)

6. **Represent** Use digits and symbols to show that negative nineteen is
(Inv. 1) greater than negative ninety.

246   *Saxon Math Intermediate 4*

*7. **(Connect)** Use a dollar sign and a decimal point to write the value of
(35) two dollars, one quarter, two dimes, and three nickels.

8. The clock shows the time that Brayden arrived at school.
(27) School begins at 8:15 a.m. Was Brayden early or late for
school? How many minutes early or late was he?

9. **(Connect)** **a.** Nine dimes are what fraction of a dollar?
(36)

   b. Write the value of nine dimes using a dollar sign and a
   decimal point.

10. Haruto lives about 1 kilometer from school. One kilometer is how many
(Inv. 2) meters?

*11. How many of these circles are shaded?
(35)

*12. **(Estimate)** Use a ruler to find the length of this screw to the nearest
(39) quarter inch:

Multiply:

*13. **a.** 4×3 **b.** 8×3 **c.** 8×4 **d.** 4×12
(38)

*14. **a.** 6×3 **b.** 6×4 **c.** 7×6 **d.** 6×12
(38)

*15. **a.** 7×3 **b.** 7×4 **c.** 8×6 **d.** 8×12
(38)

16. $\sqrt{64} - \sqrt{36}$
(Inv. 3)

17. $\$4.86$ **18.** $\$4.86$ **19.** 293
(22) $+ \$2.47$ (30) $- \$2.47$ (13) $+ 678$

20. 893 **21.** 463 **22.** 463
(30) $- 678$ (24) $\underline{-\ \ y}$ (24) $\underline{+\ \ q}$
                   411 527

23. This rectangle illustrates eight squared. What multiplication
fact is illustrated by the rectangle?
_(Inv. 3)

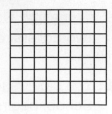

*24. **Conclude** Write the next three numbers in this counting sequence:
₍₃₎

..., 470, 480, 490, 500, ____, ____, ____, ...

25. **Represent** Draw a triangle that has three acute angles.
₍₂₃₎

*26. **Multiple Choice** Which of these does *not* equal 9 + 9?
_(27, 38)

    A 2×9 **B** 9×2

    C 3×6 **D** nine squared

*27. A realtor was writing an advertisement about houses for sale in town.
_(33, 34) The prices of five houses are listed below. Show how the realtor would
arrange the prices in order from most expensive to least expensive.

$385,900

$189,000

$1,280,000

$476,000

$299,000

28. **Justify** Lake Huron is 206 miles long. Lake Superior is 350 miles
_(14, 20) long. Anastacia estimates that Lake Superior is about 140 miles longer
than Lake Huron. Is Anastacia's estimate reasonable? Explain why or
why not.

*29. **Analyze** Kyle wants to form rectangles using straws. He has two
_(Inv. 2, 39) straws 6 inches long, two straws 4 inches long, and two straws 2 inches
long. Using four straws attached at the ends, how many different
rectangles can Kyle form? What are the perimeters of the rectangles?

*30. The table shows a relationship between feet and inches. Use the table
₍₃₈₎ below to determine the number of inches in 20 feet.

Number of Feet	1	2	3	4
Number of Inches	12	24	36	48

• Capacity

Power Up

facts	Power Up D
count aloud	Count down by fours from 40 to 4.
mental math	**a. Money:** $5.85 + $0.99
	b. Money: $8.63 + $0.98
	c. Money: $4.98 + $0.95
	d. Measurement: D'Marcus jogged 1 mile. How many feet did he jog?
	e. Time: What time will it be 10 hours after 1:35 p.m.?
	f. Time: What time will it be 11 hours after 1:35 p.m.?
	g. Estimation: Choose the more reasonable estimate for the width of a pencil: 1 centimeter or 1 inch.
	h. Calculation: 460 + 300 + 24 − 85
problem solving	The two hands of a clock are together at noon. The next time the hands of a clock are together is about how many minutes later?

Focus Strategy: Make a Model

Understand We are told that the two hands of a clock are together at noon. We are asked to find the number of minutes that pass before the hands come together again.

Plan We can *model* the situation with an analog clock (or a wristwatch).

Solve We first set our clock (or watch) to noon. Then we turn the minute hand so that it points to the numbers in order: 1, 2, 3, and so on. We watch to see whether the hour and minute hands come together at any point before the clock reaches 1:00. We notice that they do not.

When the clock shows 1:00, the hour hand points to 1 and the minute hand points to 12. At 1:05 the minute hand will point to 1. We move the minute hand of the clock to make the time 1:05 and see that the hour and minute hands are nearly together. The time, 1:05, is one hour five minutes after noon. One hour is 60 minutes, so 1:05 is **65 minutes** after noon.

(Check) We know our answer is reasonable because the minute hand moves around the clock one time each hour. During that hour, the hour hand moves forward only a little bit. This means that it takes a little more than one hour for the hands to come together again.

New Concept

Math Language

Teaspoons and tablespoons are U.S. customary units of measure for smaller amounts.

1 tablespoon = $\frac{1}{2}$ fluid ounce

1 teaspoon = $\frac{1}{6}$ fluid ounce

In the U.S. Customary System, liquids such as milk, juice, paint, and gasoline are measured in fluid ounces, cups, pints, quarts, or gallons. This table shows the abbreviations for each of these units:

**Abbreviations for
U.S. Liquid Measures**

fluid ounce	fl oz
cup	c
pint	pt
quart	qt
gallon	gal

The quantity of liquid a container can hold is the **capacity** of the container.

Activity

Measuring Capacity

Model Arrange the five containers in order from smallest to largest.

1 cup   1 pint   1 quart $\frac{1}{2}$ gallon   1 gallon

Estimate the number of cups of liquid needed to fill a 1-pint container. Estimate the number of pints needed to fill a 1-quart container, and so on. After you have estimated, fill each container with water using the next-smallest container. Answer the following questions:

a. How many cups of liquid equal a pint?

b. How many pints of liquid equal a quart?

c. How many quarts of liquid equal a half gallon?

d. How many half gallons of liquid equal a gallon?

e. How many quarters equal a dollar?

f. How many quarts of liquid equal a gallon?

g. Copy and complete this table of liquid measures from the U.S. Customary System. Notice that 8 **fluid ounces** equals 1 cup.

U.S. Liquid Measure

8 fl oz = 1 c
__ c = 1 pt
__ pt = 1 qt
__ qt = 1 gal

Liquids are also measured in **liters** (L). A liter is a metric unit of measure. Compare a one-liter container to a one-quart container (or compare a two-liter container to a half-gallon container). Which container looks larger?

Model Use a full liter (or two-liter) container to fill a quart (or half-gallon) container. Then complete these comparisons:

h. Compare: 1 quart ◯ 1 liter

i. Compare: $\frac{1}{2}$ gallon ◯ 2 liters

j. (**Estimate**) How many liters will it take to fill a gallon container?

To measure small amounts of liquid, we may use milliliters (mL). One thousand milliliters equals one liter.

Metric Liquid Measure

1000 mL = 1 L

Math Language

Droppers used for liquid medicine usually hold one or two milliliters of liquid.

k. A full 2-liter bottle of liquid contains how many milliliters of liquid?

Inspect the labels of the liquid containers used in the activity. Liquid containers often list two measures of the quantity of liquid the containers hold. For example, the label on one gallon of milk may read

1 gal (3.78 L)

The measure 3.78 L means $3\frac{78}{100}$ liters. The number 3.78 is a *decimal number.* Decimal numbers are often used in measurement, especially in metric measurement. The number 3.78 has a whole-number part and a fraction part.

3.78

Whole Number   Fraction Part

So 3.78 L means "more than three liters but a little less than four liters," just as $3.78 means "more than three dollars but not quite four dollars." We read 3.78 as "three and seventy-eight hundredths." We will learn more about decimal numbers in Investigation 4.

Lesson Practice

a. Copy and complete this table to show the relationship between gallons and quarts.

Gallons	1	2	3	4	5	6	7	8
Quarts	4	8						

b. (**Predict**) How many quarts is 12 gallons?

c. One pint is 2 cups and one cup is 8 ounces. How many ounces is one pint?

d. Estimate how many milliliters it would take to fill a $3\frac{1}{2}$-liter container.

Formulate Write and solve equations for problems **1–3.**

*1. A group of fish is called a *school*. There are twenty-five fish in the small
(31) school. There are one hundred twelve fish in the big school. How many
fewer fish are in the small school?

2. A piece of ribbon that measured 1 yard was cut into two pieces. If one
(24) piece was 12 inches long, how many inches long was the other piece?

3. Mrs. Green took forty-seven digital pictures in Hawaii. Her husband
(1, 17) took sixty-two digital pictures in Hawaii. Her son took seventy-five
digital pictures. In all, how many digital pictures did the Greens take?

*4. **Represent** Write the number 7,500,000 in expanded form. Then use
(16, 33) words to write the number.

5. Which digit in 27,384,509 is in the thousands place?
(34)

*6. **Connect** Use a dollar sign and a decimal point to write the value of
(35) three dollars, two quarters, one dime, and two nickels. Then write that
amount of money using words.

*7. A gallon of milk is how many quarts of milk?
(40)

*8. How many squares are shaded?
(35)

*9. **Estimate** Use a ruler to find the length of the line segment below to
(39) the nearest quarter inch.

_____

* 10. (**Connect**) Printed on the label of the milk container were these words
(40) and numbers:

1 gal (3.78 L)

Use this information to compare the following:

1 gallon ◯ 3 liters

11. Destiny began reading a book last night at the time shown
(27) on the clock. She read until midnight. How much time did
Destiny spend reading last night?

* 12. a. Multiple Choice What type of angle is formed by the hands of the
(23) clock shown in problem **11**?

    A acute   **B** right   **C** obtuse   **D** straight

    b. (**Justify**) How do you know that your answer to part **a** is correct?

* 13. Compare:
(Inv. 1,
36)   **a.** -29 ◯ -32 **b.** $0.75 ◯ $\frac{3}{4}$ of a dollar

14. (**Represent**) Draw a circle with a diameter of 2 centimeters. What is the
(21) radius of the circle?

Multiply:

15. a. 6×6 **b.** 7×7 **c.** 8×8 **d.** 12×12
(Inv. 3)

16. a. 7×9 **b.** 6×9 **c.** 9×9 **d.** 9×12
(32)

17. a. 7×8 **b.** 6×7 **c.** 8×4 **d.** 12×7
(38)

18. $4.98 + $7.65   **19.** $m - $6.70 = 3.30
(22)   (24)

20. $416 - z = 179$ **21.** $536 + z = 721$
(24)   (24)

22. $\sqrt{1} + \sqrt{4} + \sqrt{9}$
(Inv. 3)

* 23. **Represent** Draw an array of Xs to show 7×3.
(Inv. 3)

24. **Represent** Use words to write $10\frac{1}{10}$.
(35)

* 25. a. **Connect** Two quarters are what fraction of a dollar?
(36)

b. Write the value of two quarters using a dollar sign and a decimal point.

* 26. **Multiple Choice** A rectangle has an area of 24 square inches. Which
(Inv. 3) of these areas could be the length and width of the rectangle?

    A 6 in. by 6 in.   **B** 12 in. by 12 in.

    C 8 in. by 4 in.   **D** 8 in. by 3 in.

* 27. **Represent** Tarik measured the width of his notebook paper and said
(39) that the paper was $8\frac{2}{4}$ inches wide. What is another way to write $8\frac{2}{4}$?

* 28. **Justify** A gardener plans to build a fence around his 24-by-12-foot
(Inv. 2) rectangular vegetable garden. Fencing for the garden can be purchased
in 50-foot, 75-foot, or 100-foot rolls. Which roll of fencing should the
gardener buy? Explain why.

* 29. **Estimate** At a gardening center, one pair of gardening gloves
(22) costs $12.00, not including a sales tax of 66¢. What is a reasonable
estimate of the cost of two pairs of gloves? Explain why your estimate
is reasonable.

* 30. **Analyze** How many different three-digit numbers can you write using
(10) the digits 6, 2, and 0? Each digit may be used only once, and the digit 0
may not be used in the hundreds place. Label the numbers you write as
even or odd.

Focus on

• Tenths and Hundredths

The basic unit of our currency system is the dollar. To make fractions of a dollar, we use coins. Below the illustrated coins, we see the value of each coin expressed as a fraction of a dollar and as a decimal part of a dollar.

$\frac{1}{4}$ = $0.25 $\frac{1}{10}$ = $0.10 $\frac{1}{20}$ = $0.05 $\frac{1}{100}$ = $0.01

Notice that a dime is $\frac{1}{10}$ of a dollar and that a penny is $\frac{1}{10}$ of a dime and $\frac{1}{100}$ of a dollar.

Recall that our number system is a **base-ten system** in which the value of each place is ten times the value of the place to its right. This means that the value of each place is also $\frac{1}{10}$ (one **tenth**) of the value of the place to its left. To the right of the ones place is the $\frac{1}{10}$s place, and to the right of the $\frac{1}{10}$s place is the $\frac{1}{100}$s (**hundredths**) place.

decimal point

$$\downarrow$$

$$\underline{\qquad} \centerdot \underline{\qquad} \quad \underline{\qquad}$$

1s $\frac{1}{10}$s $\frac{1}{100}$s
place   place place

We can represent these **decimal places** with dimes and pennies as we see in the following activity.

Activity 1

Using Money Manipulatives to Represent Decimal Numbers

Materials needed:

• money manipulatives (from **Lesson Activities 2, 3, 4, 8,** and **9**)

In this activity we will use bills, dimes, and pennies to represent decimal numbers.

	Whole dollars			Parts of dollars	
100s place	10s place	1s place	$\frac{1}{10}$s place	$\frac{1}{100}$s place

decimal point

The bills and coins above can be combined to demonstrate different amounts of money. For example, we can show $234.21 like this:

$ 2   3   4   .   2   1

Model Arrange bills and coins to form the money amounts in problems **1–4.** Place each denomination of bills and coins in a separate stack. The stacks should be arranged so that the largest denomination is on the left and the smallest denomination is on the right.

1. $345.23   **2.** $0.42   **3.** $5.20   **4.** $3.02

Write the amount shown by each picture:

5.    **6.**   **7.**

Model Use money manipulatives to help compare each amount:

8.  ◯    **9.** $0.40 ◯ $0.07

Write these amounts in order from greatest to least:

10.

11. $1.09 $0.97 $1.20

Now we will use bills and coins to represent decimal numbers that are not money amounts. At right we show an example of money representing the number 4.23 (four and twenty-three hundredths).

4   .   2   3

Model Use bills and coins to represent these decimal numbers:

12. 3.42 (three and forty-two hundredths)

13. 0.24 (twenty-four hundredths)

14. 12.03 (twelve and three hundredths)

15. 1.3 (one and three tenths)

In the activity we used money to represent decimal numbers. Another model we can use to represent decimal numbers is a unit square. The whole square represents 1. Parts of the square represent fractions that can be named using decimal numbers.

The square at right is divided into ten equal parts. One tenth of the square is shaded. We may write one tenth as a fraction ($\frac{1}{10}$) or as a decimal number (0.1).

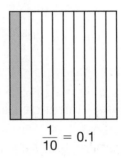

$$\frac{1}{10} = 0.1$$

Name the shaded part of each square as a fraction and as a decimal number:

16.

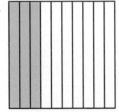

17.

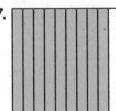

18.

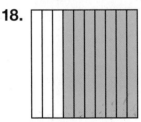

19.

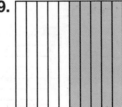

Represent Use the squares above to arrange the decimal numbers 0.5, 0.3, 0.7, and 0.8 in order from least to greatest.

The squares above were divided into ten equal parts. The squares at right and on the top of the next page are divided into 100 equal parts. Each part is one hundredth of the whole square. We may write one hundredth as a fraction ($\frac{1}{100}$) or as a decimal number (0.01).

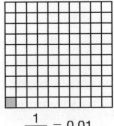

$$\frac{1}{100} = 0.01$$

Each of these squares is divided into 100 equal parts. Name the shaded part of each square as a fraction and as a decimal number.

20.

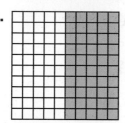

21.

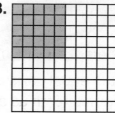

22.

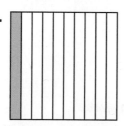

23.

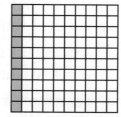

Notice in problem **21** that $\frac{10}{100}$ of the square is shaded. However, one column is one tenth of the square, so $\frac{10}{100}$ is equal to $\frac{1}{10}$, just like one dime is $\frac{10}{100}$ of a dollar and $\frac{1}{10}$ of a dollar.

In problem **22,** half of the square is shaded. We see that the fraction $\frac{50}{100}$ equals $\frac{1}{2}$. The decimal number 0.50 also equals $\frac{1}{2}$, just as $0.50 equals $\frac{1}{2}$ of a dollar. In problem **23** we see that a fourth of the square is shaded. The decimal number 0.25 equals $\frac{1}{4}$, just as $0.25 equals $\frac{1}{4}$ of a dollar.

24. Multiple Choice Which of the following numbers does *not* equal one half?

A $\frac{5}{10}$ **B** 0.5   **C** $\frac{50}{100}$ **D** 0.05

Write a decimal number to represent the shaded portion of each square. Then complete each comparison.

25.

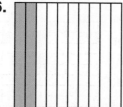 ___ ◯ ___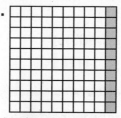

26.

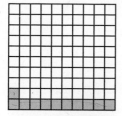 ___ ◯ ___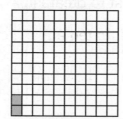

27. (**Represent**) Arrange these decimal numbers, shown in the pictures above, in order from least to greatest:

0.1   0.2   0.02

Focus on
• Relating Decimals and Fractions

Using Unit Squares to Relate Fractions and Decimal Numbers

Material needed:
- **Lesson Activity 23**

On **Lesson Activity 23,** complete the following activities:

28. Shade nine of the ten columns. Then name the shaded part of the square as a fraction, as a decimal number, and with words.

29. Shade 33 of the 100 small squares. Then name the shaded part of the square as a fraction, as a decimal number, and with words.

30. Shade two whole squares and seven of the 100 parts of the third square. Then name the number of shaded squares as a mixed number, as a decimal number, and with words.

31. Shade one column of the square on the left. Shade nine small squares of the square on the right. Then name the shaded part of each square as a fraction and as a decimal. Then compare the two decimal numbers by writing the two decimal numbers with the correct comparison symbol between them.

32. **Connect** Describe how a large square, a column or row, and a small square relate to a $1 bill, a dime, and a penny.

As we have seen, fractions and decimals are two ways to describe parts of a whole. When we write a fraction, we show both a numerator and a denominator. When we write a decimal number, the denominator is not shown but is indicated by the number of places to the right of the decimal point (the number of decimal places). Look at these examples:

one
decimal place

two
decimal places

$0.1 = \dfrac{1}{10}$ $0.12 = \dfrac{12}{100}$

To name a decimal number, we name the numerator shown by the digits and then we name the denominator indicated by the number of decimal places.

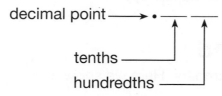

As a class, read each of these numbers:

33. a. $\dfrac{75}{100}$ **b.** 0.75

34. a. $\dfrac{7}{100}$ **b.** 0.07

35. a. $\dfrac{3}{10}$ **b.** 0.3

36. a. $\dfrac{2}{10}$ **b.** 0.2

A decimal number greater than 1 has one or more digits other than 0 to the left of the decimal point, such as 12.25. To name 12.25, we mentally split it at the decimal point and name the whole-number part and fraction part separately.

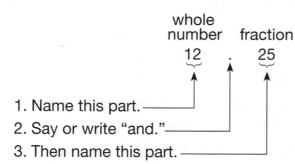

This decimal number is read as "twelve and twenty-five hundredths."

As a class, read each of these numbers. Then use words to write each number on your paper.

37. a. 10.75 **b.** 12.5

38. a. 6.42 **b.** 10.1

Use digits to write each of these decimal numbers:

39. one and three tenths

40. two and twenty-five hundredths

41. three and twelve hundredths

42. four and five tenths

 **Activity 3**

Using Decimal Numbers on Stopwatch Displays

Material needed:
- stopwatch with digital display

Use a stopwatch to generate decimal numbers. Here we show a typical stopwatch display:

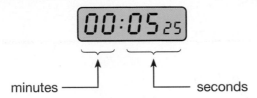

minutes —————| |————— seconds

This display shows that 5.25 seconds passed between starting and stopping the watch.

43. Start and then stop the stopwatch as quickly as possible. Record each generated time on the board, and read the times aloud. Who stopped the watch in the quickest time?

44. Test your time-estimating skills by starting the stopwatch and then, without looking, stopping the watch five seconds later. Record each generated time using digits. Determine which time is closest to 5.00 seconds.

45. As a class, arrange selected times from problem **44** in order from least to greatest.

- ## Subtracting Across Zero
- ## Missing Factors

facts	Power Up E
count aloud	We can quickly add or subtract some numbers on a calendar. On a calendar, select a number from the middle of the month. If we move straight up from one row, we subtract 7. If we move straight down one row, we add 7. We can add or subtract two other numbers if we move diagonally. Which numbers do we add or subtract when we move one row in these directions?
mental math	**a. Money:** $4.65 + 2.99
	b. Money: $3.86 + $1.95
	c. Money: $6.24 + $2.98
	d. Geometry: What is the radius of a circle that has a diameter of 1 inch?
	e. Time: Class begins at 1:05 p.m. It ends 50 minutes later. What time does class end?
	f. Measurement: Patel's kite was attached to 50 yards of string. How many feet of string is that?
	g. Estimation: The price of the new shoes was $44.85. A package of socks was $5.30. Round each price to the nearest dollar and then add to estimate the total cost.
	h. Calculation: $2 \times 9 + 9 + 6 + 66$
problem solving	Choose an appropriate problem-solving strategy to solve this problem. The hands of a clock are together at 12:00. The hands of a clock are not together at 6:30 because the hour hand is halfway between the 6 and the 7 at 6:30. The hands come together at about 6:33. Name nine more times that the hands of a clock come together.

Subtracting Across Zero

In the problem below, we must regroup twice before we can subtract the ones digits.

$$\begin{array}{r} \$405 \\ -\$126 \\ \end{array}$$

> **Reading Math**
>
> For this problem, we will regroup by exchanging one $100 bill for ten $10 bills.

We cannot exchange a ten for ones because there are no tens, so the first step is to exchange 1 hundred for 10 tens.

$$\begin{array}{r} \overset{3}{\$\cancel{4}}05 \\ -\$126 \\ \end{array}$$

Now we have 10 tens, and we can exchange 1 of the tens for 10 ones.

$$\begin{array}{r} \overset{3\ 9}{\$4\,\cancel{0}}5 \\ -\$1\,2\,6 \\ \end{array}$$

Now we subtract.

$$\begin{array}{r} \overset{3\ 9}{\$4\,\cancel{0}}5 \\ -\$1\,2\,6 \\ \hline \$2\,7\,9 \\ \end{array}$$

> **Thinking Skill**
>
> **Connect**
>
> Explain why thirty-nine $10 bills and fifteen $1 bills are equal to $405.

We can perform this regrouping in one step by looking at the numbers a little differently. We can think of the 4 and 0 as forty $10 bills (4 hundreds equals 40 tens).

$$\overset{\overbrace{\qquad}^{40\ \text{tens}}}{\$4\ 0\ 5}$$

If we exchange one of the $10 bills, then we will have thirty-nine $10 bills.

$$\begin{array}{r} \overset{3\ 9}{\$4\cancel{0}}5 \\ -\$1\,2\,6 \\ \hline \$2\,7\,9 \\ \end{array}$$

Example 1

The Vetti waterfall in Norway is 900 feet tall. The Akaka waterfall in Hawaii is 442 feet tall. How many feet taller is the Vetti waterfall?

This is a larger − smaller = difference problem. We are asked to find the difference.

$$
\begin{array}{r}
\overset{8}{\cancel{9}}\overset{9}{\cancel{0}}\overset{1}{0} \\
-\ 442 \\
\hline
458
\end{array}
$$

The Vetti waterfall is **458 feet taller** than the Akaka waterfall.

Example 2

Troy had $3.00 and spent $1.23. How much money did he have left?

We change 3 dollars to 2 dollars and 10 dimes. Then we change 10 dimes to 9 dimes and 10 pennies.

$$
\begin{array}{r}
\$3.00 \\
-\ \$1.23 \\
\end{array}
\longrightarrow
\begin{array}{r}
\overset{2}{\cancel{\$3}}\overset{1}{.}00 \\
-\ \$1.23 \\
\end{array}
\longrightarrow
\begin{array}{r}
\overset{2}{\cancel{\$3}}\overset{9}{.}\overset{1}{0}0 \\
-\ \$1.23 \\
\hline
\$1.77
\end{array}
$$

We can also think of $3 as 30 dimes. Then we exchange 1 dime for 10 pennies.

$$
\begin{array}{r}
\$3.00 \\
-\ \$1.23 \\
\end{array}
\longrightarrow
\begin{array}{r}
\overset{2}{\cancel{\$3}}\overset{9}{\underset{1}{.}}\overset{1}{0}0 \\
-\ \$1.23 \\
\hline
\$1.77
\end{array}
$$

Thinking Skill

Connect

Explain why $3.00 is the same as 29 dimes and 10 pennies.

Troy had **$1.77** left. We check our answer by adding.

$$
\begin{array}{r}
\$1.23 \\
+\ \$1.77 \\
\hline
\$3.00
\end{array}
\quad \text{check}
$$

Justify Explain why the answer is reasonable.

Missing Factors

Recall that numbers that are multiplied are called *factors* and the answer is called the *product*.

$$
\text{factor} \times \text{factor} = \text{product}
$$

If we know one factor and the product, we can find the other factor.

Example 3

> **Find the missing factors:**
>
> **a.** $5n = 40$ **b.** $a \times 4 = 36$
>
> **a.** The expression $5n$ means "$5 \times n$." Since $5 \times 8 = 40$, the missing factor is **8.**
>
> **b.** Since $9 \times 4 = 36$, the missing factor is **9.**

Lesson Practice Subtract:

a. $\begin{array}{r} \$3.00 \\ - \$1.32 \\ \hline \end{array}$ **b.** $\begin{array}{r} \$405 \\ - \$156 \\ \hline \end{array}$ **c.** $\begin{array}{r} 201 \\ - 102 \\ \hline \end{array}$

d. $\$4.00 - \$0.86$ **e.** $\$304 - \$128$ **f.** $703 - 198$

Find the missing factor in each problem:

g. $8w = 32$ **h.** $p \times 3 = 12$

i. $5m = 30$ **j.** $q \times 4 = 16$

Written Practice   *Distributed and Integrated*

*1. **Represent** The large square represents 1.
(Inv. 4) Write the shaded part of the square

   a. as a fraction.   **b.** as a decimal number.

   c. using words.

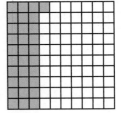

2. Takeshi had a dime, a quarter, and a penny. Write this amount using
(35) a dollar sign and a decimal point.

*3. Donna opened a 1-gallon container of milk and poured 1 quart of
(40) milk into a pitcher. How many quarts of milk were left in the
   1-gallon container?

*4. **Generalize** Describe the rule for this sequence and find the next
(3) three numbers:

   $\ldots, 4200, 4300, 4400, \underline{\hspace{0.5cm}}, \underline{\hspace{0.5cm}}, \underline{\hspace{0.5cm}}, \ldots$

*5. **Connect** Use digits and a comparison symbol to show that the
(Inv. 4) decimal number five tenths equals the fraction one half.

6. Anando fell asleep last night at the time shown on the
(27) clock. His alarm clock was set to ring eight hours later.
What time was Anando's alarm clock set to ring?

*7. Find the missing factor: $5w = 45$
(41)

*8. (Represent) The following was marked on the label of a juice container:
(Inv. 4)

$$2 \text{ qt } (1.89 \text{ L})$$

Use words to write 1.89 L.

9. What mixed number is illustrated by these shaded
(35) triangles?

10. Which letter below has no right angles?
(23)

F   E   Z   L

*11. (Connect) Rewrite this addition problem as a multiplication problem:
(27)

$$\$1.25 + \$1.25 + \$1.25 + \$1.25$$

12. (Estimate) How long is the line segment to the nearest quarter inch?
(39)

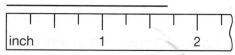

13. A meter equals how many centimeters?
(Inv. 2)

14. a. Five dimes are what fraction of a dollar?
(36)

b. Write the value of five dimes using a dollar sign and a decimal point.

*15. Compare:
(Inv. 4)

   a. 0.5 ◯ 0.50

   b. $\frac{1}{2}$ ◯ $\frac{1}{4}$

16. a. 3×8 **b.** 3×7 **c.** 3×6 **d.** 3×12
(38)

17. a. 4×8 **b.** 4×7 **c.** 4×6 **d.** 4×12
(38)

* 18.
(41)
$$\begin{array}{r} m \\ \times\ 8 \\ \hline 64 \end{array}$$

* 19.
(41)
$$\begin{array}{r} 9 \\ \times\ n \\ \hline 54 \end{array}$$

20.
(24)
$$\begin{array}{r} z \\ +\ 179 \\ \hline 496 \end{array}$$

* 21.
(41)
$$\begin{array}{r} \$3.00 \\ -\ \$1.84 \\ \hline \end{array}$$

* 22.
(41)
$$\begin{array}{r} \$500 \\ -\ \$167 \\ \hline \end{array}$$

23.
(24)
$$\begin{array}{r} w \\ -\ 297 \\ \hline 486 \end{array}$$

24. (**Conclude**) What are the next four numbers in this counting sequence?
(Inv. 1)

$$\ldots, 28, 21, 14, \underline{\quad}, \underline{\quad}, \underline{\quad}, \underline{\quad}, \ldots$$

* 25. (**Represent**) Use digits to write one million, fifty thousand.
(34)

* 26. Multiple Choice If the area of a square is 36 square inches, then how
(Inv. 3) long is each side of the square?

     A 6 in.   **B** 9 in.   **C** 12 in.   **D** 18 in.

* 27. The distance from Riley's house to school is 1.4 miles. Write 1.4
(Inv. 4) with words.

28. Nieve quickly started and stopped a stopwatch four times. Write
(Inv. 4) these times in order from fastest to slowest:

     0.27 second, 0.21 second, 0.24 second, 0.20 second

(**Formulate**) Write and solve equations for problems **29** and **30.**

* 29. (**Justify**) The Washington Monument is 153 feet taller than the
(13) City Center building in Nashville, Tennessee, which is 402 feet tall.
How tall is the Washington Monument? Explain why your answer is
reasonable.

* 30. (**Explain**) The Panther waterfall in Alberta is 600 feet tall. The Fall
(25, 41) Creek waterfall in Tennessee is 256 feet tall. How many feet taller is the
Panther waterfall? Explain how you found your answer.

42

• Rounding Numbers to Estimate

facts	Power Up E
count aloud	Count by sevens from 7 to 70.
mental math	**a. Number Sense:** 563 − 242
	b. Powers/Roots: $\sqrt{9}$
	c. Money: $5.75 − $2.50
	d. Money: $8.98 − $0.72
	e. Money: Amelia purchased a sandwich for $4.85 and soup for $1.99. What was the total cost?
	f. Measurement: How many ounces is 1 cup?
	g. Estimation: Choose the more reasonable estimate for the capacity of a drinking glass: 1 cup or 1 gallon.
	h. Calculation: $9 \times 9 + 19 + 54$

problem solving

Choose an appropriate problem-solving strategy to solve this problem. Genaro wanted to measure the length of this pencil. Instead of a ruler, he only had a piece of a broken yardstick. Genaro placed the piece of the yardstick alongside the pencil, as shown below. How long is the pencil? Describe how you found your answer.

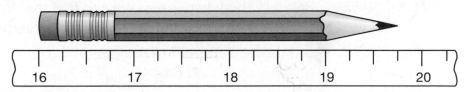

The multiples of 10 are the numbers we say when we count by 10.

$$10, 20, 30, 40, 50, \ldots$$

Likewise, the multiples of 100 are the numbers we say when we count by 100.

$$100, 200, 300, 400, 500, \ldots$$

When multiplying by multiples of 10 and 100, we focus our attention on the first digit of the multiple.

Example 1

Find the product: 3×200

We will show three ways to do this:

```
   200          2 hundred          200
   200        ×        3         ×    3
 + 200        6 hundred           600
   600
```

We will look closely at the method on the right.

```
          2 0 0  ←— Two zeros here
        ×   3
2 × 3 = 6 —→ 6 0 0  ←— Two zeros here
```

By focusing on the first digit and counting the number of zeros, we can multiply by multiples of 10 and 100 mentally.

Discuss Why can we write zeros in the ones and tens places of the product without multiplying the values of those places?

Example 2

Six buses will be used to transport students on a field trip. Each bus has seats for 40 passengers. Altogether, how many passengers can the buses transport?

We will show two ways. We can find the product mentally, whether we think of horizontal multiplication or vertical multiplication.

```
                        4 0
6 × 4 0 = 2 4 0      ×    6
                      2 4 0
```

The buses can transport a total of **240 passengers.**

Verify Before completing the multiplication, why can we write a zero in the ones place of the product?

We have practiced rounding numbers to the nearest ten. Now we will learn to round numbers to the nearest hundred. To round a number to the nearest hundred, we choose the closest multiple of 100 (number ending in two zeros). A number line can help us understand rounding to the nearest hundred.

Example 3

a. Round 472 to the nearest hundred.

b. Round 472 to the nearest ten.

Thinking Skill

Discuss

What number is halfway between 400 and 450? Explain how you know.

a. The number 472 is between 400 and 500. Halfway between 400 and 500 is 450. Since 472 is greater than 450, it is closer to 500 than it is to 400. We see this on the number line below.

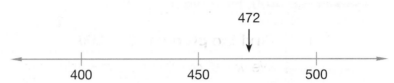

So 472 rounded to the nearest hundred is **500**.

b. Counting by tens, we find that 472 is between 470 and 480.

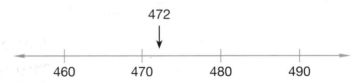

Since 472 is closer to 470 than it is to 480, we round 472 to **470**.

Example 4

Erica lives about one mile from school. A mile is 5280 feet. Round 5280 feet to the nearest hundred feet.

Counting by hundreds, we find that 5280 ft is between 5200 ft and 5300 ft. It is closer to **5300 ft** than it is to 5200 ft.

Thinking Skill

Verify

What number is halfway between 5200 and 5300?

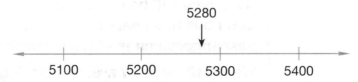

We can also round to the nearest hundred by focusing on the digit in the tens place, that is, the digit just to the right of the hundreds place.

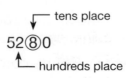

If the digit in the tens place is less than 5, the digit in the hundreds place does not change. If the digit in the tens place is 5 or more, we increase the digit in the hundreds place by one. Whether rounding up or rounding down, the digits to the right of the hundreds place become zeros.

Example 5

Round 362 and 385 to the nearest hundred. Then add the rounded numbers.

The number 362 is closer to 400 than it is to 300. The number 385 is also closer to 400 than it is to 300. Both 362 and 385 round to **400.** Now we add.

$$400 + 400 = \mathbf{800}$$

Example 6

To help prepare for the school play, the students in Mrs. Jacobsen's class arranged nine rows of chairs in the gymnasium. The students placed 44 chairs in each row. What is a reasonable estimate of the total number of chairs that were placed in the gymnasium?

To estimate, we can first round the numbers so that the arithmetic is easier. Nine rows of 44 chairs is about the same as ten rows of 40 chairs. We can multiply 10×40 to estimate the number of chairs. To multiply 40 by 10, we can simply affix a zero to 40.

$$10 \times 40 = 400$$

We estimate that there were about **400 chairs** in the gymnasium.

Lesson Practice Find each product:

a. $\begin{array}{r} 50 \\ \times\ 7 \\ \hline \end{array}$ b. $\begin{array}{r} 600 \\ \times\ \ 3 \\ \hline \end{array}$ c. 7×40 d. 4×800

Round each number to the nearest hundred:

e. 813   f. 685   g. 427   h. 2573

i. Round 297 and 412 to the nearest hundred. Then add the rounded numbers.

j. Round 623 and 287 to the nearest hundred. Then subtract the smaller rounded number from the larger rounded number.

k. A community marching band marches in 19 rows with 5 musicians in each row. What is a reasonable estimate of the number of musicians in the entire marching band? Explain why your estimate is reasonable.

l. Six months is about how many days?

Written Practice   *Distributed and Integrated*

*1. **Represent** On 1-cm grid paper, draw a square with sides 5 cm long.
(Inv. 2, Inv. 3)

    a. What is the perimeter of the square?

    b. What is the area of the square?

Formulate Write and solve equations for problems **2** and **3**.

2. Wilbur had sixty-seven grapes. Then he ate some grapes. He had
(25) thirty-eight grapes left. How many grapes did Wilbur eat?

3. The distance from Whery to Radical is 42 km. The distance
(11, 14) from Whery to Appletown through Radical is 126 km. How far is it from Radical to Appletown?

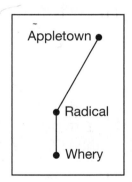

*4. Raziya arrived home from school at the time shown on the
(27) clock and began her homework half an hour later. What time did Raziya begin her homework?

*5. **Generalize** Write a rule for this sequence and find the next three
(3, Inv. 3) numbers:

$$1, 4, 9, 16, 25, 36, 49, \underline{\quad}, \underline{\quad}, \underline{\quad}, \ldots$$

*6. a. Round 673 to the nearest hundred.
(20, 42)

    b. Round 673 to the nearest ten.

7. How many squares are shaded?
(35)

*8. a. (**Estimate**) Find the length of this screw to the nearest quarter inch.
(Inv. 2, 39)

    b. Find the length of this screw to the nearest centimeter.

9. (**Connect**) Rewrite this addition problem as a multiplication problem:
(27)

$$\$2.50 + \$2.50 + \$2.50$$

*10. (**Conclude**) Are the line segments in a plus sign parallel or perpendicular?
(23)

11. (**Represent**) To what number is the arrow pointing?
(Inv. 1)

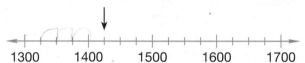

*12. (**Analyze**) Use the digits 4, 7, and 8 to write an odd number greater
(10) than 500. Each digit may be used only once.

*13. 6×80 ***14.** 7×700 ***15.** 9×80 ***16.** 7×600
(42)   (42)   (42)   (42)

17. $\begin{array}{r} z \\ +\ 338 \\ \hline 507 \end{array}$ ***18.** $\begin{array}{r} \$4.06 \\ -\ \$2.28 \\ \hline \end{array}$ ***19.** $\begin{array}{r} w \\ \times\ 6 \\ \hline 42 \end{array}$
(24)   (41)   (41)

20. $n - 422 = 305$ **21.** $55 + 555 + 378$
(24)   (17)

*22. a. Use words to write 5280.
(33)

    b. Which digit in 5280 is in the tens place?

23. a. Ten nickels are what fraction of a dollar?
(36)

    b. Write the value of ten nickels using a dollar sign and a decimal point.

*24. Compare:
(Inv. 4)

    a. 0.5 $\bigcirc$ $\frac{1}{2}$ **b.** $\frac{1}{4}$ $\bigcirc$ $\frac{1}{10}$

25. What is the sum of three squared and four squared?
(Inv. 3)

*26. Multiple Choice Which of these numbers does *not*
(Inv. 4) describe the shaded part of this rectangle?

    A $\frac{5}{10}$ **B** $\frac{1}{2}$ **C** 5.0   **D** 0.5

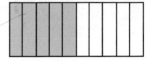

*27. The decimal number 0.25 equals $\frac{1}{4}$. Write 0.25 with words.
(Inv. 4)

*28. Anisa used a stopwatch to time herself as she ran three 50-meter
(Inv. 4) dashes. Here are her times in seconds:

9.12, 8.43, 8.57

Arrange Anisa's times in order from fastest (least time) to slowest
(greatest time).

*29. Joleen has six pieces of wood that she wants to fit together to make a
(Inv. 3, 39) picture frame. Two pieces are 8 inches long, two are 6 inches long, and
two are 4 inches long. Using four of the six pieces, how many different
rectangular frames could Joleen make? What would be the areas of the
rectangles formed?

*30. **Estimate** Each of 4 school buses can carry 52 passengers. What is
(42) a reasonable estimate of the total number of passengers the four buses
can carry? Explain why your estimate is reasonable.

Real-World Connection

The zoo's insect house has 35 glass cases. An average of 17 crickets
live in 22 of the cases and an average of 15 grasshoppers live in 13
of the cases. What is a reasonable estimate of the total number of
insects that live in the glass cases at the zoo? Explain why your answer
is reasonable.

• Adding and Subtracting Decimal Numbers, Part 1

Power Up

facts	Power Up E
count aloud	Count down by fives from 150 to 50.

mental math

  a. Number Sense: 80 − 5

  b. Number Sense: 80 − 25 (Subtract 20. Then subtract 5 more.)

  c. Powers/Roots: $\sqrt{16}$

  d. Money: Monica purchased a flashlight for $6.23 and batteries for $2.98. What was the total cost?

  e. Measurement: The perimeter of a football field is 1040 feet. Samir ran two laps along the edge of the field. How many feet did he run?

  f. Measurement: How many cups is 1 pint?

  g. Estimation: What numbers would you use to estimate the sum of $13.58 and $6.51?

  h. Calculation: $7 \times 8 + 9 + 35$

problem solving

Choose an appropriate problem-solving strategy to solve this problem. Counting by halves, we say, "one half, one, one and one half, two, ..." Write the sequence of numbers you say when you count by halves from $\frac{1}{2}$ to 10. Place the numbers along a number line. Then use your drawing to find the number that is halfway between two and five.

To add or subtract money amounts written with a dollar sign, we add or subtract digits with the same place value. We line up the digits with the same place value by lining up the decimal points.

Example 1

a. **$3.45 + $0.75**   b. **$5.35 − $2**

a. First we line up the decimal points in order to line up places with the same place value. Then we add, remembering to write the dollar sign and the decimal point.

$$\begin{array}{r} \$3.45 \\ +\ \$0.75 \\ \hline \mathbf{\$4.20} \end{array}$$

b. First we put a decimal point and two zeros behind the $2.

$2   means $2.00

Now we line up the decimal points and subtract.

$$\begin{array}{r} \$5.35 \\ -\ \$2.00 \\ \hline \mathbf{\$3.35} \end{array}$$

Model Use money manipulatives to check the answer.

Example 2

Thinking Skill

Discuss

To find the answer, explain how we could have changed each amount to cents.

At the craft store Maggie bought a pad of drawing paper for $3.75, charcoal for $4, and a clip for 15¢. What was the total price of the items before tax?

Before we add, we make sure that all the money amounts have the same form. We make these changes:

$$\$4 \longrightarrow \$4.00$$
$$15¢ \longrightarrow \$0.15$$

Then we line up the decimal points and add.

$$\begin{array}{r} \$3.75 \\ \$4.00 \\ +\ \$0.15 \\ \hline \$7.90 \end{array}$$

The total price of the three items was **$7.90.**

Model Use money manipulatives to check the answer.

We add or subtract decimal numbers that are not money amounts the same way; that is, we line up the decimal points and then add or subtract.

Adding and Subtracting Decimals

Material needed:
- **Lesson Activity 24**

Model Complete **Lesson Activity 24** to represent tenths and hundredths on a grid. Then use the representations to solve each problem in the activity.

Example 3

a. 0.2 + 0.5   **b. 3.47 − 3.41**

a. We line up the decimal points and add.

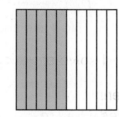

$$\begin{array}{r} 0.2 \\ + 0.5 \\ \hline \mathbf{0.7} \end{array}$$

b. We line up the decimal points and subtract.

$$\begin{array}{r} 3.47 \\ - 3.41 \\ \hline \mathbf{0.06} \end{array}$$

 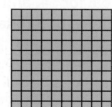 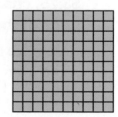 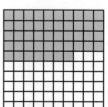

Justify Which is greater: 0.7 or 0.06? Explain your reasoning.

Example 4

One gallon of milk is about 3.78 liters. Two gallons of milk is about how many liters?

We add to find about how many liters are in two gallons.

$$\begin{array}{r} 3.78 \text{ L} \\ + 3.78 \text{ L} \\ \hline \mathbf{7.56 \text{ L}} \end{array}$$

Lesson Practice Find each sum or difference:

a. $6.32 + $5

b. $3.25 − $1.75

c. 46¢ + 64¢

d. 98¢ − 89¢

e. $1.46 + 87¢

f. 76¢ − $0.05

g. 5.6 + 5.6

h. 2.75 − 1.70

For problems **i** and **j,** use the models below to add and subtract.

i. 0.50 + 0.75

j. 0.75 − 0.50

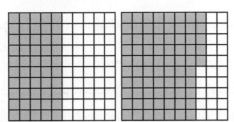 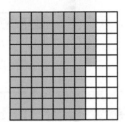

Written Practice *Distributed and Integrated*

Formulate Write and solve equations for problems **1–3.**

*1. One hundred pennies are separated into two piles. In one pile there are
(24,41) thirty-five pennies. How many pennies are in the other pile?

*2. **Estimate** Juan opened a 1-gallon bottle that held about 3.78 liters of
(25, 43) milk. He poured about 1.50 liters of milk into a pitcher. About how many
liters of milk were left in the bottle?

*3. San Francisco is 400 miles north of Los Angeles. Santa Barbara is
(11, 41) 110 miles north of Los Angeles. Stephen drove from Los Angeles to
Santa Barbara. How many miles does he still have to drive to reach
San Francisco?

*4. Draw a rectangle that is 3 cm long and 3 cm wide.
(Inv. 2,
Inv. 3)

a. What is the perimeter of the rectangle?

b. What is the area of the rectangle?

*5. a. Round 572 to the nearest hundred.
(20, 42)

b. Round 572 to the nearest ten.

*6. **(Represent)** Write the shaded part of this square
(Inv. 4)

    a. as a fraction.

    b. as a decimal number.

    c. using words.

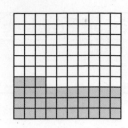

7. **(Conclude)** Are the rails of a railroad track parallel or perpendicular?
(23)

*8. **(Represent)** Draw a square to show 3×3. Then shade two ninths of
(26, Inv. 3) the square.

9. The clock shows the time Santo arrived at school. He woke
(19) up that morning at 6:05 a.m. How long after waking up did
Santo arrive at school?

10. **(Represent)** To what number is the arrow pointing?
(Inv. 1)

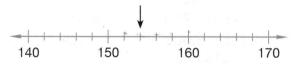

*11. $2.45 + 4.50$ ***12.** $3.25 - 2.47$
(43)   (43)

*13. $2.15 + \$3 + 7¢$ ***14.** $3.75 - 2.50$
(43)   (43)

15.   507   **16.** n ***17.**   \$5.00
(24) $-\quad n$ (24) $-\ 207$ (41) $-\ \$3.79$
    $\overline{\quad456}$ $\overline{\quad423}$

*18. 6×80 ***19.** 4×300 **20.** 7×90
(42)   (42)   (42)

*21. $8n = 32$ **22.** $\sqrt{100}$
(41)   (Inv. 3)

23. **(Represent)** Draw a line segment that is 2 inches long. Then measure
(Inv. 2) the line segment with a centimeter ruler. Two inches is about how many
centimeters?

24. (**Represent**) The population of the city was about 1,080,000. Use
(34) words to write that number.

*25. Multiple Choice Which of these metric units would probably be used
(Inv. 2) to describe the height of a tree?

   A millimeters   **B** centimeters

   C meters   **D** kilometers

*26. Multiple Choice Emily has a 2-liter bottle full of water and an empty
(40) half-gallon carton. She knows 1 liter is a little more than 1 quart. If she
pours water from the bottle into the carton, what will happen?

   A The bottle will be empty before the carton is full.

   B The carton will be full before the bottle is empty.

   C When the carton is full, the bottle will be empty.

   D The carton will be empty, and the bottle will be full.

27. Here is a list of selling prices for five houses. Arrange the prices in order
(33) from highest selling price to lowest selling price.

$$\$179,500$$
$$\$248,000$$
$$\$219,900$$
$$\$315,000$$
$$\$232,000$$

*28. Multiple Choice Which group of decimal numbers is arranged in
(43) order from least to greatest?

   A 0.23, 0.21, 0.25   **B** 0.25, 0.23, 0.21

   C 0.21, 0.23, 0.25   **D** 0.21, 0.25, 0.23

*29. An uncooked spaghetti noodle fell on the floor and broke into several
(39) pieces. Three of the pieces were $1\frac{1}{2}$ inches long, 2 inches long, and
$2\frac{1}{4}$ inches long. If two of the three pieces are lined up end to end, what
are all the possible combined lengths?

*30. (**Explain**) At an elementary school track meet, Ra'Shawn ran a
(43) 100-meter dash in 16.5 seconds. Sabrina ran 0.4 seconds faster.
What was Sabrina's time for the race? Explain why your answer is
reasonable.

• Multiplying Two-Digit Numbers, Part 1

facts   Power Up F

count aloud   Count by halves from $\frac{1}{2}$ to 10.

mental math

   a. Number Sense: $70 - 45$

   b. Number Sense: $370 - 125$

   c. Powers/Roots: $\sqrt{9} - \sqrt{1}$

   d. Money: Lisa purchased paint for $5.96 and brushes for $3.95. How much did she spend altogether?

   e. Measurement: To which number is the needle pointing on this scale?

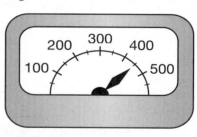

   f. Measurement: How many pints is 1 quart?

   g. Estimation: Choose the more reasonable estimate for the total capacity of a bathtub: 50 gallons or 50 milliliters.

   h. Calculation: $560 + 24 + 306$

problem solving   Choose an appropriate problem-solving strategy to solve this problem. Each time Khanh cleans his aquarium, he drains some of the old water and adds 3 liters of fresh water. Khanh has a 5-liter container and a 2-liter container. How can he use those two containers to measure 3 liters of water?

If there are 21 children in each classroom, then how many children are in 3 classrooms?

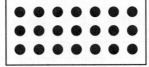 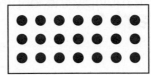 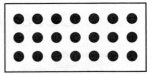

Instead of finding 21 + 21 + 21, we will solve this problem by multiplying 21 by 3. Below we show two ways to do this. The first method is helpful when multiplying mentally. The second method is a quick way to multiply using pencil and paper.

Method 1: Mental Math

Think: 21 is the same as 20 + 1.

Multiply:
$$\begin{array}{r} 20 \\ \times\ 3 \\ \hline 60 \end{array} \quad \text{and} \quad \begin{array}{r} 1 \\ \times\ 3 \\ \hline 3 \end{array}$$

Add: 60 + 3 = 63

Method 2: Pencil and Paper

Multiply ones and then multiply tens.
$$\begin{array}{r} 21 \\ \times\ 3 \\ \hline 63 \end{array}$$

three × twenty-one = sixty-three

Thinking Skill

Discuss

To find the sum of 21 + 21 + 21, we can multiply 21 × 3. Can we multiply to find the sum of 30 + 33 + 31? Why or why not?

Example 1

Multiply: 42 × 3

We write 42 on top and 3 underneath, directly below the 2. We multiply 2 by 3 to get 6. Then we multiply 4 (for 40) by 3 to get 12. The product is **126.**

$$\begin{array}{r} 4\,2 \\ \times\ 3 \\ \hline 6 \end{array} \rightarrow \begin{array}{r} 4\,2 \\ \times\ 3 \\ \hline 126 \end{array} \rightarrow \begin{array}{r} 42 \\ \times\ 3 \\ \hline 126 \end{array}$$

three × forty-two = one hundred twenty-six

Example 2

The walls of a bedroom have already been painted. The rectangular ceiling measures 12 feet by 9 feet and still needs to be painted a different color. Each quart of paint covers 120 square feet. Is one quart of paint enough to paint the ceiling?

We multiply the length and width of a rectangle to find its area.

$$12 \text{ ft} \times 9 \text{ ft} = 108 \text{ sq. ft}$$

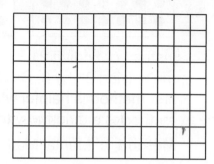

Since 108 square feet is less than 120 square feet, one quart **is enough** to paint the ceiling.

Lesson Practice

Find each product:

a. 31
     × 2

b. 31
     × 4

c. 42
     × 4

d. 30
     × 2

e. 30
     × 4

f. 24
     × 0

Written Practice

Distributed and Integrated

* 1. (Inv. 4) **Represent** The 1-gallon container of milk held 3.78 L of milk. Use words to write 3.78 L.

2. (33) **Represent** Silviano compared two numbers. The first number was forty-two thousand, three hundred seventy-six. The second number was forty-two thousand, eleven. Use digits and a comparison symbol to show the comparison.

* 3. (41, 43) **Explain** The ticket cost $3.25. Mr. Chen paid for the ticket with a $5 bill. How much change did he receive? Is your answer reasonable? Why or why not?

4. Nine squared is how much more than the square root of nine?
(Inv. 3, 31)

*5. Find the missing factor: $8m = 48$
(41)

*6. (**Connect**) Eight fluid ounces of water is one cup of water. How many
(40) fluid ounces of water is a pint of water?

7. How many circles are shaded?
(35)

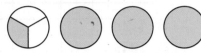

*8. (**Estimate**) Use an inch ruler to find the diameter of
(21, 39) this circle to the nearest quarter inch.

*9. Compare:
(Inv. 1, 42)   **a.** $-5 \bigcirc -2$ **b.** $4 \times 60 \bigcirc 3 \times 80$

*10. $\$4.03$ **11.** $\$4.33$ **12.** $\$5.22$ ***13.** $\$7.08$
(41) $- \$1.68$ *(43)* $+ \$5.28$ *(43)* $- \$2.46$ *(41)* $- \$0.59$

*14.   21   **15.**   40   ***16.**   73   ***17.**   51
(44) $\times\ 6$ *(42)* $\times\ 7$ *(44)* $\times\ 2$ *(44)* $\times\ 6$

18. $\$2 + 47¢ + 21¢$ **19.** $8.7 - 1.2$
(43)   *(43)*

20. $62 - n = 14$ **21.** $n - 472 = 276$
(24)   *(24)*

22. Write this addition problem as a multiplication problem:
(27)

$$2.1 + 2.1 + 2.1 + 2.1 + 2.1 + 2.1$$

*23. a. (**Connect**) Which digit in 1760 is in the hundreds place?
(33, 42)

    b. Use words to write 1760.

    c. Round 1760 to the nearest hundred.

* 24. Round 738 and 183 to the nearest hundred. Then add the rounded
(42) numbers.

* 25. (Connect) Add the decimal number one and fifty hundredths to three
(Inv. 4, and twenty-five hundredths. What is the sum?
43)

* 26. Multiple Choice If the area of this rectangle is
(Inv. 3, 6 sq. cm, then the length of the rectangle is which of
41) the following?

2 cm

    A 3 cm   **B** 4 cm

    C 10 cm   **D** 12 cm

* 27. a. Is $5.75 closer to $5 or to $6?
(20,
Inv. 4)
    b. Is 5.75 closer to 5 or to 6?

28. (Explain) How can you pay $1.23 using the fewest number of bills
(38) and coins?

(Formulate) Write and solve equations for problems **29** and **30.**

* 29. The price of the notebook was $6.59. When sales tax was added, the
(11, 41) total was $7.05. How much was the sales tax?

* 30. The Sutlej River in Asia is 900 miles long. The Po River in Europe is
(25, 41) 405 miles long. How many miles longer is the Sutlej River?

*Real-World
Connection*

The school choir is ordering new choir shirts and blouses. There are
15 girls and 11 boys in the choir. The girls' blouses cost $9 each. The
boys' shirts cost $8 each. What will be the total cost for the choir
shirts and blouses?

- **Parentheses and the Associative Property**
- **Naming Lines and Segments**

facts	Power Up E
count aloud	Count by halves from $\frac{1}{2}$ to 10.
mental math	**a. Money:** 80¢ − 35¢
	b. Money: $1.60 − $0.25
	c. Money: $4.50 − $1.15
	d. Time: What month is 14 months after March?
	e. Time: Cynthia finished her homework in 1 hour 13 minutes. If she started at 4:05 p.m., what time did she finish?
	f. Measurement: How many milliliters is 2 liters?
	g. Estimation: D'Neece had $10.97. She spent $5.92. Round each amount to the nearest dollar and then subtract to estimate the amount D'Neece has left over.
	h. Calculation: 43 + 29 + 310

problem solving

Choose an appropriate problem-solving strategy to solve this problem. This is the sequence of numbers we say when we count by fourths. Copy this sequence on your paper, and continue the sequence to the whole number 5.

$$\frac{1}{4}, \frac{1}{2}, \frac{3}{4}, 1, 1\frac{1}{4}, 1\frac{1}{2}, 1\frac{3}{4}, 2, \ldots$$

Parentheses and the Associative Property

In the following expression there are two subtractions:

$$12 - (4 - 3)$$

The parentheses show us which subtraction to perform first. The order of operations is to first subtract 3 from 4 and then to subtract that result from 12.

$$12 - (4 - 3)$$
$$12 - 1 = 11$$

Example 1

$(12 - 4) - 3$

We perform the subtraction within the parentheses first.

$$(12 - 4) - 3$$
$$8 - 3 = 5$$

Math Language

Parentheses are grouping symbols that indicate where to begin when simplifying an expression.

Compare Describe how changing the order of subtraction changes the results.

In the description and example above, we see that changing the order of subtraction changes the results. However, changing the order of addition does not change the final sum. If three numbers are to be added, it does not matter which two numbers we add first—the sum will be the same.

$$5 + (4 + 2) = 11 \qquad (5 + 4) + 2 = 11$$

This property of addition is called the **Associative Property of Addition.**

Example 2

Compare: $3 + (4 + 5) \bigcirc (3 + 4) + 5$

Both sides of the comparison equal 12.

$$3 + (4 + 5) \bigcirc (3 + 4) + 5$$
$$3 + 9 \bigcirc 7 + 5$$
$$12 \bigcirc 12$$

Math Language

The set of rules for the order in which to solve math problems is called the **order of operations**. PEMDAS is the abbreviation used to describe the order of operations (Parentheses, Exponents, Multiplication, Division, Addition, Subtraction).

Analyze Use the order of operations to solve the problem: $3 \times 4 \div (5 + 1) - 2$

We replace the circle with an equal sign.

$$3 + (4 + 5) = (3 + 4) + 5$$

This example illustrates the Associative Property of Addition.

The Associative Property also applies to multiplication. We will illustrate the **Associative Property of Multiplication** with a stack of blocks. On the left we see 12 blocks in front (3×4). There are also 12 blocks in back. We can multiply 12 by 2 to find the total number of blocks.

$(3 \times 4) \times 2 = 24$ $3 \times (4 \times 2) = 24$

On the right we see 8 blocks on top (4×2). There are 3 layers of blocks. We can multiply 8 by 3 to find the total number of blocks.

Example 3

Compare: $3 \times (2 \times 5) \bigcirc (3 \times 2) \times 5$

Both sides of the comparison equal 30.

$$3 \times (2 \times 5) \bigcirc (3 \times 2) \times 5$$
$$3 \times 10 \bigcirc 6 \times 5$$
$$30 \bigcirc 30$$

We replace the circle with an equal sign.

$$3 \times (2 \times 5) = (3 \times 2) \times 5$$

This example illustrates the Associative Property of Multiplication.

Naming Lines and Segments

Recall that a line has no end. A line goes on and on in both directions. When we draw a line, we can use arrowheads to show that the line continues. One way to identify a line is to name two points on the line.

This is line *AB*. It is also line *BA*.

This line is named "line *AB*" or "line *BA*." We can use the symbols $\overleftrightarrow{AB}$ or $\overleftrightarrow{BA}$ to write the name of this line. The small line above the letters *AB* and *BA* replaces the word *line*. To read $\overleftrightarrow{AB}$, we say, "line *AB*."

Recall that a segment is part of a line. A segment has two endpoints. We name a segment by naming its endpoints. Either letter may come first.

R •——————————————————————• S

This is segment RS. It is also segment SR.

We may use the symbols $\overline{RS}$ or $\overline{SR}$ to write the name of this segment. The small segment over the letters replaces the word *segment*. To read $\overline{RS}$, we say, "segment RS."

Example 4

Which segments in this triangle are perpendicular?

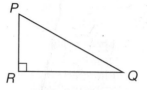

The right-angle symbol tells us this is a right triangle. $\overline{PR}$ and $\overline{RQ}$ are perpendicular because they meet and form a right angle.

Example 5

Name a pair of segments that appears to be parallel to $\overline{AB}$.

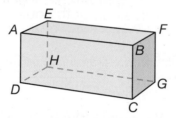

We see that $\overline{DC}$ is parallel to $\overline{AB}$. These segments are on opposite sides of the same rectangular face. $\overline{EF}$ and $\overline{HG}$ are also parallel to $\overline{AB}$.

Analyze Name two segments that appear to be perpendicular to $\overline{AB}$.

Example 6

The length of $\overline{AB}$ is 3 cm. The length of $\overline{BC}$ is 4 cm. What is the length of $\overline{AC}$?

Two short segments can form a longer segment. From A to B is one segment; from B to C is a second segment. Together they form a third segment, segment AC. We are told the lengths of $\overline{AB}$ and $\overline{BC}$. If we add these lengths, their sum will equal the length of $\overline{AC}$.

$$3 \text{ cm} + 4 \text{ cm} = 7 \text{ cm}$$

The length of $\overline{AC}$ is **7 cm.**

Lesson Practice

a. 8 − (4 + 2)   **b.** (8 − 4) + 2

c. 9 − (6 − 3)   **d.** (9 − 6) − 3

e. 10 + (2 × 3)   **f.** 3 × (10 + 20)

g. Compare: 2 + (3 + 4) ◯ (2 + 3) + 4

h. Compare: 3 × (4 × 5) ◯ (3 × 4) × 5

i. (**Analyze**) What property of addition and multiplication is shown by the comparisons in problems **g** and **h?**

j. The length of $\overline{RS}$ is 4 cm. The length of $\overline{RT}$ is 10 cm. What is the length of $\overline{ST}$? (*Hint:* You will need to subtract.)

R   S   T

k. (**Conclude**) Which segment in this figure appears to be the diameter of the circle?

l. (**Conclude**) Which segments are perpendicular?

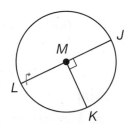

m. Refer to the figure in Example 5 and name two segments that are parallel to $\overline{BC}$.

Written Practice   *Distributed and Integrated*

*1. (**Connect**) Use the numbers 0.5, 0.6, and 1.1 to write two addition facts
(6, 43) and two subtraction facts.

2. A whole hour is 60 minutes. How many minutes is half of an hour?
(19)

3. (**Explain**) The space shuttle orbited 155 miles above the earth. The
(31) weather balloon floated 15 miles above the earth. The space shuttle was how much higher than the weather balloon? Explain why your answer is reasonable.

*4. (**Justify**) How much change should you get back if you give the
(41, 43) clerk $5.00 for a box of cereal that costs $3.85? How can you check your answer?

*5. (**Represent**) Write 12.5 using words.
(Inv. 4)

6. **Represent** Use digits and symbols to show that negative sixteen is
(Inv. 1) less than negative six.

7. The clock shows the time Joe left for work this morning. He
(27) ate breakfast 35 minutes before that time. What time did
Joe eat breakfast?

8. **Represent** Write 4060 in expanded form. Then use words to write
(16, 33) the number.

9. How many circles are shaded?
(35)

10. Compare:
(34,36)
    a. 2 quarters ◯ half dollar

    b. 2,100,000 ◯ one million, two hundred thousand

11. Find the missing factor: $6w = 42$
(41)

*12. a. **Estimate** Use an inch ruler to measure this line segment to the
(Inv. 2)   nearest inch.

    b. **Estimate** Use a centimeter ruler to measure this line segment to
    the nearest centimeter.

    _____

13. Compare: $12 - (6 - 3)$ ◯ $(12 - 6) - 3$
(45)

*14. **Explain** Look at problem **13** and your answer to the problem. Does
(45) the Associative Property apply to subtraction? Why or why not?

*15.   4.07
(43)   − 2.26
    ───

*16. $5.02
(41)   − $2.47
    ───

17. $5.83
(43)   − $2.97
    ───

18. $3.92
(43)   + $5.14
    ───

*19.   42
(44)   × 3
    ───

*20.   83
(44)   × 2
    ───

21.   40
(42)   × 4
    ───

*22.   41
(44)   × 6
    ───

23. $2.75 + 50¢ + $3
(43)

*24. 3.50 + 1.75
(43)

*25. (**Model**) Draw a rectangle that is 2 in. by 1 in.
(Inv. 2, Inv. 3)

    a. The perimeter of the rectangle is how many inches?

    b. The area of the rectangle is how many square inches?

*26. **Multiple Choice** Which of the following segments is *not* a
(21, 45) radius of the circle?

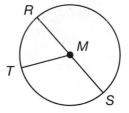

    A $\overline{RS}$ **B** $\overline{RM}$

    C $\overline{MT}$ **D** $\overline{MS}$

27. (**Formulate**) Estrella finished the first problem in 34 seconds. She
(31) finished the second problem in 28 seconds. The first problem took how much longer to finish than the second problem? Write an equation to solve the problem.

*28. Describe the order of operations in each expression. Then find the
(45) number each expression equals.

    a. $12 - (4 - 2)$

    b. $(12 - 4) - 2$

29. In Dodge City, Kansas, the average maximum temperature in July is 93°F.
(18) The average minimum temperature is 67°F. How many degrees warmer is a temperature of 93°F than a temperature of 67°F?

*30. (**Estimate**) The population density of Connecticut is 702.9 people
(25, 42) per square mile. The population density of Kentucky is 101.7 people per square mile. Round to the nearest hundred to estimate how many more people per square mile live in Connecticut than live in Kentucky.

LESSON 46

• Relating Multiplication and Division, Part 1

facts Power Up F

count aloud Count by fourths from $\frac{1}{4}$ to 5.

mental math

  a. Number Sense: 300 − 50

  b. Number Sense: 68 + 6 + 20

  c. Number Sense: 536 + 45

  d. Money: T'Wan purchased a book for $7.90 and a snack for $1.95. How much did he spend altogether?

  e. Powers/Roots: Compare: $\sqrt{81}$ ◯ 10

  f. Measurement: How many quarts is 1 gallon?

  g. Estimation: What numbers would you use to estimate the sum of $17.23 and $3.71?

  h. Calculation: $5 \times 7 + 5 + 29 + 220$

problem solving

The digits 1, 2, 3, and 4, in order, can be written with an equal sign and a times sign to form a multiplication fact.

$$12 = 3 \times 4$$

Write another multiplication fact using four different digits written in order.

Focus Strategy: Make an Organized List

(**Understand**) We are shown how the digits 1, 2, 3, and 4 can be written in order to form a multiplication fact. We are asked to find a different multiplication fact with four digits written in order.

Plan We can *make a list* of sequences of four digits written in order. Then we can look through the list to find a sequence in which we can write an equal sign and a times sign to form a multiplication fact.

Solve We list all the sequences of four digits that can be written in order:

$$1\ 2\ 3\ 4$$
$$2\ 3\ 4\ 5$$
$$3\ 4\ 5\ 6$$
$$4\ 5\ 6\ 7$$
$$5\ 6\ 7\ 8$$
$$6\ 7\ 8\ 9$$

Now we look through our list for digits that can be turned into a multiplication fact. Can we make any facts by placing a times sign between the first and second digits? We try and find that we cannot: 2×3 does not equal 45, 3×4 does not equal 56, and so on.

If we place the multiplication sign between the third and fourth digits, can we make any facts? Yes; we find that we can make two facts: $12 = 3 \times 4$ (which we were given) and **$56 = 7 \times 8$.**

Check We know that our answer is reasonable because we found a set of four digits that can be written in order to form a multiplication fact. We *made an organized list* to be sure that we considered each possibility and to save time instead of guessing and checking.

New Concept

Remember that multiplication problems have three numbers. The multiplied numbers are *factors,* and the answer is the *product.*

$$\text{Factor} \times \text{Factor} = \text{Product}$$

Visit www.
SaxonMath.com/
Int4Activities
for a calculator
activity.

If we know the two factors, we multiply to find the product. If the factors are 4 and 3, the product is 12.

$$4 \times 3 = 12$$

If we know one factor and the product, we can find the other factor.

$$4 \times w = 12 \qquad n \times 3 = 12$$

Math Language

Multiplication and division are *inverse operations*. One operation undoes the other.

We can use **division** to find a missing factor. Division "undoes" a multiplication.

We know how to use a multiplication table to find the product of 3 and 4. We locate the proper row and column, and then find the product where they meet.

	0	1	2	3	④
0	0	0	0	0	0
1	0	1	2	3	4
2	0	2	4	6	8
③	0	3	6	9	⑫
4	0	4	8	12	16

We can also use a multiplication table to find a missing factor. If we know that one factor is 3 and the product is 12, we look across the row that starts with 3 until we see 12. Then we look up to the top of the column containing 12. There we find 4, which is the missing factor.

Thinking Skill

Verify

What is the inverse of $12 \div 3 = 4$?

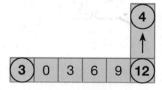

We write the numbers 3, 4, and 12 with a division box this way:

$$3{\overline{\smash{)}\,12}}^{\,4}$$

We say, "Twelve divided by three is four."

Example 1

Divide: $4\overline{)32}$

We want to find the missing factor. We think, "Four times what number is thirty-two?" We find the missing factor using the multiplication table below. First we find the row beginning with 4. Then we follow this row across until we see 32. Then we look up this column to find that the answer is **8.**

Multiplication Table

	0	1	2	3	4	5	6	7	⑧	9	10	11	12
0	0	0	0	0	0	0	0	0	0	0	0	0	0
1	0	1	2	3	4	5	6	7	8	9	10	11	12
2	0	2	4	6	8	10	12	14	16	18	20	22	24
3	0	3	6	9	12	15	18	21	24	27	30	33	36
④	0	4	8	12	16	20	24	28	㉜	36	40	44	48
5	0	5	10	15	20	25	30	35	40	45	50	55	60
6	0	6	12	18	24	30	36	42	48	54	60	66	72
7	0	7	14	21	28	35	42	49	56	63	70	77	84
8	0	8	16	24	32	40	48	56	64	72	80	88	96
9	0	9	18	27	36	45	54	63	72	81	90	99	108
10	0	10	20	30	40	50	60	70	80	90	100	110	120
11	0	11	22	33	44	55	66	77	88	99	110	121	132
12	0	12	24	36	48	60	72	84	96	108	120	132	144

Conclude Identify multiplication and division patterns that appear in the table. Explain your thinking.

Activity

Using a Multiplication Table to Divide

Use the multiplication table to perform the following divisions:

1. If 36 items are divided into 4 equal groups, we can find the number of items in each group by dividing 36 by 4. Find $4\overline{)36}$ by tracing the 4 row over to 36. What number is at the top of the column?

2. If 30 students gather in groups of 5, then we can find the number of groups by dividing 30 by 5. Find $5\overline{)30}$ by tracing the 5 row to 30. What number is at the top of the column?

3. If 108 musicians are arranged in rows and columns, and if there are 9 musicians in each row, then how many columns are there?

Example 2

A P.E. teacher divided a class of 18 students into 2 equal groups. How many students were in each group?

We search for the number that goes above the division box. We think, "Two times what number is eighteen?" We remember that $2 \times 9 = 18$, so the answer is **9 students.** We write "9" above the 18, like this:

$$2)\overline{18} = 9$$

Connect If the division problem above is reversed to show multiplication, what would the factors and the product be?

Lesson Practice Divide:

a. $2)\overline{12}$ **b.** $3)\overline{21}$ **c.** $4)\overline{20}$ **d.** $5)\overline{30}$

e. $6)\overline{42}$ **f.** $7)\overline{28}$ **g.** $8)\overline{48}$ **h.** $9)\overline{36}$

Written Practice   *Distributed and Integrated*

Formulate Write and solve equations for problems **1** and **2.**

* 1. Four hundred ninety-five oil drums were on the first train. Seven hundred
(11, 30) sixty-two oil drums were on the first two trains combined. How many oil drums were on the second train?

* 2. Workers on a Montana ranch baled 82 bales of hay on the first day.
(1, 17) They baled 92 bales of hay on the second day and 78 bales of hay on the third day. How many bales of hay did the workers bale in all three days?

* 3. The decimal number three and seventy-eight hundredths is how much
(Inv. 4, 43) more than two and twelve hundredths?

* 4. a. Round 786 to the nearest hundred.
(20, 42)

     b. Round 786 to the nearest ten.

*5. **(Represent)** Draw and shade rectangles to show the number $2\frac{1}{3}$.
(35)

*6. **(Conclude)** The first five odd numbers are 1, 3, 5, 7, and 9.
(1,
Inv. 3)

    a. What is their sum?

    b. What is the square root of their sum?

7. The clock shows a morning time. What time was it
(27) 12 hours before that time?

*8. **(Conclude)** What type of angle is formed by the hands
(23) of this clock?

*9. **(Estimate)** **a.** Use an inch ruler to find the length of this
(23, 39) rectangle to the nearest quarter inch.

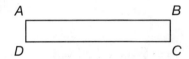

    b. Which segment is parallel to $\overline{AB}$?

10. **(Estimate)** Kita took two dozen BIG steps. About how many meters
(Inv. 2) did she walk?

*11. **(Connect)** To what mixed number is the arrow pointing?
(37)

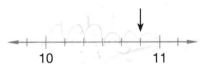

*12. $64 + (9 \times 40)$ ***13.** $\$6.25 + 39¢ + \$3$
(45)   (43)

*14. $\$4.02$ ***15.** $\$5.00$ ***16.** n
(41) $-\ \$2.47$ (41) $-\ \$2.48$ (24, 43) $+\ 2.5$
                                                                3.7

*17. 4.3 ***18.** 42 ***19.** 81
(16, 43) $-\ \ \ c$ (44) $\times\ \ 3$ (44) $\times\ \ 5$
     $\overline{\ \ 3.2\ }$

*20. $6\overline{)30}$ ***21.** $7\overline{)21}$ ***22.** $8\overline{)56}$
(46)   (46)   (46)

*23. $9\overline{)81}$ ***24.** $7\overline{)28}$ ***25.** $3\overline{)15}$
(46)   (46)   (46)

* 26. (**Model**) Draw a rectangle 3 in. long and 1 in. wide.
(Inv. 2, Inv. 3)

  a. What is its perimeter?

  b. What is its area?

* 27. Multiple Choice Rosario noticed that the distance from the pole
(21) in the center of the tetherball circle to the painted circle was about
six feet. What was the approximate radius of the tetherball circle?

  A 12 ft   **B** 4 yd   **C** 3 ft   **D** 2 yd

* 28. Tyrique, Dominic, and Tamasha checked their pockets for change.
(4, 22) Tyrique had two dimes and a penny. Dominic had three nickels and
two pennies. Tamasha had a nickel, a dime, and a penny. Using dollar
signs and decimal points list the three amounts in order from least to
greatest.

29. (**Predict**) What is the twelfth term of the sequence below?
(3, 32)

  12, 24, 36, 48, 60, . . .

30. (**Generalize**) Write a rule that describes the relationship of the data
(3) in the table.

Number of Teachers	1	2	3	4	5
Number of Students	7	14	21	28	35

Early Finishers
Real-World Connection

Cecilia's book had 58 pages. She read for 6 hours and had 4 pages left.

  a. About how many pages did Cecilia read each hour? Write a
    division problem to solve the problem.

  b. What number will go in the division box? Explain why.

LESSON

47

• Relating Multiplication and Division, Part 2

Power Up

facts	Power Up F
count aloud	As a class, count by halves from $\frac{1}{2}$ to 10.
mental math	Add hundreds, then tens, and then ones. Regroup the tens.

    a. Number Sense: 365 + 240

    b. Number Sense: 456 + 252

    c. Number Sense: 584 + 41

    d. Money: $6.00 − $1.50

    e. Money: Zakia bought a box of cereal for $4.56 and a gallon of milk for $2.99. How much did she spend?

    f. Time: Bree left her home at 7:20 a.m. She arrived at school at 7:45 a.m. How long did it take Bree to get to school?

    g. Estimation: Kaneisha estimated that each story of the building was 10 feet tall. Kaneisha counted 6 stories. Estimate the total height of the building.

    h. Calculation: $2 \times 9 + 30 + 29 + 110$

problem solving

Choose an appropriate problem-solving strategy to solve this problem. Counting by fourths we say, "one fourth, one half, three fourths, one, ..." Draw a number line from 0 to 4 that is divided into fourths. Use the quarter-inch marks on a ruler to place each tick mark on the number line. Label each tick mark. Which number is halfway between $2\frac{1}{2}$ and 3? Which number is halfway between 3 and 4?

Reading Math

Notice that we read in a different direction for each division example.

In Lesson 46 we found division answers using a multiplication table. We showed division with a division box. We can show division in more than one way. Here we show "fifteen divided by three" three different ways:

$$3\overline{)15} \qquad 15 \div 3 \qquad \frac{15}{3}$$

The first way uses a division box. The second way uses a division sign. The third way uses a division bar. The blue arrows show the order in which we read the numbers.

Example 1

Use digits and division symbols to show "twenty-four divided by six" three ways.

$$6\overline{)24} \qquad 24 \div 6 \qquad \frac{24}{6}$$

Example 2

Thinking Skill

Connect

Name the factors and the products for the multiplication problem related to each division problem.

Solve:

a. $28 \div 4$ b. $\dfrac{27}{3}$

a. We read this as "twenty-eight divided by four." It means the same thing as $4\overline{)28}$.

$$28 \div 4 = 7$$

b. We read this as "twenty-seven divided by three." It means the same thing as $3\overline{)27}$.

$$\frac{27}{3} = 9$$

Example 3

Reading Math

We cannot divide by zero.

Solve:

a. $8 \div 1$ b. $\dfrac{9}{9}$ c. $4\overline{)0}$

a. "Eight divided by one" means, "How many ones are in eight?" The answer is **8**.

b. "Nine divided by nine" means, "How many nines are in nine?" The answer is **1**.

c. "Zero divided by four" means, "How many fours are in zero?" The answer is **0**.

A multiplication fact has three numbers. We can form one other multiplication fact and two division facts with these three numbers. Together, all four facts form a multiplication and division fact family.

$$6 \times 4 = 24 \qquad 24 \div 4 = 6$$
$$4 \times 6 = 24 \qquad 24 \div 6 = 4$$

Example 4

Use the numbers 3, 5, and 15 to write two multiplication facts and two division facts.

$$3 \times 5 = 15 \qquad 15 \div 5 = 3$$
$$5 \times 3 = 15 \qquad 15 \div 3 = 5$$

Verify Why can we write a fact family of multiplication and division equations?

Example 5

For a science project, Sh'Vaughn timed the speeds at which garden snails moved. One snail moved 11 cm in 1 minute. At that rate, how far would it move in 12 minutes?

Minutes	1	2	3	4	5	6	7	8	9	10	11	12
Centimeters	11	22	33	44	?	?	?	?	?	?	?	?

We are asked to find how far the snail could move in 12 minutes. One way to find the answer is to continue the table. Another way is to multiply 11 inches per minute by 12 minutes.

$$11 \times 12 = 132$$

The snail could move **132 inches** in 12 minutes.

Generalize What division rule describes the relationship of the data in this table?

Lesson Practice Divide:

a. $49 \div 7$ **b.** $45 \div 9$ **c.** $40 \div 8$

d. $\dfrac{6}{6}$ **e.** $\dfrac{32}{8}$ **f.** $\dfrac{27}{3}$

Represent Use digits and three different division symbols to show each division:

g. twenty-seven divided by nine

h. twenty-eight divided by seven

i. **Connect** Use the numbers 12, 3, and 4 to write two multiplication facts and two division facts.

j. Write two division facts using the numbers 36, 4, and 9.

Written Practice
Distributed and Integrated

*1. **Formulate** Brand A costs two dollars and forty-three cents. Brand B
(31, 41) costs five dollars and seven cents. Brand B costs how much more than Brand A? Write an equation and solve this problem.

*2. **Connect** The numbers 3, 4, and 12 form a multiplication and division
(47) fact family.

$$3 \times 4 = 12 \qquad 12 \div 4 = 3$$
$$4 \times 3 = 12 \qquad 12 \div 3 = 4$$

Write four multiplication/division facts using the numbers 4, 5, and 20.

*3. What is the sum of the decimal numbers two and three tenths and eight
(Inv. 4, 43) and nine tenths?

*4. **Conclude** Use the digits 1, 5, 6, and 8 to write an even number
(10) greater than 8420. Each digit may be used only once.

5. a. Compare: $1\frac{1}{2} \bigcirc 1.75$
(7, Inv. 4)

b. Use words to write the greater of the two numbers you compared in part **a.**

6. **Analyze** Carlos will use square floor tiles that measure one foot on
(Inv. 3) each side to cover a hallway that is eight feet long and four feet wide. How many floor tiles will Carlos need?

7. **Represent** To what number is the arrow pointing?
(Inv. 1)

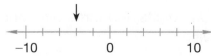

8. **a.** Five dimes are what fraction of a dollar?
(36)

    b. Write the value of five dimes using a dollar sign and a decimal point.

*9. The length of segment *PQ* is 2 cm. The length of segment *PR* is 11 cm.
(11) How long is segment *QR*?

*10. ⬭Conclude⬭ Which segment in this triangle appears to be
(23, 45) perpendicular to segment *AC*?

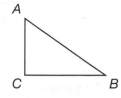

11. Round 3296 to the nearest hundred.
(42)

12. Use words to write 15,000,000.
(33)

*13. $95 - (7 \times \sqrt{64})$ **14.** $2.53 + 45¢ + $3
(Inv. 3, 45)   (43)

*15.   *n*   **16.**   40   ***17.**   51
(24, 43) $- 5.1$ (44) $\times \ 3$ (44) $\times \ 5$
       2.3

*18. $28 \div 7$ ***19.** $81 \div 9$ ***20.** $35 \div 7$ ***21.** $16 \div 4$
(47)   (47)   (47)   (47)

*22. $\dfrac{28}{4}$ ***23.** $\dfrac{42}{7}$ ***24.** $\dfrac{48}{8}$ ***25.** $\dfrac{0}{5}$
(47)   (47)   (47)   (47)

*26. **Multiple Choice** Which of these does *not* show 24 divided by 4?
(47)

    A $24\overline{)4}$ **B** $\dfrac{24}{4}$ **C** $24 \div 4$ **D** $4\overline{)24}$

27. **a.** Is $12.90 closer to $12 or to $13?
(20)

    b. Is 12.9 closer to 12 or to 13?

*28. Describe the order of operations in these expressions, and find the
   number each expression equals.
   (45)

   a. $12 \div (6 \div 2)$

   b. $(12 \div 6) \div 2$

   c. **Conclude** Does the Associative Property apply to division?
   Explain.

29. In the year 2003, each visitor to the country of Mexico spent an average
   of $540. Each visitor to the country of Canada spent an average of
   (11, 13)
   $557. How many more dollars did each visitor to Canada spend in
   2003?

*30. **Estimate** One of the largest hammerhead sharks ever caught weighed
   991 pounds. One of the largest porbeagle sharks ever caught weighed
   (25, 42)
   507 pounds. Round to the nearest hundred pounds to estimate the
   weight difference of those two sharks.

Real-World Connection

The band played for 18 minutes during halftime at the football game.
Each song was 3 minutes long. How many songs did the band play
during halftime?

   a. Write a division equation that could be used to find the answer.

   b. Write a multiplication equation that could be used to find $18 \div 3$.

   c. Explain how multiplication and division are related.

• Multiplying Two-Digit Numbers, Part 2

Power Up

facts   Power Up F

count aloud   Count by fourths from $\frac{1}{4}$ to 5.

mental math   Add hundreds, then tens, and then ones, regrouping tens.

    a. Number Sense: 466 + 72

    b. Number Sense: 572 + 186

    c. Number Sense: 682 + 173

    d. Money: $3.59 + $2.50

    e. Money: Cassie has $4.60. Victoria has $2.45. How much money do the girls have altogether?

    f. Money: Enrique has $6.24. Kalila has $2.98. How much money do they have altogether?

    g. Estimation: Estimate the total cost of items that are priced $2.98, $3.05, and $8.49.

    h. Calculation: $\sqrt{64} \times 5 + 410 + 37$

problem solving   Choose an appropriate problem-solving strategy to solve this problem. On D'Janelle's morning ride to school, she saw a sign that displayed an outdoor temperature of 29°F. On D'Janelle's afternoon ride home, the sign displayed a temperature of 4°C. Did the outdoor temperature rise or fall during the day? How can you tell?

New Concept

In Lesson 44 we practiced multiplying two-digit numbers. First we multiplied the digit in the ones place. Then we multiplied the digit in the tens place.

Multiply Ones　　**Multiply Tens**

```
   12              12
 ×  4            ×  4
    8              48
```

Often when we multiply the ones, the result is a two-digit number. When this happens, we do not write both digits below the line. Instead we write the second digit below the line in the ones column and write the first digit above the tens column.

Seven times two is 14.

We write the four below the line and write the 1 ten above the tens place.

```
   1
   12
 ×  7
    4
```

Then we multiply the tens digit and add the digit that we wrote above this column.

Seven times one is seven, plus one is eight.

```
   1
   12
 ×  7
   84
```

Model We can demonstrate this multiplication with $10 bills and $1 bills. To do this, we count out $12 seven times. We use one $10 bill and two $1 bills to make each set of $12. When we are finished, we have seven $10 bills and fourteen $1 bills.

7　　　　　　　　　14

We exchange ten $1 bills for one $10 bill. We add this bill to the stack of $10 bills, giving us a new total of eight $10 bills and four $1 bills.

8　　　　　　　　　4

Example 1

The contractor purchased 8 doors for $64 each. What was the total price of the doors before tax?

We write the two-digit number above the one-digit number. We think of $64 as 6 tens and 4 ones. We multiply 4 ones by 8 and the total is 32 ones ($32). We write the 2 of $32 below the line. The 3 of $32 is 3 tens, so we write "3" above the tens column.

$$\begin{array}{r} 3 \\ \$64 \\ \times \quad 8 \\ \hline 2 \end{array}$$

Then we multiply 6 tens by 8, which is 48 tens. We add the 3 tens to this and get a total of 51 tens. We write "51" below the line. The product is $512. The total price of the doors was **$512.**

$$\begin{array}{r} 3 \\ \$64 \\ \times \quad 8 \\ \hline \$512 \end{array}$$

Example 2

A chef uses 2 cups of milk to make one pot of soup. About how many quarts of milk does he need to make 18 pots of soup?

Each pot of soup includes 2 cups of milk, so 18 pots of soup contains 18 × 2 cups of milk. We only need an estimate, so we round 18 to 20 before multiplying.

$$20 \times 2 \text{ cups} = 40 \text{ cups}$$

The chef needs about 40 cups of milk, but we are asked for the number of quarts. Since 4 cups equals a quart, we divide 40 by 4.

$$40 \text{ cups} \div 4 = 10 \text{ quarts}$$

The chef will need a little less than **10 quarts** of milk.

Lesson Practice

Find each product:

a.
$$\begin{array}{r} 16 \\ \times \ 4 \\ \hline \end{array}$$

b.
$$\begin{array}{r} 24 \\ \times \ 3 \\ \hline \end{array}$$

c.
$$\begin{array}{r} \$45 \\ \times \ 6 \\ \hline \end{array}$$

d. 53 × 7

e. 35 × 8

f. 64 × 9

g. (**Model**) Use money manipulatives to demonstrate this multiplication:

$$\$14 \times 3$$

h. (**Estimate**) The restaurant orders 19 gallons of milk per day. Estimate the number of quarts that would equal 19 gallons. Then estimate the number of liters of milk the restaurant orders per day.

Formulate Write and solve equations for problems **1** and **2**.

*1. There were four hundred seventy-two birds in the first flock. There were
(31)   one hundred forty-seven birds in the second flock. How many fewer
birds were in the second flock?

*2. Raina hiked forty-two miles. Then she hiked seventy-five more miles.
(1, 17)   How many miles did she hike in all?

*3. **Connect** Write four multiplication/division facts using the numbers 3,
(47)   5, and 15.

*4. Use the digits 1, 3, 6, and 8 to write an odd number between 8000 and
(10)   8350. Each digit may be used only once.

*5. **Represent** Write 306,020 in expanded form. Then use words to write
(16, 33)   the number.

*6. **Represent** Draw and shade circles to show the number $2\frac{1}{8}$.
(35)

7. One mile is how many feet?
(Inv. 2)

8. What is the perimeter of this pentagon?
(Inv. 2)

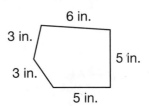

6 in.
3 in.
5 in.
3 in.
5 in.

9. A board that had a length of 1 meter was cut into two pieces. If one piece
(11,
Inv. 2)   of the board was 54 cm long, how long was the other piece?

*10. Find the length of segment *BC.*
(39)

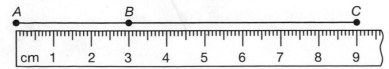

A   B   C

cm 1   2   3   4   5   6   7   8   9

*11. $100 + (4 \times 50)$
(45)

12. $3.25 + 37¢ + $3
(43)

13. $\sqrt{4} \times \sqrt{9}$
(Inv. 3)

*14.   33
(48) $\times\ 6$

*15.   24
(48) $\times\ 5$

*16.   90
(48) $\times\ 6$

*17. $42
(48) $\times\ 7$

18. $5.06
(41) $-\ 2.28

*19.   1.45
(43) $+\ 2.70$

*20.   3.25
(43) $-\ 1.50$

21.   14
(17)   28
            45
            36
            92
         $+\ 47$

*22. $28 \div 7$
(47)

23. $5\overline{)35}$
(46)

24. $6\overline{)54}$
(46)

*25. $\dfrac{63}{7}$
(47)

*26. **Multiple Choice** A rectangle has an area of 12 sq. in. Which of these
(Inv. 3) could *not* be the length and width of the rectangle?

    A 4 in. by 3 in.   **B** 6 in. by 2 in.

    C 12 in. by 1 in.   **D** 4 in. by 2 in.

*27. (**Justify**) Which property of multiplication is shown here?
(45)

$$5 \times (2 \times 7) = (5 \times 2) \times 7$$

*28. Use digits and three different division symbols to show "twenty-four
(47) divided by three."

*29. (**Estimate**) D'Ron mailed nine invitations and placed a 39¢ stamp
(48) on each invitation. Estimate the total postage cost for the 9 invitations.
Explain how you estimated the total.

*30. (**Model**) Draw a number line and show the locations of 2, 3, 1.5, and $2\frac{1}{4}$.
(Inv. 1)

• Word Problems About Equal Groups, Part 1

Power Up

facts	Power Up G
count aloud	Count by sevens from 7 to 42 and back down to 7.
mental math	Add hundreds, then tens, and then ones, regrouping tens and ones.

    a. Money: $258 + $154

    b. Money: $587 + $354

    c. Money: $367 + $265

    d. Number Sense: 480 − 115

    e. Measurement: What is the diameter of this coin?

    f. Estimation: Choose the more reasonable estimate for the length of a dollar bill: 6 inches or 6 millimeters.

    g. Calculation: 620 + 40 + 115

    h. Calculation: 95 + 50 + 19 + 110

problem solving

Choose an appropriate problem-solving strategy to solve this problem. Paige earns $2 for each day she completes her chores. Normally, Paige is paid $14 each Saturday for the entire previous week. This week, though, Paige wants to ask for an early payment so she can purchase a new game. If Paige asks to be paid for the chores she has already completed Sunday through Thursday, how much money will she ask for? Explain how you arrived at your answer.

New Concept

In this lesson we will practice solving word problems about equal groups. Problems with an **"equal groups"** plot can be solved using a multiplication formula. Consider this problem:

Azura bought 3 cartons of eggs. There were 12 eggs in each carton. Altogether, Azura bought 36 eggs.

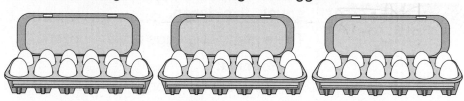

In this problem there are equal groups (cartons) of 12 eggs. Here is how we place these numbers into a multiplication formula:

Formula	Problem
Number **in** each group	12 eggs in each carton
× Number **of** groups	× 3 cartons
Total	36 eggs

Formula:
Number **of** groups × Number **in** each group = Total

Problem:
3 cartons × 12 eggs in each carton = 36 eggs

We multiply the number in each group by the number of groups to find the total. If we want to find the number of groups or the number in each group, we divide.

Reading Math

We translate the problem using a multiplication formula:

Number of groups: 3 cartons

Number in each group: 12 eggs

Total: 36 eggs

Example 1

Tyrone has 5 cans of tennis balls. There are 3 tennis balls in each can. How many tennis balls does Tyrone have?

The words *in each* are a clue to this problem. The words *in each* usually mean that the problem has an "equal groups" plot.

We write the number and the words that go with *in each* on the first line. This is the number in each group. We write the number and word *5 cans* as the number of groups. To find the total, we multiply.

Formula	Problem
Number **in** each group	3 tennis balls in each can
× Number **of** groups	× 5 cans
Total	**15 tennis balls**

Here we write the formula horizontally:

Formula:
Number **of** groups × Number **in** each group = Total

Problem:
5 cans × 3 tennis balls in each can = 15 tennis balls

Example 2

Twelve eggs equals a dozen eggs. Find the number of eggs that equals five dozen.

There are twelve eggs in each dozen.

Formula:
Number **of** groups × Number **in** each group = Total

Problem:
5 dozen × 12 eggs in each dozen = 60 eggs

We find that **60 eggs** equals five dozen.

Example 3

One human foot has 26 bones. About how many bones are in two human feet?

Since 25 is close to 26, we can estimate the total number of bones in two feet by multiplying 25 by 2.

$$2 \times 25 = 50$$

There are **about 50 bones** in two human feet.

Explain Describe how the estimate helps you find the exact number of bones in two feet.

Lesson Practice

Formulate Write and solve an equation for each "equal groups" problem.

a. There were 8 birds in each flock. There were 6 flocks. How many birds were there in all?

b. There are 6 people in each car. There are 9 cars. How many people are there in all?

c. A bakery display case contained 4 dozen muffins. How many individual muffins were in the display case?

d. **Estimate** One human hand has 27 bones. About how many bones are in two human hands? Explain how you found your answer.

Formulate Write and solve equations for problems **1** and **2**.

*1. There were 8 boys in each row. There were 4 rows. How many boys
(49) were in all 4 rows?

*2. There were 7 girls in each row. There were 9 rows. How many girls were
(49) in all 9 rows?

3. A llama weighs about 375 pounds. A coyote weighs about 75 pounds.
(31) A llama weighs about how many pounds more than a coyote?

*4. **Connect** Write four multiplication/division facts using 5, 6, and 30.
(47)

*5. **Represent** Draw and shade circles to show the number $2\frac{3}{4}$.
(35)

*6. To what mixed number and decimal number is the arrow pointing?
(37)

7. Tika is a college student. She began her homework last
(27) night at the time shown on the clock. She finished two
and one half hours later. What time did Tika finish her
homework?

*8. **Represent** Draw a rectangle that is 4 cm by 2 cm. Shade $\frac{7}{8}$ of it.
(21, 26)

9. **Represent** Use digits to write three million, seven hundred fifty thousand.
(33, 34) Which digit is in the hundred-thousands place?

*10. **Connect** Use the decimal numbers 1.4, 0.7, and 2.1 to write two
(6) addition facts and two subtraction facts.

*11. 56 ÷ 7   ***12.** 64 ÷ 8   ***13.** $\frac{45}{9}$
(47)   (47)   (47)

* 14. The length of segment *RT* is 9 cm. The length of segment *ST* is 5 cm.
 (6) What is the length of segment *RS*?

R   S   T

15. $3.07
(41) − $2.28

16. 4.78
(43) − 3.90

* 17. $(4 + 3) \times \sqrt{64}$
(Inv. 3, 45)

18. 7.07
(24, 43) − *n*
 ——
 4.85

19. *c*
(16, 43) − 2.3
 ——
 4.8

* 20. $403 − (5 \times 80)$
(45)

21. $6n = 30$
(41)

22. $(587 − 238) + 415$
(45)

* 23. 45
(48) × 6

* 24. 23
(48) × 7

* 25. $34
(48) × 8

* 26. Multiple Choice The radius of a circle is 3 ft. Which of the following
(Inv. 2, 21) is *not* the diameter of the circle?

A 36 in.   **B** 6 ft   **C** 2 yd   **D** 72 in.

* 27. Multiple Choice Which of these angles is acute?
(23)

A   **B**

C   **D**

* 28. Solve:
(47)

    a. $\dfrac{5}{5}$ **b.** $9 \div 1$ **c.** $6\overline{)0}$

29. 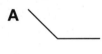 **Estimate** One human hand has 27 bones. One human foot has
(49) 26 bones. About how many bones are in two hands plus two feet? Explain
 why your estimate is reasonable.

* 30. **Estimate** The land area of Booker T. Washington National
(11, 17) Monument in Virginia is 239 acres. The land area of Cabrillo National
 Monument in California is 160 acres. What is a reasonable estimate of
 the total acreage of these two national monuments? Explain why your
 estimate is reasonable.

LESSON 50

• Adding and Subtracting Decimal Numbers, Part 2

Power Up

facts　Power Up G

count aloud　Count by fourths from $\frac{1}{4}$ to 5.

mental math　Add hundreds, then tens, and then ones, regrouping tens and ones.

　　a. Number Sense: 589 + 46

　　b. Number Sense: 375 + 425

　　c. Money: $389 + $195

　　d. Money: D'Trina paid $5.64 for a dog collar and $1.46 for a tag. Altogether, how much did D'Trina spend?

　　e. Time: Jamal started reading his book at 2:25 p.m. and read for 45 minutes. At what time did he finish reading?

　　f. Measurement: There were 4 gallons of water in the bucket. How many quarts of water is that?

　　g. Estimation: JaNeeva wants to buy a CD that costs $12.65 and a pair of headphones that costs $15.30. Round each price to the nearest 25 cents and then add to estimate the cost of the items.

　　h. Calculation: $\sqrt{36} \times 8 + 40 + 9 + 15$

problem solving　Choose an appropriate problem-solving strategy to solve this problem. Sunee is making a sequence out of money. She lined up the bills shown below. Which money amounts can she use to extend the sequence to include two more terms?

, , , . . .

We have added and subtracted decimal numbers by lining up the decimal points and then adding or subtracting the digits in each column. We line up the decimal points to ensure that we are adding and subtracting digits with the same place value.

Thinking Skill

Generalize

How does the value of the places to the left of the ones place compare to the value of the places to the right of the ones place?

The chart shows place values from hundreds to hundredths. We use the decimal point as a guide for finding the value of each place. To the left of the decimal point is the ones place, then the tens place, and then the hundreds place. To the right of the decimal point is the tenths ($\frac{1}{10}$) place and then the hundredths ($\frac{1}{100}$) place.

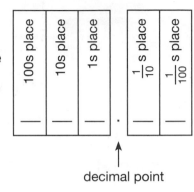

decimal point

Example 1

Name the place value of the 3 in each number:

   a. 23.4   **b. 2.34**   **c. 32.4**   **d. 4.23**

Use the chart above to find the place value.

   a. ones   **b. tenths**

   c. tens   **d. hundredths**

In this lesson we will begin adding and subtracting decimal numbers that do not have the same number of decimal places.

Example 2

Add: 3.75 + 12.5 + 2.47

To add decimal numbers with pencil and paper, we focus on lining up the decimal points—not the last digits.

Line up decimal points.

$$
\begin{array}{r}
\overset{1\ 1}{}3.75 \\
12.5 \\
+\ \ 2.47 \\
\hline
18.72
\end{array}
$$

← Treat an "empty place" like a zero.

Example 3

Subtract: 4.25 − 2.5

We line up the decimal points and subtract.

Line up decimal points.

$$
\begin{array}{r}
\overset{3}{\cancel{4}}.25 \\
-\ 2.5 \\
\hline
1.75
\end{array}
$$

← Treat an "empty place" like a zero.

Activity

Adding and Subtracting Decimals

Material needed:
- **Lesson Activity 25**

(Model) Complete **Lesson Activity 25** to represent tenths and hundredths on a grid.

Lesson Practice

a. Which digit in 23.5 is in the tenths place?

b. Which digit in 245.67 is in the hundredths place?

c. Which digit in 12.5 is in the same place as the 7 in 3.75?

Find each sum or difference:

d. 4.35 + 2.6	**e.** 4.35 − 2.6
f. 12.1 + 3.25	**g.** 15.25 − 2.5
h. 0.75 + 0.5	**i.** 0.75 − 0.7

j. Find n in the equation $n + 1.5 = 4.75$.

Written Practice

Distributed and Integrated

(Formulate) Write and solve equations for problems **1–3.**

*1. Each of the 3 boats carried 12 people. In all, how many people were in
(49) the 3 boats?

*2. The book cost $6.98. The tax was 42¢. What was the total price?
(22, 35)

* 3. Claire read six hundred twenty minutes for an afterschool reading
(31) program. Ashanti read four hundred seventeen minutes. Claire read
how many more minutes than Ashanti?

* 4. (Connect) Use the numbers 4, 12, and 48 to write two multiplication
(47) facts and two division facts.

5. Justin ran the perimeter of the block. How far did Justin run? The
(Inv. 2) measurements of the block are shown on the figure below.

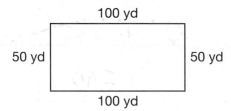

* 6. Justin ran around the block in 58.7 seconds. Write "58.7" with words.
(Inv. 4)

7. (Represent) Use digits to write twelve million, seven hundred fifty
(33, 34) thousand. Which digit is in the hundred-thousands place?

* 8. (Estimate) Round 783 and 217 to the nearest hundred. Then subtract
(42) the smaller rounded number from the larger rounded number.

9. The time shown on the clock is an evening time. Alyssa's
(19) school day begins 9 hours 30 minutes later than that time.
What time does Alyssa's school day begin?

10. (Connect) Write this addition problem as a multiplication problem:
(27)

$$\$3.75 + \$3.75 + \$3.75 + \$3.75$$

* 11. $(4 \times 50) - \sqrt{36}$
(Inv. 3, 45)

* 12. $3.6 + 4.35 + 4.2$
(50)

13. $4.63 + \$2 + 47¢ + 65¢$
(43)

* 14.   43
(48) $\times\ 6$

* 15.   54
(48) $\times\ 8$

* 16.   37
(48) $\times\ 3$

* 17. $40
(48) $\times\ \ 4$

18. 4.7 + 5.5 + 8.4 + 6.3 + 2.4 + 2.7
(43)

19. $5.00 − $4.29
(41)

*20. 7.03 − 4.2
(50)

*21.
(12, 24)

$$\begin{array}{r} n \\ -\ 27.9 \\ \hline 48.4 \end{array}$$

*22.
(24, 43)

$$\begin{array}{r} 46.2 \\ +\quad c \\ \hline 52.9 \end{array}$$

*23. $\dfrac{24}{3}$
(47)

24. $\dfrac{36}{9}$
(47)

25. The length of segment *AB* is 5 cm. The length of segment *BC* is 4 cm.
(1, 45) What is the length of segment *AC*?

A   B   C

*26. **Represent** Draw and shade circles to show the number $3\frac{3}{8}$.
(35)

27. Compare: 1 minute ◯ 58.7 seconds
(Inv. 4, 50)

*28. **Multiple Choice** Which of the following is more than one second but
(19, Inv. 4) less than two seconds?

   A 0.15 sec   **B** 1.5 sec

   C 2.1 sec   **D** 2.15 sec

*29. Write these numbers in order from least to greatest:
(33)

      250,000   47,000   9000   3,100,000   600

30. These thermometers show the average daily minimum and maximum
(18) temperatures in New York City's Central Park during the month of July.
What is the difference in degrees between the two temperatures?

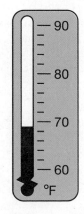

Focus on

• Percents

A part of a whole can be named with a fraction, with a decimal number, or with a percent. **Percent** means per hundred. Fifty of the 100 squares below are shaded, or $\frac{50}{100}$. This means that 50% are shaded.

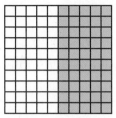

$\frac{1}{2}$ of the square is shaded.
0.50 of the square is shaded.
50% of the square is shaded.

We read 50% as "fifty percent." A percent is expressed as a fraction with a denominator of 100. The percent sign (%) represents the denominator 100.

$$50\% \text{ means } \frac{50}{100}$$

Just as 50 cents is $\frac{1}{2}$ of a whole dollar, 50 percent is $\frac{1}{2}$ of a whole. The close relationship between cents and percents can help us understand percents.

One half of a dollar is 50 cents.	One half is shaded. 50% is shaded.	
One fourth of a dollar is 25 cents.	One fourth is shaded. 25% is shaded.	
One tenth of a dollar is 10 cents.	One tenth is shaded. 10% is shaded.	

Naming Percents of a Dollar

(**Connect**) Solve:

1. A quarter is what fraction of a dollar?

2. A quarter is what percent of a dollar?

3. A dime is what fraction of a dollar?

4. A dime is what percent of a dollar?

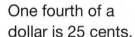

Discuss One dollar is what fraction of five dollars? Explain the relationship as a percent.

5. A penny is what fraction of a dollar?

6. A penny is what percent of a dollar?

7. A nickel is what fraction of a dollar?

8. A nickel is what percent of a dollar?

Estimating Percents of a Whole

In the picture below, the glass on the left is 100% full. The glass on the right is 50% full.

100% 50%

Multiple Choice In problems **9–12,** estimate to find the best choice for how full each glass is.

9. This glass is about what percent full?

    A 20%   **B** 40%

    C 60%   **D** 80%

10. This glass is about what percent full?

    A 25%   **B** 50%

    C 75%   **D** 100%

11. This glass is about what percent full?

    A 20%   **B** 40%

    C 60%   **D** 80%

12. This glass is about what percent full?

    A 20%   **B** 40%

    C 60%   **D** 80%

Analyze One cup is what percent of one quart?

Finding the Remaining Percent of a Whole

The parts of a whole total 100%. This means that if 25% of this circle is shaded, then 75% is *not* shaded.

25% + 75% = 100%

Analyze Write each percent:

13. If 40% of this circle is shaded, then what percent is *not* shaded?

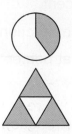

14. Seventy-five percent of the figure is shaded. What percent is *not* shaded?

15. If 80% of the answers were correct, then what percent of the answers were *not* correct?

Connect Write the answers for problems **13** and **15** as a fraction and as a decimal.

16. **Analyze** If the chance of rain is 10%, then what is the chance that it will *not* rain?

Comparing Percents to one Half

Explain Complete each comparison in problems **17–19,** and explain the reason for each of your answers.

17. Compare: 48% $\bigcirc$ $\frac{1}{2}$

18. Compare: 52% $\bigcirc$ $\frac{1}{2}$

19. Compare: 50% $\bigcirc$ $\frac{1}{3}$

20. Forty percent of the students in the class were boys. Were there more boys or girls in the class? Explain your answer.

Finding 50% of a Number

To find one half of a number, we divide the number into two equal parts. Since 50% equals $\frac{1}{2}$, we find 50% of a number by dividing it into two equal parts.

Explain Answer these questions about 50% of a number, and describe how to find each answer.

21. How many eggs is 50% of a dozen?

22. How many minutes is 50% of an hour?

23. How much money is 50% of $10?

24. How many hours is 50% of a day?

Percent

Material needed:

- **Lesson Activity 26**

Model Shade each figure to show the percent given. Then find the percent of the figure that is *not* shaded.

a. Write the shaded part of each figure below as a fraction and as a decimal.

b. Choose two figures and write an "is less than" comparison statement using fraction notation.

c. Choose two different figures and write an "is greater than" comparison statement using decimal notation.

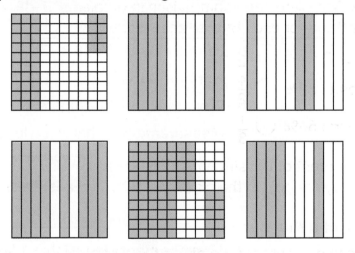

d. Write the decimal numbers in order from **least to greatest.**

e. Write the fractions in order from **greatest to least.**

- ## Adding Numbers with More Than Three Digits
- ## Checking One-Digit Division

facts	Power Up H
count aloud	Count by hundreds from 100 to 1000.
mental math	**a. Number Sense:** $100 - 40$
	b. Number Sense: $346 + 29$
	c. Number Sense: $465 + 175$
	d. Powers/Roots: Compare: $\sqrt{64} \bigcirc 100 - 36$
	e. Measurement: What is the length of this paper clip?

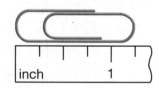

f. Measurement: Recall that 1 liter is slightly more than 1 quart. Is 1 liter slightly more than 4 pints?

g. Percent: What is 50% of $14?

h. Calculation: $21 \div 3 \times 9 + 19$

problem solving Choose an appropriate problem-solving strategy to solve this problem. On New Year's Day, 2007, M'Kayla's brother turned eighteen months old. What was the date of her brother's birth?

New Concepts

Adding Numbers with More Than Three Digits

When using pencil and paper to add numbers that have more than three digits, we add in the ones column first. Then we add in the tens column, the hundreds column, the thousands column, the ten-thousands column, and so on. When the sum of the digits in a column is a two-digit number, we record the second digit below the line. We write the first digit above (or below) the column to the left.

Example 1

A park ranger used a measuring wheel to find the length of trails in the park. Two routes to a lake from the campground measured 43,287 feet and 68,595 feet. If a hiker takes one route to the lake and takes the other route back to the campground, then the round trip is how many feet?

We add the digits in the ones column first. Then we add the digits in the other columns. When the sum is a two-digit number, we write the second digit below the line and the first digit above (or below) the column to the left. The round trip is **111,882 feet.**

$$
\begin{array}{r}
^{1}\ ^{11} \\
43{,}287 \\
+\ 68{,}595 \\
\hline
111{,}882
\end{array}
$$

Estimate   There are 5280 feet in one mile. About how many miles is 111,882 feet? Explain your thinking.

Example 2

Dale bought a used pick-up truck for his business for $4950. The taxes and registration cost $483. Then Dale paid $525 to have a toolbox installed in the bed of the truck. The tax on the toolbox was $37. Altogether, how much did Dale spend?

When we write the numbers in columns, we are careful to line up the last digit in each number. We add the digits one column at a time, starting from the right. In this example we show the carried numbers written below the columns. We find that Dale spent **$5995.**

$$
\begin{array}{r}
\$4950 \\
\$\ 483 \\
\$\ 525 \\
+\ \$\ \ 37 \\
\hline
^{1\ 1\ 1} \\
\$5995
\end{array}
$$

We can also check our answer by using a calculator. When we use our calculator, we see that the sum is $5995.

Checking One-Digit Division

Thinking Skill

Connect

Why can we use multiplication to check a division problem?

We can check a division answer by multiplying the numbers outside the division box:

$$3\overline{)12} \longrightarrow \begin{array}{r} 4 \\ \times\ 3 \\ \hline 12 \end{array} \text{ check}$$

We see that the product matches the number inside the division box. We usually show this by writing the product under the number in the division box.

$$\begin{array}{r} 4 \\ 3\overline{)12} \\ 12 \end{array}$$

← **Step 1:** Divide 12 by 3 and write "4."

← **Step 2:** Multiply 4 by 3 and write "12."

Example 3

Divide. Check the answer by multiplying.

a. $3\overline{)18}$ b. $4\overline{)32}$

First we divide and write the answer above the box. Then we multiply and write the product below the box.

a. $\begin{array}{r} 6 \\ 3\overline{)18} \\ 18 \end{array}$ b. $\begin{array}{r} 8 \\ 4\overline{)32} \\ 32 \end{array}$

Practice using multiplication to check all your division answers in the problem sets.

Lesson Practice

Add:

a. $\begin{array}{r} 4356 \\ +\ 5644 \end{array}$ b. $\begin{array}{r} 46{,}027 \\ +\ 39{,}682 \end{array}$ c. $\begin{array}{r} 360{,}147 \\ +\ 96{,}894 \end{array}$

Find each sum. Check each answer using a calculator.

d. $436 + 5714 + 88$ e. $43{,}284 + 572 + 7635$

Divide. Check each answer by multiplying.

f. $3\overline{)21}$ g. $7\overline{)42}$ h. $6\overline{)48}$

Written Practice *Distributed and Integrated*

Formulate Write and solve equations for problems **1–3.**

* **1.** In the P.E. class there were four teams. Each team had eight players.
  (49)   How many players were on all four teams?

*2. There were 7 pennies in each stack. There were 6 stacks of pennies.
$^{(49)}$ How many pennies were there in all?

*3. Lalo ran the first lap in 63.4 seconds and the second lap in 65.3 seconds.
$^{(31,\ 43)}$ Lalo ran the first lap how much faster than the second lap?

*4. (**Connect**) Write four multiplication/division facts using the numbers
$^{(47)}$ 6, 7, and 42.

5. Compare: $1 + 3 + 5 + 7 + 9$ $\bigcirc$ five squared
$^{(7,}_{Inv.\ 3)}$

6. a. Round 367 to the nearest hundred.
$^{(20,\ 42)}$

 b. Round 367 to the nearest ten.

*7. (**Represent**) Draw a circle and shade 50% of it.
$^{(Inv.\ 5)}$

8. (**Classify**) Name each type of angle shown below:
$^{(23)}$

a. **b.** **c.**

*9. A rectangle is shown at right:
$^{(Inv.\ 2,}_{Inv.\ 3)}$ **a.** What is its length?

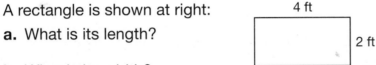

4 ft

2 ft

 b. What is its width?

 c. What is its perimeter?

 d. What is its area?

10. (**Represent**) The amount of liquid in a container is 2.75 quarts. Use
$^{(Inv.\ 4)}$ words to write that amount.

*11. (**Estimate**) The land area of Grand Portage National Monument in
$^{(30,\ 42)}$ Minnesota is 710 acres. The land area of Oregon Caves National
Monument in Arizona is 488 acres. Estimate the difference of those
areas by first rounding each area to the nearest hundred acres.

* 12. Describe the order of operations in this expression and find the number
(50) it equals.

$$15.24 + (19.6 - 1.1)$$

* 13.   63,285
(51)   + 97,642

14. $5.00
(41)   − $4.81

15. n
(24, 43)   + 39.8
                61.4

* 16.   85
(48)   × 5

17.   37
(48)   × 7

18.   40
(42)   × 8

19. f
(41)   × 8
            72

20.   47.8
(24, 43)   − c
                20.3

* 21.   462,586
(51)   +   39,728

22. z
(16, 43)   − 4.78
                2.63

Divide. Check each answer by multiplying.

* 23. 2)18
(51)

* 24. 7)21
(51)

* 25. $\dfrac{56}{8}$
(51)

26. The length of $\overline{AB}$ is 7 cm. The length of $\overline{AC}$ is 12 cm. How long is $\overline{BC}$?
(45)

A   B   C

* 27. If half the students are boys, then what percent of the students are
(Inv. 5) girls?

* 28. **Connect** If $5n = 0$, then what does $6n$ equal?
(28, 41)

* 29. Multiple Choice Which of the following does *not* name
(Inv. 4,
Inv. 5) the shaded portion of the large square?

A $\dfrac{11}{100}$ **B** 0.11   **C** 11%   **D** 11

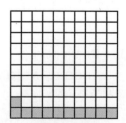

* 30. **Explain** In 1980, the median age of a resident of the United States
(50)   was 30 years. By 2000, the median age had increased 5.3 years. What
was the median age of a resident of the United States in the year 2000?
Explain why your answer is reasonable.

- **Subtracting Numbers with More Than Three Digits**
- **Word Problems About Equal Groups, Part 2**

Power Up

facts	Power Up H
count aloud	Count by hundreds from 100 to 1000 and back down to 100.
mental math	**a. Number Sense:** 200 − 30
	b. Number Sense: 400 − 90
	c. Money: $2.48 + $2.99
	d. Time: The casserole must cook in the oven for 1 hour 30 minutes. J'Meika wants the casserole to be ready to eat by 6:45 p.m. At what time does J'Meika need to put the casserole in the oven?
	e. Percent: 50% of $22
	f. Measurement: True or False: 1 liter is slightly more than 4 cups.
	g. Estimation: Choose the more reasonable estimate for the temperature of a bowl of hot soup: 120°F or 60°F.
	h. Calculation: $\sqrt{25} + 9 + 110 + 32$
problem solving	Choose an appropriate problem-solving strategy to solve this problem. A loop is worth five points, and a tip is worth three points. L'Shawn made four loops and two tips. Carlotta made three loops and five tips. How many points did each person earn?

Subtracting Numbers with More Than Three Digits

When using pencil and paper to subtract numbers with more than three digits, we begin by subtracting in the ones column. We regroup if necessary. Then we move one column to the left and subtract in the tens column, regrouping if necessary. Then we subtract in the hundreds column, the thousands column, the ten-thousands column, and so on. Sometimes we must subtract across several zeros.

Example 1

Thirty-six thousand, one hundred fifty-two tickets were sold for the first baseball game of the year. Nine thousand, four hundred fifteen fewer tickets were sold for the second game of the year. How many tickets were sold for the second game of the year?

We write the first number above the second number. We line up digits with the same place value. First we subtract in the ones column. Then we subtract in the other columns. We find that **26,737 tickets** were sold for the second game.

$$\begin{array}{r} 2\overset{1}{5}\quad\overset{1}{4}\quad\overset{1}{} \\ \cancel{3}\cancel{6},1\,\cancel{5}\,2 \\ -\quad 9,4\,1\,5 \\ \hline 2\,6,7\,3\,7 \end{array}$$

Discuss Explain how to check the answer.

Example 2

A charity received a contribution of $5000. In the first month after the contribution was received, the charity spent $2386. How much of the contribution remained after the first month?

Thinking Skill

Analyze

Explain why 5000 is equal to 499 tens + 10 ones.

We need to find some ones for the ones place before we can subtract. We may do this in one step by thinking of the "500" in 5000 as 500 tens. We exchange one of these tens for ten ones, leaving 499 tens. Then we subtract. We find that **$2614** remained.

$$\begin{array}{r} 4\,9\,9 \\ \$5\cancel{0}\cancel{0}\overset{1}{0} \\ -\ \$2\,3\,8\,6 \\ \hline \$2\,6\,1\,4 \end{array}$$

Word Problems About Equal Groups, Part 2

"Equal groups" word problems have a multiplication formula. If we know the number of groups and the number in each group, we multiply to find the total. However, if we know the total, then we need to *divide* to find the number of groups or the number in each group.

Example 3

MarVel has 21 tennis balls in cans. There are 3 tennis balls in each can. How many cans does he have?

We translate the problem using a multiplication formula:

Number in each group: 3 balls in each can

Number of groups: 7 cans

Total: 21 balls

There are two numbers in this problem. The words *in each* are a clue. They show us the number of objects in each group (3 tennis balls). The other number is 21. We need to decide whether this is the number of groups or the total. Altogether, MarVel has 21 tennis balls. This is the total.

Formula	**Problem**
Number **in each** group	3 tennis balls in each can
× Number **of** groups	× *n* cans
Total	21 tennis balls

Since we know the total, we divide the total by the number in each group to find the number of groups.

$$\begin{array}{r} 7 \\ 3\overline{)21} \\ 21 \end{array}$$

We check our answer by multiplying: 7×3 tennis balls = 21 tennis balls. Our answer is correct. MarVel has **7 cans.**

Example 4

Trushna has 5 large cans of racquetballs. She has 40 racquetballs in all. If each can contains the same number of racquetballs, how many racquetballs are in each can?

Connect

Why can we use a multiplication formula to solve a division problem?

The words *in each* show us that this is an "equal groups" problem. However, we are not given an *in each* number.

Formula

Number of groups × Number in each group = Total

Problem:

5 cans × *n* racquetballs in each can = 40 racquetballs

We may abbreviate the equation this way:

$$5n = 40$$

To find the number in each can, we divide 40 by 5.

$$\begin{array}{r} 8 \\ 5\overline{)40} \\ 40 \end{array}$$

We see that 5 times 8 racquetballs equals 40 racquetballs, so our answer is correct. There are **8 racquetballs** in each can.

Example 5

Marsha found a length of fabric marked 16 feet. She needs 4 yards of fabric to make a costume for a school play. Can the costume be made from the length of fabric Marsha found?

We can convert 16 feet to yards by dividing by 3. Since 16 does not divide evenly by 3, we look for a nearby number compatible with 3. We choose 15 and divide 15 feet by 3.

$$15 \div 3 = 5$$

We find that 16 ft is about 5 yards, so **there is enough fabric to make a costume.**

Verify Describe a different way Marsha can decide if there is enough fabric.

Lesson Practice Subtract:

a.	b.	c.
4783	4000	$20.00
− 2497	− 527	− $12.25

Formulate Write and solve equations for problems **d** and **e**.

d. There were 35 people. There were 7 cars. The number of people in each car was the same. How many people were in each car?

e. Thirty students were arranged in rows. Six students were in each row. How many rows were there?

f. Mr. Tran wants to arrange his 29 students into 5 groups. About how many students will be in each group? Explain how you found your answer.

Written Practice *Distributed and Integrated*

Write and solve equations for problems **1–5.**

*1. There were 8 buses. Each bus could seat 60 students. How many
(49) students could ride in all the buses?

*2. Each van could carry 9 students. There were 63 students. How many
(52) vans were needed to carry all of the students?

*3. The coach separated 28 players into 4 equal teams. How many
(52) players were on each team?

4. There are 10 swimmers in the race. Only 3 can be awarded medals.
(25) How many swimmers will not win a medal?

5. Hermelinda finished first in the 100-meter freestyle race with a time of
(31, 43) 57.18 seconds. Tanya finished second in 58.26 seconds. Hermelinda finished the race how many seconds sooner than Tanya?

6. (**Connect**) Write four multiplication/division facts using the numbers
(47) 7, 8, and 56.

7. Compare: $1 + 2 + 3 + 4 \bigcirc \sqrt{100}$
(Inv. 1,
Inv. 3)

*8. (**Conclude**) What are the next three numbers in this sequence?
(3)

$$\ldots, 6000, 7000, 8000, \underline{\quad}, \underline{\quad}, \underline{\quad}, \ldots$$

*9. There were two hundred sixty-seven apples in the first bin. There were
(31) four hundred sixty-five apples in the second bin. How many fewer apples were in the first bin?

*10. $8.49 + 7.3 + 6.15$ **11.** $6n = 42$
(50)   (41)

*12. $47{,}586$ **13.** $\$5.00$ **14.** n
(51) $+ 23{,}491$ (41) $- \$3.26$ (24, 43) $+ 25.8$
                                                            $\overline{60.4}$

*15. 49 **16.** 84 **17.** 70
(48) $\times\ 6$ (48) $\times\ 5$ (42) $\times\ 8$

18. 35 **19.** 400 ***20.** $\$40.00$
(48) $\times\ 9$ (24, 41) $-\ \ n$ (52) $- \$24.68$
                                $\overline{256}$

21. a. Round 639 to the nearest hundred.
(20, 42)

   b. Round 639 to the nearest ten.

*22. (**Conclude**) Which side of this triangle appears to be
(23, 45) perpendicular to $\overline{PR}$?

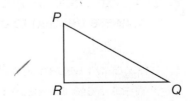

23. Compare: $49\% \bigcirc \frac{1}{2}$
(Inv. 5)

*24. Divide. Check each answer by multiplying.
(51)

　　a. $3\overline{)27}$ 　　　　**b.** $7\overline{)28}$ 　　　　**c.** $8\overline{)72}$

*25. This figure has four sides, but it is not a rectangle.
(Inv. 2) What is the perimeter of this figure?

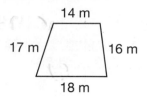

26. (**Estimate**) **a.** Is $24.10 closer to $24 or to $25?
(20,
Inv. 4)
　　b. Is 24.1 closer to 24 or to 25?

*27. Multiple Choice If $\triangle = \square$, which of these is *not* necessarily
(1, 41) true?

　　A $\triangle + 2 = \square + 2$ 　　　　　　**B** $2 \times \triangle = 2 \times \square$
　　C $\triangle - 2 = \square - 2$ 　　　　　　**D** $2 \times \triangle = \square + 2$

*28. a. What fraction of the large square is shaded?
(Inv. 4,
Inv. 5)
　　b. The shaded part of the large square represents what
　　　decimal number?

　　c. What percent of the large square is shaded?

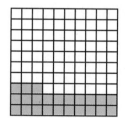

*29. (**Explain**) The answer to $33 \div 8$ is not a whole number. What whole
(52) number represents a reasonable estimate of the answer? Explain why
you chose that number.

*30. Look at these coins. List all of the different amounts you could make
(22, 43) using exactly two coins. Arrange the amounts in order from least to
greatest and write each amount with a dollar sign.

• One-Digit Division with a Remainder

Power Up

facts   Power Up I

count aloud Count by thousands from 1000 to 10,000.

mental math Nine dimes plus ten pennies totals one dollar. We can use this fact to find change back from a dollar. For example, if you pay a dollar for an item that costs 47¢, you should get 53¢ back. Notice that the 4 of 47¢ and the 5 of 53¢ equal 9 dimes. The 7 and the 3 equal 10 pennies. Find the change back from a dollar for items with these prices:

  a. Money: 46¢

  b. Money: 64¢

  c. Money: 28¢

  d. Money: 52¢

  e. Money: 17¢

  f. Money: 85¢

  g. Estimation: Is $32.45 closer to $32 or to $33?

  h. Calculation: $42 \div 7 + 26 + 110 + 38$

problem solving Choose an appropriate problem-solving strategy to solve this problem. Dakota wants to participate in two sports at her school. She can choose from four different sports that are offered—track, soccer, tennis, and basketball. What combinations of two sports can Dakota choose?

We can divide 12 objects into equal groups of four. Here we show 12 dots divided into three equal groups of four:

12 dots   3 equal groups

However, we cannot divide 13 dots into equal groups of four, because there is one dot too many. We call the extra dot the **remainder**.

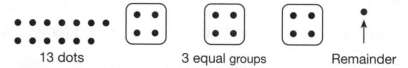

13 dots   3 equal groups   Remainder

We can show that 13 is to be divided into groups of four by writing

$$4\overline{)13}$$

As we look at this problem, we may wonder what to write for the answer. The answer is not exactly 3 because 3 × 4 is 12, which is less than 13. However, the answer cannot be 4 because 4 × 4 is 16, which is more than 13. Since we *can* make three groups of four, we write "3" as our answer. Then we multiply 3 by 4 and write "12" below the 13.

$$
\begin{array}{r}
3 \\
4\overline{)13} \\
12
\end{array}
$$
← three groups

We see that 13 is more than 12. Now we find how much is left over after making three groups of four. To do this, we subtract 12 from 13.

$$
\begin{array}{r}
3 \\
4\overline{)13} \\
-12 \\
\hline
1
\end{array}
$$
← three groups

subtract
← 1 left over (remainder)

There is one left over. The amount left over is the remainder. Using the letter R for "remainder," we write the answer to the division problem as "3 R 1."

$$
\begin{array}{r}
3 \text{ R } 1 \\
4\overline{)13} \\
-12 \\
\hline
1
\end{array}
$$

Example 1

Thinking Skill

Generalize

How can we use multiplication to check a division problem that has a remainder?

Divide: $3\overline{)16}$

This problem tells us to divide 16 into groups of three. We can use a sketch to help us with the problem. Draw 16 dots and make groups of three dots.

     ○

We can make five groups of three. One dot is not in a group of three. We write "5" above the division box, as shown below.

$$3\overline{)16}^{\,5}$$

Since three groups of five is 15, we write "15" below the 16. Then we subtract and find that the remainder is 1.

$$
\begin{array}{r}
5 \\
3\overline{)16} \\
-15 \\
\hline
1 \quad \leftarrow \text{remainder}
\end{array}
$$

We write the answer as **5 R 1.**

Verify How can we check the answer?

Activity

Finding Equal Groups with Remainders

Materials needed:

- counters

We often use division to solve problems with an "equal groups" plot. We might be looking for the number of groups of a given size, or we might be looking for the size of a given number of groups. In this activity we will solve both types of problems. Use counters (or draw dots) to illustrate each problem.

1. There are 25 students in a classroom. The teacher wants to make groups with four students in each group. How many groups can be made? Explain how to deal with the remainder.

2. In the same class, the teacher wants to make three equal groups of students. How many students will be in each group? Explain how to deal with the remainder.

Example 2

The science club will take 20 members to the museum. Vans and a car will be used to take the members to the museum. Each van can carry 6 members. How many vans can be filled? How many members will ride in the car?

First we divide 20 by 6 to find the number of groups of 6.

$$6\overline{)20}$$

We can draw 20 dots and make groups of six, or we can think, "What number times six is close to but not more than 20?" We might start by thinking, "Six times *four* equals 24"; but 24 is too much, so we think, "Six times *three* equals eighteen." Eighteen is less than 20. We write "3" as shown below.

$$\overset{3}{6\overline{)20}}$$

Next we multiply, and then we subtract.

$$
\begin{array}{r}
3 \\
6\overline{)20} \\
-18 \\
\hline
2
\end{array}
$$

← 3 groups of 6
← 20 members
← 18 members in vans
← remainder of 2 members

Three vans can be filled. If each van carries six members, then **2 members** will ride in the car.

Verify How can we check the answer?

Example 3

Lucius needs at least 18 quarts of apple cider to make punch for a school party. Apple cider is sold only in gallons. How many gallons should he buy?

Four quarts equals a gallon, so if we divide 18 by 4 we can find the number of gallons. However, 18 is not a multiple of 4, so we pick a nearby number that is compatible with 4. Both 16 and 20 are close to 18 and are multiples of 4. Lucius wants to have enough so we pick 20 and divide by 4 ($20 \div 4 = 5$). Lucius should buy **5 gallons** of apple cider.

Analyze How many 8-oz cups does Lucius need so that he can serve 18 quarts of cider mixed with 3 quarts of club soda? Explain your reasoning.

a. **Represent** Draw dots and make groups to show 14 ÷ 4. Write the answer shown by your sketch.

Divide. Write each answer with a remainder.

b. 3)17   **c.** 5)12   **d.** 4)23

e. 15 ÷ 2   **f.** 20 ÷ 6   **g.** 25 ÷ 3

h. Nina threw the shot put 28 feet. About how many yards is 28 feet? Sketch the division using dots.

Written Practice

Distributed and Integrated

Formulate Write and solve equations for problems **1** and **2**.

*1. Evita had 56 beads that she was putting into bags. She wanted to put
(52) them into equal groups of 8 beads. How many bags will she need?

*2. There were 42 children waiting for a ride. There were 7 cars available. If
(52) the same number of children rode in each car, then how many would be in each car?

*3. **Connect** Write four multiplication/division facts using the numbers 4,
(47) 7, and 28.

4. Which months have exactly 30 days?
(5)

*5. Consider this sequence:
(3)

$$..., 16,000, 17,000, 18,000, 19,000, ...$$

a. **Generalize** Write a rule that describes how to find the next term of the sequence.

b. **Predict** What is the next term of the sequence?

6. a. Round 4728 to the nearest hundred.
(20, 42)

b. Round 4728 to the nearest ten.

7. Write the time "a quarter after four in the afternoon" in digital form.
(19)

*8. **(Model)** One side of a square is 4 feet long. You may use tiles to solve.
(Inv. 2)

    a. What is the perimeter of the square?

    b. What is the area?

9. How many circles are shaded?
(35)

*10. ✏️ **(Explain)** Describe the order of operations in this expression and
(Inv. 3, find the number it equals.
45)

$$\sqrt{64} + (42 \div 6)$$

11. $6.35 + $12.49 + 42¢   ***12.** $100.00 − $59.88
(43)   (43, 52)

*13.   51,438   **14.**   60   **15.**   57
(52) − 47,495   (42, 48) × 9   (48) × 4

*16. **(Represent)** Draw dots and make groups to show 22 ÷ 5. Write the
(53) answer next to your drawing.

Divide for problems **17–19.** Write each answer with a remainder.

*17. 25 ÷ 4   ***18.** 6)39   ***19.** 7)30
(53)   (53)   (53)

20.   46   **21.**   38   **22.** z
(48) × 8   (48) × 7   (24, 43) − 16.5
                                                                       40.2

*23. 6.75 + 4.5 + 12.5
(50)

*24. **(Represent)** Use digits to write seven million, two hundred sixty
(34) thousand.

25. A half-gallon container holds about 1.89 L of fluid. Use words to
(40) write 1.89 L.

*26. Multiple Choice Shakir said, "I am thinking of two numbers. Their
(28) product is 6." The two numbers Shakir was thinking of could *not* be _____.

  A 1 and 6   **B** 2 and 3   **C** 3 and 2   **D** 6 and 0

*27. a. A quarter is what percent of a dollar?
(40,
Inv. 5) **b.** A quart is what percent of a gallon?

*28. a. What fraction of the large square is shaded?
(Inv. 4,
Inv. 5) **b.** The shaded part of the large square represents what
       decimal number?

  c. What percent of the large square is shaded?

*29. **Estimate** Brandon purchased 1 liter of juice, which is about
(53) 67.6 fluid ounces. Estimate the number of cups of juice that Brandon
  purchased. Explain your thinking.

*30. **Explain** The 900 North Michigan Avenue Building in Chicago is
(25, 30) 871 feet tall. The 181 West Madison Street Building is 680 feet tall. How
  many feet taller is the 900 North Michigan Avenue Building? Explain
  how you found your answer.

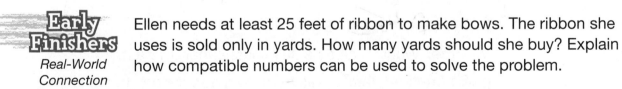

Early Finishers

Real-World Connection

Ellen needs at least 25 feet of ribbon to make bows. The ribbon she
uses is sold only in yards. How many yards should she buy? Explain
how compatible numbers can be used to solve the problem.

- # The Calendar
- # Rounding Numbers to the Nearest Thousand

Power Up

facts	Power Up I
count aloud	Count by thousands from 1000 to 10,000 and back down to 1000.
mental math	Find the change back from a dollar for items with these prices:

    a. Money: 41¢

    b. Money: 89¢

    c. Money: 34¢

    d. Money: 62¢

    e. Percent: 50% of 18

    f. Time: What is the time 30 minutes after 3:19 a.m.?

    g. Estimation: Tarana was trying to guess the number of jelly beans in the small jar. She estimated that 10 jelly beans could fit in one "layer" along the bottom of the jar. She also estimated that the jar was about 8 layers tall. What might be Tarana's estimate for the number of jelly beans?

    h. Calculation: $10 \times 7 + 35 + 53 + 134$

problem solving	Choose an appropriate problem-solving strategy to solve this problem. One way to make a dollar with seven coins is with two quarters and five dimes. Can you find three more ways to make a dollar with seven coins? (Remember to consider half-dollars.)

New Concepts

The Calendar

Math Language

Sometimes there are 7 years in a row without a leap year. This happens around "century years" that are not multiples of 400. For example, the 7-year span 1897–1903 contained no leap years, since 1900 is not a multiple of 400.

A year is the length of time it takes the Earth to travel around the sun. A day is the length of time it takes the Earth to spin around once on its axis. It takes the Earth almost exactly $365\frac{1}{4}$ days to travel around the sun. To make the number of days in every year a whole number, we have three years in a row that have 365 days each. These years are called **common years.** Then we have one year that has 366 days. A year with 366 days is called a **leap year.**

A year is divided into 12 months. The month February has 28 days in common years and 29 days in leap years. Four months have 30 days each. All the rest have 31 days. If we know the four months that have 30 days, we can remember the number of days in the other months. The following jingle helps us remember which months have 30 days:

Thirty days have September,
April, June, and November.
February has twenty-eight alone,
All the rest have thirty-one.
Excepting leap year,
That's when February's days are twenty-nine.

A **decade** is ten years. A **century** is one hundred years.

Example 1

How many days does December have?

"Thirty days have September, April, June, and November. February has twenty-eight alone" tells us that December does not have 30 days. December must have **31 days.**

Example 2

Thinking Skill

Connect

What day is the first day of the week?

According to this calendar, May 10, 2014, is what day of the week?

The letters across the top of the calendar stand for Sunday, Monday, Tuesday, Wednesday, Thursday, Friday, and Saturday. We see that May 10 is a **Saturday,** the second Saturday of the month.

MAY 2014

S	M	T	W	T	F	S
				1	2	3
4	5	6	7	8	9	10
11	12	13	14	15	16	17
18	19	20	21	22	23	24
25	26	27	28	29	30	31

Example 3

Math Language

When dates are in order from earliest to latest, they are in **chronological order.** The years 1036, 1482, 1995, and 2007 are in *chronological order.*

The Pilgrims sailed to America and landed at Cape Cod in 1620. The colonies adopted the Declaration of Independence in 1776. Write a *later − earlier = difference* equation and solve it to find the number of years between those two historic events.

This is a problem about comparing two numbers (the years 1620 and 1776). To find the amount of time between two years, we subtract. Instead of thinking "larger-smaller-difference," we think of "later-earlier-difference." We subtract the earlier date from the later date. In this problem, that means we subtract 1620 from 1776.

Formula	Problem
Later	1776
− Earlier	− 1620
Difference	156

We find that there were **156 years** from 1620 to 1776.

Rounding Numbers to the Nearest Thousand

To round a number to the nearest thousand, we find the multiple of 1000 to which the number is closest. The multiples of 1000 are the numbers in this sequence:

$$1000, 2000, 3000, \dots$$

A number line can help us understand rounding.

Example 4

Seven thousand, eight hundred thirty-six tickets were sold for the first professional indoor soccer game of the season. Round the number of tickets sold to the nearest thousand.

We know that 7836 is more than 7000 but less than 8000. Halfway from 7000 to 8000 is 7500. Since 7836 is more than halfway from 7000 to 8000, it is nearer to 8000.

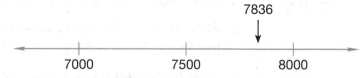

To the nearest thousand, 7836 rounds to **8000.**

Example 5

A special exhibit at a museum was seen by 34,186 visitors. To the nearest thousand, how many visitors saw the exhibit?

One way to round 34,186 is to see that 34,186 is between 34,000 and 35,000. Halfway from 34,000 to 35,000 is 34,500. Since 34,186 is less than halfway to 35,000, we know that 34,186 is nearer 34,000. **About 34,000 visitors** saw the exhibit.

Another way to round to the nearest thousand is to focus on the digit in the hundreds place.

$$34,\textcircled{1}86$$

⌐hundreds place

⌐thousands place

If the digit in the hundreds place is 5 or more, we add 1 to the digit in the thousands place. If the digit in the hundreds place is 4 or less, we leave the thousands digit unchanged. In either case, all digits to the right of the thousands place become zeros. Here the digit in the hundreds place is 1, so 34,186 rounds down to 34,000.

Example 6

Round 5486 to the nearest

    a. thousand.   **b. hundred.**   **c. ten.**

    a. To round to the nearest thousand, we look at the hundreds place.

        5486 rounds to **5000.**

    b. To round to the nearest hundred, we look at the tens place.

        5486 rounds to **5500.**

    c. To round to the nearest ten, we look at the ones place.

        5486 rounds to **5490.**

Lesson Practice

    a. How many days are in a leap year?

    b. According to the calendar in Example 2, what is the date of the fourth Friday of the month?

    c. How many years were there from 1918 to 1943? Write an equation using the *later − earlier = difference* formula.

    d. A century is how many decades?

Round each number to the nearest thousand in **e–j.**

    e. 6746   **f.** 5280   **g.** 12,327

    h. 21,694   **i.** 9870   **j.** 27,462

    k. Round 6472 to the nearest thousand, to the nearest hundred, and to the nearest ten.

* 1. In Mr. Jensen's math class, 24 students are seated in 4 rows of desks.
(52) The same number of students are in each row. Write and solve a
division equation to find the number of students in each row.

* 2. An art teacher works with 42 different students each day. During the
(44) school year, each student will complete 9 art projects. Write and solve a
multiplication equation to find the total number of projects the students
will complete.

* 3. Write and solve a subtraction equation to find the number of years from
(54) 1921 to 1938.

* 4. Multiple Choice How many years is 5 decades?
(54)   **A** 5 years   **B** 50 years   **C** 500 years   **D** 5000 years

* 5. According to this calendar, what day of the week was
(54) December 25, 1957?

| DECEMBER 1957 |||||||
S	M	T	W	T	F	S
1	2	3	4	5	6	7
8	9	10	11	12	13	14
15	16	17	18	19	20	21
22	23	24	25	26	27	28
29	30	31				

* 6. Round 5236 to the nearest thousand. Round 6929 to the nearest
(54) thousand. Then add the rounded numbers.

7. One side of a rectangle is 10 miles long. Another side is 20 miles long.
(Inv. 2, 21)
   a. Draw the rectangle and write the lengths of the sides.

   b. What is the perimeter of the rectangle?

   c. What is the area of the rectangle?

* 8. a. What fraction of this circle is shaded?
(22, Inv. 5)
   b. What percent of this circle is shaded?

*9. **Represent** To what number is the arrow pointing? Write the number
(Inv. 1) two different ways.

*10. **Analyze** When T'Von emptied his bank, he found 17 pennies,
(35) 4 nickels, 5 dimes, and 2 quarters. What was the value of the coins in
his bank?

*11. 794,150
(51) + 9,863

12. $51,786
(51) + $36,357

13. 87.6
(17, 50) 4.0
31.7
5.5
1.1
+ 0.5

*14. $20.00
(52) − $18.47

*15. 41,315
(52) − 29,418

16. 46
(48) × 7

17. 54
(48) × 8

18. 39
(48) × 9

19. 40
(42) × 9

*20. 3.68 + 2.4 + 15.2
(50)

21. 4y = 32
(41)

*22. 43 ÷ 7
(53)

*23. 9)⎺6⎺4
(53)

*24. **Represent** One inch equals 2.54 cm. Use words to write 2.54 cm.
(Inv. 4)

*25. **Explain** The answer to 52 ÷ 9 is not a whole number. What whole
(52) number represents a reasonable estimate of the answer? Explain why
you chose that number.

26. a. Which line segment is the diameter of the circle?
(21, 45)

b. **Explain** Name two intersecting line segments.
Explain your answer.

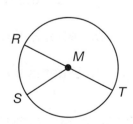

27. a. Is $136.80 closer to $136 or to $137?
(20)

b. Is 136.8 closer to 136 or to 137?

*28. **a.** What fraction of the large square is shaded?

<small>(Inv. 4, Inv. 5)</small>

    b. The shaded part of the large square represents what decimal number?

    c. What percent of the large square is shaded?

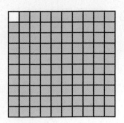

*29. **Generalize** Write a rule that describes the relationship of the data in the table.

<small>(32, 38)</small>

Number of $1 Bills	10	20	30	40	50
Number of $10 Bills	1	2	3	4	5

*30. Show all of the different ways these bills can be arranged in a row.

<small>(36)</small>

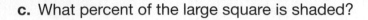

Early Finishers

Real-World Connection

Five friends played a video game. Aureli scored 7305 points, Brett scored 3595 points, Sarah scored 2039 points, Jamin scored 9861 points, and Danielle scored 1256 points.

    a. Who had the highest score?

    b. Use words to write the highest score.

    c. Round each score to the nearest thousand.

LESSON
55

• Prime and Composite Numbers

facts Power Up I

count aloud Count by halves from $\frac{1}{2}$ to 10 and back down to $\frac{1}{2}$.

mental math **Money:** Find the change back from a dollar for items with these prices:

    a. 26¢   **b.** 92¢   **c.** 31¢

    d. Time: How many years are in one decade?

    e. Money: Autumn paid $4 for the box of cereal and received 50¢ back in change. How much did the cereal cost?

    f. Measurement: Four meters is how many centimeters?

    g. Estimation: Choose the more reasonable estimate for the length of a banana: 8 inches or 8 feet.

    h. Calculation: 48 + 29 + 210

problem solving Choose an appropriate problem-solving strategy to solve this problem. Majeed was thinking of a two-digit number. He gave this clue: "You say the number when you count by threes from three, by fours from four, and by fives from five." What was Majeed's number?

New Concept

> **Math Language**
>
> A *multiple* is a product of a given number and a counting number.
>
> For example, the first four multiples of 3 are 3, 6, 9, and 12.

If we multiply 4 by the numbers 1, 2, 3, 4, 5, 6, ..., we get

$$4, 8, 12, 16, 20, 24, \ldots$$

Recall that these numbers are multiples of 4. The multiples of 4 are the numbers we say if we count by fours, starting from 4.

The following numbers are the multiples of 6:

6, 12, 18, 24, 30, 36, …

The multiples of any counting number are the products we get when we multiply the number by 1, 2, 3, 4, 5, 6, and so on.

Example 1

List the first four multiples of 7.

To find the first four multiples of 7, we multiply 7 by 1, then by 2, then by 3, and then by 4.

$$\begin{array}{cccc} 7 & 7 & 7 & 7 \\ \times\ 1 & \times\ 2 & \times\ 3 & \times\ 4 \\ \hline 7 & 14 & 21 & 28 \end{array}$$

The first four multiples of 7 are **7, 14, 21,** and **28.** The multiples of 7 are the numbers we say when we count by sevens.

Example 2

a. What is the fourth multiple of 6?

b. What is the third multiple of 8?

a. To find the fourth multiple of 6, we multiply 6 by 4. The fourth multiple of 6 is **24.**

b. To find the third multiple of 8, we multiply 8 by 3. The third multiple of 8 is **24.**

Example 3

Math Language
Since 12 is a multiple of 1, 2, 3, 4, 6, and 12, it is also **divisible** by 1, 2, 3, 4, 6, and 12.

Twelve is a multiple of which whole numbers?

A multiplication table can help us answer this question. We find 12 at each of these locations on a multiplication table:

$$1 \times 12 \qquad 12 \times 1$$
$$2 \times 6 \qquad 6 \times 2$$
$$3 \times 4 \qquad 4 \times 3$$

So 12 is a multiple of **1, 2, 3, 4, 6,** and **12.**

In Example 3, we found that 12 is a multiple of 1, 2, 3, 4, 6, and 12. Each of these numbers is a factor of 12. On a multiplication table, the factors are the numbers that may be multiplied to produce a multiple.

Multiplication Table

	factors
factors	multiples

Activity

Using Arrays to Find Factors

Materials needed:
- counters or tiles

We can find the factors of a number by forming arrays. The number of columns and rows in an array are factors of the number. For example, here we show three arrays for 12.

12 × 1   6 × 2   4 × 3

These arrays show us that 1, 2, 3, 4, 6, and 12 are factors of 12.

We can also use an area model to represent the factors of 12.

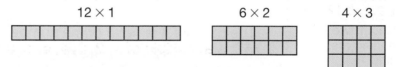

12 × 1   6 × 2   4 × 3

1. **Model** Use 24 counters or tiles to form four different arrays that show the factors of 24. List the factors you find.

2. **Represent** On grid paper, draw rectangles that outline 24 squares to show four different factor pairs for 24. Label the length and width of each rectangle.

Analyze Each rectangle drawn on the grid paper has an area of 24 square units. How do the perimeters of the four rectangles compare? What generalization can you make about the perimeters of different rectangles with the same area?

Example 4

List the four factors of 6.

Six is the multiple. We are asked to find the factors. These whole-number multiplications produce 6:

$$1 \times 6 \qquad 6 \times 1$$
$$2 \times 3 \qquad 3 \times 2$$

So the factors of 6 are **1, 2, 3,** and **6.**

Example 5

List the factors of 9.

These multiplications produce 9:

$$1 \times 9 \qquad 3 \times 3 \qquad 9 \times 1$$

So the factors of 9 are **1, 3,** and **9.**

Example 6

List the factors of 7.

We find 7 as a multiple on a multiplication table twice.

$$1 \times 7 \qquad 7 \times 1$$

So 7 has only two factors, **1** and **7.**

Math Language

A **prime number** is a counting number that has exactly two different factors, itself and 1. A counting number with more than two factors is a **composite number.**

In Example 6, we found that the number 7 has two factors: 7 and 1. Counting numbers that have exactly two different factors are **prime numbers.**

The number 1 is not a prime number because its only factor is 1. The numbers 2 and 3 are prime numbers because the only factors of 2 are 1 and 2, and the only factors of 3 are 1 and 3. The number 4 is not a prime number because 4 has three factors: 1, 2, and 4. A number with more than two factors is a **composite number.** The number 4 is a composite number.

Example 7

Which of these numbers is a prime number?

A 8 **B** 9 **C** 10 **D** 11

One way to determine that a number is prime is to decide if the number can be divided by a number other than 1 and itself without a remainder.

A Since 8 can be divided by 2 and by 4, it is composite and not prime.

B Since 9 can be divided by 3, it is composite and not prime.

C Since 10 can be divided by 2 and by 5, it is composite and not prime.

D Only 1 and 11 can divide 11, so **11** is a prime number.

Lesson Practice

a. List the first five multiples of 6.

b. List the third, fourth, and fifth multiples of 9.

c. What is the seventh multiple of 8?

d. What is the last digit of any multiple of 10?

e. What two digits appear as the last digit of the multiples of 5?

f. What five digits appear as the last digit of the multiples of 2?

g. Ten is a multiple of which whole numbers?

h. On grid paper, draw two ways to make a rectangle with an area of 8.

i. The rectangle below shows one possible way to make a rectangle with an area of 10.

Draw all the other possible arrangements.

j. List the factors of 5.

k. Write all the prime numbers less than 10.

l. True or False: If a counting number is greater than 1 and is not prime, then it is composite.

Formulate Write and solve an equation for problems **1–3.**

1. Raimi bought a toy for $1.85 and sold it for 75¢ more. For what price
(1, 43) did he sell the toy?

*2. Two thousand people entered the contest. Only seven will win prizes.
(25, 52) How many entrants will not win prizes?

*3. A recent census in Arkansas showed that 11,003 people live in Scott
(31, 52) County and 8484 people live in Newton County. How many more
people live in Scott County than in Newton County?

*4. Sixty percent of the students in the class were boys. Were there more
(Inv. 5) girls or more boys in the class?

5. Draw a rectangle that is 4 cm long and 3 cm wide.
(Inv.2,
Inv. 3)

   a. What is the perimeter of the rectangle?

   b. What is the area of the rectangle?

*6. **Analyze** Fidelia found the third multiple of 4. Then she subtracted two
(55) from this number. What was her answer?

*7. Two factors of 15 are 1 and 15 because 1 × 15 = 15. Find two more
(55) factors of 15.

8. Brenda arrived home from school 30 minutes before the
(27) time shown on the clock. What time did Brenda arrive home
from school?

*9. George Washington became the first U.S. president in 1789. The
(54) Declaration of Independence was written in 1776. How many years after
the Declaration of Independence did Washington become president?

10. What is the length of $\overline{ST}$?
(Inv. 2)

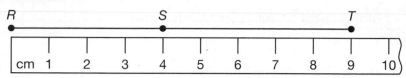

11. 4.00
(50) − 2.22

12. 70.5
(50) − 42.3

13. $45.87
(43) + $23.64

*14. $25.42
(43) − $ 7.25

*15. 64
(48) × 5

16. 70
(42) × 6

17. 89
(48) × 4

18. 63
(48) × 7

19. $\dfrac{63}{7}$
(47)

*20. $8\overline{)15}$
(53)

21. 4.68 + 12.2 + 3.75
(50)

*22. (**Model**) Draw dots and make groups to illustrate 15 ÷ 6.
(53)

23. (**Explain**) Describe the order of operations in this expression and find
(45) the number it equals.

$$\sqrt{64} \div (4 + 4)$$

*24. (**Connect**) Write this addition problem as a multiplication problem:
(27)

$$\$0.75 + \$0.75 + \$0.75 + \$0.75$$

*25. a. **Multiple Choice** Which of these numbers can be divided by
(55) 5 without leaving a remainder?

A 32 **B** 35 **C** 37 **D** 41

b. (**Explain**) How can you find the answer for part **a** just by
looking?

*26. (**Justify**) One gallon is equal to 128 fluid ounces. Garrett estimates
(40) that four gallons is about 500 fluid ounces. Is Garrett's estimate
reasonable? Explain why or why not.

27. a. Is $2.54 closer to $2 or to $3?
(20, Inv.4)

b. Is 2.54 closer to 2 or to 3?

28. a. What fraction of the large square is shaded?
(Inv. 4, Inv. 5)

b. The shaded part of the large square represents what decimal number?

c. What percent of the large square is shaded?

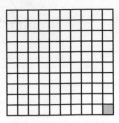

*29. Multiple Choice Which of these numbers is a composite number and *not* a prime number?
(55)

   A 2   **B** 3   **C** 4   **D** 5

30. How many different three-digit numbers can you write using the digits
(3) 8, 3, and 4? Each digit may be used only once in every number you write. Arrange the numbers in order from least to greatest.

Real-World Connection

The marching band at one school has 36 members. The members can march in any arrangement in which all the rows have the same number of people. Use counters or tiles to form arrays to show all the possible marching arrangements. List each way you find.

• Using Models and Pictures to Compare Fractions

Power Up

facts	Power Up I
count aloud	Count by fourths from $\frac{1}{4}$ to 5 and back down to $\frac{1}{4}$.
mental math	Subtract cents from dollars in **a–c**.

   a. Money: $1.00 − $0.42

   b. Money: $1.00 − $0.67

   c. Money: $2.00 − $0.25

   d. Number Sense: 370 − 125

   e. Money: The bottle of shampoo costs $3.45 and the conditioner costs $4.65. What is the total cost of the two items?

   f. Time: How many years is one century?

   g. Estimation: Estimate the sum of $7.87 and $2.14 by rounding each amount to the nearest dollar and then adding.

   h. Calculation: $\sqrt{36} + \sqrt{81} + 4 + 178$

problem solving	Choose an appropriate problem-solving strategy to solve this problem. Emiko paid a dollar for an item that cost 63 cents. If the cashier gives her back five coins, what coins should they be?

 Activity

Comparing Fractions

Model One way to compare fractions is to use manipulatives. Use your fraction manipulatives to model these exercises.

1. Show that two fourths equals one half.

2. How many eighths equals one half?

3. How many tenths equals one half?

4. How many fourths equals two eighths?

5. How many halves equals five tenths?

6. How many fourths equals six eighths?

Model Compare. Write $>$, $<$, or $=$. Use your fraction manipulatives to model each exercise.

7. $\frac{3}{4} \bigcirc \frac{6}{8}$

8. $\frac{1}{4} \bigcirc \frac{3}{10}$

9. $\frac{1}{4} \bigcirc \frac{1}{5}$

10. $\frac{2}{3} \bigcirc \frac{6}{10}$

11. Use your fraction manipulatives to model three fifths, four tenths, one half, two eighths, and three fourths.

   a. Write the numbers in order from **greatest to least** using fractions.

   b. Write the numbers in order from **least to greatest** using decimals.

   c. Write the following fractions in order from **greatest to least** using decimals: $\frac{1}{2}, \frac{2}{8}, \frac{3}{5}$.

Another way to compare fractions is to draw pictures of the fractions and then compare the pictures. To illustrate, we will draw pictures to compare $\frac{1}{2}$ and $\frac{1}{3}$. We begin by drawing two circles of the same size. Then we shade $\frac{1}{2}$ of one circle and $\frac{1}{3}$ of the other circle.

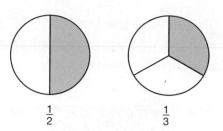

$$\frac{1}{2} \qquad \frac{1}{3}$$

We see that $\frac{1}{2}$ of a circle is larger than $\frac{1}{3}$ of the same-sized circle. So $\frac{1}{2}$ is greater than $\frac{1}{3}$.

$$\frac{1}{2} > \frac{1}{3}$$

When we draw figures to compare fractions, the figures should be **congruent**. Congruent figures have the same shape and size.

Example

Compare: $\frac{1}{4} \bigcirc \frac{1}{3}$. **Draw and shade two rectangles to show the comparison.**

We draw two congruent rectangles. We shade $\frac{1}{4}$ of one rectangle and $\frac{1}{3}$ of the other. We see that $\frac{1}{4}$ is slightly less than $\frac{1}{3}$.

$$\frac{1}{4} < \frac{1}{3}$$

Lesson Practice

Represent Compare these fractions. Draw and shade a pair of congruent figures to illustrate each comparison.

a. $\frac{1}{2} \bigcirc \frac{2}{3}$ **b.** $\frac{1}{2} \bigcirc \frac{1}{4}$

Arrange the numbers in problems **c** and **d** in order from greatest to least. You may use your fraction manipulatives.

c. 0.5, 0.2, 0.25 **d.** 0.75, 0.9, 0.7

Written Practice *Distributed and Integrated*

*1. Drew has fifty-six rolls. Seven rolls will fit on one tray. How many
(52) trays does he need to carry all of the rolls? Write an equation to solve the problem.

2. One gallon is about 3.78 L. About how many liters is two gallons? Use
(40) words to write the answer.

3. **Estimate** To estimate the sum of $6.87 and $5.92, Socorro rounded
(20) each number to the nearest dollar before adding. Write the numbers
Socorro added and their sum.

*4. **Connect** Write four multiplication/division facts using the numbers 3,
(47) 8, and 24.

*5. **List** What are the seven months of the year that have 31 days?
(54)

*6. **Analyze** Find the eighth multiple of six. Then add one. What is the
(Inv. 3) square root of the answer?

*7. **Represent** Compare these fractions. Draw and shade two congruent
(56) rectangles to show the comparison.

$$\frac{1}{4} \bigcirc \frac{1}{6}$$

*8. **Estimate** In the 2004 presidential election, 4651 residents of the state
(42, 54) of Rhode Island voted for candidate Ralph Nader. Round that number
of residents to the nearest thousand, to the nearest hundred, and to the
nearest ten.

9. a. What is the perimeter of the rectangle shown at
(Inv. 2, right?
Inv. 3)

b. What is its area?

7 mi

4 mi

*10. $10.00   ***11.**   36,024   **12.**   43,675
(43, 52) − $ 5.46   (52)   − 15,539   (51)   + 52,059

13.   73   **14.**   46   **15.**   84   **16.**   40
(48)   × 9   (48)   × 7   (48)   × 6   (42)   × 5

*17. 7)48   **18.** $\frac{63}{7}$
(53)   (46, 47)

*19. 3.75 + 2.5 + 0.4   ***20.** 42.25 − 7.5
(50)   (50)

*21. a. Multiple Choice Which of these numbers is a multiple of 10?
(55)

   A 35   **B** 40   **C** 45   **D** 101

   b. How can you find the answer for part **a** just by looking?

22. a. A dime is what fraction of a dollar?
(36,
Inv. 5)
   b. A dime is what percent of a dollar?

23. (Represent) Washington School cost about $12,350,000 to build. Use
(34)   words to write that amount of money.

*24. Two factors of 16 are 1 and 16 because $1 \times 16 = 16$. Find three more
(55)   factors of 16.

*25. (Verify) Is 16 a prime number? Why or why not?
(55)

*26. (Conclude) Refer to figure $ABCD$ to answer parts **a** and **b**.
(23, 45)

   a. Which segment appears to be parallel to $\overline{AB}$?

   b. Angle B is what type of angle?

*27. Multiple Choice Which of these numbers is a factor of 12?
(55)
   A 0   **B** 6   **C** 8   **D** 24

*28. Multiple Choice Which of these numbers is a multiple of 12?
(55)
   A 0   **B** 6   **C** 8   **D** 24

*29. a. A penny is what fraction of a dollar?
(36,
Inv. 5)
   b. Write the value of a penny as a decimal part of a dollar.

   c. A penny is what percent of a dollar?

*30. Write these numbers in order from greatest to least:
(Inv. 4)

$$\frac{3}{4} \qquad 0.09 \qquad \frac{2}{5} \qquad 0.5 \qquad \frac{1}{3}$$

• Rate Word Problems

facts   Power Up J

count aloud   Count by threes from 60 to 90.

**mental
math**
    a. Money: $1.00 − $0.85

    b. Money: $2.00 − $0.63

    c. Money: $5.00 − $1.25

    d. Number Sense: 400 − 30

    e. Measurement: What is the
    perimeter of a garden with the
    dimensions shown?

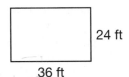

    f. Time: How many years is two
    centuries plus four decades?

    g. Estimation: Choose the more reasonable estimate for the
    distance between two cities: 120 miles or 120 feet.

    h. Calculation: 349 − 199 + 50

**problem
solving**
Alegria solved an addition problem and
then erased a digit from each number
in the problem. She gave it to Jeff as a
problem-solving exercise. Copy Alegria's
problem on your paper, and find the missing digits for Jeff.

$$\begin{array}{r} 5\_3 \\ +\ 28\_ \\ \hline \_50 \end{array}$$

Focus Strategy: Work Backwards

(**Understand**) We are shown an addition problem with some
digits missing. We are asked to find the missing digits.

(**Plan**) We will use our knowledge of addition facts to fill in the
missing digits.

Solve We can begin in the ones column just as if we were adding two numbers. We think, "3 plus what number gives us a number that ends in 0?" Since $3 + 7 = 10$, we write a 7 in the bottom addend. We must remember to regroup a 1 in the tens column. Next we think, "1 plus what number plus 8 gives a number that ends in 5?" Since $1 + 6 + 8 = 15$, we write a 6 in the top addend. Next we think, "1 (regrouped from the tens) plus 5 plus 2 equals what number?" Since $1 + 5 + 2 = 8$, we write an 8 in the sum.

Check We know our answer is reasonable because the sum of 563 and 287 is 850, which is the number we have below the line. We *worked backwards* and used our knowledge of addition facts to find the missing digits in the tens and ones columns.

$$\begin{array}{r} 56\underline{3} \\ +\ 287 \\ \hline \underline{850} \end{array}$$

New Concept

A **rate** shows a relationship between two different measurements. Here we relate the measurements "miles" and "hours":

The car went 30 miles per hour.

This statement tells us that the car's rate is 30 miles each hour. This means that for every hour the car travels at this rate, it travels 30 miles. We can make a table that shows how many miles the car travels in 1, 2, 3, and 4 hours.

Math Language

The phrase *per hour* means "in each hour."

Visit www. SaxonMath.com/ Int4Activities for a calculator activity.

Word problems about rates have the same plot as "equal groups" problems. A plan that can help us solve word problems is to make a table. We do this by writing the numbers we know into a table. Then we can find the pattern and extend it.

Distance Traveled (at 30 miles per hour)

Hours	Miles
1	30
2	60
3	90
4	120

Example 1

Liam drove the car 30 miles per hour for 4 hours. How far did Liam drive?

This is a rate problem. We do not see the words *in each* in this rate problem, but there are words that mean *in each*. The words *miles per hour* in this problem mean "miles *in each* hour."

Reading Math

We translate a rate problem using a multiplication formula:

Miles **in each** hour: 30

Number **of** hours: 4

Total: 120 miles

Formula	Problem
Number **in each** time group	30 miles per hour
× Number **of** time groups	× 4 hours
Total	120 miles

We can write another equation to solve the problem.

Formula:

Number **of** time groups × Number **in each** time group = Total

Problem:

4 hours × 30 miles per hour = 120 miles

Liam drove **120 miles.**

Example 2

Nuru earns 3 dollars a week for helping around the house. Make a table for this rate that shows how much Nuru would earn in 1, 2, and 3 weeks. Then use a formula to find how much money he would earn in 7 weeks.

Thinking Skill

Verify

What problem-solving strategies did we use to solve this problem?

The phrase *3 dollars a week* means "3 dollars each week." We make a table for this rate with "dollars" and "weeks" at the top of the two columns.

We could extend this table to 7 weeks. Instead we analyze the pattern and see that we are multiplying 3 times the number of weeks to find the dollars.

Money Earned (at $3 each week)

Weeks	Dollars
1	3
2	6
3	9

Now we know we can use a multiplication formula to find how much Nuru earns in 7 weeks.

Formula:

Number **of** groups × Number **in each** group = Total

Problem:

7 weeks × 3 dollars per week = 21 dollars

Nuru earns **21 dollars** for 7 weeks of helping around the house.

Lesson Practice

a. **Formulate** Angela drove 55 miles in one hour. At that rate, how far can she drive in 6 hours? Write an equation to solve the problem.

b. **Analyze** Barak swims 20 laps every day. How many laps will he swim in one week? Make a table to solve the problem.

*1. **Formulate** Marybeth could jump 42 times each minute. At that rate,
(57) how many times could she jump in 8 minutes? Write an equation to
solve the problem.

*2. **Analyze** Rodolfo could run 7 miles in 1 hour. At that rate, how many
(57) miles could Rodolfo run in 3 hours? Make a table to solve.

*3. **Connect** Write four multiplication/division facts using 8, 9, and 72.
(47)

4. What is the sum of $\sqrt{36}$ and $\sqrt{64}$?
(Inv. 3)

*5. Compare: $\frac{1}{3}$ ◯ 50%
(Inv. 5,
56)

*6. a. **Estimate** Round 5280 to the nearest thousand.
(42, 54)

   b. Round 5280 to the nearest hundred.

*7. This array of 12 stars shows that 4 and 3 are factors of 12.
(55) Draw a different array of 12 stars that shows two other
factors of 12.

*8. **Analyze** Find the fourth multiple of 6. Then find the third multiple of 8.
(55) Compare these two multiples.

*9. Juan Ponce de León explored the coast of Florida in 1513. In 1800,
(41, 54) the federal government of the United States moved to Washington,
DC. Write a *later − earlier = difference* equation and solve it to find the
number of years that elapsed from 1513 to 1800.

10. A square has one side that is 7 inches long.
(Inv. 2,
Inv. 3)

   a. What is the perimeter of the square?

   b. What is the area of the square?

* 11. 70,003
(52) − 36,418

12. n
(24, 43) − 4.32
_____
2.57

13. $861.34
(43, 51) + $764.87

14. 93
(48) × 5

15. 84
(48) × 6

16. 77
(48) × 7

17. 80
(42) × 8

18. $\dfrac{56}{8}$
(47)

19. $7\overline{)65}$
(53)

* 20. $45 \div 6$
(53)

21. $7n = 42$
(41)

22. $1.75 + 17.5$
(50)

23. **a.** Which segment in this figure is a diameter?
(23, 45)

    b. **Classify** Segments MW and MX form an angle. What type of angle is it? Explain.

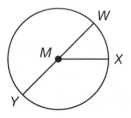

* 24. **Represent** Compare these fractions. Draw and shade two congruent
(56) rectangles to show the comparison.

$$\frac{2}{3} \bigcirc \frac{3}{4}$$

* 25. **Represent** Point X represents what mixed number and what decimal
(37) number on this number line?

* 26. One inch is 2.54 centimeters, so two inches is $2.54 + 2.54$ centimeters.
(Inv. 2) A segment that is 3 inches long is how many centimeters long?

* 27. Write this addition problem as a multiplication problem:
(27)

$$2.54 + 2.54 + 2.54$$

*28. **a.** Three pennies are what fraction of a dollar?
_(36, Inv. 5)

b. Write the value of three pennies as a decimal part of a dollar.

c. Three pennies are what percent of a dollar?

*29. **Multiple Choice** Which of these numbers is a prime number?
₍₅₅₎

    A 6   **B** 7   **C** 8   **D** 9

*30. What is the sum of these lengths? Write three answers using different
_(Inv. 2) units.

$$1 \text{ yard} + 2 \text{ feet} + 12 \text{ inches}$$

Real-World Connection

Each day Jamaal delivers 30 newspapers in 1 hr 30 min. At this rate, how many newspapers would he deliver each hour? Explain your answer.

• Multiplying Three-Digit Numbers

Power Up

facts	Power Up J
count aloud	Count by fours from 60 to 100.
mental math	**a. Money:** $5.00 − $2.25
	b. Money: $5.00 − $1.63
	c. Money: $5.00 − $3.35
	d. Number Sense: 35 + 49 + 110
	e. Measurement: Compare: 1 mile ◯ 5000 feet
	f. Time: Tupac arrived at the bus stop at 4:45 p.m. The next bus is scheduled to arrive at 4:54 p.m. How long can Tupac expect to wait for the bus?
	g. Estimation: Jazzlyn has $20. Does she have enough money to purchase three tickets that each cost $6.99?
	h. Calculation: 25 × 2 + 170 − 100

problem solving	Choose an appropriate problem-solving strategy to solve this problem. Calida baked a cake that measured 12 inches by 9 inches. If the cake is cut into square pieces that are 3 inches on each side, how many pieces will be cut?

9 in.

12 in.

New Concept

Thinking Skill

Generalize

Would we use the same multiplication algorithm if we were multiplying a number with ten digits? Why or why not?

When we multiply a three-digit number using pencil and paper, we multiply the ones digit first. Then we multiply the tens digit. Then we multiply the hundreds digit.

Multiply the ones digit.		Multiply the tens digit.		Multiply the hundreds digit.
123		123		123
× 3	→	× 3	→	× 3
9		69		369

In the problem below; we get 18 when we multiply the ones digit. We write the 8 in the ones column and carry the 1 above the tens column. Then we multiply the tens digit.

Multiply the ones digit.		Multiply the tens digit.		Multiply the hundreds digit.
1		11		11
456		456		456
× 3	→	× 3	→	× 3
8		68		1368

Three times five is 15, plus one is 16. We write the 6 below the bar and carry the 1 above the hundreds column. Then we multiply the hundreds. Three times four is 12, plus one is 13. The product is 1368.

Example 1

There are 365 days in a common year. Every fourth year is a leap year with 366 days. How many days is four years in a row?

We can multiply 4 times 365 and then add one day to the total for leap year. First we multiply the ones digit. Then we multiply the tens digit and then the hundreds digit. We write the first digit of any two-digit answer above the next column.

$$
\begin{array}{r}
22 \\
365 \\
\times \quad 4 \\
\hline
1460
\end{array}
\qquad 1460 + 1 = 1461
$$

In four years in a row, there are **1461 days.**

Example 2

Tickets to the school play were $3.75 each. How much money would 3 tickets cost?

Thinking Skill

Generalize

How is multiplying dollars and cents the same as multiplying whole numbers? How is it different?

We first multiply the pennies. Three times five pennies is 15 pennies, which equals one dime and five pennies. We write the 5 below the bar and the 1 above the dimes.

$$\begin{array}{r} 1 \\ \$3.75 \\ \times \quad 3 \\ \hline 5 \end{array}$$

Next we multiply the dimes. Three times seven dimes is 21 dimes. We add the one dime we carried to get a total of 22 dimes. Since 22 dimes equals two dollars and two dimes, we write a 2 below the bar and a 2 above the dollars.

$$\begin{array}{r} 2\ 1 \\ \$3.75 \\ \times \quad 3 \\ \hline 25 \end{array}$$

Finally, we multiply the dollars. Three times three dollars is nine dollars. We add the two dollars we carried to get a total of 11 dollars. Three tickets would cost **$11.25.**

$$\begin{array}{r} 2\ 1 \\ \$3.75 \\ \times \quad 3 \\ \hline \$11.25 \end{array}$$

Example 3

When the gate of a stadium was opened for a concert, people passed through the gate at a rate of 100 people per minute. At that rate, how many people passed through the gate in 10 minutes?

To find the answer, we can continue a table or we can multiply 100 by 10.

Minute	1	2	3	4	5	6	7	8	9	10
People	100	200	300	400						

$$10 \times 100 = 1000$$

Using either method, we find that **1000 people** could pass through the stadium gate in 10 minutes.

Generalize How could you write a rule for this pattern using a multiplication equation? How could you write a rule using a division equation?

Example 4

A landscape architect is designing a border of plants and trees for a parking area that has a perimeter of 256 yards. What is the approximate perimeter of the parking area in feet?

We will use mental math to estimate the number of feet. Each yard is 3 feet, so we multiply the number of yards by 3. A compatible number close to 256 that we can multiply mentally is 250.

$$250 \times 3 = 750$$

Since 256 yd is a little more than 250 yd, the actual perimeter is a little more than **750 ft.**

Estimate The parking area is shaped like a square. Estimate the length of each side of the parking area in feet. Explain your reasoning.

Lesson Practice Multiply:

a. 234
    × 3

b. $340
    × 4

c. $4.25
    × 5

d. Explain the steps of multiplying 5 by $4.25, using the words *dollars, dimes,* and *pennies* (as in Example 2).

e. At $2.47 per gallon, what is the approximate cost of four gallons of milk?

Written Practice *Distributed and Integrated*

*1. Chazz pays $7.50 every week for a bus pass. How much does she pay
(57) for 4 weeks of bus passes? Write an equation to solve the problem.

*2. It takes 4 apples to make 1 pint of applesauce. How many apples
(49) does it take to make 5 pints? Make a table to solve the problem.

3. Calvin has to get up at 6 a.m. By what time should he go to bed in
(27) order to get 8 hours of sleep?

*4. **Explain** The store sells paint in quart cans, gallon cans, and
(40) 5-gallon cans. The price per quart is lower with larger cans. Hosni needs 8 quarts of paint. What containers of paint should he buy? Explain.

*5. **Represent** Write 8402 in expanded form. Then use words to write
(16, 33) the number.

*6. **Analyze** Find the fourth multiple of 7. Then find the sixth multiple of 6.
(Inv. 3, 55) Add these multiples. What is the square root of the answer?

*7. According to this calendar, what is the date of the second
(54) Tuesday in September 2042?

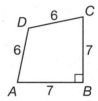

SEPTEMBER 2042

S	M	T	W	T	F	S
		1	2	3	4	5	6
7	8	9	10	11	12	13
14	15	16	17	18	19	20
21	22	23	24	25	26	27
28	29	30				

8. If $5 + n = 23$, then what number does $n - 5$ equal?
(24)

*9. a. What is the perimeter of this figure? Measurements
(Inv. 2, 23) are in feet.

    b. **Classify** Describe each angle as acute, obtuse, or
    right.

*10. **Represent** Compare these fractions. Draw and shade two congruent
(26, 56) circles to show the comparison.

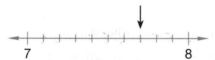

$$\frac{1}{2} \bigcirc \frac{2}{4}$$

11. To what mixed number is the arrow pointing?
(37)

*12. Which segment appears parallel to $\overline{AB}$?
(23)

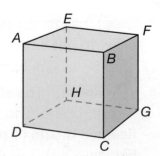

13. $0.47 + 3.62 + 0.85 + 4.54$
(50)

14. $3 + $4.39 + $12.62
(43)

15. $36.47 - (3.5 + 12.6)$
(45, 50)

*16. $20.00 - (29¢ + $7)$
(45, 52)

*17. $41,059 - 36,275$
(52)

*18. $\begin{array}{r} 768 \\ \times \quad 3 \\ \hline \end{array}$
(58)

*19. $\begin{array}{r} \$2.80 \\ \times \quad 4 \\ \hline \end{array}$
(58)

20. $\begin{array}{r} 436 \\ - \quad z \\ \hline 252 \end{array}$
(24, 30)

*21. $5\overline{)36}$
(53)

22. $7\overline{)45}$
(53)

23. $4\overline{)35}$
(53)

24. ✏️ **Explain** How can you find the product of 4×100 using only
(42, 55) mental math?

*25. **Analyze** Two factors of 20 are 1 and 20 because $1 \times 20 = 20$.
(55) Find four more factors of 20.

*26. According to the census, the population of South Fork was 6781.
(42, 54)

    a. Round 6781 to the nearest thousand.

    b. Round 6781 to the nearest hundred.

*27. **Multiple Choice** If $4n = 24$, then which of these equations is *not*
(47) true?

    A $\dfrac{24}{4} = n$ **B** $\dfrac{24}{n} = 4$

    C $2n = 12$ **D** $4n = 6$

28. **a.** Seven pennies are what fraction of a dollar?
(36,
Inv. 5)

    b. Write the value of seven pennies as a decimal part of a dollar.

    c. Seven pennies are what percent of a dollar?

*29. **Multiple Choice** Which of these even numbers is a prime number?
(55)

    A 2   **B** 4   **C** 6   **D** 8

*30. **Estimate** On a road trip across the country, Kwan drove 387 miles
(58) the first day and 409 miles the second day. If he drives about the same
distance each day, approximately how many miles will Kwan drive in
5 days?

• Estimating Arithmetic Answers

facts   Power Up J

count aloud   Count down by hundreds from 2000 to 100.

mental math
a. **Money:** $5.00 − $3.95

b. **Money:** $5.00 − $1.39

c. **Money:** $10.00 − $8.75

d. **Number Sense:** 46 + 320 + 200

e. **Measurement:** Find the length of the paper clip shown below.

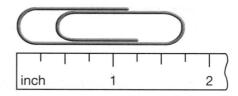

f. **Percent:** 50% of 50

g. **Estimation:** Carter has $8.56. Cadric has $1.61. Round each amount to the nearest 25 cents and then add to estimate the total amount the boys have.

h. **Calculation:** $\sqrt{36}$ + 75 + 319 + 223

problem solving
Choose an appropriate problem-solving strategy to solve this problem. Can you find three ways to make a dollar with eight coins?

We can estimate arithmetic answers by rounding the numbers before doing the arithmetic. Estimating does not give us the exact answer, but it can give us an answer that is close to the exact answer. For some problems, an estimate is all that is necessary to solve the problem. When an exact answer is needed, estimating is a way to decide whether our exact answer is *reasonable.* Estimating is useful for many purposes, such as mentally adding price totals when shopping.

Example 1

Estimate the sum of 396 and 512.

To estimate, we first round the number to the nearest hundred. We round 396 to 400 and 512 to 500. Then we find the estimated sum by adding 400 and 500.

$$\begin{array}{r} 400 \\ + 500 \\ \hline 900 \end{array}$$

The estimated sum of 396 and 512 is **900.** The exact sum of 396 and 512 is 908. The estimated answer is not equal to the exact answer, but it is close.

Thinking Skill

Discuss

Which place is used to round a 3-digit number to the nearest hundred?

Example 2

Estimate the product of 72 and 5.

We round the two-digit number, but we generally do not round a one-digit number when estimating. The estimated product of 72 and 5 is **350.**

$$\begin{array}{r} 70 \\ \times\ 5 \\ \hline 350 \end{array}$$

The exact product of 72 and 5 is 360. The estimated product is a little less than the exact answer, 360, because 72 was rounded down to 70 for the estimate.

Thinking Skill

Connect

Which place is used to round a 2-digit number to the nearest ten?

Example 3

To estimate 7 × 365, Towanda multiplied 7 by 400. Was Towanda's estimate more than, equal to, or less than the actual product of 7 and 365?

Towanda's estimate was **more than the actual product** of 7 and 365 because she rounded 365 up to 400 before multiplying.

Example 4

Estimate the answer to 43 ÷ 8.

To estimate division answers, we want to use numbers that divide easily. So we change the problem slightly. We keep the number we are dividing by, which is 8, and we change the number that is being divided, which is 43, to a compatible number. We change 43 to a nearby number that can be divided easily by 8, such as 40 or 48. Using 40, we find that the estimated answer is **5.** Using 48, we find that the estimated answer is **6.** Since 43 is between 40 and 48, the actual answer is more than 5 but less than 6—that is, the exact answer is 5 plus a remainder.

Example 5

Nicola bought a box of cereal for $5.89, a gallon of milk for $3.80, and a half gallon of juice for $2.20. Estimate Nicola's grocery bill.

We round the prices of each item to the nearest dollar.

The cereal cost $5.89, which is closer to $6 than to $5.

The milk cost $3.80, which is closer to $4 than to $3.

The juice cost $2.20, which is closer to $2 than to $3.

Thinking Skill

Verify

How do we round $3.80 to the nearest dollar? Explain your thinking.

Item	Price	Rounded to the Nearest Dollar
Cereal	$5.89	$6
Milk	$3.80	$4
Juice	$2.20	$2

To estimate the total, we add the rounded numbers.

$$\$6 + \$4 + \$2 = \$12$$

Nicola's estimated grocery bill was **about $12.**

Evaluate Suppose that Nicola wanted to be sure he had enough money to purchase all of the items *before* he reached the checkout line. How should he round the prices? Explain your reasoning.

Lesson Practice

Estimate the answer to each arithmetic problem. Then find the exact answer.

a. 59 + 68 + 81   **b.** 607 + 891

c. 585 − 294   **d.** 82 − 39

e. 59 × 6   **f.** 397 × 4

g. 42 ÷ 5   **h.** 29 ÷ 7

i. **Explain** Dixie estimated the product of 5 and 5280 by multiplying 5 by 5000. Was Dixie's estimate more than, equal to, or less than the actual product? Why?

j. Mariano would like to purchase a notebook computer, a wireless mouse, and an accessory carrying bag. The cost of each item is shown in the table.

Item	Cost
Notebook computer	$845
Wireless mouse	$27.50
Accessory bag	$39.95

What is a reasonable estimate of the total cost? Explain your thinking.

Written Practice   *Distributed and Integrated*

*1. **Analyze** A comfortable walking pace is about 3 miles per hour. How
(57) far would a person walk in 4 hours at a pace of 3 miles per hour? Make a table to solve the problem.

*2. There were forty-eight pears in all. Six pears were in each box. How
(52) many boxes were there? Write an equation to solve the problem.

3. One mile is about 1.61 km.
(Inv. 2,
Inv. 4)
    a. Use words to write 1.61 km.

    b. Compare: 1 mi $\bigcirc$ 1 km

*4. **Estimate** To estimate the product of 5 and 193, round 193 to the
(59) nearest hundred before multiplying.

5. Compare: 50% of 16 $\bigcirc$ $\sqrt{16}$
(Inv. 3,
Inv. 5)

*6. **Analyze** Subtract the third multiple of four from the second multiple
(55) of six. What is the difference?

*7. In 1587, Virginia Dare was the first infant born to English parents in
(54) North America. Write a *later − earlier = difference* equation and solve it
to find the number of years that have elapsed from 1587 to the year of
your birth.

*8. a. (**Classify**) Which angle in this figure appears to be a
(23, 45) right angle?

   b. Which segment in this figure does not appear to be
   perpendicular to $\overline{AB}$?

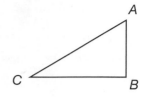

*9. Compare these fractions. Draw and shade two congruent rectangles to
(56) show the comparison.

$$\frac{2}{5} \bigcirc \frac{1}{4}$$

*10. Safara could pack 40 packages in 1 hour. At that rate, how many
(57) packages could she pack in 5 hours?

*11. (**Represent**) Use digits to write fifteen million, two hundred ten thousand.
(34)

12. (**Represent**) A town was on a rectangular plot of land 3 miles long and
(Inv. 2, 21) 2 miles wide. Draw the rectangle and show the length of each side.

   a. What is the perimeter of the rectangle?

   b. What is the area?

13. $37.75
(43, 51) + $45.95

14.   43,793
(51)   + 76,860

15.   48.0
(50)   9.7
            12.6
            5.3
         + 236.2

*16. $50.00
(52)   − $42.87

*17.   43,793
(52)   − 26,860

*18. 483 × 4
(58)

*19. 360 × 4
(58)

*20. 207 × 8
(58)

21. 8)‾43‾
(53)

22. 5)‾43‾
(53)

23. 7)‾43‾
(53)

24. a. The thermometer at right shows the temperature at 3 p.m.
(18)   What was the temperature at 3 p.m.?

b. From 3 p.m. to 6 p.m., the temperature rose 4 degrees.
What was the temperature at 6 p.m.?

25. (Represent) Use a ruler to draw a line segment 4 in. long. Then draw a
(Inv. 2, 23) parallel segment 10 cm long.

* 26. Each engine oil change in Francisco's car requires $3\frac{1}{2}$ quarts of new oil.
(40, 43) That number of quarts is the same as what number of pints?

* 27. (Explain) On a playground, a rectangular basketball court measures
(Inv. 2) 58.5 feet long by 42.5 feet wide. What is a reasonable estimate of the
perimeter of the court? Explain your thinking.

* 28. Write each decimal number illustrated, and then write the sum and the
(Inv. 4, Inv. 5) difference of the numbers.

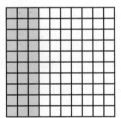   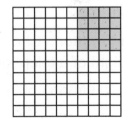

* 29. a. Multiple Choice Which of these odd numbers is a composite
(55)   number and *not* a prime number?

   A 5 **B** 7 **C** 9 **D** 11

b. (Verify) Explain your answer in part **a.**

30. (Estimate) J'Neane would like to purchase a pair of in-line skates
(59) and accessories, including a helmet, knee pads, elbow pads, and wrist
guards. The skates cost $59.95, and the total cost of the accessories
is $44.50. What is a reasonable estimate of how much more the skates
cost than the accessories? Explain your thinking.

LESSON
60

• Rate Problems with a Given Total

facts   Power Up J

count aloud   Count by sevens from 7 to 70.

mental math

a. **Money:** $10.00 − $3.24

b. **Money:** Jade purchased a book that cost $7.25. She paid with a $10 bill. How much change should she receive?

c. **Money:** Lilah had $10.00. She spent $8.67. How much money does she have left?

d. **Fractional Parts:** How many inches is $\frac{1}{2}$ of a foot?

e. **Powers/Roots:** Compare: $\sqrt{81}$ ◯ 200 − 190

f. **Time:** How many years is 5 centuries?

g. **Estimation:** Choose the more reasonable estimate for the height of a telephone pole: 30 feet or 30 inches.

h. **Calculation:** 50 × 2 + 26 + 49

problem solving   Choose an appropriate problem-solving strategy to solve this problem. The question below is written in a code where 1 is A, 2 is B, 3 is C, and so on. After you decode the question, write the answer using the same code.

23-8-1-20   4-1-25   9-19   20-8-9-19?

Rate problems involving time consist of three quantities: a rate, an amount of time, and a total. If we know two of the quantities in a rate problem, we can find the third. We have practiced problems in which we were given the rate and the amount of time. We multiplied to find the total. In this lesson we will practice problems in which we are given the total. We will divide to find either the rate or the amount of time.

Example 1

Zariali can read 2 pages in 1 minute. How long will it take him to read 18 pages?

This is a rate problem. A rate problem is an "equal groups" problem.

We are told that Zariali can read 2 pages in 1 minute. This means the rate is 2 pages each minute. The total number of pages is 18. We are asked for the amount of time.

Formula	Problem
Number **in each** time group	2 pages each minute
$\times$ Number **of** time groups	$\times$ n minutes
Total	18 pages

Now we find the missing number. **To find the first or second number in an "equal groups" pattern, we divide.**

$$2)\overline{18} \quad \frac{9}{}$$

It will take Zariali **9 minutes** to read 18 pages.

Reading Math

We translate a rate problem using a multiplication formula:

Pages **in each** minute: 2
Number **of** minutes: 9
Total: 18 pages

Example 2

Yolanda rode her bike 24 miles in 3 hours. Yolanda's average riding rate was how many miles per hour?

We are given the total distance Yolanda rode (24 miles) and the amount of time it took her (3 hours). We are asked for the average number of miles Yolanda rode in each hour.

Formula	Problem
Number **in each** time group	m miles each hour
$\times$ Number **of** time groups	$\times$ 3 hours
Total	24 miles

To find the missing factor, we divide.

$$24 \div 3 = 8$$

Rebecca's average riding rate was **8 miles per hour.** Rebecca actually may have ridden more than 8 miles during one hour and less than 8 miles during another hour, but her *average* rate was 8 miles per hour.

Connect Explain how to solve the equation $3m = 24$.

Lesson Practice

Formulate Write and solve an equation for each problem.

a. Javier can sharpen 5 pencils in a minute. How long will it take Javier to sharpen 40 pencils?

b. The troop hiked 12 miles in 4 hours. The troop's average rate was how many miles per hour?

c. Alexis was paid $48 for 6 hours of work. How much money was Alexis paid for each hour of work?

Written Practice

Distributed and Integrated

Formulate Write and solve equations for problems **1** and **2**.

* 1. There were two hundred fourteen parrots, seven hundred fifty-two
(1, 33, 51) crows, and two thousand, forty-two blue jays. How many birds were there in all?

* 2. K'Shella used one bag of soil to pot 8 plants. How many bags of soil
(52) would she need to pot 2 dozen plants?

* 3. Yachi could paint 12 signs in 1 hour. At that rate, how many signs could
(57) he paint in 3 hours? Make a table to solve this problem.

4. Fifty percent of an hour is how many minutes?
(Inv. 5)

* 5. **Estimate** Mount St. Helens is a volcano in Washington State. After
(51) erupting in May 1980, the peak of the volcano was 8363 feet above sea level. During the eruption, the volcano lost 1314 feet of its height. What is a reasonable estimate of the height of the volcano before its eruption? Explain your thinking.

*6. Multiple Choice Which of these numbers is *not* a multiple of 2?
(55)

    A 23   **B** 24   **C** 32   **D** 46

7. Write the time "a quarter to seven in the morning" in digital form.
(19)

8. Solve for *n:* $3n = 3 \times 5$
(41)

*9. The product of 6 and 7 is how much greater than the sum of 6
(31) and 7?

10. What is the length of segment *BC?*
(Inv. 2)

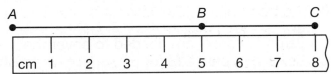

11. Compare: $(32 \div 8) \div 2 \bigcirc 32 \div (8 \div 2)$
(45)

12. $6.49 + $12 + $7.59 + 8¢
(43)

13. $6.5 + 4.75 + 11.3$ **14.** $12.56 - 4.3$
(50)   (50)

*15.   350   ***16.**   204   ***17.**   463
(58) $\times$ 5   (58) $\times$ 7   (58) $\times$ 6

18. $4\overline{)37}$ **19.** $6\overline{)39}$ **20.** $3\overline{)28}$
(53)   (53)   (53)

21. a. A nickel is what fraction of a dollar?
(36, Inv. 5)

    b. A nickel is what percent of a dollar?

*22. Perfect squares have an odd number of factors. The numbers 9 and 25
(Inv. 3, 55) are perfect squares. The three factors of 9 are 1, 3, and 9. What are the
three factors of 25?

23. Compare: 5% $\bigcirc \dfrac{1}{2}$
(Inv. 5)

*24. (Classify) Refer to figure ABCD to answer parts **a** and **b**.
(23)

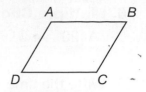

    a. What type of angle are angles *A* and *C*?

    b. What type of angle are angles *B* and *D*?

*25. (Analyze) The rectangular room is 5 yards long and 4 yards wide.
(Inv. 2, Inv. 3)

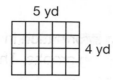

5 yd

4 yd

    a. How many yards of molding are needed to go around the room?

    b. How many square yards of carpet are needed to cover the floor?

*26. Multiple Choice If $n + 10 = 25$, then which of these equations is *not* true?
(24)

    A $n + 11 = 26$ **B** $n + 12 = 27$

    C $n - 5 = 20$ **D** $n + 9 = 24$

27. a. Compare: $8 \div (4 \div 2) \bigcirc (8 \div 4) \div 2$
(45, 47)

    b. Look at your answer to part **a.** Does the Associative Property apply to division?

28. a. Nineteen pennies are what fraction of a dollar?
(36, Inv. 5)

    b. Nineteen pennies are what percent of a dollar?

    c. Write the value of nineteen pennies as a decimal part of a dollar.

*29. (Estimate) At the restaurant Jackson ordered a meal for $7.95, a glass of milk for $1.75, and a dessert for $3.95. Estimate Jackson's restaurant bill.
(59)

*30. a. (Conclude) Name a segment that is parallel to $\overline{EF}$.
(23)

    b. Name a segment that is perpendicular to $\overline{BF}$.

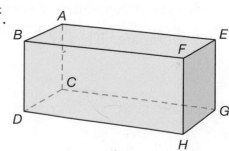

Focus on

• Displaying Data Using Graphs

In this investigation we will practice finding information in different types of **graphs**. Then we will practice making graphs. The four types of graphs we will study are **pictographs, bar graphs, line graphs,** and **circle graphs.** The first three types usually have a rectangular shape. On these graphs look for titles, labels, scales, and units. You might also find a **legend,** or **key,** that tells what the symbols on the graph stand for.

Pictographs

We begin with a pictograph, which uses pictures to display information. The following pictograph shows the results of a survey of some students at Thompson School. The cafeteria manager wanted to know the favorite lunches of Thompson School students, so each student in Room 12 was asked to name his or her favorite lunch from the school menu. Each student could name one lunch. The pictograph shows how students in the class answered the question.

Visit www. SaxonMath.com/ Int4Activities for a calculator activity.

**Favorite School Lunches
of Students in Room 12**

Chicken	◯ ◯ ◯
Tuna	◯ ◯ ◯ ◯ ◖
Turkey	◯ ◯ ◖
Pizza	◯ ◯ ◯ ◯ ◯

◯ represents the choice of 2 students

1. What is the title of the pictograph?

2. How many different types of lunches are shown in the graph?

3. **Explain** How can you tell how many students chose a particular lunch as their favorite lunch?

4. How many students named chicken as their favorite lunch? How did you find your answer?

5. ✏️ (Explain) How many students named tuna as their favorite lunch? How did you find your answer?

6. ✏️ (Represent) The pictograph shows the favorite lunches of how many students? How did you find your answer?

Bar Graphs

The information in the pictograph can also be shown in a bar graph like the one below. In this graph the bars are vertical (they go up and down). In some bar graphs, the bars are horizontal (they go sideways). The words along the sides of the graph are labels. The labels tell what other words or numbers along the sides mean.

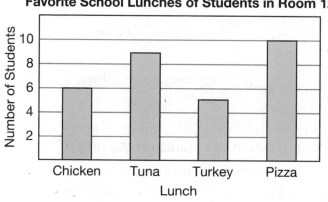

Favorite School Lunches of Students in Room 12

7. What is the label along the vertical left side of the graph?

8. Along the vertical left side of the graph are marks and numbers. What does the number 8 stand for?

9. ✏️ (Explain) Which bar is the tallest, and what does that mean?

10. ✏️ (Explain) The bar for tuna is taller than the bar for turkey, so more students named tuna as their favorite lunch than turkey. How many more students named tuna than named turkey? How did you find the answer?

Line Graphs

The following graph is a line graph. Line graphs are often used to show information or data that change over time. The data are **continuous,** which means that the data are assembled between the points on the graph. This graph shows Jamil's height from his birth until he was 10 years old. Notice that there is a vertical scale and a horizontal scale. The labels along these scales show the units (in parentheses) for the numbers along the scales. The change in Jamil's height is shown by the segments connecting the dots. The background grid makes the chart easier to read.

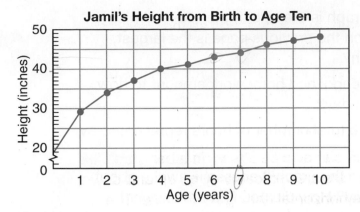

Jamil's Height from Birth to Age Ten

Height (inches) — vertical axis: 0, 20, 30, 40, 50

Age (years) — horizontal axis: 1 2 3 4 5 6 7 8 9 10

11. What does the 8 on the horizontal scale mean?

12. **Explain** How tall was Jamil on his fourth birthday? How did you find your answer?

13. **Analyze** During which year did Jamil become 45 inches tall? How did you find the answer?

14. **Interpret** The graph of Jamil's height is steep during the first few years and then becomes less steep. What does the change in steepness mean about Jamil's growth?

Analyze What data are accumulating between the points on the graph?

Circle Graphs

We have looked at three rectangular graphs. Now we will look at a circle graph. A circle graph shows how a whole is divided into parts. A circle graph is sometimes called a *pie graph.* The "pie" is cut into "slices" that show the size of the parts. In this circle graph we see how Vanessa usually spends a whole school day.

How Vanessa Spends a School Day

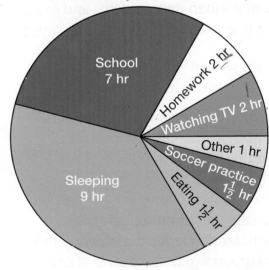

School 7 hr

Homework 2 hr

Watching TV 2 hr

Other 1 hr

Soccer practice $1\frac{1}{2}$ hr

Eating $1\frac{1}{2}$ hr

Sleeping 9 hr

15. The "scale" on a circle graph is the size of the slices. Which slice of the circle graph on the previous page is the largest, and what does that mean?

16. **Analyze** Together, school and homework amount to how many hours of Vanessa's day?

17. **Interpret** What is the total number of hours represented by the entire circle graph?

18. **Explain** According to the graph, Vanessa is awake about how many hours each day? How did you find the answer?

Activity

Displaying Information on Graphs

Materials needed:
- **Lesson Activities 27** and **28**

Lesson Activities 27 and **28** are patterns for making the four kinds of graphs we have studied in this investigation. Use these patterns to make graphs for the following information.

Make a Pictograph:

Represent The students in Room 12 were asked to name the drink they most like to have with lunch. Eight students said "punch," six said "water," nine said "milk," and seven said "juice."

Display this information in a pictograph. Title the graph. List the drink choices along the vertical left side of the graph. Draw an object, like a cup, to represent the students' drink preferences. You may use the same object for each category. Decide whether the picture will represent the choice of one student or more than one student, and show that information in a legend. Here is an example:

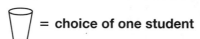
= **choice of one student**

Make a Bar Graph:

Represent Carmen asked the students in Room 15 how they travel to school in the morning. She found that six students walk, seven ride bikes, three ride skateboards, six travel by car, and seven ride the bus.

Display this information in a bar graph. Title the graph. Label the vertical and horizontal sides of the graph. Mark a scale and draw the bars.

Make a Line Graph:

Represent Mr. Lopez ran a six-mile race. As he passed each mile mark of the race, he looked at his stopwatch to see how long he had been running. Here are the times Mr. Lopez read on his stopwatch at each mile mark:

1 mile	6 minutes
2 miles	13 minutes
3 miles	20 minutes
4 miles	28 minutes
5 miles	36 minutes
6 miles (finished race)	45 minutes

On a line graph, make the vertical scale represent the distance run in miles. Make the horizontal scale represent the time run in minutes. Let the lower left corner of the scale be zero miles and zero minutes. Mark each scale with a sequence of numbers that allows the information to fit well on the graph. (For instance, let the distance between marks on the horizontal scale be 5 minutes.) Remember to title the graph.

Now make seven dots on the graph. One dot will be at the lower left corner to show the start of the race. The other six dots will show the elapsed time at each mile mark. On the one-mile level of the graph, mark a dot at your best estimate for 6 minutes. On the two-mile level, mark a dot for 13 minutes. Continue marking dots to the end of the race. After marking the dots, draw line segments from dot to dot, beginning at the lower left corner and stopping at the dot for the end of the race. Every point along the line graph shows the approximate running time and distance run by Mr. Lopez at that point in the race.

Analyze What data are accumulating between the points on your graph?

Make a Circle Graph:

Represent Jared made a schedule for school days. His schedule is shown on the following page. Notice that the schedule has seven sections. Use the information in this schedule to make a circle graph of how Jared spends his day. Your circle graph should also have seven sections. The size of the sections should show the number of hours Jared spends on each activity. (The circle graph pattern on **Lesson Activity 28** has 24 marks to make it easier to divide the circle into sections. The distance from one mark to the next represents one hour.) Choose a title for the graph, and label each section with

Jared's activity and the amount of time spent on that activity. Below we show an example with three of the seven sections completed.

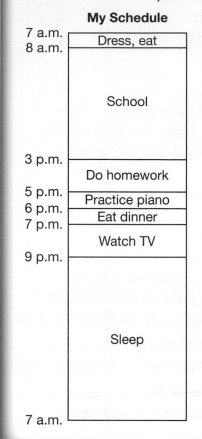

My Schedule

Time	Activity
7 a.m.–8 a.m.	Dress, eat
	School
3 p.m.	
	Do homework
5 p.m.	
6 p.m.	Practice piano
	Eat dinner
7 p.m.	
	Watch TV
9 p.m.	
	Sleep
7 a.m.	

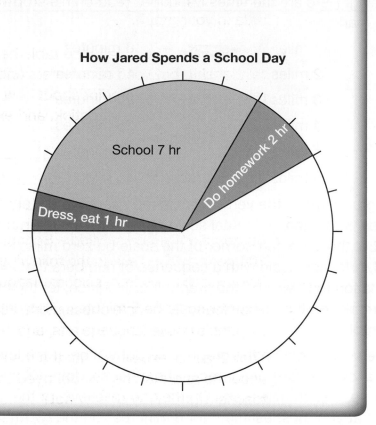

How Jared Spends a School Day

School 7 hr

Do homework 2 hr

Dress, eat 1 hr

Investigate Further

a. (**Represent**) Look for examples of graphs in newspapers, magazines, or Web sites to show how different types of graphs are used to display information.

b. (**Model**) Generate or collect information (data) and make graphs to display the information.

c. (**Represent**) Round the population of each town to the nearest thousand.

Town	Population
Roosevelt, UT	4404
Lincoln, CA	1860
Washington, KS	1168
Adams, WI	1840

Town	Population
Johnson, TX	1274
Clinton, CT	3516
Monroe, OH	8821
Jefferson, IA	4440

d. Choose five towns from problem **c.** Then choose an appropriate graph for graphing the rounded populations of those towns. Decide whether to use a bar graph, a pictograph, or a line graph. Make the graph, and then write a statement that describes the data in your graph.

e. **Analyze** The data in the table below show an estimated relationship between centimeters and inches. Describe the relationship. Then predict about how many centimeters are equal to a yard on a yardstick, and explain how you made your estimate.

Inches	1	2	3	4	5	6
Centimeters	2.5	5	7.5	10	12.5	15

f. Students at Parkcrest Middle School conducted a survey of 100 people. They asked the following question: What is your favorite subject: math, science, language arts, or social studies?

They found 27 people chose math, 26 people chose science, 21 people chose language arts, and 18 people chose social studies.

Their teacher explained that the results of their survey were not accurate and that they would need to do it again. Was their teacher right? Why or why not?

- **Remaining Fraction**
- **Two-Step Equations**

 **Power Up**

facts	Power Up I
count aloud	Count by halves from $\frac{1}{2}$ to 6 and back down to $\frac{1}{2}$.
mental math	In problems **a–c,** multiply a number by 10.

    a. Number Sense: 12×10

    b. Number Sense: 120×10

    c. Number Sense: 10×10

    d. Money: Jill paid for a pencil that cost 36¢ with a $1 bill. How much change should she receive?

    e. Money: One container of motor oil costs $3.75. How much do 2 containers cost?

    f. Percent: The whole circle has been divided into quarters. What percent of the circle is shaded? What percent is not shaded?

    g. Estimation: Phil plans to buy lasagna for $5.29 and a drink for $1.79. Round each price to the nearest 25 cents and then add to estimate the total cost.

    h. Calculation: $48 + 250 + 6 + 6$

problem solving   Choose an appropriate problem-solving strategy to solve this problem. Garcia is packing his clothes for summer camp. He wants to take three pairs of shorts. He has four different pairs of shorts from which to choose—tan, blue, white, and black. What are the different combinations of three pairs of shorts that Garcia can pack?

Remaining Fraction

The whole circle in Example 1 below has a shaded portion and an unshaded portion. If we know the size of one portion of a whole, then we can figure out the size of the other portion.

Example 1

a. **What fraction of the circle is shaded?**

b. **What fraction of the circle is not shaded?**

We see that the whole circle has been divided into eight equal parts. Three of the parts are shaded, so five of the parts are not shaded.

a. The fraction that is shaded is $\frac{3}{8}$.

b. The fraction that is not shaded is $\frac{5}{8}$.

Represent Compare the shaded part to the part not shaded using $>$, $<$, or $=$.

Example 2

The pizza was cut into eight equal slices. After Willis, Hunter, and Suelita each took a slice, what fraction of the pizza was left?

The whole pizza was cut into eight equal parts. Since three of the eight parts were taken, five of the eight parts remained. The fraction that was left was $\frac{5}{8}$.

Example 3

Two fifths of the crowd cheered. What fraction of the crowd did not cheer?

We think of the crowd as though it were divided into five equal parts. We are told that two of the five parts cheered. So there were three parts that did not cheer. The fraction of the crowd that did not cheer was $\frac{3}{5}$.

Two-Step Equations	The equation below means, "2 times what number equals 7 plus 5?"

$$2n = 7 + 5$$

It takes two steps to solve this equation. The first step is to add 7 and 5 ($7 + 5 = 12$), which gives us this equation:

$$2n = 12$$

The second step is to find n. Since $2 \times 6 = 12$, we know that n is 6.

$$n = 6$$

Verify How can we check the answer?

Example 4

Find m in the following equation: $3m = 4 \cdot 6$

Reading Math

We read this equation as "3 times what number equals 4 times 6?"

A dot is sometimes used between two numbers to indicate multiplication. So $4 \cdot 6$ means "4 times 6." The product of 4 and 6 is 24.

$$3m = 4 \cdot 6$$
$$3m = 24$$

Now we find m. Three times 8 equals 24, so m equals 8.

$$3m = 24$$
$$m = \mathbf{8}$$

Verify How can we check the answer?

Lesson Practice

a. What fraction of this rectangle is not shaded?

b. Three fifths of the race was over. What fraction of the race was left?

Find each missing number:

c. $2n = 2 + 8$ **d.** $2 + n = 2 \cdot 8$

Written Practice   *Distributed and Integrated*

*1. **Explain** The diameter of Filomena's bicycle tire is 24 inches. What
(21)   is the radius of the tire? Explain how you know.

2. There are five apple slices in each school lunch. If 35 students buy a
(49)
school lunch, how many apple slices are there? Write an equation for
this problem.

3. a. Two nickels are what fraction of a dollar?
(36,
Inv. 4)
b. Two nickels are what decimal part of a dollar?

*4. The Gilbreth family drank 39 cups of milk in 3 days. That averages to
(60)
how many cups of milk each day?

*5. Maya drove 28 miles to Ariana's house. That afternoon the two friends
(1, 17)
drove 3 miles to a restaurant and then drove back to Ariana's house.
That evening Maya drove 28 miles to return home. Altogether, how
many miles did Maya travel that day?

*6. What fraction of this rectangle is *not* shaded?
(61)

*7. Multiple Choice Which of these numbers is *not* a factor of 10?
(55)
   A 2   **B** 5   **C** 10   **D** 20

*8. (**Verify**) The loaf of bread was sliced into 6 equal pieces. After 1 piece
(61)
was taken, what fraction of the loaf was left?

*9. (**Represent**) Compare these fractions. Draw and shade two congruent
(56)
circles to show the comparison.

$$\frac{2}{3} \bigcirc \frac{3}{4}$$

*10. (**Estimate**) Find the sum of 5070 and 3840 by rounding each number
(54, 59)
to the nearest thousand before adding.

11. If 60% of the answers were true, then were there more true answers or
(Inv. 5)
more false answers?

12. a. What is the perimeter of this rectangle?
(Inv. 2,
Inv. 3)
b. What is the area of this rectangle?

4 cm

8 cm

13.
(43, 51)
$62.59
+ $17.47

*14. $5n = 12 + 18$
(61)

*15. $1000 - (110 \times 9)$
(45, 58)

16. $3.675 - 1.76$
(50)

*17. $6.70
(58) $\times\ \ \ \ 4$

*18.   703
(58) $\times\ \ \ 6$

*19. $346
(58) $\times\ \ \ \ 9$

*20. $5\overline{)39}$
(53)

*21. $7\overline{)39}$
(53)

22. $4\overline{)39}$
(53)

23. $16 \div 3$
(53)

24. $26 \div 6$
(53)

25. $36 \div \sqrt{36}$
(Inv. 3, 47)

*26. (Represent) Point *A* represents what number on this number line?
(Inv. 1)

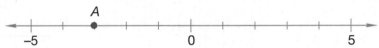

27. Compare:
(33)

    a. 745 ◯ 754   **b.** 132 ◯ 99

28. a. What fraction of the large square is not shaded?
(Inv. 4, Inv. 5)

    b. The unshaded part of the large square represents what decimal number?

    c. What percent of the large square is not shaded?

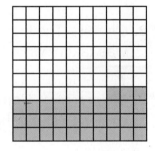

*29. (Classify) Name the parallel and perpendicular segments in this figure. Describe the angles as acute, obtuse, or right.
(52)

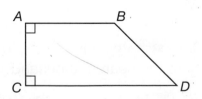

*30. In 1847 the first adhesive postage stamps were sold in the United States. In 1873 the first postcards were issued. What is the elapsed time in years between those two events?
(23, 45)

• Multiplying Three or More Factors
• Exponents

facts　　Power Up I

count aloud　　Count by fourths from $5\frac{1}{4}$ to 10.

mental math

a. Number Sense: 14×10

b. Money: Sean bought a ream of paper for $6.47 and a box of staples for $1.85. What was the total cost?

c. Percent: Compare: $25\% \bigcirc \frac{1}{2}$

d. Geometry: What is the perimeter of a square that is 6 inches on each side?

e. Time: Crystal phoned her friend at 4:05 p.m. They talked for 22 minutes. What time did Crystal's phone call end?

f. Measurement: Ray cut a 1-foot length of string from a larger piece that was 22 inches long. How many inches of string remained?

g. Estimation: Washington School has 258 students. Lincoln School has 241 students. Round each number to the nearest ten and then add to estimate the total number of students.

h. Calculation: $400 + 37 + 210 - 17$

problem solving　　Choose an appropriate problem-solving strategy to solve this problem. The following page shows a sequence of triangular numbers. The third term in the sequence, 6, is the number of dots in a triangular arrangement of dots with three rows. Notice that in this sequence the count from one number to the next increases. Find the number of dots in a triangular arrangement with 8 rows. Explain how you arrived at your answer and how you can verify your answer.

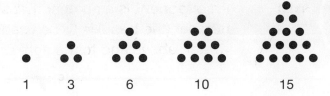

1   3   6   10   15

New Concepts

Multiplying Three or More Factors

To find the product of three numbers, we first multiply two of the numbers. Then we multiply the answer we get by the third number. To multiply four numbers, we must multiply once more. In any multiplication we continue the process until no factors remain.

Example 1

Multiply: $3 \times 4 \times 5$

First we multiply two of the numbers to get a product. Then we multiply that product by the third number. If we multiply 3 by 4 first, we get 12. Then we multiply 12 by 5 and get 60.

Step 1	Step 2
3	12
$\times\ 4$	$\times\ 5$
12	**60**

It does not matter which two numbers we multiply first. If we multiply 5 by 4 first, we get 20. Then we multiply 20 by 3 and again get 60.

Step 1	Step 2
5	20
$\times\ 4$	$\times\ 3$
20	**60** ← same answer

The order of the multiplications does not matter because of the Associative Property of Multiplication, which we studied in Lesson 45.

Example 2

Multiply: $4 \times 5 \times 10 \times 10$

We may perform this multiplication mentally. If we first multiply 4 by 5, we get 20. Then we multiply 20 by 10 to get 200. Finally, we multiply 200 by 10 and find that the product is **2000.**

Exponents

An **exponent** is a number that shows how many times another number (the **base**) is to be used as a factor. An exponent is written above and to the right of the base.

$$\text{base} \longrightarrow 5^2 \longleftarrow \text{exponent}$$

$$5^2 \text{ means } 5 \times 5.$$

$$5^2 \text{ equals } 25.$$

If the exponent is 2, we say "squared" for the exponent. So 5^2 is read as "five squared." If the exponent is 3, we say "cubed" for the exponent. So 2^3 is read as "two cubed."

Example 3

Simplify: $5^2 + 2^3$

We will add five squared and two cubed. We find the values of 5^2 and 2^3 before adding.

$$5^2 \text{ means } 5 \times 5, \text{ which is } 25.$$

$$2^3 \text{ means } 2 \times 2 \times 2, \text{ which is } 8.$$

Now we add 25 and 8.

$$25 + 8 = \mathbf{33}$$

Example 4

Math Language

An **exponential expression** indicates that the base is to be used as a factor the number of times shown by the exponent.

$$4^3 = 4 \times 4 \times 4$$

Rewrite this expression using exponents:

$$\mathbf{5 \times 5 \times 5}$$

Five is used as a factor three times, so the exponent is 3.

$$\mathbf{5^3}$$

Exponents are sometimes used in formulas. The formula for the area of a square shows that the length of a side (s) is squared.

$$A = s^2$$

$$\text{Area of a square} = (\text{length of side})^2$$

Example 5

Reading Math

We read s^2 as "s squared" which means $s \times s$.

Use the formula for the area of a square to find the area of this square.

The formula for the area of a square is $A = s^2$. The length of each side is 5 in. Replace the "*s*" in the formula with 5 in.

$$A = (5 \text{ in.})^2$$

Multiplying 5 in. $\times$ 5 in., we find the area of the square is 25 sq. in.

We can write the answer as **25 in.^{2}** or **25 sq. in.**

Simplify:

a. $2 \times 3 \times 4$ **b.** $3 \times 4 \times 10$

c. 8^2 **d.** 3^3

e. $10^2 - 6^2$ **f.** $3^2 - 2^3$

g. Rewrite this expression using exponents:

$$4 \times 4 \times 4$$

h. Write a formula for finding the area of a square. Then use the formula to find the area of a square with each side 6 inches long.

Written Practice

Distributed and Integrated

Formulate Write and solve equations for problems **1** and **2**.

*1.
(52)
There were twice as many peacocks as there were hens. If there were 12 peacocks, then how many hens were there?

*2.
(43, 59)
Mae-Ying bought a package of paper priced at $1.98 and 2 pens priced at $0.49 each. The tax on the entire purchase was 18¢. What was the total cost of the items? Explain why your answer is reasonable.

3.
(27)
Raquel's dance class begins at 6 p.m. It takes 20 minutes to drive to dance class. What time should she leave home to be on time for dance class?

*4.
(57)
Analyze Glenda drove across the desert at an average speed of 60 miles per hour. At that rate, how far would she drive in 4 hours? Make a table to solve the problem.

*5.
(61)
Two thirds of the race was over. What fraction of the race was left?

*6.
(59)
Estimate Otieno bought a notebook for $8.87 and paper for $2.91. Estimate the total by rounding each amount to the nearest dollar, then add.

*7.
(61)
In the equation $9 \times 11 = 100 - y$, the letter y stands for what number?

*8. (Represent) Compare: $\frac{2}{4} \bigcirc \frac{4}{8}$. Draw and shade two congruent circles
(56) to show the comparison.

*9. Multiple Choice Recall that a prime number has exactly two factors.
(55) Which of these numbers has exactly 2 factors?

    A 7   **B** 8   **C** 9   **D** 10

10. According to this calendar, July 4, 2014 is what day of the
(54) week?

JULY 2014
S M T W T F S
1 2 3 4 5
6 7 8 9 10 11 12
13 14 15 16 17 18 19
20 21 22 23 24 25 26
27 28 29 30 31

*11. (Connect) Write four multiplication/division facts using the numbers 6,
(47) 3, and 18.

*12. $5 \times 6 \times 7$
(62)

*13. 4^3
(62)

14.   476,385
(51) + 259,518

15. $20.00
(52) − $17.84

16. c
(24) − 19,434
    45,579

*17. $4.17
(58) ×   8

*18. $470
(58) ×   7

*19.   608
(58) ×   4

20. $4\overline{)29}$
(53)

21. $8\overline{)65}$
(53)

22. $5\overline{)29}$
(53)

23. $65 \div 7$
(53)

24. $29 \div 5$
(53)

25. $65 \div 9$
(53)

26. If 40% of the students are boys, then what percent of the students
(Inv. 5) are girls?

*27. a. What is the perimeter of this square shown at right?
(Inv. 2,
Inv. 3)   **b.** Use a formula to find the area of the square.

6 in

*28. Multiple Choice What type of angle is each angle of a square?
₍₂₃₎

    A acute   **B** right   **C** obtuse   **D** straight

*29. This bar graph shows the number of colored candles in a package. Use
_(Inv. 6) the bar graph to answer each question.

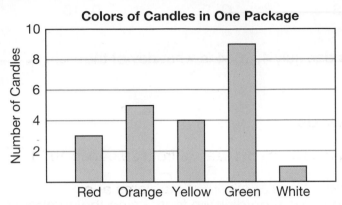

Colors of Candles in One Package

a. How many red candles were there?

b. There were how many more green candles than orange candles?

*30. (**Model**) Draw a number line from 1 to 2, and show the locations of $1\frac{1}{2}$,
_(37, 50) 1.25, and $1\frac{3}{4}$.

Real-World Connection

A square with 1-inch sides has an area of 1 square inch. A square with 2-inch sides has an area of 4 square inches. Review the squares shown below.

 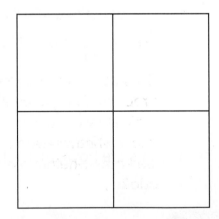

1 × 1 = 1 square inch   2 × 2 = 4 square inches

a. What is the area of a square with sides that are 3 inches long?

b. What is the area of a square with sides that are 4 inches long?

c. What is the area of a square with sides that are 5 inches long?

d. Draw and label each of the squares in parts **a–c.**

• Polygons

Power Up

facts   Power Up J

count aloud   Count down by thousands from 20,000 to 1000.

mental math   Multiply three numbers in problems **a–c.**

    a. Number Sense: $6 \times 7 \times 10$

    b. Number Sense: $5 \times 8 \times 10$

    c. Number Sense: $12 \times 10 \times 10$

    d. Money: $\$7.59 + \$0.95$

    e. Money: Sydney had $5.00. Then she spent $3.25 on photocopies. How much money does she have left?

    f. Geometry: Compare: $4\frac{1}{2}$ in. $\bigcirc$ radius of a circle with a 10 in. diameter

    g. Estimation: Henry estimated that his full drinking glass contained 400 mL of water. Is this a reasonable estimate?

    h. Calculation: $470 - 30 + 62 + 29$

problem solving   Choose an appropriate problem-solving strategy to solve this problem. Fifty percent of the students in Gabriel's class are girls. Do we know how many students are in this class? Do we know whether there are more boys or more girls in the class? Do we know whether the number of students in the class is even or odd?

New Concept

Polygons are closed, flat shapes formed by line segments.

Example 1

Which of these shapes is a polygon?

A B C D

Figure A is not a polygon because it is not closed. Figure B is not a polygon because it is not flat. Figure C is not a polygon because not all of its sides are straight. **Figure D** is a polygon. It is closed and flat, and each of its sides is a line segment.

Thinking Skill

Verify

What is a regular rectangle called?

Polygons are named according to the number of sides they have. The lengths of the sides may or may not be the same. If a polygon's sides are all the same length and its angles are all the same size, it is called a **regular polygon.** The figure to the right in each row below is a regular polygon.

 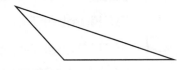

Three-sided polygons are **triangles.**

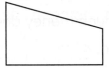 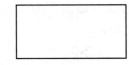

Four-sided polygons are **quadrilaterals.**

 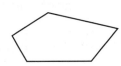

Five-sided polygons are **pentagons.**

 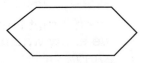

Six-sided polygons are **hexagons.**

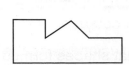 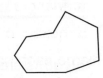

Eight-sided polygons are **octagons.**

Ten-sided polygons are **decagons.**

(**Classify**) Describe the angles that form a regular triangle, a rectangle, and a regular hexagon.

Example 2

What kind of a polygon is a square?

A square has four sides, so a square is a **quadrilateral.** In fact, a square is a regular quadrilateral.

Each corner of a polygon is called a *vertex* (plural: *vertices*). A polygon has as many vertices as it has sides.

(**Classify**) Describe the line segments that form a square.

Example 3

An octagon has how many more vertices than a pentagon?

An octagon has eight sides and eight vertices. A pentagon has five sides and five vertices. So an octagon has **3 more vertices** than a pentagon.

(**Classify**) Describe the line segments that form a regular pentagon and a regular hexagon.

Example 4

Name the polygons that form this pyramid.

This pyramid has 5 faces. The base is a **square.** The other four faces are **triangles.**

(**Analyze**) Describe the angles and the line segments that form this pyramid.

(**Lesson Practice**) Draw an example of each of these polygons:

    a. triangle   **b.** quadrilateral   **c.** pentagon

    d. hexagon   **e.** octagon   **f.** decagon

Name each polygon shown and describe its angles:

    g.    **h.**

i.

j.

k. Which figures in problems **g–j** appear to be regular polygons?

l. What common street sign has the shape of the polygon in problem **j?**

m. A decagon has how many more vertices than a hexagon?

Written Practice · Distributed and Integrated

1. Three feet equals 1 yard. A car that is 15 feet long is how many yards long?
(Inv. 2)

*2. **Connect** Write four multiplication/division facts using the numbers 3, 10, and 30.
(47)

*3. **Analyze** Nevaeh had six quarters, three dimes, and fourteen pennies. How much money did she have in all?
(35)

4. What is the sum of the even numbers that are greater than 10 but less than 20?
(1, 10)

*5. **Estimate** Round $7.15 and $5.94 to the nearest dollar, and then add.
(59)

*6. **Model** Erin opened 1 gallon of milk and began filling glasses. Each glass held 1 cup of milk. Two cups equals a pint. Two pints equals a quart. Four quarts equals a gallon. How many glasses could Erin fill? Use containers to solve.
(40)

7. To what mixed number is the arrow pointing?
(37)

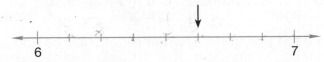

*8. The cornbread was cut into 12 equal pieces. Seven of the pieces were eaten. What fraction of the cornbread was left?
(61)

*9. The product of 4 and 3 is how much greater than the sum of 4 and 3?
(31, 38)

*10. What is the sum of 92 and $\sqrt{9}$?
(Inv. 3, 62)

*11. a. **Classify** What is the name of this polygon?
(Inv. 2, 63)

    b. Each side is the same length. What is the perimeter of this polygon?

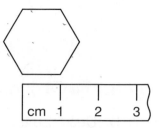

*12. Roger picked 56 berries in 8 minutes. At that rate, how many berries did he pick in 1 minute?
(60)

*13. Chanisse picked 11 berries in 1 minute. At that rate, how many berries could she pick in 5 minutes?
(57)

14. $40.00 − d = $2.43
(24, 52)

*15. $5 \times n = 15 + \sqrt{25}$
(Inv. 3, 61)

*16. $6 \times 4 \times 10$
(62)

*17. 5^3
(62)

18. $3.5 + 2.45$
(50)

19. $1.95 − 0.4$
(50)

20. $1.00 − ($0.36 + $0.57)
(43, 45)

*21. 349×8
(58)

*22. 7.60×7
(58)

23. $6\overline{)34}$
(53)

24. $8\overline{)62}$
(53)

25. $5\overline{)24}$
(53)

26. $\dfrac{63}{7}$
(47)

*27. **Explain** Vans will be used to carry 22 soccer players to a game. Each van can carry 5 players. Write and solve an equation to find the least number of vans that will be needed. Then explain your answer.
(53)

*28. **Multiple Choice** Which of these numbers is a multiple of 10?
(55)

    A 3   **B** 5   **C** 15   **D** 40

29. **a.** What fraction of the large square is shaded?
(*Inv. 4,*
Inv. 5)
    b. What decimal of the whole grid is not shaded?

    c. What percent of the large square is not shaded?

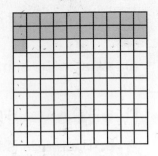

*30. **a.** (Classify) What polygons form this figure?
(*23, 63*)
    b. Describe the angles and line segments of this figure.

Early Finishers
Real-World Connection

Find three classroom objects that are examples of different types of polygons.

    a. Name each object.

    b. Draw a picture of each object. Each picture should show the number of sides each object has.

    c. Label each drawing with the name of the polygon it represents.

• Division with Two-Digit Answers, Part 1

Power Up

facts   Power Up J

count aloud   When we count by fives from 1, we say the numbers 1, 6, 11, 16, and so on. Count by fives from 1 to 51.

mental math   Multiply four numbers in problems **a–c.**

   a. Number Sense: $6 \times 4 \times 10 \times 10$

   b. Number Sense: $3 \times 4 \times 10 \times 10$

   c. Number Sense: $4 \times 5 \times 10 \times 10$

   d. Money: Alex had $10.00. Then he bought a cap for $6.87. How much money does Alex have left?

   e. Time: J'Narra must finish the test by 2:30 p.m. If it is 2:13 p.m., how many minutes does she have left to finish?

   f. Measurement: Five feet is 60 inches. How many inches tall is a person whose height is 5 feet 4 inches?

   g. Estimation: Choose the more reasonable estimate for the width of a computer keyboard: 11 inches or 11 feet.

   h. Calculation: $\sqrt{49} + 6 + 37 + 99$

problem solving

Choose an appropriate problem-solving strategy to solve this problem. Shamel is making lemonade for her lemonade stand. The package of powdered lemonade says that each package makes 1 quart of lemonade. If Shamel wants to make $1\frac{1}{2}$ gallons of lemonade, how many packages of powdered lemonade will she need? Explain how you found your answer.

In this lesson we will learn a pencil-and-paper method for dividing a two-digit number by a one-digit number. We will demonstrate the method as we solve this problem:

The seventy-eight fifth-graders at Washington School will be divided equally among three classrooms. How many students will be in each room?

There are three numbers in this "equal groups" problem: the total number of students, the number of classrooms, and the number of students in each classroom.

Formula:
Number of groups × Number in each group = Total

Problem:
3 classrooms × *n* students in each classroom = 78 students

To find the number of students in each classroom, we divide 78 by 3.

$$3\overline{)78}$$

For the first step we ignore the 8 and divide 7 by 3. We write "2" above the 7. Then we multiply 2 by 3 and write "6" below the 7. Then we subtract and write "1."

$$\begin{array}{r} 2 \\ 3\overline{)78} \\ \underline{6} \\ 1 \end{array}$$

Next we "bring down" the 8, as shown here. Together, the 1 and 8 form 18.

$$\begin{array}{r} 2 \\ 3\overline{)78} \\ \underline{6}\downarrow \\ 18 \end{array}$$

Now we divide 18 by 3 and get 6. We write the 6 above the 8 in 78. Then we multiply 6 by 3 and write "18" below the 18.

$$\begin{array}{r} 26 \\ 3\overline{)78} \\ \underline{6} \\ 18 \\ \underline{18} \\ 0 \end{array}$$

Reading Math

We can write the related equation 78 ÷ 3 = *n* to represent this problem.

Thinking Skill

Discuss

Why do we write the first digit of the quotient in the tens place?

Thinking Skill

Verify

Why do we write the second digit of the quotient in the ones place?

We subtract and find that the remainder is zero. This means that if the students are divided equally among the classrooms, there will be 26 students in each classroom.

$$78 \div 3 = 26$$

Since division facts and multiplication facts form fact families, we may arrange these three numbers to form a multiplication fact.

$$3 \times 26 = 78$$

We can multiply 3 by 26 to check our work.

$$
\begin{array}{r}
1 \\
26 \\
\times\ \ 3 \\
\hline
78\ \ \text{check}
\end{array}
$$

Example 1

> **An 87-acre field is divided into 3 equal parts. A different crop will be planted in each part. How many acres is one part of the field?**
>
> For the first step, we ignore the 7. We divide 8 by 3, multiply, and then subtract. Next we bring down the 7 to form 27. Now we divide 27 by 3, multiply, and subtract again.
>
> $$
> \begin{array}{r}
> 29 \\
> 3\overline{)87} \\
> 6\downarrow \\
> \hline
> 27 \\
> 27 \\
> \hline
> 0
> \end{array}
> $$
>
> The remainder is zero, so we see that one part of the field is **29 acres.**

Now we multiply 3 by 29 to check our work. If the product is 87, we can be confident that our division was correct.

$$
\begin{array}{r}
2 \\
29 \\
\times\ \ 3 \\
\hline
87\ \ \text{check}
\end{array}
$$

Notice that there is no remainder when 87 is divided by 3; there is no remainder because 87 is a multiple of 3. We cannot identify the multiples of 3 by looking at the last digit because the multiples of 3 can end with any digit. However, adding the digits of a number can tell us whether a number is a multiple of 3. If the sum is a multiple of 3, then so is the number. For example, adding the digits in 87 gives us 15 ($8 + 7 = 15$). Since 15 is a multiple of 3, we know that 87 is a multiple of 3.

Example 2

Four students can sit in each row of seats in a school bus. Thirty-eight students are getting on the bus. If each student sits in the first available seat, what is a reasonable estimate of the number of rows of seats that will be filled?

We are asked for a reasonable estimate, so we can use compatible numbers. Since 38 and 4 are not compatible for division, we choose a number near 38 that divides evenly by 4. Nearby multiples of 4 are 36 and 40. Using one of these multiples, we find that a reasonable estimate of the number of rows that will be filled is **9** or **10.**

Example 3

Which of these numbers can be divided by 3 with no remainder?

  A 56   **B** 64   **C** 45   **D** 73

We add the digits of each number:

  A $5 + 6 = 11$ **B** $6 + 4 = 10$ **C** $4 + 5 = 9$ **D** $7 + 3 = 10$

Of the numbers 11, 10, and 9, only 9 is a multiple of 3. So the only choice that can be divided by 3 with no remainder is **45.**

Lesson Practice

Divide:

  a. $3\overline{)51}$ **b.** $4\overline{)52}$ **c.** $5\overline{)75}$

  d. $3\overline{)72}$ **e.** $4\overline{)96}$ **f.** $2\overline{)74}$

  g. (**Connect**) Find the missing factor in this equation: $3n = 45$

  h. Multiple Choice Which of these numbers can be divided by 3 with no remainder? How do you know?

    A 75   **B** 76

    C 77   **D** 79

  i. Each row of desks in a classroom can seat six students. Twenty-nine students are entering the classroom. If each student sits in the first available seat, what is a reasonable estimate of the number of rows of seats that will be filled? Explain your answer.

*1. A square mile is twenty-seven million, eight hundred seventy-eight
(34) thousand, four hundred square feet. Use digits to write this number.

2. The tree was one hundred thirteen paces away. If each pace was 3 feet,
(49) how many feet away was the tree?

3. Tracey's baseball-card album will hold five hundred cards. Tracey has
(25, 41) three hundred eighty-four cards. How many more cards will fit into the
album? Write an equation.

4. The trip lasted 21 days. How many weeks did the trip last?
(52, 54)

*5. A stop sign has the shape of an octagon. How many sides do seven
(49) stop signs have?

*6. Find the length of this hairpin to the nearest quarter inch.
(39)

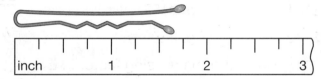

7. Write 406,912 in expanded form. Then use words to write the number.
(16, 33)

*8. One foot equals 12 inches. If each side of a square is 1 foot long, then
(Inv. 2) what is the perimeter of the square in inches?

*9. **Estimate** During a school fundraiser, a group of students worked
(59) for 90 minutes and washed 8 cars. What is a reasonable estimate of the
number of minutes the students spent washing each car? Explain why
your answer is reasonable.

*10. **Represent** Compare: $\frac{3}{6} \bigcirc \frac{1}{2}$. Draw and shade two congruent circles
(56) to show the comparison.

11. Compare:
(33)
    a. 614 $\bigcirc$ 609   **b.** 88 $\bigcirc$ 106

*12. (11, 30) ✏️ **Explain** Last week Ms. Willyard graded some papers. This week she graded 47 more papers. In these two weeks, Ms. Willyard graded 112 papers altogether. How many papers did she grade last week? Explain why your answer is reasonable.

13. (43, 51)
$$\begin{array}{r} \$32.47 \\ + \$67.54 \\ \hline \end{array}$$

14. (52)
$$\begin{array}{r} 51{,}036 \\ - 7{,}648 \\ \hline \end{array}$$

15. (50)
$$\begin{array}{r} 53.6 \\ 2.9 \\ 97.4 \\ 8.8 \\ + 436.1 \\ \hline \end{array}$$

*16. (41) $5n = 75$

*17. (64) $3\overline{)84}$

*18. (64) $4\overline{)92}$

19. (53) $6\overline{)58}$

*20. (58)
$$\begin{array}{r} 257 \\ \times 5 \\ \hline \end{array}$$

*21. (58)
$$\begin{array}{r} \$7.09 \\ \times 3 \\ \hline \end{array}$$

22. (58)
$$\begin{array}{r} \$334 \\ \times 9 \\ \hline \end{array}$$

*23. (64) $2\overline{)36}$

24. (41) $4n = 36$

*25. (62) $4^2 + 2^3$

26. (43, 45) $3.5 - (2.4 - 1.3)$

*27. (36) Look at these bills. List all of the different ways to pair two bills.

*28. (61) Three fourths of the game was over. What fraction of the game remained?

29. (Inv. 4, Inv. 5) **a.** What fraction of the large square is shaded?

b. What decimal number is represented by the shaded part of the square?

c. What percent of the large square is not shaded?

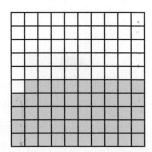

*30. (55) **Multiple Choice** The first two prime numbers are 2 and 3. The next two prime numbers are ____.

A 4 and 5 **B** 5 and 6 **C** 5 and 7 **D** 7 and 9

• Division with Two-Digit Answers, Part 2

Power Up

facts   Power Up J

count aloud   Count by fives from 1 to 51.

mental math   Multiply two numbers ending in zero in problems **a–d.** (Example: 30 × 40 equals 3 × 10 times 4 × 10. We rearrange the factors to get 3 × 4 × 10 × 10, which is 1200.)

    a. Number Sense: 40 × 40

    b. Number Sense: 30 × 50

    c. Number Sense: 60 × 70

    d. Number Sense: 40 × 50

    e. Powers/Roots: $2^2 + 2$

    f. Money: $6.48 + $2.39

    g. Estimation: Each bottled water costs 99¢. If Ms. Hathcoat buys 1 bottle for each of her 24 students, about how much money will she spend?

    h. Calculation: $\sqrt{64} - 6 + 37 + 61$

problem solving   Choose an appropriate problem-solving strategy to solve this problem. Jamisha paid a dollar for an item that cost 44¢. If she got back four coins in change, what should the four coins have been?

New Concept

The numbers in a division problem are named the **divisor,** the **dividend,** and the **quotient.**

$$\overset{\text{quotient}}{\text{divisor}\,)\overline{\text{dividend}}} \qquad \text{dividend} \div \text{divisor} = \text{quotient}$$

$$\frac{\text{dividend}}{\text{divisor}} = \text{quotient}$$

If we calculate how to divide 78 students among 3 classrooms, then 78 becomes the dividend and 3 becomes the divisor. The result, 26, is the quotient.

$$\begin{array}{r} 26 \leftarrow \text{quotient} \\ \text{divisor} \longrightarrow 3\overline{)78} \leftarrow \text{dividend} \end{array}$$

The dividend is the number being divided. The divisor is the number by which the dividend is divided. The quotient is the result of the division.

Example 1

Identify the 8 in each of these problems as the *divisor, dividend,* or *quotient:*

a. $8 \div 2 = 4$ b. $8\overline{)24}^{\,3}$ c. $\frac{40}{5} = 8$

a. dividend   b. divisor   c. quotient

Analyze Write a multiplication equation and a division equation using the words divisor, dividend, and quotient.

We solve the following problem by dividing:

On a three day bike trip Hans rode 234 kilometers. Hans rode an average of how many kilometers each day?

We find the answer by dividing 234 by 3.

$$3\overline{)234}$$

To perform the division, we begin by dividing $3\overline{)23}$. We write "7" above the 3 of 23. Then we multiply and subtract.

$$\begin{array}{r} 7 \\ 3\overline{)234} \\ \underline{21} \\ 2 \end{array}$$

Next we bring down the 4.

$$\begin{array}{r} 7 \\ 3\overline{)234} \\ \underline{21\downarrow} \\ 24 \end{array}$$

Now we divide 24 by 3. We write "8" above the 4. Then we multiply and finish by subtracting.

Thinking Skill

Discuss

Why do we write the first digit of the quotient in the tens place?

Thinking Skill

Verify

Why do we write the second digit of the quotient in the ones place?

$$\begin{array}{r} 78 \\ 3\overline{)234} \\ \underline{21} \\ 24 \\ \underline{24} \\ 0 \end{array}$$

We find that Hans rode an average of 78 kilometers each day.

We can check our work by multiplying the quotient, 78, by the divisor, 3. If the product is 234, then our division answer is correct.

$$\begin{array}{r} 78 \\ \times\ 3 \\ \hline 234 \end{array} \quad \text{check}$$

Example 2

On a 9-day bike trip through the Rocky Mountains, Vera and her companions rode 468 miles. They rode an average of how many miles per day?

Vera and her companions probably rode different distances each day. By dividing 468 miles by 9, we find how far they traveled if they rode the same distance each day. This is called the *average distance.* We begin by finding $9\overline{)46}$. We write "5" above the 6 in 46. Then we multiply and subtract.

$$\begin{array}{r} 5 \\ 9\overline{)468} \\ \underline{45} \\ 1 \end{array}$$

Next we bring down the 8. Now we divide 18 by 9.

$$\begin{array}{r} 52 \\ 9\overline{)468} \\ \underline{45}\downarrow \\ 18 \\ \underline{18} \\ 0 \end{array}$$

We find that they rode an average of **52 miles** per day.

We check the division by multiplying 52 by 9, and we look for 468 as the answer.

$$\begin{array}{r} {\scriptstyle 1} \\ 52 \\ \times\ 9 \\ \hline 468 \end{array} \quad \text{check}$$

Connect Why can we use multiplication to check a division problem?

Notice in Example 2 that there is no remainder when 468 is divided by 9. That is because 468 is a multiple of 9. Just as we identified multiples of 3 by adding the digits of a number, we can identify multiples of 9 by adding the digits of a number. For the number 468, we have

$$4 + 6 + 8 = 18$$

The sum 18 is a multiple of 9, so 468 is a multiple of 9.

Example 3

Which of these numbers is a multiple of 9?

A 123   **B** 234   **C** 345   **D** 456

We add the digits of each number:

A $1 + 2 + 3 = 6$ **B** $2 + 3 + 4 = 9$

C $3 + 4 + 5 = 12$ **D** $4 + 5 + 6 = 15$

The sums 6, 9, and 12 are all multiples of 3, but only 9 is a multiple of 9. Therefore, only **234** is a multiple of 9 and can be divided by 9 without a remainder.

Example 4

Each day, some of the students in Montrelyn's class order milk at snack time and at lunch time. Each month, a total of 192 pints of milk are delivered to Montrelyn's classroom. About how many quarts of milk are delivered each month? Explain why your answer is reasonable.

We are given a number of pints and asked for a number of quarts. Since there are 2 pints in a quart, we divide 192 pints by 2. We are not asked for an exact answer, so we can estimate. Since 192 is nearly 200, we can arrange 200 pints into groups of 2 pints by dividing. The answer is **about 100 quarts.**

Analyze About how many gallons is 192 pints? Explain your reasoning.

Lesson Practice   In the division fact 32 ÷ 8 = 4,

      a. what number is the divisor?

      b. what number is the dividend?

      c. what number is the quotient?

Divide:

d. $3\overline{)144}$ **e.** $4\overline{)144}$ **f.** $6\overline{)144}$

g. $225 \div 5$ **h.** $455 \div 7$ **i.** $200 \div 8$

j. Multiple Choice Which of these numbers can be divided by 9 without a remainder? How do you know?

  A 288   **B** 377   **C** 466   **D** 555

k. Find the missing factor in this equation:

$$5m = 125$$

l. An oil-change business changes the motor oil in cars and trucks. On Saturday, the business sold 157 quarts of new motor oil. About how many gallons of new motor oil were sold that day? Explain your answer.

Written Practice   *Distributed and Integrated*

Formulate Write and solve equations for problems **1** and **2**.

1. The chef uses 3 eggs for each omelette. How many omelettes can
(52) he make with two dozen eggs?

*2. Aaliyah looked at the clock and realized that her next class would
(25) begin in 27 minutes and end in 72 minutes. How many minutes long is Aaliyah's next class?

*3. Alvaro is turning three years old today. How many months old is
(54) Alvaro?

*4. **Estimate** Madeline's favorite orange juice is sold in half-gallon
(40, 65) containers. Each month, Madeline estimates that she purchases 7 containers of juice. Estimate the number of gallons of juice Madeline purchases each month. Explain your reasoning.

*5. Trudy rode her bike 36 miles in 4 hours. She rode at an average
(60) rate of how many miles per hour?

*6. **Analyze** The wagon train traveled at an average rate of 20 miles
(57) per day. At that rate, how many miles would the wagon train travel in 5 days? Make a table to solve the problem.

*7. a. What fraction of this hexagon is *not* shaded?
(61)

b. Each side of the hexagon is 1 cm long. What is its
(Inv. 2)   perimeter?

*8. (Inv. 6)   **Interpret** The average amount of precipitation received each year
in each of four cities is shown in the table below:

Average Annual Precipitation

City and State	Amount (to the nearest inch)
Phoenix, AZ	8
Reno, NV	7
Boise, ID	12
Albuquerque, NM	9

Display the data in a bar graph. Write one statement that describes
the data.

*9. J'Raa started jogging early in the morning and did not stop until he
(27)   returned home. How much time did J'Raa spend jogging?

Started jogging   Stopped jogging

a.m.   a.m.

10. Nigel drew a circle with a radius of 18 inches. What was the diameter of
(21)   the circle?

11. How long is segment *BC*?
(45)

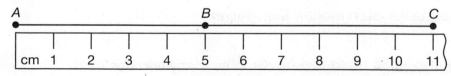

*12. Multiple Choice Which of these words is the answer to a division
(65)   problem?

A product   **B** dividend   **C** divisor   **D** quotient

*13. Compare: $27 \div 3^2 \bigcirc 27 \div \sqrt{9}$
(Inv. 3, 62)

14. $97.56
(43, 51)   + $ 8.49

15. $60.00
(52)   − $54.78

16.   37.64
(43)   29.45
       3.01
    + 75.38

*17. $168 \div 3$
(65)

*18. $378 \div 7$
(65)

19. 840×3
(58)

20. 4×564
(58)

*21. 304×6
(58)

*22. $4\overline{)136}$
(65)

*23. $2\overline{)132}$
(65)

*24. $6\overline{)192}$
(65)

*25. **Explain** Describe the steps for solving the equation and then
(61, 65) solve the equation to find *n*.

$$7n = 50 + 34$$

*26. $12 \times 7 \times 10$
(62)

27. Dimitri woke up on a cold morning and glanced out the
(18) window at the thermometer. What temperature is shown
on this thermometer?

28. a. Three quarters is what fraction of a dollar?
(36,
Inv. 5)
    b. Three quarters is what percent of a dollar?

*29. Draw a quadrilateral. A quadrilateral has how many vertices?
(63)

*30. a. Which side of this quadrilateral is parallel to
(23, 45)   side *CB?*

    b. Which angle appears to be an obtuse
      angle?

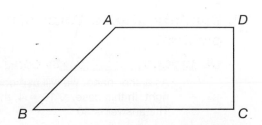

• Similar and Congruent Figures

Power Up

facts	Power Up J
count aloud	Count down by fives from 51 to 1.
mental math	Multiply three numbers, including numbers ending in zero, in **a–c**.

    a. Number Sense: $3 \times 10 \times 20$

    b. Number Sense: $4 \times 20 \times 30$

    c. Number Sense: $3 \times 40 \times 10$

    d. Powers/Roots: $2^2 + 5^2$

    e. Geometry: Altogether, how many sides do 3 hexagons have?

    f. Money: Logan owes $10.00 for his club dues. He has $9.24. How much more money does Logan need?

    g. Estimation: Lieu wants to buy 6 stickers that each cost 21¢. Lieu has $1.15. Does she have enough money to buy 6 stickers?

    h. Calculation[1]: $\sqrt{16}$, $\times 2$, $\times 2$, $+ 4$, $\times 2$

problem solving

Choose an appropriate problem-solving strategy to solve this problem. Dasha plans to use only four different colored pencils to color the states on a United States map. She has five different colored pencils from which to choose—red, orange, yellow, green, and blue. What are the combinations of four colors Dasha can choose? (There are five combinations.)

---

[1] As a shorthand, we will use commas to separate operations to be performed sequentially from left to right. In this case, $\sqrt{16} = 4$, then $4 \times 2 = 8$, then $8 \times 2 = 16$, then $16 + 4 = 20$, then $20 \times 2 = 40$. The answer is 40.

Look at these four triangles:

Figures that are the same shape are **similar.** Figures that are the same shape and the same size are *congruent.*

Triangles *A* and *B* are both similar and congruent.

Triangles *B* and *C* are not congruent because they are not the same size. However, they are similar because they are the same shape. We could look at triangle *B* through a magnifying glass to make triangle *B* appear to be the same size as triangle *C*.

Triangle *A* and triangle *D* are not congruent and they are not similar. Neither one is an enlarged version of the other. Looking at either triangle through a magnifying glass cannot make it look like the other because their sides and angles do not match.

Example

a. **Which of these rectangles are similar?**

b. **Which of these rectangles are congruent?**

a. **Rectangles *B, C,*** and ***D*** are similar. Rectangle *A* is not similar to the other three rectangles because it is not a "magnified" version of any of the other rectangles.

b. **Rectangle *B*** and **rectangle *D*** are congruent because they have the same shape and size.

Activity

Determining Similarity and Congruence

Material needed:
- **Lesson Activity 29**

Model Look at the shapes on the left side of **Lesson Activity 29.** Compare each shape to the figure next to it on the right, and answer each question below.

1. Is the first shape similar to the bike sign? Is the shape congruent to the bike sign? Check your answers by cutting out the shape on the left and placing it on top of the bike sign. Describe and record the result.

2. Is the triangle similar to the yield sign? Is the triangle congruent to the yield sign? Check your answers by cutting out the triangle and placing it on top of the yield sign. Describe and record the result.

3. **Discuss** How can you tell if the octagon on the left is congruent to the stop sign? Are these shapes similar?

Lesson Practice Refer to the figures below to answer problems **a** and **b**.

a. Which of these triangles appear to be similar?

b. Which of these triangles appear to be congruent?

Written Practice — *Distributed and Integrated*

Formulate Write and solve equations for problems **1** and **2.**

1. Lobo works 8 hours each day and earns $18 for each hour he works. What amount of income does Lobo earn each day?
   (48)

* **2.** Every third bead on the necklace was red. There were one hundred forty-one beads in all. How many beads were red? (Make equal groups of three.)
   (52, 65)

3. Twenty-five percent of this square is shaded. What percent of
(Inv. 5) the square is not shaded?

* 4. (**Represent**) In one day, Liliana drove 20 kilometers north and then
(25) 15 kilometers south. How far was Liliana from where she started?
Draw a diagram to solve the problem.

5. At 11:45 a.m. Dequon glanced at the clock. His doctor's appointment
(27) was in $2\frac{1}{2}$ hours. At what time was his appointment?

* 6. a. (**Analyze**) In the figure below, we do not state the size of the units
(Inv. 2, used to measure the rectangle. Find the perimeter and area of the
Inv. 3) rectangle. Label your answers with *units* or *square units.*

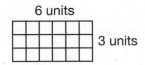

6 units

3 units

b. (**Represent**) The rectangle has 3 rows of 6 squares, showing
that 3 and 6 are factors of 18. Draw a rectangle arranged in two
rows to show two other factors of 18.

* 7. (**Explain**) The car could go 30 miles on 1 gallon of gas. How far
(57) could the car go on 8 gallons of gas? Explain your thinking.

* 8. Two sevenths of the crowd cheered wildly. The rest of the crowd stood
(61) quietly. What fraction of the crowd stood quietly?

9. How many different three-digit numbers can you write using the digits
(3, 10) 4, 2, and 7? Each digit may be used only once. Label the numbers you
write as even or odd.

* 10. (**Represent**) Compare: $\frac{1}{2} \bigcirc \frac{2}{5}$. Draw and shade two congruent
(56) rectangles to show the comparison.

11. $n + 2 = 3 \times 12$ **12.** $6.42 - (3.3 - 1.5)$
(61)   *(45, 50)*

* 13. $\sqrt{81} + 82 + 3^2$ **14.** $\$10 - 10¢$
(Inv. 3,   *(43)*
62)

15. $43,016 - 5987$ *** 16.** $24 \times 3 \times 10$
(52)   *(62)*

17. $4.86 × 7
(58)

18. 307 × 8
(58)

19. $460 × 9
(58)

*20. 2)152
(65)

*21. 6)264
(65)

*22. $4w = 56$
(41, 64)

*23. 230 ÷ 5
(65)

*24. 91 ÷ 7
(64)

*25. 135 ÷ 3
(65)

26. **a.** Write 8¢ using a dollar sign and a decimal point.
(20, 35)

b. Round $11.89 to the nearest dollar.

*27. (Represent) Use words to name each number:
(35, Inv. 4)

a. $2\frac{3}{10}$

b. 2.3

*28. **a. Multiple Choice** Which two triangles are congruent?
(66)

A   B   C   D

b. ✎ (Explain) Explain your answer to part **a.**

*29. (Represent) Draw a pentagon. A pentagon has how many vertices?
(63)

*30. ✎ (Conclude) Are all squares similar? Why or why not?
(66)

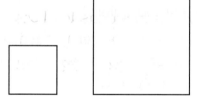

Early Finishers

Real-World Connection

Road signs often have the same shape, but they may not have the same size. Look at the road signs below. Find two signs that are congruent and two other signs that are similar but not congruent.

• Multiplying by Multiples of 10

Power Up

facts   Power Up I

count aloud   When we count by fives from 2, we say the numbers 2, 7, 12, 17, and so on. Count by fives from 2 to 52.

mental math   Multiply numbers ending in two zeros by numbers ending in one zero in **a–c.**

    a. Number Sense: 200×10

    b. Number Sense: 300×20

    c. Number Sense: 400×50

    d. Percent: 50% of $10

    e. Percent: 25% of $10

    f. Percent: 10% of $10

    g. Estimation: Estimate the total cost of two items priced at $3.88 each and one item priced at $5.98.

    h. Calculation: $4^2, + 34, + 72, - 24$

problem solving   Choose an appropriate problem-solving strategy to solve this problem. Mathea exercised for 50% of an hour. For 50% of her exercise time, she was running. For how many minutes was Mathea exercising? For how many minutes was she running?

New Concept

We remember that the multiples of 10 are the numbers we say when we count by tens starting from 10. The last digit in every multiple of 10 is a zero. The first five multiples of 10 are 10, 20, 30, 40, and 50.

We may think of 20 as 2 × 10. So to find 34 × 20, we may look at the problem this way:

$$34 \times 2 \times 10$$

We multiply 34 by 2 and get 68. Then we multiply 68 by 10 and get 680.

Example 1

Write 25 × 30 as a product of 10 and two other factors. Then multiply.

Since 30 equals 3 × 10, we may write 25 × 30 as

25 × 3 × 10

Three times 25 is 75, and 75 times 10 is **750**.

Analyze Is 25 × (3 × 10) the same as 25 × (10 × 10 × 10)? Why or why not?

To multiply a whole number or a decimal number by a multiple of 10, we may write the multiple of 10 so that the zero "hangs out" to the right. Below we use this method to find 34 × 20.

$$\begin{array}{r} 34 \\ \times\ 20 \end{array} \leftarrow \text{zero "hangs out" to the right}$$

We first write a zero in the answer directly below the "hanging" zero.

$$\begin{array}{r} 34 \\ \times\ 20 \\ \hline 0 \end{array}$$

Then we multiply by the 2 in 20.

$$\begin{array}{r} 34 \\ \times\ 20 \\ \hline 680 \end{array}$$

Verify Is 20 the same as 10 × 10? Why or why not?

Example 2

To complete a spelling test, 30 students each wrote 34 different words. How many spelling words will the teacher check altogether?

We write the multiple of 10 as the bottom number and let the zero "hang out."

$$\begin{array}{r} 34 \\ \times\ 30 \end{array}$$

Next we write a zero in the answer directly below the zero in 30. Then we multiply by the 3. The teacher will check **1020 words**.

$$\begin{array}{r} \overset{1}{3}4 \\ \times\ 30 \\ \hline 1020 \end{array}$$

Justify How could you check the answer?

Example 3

A member of a school support staff ordered 20 three-ring binders for the school bookstore. If the cost of each binder was $1.43, what was the total cost of the order?

We write the multiple of 10 so that the zero "hangs out." We write a zero below the bar, and then we multiply by the 2. We place the decimal point so that there are two digits after it. Finally, we write a dollar sign in front. The cost of the order was **$28.60.**

$$\begin{array}{r} \$1.43 \\ \times \quad 20 \\ \hline \$28.60 \end{array}$$

Lesson Practice

In problems **a–f,** multiply the factors.

a. 75×10

b. 10×32

c. $10 \times 53¢$

d. $\begin{array}{r} 26 \\ \times \ 20 \\ \hline \end{array}$

e. $\begin{array}{r} \$1.64 \\ \times \quad 30 \\ \hline \end{array}$

f. $\begin{array}{r} 45 \\ \times \ 50 \\ \hline \end{array}$

g. Write 12×30 as a product of 10 and two other factors. Then multiply.

Written Practice   *Distributed and Integrated*

* 1. Seventy-five beans were equally divided into five pots. How many beans were in each pot?
(52, 65)

* 2. a. **Analyze** Find the perimeter and area of this rectangle. Remember to label your answer with *units* or *square units*.
(Inv. 2, Inv. 3)

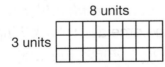

8 units

3 units

b. **Represent** Sketch a rectangle that is four units wide with the same area as the rectangle in part **a.** What is the perimeter of this new rectangle?

3. **Multiple Choice** The server placed a full pitcher of water on the table. Which of the following is a reasonable estimate of the amount of water in the pitcher?
(40)

A 2 gallons   **B** 2 quarts   **C** 2 cups   **D** 2 ounces

*4. Multiple Choice Which of these numbers is *not* a factor of 12?
(55)
    A 6   **B** 5   **C** 4   **D** 3

5. The starting time was before dawn. The stopping time was in the
(27)
afternoon. What was the difference in the two times?

Starting time   Stopping time

*6. (Represent) One square mile is 3,097,600 square yards. Use words
(34)
to write that number of square yards.

7. a. What fraction of this pentagon is *not* shaded?
(Inv. 5, 61)
   b. Is the shaded part of this pentagon more than 50% or
less than 50% of the pentagon?

8. According to this calendar, what is the date of the last
(54)
Saturday in July 2019?

| **JULY 2019** | | | | | | |
S	M	T	W	T	F	S
	1	2	3	4	5	6
7	8	9	10	11	12	13
14	15	16	17	18	19	20
21	22	23	24	25	26	27
28	29	30	31			

*9. (Estimate) To estimate the product of two factors, a student
(59)
rounded one factor down and left the other factor unchanged. Was the
estimate greater than the exact product or less than the exact product?
Give an example to support your answer.

10. (Represent) To what mixed number is the arrow pointing?
(37)

* 11. **Justify** Sofia estimated that the exact product of 4 × 68 is close to
(59) 400 because 68 rounded to the nearest hundred is 100, and 4 × 100 =
400. Was Sofia's estimate reasonable? Explain why or why not.

* 12. Compare: 2^3 ◯ 2 × 3
(Inv. 1, 62)

13. $6.25 + $4 + $12.78
(43)

14. 3.6 + 12.4 + 0.84
(50)

15. $30.25
(24, 52) − _____ b
         ───────
           $13.06

16.   149,384
(52)   −   98,765

17.   409
(67)   ×   70

18. 5 × $3.46
(58)

19. $0.79 × 6
(58)

* 20. 10 × 39¢
(67)

* 21. 6)‾90‾
(64)

* 22. 4w = 96
(41, 64)

* 23. 8)‾456‾
(65)

* 24. 95 ÷ 5
(64)

* 25. 234 ÷ 3
(65)

* 26. Name the shaded part of this rectangle as a fraction and
(Inv. 4) as a decimal.

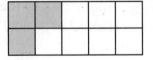

* 27. a. Multiple Choice Which two figures are congruent?
(66)

A    B   C   D

b. **Conclude** Explain how you know.

28. How much money is $\frac{1}{4}$ of a dollar?
(36)

* 29. **Represent** Draw a hexagon. A hexagon has how many vertices?
(63)

*30. **Interpret** The line graph shows the temperature at different times
(Inv. 6) on a winter morning at Hayden's school. Use the graph to answer the
questions that follow.

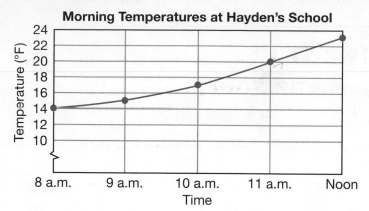

a. At what time was the first temperature of the morning recorded?
What was that temperature?

b. Was the noon temperature warmer or colder than the 10 a.m.
temperature? How many degrees warmer or colder was the
noon temperature?

Early Finishers

Real-World Connection

Marla bought a new protein shake with ten times the amount of protein
as her old protein shake.

a. If the old protein shake has 3.25 grams of protein,
how many grams of protein does Marla's new shake
have?

b. What equation did you use to solve?

LESSON 68

• Division with Two-Digit Answers and a Remainder

Power Up

facts   Power Up I

count aloud Count down by fives from 52 to 2.

mental math
- **a. Number Sense:** $10 \times 20 \times 30$
- **b. Number Sense:** 250×10
- **c. Money:** Shatavia had $5.00. Then she spent $3.79. How much did she have left?
- **d. Money:** Tan bought a scorebook for $6.48 and a whistle for $2.84. How much did he spend?
- **e. Geometry:** What is the perimeter of a square with 9-inch sides? Express your answer in feet.
- **f. Time:** How many years is 1 century plus 4 decades?
- **g. Estimation:** Estimate 193×5 by rounding 193 to the nearest hundred and then multiplying.
- **h. Calculation:** $18 \div 9$, $\times 6$, $\times 6$

problem solving

Choose an appropriate problem-solving strategy to solve this problem. Stephanie solved an addition problem and then erased some of the digits from the problem. She gave it to Ian as a problem-solving exercise. Copy Stephanie's problem on your paper, and find the missing digits for Ian.

$$\begin{array}{r} 7\_6 \\ +\ \_4\_ \\ \hline \_45 \end{array}$$

New Concept

The pencil-and-paper method we use for dividing has four steps: divide, multiply, subtract, and bring down. These steps are repeated until the division is complete.

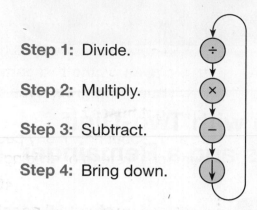

Step 1: Divide.

Step 2: Multiply.

Step 3: Subtract.

Step 4: Bring down.

For each step we write a number. When we finish Step 4, we go back to Step 1 and repeat the steps until there are no more digits to bring down. The number left after the last subtraction is the remainder. We show the remainder in the division answer by writing it with an uppercase "R" in front.

Example 1

Thinking Skill

Verify

Why do we write the first digit of the quotient in the tens place?

Divide: $5\overline{)137}$

Step 1: Divide 13 by 5 and write "2."

Step 2: Multiply 2 by 5 and write "10."

Step 3: Subtract 10 from 13 and write "3."

Step 4: Bring down 7 to make 37.

$$\begin{array}{r} 2 \\ 5\overline{)137} \\ 10\!\downarrow \\ \hline 37 \end{array}$$

Now we repeat the same four steps:

Step 1: Divide 37 by 5 and write "7."

Step 2: Multiply 7 by 5 and write "35."

Step 3: Subtract 35 from 37 and write "2."

Step 4: There are no more digits to bring down, so we will not repeat the steps. The remainder is 2. Our answer is **27 R 2.**

$$\begin{array}{r} 27 \\ 5\overline{)137} \\ 10 \\ \hline 37 \\ 35 \\ \hline 2 \end{array}$$

If we divide 137 into 5 equal groups, there will be 27 in each group. There will also be 2 extra.

To check a division answer that has a remainder, we multiply the quotient (without the remainder) by the divisor and then add the remainder. For this example, we multiply 27 by 5 and then add 2.

$$\begin{array}{r} 27 \\ \times\ 5 \\ \hline 135 \end{array} \qquad \begin{array}{r} 135 \\ +\ 2 \\ \hline 137 \end{array} \text{ check}$$

Example 2

> Three hundred seventy-five fans chartered eight buses to travel to a playoff basketball game. About how many fans were on each bus if the group was divided as evenly as possible among the eight buses?
>
> To find "about how many people," we can estimate with compatible numbers. Instead of dividing 375 by 8, we will divide 400 by 8.
>
> $$400 \div 8 = 50$$
>
> There will be **about 50 people** on each bus.

Lesson Practice   Divide:

a. $3\overline{)134}$ **b.** $7\overline{)240}$ **c.** $5\overline{)88}$

d. $259 \div 8$ **e.** $95 \div 4$ **f.** $325 \div 6$

g. Shou divided 235 by 4 and got 58 R 3 for her answer. Describe how to check Shou's calculation.

h. A wildlife biologist estimates that 175 birds live in the 9-acre marsh. What is a reasonable estimate of the number of birds in each acre of the marsh? Explain why your estimate is reasonable.

Written Practice   *Distributed and Integrated*

*1. **(Analyze)** Alphonso ran 6 miles per hour. At that rate, how far could he run in 3 hours? Make a table to solve this problem.
(57)

*2. Find the perimeter and area of this rectangle:
(Inv. 2, Inv. 3)

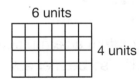

6 units

4 units

3. **(Represent)** Aletta ran 100 meters in twelve and fourteen hundredths seconds. Use digits to write her time.
(Inv. 4)

*4. Taydren drew an octagon and a pentagon. How many sides did the two polygons have altogether?
(63)

*5. 47×30 ***6.** 60×39 ***7.** 85×40
(67)   (67)   (67)

*8. a. Maura ran $\frac{3}{5}$ of the course but walked the rest of the way. What
(Inv. 5, 61) fraction of the course did she walk?

b. Did Maura run more than 50% of the course or less than 50% of the course?

9. (**Represent**) To what mixed number is the arrow pointing?
(37)

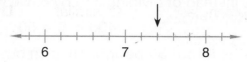

*10. (**Model**) Draw a number line and show the locations of 0, 1, 2, $1\frac{2}{3}$,
(37) and $2\frac{1}{3}$.

11. (**Represent**) Mount Rainier stands four thousand, three hundred
(33) ninety-two meters above sea level. Use digits to write that number.

*12. Mo'Nique could make 35 knots in 7 minutes. How many knots could
(60) she make in 1 minute?

13. Estimate the sum of 6810 and 9030 by rounding each number to the
(59) nearest thousand before adding.

*14. Estimate the sum of $12.15 and $5.95. Then find the exact sum.
(43, 59)

15. $20 − ($8.95 + 75¢)   **16.** 23.64 − 5.45
(43, 45)   (43)

17.   43¢   **18.** $3.05   **19.** $2.63
(48) × 8   (58) ×   5   (58) ×   7

20. (**Connect**) Rewrite this addition problem as a multiplication problem
(27) and find the answer:

$$64 + 64 + 64 + 64 + 64$$

*21. $5\overline{)96}$ ***22.** $7\overline{)156}$ ***23.** $3\overline{)246}$
(68)   (68)   (65)

*24. $\frac{216}{6}$ ***25.** $4r = 156$ ***26.** $195 \div 8$
(65)   (41, 65)   (68)

*27. **Model** Use an inch ruler to find the lengths of segments *AB, BC,* and *AC.*
(39, 45)

A   B   C

*28. a. **Multiple Choice** Which word makes the following sentence untrue?
(63, 66)

All squares are _____.

A polygons   **B** rectangles   **C** similar   **D** congruent

b. **Explain** Explain your choice.

29. Compare: 2 quarts $\bigcirc$ $\frac{1}{2}$ gallon
(40)

*30. **Interpret** The lengths of three land tunnels in the United States are
(Inv. 6) shown in the graph. Use the graph to answer parts **a–c.**

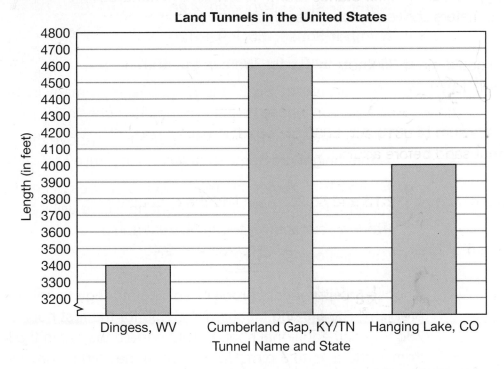

a. Write the names of the tunnels in order from shortest to longest.

b. How many feet longer is the Hanging Lake Tunnel than the Dingess Tunnel?

c. One mile is equal to 5280 feet. Are the combined lengths of the tunnels more than or less than 2 miles?

• Millimeters

facts   Power Up I

count aloud   Count down by threes from 60 to 3.

mental math

   a. Number Sense: $12 \times 2 \times 10$

   b. Number Sense: $20 \times 20 \times 20$

   c. Number Sense: $56 + 9 + 120$

   d. Fractional Parts: What is $\frac{1}{2}$ of $60?

   e. Measurement: Six feet is 72 inches. How many inches tall is a person whose height is 5 feet 11 inches?

   f. Measurement: The airplane is 5500 feet above the ground. Is that height greater than or less than 1 mile?

   g. Estimation: Xavier can read about 30 pages in one hour. If Xavier must read 58 pages, about how long will it take him? (Round your answer to the nearest hour.)

   h. Calculation: 6^2, $- 18$, $\div 9$, $\times 50$

problem solving   Choose an appropriate problem-solving strategy to solve this problem. The parking lot charged $1.50 for the first hour and 75¢ for each additional hour. Harold parked the car in the lot from 11:00 a.m. to 3 p.m. How much money did he have to pay? Explain how you found your answer.

This line segment is one centimeter long:

———

If we divide a centimeter into ten equal lengths, each equal length is **1 millimeter** long. A dime is about 1 millimeter thick.

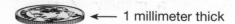 ← 1 millimeter thick

The words *centimeter* and *millimeter* are based on Latin words. *Centum* is the Latin word for "hundred." A centimeter is one hundredth ($\frac{1}{100}$) of a meter, just as a cent is one hundredth of a dollar. *Mille* is the Latin word for "thousand." A millimeter is one thousandth ($\frac{1}{1000}$) of a meter, just as a milliliter is one thousandth of a liter.

Here we show a millimeter scale and a centimeter scale:

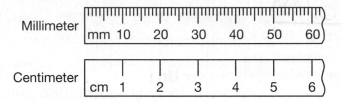

We can see from the scales that each centimeter equals ten millimeters.

Math Symbols

The abbreviation for centimeter is cm. The abbreviation for millimeter is mm.

Example 1

The segment below is how many millimeters long?

The length of the segment is **35 mm.**

Example 2

This paper clip is 3 cm long. How many millimeters long is it?

Each centimeter is 10 mm. We multiply 10 mm by 3 to find that the length of the paper clip is **30 mm.**

Using the scales below, we see that a segment that is 25 mm long is $2\frac{5}{10}$ cm long.

We usually write metric measures as decimal numbers instead of fractions. So a 25-mm segment is 2.5 cm long.

Example 3

Write the length of this segment

    a. in millimeters.

    b. in centimeters.

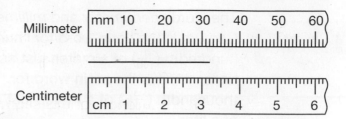

Millimeter

Centimeter

a. 32 mm

b. 3.2 cm

(Connect) Write 3.2 cm as a mixed number.

Example 4

Write a decimal subtraction problem that shows how to find the length of segment *BC.*

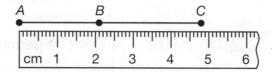

Segment *AC* is 4.8 cm long. Segment *AB* is 2.1 cm long. If we "take away" segment *AB* from segment *AC,* segment *BC* is left. We subtract 2.1 cm from 4.8 cm to find the length of segment *BC.*

4.8 − 2.1 = 2.7

We find that segment *BC* is 2.7 cm long.

(Connect) Write 2.7 cm as a mixed number.

Activity

Measuring with Metric Units

(Model) Use a ruler to estimate the length of real-world items.

1. (Estimate) Find an item in your classroom that is about 280 mm long. How many centimeters is 280 mm?

2. (Estimate) Find an item in your classroom that is about 170 mm long. How many centimeters is 170 mm?

3. Find two other items in your classroom and estimate each length in millimeters and centimeters. Record your estimates. Then measure the items to see how close your estimate is to the actual measurement.

(Discuss) When measuring the length of an object in millimeters and in centimeters, which number is greater, the number of millimeters or the number of centimeters? Explain why.

Lesson Practice

a. The thickness of a dime is about 1 mm. Estimate the number of dimes it would take to form a stack that is about 1 cm high.

b. Write the length of this segment twice, once in millimeters and once in centimeters.

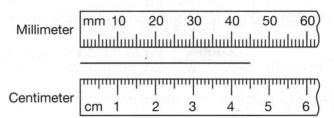

c. Each side of this square is 1 cm long. What is the perimeter of this square in millimeters?

d. The diameter of a penny is about 19 mm. How many centimeters is that?

e. Write a decimal subtraction equation that shows how to find the length of segment *XY*.

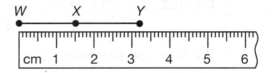

f. Write 3.4 cm as a fraction.

Written Practice *Distributed and Integrated*

Formulate Write and solve equations for problems **1** and **2**.

*1. Celeste has three hundred eighty-four baseball cards. Will has two hundred sixty baseball cards. Celeste has how many more cards than Will?
(25, 30)

*2. Forty-two students could ride in one bus. There were 30 buses. How many students could ride in all the buses?
(49, 67)

*3. Kya's house key is 5.2 cm long. How many millimeters long is her house key?
(69)

*4. **Represent** Write a decimal and a fraction (or a mixed number) to
(Inv. 1, 37) represent each point.

A   B   C

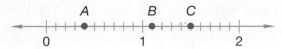

0   1   2

*5. **Represent** Copy this hexagon and shade one sixth of it.
(26)

*6. a. This toothpick is how many centimeters long?
(69)

   b. This toothpick is how many millimeters long?

7. Twenty-five percent of the students in a class completed the science
(Inv. 5) project on Thursday. All of the other students in the class completed the
project on Friday. What percent of the students completed the project on
Friday?

8. **Analyze** One yard equals 3 feet. If each side of a square is 1 yard
(Inv. 2, 49) long, then what is the perimeter of the square in feet?

*9. **Explain** The number of students enrolled at each of three elementary
(59) schools is shown in the table below.

Elementary School Enrollment

School	Number of Students
Van Buren	412
Carter	495
Eisenhower	379

Use rounding to make a reasonable estimate of the total number of
students enrolled at the three schools. Explain your answer.

*10. Segment *AB* is 3.5 cm long. Segment *AC* is 11.6 cm long. How long
(45, 69) is segment *BC*? Write a decimal subtraction equation and find the
answer.

A   B   C

11. a. Hugo rode 125 miles in 5 hours. His average speed was how many
(57, 60) miles per hour?

b. Levi could ride 21 miles in 1 hour. At that rate, how many miles
could Levi ride in 7 hours?

* **12.** The first three prime numbers are 2, 3, and 5. What are the next three
(55) prime numbers?

13. **Estimate** Claudio's meal cost $7.95. Timo's meal cost $8.95.
(20, 59) Estimate the total price for both meals by rounding each amount to the
nearest dollar before adding.

* **14.** 250 ÷ 6   * **15.** 100 ÷ 9   **16.**   36.2
(68)   (68)   (43)   4.7
                                                                    15.9
* **17.** $\dfrac{256}{8}$ * **18.** 4w = 60   148.4
(65)   (41, 64)   30.5
                                                              +   6.0
19. 9 × $4.63   * **20.** 80 × 29¢
(58)   (67)

21. $10.00   **22.**   36,428   * **23.**   78
(52)   − $ 1.73   (52)   − 27,338   (67)   ×   60

* **24.** 4)‾328‾   * **25.** 7)‾375‾   * **26.** 5)‾320‾
(65)   (68)   (65)

27. a + 5 = 25 + 25
(61)

* **28.** **Explain** Solve the equation below and describe the steps in the
(43, 45) order you completed them.

$$4.7 − (3.6 − 1.7)$$

* **29. a.** Find the perimeter of this rectangle in millimeters.
(Inv. 2,
Inv. 3) **b.** Find the area of this rectangle in square centimeters.

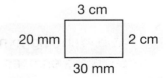
3 cm
20 mm   2 cm
30 mm

* **30.** **Multiple Choice** Each angle of this triangle is _____.
(23)
    A acute   **B** right
    C obtuse   **D** straight

• Word Problems About a Fraction of a Group

Power Up

facts	Power Up I
count aloud	Count by fives from 1 to 51.
mental math	**a. Number Sense:** $21 \times 2 \times 10$
	b. Number Sense: $25 \times 2 \times 10$
	c. Number Sense: $12 \times 4 \times 10$
	d. Money: $\$5.36 + \$1.98$
	e. Measurement: Ten feet is how many inches?
	f. Estimation: Round the prices $\$2.58$ and $\$6.54$ to the nearest dollar and then add to estimate the total.
	g. Estimation: Round the prices $\$2.58$ and $\$6.54$ to the nearest 25 cents and then add to estimate the total.
	h. Calculation: $9^2 + 125 + 37$
problem solving	Choose an appropriate problem-solving strategy to solve this problem. Tazara has ten coins that total one dollar, but only one of the coins is a dime. What are the other nine coins? (There are two possibilities.)

New Concept

Reading Math

We can use fractions to name part of a whole, part of a group or number, and part of a distance.

We know that the fraction $\frac{1}{2}$ means that a whole has been divided into 2 parts. To find the number in $\frac{1}{2}$ of a group, we divide the total number in the group by 2. To find the number in $\frac{1}{3}$ of a group, we divide the total number in the group by 3. To find the number in $\frac{1}{4}$ of a group, we divide the total number in the group by 4, and so on.

Example 1

One half of the carrot seeds sprouted. If 84 seeds were planted, how many seeds sprouted?

We will begin by drawing a picture. The large rectangle stands for all the seeds. We are told that $\frac{1}{2}$ of the seeds sprouted, so we divide the large rectangle into 2 equal parts (into halves). Then we divide 84 by 2 and find that **42 seeds** sprouted.

84 seeds

$\frac{1}{2}$ sprouted. { | 42 seeds |

$\frac{1}{2}$ did not { | 42 seeds |
sprout.

$$\begin{array}{r} 42 \text{ seeds} \\ 2\overline{)84 \text{ seeds}} \end{array}$$

Discuss How can we use addition to check the answer?

Example 2

On Friday, one third of the 27 students purchased lunch in the school cafeteria. How many students purchased lunch on Friday?

We start with a picture. The whole rectangle stands for all the students. Since $\frac{1}{3}$ of the students purchased lunch, we divide the rectangle into 3 equal parts. To find how many students are in each part, we divide 27 by 3 and find that **9 students** purchased a lunch on Friday.

27 students

$\frac{1}{3}$ purchased lunch. { | 9 students |

$\frac{2}{3}$ did not { | 9 students |
purchase lunch. { | 9 students |

$$\begin{array}{r} 9 \text{ students} \\ 3\overline{)27 \text{ students}} \end{array}$$

Justify Explain why the answer is correct.

Example 3

One fourth of the team's 32 points were scored by Thi. How many points did Thi score?

We draw a rectangle. The whole rectangle stands for all 32 points. Thi scored $\frac{1}{4}$ of the points, so we divide the rectangle into 4 equal parts. We divide 32 by 4 and find that each part is 8 points. Thi scored **8 points.**

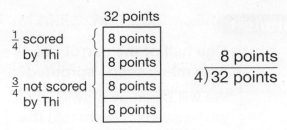

$\frac{1}{4}$ scored by Thi

$\frac{3}{4}$ not scored by Thi

32 points

| 8 points |
| 8 points |
| 8 points |
| 8 points |

$$\frac{8 \text{ points}}{4)\overline{32 \text{ points}}}$$

Justify Explain why the answer is correct.

Example 4

What is $\frac{1}{5}$ of 40?

We draw a rectangle to represent 40. We divide the rectangle into five equal parts, and we divide 40 by 5. Each part is 8, so $\frac{1}{5}$ of 40 is **8.**

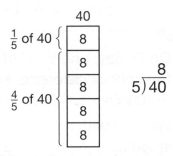

$\frac{1}{5}$ of 40

$\frac{4}{5}$ of 40

40

| 8 |
| 8 |
| 8 |
| 8 |
| 8 |

$$\frac{8}{5)\overline{40}}$$

Lesson Practice

Draw a picture to solve each problem:

a. What is $\frac{1}{3}$ of 60? **b.** What is $\frac{1}{2}$ of 60?

c. What is $\frac{1}{4}$ of 60? **d.** What is $\frac{1}{5}$ of 60?

e. One half of the 32 children were boys. How many boys were there?

f. One third of the 24 coins were quarters. How many quarters were there?

Written Practice   *Distributed and Integrated*

Formulate Write and solve equations for problems **1** and **2**.

*1. There were 150 seats in the cafeteria. If 128 seats were filled, how
(31) many seats were empty?

*2. **Analyze** Anaya ran 100 meters in 12.14 seconds. Marion ran
(Inv 4, 43) 100 meters in 11.98 seconds. Marion ran 100 meters how many seconds faster than Anaya?

3. Forty-two million is how much greater than twenty-four million?
(31, 34)

4. Keenan bought his lunch Monday through Friday. If each lunch cost
(49) $1.25, how much did he spend on lunch for the week?

* 5. Find the perimeter and area of this rectangle:
(Inv. 2,
Inv. 3)

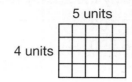

5 units

4 units

* 6. ✏️ **Explain** Re'Bekka read 30 pages a day on Monday, Tuesday, and
(22) Wednesday. She read 45 pages on Thursday and 26 pages on Friday.
How many pages did she read in all? Explain why your answer is
reasonable.

* 7. a. Represent One half of the cabbage seeds sprouted. If 74 seeds
(Inv. 5, were planted, how many sprouted? Draw a picture to solve the
70) problem.

b. What percent of the seeds sprouted?

8. Represent Show all of the different ways these bills can be arranged
(36) in a row.

* 9. Represent What is $\frac{1}{6}$ of 60? Draw a picture to solve the problem.
(70)

* 10. Analyze Driving at a highway speed limit of 65 miles per hour, how
(57) far can a truck travel in 3 hours? Make a table to solve this problem.

* 11. Formulate If a truck traveled 248 miles in 4 hours, then the truck
(60, 65) traveled an average of how many miles each hour? Write an equation
to solve this problem.

* 12. a. What is the diameter of this shirt button in
(69) centimeters?

b. What is the radius of this shirt button in millimeters?

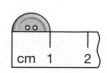

cm   1   2

*13. Segment *AB* is 2.7 cm long. Segment *BC* is 4.8 cm long. How long is
(45, 69) segment *AC?* Write a decimal addition equation and find the answer.

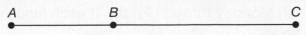

A   B   C

14. $8 + $9.48 + 79¢
(43)

15. 5.36 + 2.1 + 0.43
(50)

16. $100.00
(52)   − $ 59.47

17.   37,102
(52)   − 18,590

18. $\sqrt{49} \times 2^3$
(Inv. 3, 62)

*19. $1.63 × 40
(67)

*20. 60 × 39
(67)

21. 7 × $2.56
(58)

*22. 3$\overline{)89}$
(68)

*23. 9$\overline{)234}$
(65)

24. $\dfrac{90}{6}$
(64)

*25. 243 ÷ 7
(68)

*26. $5m = 355$
(41, 65)

27. $7 + n = 28$
(2)

28. (Represent) Write twelve and three tenths as a mixed number and as a
(35, Inv. 4) decimal number.

*29. Multiple Choice Which of these numbers is a factor of both 12
(55) and 20?

   A 3   **B** 4   **C** 5   **D** 6

*30. (Represent) Draw a triangle that has one right angle.
(23)

Real-World Connection

Leroy's class took a field trip to the aquarium. A total of 35 students
and adults went on the trip. Five sevenths of the group were students.

   a. How many students went on the field trip?

   b. Draw a diagram to show that your answer is reasonable.

Focus on

• Collecting Data with Surveys

In Investigation 6, a pictograph displayed the favorite lunches of the students in Room 12. The information in the graph was gathered by asking students to name their favorite lunch from the school menu. The students who answered the question were participating in a **survey.** A survey is an effort to gather specific information about a group, or a **population.** People who make surveys collect information about part of the population. This part is called a **sample.** Then they draw conclusions about how the results of the survey apply to the whole population. In the favorite-lunch survey, the students in Room 12 were the sample, while all Thompson School students were the population.

Visit www.
SaxonMath.com/
Int4Activities for
an online activity.

In this investigation you will conduct a survey of students in your class. You will need to write questions for the survey, ask the questions fairly, record the answers, and display the results of the survey. From the survey you may be able to draw conclusions about a larger population.

The way survey questions are asked can affect the results of a survey. Here are two survey questions. Describe how the answers to these questions might be different.

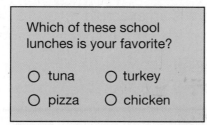

Which of these school
lunches is your favorite?

○ tuna   ○ turkey

○ pizza   ○ chicken

Which lunch from
the school menu
is your favorite?

_____

Notice that one of the questions is a multiple-choice question. The answer is limited to the choices that are provided. The other question is open to many answers.

1. **Formulate** Write two questions that you could ask to determine students' favorite drink to have with lunch. For one question, provide options to choose from. For the other, leave the question open (do not list options). You may use the favorite-lunch questions as models.

Survey questions should be phrased without **bias;** that is, without favoring one choice over another.

2. Describe the bias in the following question:

Which drink do you prefer with lunch: cool, sweet lemonade or milk that has been out of the refrigerator for an hour?

3. **Formulate** Rewrite the question in problem **2** so that the bias is removed.

When we use a sample to find information about a larger population, we need to make sure that the sample is very similar to the population. For example, if we wanted to know the favorite TV show of kindergarten students, we would not survey a group of fourth grade students.

4. a. Multiple Choice For your survey, you will collect answers from students in your class. This means that your class is the sample. Which of these larger populations will probably be best represented by your survey results?

   A all the students in the school

   B all the school children your age in your community

   C all the children your age in the country

   D all the parents of the students in the class

b. **Explain** For each choice, explain why each population could or could not be represented by your sample.

When we ask our survey questions, we need to have a way to record the answers. One way to keep track of answers is with a tally sheet. On a tally sheet we make **tally marks.** A tally mark is a short vertical mark that counts as one. Two marks count as two. Four marks with a fifth, diagonal mark crossing them counts as five. Here is an example of a tally sheet for the favorite-lunch question:

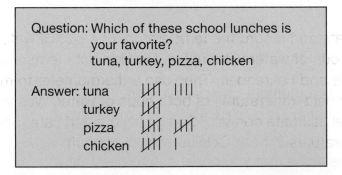

The question was written on the tally sheet so that it could be read to the person being interviewed. By reading the question from a sheet, we make sure that we ask the question the same way each time.

5. **Interpret** Each time a person answers the question, a tally mark is placed by the answer. Look at the tally marks for tuna. According to the tally marks, how many students named tuna as their favorite lunch?

6. **Represent** Create a tally sheet similar to the one above to show favorite drinks to have with lunch. Write a question with choices. Then list the possible answers, leaving room on the paper to tally the answers. One of the options may be "no opinion."

While gathering or combining data, we need to avoid duplicating or omitting data. Duplicating data occurs when information is counted more than once or repeated. Omitting data occurs when necessary information is left out.

7.  **Analyze** Brad found that 11 students in his class had dogs for pets. Dena found that 9 students in the same class had cats for pets. Brad and Dena concluded that 20 students in the class had dogs or cats for pets. Do you think their conclusion is correct? Why or why not?

8. **Analyze** Brad and Dena also concluded that 20 students in the class have pets. Do you think this conclusion is correct? Why or why not?

Activity

Class Survey

Represent With your group, think of a survey question to ask other students.[1] Your question should not have bias. Provide at least two answer options from which the other students may choose. Make a tally sheet that contains your question and answer choices. Ask the other students your survey question. Be sure to tally the other students' answers on your tally sheet. When you have finished your survey, choose and make the appropriate graph to display the results of your survey.

Investigate Further

a. Estimate and record the temperature of a cup of water with ice and a cup of water without ice. Provide both temperatures in Celsius and Fahrenheit. Then use a thermometer to measure the actual temperatures of both cups of water. Was your original estimate correct? Compare your estimate to the actual temperatures in both Celsius and Fahrenheit.

---

[1] Sample topics for surveys:
- favorite sport or sports team
- favorite television show
- favorite school subject
- number of siblings in family
- how students get to school
- favorite season of the year

b. Before you start this activity, look at the clock and find your starting time. Use paper to write each multiple of 4 from 4 to 100. After you are finished, write your ending time. How much time did it take you to complete the activity? Repeat the activity by writing the multiples of 2 from 2 to 100. Which activity took longer? How much longer did it take?

c. Time yourself saying the alphabet. Look at the clock. Write down the beginning time. Then say the alphabet twice. Write down the ending time. Find the time that elapsed while you said the alphabet two times.

• Division Answers Ending with Zero

Power Up

facts Power Up H

count aloud Count by fives from 2 to 52.

mental math

  a. Number Sense: 300×30

  b. Number Sense: 240×10

  c. Number Sense: Counting by 5s from 5, every number Cailey says ends in 0 or 5. If she counts by 5s from 6, then every number she says ends in what digits?

  d. Percent: 50% of 120

  e. Powers/Roots: $\sqrt{64} \div 4$

  f. Money: Cantrice bought peanuts for $3.75 and a drink for $2.95. What was the total cost?

  g. Estimation: Estimate the cost of 8 action figures that are each priced at $4.95.

  h. Calculation: 9^2, $- 60$, $\div 7$, $\times 20$

problem solving Choose an appropriate problem-solving strategy to solve this problem. Cuintan finished his 150-page book on Friday. The day before he had put the book down after reading page 120. If Cuintan read the same number of pages each day, on what day did Cuintan begin reading his book? Explain how you found your answer.

New Concept

Sometimes division answers end with a zero. It is important to continue the division until all the digits inside the division box have been used. Look at the problem at the top of the next page.

Two hundred pennies are separated into 4 equal piles. How many pennies are in each pile?

This problem can be answered by dividing 200 by 4. First we divide 20 by 4. We write a 5 in the quotient. Then we multiply and subtract.

Thinking Skill

Verify

Why do we write the first digit of the quotient in the tens place?

$$\begin{array}{r} 5 \\ 4\overline{)200} \\ \underline{20} \\ 0 \end{array}$$

The division might look complete, but it is not. The answer is not "five pennies in each pile." That would total only 20 pennies. There is another zero inside the division box to bring down. So we bring down the zero and divide again. Zero divided by 4 is 0. We write 0 in the quotient, multiply, and then subtract. The quotient is 50.

$$\begin{array}{r} 50 \\ 4\overline{)200} \\ \underline{20}\downarrow \\ 00 \\ \underline{0} \\ 0 \end{array}$$

Check:

$$\begin{array}{r} 50 \\ \times\ 4 \\ \hline 200 \end{array}$$

We check our work by multiplying the quotient, 50, by the divisor, 4. The product should equal the dividend, 200. The answer checks. We find that there are 50 pennies in each pile.

Sometimes there will be a remainder with a division answer that ends in zero. We show this in the following example.

Example 1

Thinking Skill

Verify

Why do we write the first digit of the quotient in the tens place?

Divide: $3\overline{)121}$

We begin by finding $3\overline{)12}$. Since 12 divided by 3 is 4, we write "4" above the 2. We multiply and subtract, getting 0, but we are not finished. We bring down the last digit of the dividend, which is 1. Now we divide 01 (which means 1) by 3. Since we cannot make an equal group of 3 if we have only 1, we write "0" on top in the ones place. We then multiply zero by 3 and subtract. The remainder is 1.

$$\begin{array}{r} 4 \\ 3\overline{)121} \\ \underline{12} \\ 0 \end{array}$$

$$\begin{array}{r} \textbf{40 R 1} \\ 3\overline{)121} \\ \underline{12} \\ 01 \\ \underline{0} \\ 1 \end{array}$$

Example 2

Mr. Griffith drove 254 miles in 5 hours. About how many miles did he drive each hour?

To find "about how many miles" Mr. Griffith drove each hour, we can use compatible numbers to estimate. Since 250 is close to 254 and is divisible by 5, we divide 250 by 5 to estimate.

250 miles ÷ 5 hours = 50 miles each hour

Mr. Griffith drove **about 50 miles** each hour.

Lesson Practice Divide:

a. $3\overline{)120}$ b. $4\overline{)240}$ c. $5\overline{)152}$

d. $4\overline{)121}$ e. $3\overline{)91}$ f. $2\overline{)41}$

g. **Estimate** The employees in the shipping department of a company loaded 538 boxes into a total of 6 railcars. They put about the same number of boxes into each railcar. About how many boxes are in each railcar? Explain how you found your answer.

Written Practice *Distributed and Integrated*

*1. A rectangular ceiling is covered with square tiles. The ceiling is 40 tiles
(Inv. 3, 67) long and 30 tiles wide. In all, how many tiles are on the ceiling?

2. There were two hundred sixty seats in the movie theater. All but forty-three
(30) seats were occupied. How many seats were occupied?

3. At the grand opening of a specialty food store, five coupons were
(49, 58) given to each customer. One hundred fifteen customers attended the grand opening. How many coupons were given to those customers altogether?

*4. A recipe for making fruit punch calls for a cup of pineapple juice for
(40) each quart of fruit punch. How many cups of pineapple juice are needed to make a gallon of fruit punch?

*5. **Analyze** What is the value of 5 pennies, 3 dimes, 2 quarters, and
(35) 3 nickels?

*6. a. **(Represent)** On the last Friday in May, one fourth of the 280
(Inv. 5, 70) students in a school were away on a field trip. How many
students were on the field trip? Draw a picture to solve the
problem.

   b. What percent of the students were on the field trip?

*7. **(Represent)** What is $\frac{1}{2}$ of 560? Draw a picture to solve the problem.
(70)

*8. a. The line segment shown below is how many centimeters long?
(69)
   b. The segment is how many millimeters long?

*9. The first four multiples of 9 are 9, 18, 27, and 36. What are the first four
(55) multiples of 90?

10. **(Represent)** Compare: $\frac{2}{3} \bigcirc \frac{2}{5}$. Draw and shade two congruent
(56) rectangles to show the comparison.

*11. Badu can ride her bike an average of 12 miles per hour. At that
(57) rate, how many miles could she ride in 4 hours? Make a table to
solve this problem.

12. $375.48
(43, 51)   + $536.70

13.   367,419
(51)   + 90,852

14.   42.3
(50)   57.1
            28.9
            96.4
         + 38.0

15. $20.00
(52)   − $19.39

16.   310,419
(52)   − 250,527

17. $6.08
(58)   ×   7

18.   86
(67)   ×   40

19.   59¢
(48)   ×   8

*20. 3)‾180‾
(71)

*21. 8)‾241‾
(71)

*22. 5)‾323‾
(68)

*23. 184 ÷ 6
(71)

*24. 423 ÷ 7
(71)

*25. $\sqrt{36} + 4^2 + 10^2$
(Inv. 3, 62)

26. $9 + m = 27 + 72$
(61)

27. $6n = 90$
(41, 64)

28. **Model** Use an inch ruler to find the lengths of segments *AB*, *BC*,
(39) and *AC*.

A   B   C

*29. If the diameter of a coin is 2 centimeters, then its radius is how many
(21, 69) millimeters?

*30. **Estimate** From 7 a.m. until noon, the employees in a customer
(71) service department received 147 phone calls. What is a reasonable
estimate of the number of calls that were received each hour? Explain
how you found your answer.

Early Finishers

Real-World Connection

Maddox has a roll of film with 32 photos and another roll with
12 photos. He developed both rolls of film. He decided to put all of his
photos into two scrapbooks. Each scrapbook will hold 20 pictures.

  a. How many pictures does Maddox have altogether?

  b. Will Maddox be able to place all of his photos into the two
     scrapbooks? Explain your answer.

• Finding Information to Solve Problems

Power Up

facts   Power Up H

count aloud   When we count by fives from 3, we say the numbers 3, 8, 13, 18, and so on. Count by fives from 3 to 53.

mental math
a. **Number Sense:** 12 × 20
b. **Number Sense:** 12 × 30
c. **Number Sense:** 12 × 40
d. **Number Sense:** 36 + 29 + 230
e. **Money:** Lucas bought a roll of film for $4.87 and batteries for $3.98. What was the total cost?
f. **Time:** The baseball game started at 7:05 p.m. and lasted 1 hour 56 minutes. What time did the game end?
g. **Estimation:** One mile is about 1609 meters. Round this length to the nearest hundred meters.
h. **Calculation:** $\frac{1}{2}$ of 6, × 2, × 5, − 16

problem solving
Levon has three colors of shirts—red, white, and blue. He has two colors of pants—black and tan. What combinations of one shirt and one pair of pants can Levon make?

Focus Strategy: Make a Diagram

Understand We are told that Levon has three colors of shirts and two colors of pants. We are asked to find the possible combinations of shirts and pants that Levon can wear.

Plan We can *make a diagram* to find all the combinations of shirt and pants colors.

Solve For each shirt, there are two colors of pants Levon can wear. We can list each shirt color and then draw two branches from each color. At the ends of the branches, we can write the color of the pants, like this:

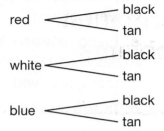

Now we can list the combinations formed by the diagram. We have a total of six branches, so we find that Levon can make six different combinations of shirt and pants colors:

red, black; red, tan; white, black; white, tan; blue, black; blue, tan

Check We found six combinations that Levon can make with three different shirt colors and two different pants colors. We know our answer is reasonable because there are two combinations possible for each shirt color. There are 2 + 2 + 2, or 6 combinations for three different shirt colors.

We call the diagram we made in this problem a *tree diagram*, because each line we drew to connect a shirt color with a pants color is like a branch of a tree.

New Concept

Part of the problem-solving process is finding the information needed to solve a problem. Sometimes we need to find information in graphs, tables, pictures, or other places. In some cases, we might be given more information than we need to solve a problem. In this lesson we will be finding the information we need to solve a problem.

Example 1

Read this information. Then answer the questions that follow.

The school elections were held on Friday, February 2. Tejana, Lily, and Taariq ran for president. Lily received 146 votes, and Tejana received 117 votes. Taariq received 35 more votes than Tejana.

Reading Math

Sometimes problems contain too much information. We need to look for the information that is necessary to solve a problem.

a. How many votes did Taariq receive?

b. Who received the most votes?

c. Speeches were given on the Tuesday before the elections. What was the date on which the speeches were given?

a. Taariq received 35 more votes than Tejana, and Tejana received 117 votes. So we add 35 to 117 and find that Taariq received **152 votes.**

b. **Taariq** received the most votes.

c. The elections were on Friday, February 2. The Tuesday when the speeches were presented was 3 days before that. We count back 3 days: February 1, January 31, January 30. The speeches were given on Tuesday, **January 30.**

Example 2

Alyssa collects key chains from the different states she has visited and displays them on a pegboard.

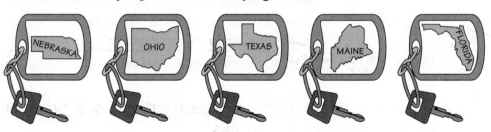

Since Alyssa lives in Nebraska and her grandmother lives in Ohio, she always keeps the Nebraska and Ohio key chains on the first two pegs. How many different ways can Alyssa arrange the key chains in one row?

If the Nebraska key chain is first and the Ohio key chain is second, then the other three chains can be arranged six ways:

Florida, Texas, Maine

Florida, Maine, Texas

Texas, Florida, Maine

Texas, Maine, Florida

Maine, Florida, Texas

Maine, Texas, Florida

If the Ohio key chain is first and the Nebraska key chain is second, then the other three chains can be arranged in the same six ways. Altogether, there are **12 different ways** to arrange the key chains.

Lesson Practice Read this information. Then solve the problems that follow.

Terell did yard work on Saturday. He worked for 3 hours in the morning and 4 hours in the afternoon. He was paid $6 for every hour he worked.

a. How many hours did Terell work in all?

b. How much money did Terell earn in the morning?

c. How much money did Terell earn in all?

d. How many different amounts of money could you make using any two of the three coins shown below? Name the amounts.

Written Practice *Distributed and Integrated*

1. Christie's car travels 18 miles on each gallon of gas. How many miles
(57) can it travel on 10 gallons of gas?

*2. Analyze Alejandro's front yard was 50 feet wide. Each time he
(Inv. 2, pushed the mower along the length of the yard, he mowed a path
52) 24 inches wide. To mow the entire yard, how many times did Alejandro need to push the mower along the length of the yard?

*3. A gift of $160 is to be divided equally among 8 children. What amount
(64, 71) of money will each child receive?

4. Soccer practice lasts for an hour and a half. If practice starts at
(27) 3:15 p.m., at what time does it end?

*5. Represent One third of the team's 36 points were scored by
(70) Chinara. How many points did Chinara score? Draw a picture to help you solve the problem.

6. Find the perimeter and area of the rectangle at right.
(Inv. 2, Inv. 3)

4 units

3 units

*7. (Estimate) This key is 60 mm long. The key is how many centimeters long?
(69)

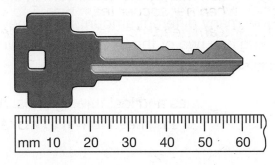

mm 10   20   30   40   50   60

*8. According to this calendar, the year 1902 began on what day of the week?
(54)

DECEMBER 1901

S	M	T	W	T	F	S
1	2	3	4	5	6	7
8	9	10	11	12	13	14
15	16	17	18	19	20	21
22	23	24	25	26	27	28
29	30	31				

*9. Jocelyn is the first person in line at the school cafeteria. Antonio, Bryan, and Caroline are standing in line behind Jocelyn. In how many different orders could Antonio, Bryan, and Caroline be arranged behind Jocelyn? Name the ways.
(72)

10. A meter equals 100 centimeters. If each side of a square is 1 meter long, then what is the perimeter of the square in centimeters?
(Inv. 2)

*11. List the first four multiples of 90.
(55)

12. $1.68 + 32¢ + $6.37 + $5
(43)

13. 4.3 + 2.4 + 0.8 + 6.7
(43)

14. (Explain) Find $10 − ($6.46 + $2.17). Describe the steps you used.
(43, 45)

15. 5 × 4 × 5   **16.** 359 × 70   **17.** 50 × 74
(62)   *(67)*   *(67)*

*18. $2\overline{)161}$
(71)

*19. $5\overline{)400}$
(71)

*20. $9\overline{)462}$
(68)

21. $\dfrac{216}{3}$
(65)

*22. $159 \div 4$
(68)

*23. $\dfrac{490}{7}$
(71)

24. $\dfrac{126}{3}$
(65)

*25. $360 \div \sqrt{36}$
(Inv. 3, 71)

26. $5n = 120$
(41, 65)

*27. (Analyze) Use the information below to answer parts **a** and **b**.
(72)

> Kamili scored two goals when her soccer team won 5 to 4 on November 3. To make the playoffs, her team needs to win two of the next three games.

    a. How many goals were scored by Kamili's teammates?

    b. Kamili's team has won four games and lost three games. Altogether, how many games does Kamili's team need to win to make the playoffs?

28. a. (Classify) Angles C and D of this polygon are right angles. Which angle appears to be an obtuse angle?
(23)

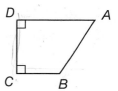

    b. (Classify) Which segments are perpendicular?

    c. (Classify) Which segments are parallel?

*29. Multiple Choice Which two of these figures appear to be congruent?
(66)

  A   **B**   **C**   **D**

*30. (Represent) The average weights of some animals are shown in the table. Make a bar graph to display the data.
(Inv. 6)

Average Weights of Animals

Animal	Weight (in pounds)
Domestic Rabbit	8
Otter	13
Ringtail Monkey	6
Chicken	7

• Geometric Transformations

facts   Power Up H

count aloud Count down by fives from 53 to 3.

mental math
  a. Number Sense: 21×20

  b. Number Sense: 25×30

  c. Number Sense: 25×20

  d. Number Sense: $48 + 19 + 310$

  e. Money: Julia has a gift card that is worth $50. She has used the card for $24.97 in purchases. How much value is left on the card?

  f. Time: The track meet started at 9:00 a.m. and lasted 4 hours 30 minutes. What time did the track meet end?

  g. Estimation: At sea level, sound travels about 1116 feet in one second. Round this distance to the nearest hundred feet.

  h. Calculation: $\sqrt{25}$, $\times 7$, $+ 5$, $+ 10$, $\div 10$

problem solving
Choose an appropriate problem-solving strategy to solve this problem. The charge for the taxi ride was $2.50 for the first mile and $1.50 for each additional mile. What was the charge for an 8-mile taxi ride? Explain how you solved the problem.

Geometry is a branch of mathematics that deals with such figures as lines, angles, polygons, circles, and solid objects. One concept from geometry that we have practiced is congruent figures. Recall that figures are congruent if they have the same shape and size. However, congruent figures may be in different

orientations (positions). For example, all four of these triangles are congruent:

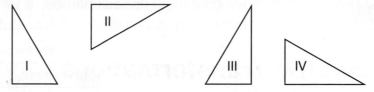

The right angle of △I ("triangle one") is at the lower left of the triangle. The other triangles may be reoriented to match △I.

To reorient △II, we may *turn* the triangle so that its right angle is at the lower left.

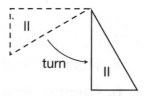

To reorient △III, we may *flip* the triangle as we might flip a pancake or flip a page in a book. (Imagine flipping △III so that its right angle is at the lower left.)

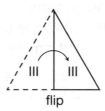

To reorient △IV, we may both turn and flip the triangle. (Imagine turning △IV so that it is oriented like △III. After turning the triangle, flip the triangle to match △I.)

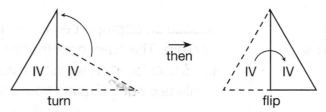

To put each of triangles II, III, and IV in the same location as △I requires an additional step. Each reoriented triangle needs to *slide* to the location of △I.

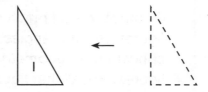

Turns, flips, and slides are three ways of moving figures. In geometry we call these movements **transformations,** and we give them special names: a turn is a **rotation,** a flip is a **reflection,** and a slide is a **translation.**

Transformations

Movement	Name
Slide	Translation
Turn	Rotation
Flip	Reflection

Example 1

Which transformations would move △II to the same orientation and location as △I?

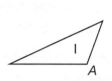

We may move △II to the location of △I with two transformations: **a turn and a slide.** The order of the transformations does not matter. We may slide △II so that point *B* is on point *A*. Then we may turn △II around point *B* so that the sides and angles align with △I. We call a slide a **translation,** and we call a turn a **rotation.**

Activity

Using Transformations

Model Use classroom objects to act out the activities below.

a. Place two books in the positions shown below. Describe the transformations you would use to move one book into the same position as the other. Are the books congruent? Explain.

b. Place two pencils in the positions shown below. Describe the transformations you would use to move one pencil to the same position as the other. Are the pencils the same size and shape? Explain.

c. Place two rulers on a desk and describe the transformations that are needed to move one ruler to the same position as the other. Arrange the rulers so that a translation, a reflection, and a rotation are needed to move one ruler to the same position as the other.

Lesson Practice

a. Congruent figures may be repositioned through transformations so that all corresponding sides and angles are aligned. Name the three transformations described in this lesson. Give the common name and the geometric name for each transformation.

b. (**Conclude**) Which transformations would position △ABC on △DEC?

c. (**Model**) Use a color tile to model a turn, a flip, and a slide.

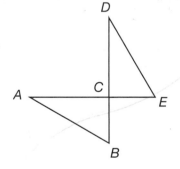

Written Practice *Distributed and Integrated*

*1. (**Represent**) Half of the 48 pencils were sharpened. How many were *(Inv. 5, 70)* *not* sharpened? What percent of the pencils were not sharpened? Draw a picture to solve the problem.

*2. (**Represent**) What number is $\frac{1}{4}$ of 60? Draw a picture to solve the *(70)* problem.

*3. Use this information to answer parts **a–c:**
(52, 72)

> Thirty students are going on a field trip. Each car can hold
> five students. The field trip will cost each student $5.

    a. How many cars are needed for the field trip?

    b. Altogether, how much money will be needed?

    c. Diego has saved $3.25. How much more does he need to go on
       the field trip?

4. (**Analyze**) During the summer, the swim team practiced $3\frac{1}{2}$ hours a day.
(27) If practice started at 6:30 a.m., at what time did it end if there were no
breaks?

5. One gallon of water will be poured into 1-quart bottles.
(40) How many 1-quart bottles will be filled?

1 gal   1 qt

*6. Each side of a regular polygon has the same length. A regular hexagon
(69) is shown below. How many millimeters is the perimeter of this
hexagon?

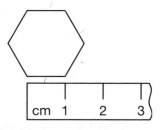

7. A mile is five thousand, two hundred eighty feet. The Golden Gate
(31, 52) Bridge is four thousand, two hundred feet long. The Golden Gate
Bridge is how many feet less than 1 mile long?

*8. Multiple Choice Which of these numbers is *not* a multiple of 90?
(55)
   A 45   **B** 180   **C** 270   **D** 360

9. What number is halfway between 300 and 400?
(Inv. 1)

10. $37.56 - 4.2$
(50)

11. $4.2 + 3.5 + 0.25 + 4.0$
(50)

12. $\begin{array}{r} \$100.00 \\ - \ \$ \ 31.53 \\ \hline \end{array}$
(52)

13. $\begin{array}{r} 251{,}546 \\ - \ 37{,}156 \\ \hline \end{array}$
(52)

14. $\begin{array}{r} n \\ + \ 423 \\ \hline 618 \end{array}$
(24)

15. $\begin{array}{r} \$3.46 \\ \times \quad 7 \\ \hline \end{array}$
(58)

16. $\begin{array}{r} 96 \\ \times \ 30 \\ \hline \end{array}$
(67)

17. $\begin{array}{r} \$0.59 \\ \times \quad 8 \\ \hline \end{array}$
(58)

*18. $7\overline{)633}$
(71)

*19. $5\overline{)98}$
(68)

*20. $3\overline{)150}$
(71)

*21. $329 \div 6$
(68)

*22. $274 \div 4$
(68)

*23. $247 \div 8$
(71)

24. $\sqrt{25} \times m = 135$
(41, 65)

25. $z - 476 = 325$
(24)

26. $6a = 12 + 6$
(61)

*27. (**Connect**) Segment AB is 2.3 cm long. Segment BC is 3.5 cm long.
(45, 69) How long is segment AC? Write a decimal addition problem and find
the answer.

*28. (**Conclude**) Which transformation would position $\triangle ABC$
(73) on $\triangle ABD$?

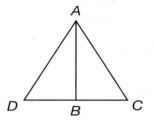

29. (**Estimate**) Using rounding or compatible numbers, which numbers
(59) would you choose to estimate the exact product of 25×25? Explain
your reasoning.

*30. ![pencil icon] **Interpret** This pictograph shows the maximum speeds that
(Inv. 6) animals can run for a short distance. Use the pictograph to answer the
questions that follow.

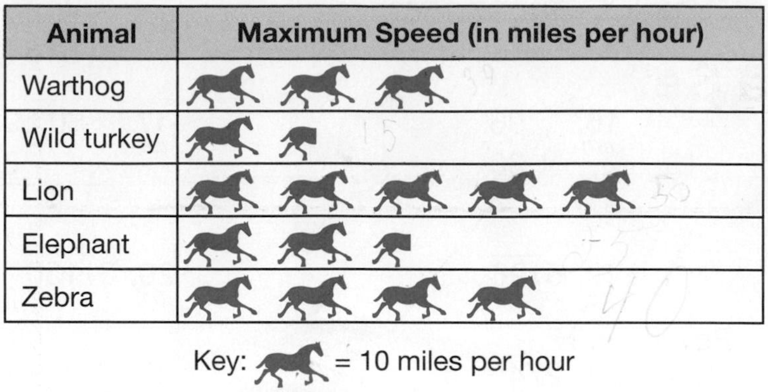

Animal	Maximum Speed (in miles per hour)
Warthog	🐎 🐎 🐎
Wild turkey	🐎 🐎
Lion	🐎 🐎 🐎 🐎 🐎
Elephant	🐎 🐎 🐎
Zebra	🐎 🐎 🐎 🐎

Key: 🐎 = 10 miles per hour

a. Which animals can run at a speed of at least 30 miles per hour?

b. A squirrel can run at a maximum speed of 12 miles per hour. About
how many times greater is the maximum speed of a lion? Explain
your reasoning.

c. Some athletes can run at a maximum speed of about 28 miles per
hour for short distances. Could some athletes run faster than an
elephant? Explain your answer.

Early Finishers

Real-World Connection

Mr. Mikel drew the figure shown below. His students said the answer
was "flip." What questions did Mr. Mikel ask the students?

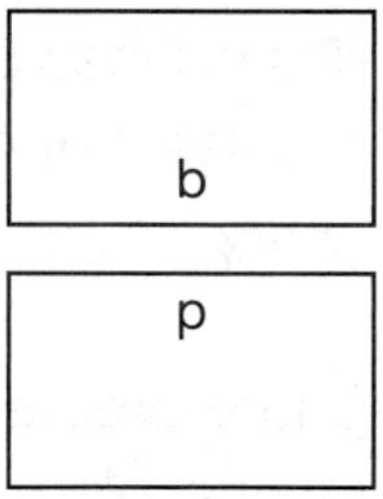

```
┌─────────────┐
│             │
│      b      │
│             │
└─────────────┘
┌─────────────┐
│      p      │
│             │
└─────────────┘
```

LESSON 74

• Fraction of a Set

facts	Power Up H
count aloud	When we count by fives from 4, we say the numbers 4, 9, 14, 19, and so on. Count by fives from 4 to 54.
mental math	**a. Number Sense:** 25 × 100

a. Number Sense: 25 × 100

b. Number Sense: 100 × 40

c. Number Sense: 12 × 3 × 100

d. Number Sense: Counting by 5s from 5, every number Raven says ends in 0 or 5. If she counts by 5s from 7, then every number she says ends in which digit?

e. Powers/Roots: $\sqrt{4} + 3^2 + 1^2$

f. Measurement: Abdul needs 6 quarts of water to make enough lemonade for the team. How many cups is 6 quarts?

g. Estimation: Rahoul has $28. Does he have enough money to buy three T-shirts that cost $8.95 each?

h. Calculation: 50% of 44, + 6, ÷ 7, − 4

problem solving

Choose an appropriate problem-solving strategy to solve this problem. M'Keisha solved a subtraction problem and then erased two of the digits from the problem. She gave the problem to Mae as a problem-solving exercise. Copy M'Keisha's problem on your paper, and fill in the missing digits for Mae.

$$\begin{array}{r} 123 \\ -\ \ 4\_ \\ \hline \_4 \end{array}$$

Thinking Skill

Discuss

How can we check the answer?

There are seven circles in the set below. Three of the circles are shaded. The fraction of the set that is shaded is $\frac{3}{7}$.

$\frac{3}{7}$ Three circles are shaded.
There are seven circles in all.

The total number of members in the set is the denominator (bottom number) of the fraction. The number of members named is the numerator (top number) of the fraction.

Example 1

What fraction of the triangles is not shaded?

Thinking Skill

Verify

How can we check the answer?

The denominator of the fraction is 9, because there are 9 triangles in all.
The numerator is 5, because 5 of the 9 triangles are not shaded. So the fraction of triangles that are not shaded is $\frac{5}{9}$.

Example 2

In a class of 25 students, there are 12 girls and 13 boys. What fraction of the class is girls?

Twelve of the 25 students in the class are girls. So the fraction of the class that is girls is $\frac{12}{25}$.

Lesson Practice

a. What fraction of the set is shaded?

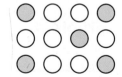

b. What fraction of the set is not shaded?

c. In a class of 27 students, there are 14 girls and 13 boys. What fraction of the class is boys?

d. In the word ALABAMA, what fraction of the letters are As?

1. Milagro volunteered for sixty-two hours last semester. Michael
_(1, 17) volunteered for seven hours. Mitsu and Michelle each volunteered for
twelve hours. Altogether, how many hours did they volunteer?

*2. The Matterhorn is fourteen thousand, six hundred ninety-one feet high.
_(31, 52) Mont Blanc is fifteen thousand, seven hundred seventy-one feet high.
How much taller is Mont Blanc than the Matterhorn?

3. There are 25 squares on a bingo card. How many squares are on
₍₄₉₎ 4 bingo cards?

*4. (Analyze) Ninety-six books were placed on 4 shelves so
₍₇₀₎ that the same number of books were on each shelf. How
many books were on each shelf?

96 books

*5. One half of the 780 fans stood and cheered. How many fans stood and
_(Inv. 5, 70) cheered? What percent of the fans stood and cheered?

6. How many years is ten centuries?
₍₅₄₎

*7. (Estimate) A package of José's favorite trading cards costs $1.75.
₍₅₉₎ What is a reasonable estimate of the number of packages José could
purchase with $10.00? Explain your answer.

*8. What fraction of this set is not shaded?
₍₇₄₎

9. This 2-liter bottle contains how many milliliters of juice?
₍₄₀₎

10. **a.** What is the perimeter of the rectangle shown at right?
(Inv. 2, Inv. 3)

b. How many 1-inch squares would be needed to cover this rectangle?

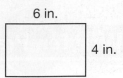
6 in.

4 in.

*11. **Predict** How many millimeters are equal to 10 centimeters? Use the table to decide.
(32)

Millimeters	10	20	30	40	50
Centimeters	1	2	3	4	5

12. Which transformation(s) would position $\triangle STR$ on $\triangle PQR$?
(73)

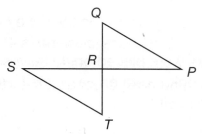

13. $6.15 − ($0.57 + $1.20)
(43, 45)

14. 43,160 − 8459
(52)

*15. 8 × 8 × 8
(62)

16. $3.54 × 6
(58)

17. 80 × 57
(67)

*18. 704 × 9
(58)

*19. 9)354
(68)

*20. 7)285
(71)

*21. 5)439
(68)

*22. 515 ÷ 6
(68)

*23. $\frac{360}{4}$
(71)

24. 784 ÷ 8
(65)

*25. $\sqrt{36} + n = 6^2$
(Inv. 3, 62)

26. 462 − y = 205
(24)

27. 50 = 5r
(41)

*28. **Conclude** Find the next number in this counting sequence:
(3)

..., 90, 180, 270, ____, ...

*29. **Explain** Sierra's arm is 20 inches long. If Sierra swings her arm in a circle, what will be the diameter of the circle? Explain your answer.
(21)

*30. **Multiple Choice** Which of these numbers is a prime number?
(55)

A 1 **B** 2 **C** 4 **D** 9

• Measuring Turns

facts	Power Up H
count aloud	Count down by fives from 54 to 4.
mental math	The sum of 38 and 17 is 55. If we make 38 larger by 2 and 17 smaller by 2, then the addition is 40 + 15. The sum is still 55, but the mental addition is easier. Before finding the following sums, make one number larger and the other smaller so that one of the numbers ends in zero.

    a. Number Sense: 38 + 27

    b. Number Sense: 48 + 24

    c. Number Sense: 59 + 32

    d. Number Sense: 57 + 26

    e. Money: $6.49 + $2.99

    f. Measurement: How many cups is one pint?

    g. Estimation: Choose the more reasonable estimate for the temperature inside a refrigerator: 3°C or 30°C.

    h. Calculation: $2 \times 9, + 29, + 53, \div 10$

problem solving	Choose an appropriate problem-solving strategy to solve this problem. Sid wants to know the circumference of (distance around) the trunk of the big oak tree at the park. He knows the circumference of the trunk is more than one yard. Sid has some string and a yardstick. How can he measure the circumference of the trunk of the tree in inches?

As Micah rides a skateboard, we can measure his movements. We might use feet or meters to measure the distance Micah travels. To measure Micah's turns, we may use **degrees.** Just as for temperature measurements, we use the degree symbol (°) to stand for degrees.

If Micah makes a **full turn,** then he has turned 360°. If Micah makes a **half turn,** he has turned 180°. A **quarter turn** is 90°.

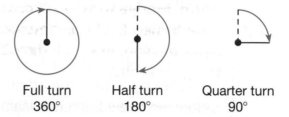

Full turn   Half turn   Quarter turn
360°   180°   90°

Besides measuring the amount of turn, we may also describe the direction of a turn as **clockwise** or **counterclockwise.**

Clockwise turn   Counterclockwise turn

For instance, we tighten a screw by turning it clockwise, and we loosen a screw by turning it counterclockwise.

 **Activity 1**

Rotations and Degrees

Stand and perform these activities as a class.

Model Face the front of the room and make a quarter turn to the right.

Discuss How many degrees did you turn? Did you turn clockwise or counterclockwise?

Return to your original position by turning a quarter turn to the left.

How many degrees did you turn? Did you turn clockwise or counterclockwise?

Face the front of the room, and make a half turn either to the right or to the left.

How many degrees did you turn? Is everyone facing the same direction?

Start by facing the front. Then make a three-quarter turn clockwise.

How many degrees did you turn? How many more degrees do you need to turn clockwise in order to face the front?

Example 1

Mariya and Irina were both facing north. Mariya turned 90° clockwise and Irina turned 270° counterclockwise. After turning, in which directions were the girls facing?

Below we show the turns Mariya and Irina made.

90°

Mariya   270°   Irina

After turning 90° clockwise, Mariya was facing east. After turning 270° counterclockwise, Irina was also facing east. (Each quarter turn is 90°, so 270° is three quarters of a full turn.) Both girls were facing **east** after their turns.

Example 2

Describe the amount and the direction of a turn around point A that would position △II on △I.

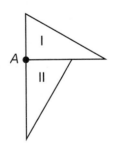

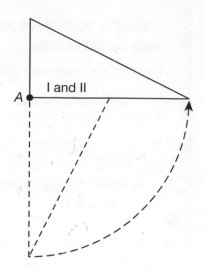

Point *A* does not move, but the rest of △II is turned to align with △I. One solution is to rotate △II **90° counterclockwise.** The fact that the triangles perfectly match after the rotation shows that they are congruent.

Conclude Describe an alternate way to rotate △II to the position of △I.

Activity 2

Rotations and Congruence

One way to show that two figures are congruent is to move one figure to the position of the other figure to see if the two figures perfectly match.

a. **Model** Fold a sheet of paper in half and cut a shape from the doubled sheet of paper so that two congruent shapes are cut out at the same time. Then position the two figures on your desk so that a rotation is the only movement necessary to move one shape onto the other shape. Perform the rotation to show that the shapes are congruent.

b. **Represent** On another sheet of paper, draw or trace the two shapes you cut out. Draw the shapes in such a position that a 90° rotation of one shape would move it to the position of the other shape.

Lesson Practice

a. **Predict** Wakeisha skated east, turned 180° clockwise, and then continued skating. In what direction was Wakeisha skating after the turn?

13. $86.47
(43, 51)   + $47.98

14. 36.7
(50)   − 18.5

15. 2358
(51)   4715
       317
       2103
     + 62

* **16.** 8)‾716‾
(68)

* **17.** 2)‾161‾
(71)

18. 7)‾434‾
(65)

* **19.** 513 ÷ 6
(68)

* **20.** $\dfrac{270}{9}$
(71)

21. $\dfrac{267}{3}$
(65)

22. $n - 7.5 = 21.4$
(24, 50)

23. $6.95
(58)   ×   8

24. 46
(67)   × 70

25. 460
(58)   ×   9

26. $3a = 30 + 30$
(61)

27. $3^2 - 2^3$
(62)

* **28.** A quarter turn is 90°. How many degrees is a three-quarter turn?
(75)

29. (**Conclude**) **a.** Which segment appears to be
(23, 66)   perpendicular to segment *BC*?

b. Draw a triangle similar to, but not congruent to,
   △*ABC*.

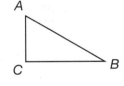

30. ✎ (**Explain**) During their professional baseball careers, pitcher
(52)   Nolan Ryan struck out 5714 batters. Pitcher Steve Carlton struck
       out 4136 batters. How many more batters did Nolan Ryan strike out?
       Explain why your answer is reasonable.

Early Finishers
Real-World Connection

Alba glanced at the clock and saw that it was 3:00 p.m. When Alba glanced at the clock again, it was 3:45 p.m.

a. During this time, how many degrees did the minute hand turn?

b. Draw a picture to solve the problem.

• Division with Three-Digit Answers

Power Up

facts   Power Up G

count aloud Count _____ from 1 to 51.

mental math Before adding, make one number larger and the other number smaller.

  a. **Number Sense:** 49 + 35

  b. **Number Sense:** 57 + 35

  c. **Number Sense:** 28 + 44

  d. **Number Sense:** 400 × 30

  e. **Money:** KaNiyah owes her brother $10.00. She only has $4.98. How much more money does she need to repay her brother?

  f. **Measurement:** Seven feet is 84 inches. A dolphin that is 7 feet 7 inches long is how many inches long?

  g. **Estimation:** Each half-gallon of milk costs $2.47. Round this price to the nearest 25 cents. Then estimate the cost of 3 half-gallon containers of milk.

  h. **Calculation:** $\sqrt{25}$, × 2, ÷ 5, × 15, + 48

problem solving   Choose an appropriate problem-solving strategy to solve this problem. The map of a park's trails is shown at right. LaDonna will start at the point labeled "Start." She wants to visit both Eagle Lookout and Slippery

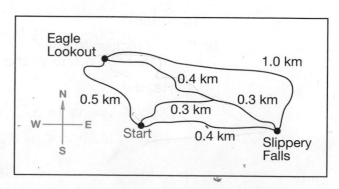

Falls. What is the shortest distance she can hike in order to visit both points and then return to where she started?

New Concept

We have practiced division problems that have two-digit answers. In this lesson we will practice division problems that have three-digit answers. Remember that the pencil-and-paper method we have used for dividing has four steps.

Step 1: Divide.

Step 2: Multiply.

Step 3: Subtract.

Step 4: Bring down.

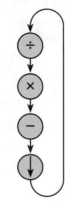

For each step we write a number. When we finish Step 4, we go back to Step 1 and repeat the steps until no digits remain to bring down.

Example 1

Divide: 3)794

Step 1: Divide 3)7 and write "2."

Step 2: Multiply 2 by 3 and write "6."

Step 3: Subtract 6 from 7 and write "1."

Step 4: Bring down the 9 to make 19.

Repeat:

Step 1: Divide 19 by 3 and write "6."

Step 2: Multiply 6 by 3 and write "18."

Step 3: Subtract 18 from 19 and write "1."

Step 4: Bring down the 4 to make 14.

Repeat:

Step 1: Divide 14 by 3 and write "4."

Step 2: Multiply 4 by 3 and write "12."

Thinking Skill

Discuss

Why do we write the digit 2 in the hundreds place of the quotient?

```
      264 R 2
  3)794
      6
      19
      18
      14
      12
       2
```

Check:
```
    264
  ×   3
    792
```

Step 3: Subtract 12 from 14 and write "2."

Step 4: There are no digits to bring down. We are finished dividing. We write "2" as the remainder for a final answer of **264 R 2.**

$$\begin{array}{r} 792 \\ + 2 \\ \hline 794 \end{array}$$

To divide dollars and cents by a whole number, we divide the digits just like we divide whole numbers. **The decimal point in the answer is placed directly above the decimal point inside the division box.** We write a dollar sign in front of the answer.

Example 2

Thinking Skill

Justify

How can we check the answer?

The total cost of three identical items is $8.40. What is the cost of each item?

The decimal point in the quotient is directly above the decimal point in the dividend. We write a dollar sign in front of the quotient.

The cost of each item is **$2.80.**

$$\begin{array}{r} \$2.80 \\ 3\overline{)\$8.40} \\ \underline{6} \\ 2\,4 \\ \underline{2\,4} \\ 00 \\ \underline{00} \\ 0 \end{array}$$

Example 3

At 4 p.m. there were about 500 cars waiting in lines at 7 highway tollbooths. About the same number of cars were in each line. What is a reasonable estimate of the number of cars in each line?

We separate 500 cars into 7 equal groups by dividing 500 by 7. To estimate, we choose a compatible number close to 500 that is divisible by 7. We choose 490.

$$490 \div 7 = 70$$

About 70 cars were in each line.

Lesson Practice

a. Copy the diagram at right. Then name the four steps of pencil-and-paper division.

Divide:

b. $4\overline{)974}$

c. $\$7.95 \div 5$

d. $6\overline{)1512}$

e. $8\overline{)\$50.00}$

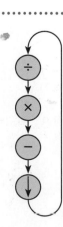

f. Altogether, 878 people attended three showings of a movie on Thursday. About the same number of people attended each showing. What is a reasonable estimate of the attendance at each showing? Explain your answer.

Written Practice   *Distributed and Integrated*

*1. **(Analyze)** Brett can type at a rate of 25 words per minute. At that rate, how many words can he type in 5 minutes? Make a table to solve this problem.
(57)

*2. Shakia has five days to read a 200-page book. If she wants to read the same number of pages each day, how many pages should she read each day?
(52, 71)

*3. **(Estimate)** Jira ordered a book for $6.99, a dictionary for $8.99, and a set of maps for $5.99. Estimate the price for all three items. Then find the actual price.
(43, 59)

4. Patrick practiced the harmonica for 7 weeks before his recital. How many days are equal to 7 weeks?
(49)

5. One third of the books were placed on the first shelf. What fraction of the books were not placed on the first shelf ?
(61)

*6. **(Represent)** To what decimal number is the arrow pointing? What mixed number is this?
(Inv. 1)

*7. In the word HIPPOPOTAMI, what fraction of the letters are Ps?
(74)

*8. **Multiple Choice** Deunoro ran a 5-kilometer race. Five kilometers is how many meters?
(Inv. 2)

    A 5 m   **B** 50 m   **C** 500 m   **D** 5000 m

9. What is the perimeter of this triangle?
(Inv. 2)

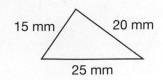
15 mm   20 mm
25 mm

*10. ✏️ **Estimate** Altogether, 117 students attend 6 different grades of a
(76) small elementary school. About the same number of students attend
each grade. What is a reasonable estimate of the number of students in
each grade? Explain your answer.

*11. **Connect** The length of segment *AB* is 3.6 cm. The length of segment
(45, 69) *AC* is 11.8 cm. What is the length of segment *BC*? Write and solve a
decimal addition equation and a decimal subtraction equation.

A   B   C

12. $25 − ($19.71 + 98¢)
(43, 45)

13. $12 + 13 + 5 + n = 9 \times 8$
(2, 24)

14. $5.00 − $2.92
(43)

15. $36.21 − 5.7$
(50)

16. $5 \times 6 \times 9$
(62)

17. 50×63
(67)

18. 478×6
(58)

*19. $3\overline{)435}$
(76)

*20. $7\overline{)867}$
(76)

*21. $5\overline{)\$13.65}$
(76)

22. $453 \div 6$
(68)

*23. $543 \div 4$
(76)

*24. $4.72 \div 8$
(76)

25. $n + 6 = 120$
(24)

26. $4w = 132$
(41, 65)

*27. $4 + 8 + 7 + 6 + 4 + n + 3 + 6 + 5 = 55$
(2)

*28. **Predict** Mieko was facing east. If Mieko turned 90° clockwise, in
(75) which direction would she be facing?

29. If the diameter of a playground ball is one foot, then its radius is how
(21) many inches?

*30. **Conclude** Which transformations would move △*ABC*
(73) to position *RST*?

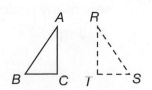

LESSON
77

• **Mass and Weight**

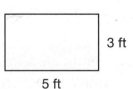

facts	Power Up G
count aloud	Count by fives from 2 to 52.
mental math	Before adding, make one number larger and the other number smaller.

    a. Number Sense: $55 + 47$

    b. Number Sense: $24 + 48$

    c. Number Sense: $458 + 33$

    d. Number Sense: 15×30

    e. Money: Renee bought a pair of gloves for $14.50 and a hat for $8.99. What was the total cost of the items?

    f. Measurement: Compare: 2 miles $\bigcirc$ 10,000 feet

    g. Estimation: An *acre* is a measurement of land. A square plot of land that is 209 feet on each side is about 1 acre. Round 209 feet to the nearest hundred feet.

    h. Calculation: 7^2, $- 1$, $\div 8$, $+ 4$, $- 4$, $\div 6$

problem solving

Choose an appropriate problem-solving strategy to solve this problem. Colby wants to cover his bulletin board with square sheets of paper that are 1 foot on each side. His bulletin board is 5 feet wide and 3 feet tall. If Colby has already cut 12 squares of paper, how many more squares does he need to cut? Explain how you found your answer.

There is a difference between *weight* and *mass*. The **mass** of an object is how much matter an object has. **Weight** is the measure of the force of gravity on that object. Though an object's weight depends on the force of gravity, its mass does not. For example, the force of gravity on the moon is less than it is on Earth, so the weight of an object on the moon is less, but its mass remains the same.

The units of *weight* in the U.S. Customary System are **ounces, pounds,** and **tons.** Remember that in Lesson 40, we used the word *ounce* to describe an amount of fluid. However, *ounce* can also describe an amount of weight. A fluid ounce of water weighs about one ounce.

As we see in the table below, one *pound* is 16 ounces, and one *ton* is 2000 pounds. Ounce is abbreviated **oz.** Pound is abbreviated **lb.**

$$16 \text{ oz} = 1 \text{ lb}$$
$$2000 \text{ lb} = 1 \text{ ton}$$

A box of cereal might weigh 24 ounces. Some students weigh 98 pounds. Many cars weigh 1 ton or more.

24 ounces   98 pounds   1 ton

Example 1

Mallory's book weighs about 2 pounds. Two pounds is how many ounces?

Each pound is 16 ounces. This means that 2 pounds is 2 × 16 ounces, which is **32 ounces.**

Example 2

The rhinoceros weighed 3 tons. Three tons is how many pounds?

Each ton is 2000 pounds. This means 3 tons is 3 × 2000 pounds, which is **6000 pounds.**

Customary Weight

Materials needed:
- **Lesson Activity 30**
- balance scale
- #2 pencils (unsharpened, taped in bundles of 5)

Use a balance scale and pencils to perform these activities. Use the U.S. Customary Weights table on **Lesson Activity 30** to record your answers.

a. Each bundle of 5 pencils is equal to 1 ounce. Using this information, how many pencils would weigh a pound?

b. Find a small object in the classroom to weigh, such as a ruler or tape. Use the bundle of pencils to estimate the weight of this object in ounces, and then place the object on a balance scale. Record the name of the object, your estimate, and the measured weight in ounces. Was your estimate reasonable? Why or why not?

c. Find two different objects that you estimate to be the same weight. Place the two objects on the balance scale to see if the scale is balanced. Record the names of the two objects, and state which object is heavier or if the weights are equal.

Grams and *kilograms* are metric units of mass. Recall that the prefix *kilo-* means "thousand." This means a kilogram is 1000 grams. Gram is abbreviated **g**. Kilogram is abbreviated **kg.**

$$1000 \text{ g} = 1 \text{ kg}$$

A dollar bill has a mass of about 1 gram. This book has a mass of about 1 kilogram. Since this book has fewer than 1000 pages, each page is more than 1 gram.

Example 3

Choose the more reasonable measure for parts a–c.

    a. pair of shoes: 1 g or 1 kg

    b. cat: 4 g or 4 kg

    c. quarter: 5 g or 5 kg

    a. A pair of shoes is about **1 kg.**

    b. A cat is about **4 kg.**

    c. A quarter is about **5 g.**

Example 4

Delores's rabbit has a mass of 4 kilograms. Four kilograms is how many grams?

Each kilogram is 1000 grams. So 4 kilograms is 4 × 1000 grams, which is **4000 grams.**

Activity 2

Metric Mass

Materials needed:
- **Lesson Activity 30**
- balance scale
- gram masses

Use a balance scale and gram masses to perform these activities. Use the "Metric Mass" table on **Lesson Activity 30** to record your answer.

    a. Select an object such as a pencil or ruler and estimate its mass in grams. Then balance the object on a balance scale with gram masses to find its mass. Record the name of the object, your estimate, and the measured mass.

    b. Estimate how many pencils would equal a kilogram. Then weigh a number of pencils to improve your estimate. Describe how you can make a close estimate of the number of pencils that would equal a kilogram.

    c. Find a small book and estimate its weight in grams. Use a balance scale to find the actual weight of the book. How close was your estimate to the actual weight?

a. Dave's pickup truck can haul a half ton of cargo. How many pounds is a half ton?

b. The newborn baby weighed 7 lb 12 oz. The baby's weight was how much less than 8 pounds?

Estimate Choose the more reasonable measure in problems **c–h:**

c. tennis ball: 57 g or 57 kg   **d.** tennis ball: 5 oz or 5 lb

e. dog: 6 g or 6 kg   **f.** dog: 11 oz or 11 lb

g. bowling ball: 7 g or 7 kg   **h.** bowling ball: 13 oz or 13 lb

i. Seven pounds is how many ounces?

j. Which depends on the force of gravity: mass or weight?

k. Nancy had 4 pounds of peaches. To make a peach cobbler, she needs 24 ounces of peaches. After making the cobbler, how many ounces of peaches will Nancy have left?

Written Practice *Distributed and Integrated*

*1. Use the information in the pictograph below to answer parts **a–c.**
(40, Inv. 6)

Consumed by Matt in One Day	
Water	🥤🥤🥤🥤🥤🥤
Tea	🥤
Milk	🥤🥤🥤🥤
Juice	🥤🥤🥤

Key: 🥤 = 1 cup = 8 ounces

a. How many pints of liquid did Matt drink in 1 day?

b. Matt drank twice as much water as he did what other beverage?

c. He drank exactly 1 quart of which beverage?

*2. **Analyze** There were 4 rooms. One fourth of the 56 guests gathered in
(Inv. 5, 70) each room. How many guests were in each room? What percent of the guests were in each room?

3. **Estimate** Which of these arrows could be pointing to 2500?
(Inv. 1)

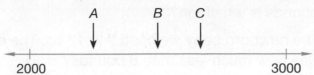

A   B   C

2000   3000

*4. **Estimate** Zoe estimated the sum of 682 + 437 + 396 by first
(59) rounding each addend to the nearest hundred. What was Zoe's
estimate of the actual sum?

*5. What fraction of this set is shaded?
(74)

*6. **Connect** Jevonte weighed 9 pounds when he was born. How many
(77) ounces is that?

*7. a. **Estimate** The segment below is how many centimeters long?
(69)

b. The segment is how many millimeters long?

cm 1   2   3   4   5   6

*8. **Represent** A company was sold for $7,450,000. Use words to
(33) write that amount of money.

9. If each side of a hexagon is 1 foot long, then how many inches is its
(Inv. 2,
63) perimeter?

10.   93,417
(51)   + 8,915

11.   42,718
(24, 52)   −   k
─────────
26,054

12.   1307
(51)   638
5219
138
+   16
─────

13. $100.00
(41, 52) − $ 86.32

14.   405,158
(52) − 396,370

15. 567 × 8
(58)

16. 30 × 84¢
(67)

17. $2.08 × 4
(58)

*18. 4)$15.00
(76)

*19. $\frac{936}{6}$
(76)

*20. 8)4537
(76)

*21. 452 ÷ 5
(71)

22. 378 ÷ 9
(65)

*23. 960 ÷ 7
(76)

24. $\sqrt{16} \times n = 100$
(Inv. 3, 41)

25. $5b = 10^2$
(61, 62)

*26. **Represent** To what decimal number is the arrow pointing? What mixed number is this?
(Inv. 1)

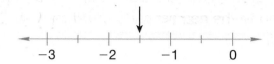

*27. **Conclude** Mona turned a quarter turn clockwise, and then she turned two more quarter turns clockwise. Altogether, Mona turned how many degrees?
(75)

28. Find the perimeter and area of the rectangle shown at right.
(Inv. 2, Inv. 3)

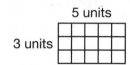
5 units
3 units

29. The relationship between feet and inches is shown in the table below:
(3, 32)

Inches	12	24	36	48	60
Feet	1	2	3	4	5

    a. **Generalize** Write a rule that describes the relationship.

    b. **Predict** How many inches are equal to 12 feet?

*30. **Verify** The weight of an object on the moon is about $\frac{1}{6}$ of its weight on Earth. Obi's golden retriever weighs 84 pounds. What would the golden retriever weigh on the moon?
(77)

Early Finishers

Real-World Connection

The great white shark is found in oceans all over the world. It is the world's largest predatory fish. The average weight of the great white is 2500 pounds.

    a. Does the average great white shark weigh more or less than a ton? Explain your answer.

    b. Does the average great white shark weigh more or less than two tons? Explain your answer.

• Classifying Triangles

facts	Power Up G
count aloud	Count by fives from 3 to 53.
mental math	**a. Number Sense:** 35×100
	b. Number Sense: Counting by 5s from 5, every number Ramon says ends in 0 or 5. If he counts by 5 s from 8, then every number he says ends in which digit?
	c. Percent: 50% of $31.00
	d. Measurement: Jenna jogged 3 kilometers. How many meters is that?
	e. Money: The box of cereal cost $4.36. Tiana paid with a $5 bill. How much change should she receive?
	f. Time: Rodrigo's school day lasts 7 hours. If Rodrigo attends school Monday through Friday, how many hours is he at school each week?
	g. Estimation: Each CD costs $11.97. Estimate the cost of 4 CDs.
	h. Calculation: 50% of 88, + 11, ÷ 11
problem solving	Choose an appropriate problem-solving strategy to solve this problem. V'Nessa is mailing an envelope that weighs 6 ounces. The postage rates are 39¢ for the first ounce and 24¢ for each additional ounce. If V'Nessa pays the postal clerk $2.00 for postage, how much money should she get back?

One way to classify (describe) a triangle is by referring to its largest angle as either obtuse, right, or acute. An obtuse angle is larger than a right angle. An acute angle is smaller than a right angle.

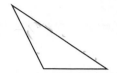

Thinking Skill

Conclude

Describe two different characteristics of the angles of an equilateral triangle.

Obtuse triangle
(One angle is obtuse.)

Right triangle
(One angle is right.)

Acute triangle
(All angles are acute.)

Another way to classify a triangle is by comparing the lengths of its sides. If all three sides are equal in length, the triangle is *equilateral.* If at least two sides are equal in length, the triangle is **isosceles.** If all three sides have different lengths, the triangle is **scalene.**

Equilateral triangle   Isosceles triangle   Scalene triangle

Represent Can an isosceles triangle have an obtuse angle? Draw a triangle to support your conclusion.

Notice that the three angles of the equilateral triangle are the same size. This means an equilateral triangle is also **equiangular.** Now notice that two angles of the isosceles triangle are the same size. In a triangle, the number of angles with the same measure equals the number of sides with the same measure.

Example

Draw a triangle that is both a right triangle and an isosceles triangle.

A right triangle contains one right angle. An isosceles triangle has two sides of equal length. We begin by drawing a right angle with equal-length sides.

Then we draw the third side of the triangle.

Discuss Describe different triangles that have acute, right, and obtuse angles.

Transformations and Congruent Triangles

Material needed:
* **Lesson Activity 31**

Formulate For this activity, you will develop a plan to predict the movement of a triangle to determine **congruence.**

a. Cut out the two right triangles from **Lesson Activity 31,** or use triangle manipulatives.

b. **Predict** Place the two triangles in the positions shown below. Plan a way to move one triangle using a translation and a rotation to show that the triangles are congruent. Remember that one triangle must be on top of the other in the final position. Write your conclusion. Include direction and degrees in your answer.

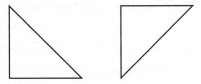

c. **Predict** Place the two triangles in the positions shown below. Plan a way to move one triangle to show that the triangles are congruent. Remember that one triangle must be on top of the other in the final position. Write your conclusion. Include direction and degrees in your answer.

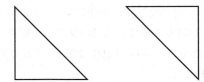

Lesson Practice

a. **Conclude** Can a right triangle have two right angles? Why or why not?

b. What is the name for a triangle that has at least two sides equal in length?

c. **Model** Use a color tile to model a translation, reflection, and rotation.

1. Jarell bought pencils on sale for 5 cents each. He spent 95 cents. How
(52, 64) many pencils did Jarell buy?

2. **Estimate** Clanatia went to the store with $9.12. She spent $3.92.
(25, 30) About how much money did Clanatia have left?

3. Pamela listened to half of a 90-minute tape. How many minutes of the
(70) tape did she hear?

*4. One fourth of the guests gathered in the living room. What fraction
(Inv. 5, of the guests did not gather in the living room? What percent of the
61) guests did not gather in the living room?

*5. If one side of an equilateral triangle is 3 centimeters long, then what is
(69, 78) its perimeter in

    a. centimeters?   **b.** millimeters?

*6. **Represent** To what decimal number is the arrow pointing? What
(Inv. 1) mixed number is this?

$$-8.9 \qquad\qquad -8.8$$

*7. **Analyze** Half of a gallon is a half gallon. Half of a half gallon is a
(40, 74) quart. Half of a quart is a pint. Half of a pint is a cup. A cup is what
fraction of a quart?

*8. A baby deer is called a fawn. Most fawns weigh about 3 kilograms
(77) when they are born. How many grams is that?

*9. **Explain** Isabella estimated the product of 389 × 7 to be 2800.
(59) Explain how Isabella used rounding to make her estimate.

*10. Multiple Choice It is late afternoon. When the minute
(27, 75) hand turns 360°, what time will it be?

    A 11:25 a.m.   **B** 5:56 a.m.

    C 4:56 p.m.   **D** 5:56 p.m.

*11. (**Represent**) Compare: $\frac{3}{4}$ ◯ $\frac{4}{5}$. Draw and shade two congruent
(56) rectangles to show the comparison.

12. $4.32 - 2.5$ **13.** $3.65 + 5.2 + 0.18$
(50)   (50)

14. $\$50.00 - \$42.60$ **15.** $\$17.54 + 49¢ + \$15$
(50)   (43)

*16. $2\overline{)567}$ ***17.** $6\overline{)\$34.56}$ ***18.** $4\overline{)978}$
(76)   (76)   (76)

19. 398×6 **20.** 47×60 **21.** $8 \times \$6.25$
(58)   (67)   (58)

*22. $970 \div \sqrt{25}$ ***23.** $\dfrac{372}{3}$ **24.** $491 \div 7$
(Inv. 3,   (76)   (71)
76)

25. $8n = 120$ **26.** $f \times 3^2 = 108$
(41, 65)   (62, 65)

27. $7 + 8 + 5 + 4 + n + 2 + 7 + 3 = 54$
(2)

*28. Find the perimeter and area of this rectangle:
(Inv. 2,
Inv. 3)

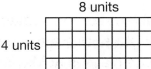

8 units

4 units

*29. Name the transformation(s) that would move $\triangle ABC$ to position *WXY.*
(73)

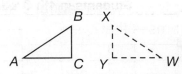

*30. The first four multiples of 18 are 18, 36, 54, and 72. What are the first
(55) four multiples of 180?

• **Symmetry**

Power Up

facts   Power Up G

count aloud   Count by fives from 4 to 54.

mental
math

Before adding, make one number larger and the other number smaller in **a–c.**

   a. Number Sense: 48 + 37

   b. Number Sense: 62 + 29

   c. Number Sense: 135 + 47

   d. Percent: 50% of $20

   e. Percent: 25% of $20

   f. Percent: 10% of $20

   g. Estimation: Masoud earns $8.95 for each hour he works. About how much does Masoud earn for working 6 hours?

   h. Calculation: $\sqrt{64}$, × 3, + 1, × 2, + 98

problem
solving

Choose an appropriate problem-solving strategy to solve this problem. The bar graph at right shows the number of students in each of the three fourth grade classes at Mayfair School. If seven new fourth graders were to start attending the school, how could they be assigned to the classes to make each class equal in size?

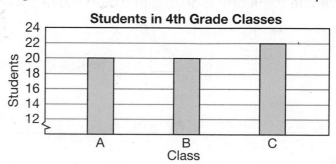

Thinking Skill

Discuss

Name several real-world examples of line symmetry.

In nature, we often find balance in the appearance and structure of objects and living things. For example, we see a balance in the wing patterns of moths and butterflies. We call this kind of balance **reflective symmetry,** or just **symmetry.**

The dashes across this drawing of a moth indicate a **line of symmetry.** The portion of the figure on each side of the dashes is the *mirror image* of the other side. If we stood a mirror along the dashes, the reflection in the mirror would appear to complete the figure.

Visit www. SaxonMath.com/ Int4Activities for an online activity.

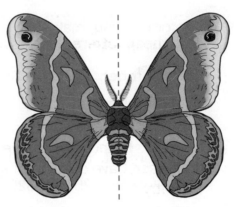

Some polygons and other figures have one or more lines of symmetry.

Example 1

Which of these polygons does *not* have a line of symmetry?

A B C D

The rectangle has two lines of symmetry.

The isosceles triangle has one line of symmetry.

The square has four lines of symmetry.

The third polygon has no line of symmetry. The answer is **C.**

Conclude Will every regular polygon always have at least one line of symmetry? Explain why or why not.

About half of the uppercase letters in the alphabet have lines of symmetry.

Example 2

Copy these letters and draw each line of symmetry, if any.

C H A I R

The letters **H** and **I** each have two lines of symmetry. The letters **C** and **A** each have one line of symmetry. The letter **R** has no lines of symmetry.

C H A I R

Represent Print the letters of your first name and describe any lines of symmetry those letters have.

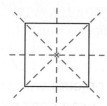

Reflections and Lines of Symmetry

Materials needed:
- **Lesson Activity 32**
- mirror

Use a mirror to find lines of symmetry in the figures on **Lesson Activity 32.**

The symmetry illustrated in Examples 1 and 2 is reflective symmetry. Another type of symmetry is *rotational symmetry*. A figure has rotational symmetry if it matches its original position as it is rotated.

For example, a square has rotational symmetry because it matches itself every quarter turn (90°).

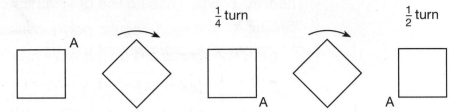

Likewise, the uppercase letter H has rotational symmetry because it matches its original position every half turn (180°).

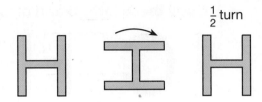

Example 3

Which figures do *not* have rotational symmetry?

A

B

C

D

Figure A has rotational symmetry because it matches its original position every $\frac{1}{3}$ of a turn (120°).

Figure B has rotational symmetry because it matches its original position in one half of a turn (180°).

Figure C has rotational symmetry because it matches its original position every $\frac{1}{6}$ of a turn (60°).

Figure D does not have rotational symmetry because it requires a full turn (360°) to match its original position.

Lesson Practice Copy each figure and draw the lines of symmetry, if any.

a. [figure]

b. [parallelogram figure]

c. [triangle figure]

d. W

e. X

f. Z

g. Which figures **a–f** do *not* have rotational symmetry?

h. Which figures in **a–f** have reflective symmetry?

i. Which of these polygons have reflective symmetry?

A [octagon figure]

B [hexagon figure]

C [trapezoid figure]

D [L-shaped figure]

Written Practice *Distributed and Integrated*

*1. **Interpret** Use this circle graph to answer parts **a–d.**
(Inv. 6, 74)

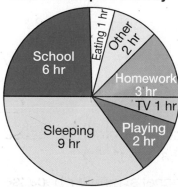

How Franz Spent His Day

School 6 hr
Eating 1 hr
Other 2 hr
Homework 3 hr
TV 1 hr
Sleeping 9 hr
Playing 2 hr

a. What is the total number of hours shown in the graph?

b. What fraction of Franz's day was spent watching TV?

c. If Franz's school day starts at 8:30 a.m., at what time does it end?

d. **Multiple Choice** Which two activities together take more than half of Franz's day?

   A sleeping and playing

   B school and homework

   C school and sleeping

   D school and playing

2. One fifth of the 60 eggs were placed in each box. How
(70) many eggs were placed in each box?

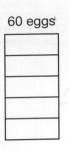

60 eggs

3. (Estimate) Which of these arrows could be pointing to 2250?
(Inv. 1)

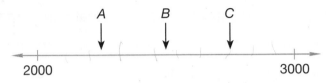

*4. (Estimate) Find a reasonable estimate of $4.27, $5.33, and $7.64 by
(59) rounding each amount to the nearest dollar before adding.

*5. a. What fraction of this set is *not* shaded?
(74)

b. What decimal of this set is shaded?

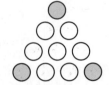

*6. Kurt drove across the state at 90 kilometers per hour. At that rate,
(57) how far will Kurt drive in 4 hours? Make a table to solve the problem.

7. (Verify) Is the product of 3 and 7 a prime number? How do you
(55) know?

*8. a. What is the perimeter of this square?
(Inv. 2,
Inv. 3)

b. If the square were to be covered with 1-inch squares,
how many squares would be needed?

5 inches

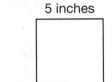

*9. (Represent) Draw the capital letter E rotated 90° clockwise.
(73)

E

10. $20.10
(43, 51) − $16.45

11. $98.54
(43, 51) + $ 9.85

12. 380 × 4
(58)

13. 97 × 80
(67)

*14. 5)3840
(76)

15. $8.63 × 7
(58)

16. 4.25 − 2.4
(50)

*17. 8)$70.00
(76)

*18. 6)3795
(76)

19. $4p = 160$
(41, 71)

20. $\dfrac{\sqrt{64}}{\sqrt{16}}$
(Inv. 3)

21. $\dfrac{287}{7}$
(65)

*22. $10 × (6^2 + 2^3)$
(45, 62)

23. (**Analyze**) Find the perimeter of this rectangle
(Inv. 2, 69)

    a. in centimeters.

    b. in millimeters.

1.5 cm

0.8 cm

24. The thermometer shows the outside temperature on a cold,
(18) winter day in Cedar Rapids, Iowa. What temperature does
the thermometer show?

*25. Mulan spun completely around twice on a skateboard. How many
(75) degrees did Mulan spin?

*26. a. (**Conclude**) Which of these letters does *not* have a line
(79) of symmetry?

T N V W

    b. Which of these letters has rotational symmetry?

*27. a. Multiple Choice Sketch each of the triangles below. Which of
(78) these triangles does *not* exist?

    A a scalene right triangle   **B** an isosceles right triangle

    C an equilateral right triangle   **D** an equilateral acute triangle

    b. (**Justify**) Explain why the triangle you chose does not
exist.

*28. **Analyze** How many different amounts of money could you make
(22) using any two of the four coins shown below? Name the amounts.

*29. **Estimate** Cora estimated the quotient of $261 \div 5$ to be 50. Explain
(65) how Cora used a compatible number to make her estimate.

*30. **Formulate** Write and solve a subtraction word problem for the
(25) equation $175 - t = 84$.

Early Finishers

Real-World Connection

a. Draw a capital letter that has rotational symmetry and line symmetry.

b. Draw a capital letter that has line symmetry but does *not* have rotational symmetry.

c. What is the difference between the two figures you have drawn?

• Division with Zeros in Three-Digit Answers

facts	Power Up G
count aloud	Count by fourths from $2\frac{1}{2}$ to $7\frac{1}{2}$.
mental math	Subtracting two-digit numbers mentally is easier if the second number ends in zero. By increasing both numbers in a subtraction by the same amount, we can sometimes make the subtraction easier while keeping the difference the same. For example, instead of $45 - 28$, we can think $47 - 30$. We added two to 28 to make it end in zero and then added two to 45 to keep the difference the same. Use this strategy in **a–d**.

   a. Number Sense: $45 - 39$

   b. Number Sense: $56 - 27$

   c. Number Sense: $63 - 48$

   d. Number Sense: $82 - 35$

   e. Powers/Roots: Compare: $\sqrt{16} - \sqrt{9} \bigcirc 1^2$

   f. Measurement: The high temperature was 84°F. The low temperature was 68°F. The difference between the high and low temperatures was how many degrees?

   g. Estimation: Each candle costs $3.05. If Miranda has $12, does she have enough to buy 4 candles?

   h. Calculation: $\frac{1}{4}$ of 24, $\times\, 9$, $-\, 15$, $+\, 51$

problem solving	Choose an appropriate problem-solving strategy to solve this problem. Tahlia's soccer team, the Falcons, won their match against the Eagles. There were 11 goals scored altogether by both teams. The Falcons scored 3 more goals than the Eagles. How many goals did each team score?

New Concept

Recall that the pencil-and-paper method we have used for dividing numbers has four steps:

Step 1: Divide.

Step 2: Multiply.

Step 3: Subtract.

Step 4: Bring down.

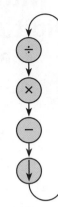

Every time we bring a number down, we return to Step 1. Sometimes the answer to Step 1 is zero, and we will have a zero in the answer.

Example 1

Each weekday afternoon in a small town, 618 newspapers are delivered to customers. The task of delivering the newspapers is divided equally among 3 drivers. How many newspapers does each driver deliver?

Step 1: Divide $3\overline{)6}$ and write "2."

Step 2: Multiply 2 by 3 and write "6."

Step 3: Subtract 6 from 6 and write "0."

Step 4: Bring down the 1 to make 01 (which is 1).

$$\begin{array}{r} 2 \\ 3\overline{)618} \\ \underline{6} \\ 01 \end{array}$$

Repeat:

Step 1: Divide 3 into 01 and write "0."

Step 2: Multiply 0 by 3 and write "0."

Step 3: Subtract 0 from 1 and write "1."

Step 4: Bring down the 8 to make 18.

Repeat:

Step 1: Divide 3 into 18 and write "6."

Step 2: Multiply 6 by 3 and write "18."

Step 3: Subtract 18 from 18 and write "0."

Step 4: There are no more digits to bring down, so the division is complete. The remainder is zero.

$$\begin{array}{r} 206 \\ 3\overline{)618} \\ \underline{6} \\ 01 \\ \underline{0} \\ 18 \\ \underline{18} \\ 0 \end{array}$$

Each driver delivers **206 papers.**

Thinking Skill

Verify

Why do we write the digit 2 in the hundreds place of the quotient?

Thinking Skill

Discuss

Why do we write the digit 0 in the tens place of the quotient?

Example 2

Divide: $4\overline{)1483}$

Step 1: Divide $4\overline{)14}$ and write "3."

Step 2: Multiply 3 by 4 and write "12."

Step 3: Subtract 12 from 14 and write "2."

Step 4: Bring down the 8 to make 28.

Repeat:

Step 1: Divide 4 into 28 and write "7."

Step 2: Multiply 7 by 4 and write "28."

Step 3: Subtract 28 from 28 and write "0."

Step 4: Bring down the 3 to make 03 (which is 3).

Repeat:

Step 1: Divide 4 into 03 and write "0."

Step 2: Multiply 0 by 4 and write "0."

Step 3: Subtract 0 from 3 and write "3."

Step 4: There are no digits to bring down, so the division is complete. We write "3" as the remainder.

$$\begin{array}{r} 370 \text{ R } 3 \\ 4\overline{)1483} \\ \underline{12} \\ 28 \\ \underline{28} \\ 03 \\ \underline{0} \\ 3 \end{array}$$

Use a calculator to divide the example.

Discuss How is the answer displayed on the calculator different from the answer displayed in the solution?

Example 3

The same number of landscaping bricks are stacked on each of 4 pallets. The total weight of the pallets is 3 tons. What is the weight in pounds of each pallet?

First we find the number of pounds in 3 tons. Each ton is 2 thousand pounds, so 3 tons is 6 thousand pounds. Now we find the weight of each pallet of bricks by dividing 6000 by 4.

We find that each pallet of bricks weighs **1500 pounds.**

$$\begin{array}{r} 1500 \\ 4\overline{)6000} \\ \underline{4} \\ 20 \\ \underline{20} \\ 000 \end{array}$$

Lesson Practice

a. List the four steps of division and draw the division diagram.

Divide:

b. $4\overline{)815}$

c. $5\overline{)4152}$

Divide using a calculator. Show your answer as a decimal number.

d. 6)$\overline{5432}$ **e.** 7)$\overline{845}$

Divide mentally:

f. 5)$\overline{1500}$ **g.** 4)$\overline{2000}$

h. Find the missing factor in the equation $3m = 1200$.

Written Practice

Distributed and Integrated

1. If the chance of rain is 30%, then is it more likely that it will rain or that
(Inv. 5) it will not rain?

*2. (**Analyze**) Monty ran the race 12 seconds faster than Ivan. Monty ran
(31) the race in 58 seconds. Ivan ran the race in how many seconds?

3. The whole rectangle is divided into 5 equal parts.
(70) Each part is what percent of the rectangle?
(*Hint:* Divide 100 by 5.)

100%

4. (**Analyze**) How many 6-inch-long sticks can be cut from a 72-inch-long
(52) stick?

*5. Multiple Choice One fifth of the leaves had fallen. What fraction of
(61) the leaves had *not* fallen?

A $\frac{2}{5}$ **B** $\frac{3}{5}$ **C** $\frac{4}{5}$ **D** $\frac{5}{5}$

6. (**Estimate**) Which of these arrows could be pointing to 5263?
(Inv. 1)

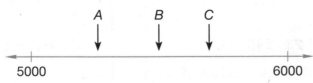

*7. What fraction of the months of the year have 31 days?
(54, 74)

*8. The prefix *kilo-* means what number?
(77)

9. **Explain** Cleon would like to estimate the difference between $579
(52) and $385. Explain how Cleon could use compatible numbers to make
an estimate.

*10. The triangle at right is equilateral.
(Inv. 2,
78)   **a.** How many millimeters is the perimeter of the
triangle?

   b. **Classify** Describe the angles.

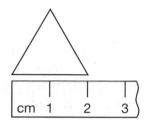

11. Three liters equals how many milliliters?
(40)

*12. Wilma runs 5 miles every day. At that rate, how many days would it take
(60) her to run 40 miles? Make a table to solve the problem.

13. $2n = 150$
(41, 65)

14. $24.25 - (6.2 + 4.8)$
(45, 50)

15.   103,279
(51) $+ 97,814$

16. $36.14
(43, 51) $+ \ 27.95

17.   39,420
(52) $- \ 29,516$

18. $60.50
(24, 52) $- n$
            $\overline{\$43.20}$

19.   604
(58) $\times 9$

20.   87
(67) $\times 60$

21. $6.75
(58) $\times 4$

*22. $3\overline{)618}$
(80)

*23. $5\overline{)\$21.50}$
(76, 80)

*24. n
(24, 52) $+ \ 1467$
            $\overline{2459}$

*25. $\dfrac{600}{4}$
(80)

26. $543 \div 6$
(71)

27. $472 \div 8$
(65)

*28. $9w = 9^2 + (9 \times 2)$
(61, 62)

*29. Divide mentally: $5\overline{)3000}$
(80)

*30. a. **Represent** Draw a triangle that is congruent to this
(66, 79)   isosceles triangle. Then draw its line of symmetry.

   b. Draw the triangle when it is rotated 180°.

Focus on

• Analyzing and Graphing Relationships

In Lesson 57 we learned to make a table to display a relationship between two sets of data. Now we will learn how to write an equation to represent the relationship in the table.

Mrs. Cooke writes the percent of correct answers on each 10-question quiz she grades. Look at the data in each column. On the quiz, 100 points is equal to 100%. If a student has 8 correct answers, the score is 80%. This means 80 out of 100 points are earned for correct answers.

Quiz: 10 Questions

Number of Correct Answers	Score
1	10%
2	20%
3	30%
4	40%
5	50%
6	60%
7	70%
8	80%
9	90%
10	100%

Interpret Use the table above to answer problems **1–4.**

1. Seven correct answers will earn what percent?

2. A score of 90% means how many questions were answered correctly?

3. **Analyze** Each quiz question represents what number of points?

4. a. (Analyze) What multiplication formula could you write to represent the relationship between the two columns of data?

b. (Represent) Mrs. Cooke also writes the percent of correct answers on each 20-question test she grades. Copy the table for the 20-question test. Extend the table to show the scores for each number of correct answers up to 20.

Test: 20 Questions

Number of Correct Answers	Score
1	5%
2	10%
3	15%
4	20%
5	25%
6	30%
7	35%
8	40%
9	45%
10	50%
11	55%

(Interpret) Use your table to answer problems **5–8**.

5. Sonia answered 18 questions correctly. What was her score?

6. Litzel scored 70%. How many questions did Litzel answer correctly?

7. (Analyze) Each test question represents what number of points?

8. (Analyze) What multiplication equation could you write to represent the relationship between the two columns of data?

Graphs can also be used to display relationships between two quantities, such as pay and time worked.

Suppose Dina has a job that pays $10 per hour. This table shows the total pay Dina would receive for 1, 2, 3, or 4 hours of work.

9. (Represent) Copy the table. Extend the table to show Dina's pay for each hour up to 8 hours of work.

Pay Schedule

Hours Worked	Total Pay
1	$10
2	$20
3	$30
4	$40

The graph below shows the same relationship between hours worked and total pay. Each dot on the graph represents both a number of hours and an amount of pay.

If Dina works more hours, she earns more pay. We say that her total pay is a function of the number of hours she works. Since Dina's total pay depends on the number of hours she works, we make "Total Pay" the vertical scale and "Total Hours" the horizontal scale.

Total Pay for Hours Worked

10. **(Represent)** Copy the graph. Extend the sides of the graph to include 8 hours and $80. Then graph (draw) the dots for Dina's total pay for each hour up to 8 hours.

The following table and graph show how many miles Rosita hiked at 4 miles per hour.

Miles Hiked
(at 4 mi per hr)

Hours	Miles
1	4
2	8
3	12

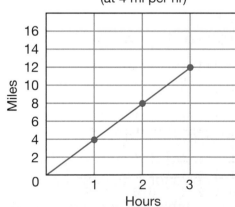

Miles Hiked
(at 4 mi per hr)

The dots indicate how far Rosita hiked in one, two, and three hours. However, every second Rosita hiked, she was hiking a small part of a mile. We show this progress by drawing a line through the dots. Every point on a line represents a distance hiked for a given time.

For example, straight up from $1\frac{1}{2}$ hours is a point on the line at 6 miles.

11. **Interpret** Use the graph to find the distance Rosita hiked in $2\frac{1}{2}$ hours.

12. **Analyze** What multiplication formula could you write to represent the relationship between the two sets of data?

13. **Verify** Use your formula to find the number of miles Rosita would hike in 5 hours.

Activity 1

Graphing Pay Rates

Formulate Work with a partner and agree on an hourly rate of pay for a selected job. Then create a table to display a pay schedule showing the total pay for 1, 2, 3, 4, 5, 6, 7, and 8 hours of work at the agreed rate of pay. Use the pay schedule to create a graph that shows the relationship represented by the table. Write an equation to represent the data.

Graphing Points on a Coordinate Plane

Sometimes we want to name points on a grid. Below we show how to name points using pairs of numbers called **coordinates.** The first number in each coordinate pair is taken from the horizontal scale. The second number in each pair is taken from the vertical scale. We write the coordinates in parentheses.

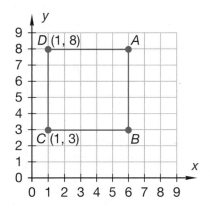

14. Write the coordinates of point *A*.

15. Write the coordinates of point *B*.

To draw this rectangle, we connect points by using segments. We start at point *A*, draw a segment to point *B*, and then continue in order to points *C* and *D* before going back to point *A*.

Activity 2

Graphing on a Coordinate Grid

Material needed:

- **Lesson Activity 34**

Practice graphing points on a grid and connecting the points to complete a design.

Investigate Further

a. Use a large container or bucket. Estimate the number of pints that would fill the container. Use water or sand to determine how close your estimate was. Make a table to show the relationship between pints and 1, 2, 3, 4, and 5 containers or buckets. Then write an equation to represent the relationship.

b. Use a large container or bucket. Estimate the number of liters that would fill the container. Use water or sand to determine how close your estimate was. Make a table to show the relationship between liters and 1, 2, 3, 4, and 5 containers or buckets. Then write an equation to represent the relationship.

c. Estimate the mass and weight of an object of your choosing. Then use a scale to find the actual mass and weight. Research the force of gravity on other planets. Make a table that shows how the weight/mass of the object would or would not change on other planets.

d. Use a stopwatch to time how many seconds it takes you to write your first and last names. Use the data to make a table to represent the relationship of the amount of time and the number of times you wrote your name (up to four times). Then graph the relationship represented by the table.

e. Copy the table of *x*- and *y*-coordinates of the set of data in Rosita's hiking table and extend the table to five hours. Then list the five ordered pairs.

LESSON
81

• Angle Measures

facts   Power Up I

count aloud   Count by fours from 80 to 120.

mental math   Find each difference by first increasing both numbers so that the second number ends in zero in **a–c.**

    a. Number Sense: 63 – 28

    b. Number Sense: 45 – 17

    c. Number Sense: 80 – 46

    d. Money: Noah had $10.00. Then he spent $5.85 on lunch. How much money did he have left over?

    e. Measurement: How many inches is $\frac{1}{2}$ of a foot?

    f. Measurement: How many inches is $\frac{1}{4}$ of a foot?

    g. Estimation: The total cost for 4 movie rentals was $15.92. Round this amount to the nearest dollar and then divide by 4 to estimate the cost per rental.

    h. Calculation: 5^2, × 2, × 2, × 2, × 2

problem solving   Choose an appropriate problem-solving strategy to solve this problem. In the diagram at right, the circle represents students who have one or more pets at home. A letter inside the circle represents a particular student who has a pet. A letter outside the circle represents a student who does not have any pets. The letter *A* represents Adrian, who has a dog. The letter *B* represents Beth, who does not have any pets. Copy the graph on your paper. On the graph, place the letter *C* for Clarissa, who keeps a goldfish, and *D* for David, who does not have pets.

Students with Pets

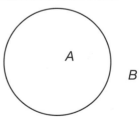

Thinking Skill

Discuss

Name a time on a clock when the hour hand and the minute hand form

a. an acute angle.

b. an obtuse angle.

In one hour the minute hand of a clock turns all the way around once. Recall from Lesson 75 that one full turn measures 360°.

As the minute hand moves, it forms changing angles with the hour hand. At 3 o'clock the angle formed is a right angle, which measures 90°. At 6 o'clock the angle formed is a **straight angle** because the two sides of the angle form a straight line. A straight angle measures 180°.

right angle, 90°   straight angle, 180°

Here we show some angles and their measures in degrees:

45°   90°   135°   180°

Notice that a 45° angle is half the size of a 90° angle. Also notice that a 135° angle is the size of a 90° angle plus a 45° angle. A 180° angle is twice the size of a 90° angle.

Activity

Angle Measurement Tool

Material needed:
• 3-by-5-inch rectangle of unlined paper

Create your own angle measurement tool.

Step 1: Fold the paper in half, making sure the sides are aligned before creasing. Draw a square corner at the fold and write "90°" as shown. Use the edge of your pencil point to shade the sides of the 90° angle.

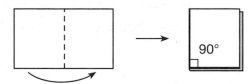

Step 2: Fold the paper again so that the left side aligns with the bottom side before creasing. Write "45°" as shown. Shade the sides of the 45° angle.

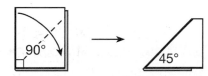

Step 3: Unfold the paper. Turn the paper over so that the 90° and 45° labels are on the back and the folds appear as shown. Write "180°" where the folds meet. Shade the 180° angle across the bottom of the card.

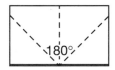

Step 4: Fold up the right-hand corner of the paper, and write "135°" as shown. Shade the remaining side of the 135° angle.

(**Model**) Find three angles to measure in the classroom using your tool. If the angle does not match one of the angles on your tool, then estimate its measure. Sketch the three angles on your paper and write your estimate of the measure of each angle.

(**Lesson Practice**)

Using the paper you folded in this lesson, estimate the measure of each angle in problems **a–d.** First find an angle on the paper that is a close match to the angle you are measuring. Then match the corner and one side of the paper with the corner and one side of the angle. If the angle is larger or smaller than the paper angle, estimate how much larger or smaller. Add or subtract from your paper measurement to get a final estimate.

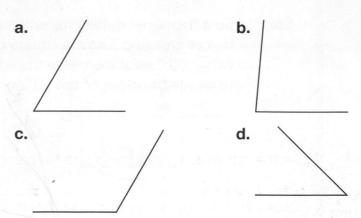

a.

b.

c.

d.

e. At 9 o'clock the hands of a clock form an angle of how many degrees?

Written Practice · Distributed and Integrated

1. Cecilia skated 27 times around the rink forward and 33 times around the rink
(1) backward. How many times did she skate around the rink altogether?

2. Nectarines cost 68¢ per pound. What is the price for 3 pounds of
(49) nectarines?

*3. (**Analyze**) In bowling, the sum of Amber's score and Bianca's score
(72) was equal to Consuela's score. If Consuela's score was 113 and
Bianca's score was 55, what was Amber's score?

*4. One third of the 84 students were assigned to each room. How many
(70) students were assigned to each room? Draw a picture to explain how
you found your answer.

5. Round 2250 to the nearest thousand.
(54)

*6. In the word ARIZONA, what fraction of the letters are *not* As?
(74)

*7. **Multiple Choice** The African elephant weighed 7 tons. How many
(77) pounds is that?

    A 7000   **B** 140   **C** 14,000   **D** 2000

*8. **Estimate** The tip of this shoelace is how many millimeters long?
(69)

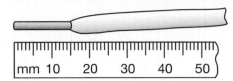

*9. **Conclude** Choose the more reasonable measure for parts **a** and **b.**
(40, 77)

    a. a new box of cereal: 2 lb or 2 oz

    b. a full pail of water: 1 pt or 1 gal

*10. According to this calendar, what is the date of the last
(54) Tuesday in February 2019?

FEBRUARY 2019						
S	M	T	W	T	F	S
					1	2
3	4	5	6	7	8	9
10	11	12	13	14	15	16
17	18	19	20	21	22	23
24	25	26	27	28		

11. **Represent** Forty-two thousand, seven hundred is how much greater
(31, 52) than thirty-four thousand, nine hundred?

12. Find the perimeter and area of this rectangle:
(Inv. 2,
Inv. 3)

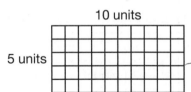

10 units

5 units

*13. **Analyze** Sh'Reese was riding north. Then she turned 90° to the left.
(75) After turning, in what direction was Sh'Reese riding? Explain how you
know.

14. 6743 − (507 × 6)   **15.** $70.00 − $63.17
(52, 58)   (43)

16. 3 × 7 × 0   **17.** $8.15 × 6
(62)   (58)

18. 67¢ × 10   **19.** 4.5 + 0.52 + 1.39
(67)   (50)

*20. 2)$12.16   ***21.** 6)4321   ***22.** 8)4800
(76, 80)   (80)   (80)

*23. $963 \div \sqrt{9}$
(Inv. 3, 76)

*24. $5^3 \div 5$
(62, 65)

*25. $\$6.57 \div 9$
(76)

26. $4n = 200$
(41, 71)

27. $7d = 105$
(41, 65)

28.
(17, 24)
$$
\begin{array}{r}
473 \\
286 \\
+\ \ n \\
\hline
943
\end{array}
$$

29. $1 + 12 + 3 + 14 + 5 + 26$
(1)

*30. The bar graph shows the average life span in years of several animals.
(Inv. 6) Use the graph to solve parts **a–c.**

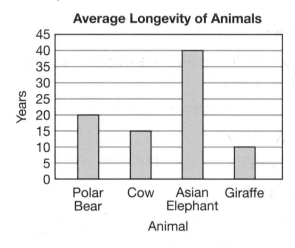

Average Longevity of Animals

a. Write the names of the animals in order from longest to shortest average life span.

b. What fraction of the average life span of an Asian elephant is the average life span of a polar bear?

c. When compared to the average life span of a giraffe, how many times greater is the average life span of an Asian elephant?

Early Finishers

Real-World Connection

a. Use the angle measurement tool you created in the activity to draw a polygon. Use all the angles on your tool at least once.

b. For each angle of the polygon, label the type of angle as obtuse, right, or acute.

c. Then label each angle with the number of degrees.

• Tessellations

facts   Power Up I

count aloud   Count by fives from 3 to 63.

mental math   Before adding, make one number larger and the other number smaller in **a–e.**

> **a. Number Sense:** 38 + 46
>
> **b. Number Sense:** 67 + 24
>
> **c. Number Sense:** 44 + 28
>
> **d. Number Sense:** 3 × 50 × 10
>
> **e. Number Sense:** Counting by 5s from 5, every number Julio says ends in 0 or 5. If he counts by 5s from 9, then every number he says ends in which digit?
>
> **f. Geometry:** The radius of the truck tire was 15 inches. The diameter of the tire was how many inches?
>
> **g. Estimation:** The total cost for 6 boxes of snack bars was $17.70. Round this amount to the nearest dollar and then divide by 6 to estimate the cost per box.
>
> **h. Calculation:** 25% of 40, × 2, ÷ 10, × 8, + 59

problem solving   Choose an appropriate problem-solving strategy to solve this problem. Landon is packing a lunch for the park. He will take one bottle of water, a sandwich, and a fruit. He will choose either a ham sandwich or a peanut butter and jelly sandwich. For the fruit, Landon will choose an apple, an orange, or a banana. Make a tree diagram to find the possible combinations of lunches that Landon can pack. Then list each possible combination.

Archeologists have found that people used tiles to make mosaics and to decorate homes and other buildings as long ago as 4000 B.C. The Romans called these tiles *tesselae,* from which we get the word **tessellation.** A tessellation, also called a *tiling,* is the repeated use of shapes to fill a flat surface without gaps or overlaps. Below are examples of tessellations and the name of the shape that produced each one.

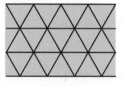

triangle

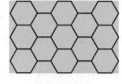

hexagon

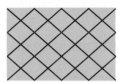

quadrilateral

(**Connect**) Starting with any tile, how might you move that tile to continue each tessellation above? That is, what transformations can be used to go from one tile to another?

- For the triangle tessellation, rotate a tile 180° and then translate it up, down, right, or left.

- For the hexagon tessellation, translate a tile until one of its sides aligns with the side of another hexagon.

- For the quadrilateral tessellation, translate a tile to continue the pattern. The translation can be up, down, left, right, or diagonal.

Not all polygons tessellate, or fill a flat surface. However, every triangle and every quadrilateral can fill a flat surface. Here we show two examples:

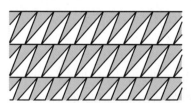

triangle

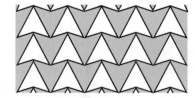

quadrilateral

Activity 1

Tessellations

Materials needed:
- **Lesson Activity 35**
- scissors
- mirror

1. **Model** Cut out the triangles and quadrilaterals on **Lesson Activity 35.** Then use the figures to form two tessellations: one with the triangles and one with the quadrilaterals. You may want to color the figures before cutting them out and then put them together in a way that creates a colorful design.

2. **Analyze** Use a mirror to decide if your design has a line of symmetry. If it does, draw the line of symmetry.

Activity 2

Tessellations With Multiple Shapes

Materials needed:
- **Lesson Activity 36**
- scissors

Use **Lesson Activity 36** to cut out the same shapes as those shown below.

Model Look for pairs of shapes that will tessellate. Make a list to show the combinations of each pair of shapes.

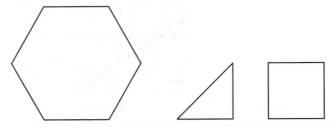

a. Trace this figure on your paper a few times, turning your paper as you trace, to show that the figure will fill a flat surface.

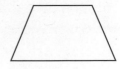

b. Does this figure tessellate?

c. Look at the three shapes below. Find pairs of shapes that will tessellate. Make a list to show the combinations of each pair of shapes.

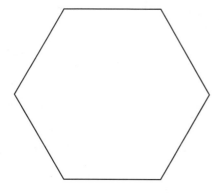
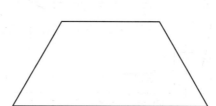
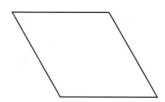

Written Practice   *Distributed and Integrated*

Formulate   Write and solve equations for problems **1–4.**

1. There were 35 students in the class but only 28 math books. How many
(31) more math books are needed so that every student in the class has a math book?

2. Each of the 7 children slid down the water slide 11 times. How many
(49) times did they slide in all?

*3. A bowling lane is 60 feet long. How many yards is 60 feet?
(Inv. 2, 52)

*4. Wei carried the baton four hundred forty yards. Eric carried it eight
(1, 51) hundred eighty yards. Jesse carried it one thousand, three hundred twenty yards, and Bernardo, carried it one thousand, seven hundred sixty yards. Altogether, how many yards was the baton carried?

5. One third of the members voted "no." What fraction of the members
(61) did not vote "no"?

*6. **Explain** Marissa would like to estimate the sum of 6821 + 4963.
(59) Explain how Marissa could use rounding to make an estimate.

7. What fraction of the days of the week start with the letter S?
(74)

*8. Together, Bob's shoes weigh about 1 kilogram. Each shoe weighs
(77) about how many grams?

*9. **Interpret** Use the line graph below to answer parts **a–c.**
(Inv. 6)

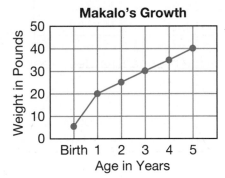

Makalo's Growth

a. About how many pounds did Makalo weigh on his second
birthday?

b. About how many pounds did Makalo gain between his third and
fifth birthdays?

c. Copy and complete this table using information from the line graph:

Makalo's Growth

Age	Weight
At birth	6 pounds
1 year	
2 years	

10. If 65% of the lights are on, then what percent of the lights are off?
(Inv. 5)

*11. **Analyze** Kerry is thinking about names for a baby girl. She likes Abby
(39) or Bekki for the first name and Grace or Marie for the middle name.
What combinations of first and middle names are possible with these
choices?

*12. The table shows the number of vacation days Carson earns at work:
(Inv. 8)

Days Worked	Vacation Days Earned
30	1
60	2
90	3
120	4
150	5
180	6

a. **Generalize** Write a word sentence that describes the relationship
of the data.

b. **Predict** Use the word sentence you wrote to predict the number
of vacation days Carson will earn by working 300 days.

13. $60.75
(43, 51) + $95.75

14. $16.00
(43, 52) − $15.43

15.   3.15
(50) − 3.12

16.   320
(67) × 30

17.   465
(58) × 7

18. $0.98
(58) × 6

19. 425 ÷ 6
(71)

*20. $6.00 ÷ 8
(76)

*21. 625 ÷ 5
(76)

22. $3r = 150$
(41, 71)

23. $10^2 + t = 150$
(24, 62)

24. $1 + 7 + 2 + 6 + 9 + 4 + n = 37$
(2)

25. a. If the 3-inch square is covered with 1-inch squares, how
(Inv. 3)   many of the 1-inch squares are needed?

b. What is the area of the larger square?

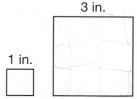
3 in.

1 in.

26. a. What is the perimeter of this triangle?
(Inv. 2, 78)

    b. Is the triangle a right triangle, an acute triangle, or an obtuse triangle?

1.2 cm   2.0 cm

1.6 cm

* 27. a. <u>Conclude</u> Which of these letters has only one line of symmetry?
(79)

Q R H T

    b. Which of these letters has rotational symmetry?

* 28. Write the capital letter P rotated 90° counterclockwise.
(75)

* 29. Multiple Choice Three of these triangles are congruent. Which
(66)   triangle is *not* one of the three congruent triangles?

A   B   C   D

* 30. The radius of this circle is 1.2 cm. What is the diameter
(21, 43)   of the circle?

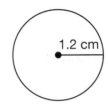

1.2 cm

Real-World Connection

In science Nam learned that a bee's honeycomb is a tessellation of hexagons. Nam is putting tile in his bathroom, and he wants to use a tessellation design on the floor. He decides to use 6-inch square tiles to cover part of the floor.

    a. Using the measurements of the rectangle below, how many 6-inch tiles does he need?

    b. Choose a different shape, and then draw a different tessellation that Nam could use on his bathroom floor.

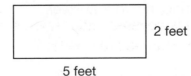

2 feet

5 feet

LESSON 83

• Sales Tax

facts Power Up I

count aloud Count down by halves from 10 to $\frac{1}{2}$.

mental math Before subtracting, make both numbers larger in **a–c.**

   a. Number Sense: 56 − 29

   b. Number Sense: 43 − 18

   c. Number Sense: 63 − 37

   d. Money: Jabulani bought a vegetable tray for $7.52 and a bottle of fruit punch for $1.98. What was the total cost?

   e. Time: Compare: 72 hours ◯ 2 days

   f. Time: How many days are in 10 common years?

   g. Estimation: The total cost for 3 boxes of cereal is $11.97. Round this amount to the nearest dollar and then divide by 3 to estimate the cost per box.

   h. Calculation: $\frac{1}{2}$ of 70, ÷ 7, × 2, + 8, ÷ 9, ÷ 2

problem solving Choose an appropriate problem-solving strategy to solve this problem. Twenty-one students went on a train tour of the zoo. Five students rode in the first train car with the engineer. The other students were divided equally among the last four train cars. How many students were in each of the last four train cars? Explain how you found your answer.

New Concept

Sales tax is an extra amount of money that sometimes must be paid when items are purchased. The amount of tax depends upon the amount purchased and the local sales-tax rate. In the United States, sales-tax rates vary by city, by county, and by state.

Example 1

Yin bought six bolts priced at 89¢ each. The total sales tax was 32¢. How much did Yin spend in all?

First we find the cost of the six bolts by multiplying.

$$\begin{array}{r} \overset{5}{89¢} \\ \times \quad 6 \\ \hline 534¢ = \$5.34 \end{array}$$

The six bolts cost $5.34. Now we add the sales tax.

$$\begin{array}{rl} \$5.34 & \text{price of bolts} \\ + \ \$0.32 & \text{sales tax} \\ \hline \$5.66 & \text{total cost} \end{array}$$

The total cost, including tax, was **$5.66.**

Thinking Skill

Verify

Why are there two decimal places in the answer?

Example 2

Taeko bought a blouse priced at $25. The sales-tax rate was 8¢ per dollar. How much tax did Taeko pay?

Finding the amount of tax on a purchase is similar to solving an "equal groups" problem.

Formula: Price × Tax rate = Tax

Problem: 25 × 8¢ = 200 cents

Since 200¢ is two dollars, Taeko paid a tax of **$2.00.**

If we do not have the exact amount of money needed to buy something at a store, we pay more than the total cost and then we get change back. To find how much change we should get back, we subtract the total cost from the amount we paid.

Example 3

Morgan bought a pair of pants priced at $23.99. The sales tax was $1.56. Morgan paid the clerk $40.00. How much money should she get back in change?

First we figure out the total cost.

$$\begin{array}{rl} \$23.99 & \text{price of pants} \\ + \ \$ \ 1.56 & \text{sales tax} \\ \hline \$25.55 & \text{total cost} \end{array}$$

Now we subtract the total cost from the amount she paid.

$$\begin{array}{rl} \$40.00 & \text{amount paid} \\ - \ \$25.55 & \text{total cost} \\ \hline \$14.45 & \text{change back} \end{array}$$

Thinking Skill

Discuss

Suppose Morgan gave the clerk $40.55 instead of $40 to pay for her purchase. Why would she do that?

Morgan should get **$14.45** back from the clerk.

Justify How can we count to check the answer?

Example 4

Mrs. Benson has coupons that can be used at her favorite restaurant. Some coupons are for a beverage and other coupons are for a main course. How many different ways can she combine one beverage coupon and one main-course coupon?

Each beverage coupon can be linked with one main-course coupon. We will use a tree diagram to show the combinations.

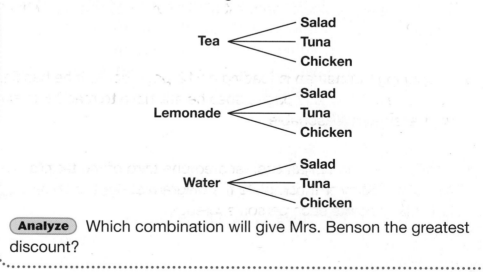

Analyze Which combination will give Mrs. Benson the greatest discount?

a. Serena bought three pairs of socks. Each pair was priced at $2.24. The sales tax was 34¢. Altogether, how much did Serena spend on socks?

b. Hakim paid $10.00 for a tape that cost $6.95. The sales tax was 49¢. How much money should Hakim get back in change?

c. At a "no sales tax" sale at the hardware store, Beatriz is deciding which of two paint brushes to buy. One costs $3.99 and a better one costs $4.49. Beatriz has a $5 bill, a $10 bill, and a $20 bill. If she buys one of the brushes and pays with one of the bills, what combinations are possible and how much will she get back in change? Use a tree diagram to find the combinations.

Written Practice

Distributed and Integrated

*1. **Multiple Choice** To prepare for a move to a new building, the
(49, 67) employees of a library spent an entire week packing books in boxes. On Monday the employees packed 30 books in each of 320 boxes. How many books did those boxes contain?

A 9600 books **B** 960 books **C** 320 books **D** 350 books

2. The movie was 3 hours long. If it started at 11:10 a.m., at what time did
(27) it end?

3. **Explain** Jonathan is reading a 212-page book. If he has finished
(25, 30) 135 pages, how many pages does he still have to read? Explain why your answer is reasonable.

4. Khalil, Julian, and Elijah each scored one third of the team's
(70) 42 points. Copy and complete the diagram at right to show how many points each person scored.

42 points

5. **Estimate** A family has $4182 in a savings account. Round the
(54) number of dollars in the account to the nearest thousand.

*6. **Explain** The shirt was priced at $16.98. The tax was $1.02. Sam
(83)   paid the clerk $20. How much money should Sam get back? Explain
          your thinking.

*7. What fraction of the letters in the following word are Is?
(74)

S U P E R C A L I F R A G I L I S T I C E X P I A L I D O C I O U S

8. Compare: $3 \times 4 \times 5 \bigcirc 5 \times 4 \times 3$
(Inv. 1,
62)

9. $m - 137 = 257$ **10.** $n + 137 = 257$
(24)   (24)

11. $1.45 + 2.4 + 0.56 + 7.6$ **12.** $5.75 - (3.12 + 0.5)$
(50)   (45, 50)

*13. **Analyze** Use the information below to answer parts **a–c.**
(72)
          In the first 8 games of this season, the Rio Hondo football team
          won 6 games and lost 2 games. They won their next game by a
          score of 24 to 20. The team will play 12 games in all.

   a. In the first nine games of the season, how many games did Rio
          Hondo win?

   b. Rio Hondo won its ninth game by how many points?

   c. What is the greatest number of games Rio Hondo could win this
          season?

14.   638   **15.**   472   **16.** $6.09
(67) $\times$ 50   (58) $\times$ 9   (58) $\times$ 6

*17. $3\overline{)921}$ ***18.** $5\overline{)678}$ ***19.** $4\overline{)2400}$
(80)   (76)   (80)

20. $12.60 \div 5$ **21.** $14.34 \div 6$ ***22.** $46.00 \div 8$
(76)   (76)   (76)

23. $9^2 = 9n$ **24.** $5w = 5 \times 10^2$
(61, 62)   (61, 62)

25. The names of one fourth of the months begin with the letter J. What
(Inv. 5) percent of the months begin with the letter J?

* 26. **a.** (**Model**) Use a ruler to find the perimeter of the rectangle at right in millimeters.
_(Inv. 2, 69)

b. (**Analyze**) Draw a rectangle that is similar to the rectangle in part **a** and whose sides are twice as long. What is the perimeter in centimeters of the rectangle you drew?

27. Barton turned around three times. How many degrees did Barton turn?
₍₇₅₎

28. Rachel wants to determine if two right triangles are congruent, so she moves △1 to the position of △2 to see if they match. Name two transformations Rachel uses to move △1.
₍₇₃₎

29. Below we show an equilateral triangle, an isosceles triangle, and a scalene triangle. Name the triangle that does not have reflective symmetry.
_(78, 79)

* 30. Four students wrote their names on slips of paper. The names were then placed in a paper bag and picked one at a time.
₍₃₆₎

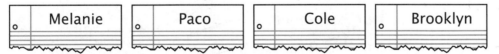

List the different ways the second, third, and fourth names could have been chosen if Cole's name was chosen first.

Early Finishers
Real-World Connection

Before taxes were calculated, Crystal spent $34.00 on school supplies. After adding tax, she paid the clerk $37.40.

a. What was the tax on Crystal's purchase?

b. How many cents per dollar of tax did Crystal pay?

• Decimal Numbers to Thousandths

Power Up

facts   Power Up I

count aloud   Count down by quarters from 4 to $\frac{1}{4}$.

mental math   Counting by fives from 1, 2, 3, 4, or 5, we find five different final-digit patterns: 1 and 6; 2 and 7; 3 and 8; 4 and 9; and 5 and 0. When a number ending in 5 is added to or subtracted from another number, the final digit of that number and of the answer will fit one of the five patterns. Look for the final-digit patterns as you solve **a–f.**

  a. Number Sense: $22 + 5$

  b. Number Sense: $22 - 5$

  c. Number Sense: $38 + 5$

  d. Number Sense: $38 - 5$

  e. Number Sense: $44 + 5$

  f. Number Sense: $44 - 5$

  g. Estimation: Estimate the percent of this circle that is shaded:

  h. Calculation: $\sqrt{36}$, $\times\,3$, $+\,10$, $\div\,4$, $-\,1$, $\div\,3$

problem solving   Choose an appropriate problem-solving strategy to solve this problem. Tanner has three homework assignments to complete. One assignment is in math, one is in science, and one is in vocabulary. Tanner plans to finish one assignment before starting the next. What are the possible sequences in which he could complete the assignments?

In Investigation 4, we practiced writing fractions with a denominator of 10 as decimal numbers with one decimal place.

$$\frac{7}{10} = 0.7 \qquad \text{Both numbers are } \textit{seven tenths.}$$

Thinking Skill

Discuss

Name the order of the fractions from least to greatest.

We also wrote fractions with a denominator of 100 as decimal numbers with two decimal places.

$$\frac{12}{100} = 0.12 \qquad \text{Both numbers are } \textit{twelve hundredths.}$$

In this lesson, we will write fractions with a denominator of 1000 as decimal numbers with three decimal places.

$$\frac{125}{1000} = 0.125 \qquad \text{Both numbers are } \textit{one hundred twenty-five thousandths.}$$

$$\frac{25}{1000} = 0.025 \qquad \text{Both numbers are } \textit{twenty-five thousandths.}$$

Example 1

Visit www. SaxonMath.com/ Int4Activities for a calculator activity.

Write $\frac{375}{1000}$ as a decimal number. Then use words to name both numbers.

The denominator of the fraction is 1000, so we use three decimal places to write the fraction as a decimal number.

$$\frac{375}{1000} = \mathbf{0.375} \qquad \textbf{three hundred seventy-five thousandths}$$

Working in the reverse, we see that a decimal number with three decimal places may be written as a fraction with a denominator of 1000.

Example 2

Write each decimal number as a fraction or mixed number. Then use words to name the numbers.

    a. 0.625   **b. 3.125**

a. Since there are three places that follow the decimal point, we will use the denominator 1000 for our fraction. We write the digits that follow the decimal point as the numerator of the fraction.

$$0.625 = \frac{625}{1000} \qquad \textbf{six hundred twenty-five thousandths}$$

b. Since there is a whole number, 3, we may write the decimal number as a mixed number. Only the digits that follow the decimal point become part of the fraction.

$$3.125 = \frac{125}{1000}$$ three and one hundred twenty-five thousandths

Verify Explain why $\frac{625}{1000}$ is greater than $\frac{325}{1000}$.

Lesson Practice Write each fraction or mixed number as a decimal number:

a. $\frac{425}{1000}$

b. $3\frac{875}{1000}$

c. $\frac{35}{1000}$

d. $2\frac{7}{1000}$

Write each decimal number as a fraction or mixed number. Then use words to name the numbers.

e. 0.214

f. 4.321

g. 0.025

h. 5.012

i. 0.003

j. 9.999

Written Practice *Distributed and Integrated*

*1. If it is not a leap year, what is the total number of days in January,
(54) February, and March?

2. A tailor made each of 12 children a pair of pants and 2 shirts. How
(49) many pieces of clothing did the tailor make?

*3. Ariel did seven more chin-ups than Burke did. If Ariel did eighteen
(31) chin-ups, how many chin-ups did Burke do?

4. Kadeeja drove 200 miles on 8 gallons of gas. Her car averaged how
(60) many miles on each gallon of gas?

*5. Melinda paid the clerk $20.00 for a book that was priced at $8.95. The
(83) tax was 54¢. How much money should she get back?

*6. a. Which two prime numbers are factors of 15?
(55)

   b. **Explain** Is 15 a prime number? Why or why not?

7. If each side of an octagon is 1 centimeter long, what is the octagon's
(69) perimeter in millimeters?

8. (**Represent**) One third of the 18 marbles were blue. How many
(70) of the marbles were blue? Draw a picture to solve the problem.

9. a. (**Analyze**) The Mendez family hiked 15 miles in 1 day. At that
(57) rate, how many miles would they hike in 5 days? Make a table to
solve the problem.

b. (**Formulate**) Write an equation to represent the data in the table.

*10. (**Explain**) Mylah picked 3640 peaches in 7 days. She picked an
(60, 80) average of how many peaches each day? Explain why your answer is
reasonable.

*11. a. (**Analyze**) Zachary did 1000 push-ups last week. He did 129 of
(74, 84) those push-ups last Wednesday. What fraction of the 1000 push-ups
did Zachary do last Wednesday?

b. (**Represent**) Write the answer to part **a** as a decimal number.
Then use words to name the number.

*12. (**Explain**) Suppose that an object on Earth has a known mass of
(77) 80 kilograms. Will the mass of that object be less than, more than, or the
same as on the other planets in our solar system? Explain your answer.

13. $4.56 - (2.3 + 1.75)$
(45, 50)

14. $\sqrt{36} + n = 7 \times 8$
(Inv. 3, 61)

15. $3 \times 6 \times 3^2$
(62)

16. $462 \times \sqrt{9}$
(Inv. 3, 58)

17. $7^2 - \sqrt{49}$
(Inv. 3, 62)

18. $\begin{array}{r} 36 \\ \times\ 50 \\ \hline \end{array}$
(67)

19. $\begin{array}{r} \$4.76 \\ \times\ \ \ \ 7 \\ \hline \end{array}$
(58)

20. $\begin{array}{r} 4 \\ 3 \\ 2 \\ 7 \\ 6 \\ 8 \\ +\ n \\ \hline 47 \end{array}$
(2)

21. $\dfrac{524}{4}$
(76)

*22. $6\overline{)4200}$
(80)

23. $5\overline{)\$26.30}$
(76)

24. $2n = \$3.70$
(41, 76)

25. $786 \div 3$
(76)

*26. $4902 \div 7$
(80)

* 27. Write 0.321 as a fraction.
(84)

28. Find the perimeter and area of this square:
(Inv. 2, Inv. 3)

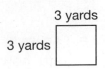

3 yards

3 yards

29. Which transformations would move figure *ABCD* to
(73) position *WXYZ*?

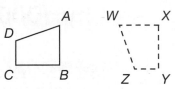

30. **Estimate** Which angle in this figure looks like it measures about 45°?
(23, 81)

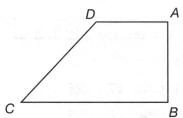

Early Finishers

Real-World Connection

The Republic of Malta is a group of small islands in the Mediterranean Sea. It is directly south of Sicily and north of Libya. From 1972 to 1994, the currency used in the Republic of Malta included a 2-mil coin, a 3-mil coin, and a 5-mil coin. A mil was $\frac{1}{1000}$ (or 0.001) of a lira, another Maltese money amount.

a. Write the value of each mil coin in both decimal and fraction form as it relates to the lira.

b. Use words to name each fraction in part **a.**

c. If you were to add a 2-mil coin, a 3-mil coin, and a 5-mil coin together, how many mils would you have?

d. How many lira would equal the total in part **c?** Write the total as a decimal and than as a fraction in lowest terms.

• Multiplying by 10, by 100, and by 1000

Power Up

facts　　Power Up G

mental math

Use the 5s pattern as you add in **a–c.**

　a. Number Sense: 36 + 15

　b. Number Sense: 47 + 25

　c. Number Sense: 28 + 35

　d. Number Sense: 40 × 40 × 10

　e. Money: $10.00 − $2.75

　f. Time: How many days is 8 weeks?

　g. Estimation: Each bracelet costs $2.99. Tatiana has $11. Does she have enough money to buy 4 bracelets?

　h. Calculation: 50% of 42, ÷ 3, + 10, − 3, ÷ 2, × 7

problem solving

Choose an appropriate problem-solving strategy to solve his problem. The diagram at right is called a *Venn diagram*. The circle on the left stands for fruit, and the circle on the right stands for vegetables. The *A* represents apples, which are fruit, and the *B* represents broccoli, which is a vegetable. The *C* stands for cheese, which is not a fruit or a vegetable. Copy the diagram on your paper and place abbreviations for eggs, oranges, and green beans.

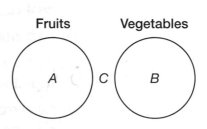

To multiply a whole number by 10, we simply attach a zero to the end of the number.

$$\begin{array}{r} 123 \\ \times\ \ \ 10 \\ \hline 1230 \end{array}$$

Thinking Skill

Generalize

If we were to multiply 15 by 1 million, how many zeros would we attach to the right of the product of 15 and 1?

When we multiply a whole number by 100, we add two zeros to the end of the number.

$$\begin{array}{r} 123 \\ \times\ \ \ 100 \\ \hline 12{,}300 \end{array}$$

When we multiply a whole number by 1000, we add three zeros to the end of the number.

$$\begin{array}{r} 123 \\ \times\ \ \ 1000 \\ \hline 123{,}000 \end{array}$$

When we multiply dollars and cents by a whole number, we remember to insert the decimal point two places from the right side of the product.

$$\begin{array}{r} \$1.23 \\ \times\ \ \ 100 \\ \hline \$123.00 \end{array}$$

Example

Thinking Skill

Discuss

Why is the product of 100 and $6.12 *not* written as $6.1200?

Multiply mentally:

a. 37×10 **b.** $\$6.12 \times 100$ **c.** $45¢ \times 1000$

a. The answer is "37" with one zero at the end:

370

b. The answer is "612" with two zeros at the end. We remember to place the decimal point and dollar sign:

$612.00

c. The answer is "45" with three zeros at the end. This makes 45,000¢, which in dollar form is

$450.00

Lesson Practice   Multiply mentally:

    a. 365 × 10   **b.** 52 × 100   **c.** 7 × 1000

    d. $3.60 × 10   **e.** 420 × 100   **f.** $2.50 × 1000

    g. The table below shows the relationship between dimes and dollars. Write a formula to represent the relationship.

Number of Dollars	1	2	3	4	5
Number of Dimes	10	20	30	40	50

Written Practice   *Distributed and Integrated*

---

*1. **(Interpret)** Use the information in the graph below to answer parts **a–c**.
(49, Inv. 6)

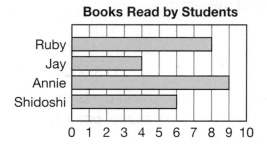

Books Read by Students

Ruby, Jay, Annie, Shidoshi

0 1 2 3 4 5 6 7 8 9 10

    a. Which student has read exactly twice as many books as Jay?

    b. Shidoshi's goal is to read 10 books. How many more books does he need to read to reach his goal?

    c. If the books Annie has read have an average of 160 pages each, how many pages has she read?

*2. Dala saw some pentagons. The pentagons had a total of 100 sides.
(52, 63) How many pentagons did Dala see?

*3. Mariah bought a rectangular piece of land that was 3 miles long and
(Inv. 3, Inv. 5) 2 miles wide. Fifty percent of the land could be farmed. How many square miles could be farmed?

*4. Max bought 10 pencils for 24¢ each. The tax was 14¢. What was the
(83) total cost of the pencils?

*5. Multiple Choice A full pitcher of orange juice contains about how
(40) much juice?

    A 2 ounces   **B** 2 liters   **C** 2 gallons   **D** 2 cups

6. **(Represent)** Draw a triangle that has two perpendicular sides. What
(23, 78) type of triangle did you draw?

7. a. **(Represent)** One fourth of the 48 gems were rubies. How many of
(Inv. 5, 70) the gems were rubies? Draw a picture to solve the problem.

b. What percent of the gems were not rubies?

*8. a. **(Represent)** One thousand fans attended the game, but only
(74, 84) 81 fans cheered for the visiting team. What fraction of the fans who
attended the game cheered for the visiting team?

b. Write the answer in part **a** as a decimal number. Then use words to
name the number.

9. $46.01 - (3.68 + 10.2)$
(45, 50)

10. $728 + c = 1205$
(24)

11. 36×10 **12.** 100×42 **13.** $\$2.75 \times 1000$
(85)   (85)   (85)

14. $\$3.17$ **15.** 206 **16.** 37
(58) $\underline{\times \quad 4}$ (58) $\underline{\times \quad 5}$ (67) $\underline{\times \quad 40}$

17. $3\overline{)492}$ **18.** $5\overline{)860}$ **19.** $6m = \$9.30$
(76)   (76)   (41, 76)

20. $168 \div 2^3$ ***21.** $\$20.00 \div 8$ ***22.** $1600 \div \sqrt{16}$
(62, 65)   (76, 80)   (Inv. 3, 80)

23. Find the perimeter and area of this rectangle:
(Inv. 2, Inv. 3)

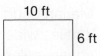

10 ft

6 ft

*24. **a.** (**Verify**) Which of these letters has two lines of symmetry?
(79)

H A P P Y

b. Which of these letters has rotational symmetry?

*25. (**Estimate**) Which angle in this figure looks like it
(23, 81) measures about 135°?

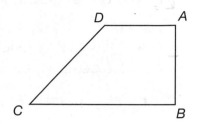

*26. **Multiple Choice** Luz wants to cover a floor with tiles. Which of these
(82) tile shapes will *not* tessellate, or will not completely cover the floor?

A   **B**   **C**   **D**

*27. The table shows the relationship between meters and centimeters:
(Inv. 8)

Number of Meters	1	2	3	4	5
Number of Centimeters	100	200	300	400	500

    a. (**Formulate**) Write a formula to represent the relationship.

    b. (**Predict**) Use your formula to find the number of centimeters in 10 meters.

28. In Dodge City, Kansas, the average maximum temperature in January
(18) is 41°F. The average minimum temperature is 19°F. How many degrees cooler is 19°F than 41°F?

29. The Peace River is 1210 miles long, and its source is in British Columbia.
(52) The Red River is 1290 miles long, and its source is in New Mexico. Which river is longer?

*30. (**Model**) Draw a number line from 6 to 7 divided into tenths. On it show the
(Inv. 1) locations of 6.1, $6\frac{3}{10}$, 6.6, and $6\frac{9}{10}$.

• Multiplying Multiples of 10 and 100

Power Up

facts   Power Up G

mental math   Use the 5s pattern as you subtract in **a–c.**

   a. Number Sense: $41 - 15$

   b. Number Sense: $72 - 25$

   c. Number Sense: $84 - 45$

   d. Number Sense: 25×30

   e. Money: Bridget spent $6.54. Then she spent $2.99 more. Altogether, how much did Bridget spend?

   f. Time: Mirabel's speech lasted 2 minutes 20 seconds. How many seconds is that?

   g. Estimation: Kione purchased two DVDs for $18.88 each. Estimate the total cost of the DVDs.

   h. Calculation: $\frac{1}{10}$ of 60, $\times\, 4$, $\div\, 2$, $\times\, 5$

problem solving   Choose an appropriate problem-solving strategy to solve this problem. Josh will flip a coin three times in a row. On each flip, the coin will either land on "heads" or "tails." If the coin were to land heads up each time, the combination of flips would be heads, heads, heads, which can be abbreviated as HHH. Find all the possible combinations of heads and tails Josh can get with three coin flips.

New Concept

Once we have memorized the multiplication facts, we can multiply rounded numbers "in our head." To do this, we multiply the first digits of the factors and count zeros. Study the multiplication on the next page.

Thinking Skill

Analyze

Is the product of 40 and 50 written as 200, 2000, or 20,000? Explain your reasoning.

To find the product of 40 and 30, we multiply 4 by 3 and then attach two zeros.

Example 1

In the weight-lifting room, a group of football players lifted 80 pounds of weights 60 different times. How many pounds of weight did the players lift altogether?

We think, "Six times eight is 48." Since there is one zero in 60 and one zero in 80, we attach two zeros to 48. The product is 4800, so the total weight lifted was **4800 pounds.**

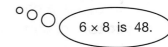

6 × 8 is 48.

Example 2

Thinking Skill

Verify

Why do we attach three zeros when we multiply 30 by $7.00?

A store has 30 ping-pong paddles for sale at $7.00 each. How much money will the store receive if all of the paddles are sold?

We think, "Three times seven is 21." There are three zeros in the problem, so we attach three zeros to 21 to get 21,000. Since we multiplied dollars and cents, we insert the decimal point two places from the right and add a dollar sign. The product is $210.00, so the income will be **$210.**

3 × 7 is 21.

Example 3

Multiply mentally: 400 × 700

We think, "Four times seven is 28." We attach four zeros and get **280,000.**

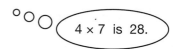

4 × 7 is 28.

Lesson Practice

Multiply mentally:

a. 70 × 80

b. 40 × 50

c. 40 × $6.00

d. 30 × 800

1. It takes Tempest 20 minutes to walk to school. At what time should she
(27) start for school if she wants to arrive at 8:10 a.m.?

*2. A container and its contents weigh 125 pounds. The contents of the
(25, 30) container weigh 118 pounds. What is the weight of the container?

*3. Anjelita is shopping for art supplies and plans to purchase a sketchpad
(83) for $4.29, a charcoal pencil for $1.59, and an eraser for 69¢. If the
amount of sales tax is 43¢ and Anjelita pays for her purchase with a
$10 bill, how much change should she receive?

4. According to this calendar, October 30, 1904,
(54) was what day of the week?

OCTOBER 1904

S	M	T	W	T	F	S
						1
2	3	4	5	6	7	8
9	10	11	12	13	14	15
16	17	18	19	20	21	22
23	24	25	26	27	28	29
30	31					

*5. **Explain** From 3:00 p.m. to 3:45 p.m., the minute hand of a clock
(75) turns how many degrees? Explain your thinking.

6. Round three thousand, seven hundred eighty-two to the nearest
(34, 54) thousand.

7. The limousine weighed 2 tons. How many pounds is 2 tons?
(77)

*8. **Represent** One fifth of the 45 horses were pintos. How many of the
(70) horses were pintos? Draw a picture to illustrate the problem.

9. What percent of the horses in problem **8** were pintos?
(Inv. 5, 70) (*Hint:* Find $\frac{1}{5}$ of 100%.)

100%

10. (Inv. 1) **Represent** Which point on the number line below could represent 23,650?

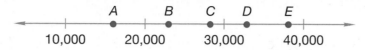

*11. (Inv. 4, 84) **Connect** Write each decimal number as a fraction:

  a. 0.1 **b.** 0.01 **c.** 0.001

12. (43, 51)
$36.47
+ $ 9.68

13. (52)
$30.00
− $13.45

14. (17)
  6
  8
  17
  23
  110
  25
+ 104

15. (58)
  476
× 7

16. (58)
  804
× 5

17. (45, 50) $12.65 - (7.43 - 2.1)$

18. (61, 62) $5^2 + 5^2 + n = 10^2$

19. (35, Inv. 4) **Represent** Write each of these numbers with words:

  a. $2\frac{1}{10}$ **b.** 2.1

*20. (85) $100 \times 23¢$

*21. (86) 60×30

*22. (86) $70 \times \$2.00$

*23. (76, 80) $3\overline{)\$6.27}$

24. (76) $7\overline{)820}$

25. (68) $6\overline{)333}$

26. (Inv. 3, 76) $625 \div \sqrt{25}$

*27. (62, 80) $4000 \div 2^3$

28. (41, 76) $2w = 1370$

29. (Inv. 2, Inv. 3) Find the perimeter and area of this square.

10 m

*30. a. (63, 82) **Analyze** Some combinations of shapes will fit together to cover a flat surface. What two types of polygons are used in the pattern at right?

  b. Does this tessellation have line symmetry?

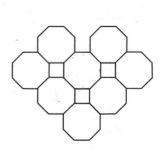

• Multiplying Two Two-Digit Numbers, Part 1

Power Up

facts　　Power Up G

mental math　　Use the 5s pattern as you add or subtract in **a–c.**

　　a. Number Sense: 83 − 15

　　b. Number Sense: 29 + 35

　　c. Number Sense: 76 + 15

　　d. Percent: Cory figures that about 50% of the calories he consumes are from carbohydrates. Cory consumes about 2000 calories each day. About how many of those calories are from carbohydrates?

　　e. Measurement: How many inches is one yard?

　　f. Time: Which day of the week is 71 days after Monday?

　　g. Estimation: Jayla has run $\frac{1}{2}$ mile in 4 minutes 57 seconds. If she can continue running at the same pace, about how long will it take Jayla to run one full mile?

　　h. Calculation: $5^2 + 5^2$, + 6, ÷ 8

problem solving　　Choose an appropriate problem-solving strategy to solve this problem. Sandra bought a CD priced at $12.95. Sales tax was $1.10. She paid for her purchase with a $10 bill and a $5 bill. Sandra got back five coins (not including a half-dollar). What were the coins Sandra should have received in change?

We use three steps to multiply by a two-digit number. First we multiply by the ones digit. Next we multiply by the tens digit. Then we add the products. To multiply 34 by 12, for example, we multiply 34 by 2 and then multiply 34 by 10. Then we add the products.

$$34 \times 2 = 68 \quad \text{partial product}$$
$$34 \times 10 = 340 \quad \text{partial product}$$
$$34 \times 12 = 408 \quad \text{total product}$$

Thinking Skill

Evaluate

Can the expression (2 × 34) + (10 × 34) be used to represent the vertical form of 34 × 12? Explain why or why not.

Multiple Methods: It is easier to write the numbers one above the other when we multiply, like this:

$$\begin{array}{r} 34 \\ \times\ 12 \\ \hline \end{array}$$

Method 1: First we multiply 34 by 2 and write the answer.

$$\begin{array}{r} 34 \\ \times\ 12 \\ \hline 68 \end{array}$$

Next we multiply 34 by 1. This 1 is actually 10, so the product is 340. We write the answer, and then we add the results of the two multiplication problems and get 408.

$$\begin{array}{r} 34 \\ \times\ 12 \\ \hline 68 \\ +\ 340 \\ \hline 408 \end{array}$$

Visit www. SaxonMath.com/ Int4Activities for a calculator activity.

Method 2: An alternate method would be to omit the zero from the second multiplication. Using this method, we position the last digit of the second multiplication in the second column from the right. The empty place is treated like a zero when adding.

$$\begin{array}{r} 34 \\ \times\ 12 \\ \hline 68 \\ +\ 34 \\ \hline 408 \end{array}$$

Multiply: 31
       × **23**

First we multiply 31 by 3.

$$
\begin{array}{r}
31 \\
\times\ 23 \\
\hline
93
\end{array}
$$

Now we multiply 31 by 2. Since this 2 is actually 20, we write the last digit of the product in the tens column. Then we add to get **713**.

$$
\begin{array}{r}
31 \\
\times\ 23 \\
\hline
93 \\
+\ 62 \\
\hline
713
\end{array}
\quad \text{or} \quad
\begin{array}{r}
31 \\
\times\ 23 \\
\hline
93 \\
+\ 620 \\
\hline
713
\end{array}
$$

Lesson Practice Multiply:

a. 32 × 23

b. 23 × 32

c. 43 × 12

d. 34 × 21

e. 32 × 32

f. 22 × 14

g. 13 × 32

h. 33 × 33

Written Practice *Distributed and Integrated*

*1. **(Analyze)** Use the following information to answer parts **a–c.**
(27, 72)

Freeman rode his bike 2 miles from his house to Didi's house. Together they rode 4 miles to the lake. Didi caught 8 fish. At 3:30 p.m. they rode back to Didi's house. Then Freeman rode home.

a. Altogether, how far did Freeman ride his bike?

b. It took Freeman an hour and a half to get home from the lake. At what time did he get home?

c. Didi caught twice as many fish as Freeman. How many fish did Freeman catch?

*2. Saraj bought some feed priced at $12.97. Tax was 91¢. He paid with a
(83) $20 bill. How much change should he receive?

3. (**Estimate**) Find a reasonable sum of 4876 and 3149 by rounding each
(59) number to the nearest thousand and then adding.

4. (**Estimate**) What is the perimeter of a pentagon if each side is
(Inv. 2,
63) 20 centimeters long? Explain your reasoning.

*5. (**Estimate**) Find the length of this segment to the nearest quarter inch:
(39)

6. (**Represent**) One half of the 18 players were on the field. How many
(70) players were on the field? Draw a picture to illustrate the problem.

7. A dime is $\frac{1}{10}$ of a dollar. What fraction of a dollar is a penny?
(36)

8. A dime is what percent of a dollar?
(Inv. 5)

9. Find 13^2 by multiplying 13×13.
(87)

10. (**Represent**) One millimeter is $\frac{1}{1000}$ of a meter. Write that number as a
(84) decimal number. Then use words to write the number.

*11.   31
(87) $\times 21$

*12.   32
(87) $\times 31$

*13.   13
(87) $\times 32$

*14.   11
(87) $\times 11$

*15.   12
(87) $\times 14$

*16. 30×800
(86)

17. $7\overline{)1000}$
(76)

18. $3\overline{)477}$
(76)

19. $5\overline{)2535}$
(80)

20. $64.80 \div 9$
(76, 80)

21. $716 \div 4$
(76)

22. $8x = 352$
(41, 65)

*23. How many different three-digit numbers can you write using the digits
(36)   1, 5, and 0? Each digit may be used only once, and the digit 0 may not
be used in the hundreds place.

*24. Find the perimeter and area of this rectangle:
(Inv. 3, 86)

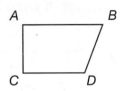
20 in.

10 in.

*25. **Represent** Draw an equilateral triangle with sides 2 cm long.
(78)

26. What is the perimeter in millimeters of the triangle you drew in
(Inv. 2, 69)   problem **25?**

*27. a. **Conclude** In this polygon, which side appears to be parallel to
(23, 81)   side *AB?*

b. **Estimate** Which angle looks as if it might measure
110°?

A   B

C   D

28. This graph shows the relationship between Rudy's age and Neelam's
(Inv. 8)   age. How old was Neelam when Rudy was 4 years old?

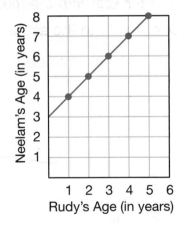

29. 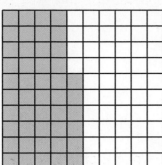 **Represent** Each grid represents a decimal number.
(Inv. 4)

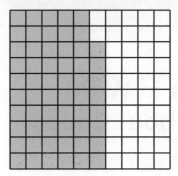

Write each decimal number. Then write the sum and the difference of those numbers.

30.  **Estimate** A mail carrier worked from 8 a.m. to noon and from 1 p.m.
(76) to 4 p.m. During those times, the carrier delivered mail to 691 homes. About how many deliveries did the carrier make each hour? Explain your answer.

Early Finishers

Real-World Connection

Murals are pictures painted on walls. In 2005, archaeologists revealed the last wall of a room-sized mural that was painted more than 2000 years ago in the ancient Mayan city of San Bartolo, Guatemala.

a. Estimate the area of a mural that measures 23 feet by 84 feet.

b. Find the actual area of a mural with the measurements given.

c. How close was your estimate to the actual area?

• Remainders in Word Problems About Equal Groups

Power Up

facts   Power Up G

**mental
math**

a. **Number Sense:** $85 - 38$

b. **Number Sense:** $4 \times 20 \times 10$

c. **Percent:** 10% of $20

d. **Measurement:** How many pints is a gallon?

e. **Powers/Roots:** $9^2 - \sqrt{9}$

f. **Time:** Which day of the week is 699 days after Monday?

g. **Estimation:** Estimate what percent of the circle is shaded.

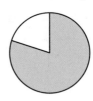

h. **Calculation:** $\sqrt{81}$, $\div 3$, $\times 25$, $+ 75$, $\times 2$

**problem
solving**

Choose an appropriate problem-solving strategy to solve this problem. Tandy wants to know the circumference of (the distance around) her bicycle tire. She has some string and a meterstick. How can Tandy measure the circumference of the tire in centimeters?

New Concept

We have practiced solving "equal groups" problems using division. In these problems, there were no remainders from the division. In this lesson we will begin practicing division word problems that involve remainders. When solving these problems, we must be careful to identify exactly what the question is asking.

Example

Lilly needs to place 100 bottles into boxes that hold 6 bottles each.

> **a. How many boxes can be filled?**
>
> **b. How many bottles will be left over?**
>
> **c. How many boxes are needed to hold all the bottles?**

Each of these questions asks for different information. To answer the questions, we begin by dividing 100 by 6.

$$\begin{array}{r} 16\text{ R }4 \\ 6\overline{)100} \\ \underline{6} \\ 40 \\ \underline{36} \\ 4 \end{array}$$

The result "16 R 4" means that the 100 bottles can be separated into 16 groups of 6 bottles. There will be 4 extra bottles.

a. The bottles can be separated into 16 groups of 6 bottles, so **16 boxes** can be filled.

b. The 4 remaining bottles do not completely fill a box. So after filling 16 boxes, there will still be **4 bottles** left over.

c. Although the 4 remaining bottles do not completely fill a box, another box is needed to hold them. Thus, **17 boxes** are needed to hold all the bottles.

Lesson Practice

Interpret Use the statement below to answer problems **a–b.**

Tomorrow 32 students are attending an awards ceremony. Each table will seat 5 students.

a. How many tables can be filled?

b. How many tables will be needed?

Interpret Use the statement below to answer problems **c–e.**

Tendai found 31 quarters in his bank. He made stacks of 4 quarters each.

c. How many stacks of 4 quarters did he make?

d. How many extra quarters did he have?

e. If Tendai made a short stack with the extra quarters, how many stacks would he have in all?

*1. (**Interpret**) Taryn packed 6 table-tennis balls in each package. There
(88) were 100 table-tennis balls to pack.

    a. How many packages did he fill?

    b. How many table-tennis balls were left over?

*2. Write the formula for the area of a square. Then find the area of a
(62, 87) square with sides 12 inches long.

*3. ✏ (**Estimate**) Paola bought four pretzels priced at 59¢ each. The
(83) sales tax was 16¢. Estimate the total cost of the pretzels. Explain your
thinking.

4. Twenty-four inches is how many feet?
(Inv. 2)

*5. a. Segment *YZ* is how many millimeters long?
(45, 69)

    b. Segment *YZ* is how many centimeters long?

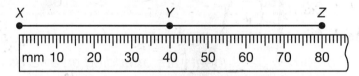

6. Jorge finished eating breakfast at the time shown on the
(27) clock. He finished eating lunch 5 hours 20 minutes later.
What time did Jorge finish eating lunch?

7. (**Represent**) Write the number 7528 in expanded form. Then use
(16, 33) words to write the number.

*8. a. (**Represent**) One fifth of the 25 band members missed the note.
(Inv. 5, How many band members missed the note? Draw a picture to
70) illustrate the problem.

    b. What percent of the band members missed the note?

*9. Nikki cut a rectangular piece of paper along a diagonal to
(73) make two triangles. What transformation can Nikki use to
find out if the triangles are congruent?

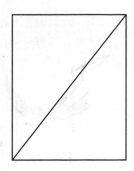

10. $6.35 + $14.25 + $0.97 + $5
(43, 51)

*11. 4.60 − (1.4 + 2.75)   **12.** $10.00 − (46¢ + $1.30)
(43, 50)   (43, 45)

*13. 28 × 1000   ***14.**   13   ***15.**   12
(85)   (87)   × 13   (87)   × 11

16. $8.67   ***17.**   31   ***18.**   12
(58)   ×   9   (87)   × 31   (87)   × 31

19. 7)‾3542   **20.** 6)‾$33.00   **21.** 8)‾4965
(80)   (76, 80)   (80)

22. 482 ÷ 5   **23.** 2700 ÷ 9   **24.** 2700 ÷ √9
(68)   (80)   (Inv. 3,
                                                                                    80)

25. 7 + 7 + $n = 7^2$ **26.** $3n = 6^2$
(61, 62)   (61, 62)

*27. a. (**Represent**) Draw an obtuse triangle.
(78)

    b. (**Explain**) Describe the segments of the obtuse angle. Explain
your thinking.

28. The classroom was 40 feet long and 30 feet wide. How
(Inv. 3, many 1-foot square floor tiles were needed to cover the
86) floor?

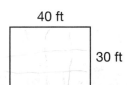

*29. a. In polygon *ABCD,* which side appears to be parallel to
(23) side *AD?*

    b. (**Classify**) Describe the angles.

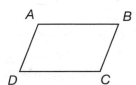

*30. **Interpret** This table shows the heights of several tall buildings.
(Inv. 6)   Make a bar graph to display the data.

Tall Buildings in the United States

Building	Location	Height (stories)
The Pinnacle	Chicago, IL	48
Interstate Tower	Charlotte, NC	32
Two Union Square	Seattle, WA	56
28 State Street	Boston, MA	40

Real-World Connection

George's Peach Pit Stop sells peaches in paper packages. Each package holds 25 peaches. George has an order for 346 peaches.

a. How many packages can be filled?

b. How many packages will he actually need?

c. How many peaches will be in the partially filled package?

LESSON 89

• Mixed Numbers and Improper Fractions

 **Power Up**

facts

Power Up G

mental math

a. **Number Sense:** 25×1000

b. **Number Sense:** $58 + 35$

c. **Percent:** Alonso needs to collect 25% of $40. What is 25% of $40?

d. **Time:** What day is 71 days after Wednesday?

e. **Measurement:** How many feet is 6 yards?

f. **Money:** The book cost $6.75. If Daina paid for the book with a $10 bill, then how much change should she receive?

g. **Estimation:** The total cost for 6 picture frames was $41.94. Round this amount to the nearest dollar and then divide by 6 to estimate the cost of each frame.

h. **Calculation:** $\sqrt{1}$, $\times 1$, $\div 1$, $- 1 + 1$

problem solving

Choose an appropriate problem-solving strategy to solve this problem. In this Venn diagram, the circle on the left stands for multiples of 3. The circle on the right stands for even numbers. The number 6 is both a multiple of 3 and an even number, so it is placed within the space created by the overlap of the two circles. The number 4 is placed within the circle for even numbers but outside the overlap, since 4 is not a multiple of 3. The number 1 is placed outside both circles because it is not a multiple of 3 and it is not even. Copy the Venn diagram on your paper, and place the numbers 9, 10, 11, and 12.

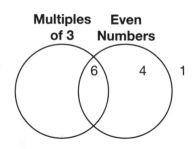

Here we show a picture of $1\frac{1}{2}$ shaded circles. Each whole circle has been divided into two half circles.

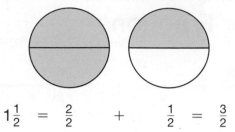

$$1\frac{1}{2} \quad = \quad \frac{2}{2} \quad + \quad \frac{1}{2} \quad = \quad \frac{3}{2}$$

Math Language

A **proper fraction** is a fraction whose numerator is less than the denominator.

We see from the picture that $1\frac{1}{2}$ is the same as *three halves,* which is written as $\frac{3}{2}$. The numerator is greater than the denominator, so the fraction $\frac{3}{2}$ is greater than 1. Fractions that are greater than or equal to 1 are called **improper fractions.** In this lesson we will draw pictures to show mixed numbers and their equivalent improper fractions.

Example

Draw circles to show that $2\frac{3}{4}$ equals $\frac{11}{4}$.

We begin by drawing three circles. The denominator of the fraction part of $2\frac{3}{4}$ is four, so we divide all the circles into fourths and shade $2\frac{3}{4}$ of them.

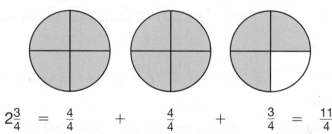

$$2\frac{3}{4} \quad = \quad \frac{4}{4} \quad + \quad \frac{4}{4} \quad + \quad \frac{3}{4} \quad = \quad \frac{11}{4}$$

We count 11 shaded fourths. The drawing shows that $2\frac{3}{4}$ equals $\frac{11}{4}$.

Modeling Mixed Numbers and Improper Fractions

Material needed:
* fraction manipulatives from **Lesson Activities 37** and **38**

Use fraction manipulatives to perform the following activities:

a. Place five $\frac{1}{2}$ circles on a desk. Then arrange four of the $\frac{1}{2}$ circles to form whole circles. Draw a picture of the whole and part circles you formed, and write the improper fraction and mixed number represented by the five $\frac{1}{2}$ circles.

b. Place one more $\frac{1}{2}$ circle on the desk to complete another circle. Write the improper fraction and whole number represented.

c. Clear the desk of $\frac{1}{2}$ circles and place seven $\frac{1}{4}$ circles on the desk. Fit the pieces together to form a whole circle and part of a circle. Draw a picture, and write the improper fraction and mixed number represented.

d. Place one more $\frac{1}{4}$ circle on the desk to complete another circle. Write the improper fraction and whole number represented.

Lesson Practice

a. Draw circles to show that $1\frac{3}{4} = \frac{7}{4}$.

b. Draw circles to show that $2\frac{1}{2} = \frac{5}{2}$.

c. Draw circles to show that $1\frac{1}{3} = \frac{4}{3}$.

Written Practice   *Distributed and Integrated*

*1. **(Interpret)** The coach divided 33 players as equally as possible into
(88)   4 teams.

    a. How many teams had exactly 8 players?

    b. How many teams had 9 players?

2. **(Justify)** On the package there were two 39¢ stamps, two 20¢
(1, 43)   stamps, and one 15¢ stamp. Altogether, how much did the stamps on the package cost? Explain why your answer is reasonable.

3. Daniella read 20 pages each day. How many pages did she read in
(49, 67)   2 weeks?

4. In the first track meet of the season, Wyatt's best triple jump measured
(Inv. 2)   36 feet. What was the distance of that jump in yards?

*5. What is the perimeter of this isosceles triangle in centimeters?
(Inv. 2, 69)

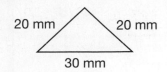

20 mm   20 mm
30 mm

*6. **Multiple Choice** Which of these tallies represents a prime number?
(55, Inv. 7)

A ⅢⅢ ||| B ⅢⅢ ⅢⅢ

C ⅢⅢ ⅢⅢ | D ⅢⅢ ⅢⅢ ||

*7. **Multiple Choice** About how much liquid is in this medicine dropper?
(40)

A 2 milliliters   B 2 liters

C 2 pints   D 2 cups

8. Solve for n: $87 + 0 = 87 \times n$
(61)

*9. **Represent** One third of the 24 students finished early. How many students finished early? Draw a picture to illustrate the problem.
(70)

10. What percent of a dollar is a quarter?
(Inv. 5)

11. $478.63
(43, 51) $+ \$\ 32.47$

12.   137,140
(52) $-\ 129,536$

13. $60.00
(52) $-\ \$24.38$

*14. 70×90
(86)

15.   11
(87) $\times\ 13$

*16.   12
(87) $\times\ 12$

17. $4.76
(58) $\times\ \ \ \ 8$

*18.   21
(87) $\times\ 13$

*19.   21
(87) $\times\ 21$

20. $4\overline{)3000}$
(80)

21. $5n = 635$
(41, 76)

22. $7\overline{)426}$
(71)

23. $8\overline{)3614}$
(76)

24. $\dfrac{2736}{6}$
(76)

25. How much is one fourth of $10.00?
(70)

*26. **Represent** Draw and shade circles to show that $1\frac{1}{2}$ equals $\frac{3}{2}$.
(89)

*27. a. (**Represent**) Draw a rectangle that is 5 cm long and 4 cm wide.
(Inv. 2, Inv. 3)

    b. What is the perimeter and area of the rectangle you drew?

*28. a. (**Conclude**) In this polygon, which side appears to be parallel to side *BC?*
(23, 79)

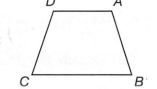

    b. Copy this figure and draw its line of symmetry.

    c. Does this figure have rotational symmetry?

*29. (**Analyze**) Which two-digit number less than 20 is a multiple of both 4 and 6?
(55)

*30. (**Interpret**) This circle graph shows the results of an election for class president. Use the graph to answer the questions that follow.
(Inv. 6)

Class Election Results

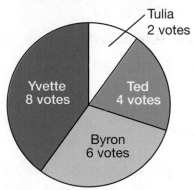

    a. Which candidate won the election? How many votes did that candidate receive?

    b. Altogether, how many votes were cast in the election?

    c. Which number is greater: the number of votes received by the winner, or the sum of the number of votes received by all of the other candidates?

• Multiplying Two Two-Digit Numbers, Part 2

Power Up

facts   Power Up I

mental math   Find half of each number in **a–d.**

  a. Number Sense: 40

  b. Number Sense: 48

  c. Number Sense: 64

  d. Number Sense: 86

  e. Number Sense: 75 + 37

  f. Money: Taylor bought scissors for $3.54 and glue for $2.99. What was the total cost?

  g. Estimation: Choose the more reasonable estimate for the mass of 500 sheets of copy paper: 2 grams or 2 kilograms.

  h. Calculation: $\sqrt{49}$, × 2, + 7, ÷ 3, × 7

problem solving   Choose an appropriate problem-solving strategy to solve this problem. A half-ton pickup truck can carry a load weighing half of a ton. How many 100-pound sacks of cement can a half-ton pickup truck carry?

New Concept

Recall the three steps for multiplying two two-digit numbers:

Step 1: Multiply by the ones digit.

Step 2: Multiply by the tens digit.

Step 3: Add to find the total.

Example 1

A college auditorium has 27 rows of seats and 46 seats in each row. How many people can be seated in the auditorium?

The first step is to multiply 46 by 7. The result is 322. This is not the final product. It is called a *partial product.*

$$
\text{Step 1} \quad
\begin{array}{r}
\overset{4}{4}6 \\
\times\ 27 \\
\hline
322
\end{array}
$$

The second step is to multiply 46 by the 2 of 27. Since we are actually multiplying by 20, we place a zero in the ones place or shift this partial product one place to the left.

$$
\text{Step 2}\quad
\begin{array}{r}
\overset{1}{\overset{4}{4}}6 \\
\times\ 27 \\
\hline
322 \\
92 \\
\end{array}
\quad\text{or}\quad
\begin{array}{r}
\overset{1}{\overset{4}{4}}6 \\
\times\ 27 \\
\hline
322 \\
920 \\
\end{array}
$$

$$
\text{Step 3}\quad
\begin{array}{r}
\hline
1242
\end{array}
\qquad
\begin{array}{r}
\hline
1242
\end{array}
$$

The third step is to add the partial products. The final product is 1242.

We find that **1242 people** can be seated.

Example 2

A golf course has 46 different spectator mounds. Each mound can seat an average of 72 spectators. How many spectators can be seated on the mounds altogether?

First we multiply 46 by 2.

$$
\begin{array}{r}
\overset{1}{4}6 \\
\times\ 72 \\
\hline
92
\end{array}
$$

Next we multiply 46 by 7 and then add the partial products.

$$
\begin{array}{r}
\overset{4}{\overset{1}{4}}6 \\
\times\ 72 \\
\hline
92 \\
322 \\
\hline
3312
\end{array}
\quad\text{or}\quad
\begin{array}{r}
\overset{4}{\overset{1}{4}}6 \\
\times\ 72 \\
\hline
92 \\
3220 \\
\hline
3312
\end{array}
$$

We find that **3312 spectators** can be seated.

Example 3

Adelio estimated the product of 86 × 74 to be 6300. Did Adelio make a reasonable estimate?

Before multiplying, we round 86 to 90 and round 74 to 70. Since 90 × 70 = 6300, Adelio's estimate is reasonable. (The exact product is 6364.)

Lesson Practice   Multiply:

a. 38	**b.** 49	**c.** 84	**d.** 65
× 26	× 82	× 67	× 48

e. Mya is renting 21 tables for a reception. The rental charge is $29 per table. Explain how Mya can make a reasonable estimate of the total cost.

Written Practice   *Distributed and Integrated*

* 1.
(Inv. 6)   **Interpret**   The line graph shows the average monthly temperatures during spring in Jacksonville, Florida. Use the graph to answer the questions that follow.

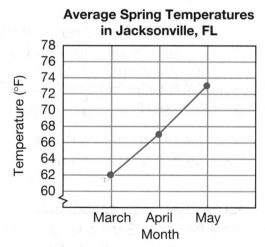

Average Spring Temperatures in Jacksonville, FL

a. What is the average temperature during March in Jacksonville, Florida? During April? During May?

b. Write a sentence that compares the average March temperature to the freezing temperature of water.

c. In Salt Lake City, Utah, the average May temperature is 14 degrees cooler than the average May temperature in Jacksonville, Florida. What is the average May temperature in Salt Lake City?

2. The 3-pound melon cost $1.44. What was the cost per pound?
(52)

3. Jin spun all the way around in the air and dunked the basketball. Jin
(75) turned about how many degrees?

*4. Shunsuke bought a pair of shoes priced at $47.99. The sales tax was
(83) $2.88. Shunsuke gave the clerk $60.00. How much change should he
receive?

5. (**Analyze**) If the perimeter of a square is 1 foot, how many inches long
(Inv. 2) is each side?

*6. a. The mass of a dollar bill is about 1 gram. Use this information to
(77) estimate the number of dollar bills it would take to equal 1 kilogram?

b. Would the mass of a dollar bill still be about 1 gram on the moon?
Why or why not?

7. a. (**Represent**) One fourth of the 64 balloons were red. How many
(Inv. 5, balloons were red? Draw a picture to illustrate the problem.
70)

b. What percent of the balloons was not red?

*8. a. T'Marra knew that her trip would take about 7 hours. If she left
(27) at half past nine in the morning, around what time should she arrive?

b. If T'Marra traveled 350 miles in 7 hours, then she traveled an
average of how many miles each hour?

c. Using your answer to part **b**, make a table to show how far T'Marra
would travel at her average rate in 1, 2, 3, and 4 hours.

*9. (**Explain**) On the last Wednesday in May, school buses
(88) will transport 116 students on a field trip. Each bus can seat
40 passengers. How many buses will be needed to transport the
students, 8 teachers, and 13 adult volunteers? Explain your answer.

10. Compare: 3049 $\bigcirc$ 3049.0
(33)

* 11. **Estimate** Shakura purchased a birthday present for each of
(22)   two friends. Including sales tax, the cost of one present was $16.61
and the cost of the other present was $14.37. What is a reasonable
estimate of the total cost of the presents? Explain your answer.

* 12. **Represent** Manuel is deciding what to wear. He must choose
(83)   between blue pants and black pants, and between a red shirt, a green
shirt, and a yellow shirt. Draw a tree diagram to show all of the different
ways to combine two pairs of pants and three shirts.

* 13. Eighty-eight horseshoes are enough to shoe how many horses?
(52, 64)

* 14. a. **Conclude** Triangles *ABC* and *DEF* are congruent. Which
(73, 78)   transformations would move △*ABC* to the same position as △*DEF*?

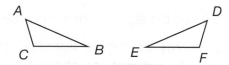

b. Multiple Choice Which of these words does *not* describe
triangles *ABC* and *DEF*?

   A similar   **B** obtuse   **C** scalene   **D** isosceles

15. Find $0.625 - (0.5 + 0.12)$. Describe the steps in order.
(45, 50)

16. Mentally find the product of 47×100.
(85)

17.   328   *** 18.**   43   *** 19.**   25
(58) $\times$ 4   (87) $\times$ 32   (90) $\times$ 35

20. $5\overline{)4317}$ **21.** $8\overline{)\$40.00}$ **22.** $6\overline{)3963}$
(76)   (80)   (80)

23. $3a = 426$ **24.** $2524 \div 4$ *** 25.** 60×700
(76)   (76)   (86)

26. **Represent** Draw and shade circles to show that $2\frac{1}{2}$ equals $\frac{5}{2}$.
(89)

27. $4 + 3 + 27 + 35 + 8 + n = 112$
(2)

* 28. a. Segment *BC* is 1.7 cm long. How many centimeters long is
(69)   segment *AB*?

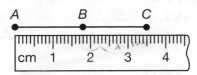

b. Write a decimal addition problem that is illustrated by the lengths of
segments *AB, BC,* and *AC.*

* 29. a. Name a pair of parallel edges in the figure at
(45)   right.

b. Name a pair of perpendicular edges.

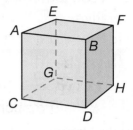

* 30. Before multiplying two numbers, Ashley estimated the product. After
(90)   multiplying the numbers, she used the estimate to check her work. Explain
how Ashley can estimate the product of 32 × 57.

*Real-World
Connection*

a. Describe the error Julio made on his homework.

$$
\begin{array}{r}
67 \\
\times\ 38 \\
\hline
536 \\
201 \\
\hline
737
\end{array}
$$

b. What is the correct answer?

Focus on

• Investigating Fractions with Manipulatives

Fraction manipulatives can help us better understand fractions. In this investigation we will make and use a set of fraction manipulatives.

Activity 1

Using Fraction Manipulatives

Materials needed:

- **Lesson Activities 37, 38,** and **39**
- scissors
- envelopes or locking plastic bags (optional)

Model Use your fraction manipulatives to complete the following exercises:

1. Another name for $\frac{1}{4}$ is a *quarter*. How many quarters of a circle does it take to form a whole circle? Show your work.

2. Fit two quarter circles together to form a half circle; that is, show that $\frac{2}{4}$ equals $\frac{1}{2}$.

3. How many fourths equal $1\frac{1}{4}$?

4. This number sentence shows how to make a whole circle using half circles:

$$\frac{1}{2} + \frac{1}{2} = 1$$

   Write a number sentence that shows how to make a whole circle using only quarter circles.

5. How many half circles equal $1\frac{1}{2}$ circles?

6. Four half circles make how many whole circles?

Model Manipulatives can help us compare and order fractions. Use your fraction manipulatives to illustrate and answer these problems:

7. Arrange $\frac{1}{2}$, $\frac{1}{8}$, and $\frac{1}{4}$ in order from least to greatest.

8. Arrange $\frac{3}{8}$, $\frac{3}{4}$, and $\frac{1}{2}$ in order from greatest to least.

9. $\frac{2}{2} \bigcirc \frac{2}{4}$

10. $\frac{4}{8} \bigcirc \frac{3}{8}$

11. (Generalize) If the denominators of two fractions are the same, how can we determine which fraction is larger and which is smaller?

12. (Generalize) If the numerators of two fractions are the same, how can we determine which fraction is larger and which is smaller?

Manipulatives can also help us **reduce** fractions. When we reduce a fraction, we do not change the size of the fraction. We just use smaller numbers to name the fraction. (With manipulatives, we use fewer pieces to form the fraction.) For example, we may reduce $\frac{2}{4}$ to $\frac{1}{2}$. Both $\frac{2}{4}$ and $\frac{1}{2}$ name the same portion of a whole, but $\frac{1}{2}$ uses smaller numbers (fewer pieces) to name the fraction. If a fraction cannot be reduced, it is in **lowest terms.**

Use your fraction manipulatives to reduce the fractions in problems **13–16.** Show how the two fractions match.

13. $\frac{2}{4}$

14. $\frac{2}{8}$

15. $\frac{4}{8}$

16. $\frac{6}{8}$

Manipulatives can also help us add and subtract fractions. Illustrate each addition below by combining fraction manipulatives. Record each sum.

17. $\frac{1}{4} + \frac{2}{4}$

18. $\frac{2}{8} + \frac{3}{8}$

To illustrate each subtraction in problems **19–21,** form the first fraction using your fraction manipulatives; then separate the second fraction from the first fraction. Record what is left of the first fraction as your answer.

19. $\frac{3}{4} - \frac{2}{4}$

20. $\frac{4}{8} - \frac{1}{8}$

21. $\frac{2}{2} - \frac{1}{2}$

Activity 2

Understanding How Fractions, Decimals, and Percents Are Related

Fraction manipulatives can help us understand how fractions and percents are related. Use the percent labels on your manipulatives to answer these problems:

22. One half of a circle is what percent of a circle?

23. What percent of a circle is $\frac{1}{4}$ of a circle?

24. What percent of a circle is $\frac{3}{4}$ of a circle?

Fraction manipulatives can help us understand how fractions and decimals are related. Use the decimal labels on your manipulatives to answer these problems:

25. What decimal number is equivalent to $\frac{1}{2}$?

26. What decimal number is equivalent to $\frac{1}{4}$?

27. What decimal number is equivalent to $\frac{1}{8}$?

Complete each comparison.

28. 0.5 $\bigcirc$ 0.2

29. 0.2 $\bigcirc$ 0.25

30. Compare: 0.125 $\bigcirc$ 0.25

31. Arrange the decimal numbers 0.5, 0.125, and 0.25 in order from greatest to least.

32. Form a half circle using two $\frac{1}{4}$ pieces. Here is a fraction number sentence for the model:

$$\frac{1}{4} + \frac{1}{4} = \frac{1}{2}$$

Write an equivalent number sentence using the decimal numbers on the pieces.

33. Compare: 0.50 $\bigcirc$ 0.5

34. Form a half circle using four $\frac{1}{8}$ pieces. Here is a fraction number sentence for the model:

$$\frac{1}{8} + \frac{1}{8} + \frac{1}{8} + \frac{1}{8} = \frac{1}{2}$$

Write an equivalent number sentence using the decimal numbers on the pieces.

35. Compare: 0.500 $\bigcirc$ 0.5

36. Form $\frac{3}{4}$ of a circle two ways. First use three $\frac{1}{4}$ pieces. Then use a $\frac{1}{2}$ piece and a $\frac{1}{4}$ piece. Here are the two fraction number sentences for these models:

$$\frac{1}{4} + \frac{1}{4} + \frac{1}{4} = \frac{3}{4} \qquad \frac{1}{2} + \frac{1}{4} = \frac{3}{4}$$

Write equivalent number sentences using the decimal numbers on these pieces.

37. Form a whole circle using four $\frac{1}{4}$ pieces. Then take away one of the $\frac{1}{4}$ pieces. A fraction number sentence for this subtraction is shown below. Write an equivalent number sentence using the decimal numbers on the pieces.

$$1 - \frac{1}{4} = \frac{3}{4}$$

38. Form a half circle using four $\frac{1}{8}$ pieces. Then take away one of the pieces. A fraction number sentence for this subtraction is shown below. Write an equivalent number sentence using the decimal numbers on the pieces.

$$\frac{1}{2} - \frac{1}{8} = \frac{3}{8}$$

39. Here we show $\frac{3}{4}$ of a circle and $\frac{1}{2}$ of a circle:

We see that $\frac{3}{4}$ is greater than $\frac{1}{2}$. In fact, we see that $\frac{3}{4}$ is greater than $\frac{1}{2}$ by a $\frac{1}{4}$ piece. Here we show a larger-smaller-difference number sentence for this comparison:

$$\frac{3}{4} - \frac{1}{2} = \frac{1}{4}$$

Write an equivalent number sentence using the decimal numbers on the pieces.

Investigate Further

Instead of using fraction circles, we can use squares divided into 10 or 100 parts to represent decimal numbers. Each large square represents the whole number 1. Each row or column represents the fraction $\frac{1}{10}$ and the decimal 0.1. Each small square represents the fraction $\frac{1}{100}$ and the decimal 0.01. Use **Lesson Activity 40** to complete the following activities:

a. In the first row of squares, shade all of the first square, one column of the second square, and one small square of the third square. Name the shaded part of each square as a fraction and as a decimal. Look at the three numbers in the decimals row and arrange the decimal numbers in order from least to greatest.

b. In the second row of squares, shade three rows of the first square and 27 small squares of the second square. Name the shaded part of each square as a fraction and as a decimal. Write a comparison statement that compares the two decimal numbers.

c. In the third row, shade the first five columns in the first square and the first fifty small squares in the second square. Name the shaded part of each square as a fraction and as a decimal. Write a comparison statement that compares the two decimal numbers.

• Decimal Place Value

facts   Power Up I

mental math   Find half of each number in **a–d**.

   a. Number Sense: 24

   b. Number Sense: 50

   c. Number Sense: 46

   d. Number Sense: 120

   e. Money: The apples cost $3.67. Lindsay paid for them with a $5 bill. How much change should she receive?

   f. Estimation: About how many feet is 298 yards? (*Hint:* Round the number of yards to the nearest hundred yards before mentally calculating.)

   g. Calculation: $6 \times 7, - 2, + 30, + 5, \div 3$

   h. Roman Numerals[1]: Write 12 in Roman numerals.

problem solving   Choose an appropriate problem-solving strategy to solve this problem. There were two gallons of punch for the class party. The punch was served in 8-ounce cups. Two gallons of punch was enough to fill how many cups? (Remember that 16 ounces is a pint, two pints is a quart, two quarts is a half gallon, and two half gallons is a gallon.)

---

[1] In Lessons 91–105, the Mental Math section "Roman Numerals" reviews concepts from Appendix Topic A. You may skip these Mental Math problems if you have not covered Appendix Topic A.

New Concept

Visit www. SaxonMath.com/ Int4Activities for a calculator activity.

Math Language

The **mill** was first introduced in 1786 by the Continental Congress as a money amount worth 1/1000 of the federal dollar. Some states issued a token in this amount as a way to pay sales tax, but by 1960 the mill was no longer made. Today, the cost of gasoline is still represented in tenths of a cent. For example, $3.019 per gallon is three dollars, one penny, and nine mills.

Thinking about money can help us understand decimal place value.

| hundreds | tens | ones | . decimal point | tenths | hundredths | thousandths |

We have used $100, $10, and $1 bills to represent place values to the left of the decimal point. To the right of the decimal point, we see the tenths, hundredths, and thousandths places. Since a dime is $\frac{1}{10}$ of a dollar, the tenths place is for dimes. The number of pennies goes in the hundredths place because a penny is $\frac{1}{100}$ of a dollar. The third place to the right of the decimal point is the thousandths place. We do not have a coin for a thousandth of a dollar, but we do have a name for it. A thousandth of a dollar is a *mill,* so one mill is $\frac{1}{1000}$ of a dollar. Ten mills equals one cent.

Example 1

Which digit in 12.875 is in the tenths place?

To identify decimal place value, we use the decimal point as our reference point instead of the last number to the right. The tenths place is the first place to the right of the decimal point. The digit in the tenths place is **8.**

Example 2

Which digit is in the hundredths place in each of these two decimal numbers?

  a. 4.37   b. 4.370

We focus on the decimal point. The hundredths place is the second place to the right of the decimal point.

  a. The second place to the right of the decimal point in 4.37 is **7.**

  b. The second place to the right of the decimal point in 4.370 is also **7.**

Notice in Example 2 that each digit in 4.37 holds the same place in 4.370.

```
      ones tenths hundredths thousandths
      4  .  3    7
      4  .  3    7        0
```

Because the zero in the thousandths place of 4.370 does not add value, 4.37 and 4.370 are equal.

$$4.37 = 4.370$$

Example 3

Compare: 23.25 ◯ 23.250

We will write the numbers with the decimal points lined up and will compare the numbers place by place.

23.25

23.250

Both numbers have the same digits in the same places. The zero in the thousandths place of 23.250 adds no value, so the numbers are equal.

23.25 = 23.250

When performing decimal arithmetic, it is often helpful to attach one or more zeros to the end of a decimal number, as we see below. The attached zeros do not add value, so the original problem remains the same.

Example 4

Subtract: 4.37 − 1.146

We line up the decimal points whenever we add or subtract decimal numbers. This ensures that we add or subtract digits with the same place values. In this example, notice that there is no digit to subtract the 6 from. We may fill the empty place with a zero because 4.370 equals 4.37. Then we can subtract. The answer is **3.224.**

```
    4.37
  − 1.146
```

```
       6 1
    4.3 7̶ 0
  − 1.1 4 6
    3.2 2 4
```

Lesson Practice

a. Which digit in 4.370 is in the hundredths place?

b. Which digit in 4.370 is in the same place as the 2 in 15.24?

c. Name the place value of the 4 in the number 1.234.

d. Multiple Choice Which two numbers below are equal?

   A 12.34   **B** 12.340   **C** 1.234   **D** 123.4

   e. Compare: 3.25 ◯ 32.50

   f. Compare: 3.250 ◯ 3.25

   Subtract. Show your work for each problem.

   g. 12.34 − 1.234   **h.** 1.2 − 0.12

Written Practice

Distributed and Integrated

*1. **(Analyze)** Three quarters, four dimes, two nickels, and seven pennies
(35)   is how much money?

*2. **(Analyze)** Colvin separated the 37 math books as equally as possible
(88)   into 4 stacks.

   a. How many stacks had exactly 9 books?

   b. How many stacks had 10 books?

*3. **(Explain)** Gregory paid $1 for a folder and received 52¢ in change. If
(83)   the tax was 3¢, how much did the folder cost without tax? Explain your
   thinking.

4. Ryan wrote each of his 12 spelling words five times. In all, how many
(49)   words did he write?

5. **(Estimate)** In the 2004 presidential election, 5992 voters in Blaine
(59)   County, Idaho, voted for candidate John Kerry, and 4034 voters voted
   for candidate George Bush. Estimate the total number of votes those
   two candidates received and explain your estimate.

6. What is the tally for 10?
(Inv. 7)

7. Name the shaded part of this square
(Inv. 4)
   a. as a fraction.

   b. as a decimal number.

8. **Represent** One sixth of the 48 crayons is in the box. How many
(70) crayons are in the box? Draw a picture to illustrate the problem.

*9. Segment *AB* is 32 mm long. Segment *BC* is 26 mm long. Segment
(45, 69) *AD* is 91 mm long. How many millimeters long is segment *CD*?

$$\overset{A}{\bullet}\rule{2cm}{0.4pt}\overset{B}{\bullet}\rule{2cm}{0.4pt}\overset{C}{\bullet}\rule{2cm}{0.4pt}\overset{D}{\bullet}$$

*10. Which digit in 6.125 is in the hundredths place?
(91)

11. **Estimate** If a pint of water weighs about one pound, then about how
(40, 77) many pounds does a quart of water weigh?

*12. $4.32 - 0.432$ **13.** $5^2 + \sqrt{25} + n = 30$
(91)   (Inv. 3, 62)

14. $\$6.08$ ***15.** 47 ***16.** 36
(58) $\underline{\times\quad 8}$ (90) $\underline{\times\ 24}$ (90) $\underline{\times\ 62}$

17. 53×30 ***18.** 63×37
(67)   (90)

19. 100×32 **20.** $4\overline{)3456}$
(85)   (76)

21. $8n = 6912$ **22.** $7\overline{)\$50.40}$
(76)   (76, 80)

*23. **Represent** Draw and shade circles to show that $1\frac{1}{4}$ equals $\frac{5}{4}$.
(89)

*24. **a.** **Represent** Draw a square with sides 4 cm long.
(21, Inv. 5)

   b. Shade 50% of the square you drew. How many square centimeters
   did you shade?

*25. **Represent** Write twenty-one thousandths as a fraction and as a
(84) decimal number.

*26. **Explain** Emma mixed two quarts of orange juice from frozen
(40, 88) concentrate. She knows 1 quart is equal to 32 fluid ounces. The small
juice glasses Emma is filling each have a capacity of 6 fluid ounces.
How many juice glasses can Emma fill? Explain your answer.

*27. Multiple Choice Use the polygons below to answer parts **a–c.**
(63, 79)

A △   B ⏢   C ▢   D ⏢

    a. Which of these polygons has no lines of symmetry?

    b. Which two of these polygons have rotational symmetry?

    c. Which polygon is *not* a quadrilateral?

*28. How many degrees does the minute hand of a clock turn in half
(75) an hour?

*29. Compare: 4.2 ◯ 4.200
(91)

*30. Use the pictograph below to answer parts **a–c.**
(Inv. 6)

Animal	Typical Weight (in pounds)
Alligator	⊝—⊝ ⊝—
Porpoise	⊝—⊝
Wild Boar	⊝—⊝ ⊝—⊝ ⊝—⊝
Seal	⊝—⊝ ⊝—⊝

Key: ⊝—⊝ = 100 pounds

    a. What amount of weight does each symbol represent?

    b. Write the typical weights of the animals in order from least to
       greatest.

    c. **Connect** Write a sentence that compares the weights of
       two animals.

Early Finishers
Real-World Connection

Gas is sold in amounts to the tenth of a penny, which is the same as
the thousandth of a dollar. Gus's Grand Gas Station is selling gas for
$2.679 per gallon.

    a. Which digit is in the thousandths place? Which digit is in the tenths
       place?

    b. Which is more: 2.679 or 2.67?

    c. If you were to buy ten gallons of gas, how much would you spend?
       If you were to pay $30 for the gas, what would your change be?

• Classifying Quadrilaterals

facts   Power Up I

mental math   Find half of a product in **a–c**.

    a. Number Sense: half of 10 × 12

    b. Number Sense: half of 10 × 24

    c. Number Sense: half of 10 × 480

    d. Money: The art supplies cost $17.50. Adam paid with a $20 bill. How much change should he receive?

    e. Estimation: About what percent of the circle is shaded? About what percent of the circle is not shaded?

    f. Calculation: 25% of 40, × 2, + 4, ÷ 3

    g. Roman Numerals: Write XI in our number system.

problem solving

Choose an appropriate problem-solving strategy to solve this problem. Below we show the first five terms of a sequence. The terms of the sequence increase from left to right. Estimate how many terms will be in the sequence when it reaches a number that is 500 or greater. Then check your estimate by continuing the sequence until you reach a number that is 500 or greater.

1, 2, 4, 8, 16, …

Recall from Lesson 63 that a quadrilateral is a polygon with four sides. In this lesson we will practice recognizing and naming different types of quadrilaterals. On the following page, we show four different types.

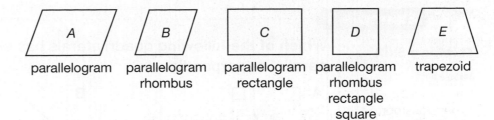

A   B   C   D   E

parallelogram   parallelogram rhombus   parallelogram rectangle   parallelogram rhombus rectangle square   trapezoid

A **parallelogram** is a quadrilateral with **two** pairs of parallel sides. Figures *A, B, C,* and *D* each have two pairs of parallel sides, so all four figures are parallelograms. A **trapezoid** is a quadrilateral with exactly **one** pair of parallel sides. Figure *E* is not a parallelogram; it is a trapezoid.

A **rectangle** is a special type of parallelogram that has four right angles. Figures *C* and *D* are rectangles. A **rhombus** is a special type of parallelogram whose sides are equal in length. Figure *B* is a rhombus, as is figure *D*. A **square** is a regular quadrilateral. Its sides are equal in length, and its angles are all right angles. Figure *D* is a square. It is also a parallelogram, a rhombus, and a rectangle.

Example 1

Which of these quadrilaterals is *not* a parallelogram?

We look for pairs of parallel sides. A parallelogram has two pairs of parallel sides. Figures *F, G,* and *I* each have two pairs of parallel sides. **Figure H** has only one pair of parallel sides, so it is a trapezoid, not a parallelogram.

Example 2

Draw two parallel line segments of different lengths. Then form a quadrilateral by drawing two line segments that connect the endpoints. What type of quadrilateral did you make?

First we draw two parallel line segments of different lengths.

Then we connect the endpoints with line segments to form a quadrilateral.

We see that this quadrilateral is a **trapezoid.**

Example 3

Thinking Skill

Model

Find a quadrilateral in your classroom. Identify and describe the parallel, perpendicular, and intersecting segments in the quadrilateral.

Which of the following quadrilaterals has sides that are *not* parallel or perpendicular?

A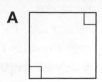

B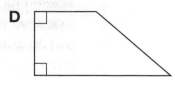

C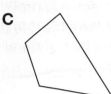

D

We will consider the relationships between the sides of each quadrilateral.

A The opposite sides are parallel, and the adjacent sides are perpendicular.

B The opposite sides are parallel, and the adjacent sides intersect but are not perpendicular.

C There are no parallel or perpendicular sides.

D One pair of opposite sides is parallel, and another side is perpendicular to the parallel sides.

Only **figure C** has sides that are not parallel or perpendicular.

Example 4

Describe the angles in each of the quadrilaterals in Example 3.

Figure **A** is a square; it has **four right angles.**

Figure **B** is a parallelogram; it has **two acute angles and two obtuse angles.**

Figure **C** is a quadrilateral; it has **two obtuse angles and two acute angles.**

Figure **D** is a trapezoid; it has **two right angles, one acute angle, and one obtuse angle.**

Activity 1

Quadrilaterals in the Classroom

Look around the room for quadrilaterals. Find examples of at least three different types of quadrilaterals illustrated in the beginning of this lesson. Draw each example you find, and next to each picture, name the object you drew and its shape. Then describe how you know that the object is the shape you named and describe the relationships of the sides of each quadrilateral.

Activity 2

Symmetry and Quadrilaterals

Materials needed:
- **Lesson Activity 41**
- mirror or reflective surface

If a figure can be divided into mirror images by a line of symmetry, then the figure has reflective symmetry. A mirror can help us decide if a figure has reflective symmetry. If we place a mirror upright along a line of symmetry, the half of the figure behind the mirror appears in the reflection of the other half. Use a mirror to discover which figures in **Lesson Activity 41** have reflective symmetry. If you find a figure with reflective symmetry, draw its line (or lines) of symmetry.

Lesson Practice

Classify Describe each quadrilateral as a trapezoid, parallelogram, rhombus, rectangle, or square. (More than one description may apply to each figure.)

a. 　　b. 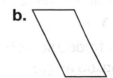　　c. 　　d.

e. Describe the angles in figures **a–d** and the relationships between the sides.

f. Draw two parallel line segments that are the same length. Then make a quadrilateral by drawing two more parallel line segments that connect the endpoints. Is your quadrilateral a parallelogram? Why or why not?

Written Practice   *Distributed and Integrated*

* 1. **(Analyze)** Use this information to answer parts **a–c.**
(72, 88)

Lanisha invited 14 friends over for lunch. She plans to make 12 tuna sandwiches, 10 bologna sandwiches, and 8 chicken sandwiches.

   a. How many sandwiches will Lanisha make in all?

   b. Including Lanisha, each person can have how many sandwiches?

   c. If Lanisha cuts each tuna sandwich in half, how many halves will there be?

2. Five pounds of grapes cost $2.95. What is the cost per pound?
(53)

* 3. If each side of a hexagon is 4 inches long, what is the perimeter of the
(Inv. 2, 63) hexagon in feet?

4. **(Represent)** Nine million, four hundred thousand is how much greater
(31, 52) than two million, seven hundred thousand?

* 5. Three brands of whole grain cereal cost $4.68, $4.49, and $4.71.
(30) Arrange these prices in order from least to greatest.

* 6. **(Estimate)** Lauren saw that a package of 50 blank CDs costs $9.79.
(58) Estimate the cost for Lauren to buy 100 blank CDs. Explain your answer.

7. Name the shaded part of the large square
(Inv. 4)
   a. as a fraction.

   b. as a decimal number.

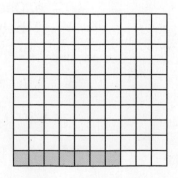

8. (Represent) Use words to write $7572\frac{1}{8}$.
(35)

*9. (Represent) At Kelvin's school, one fifth of the 80 fourth grade
(70) students ride the bus to and from school each day. How many
fourth grade students ride the bus? Draw a picture to illustrate
the problem.

10. How many different three-digit numbers can you write using the digits
(3) 9, 1, and 5? Each digit may be used only once in every number you
write.

11. Franca's trip only lasted for a couple of hours. According to the clocks
(27) shown below, exactly how long did the trip take?

Began   Finished

*12. (Justify) James traveled 301 miles in 7 hours. He traveled an
(60) average of how many miles per hour? Explain why your answer is
reasonable.

*13. Martino bought 3 folders priced at $1.99 each. Sales tax was 33¢. He
(83) paid with a $20 bill. How much money should he get back?

14. $25 + $2.75 + $15.44 + 27¢
(43, 51)

*15. $m + 0.26 = 6.2$ **16.** $100 − $89.85
(91)   (43, 52)

17. 60 × 900   **18.** 42 × 30   **19.** 21 × 17
(86)   (67)   (87)

*20.   36   ***21.**   48   **22.** $4.79
(90)   × 74   (90) × 25   (58) ×   6

23. 9)918   **24.** 5r = 485
(80)   (41)

25. 6)482   **26.** $50.00 ÷ 8
(53)   (76)

27. 2100 ÷ 7
(80)

28. 0.875 − (0.5 + 0.375)
(45, 50)

* **29.** 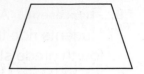 **Classify** This polygon is what type of quadrilateral?
(92)   How do you know?

* **30.** **Represent** Draw and shade rectangles to show that $1\frac{2}{3}$ equals $\frac{5}{3}$.
(89)

Real-World Connection

Stephanie's class has to identify polygons for math class.

a. Draw and label a picture for each of the following shapes that her class could use as examples: square, rectangle, rhombus, trapezoid, and parallelogram.

b. Explain why each drawing fits its name.

LESSON
93

- ## Estimating Multiplication and Division Answers

Power Up

facts   Power Up I

mental math   Find half of a product in **a–c.**

  a. Number Sense: half of 10 × 18

  b. Number Sense: half of 10 × 44

  c. Number Sense: half of 10 × 260

  d. Time: How many minutes are in $1\frac{1}{2}$ hours?

  e. Measurement: How many quarts is 3 gallons?

  f. Estimation: About how many feet is 1989 yards?

  g. Calculation: 3^2, + 1, × 5, − 1, $\sqrt{}$

  h. Roman Numerals: Write 9 in Roman numerals.

problem solving

Choose an appropriate problem-solving strategy to solve this problem. In this Venn diagram, the circle on the left stands for animals with the ability to fly, and the circle on the right stands for birds. The *R* in the overlapping portion of the circles stands for robins, which are birds that can fly. The *O* stands for ostriches, which are birds that cannot fly. The *B* stands for bats, which can fly but are not birds. The *W* stands for whales, which are not birds and cannot fly. Copy the Venn diagram on your paper, and place an abbreviation for a penguin, eagle, goldfish, and cat.

Animals with Ability to Fly   Birds

B R O W

Estimation can help prevent mistakes. If we estimate the answer before we multiply, we can tell whether our answer is reasonable.

Example 1

Luke multiplied 43 by 29 and got 203. Is Luke's answer reasonable?

We estimate the product of 43 and 29 by multiplying the rounded numbers 40 and 30.

$$40 \times 30 = 1200$$

Luke's answer of 203 and our estimate of 1200 are very different, so Luke's answer is **not reasonable.** He should check his work.

(Discuss) What is the exact product? Is the exact product close to 1200?

Example 2

Estimate the product of 38 and 53. Then find the exact answer.

We estimate the product by multiplying the rounded numbers 40 and 50.

$$40 \times 50 = 2000$$

Then we find the exact answer.

$$
\begin{array}{r}
38 \\
\times\ 53 \\
\hline
114 \\
+\ 190 \\
\hline
2014 \\
\end{array}
$$

Our estimate of the product was **2000,** so our answer of **2014** is reasonable.

Example 3

Thinking Skill

Estimate

How would you estimate the quotient of 184 ÷ 6?

Estimate the quotient of 1845 divided by 6.

We choose a number close to 1845 that can easily be divided by 6. We know that 18 is a multiple of 6, so 1800 is a compatible dividend. We can calculate mentally: "18 hundred divided by 6 is 3 hundred."

$$1800 \div 6 = \mathbf{300}$$

Estimate First estimate each product or quotient. Then find the exact answer.

    a. 58 × 23   **b.** 49 × 51   **c.** 61 × 38   **d.** 1845 ÷ 9

Written Practice   *Distributed and Integrated*

* 1. Ninety-one students are divided as equally as possible among
(88) 3 classrooms.

    a. How many classrooms have exactly 30 students?

    b. How many classrooms have 31 students?

* 2. a. **Analyze** In 1970 it cost 6¢ to mail a letter. How much did it cost to
(49) mail twenty letters in 1970?

    b. How much does it cost to mail twenty letters today?

3. **Represent** Point *A* represents what number on this number
(Inv. 1) line?

```
        A
+--+--+--+--+--+--+--+--+
0      100     200
```

4. George Washington was born in 1732. How old was he when he
(54) became the first president of the United States in 1789?

5. A $1 bill weighs about 1 gram. How much would a $5 bill weigh?
(77)

* 6. Draw a quadrilateral that has two pairs of parallel sides.
(92)

7. Name the shaded part of the large square
(Inv. 4)
    a. as a fraction.

    b. as a decimal number.

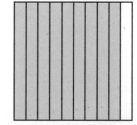

8. **Estimate** Jon used rounding and decided that 54,000 was a good
(93) estimate of the product 58 × 87. Was Jon's estimate reasonable?
Explain why or why not.

*9. (Represent) One half of the 32 chess pieces were still on the board.
(70) How many chess pieces were still on the board? Draw a picture to
illustrate the problem.

10. Miriam left home at 10:30 a.m. She traveled for 7 hours. What time was
(27) it when she arrived?

11. Maureo traveled 42 miles in 1 hour. If he kept going at the same speed,
(57, 67) how far would he travel in 20 hours?

*12. Violet gave the cashier $40 for a toaster that cost $29.99 plus $1.80 in
(83) tax. What was her change? Write one equation to solve the problem.

*13. Alvin faced the sun as it set in the west, then turned 90°
(75) counterclockwise and headed home. In what direction was
Alvin heading after the turn?

14. $n + 8 + 2 + 3 + 5 + 2 = 24$
(2)

15. $4.12 - (3.6 + 0.2 + 0.125)$
(45, 91)

16. $18 - 15.63
(43, 52)

17. $15.27 + 85.75
(43, 51)

18. $2^3 \times \sqrt{25}$
(Inv. 3, 62)

19. 30×90
(86)

20. 7.50×8
(58)

*21. $\quad 49$
(90) $\quad \times\ 62$

*22. $\quad 54$
(90) $\quad \times\ 23$

23. $\quad 74$
(67) $\quad \times\ 40$

24. $4\overline{)\$6.36}$
(76)

25. $5\overline{)800}$
(80)

26. $473 \div 8$
(53)

27. $3m = 1800$
(41, 80)

*28. Estimate the quotient when 1520 is divided by 5. Then find the exact quotient.
(53, 93)

*29. (Represent) Draw and shade circles to show that $2\frac{1}{4}$ equals $\frac{9}{4}$.
(89)

30. Find the perimeter and area of this rectangle.
(Inv. 2, Inv. 3)

50 ft

20 ft

• Two-Step Word Problems

facts	Power Up H
mental math	Five is half of 10. To multiply by 5, we can multiply by half of 10. For example, 5 × 12 equals half of 10 × 12. Find each product by multiplying by "half of 10" in **a–d**.

  a. **Number Sense:** 5 × 16

  b. **Number Sense:** 5 × 24

  c. **Number Sense:** 5 × 28

  d. **Number Sense:** 5 × 64

  e. **Measurement:** A *stone* is a British unit of weight equal to 14 pounds. Two stone is 28 pounds, 3 stone is 42 pounds, and so on. How many pounds is 10 stone?

  f. **Estimation:** Lydia walked 1 km in 608 seconds. About how many minutes did it take her to walk 1 km?

  g. **Calculation:** 10% of 40, × 10, + 5, ÷ 5

  h. **Roman Numerals:** Write XIV in our number system.

problem solving

Choose an appropriate problem-solving strategy to solve this problem. Find the next five numbers in this sequence. Then describe the sequence in words.

..., 64, 32, 16, 8, ____, ____, ____, ____, ____, ...

New Concept

We have practiced two-step word problems that involve finding total costs (including tax) and change back. Starting with this lesson, we will practice other kinds of two-step problems. Writing down the given information and using problem-solving strategies is often helpful in solving these problems.

Example 1

Reading Math

When we translate a problem, we identify the goal and list the steps.

Goal: Find Jim's age.

Step 1: Find Ali's age.

Step 2: Find Jim's age.

Then we use the steps to make a plan.

Jim is 5 years older than Ali. Ali is 2 years younger than Blanca. Blanca is 9 years old. How old is Jim?

We will use two steps to solve the problem. First we will use Blanca's age to find Ali's age. Then we will use Ali's age to calculate Jim's age. We write down the given information.

> Blanca is 9 years old.
>
> Ali is 2 years younger than Blanca.
>
> Jim is 5 years older than Ali.

We know that Blanca is 9 years old. Ali is 2 years younger than Blanca, so Ali is 9 − 2, or 7 years old. Jim is 5 years older than Ali, so Jim is 7 + 5, or **12 years old.**

Example 2

Thinking Skill

Verify

What are the two steps needed to find the cost of each pound?

Ja'Von paid for 5 pounds of apples with a $10 bill. His change was $6. What was the cost of each pound of apples?

We begin by finding how much all 5 pounds of apples cost. If Ja'Von paid for the apples with a $10 bill and received $6 in change, then all 5 pounds must have cost $4.

$$
\begin{array}{rl}
\$10 & \text{amount paid} \\
-\ \$\ 6 & \text{change} \\
\hline
\$\ 4 & \text{cost of 5 pounds of apples}
\end{array}
$$

To find the cost of each pound of apples, we divide $4 by 5.

$$
\begin{array}{r}
\$0.80 \\
5\overline{)\$4.00} \\
\underline{4\ 0} \\
00 \\
\underline{0} \\
0
\end{array}
$$

Each pound of apples cost **$0.80.**

Example 3

One of the foods that Maribella feeds her pet rabbit is 2 ounces of lettuce each day. In how many days does her rabbit eat a pound of lettuce? How many pounds of lettuce does the rabbit eat in 4 months?

A pound is 16 ounces. At 2 ounces per day, the rabbit eats a pound of food every **8 days.**

$$16 \div 2 = 8$$

A month is about 30 days, so 4 months is 4 × 30 days, which is 120 days. We divide 120 days into groups of 8 days to find the number of pounds of lettuce the rabbit eats.

$$120 \div 8 = 15$$

In 4 months, the rabbit eats about **15 pounds** of lettuce.

Example 4

Point *B* represents which number on this number line?

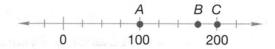

Sometimes two-step problems are not word problems. We can solve problems like this with two or three steps of arithmetic.

We see that the distance from point *A* to point *C* is 100.

Step 1: $200 - 100 = 100$

The distance is divided into 4 segments. By dividing 100 by 4, we find that each segment is 25.

Step 2: $100 \div 4 = 25$

Step 3: If we count by 25s from 100, point *A* to point *B,* we find that point *B* represents **175.** Since point *B* is one segment from point *C,* we can check the answer by counting back 25 from 200. The result is 175, which is our original answer.

(**Discuss**) How could we use the *guess and check* strategy to solve this problem?

Example 5

If *y* = 2*x* + 1, then what is *y* when *x* = 3?

The equation $y = 2x + 1$ shows us how to find the number that *y* equals when we know what the number *x* equals.

The equation means, "To find *y,* multiply *x* by 2 and then add 1."

In this equation *x* is 3, so we multiply 2 times 3 and then add 1.

$$y = (2 \times 3) + 1$$
$$y = \quad 6 \quad + 1$$
$$y = 7$$

When *x* is 3, *y* is **7.**

(**Represent**) What is *y* when *x* is 5?

We can write these values in a table to find the answer.

$2x + 1 = y$	
x	y
3	7
4	9
5	11

When x is 5, y is **11**.

Predict What is y when $x = 10$? Explain how you know.

Lesson Practice

a. Kim paid for 4 pounds of peaches with a $5 bill. She got $3 back. What was the cost of each pound of peaches? (*Hint:* First find the cost of 4 pounds of peaches.)

b. The perimeter of this square is 12 inches. What is the area of the square? (*Hint:* First find the length of each side.)

c. Orlando is 10 years younger than Gihan, and Gihan is 2 years older than Shaniqua. If Orlando is 13 years old, how old is Shaniqua? (*Hint:* First find how old Gihan is.)

d. Point N represents what number on this number line?

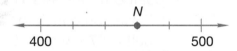

e. If $y = 3x + 2$, what is y when x is 4?

f. Mr. Simmons is 5 ft 10 in. tall. How many inches is 5 ft 10 in.?

Written Practice   *Distributed and Integrated*

1. Joel gave the clerk a $5 bill to pay for a half gallon of milk that cost
(83) $1.06 and a box of cereal that cost $2.39. How much change should he receive?

*2. Eighty-one animals live at the zoo. One third of them are not mammals.
(70, 94) The rest are mammals. How many mammals live at the zoo? (*Hint:* First find the number of animals that are not mammals.)

3. Ciante planted 8 rows of apple trees. There were 15 trees in each row.
(49) How many trees did she plant?

4. A ruble is a Russian coin. If four pounds of bananas costs one hundred
(52, 65) and fifty-six rubles, what is the cost in rubles of each pound of bananas?

*5. a. This scale shows a mass of how many grams?
(77)

    b. **Explain** Would this fruit have the same mass on
    another planet? Explain why.

*6. Felix is ten years younger than Zatravian. Zatravian wrote this formula
(94) for finding Felix's age: $F = Z - 10$. Find F when Z is 27.

7. Name the shaded part of the large square
(Inv. 4)
    a. as a fraction.

    b. as a decimal number.

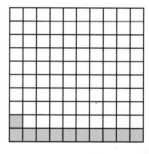

*8. Estimate the product of 32 and 48. Then find the exact product.
(93)

9. **Represent** Bactrian camels have 2 humps. One third of the
(70) 24 camels were Bactrian. How many camels were Bactrian? Draw
a picture to illustrate the problem.

10. A quart is a quarter of a gallon. A quart is what percent of a gallon?
(40,
Inv. 5)

*11. **Classify** For each statement, write either "true" or "false."
(92)
    a. Every square is also a rectangle.

    b. Every rectangle is also a square.

* 12. a. (Represent) Four hundred seventy-one of the one thousand
(Inv. 4, 84) students in the school were girls. Girls made up what fraction of the
students in the school?

b. (Represent) Write your answer for part **a** as a decimal number.
Then use words to name the number.

* 13. Which digit in 1.875 is in the tenths place?
(91)

* 14. If $y = 2x - 3$, what is y when x is 5?
(94)

15. Tyler traveled 496 miles in 8 hours. He traveled an average of how
(60) many miles per hour?

* 16. Find $8.3 - (1.74 + 0.9)$. Describe the steps in order.
(45, 91)

17. 63×1000 **18.** $80 \times 50¢$ **19.**   37
(85)   (86)   (17)   81
                                                                            45
* 20.   52   *** 21.**   36   139
(90) $\times 15$ (90) $\times 27$ 7
                                                                            15
                                                                          $+ 60$

22. $2\overline{)714}$ **23.** $6\overline{)789}$
(76)   (53, 76)

24. $3n = 624$ **25.** $5 + w = 5^2$
(41, 80)   (61, 62)

* 26. (Represent) Draw and shade rectangles to show that $1\frac{2}{5}$ equals $\frac{7}{5}$.
(89)

27. A room is 5 yards long and 4 yards wide. How many square yards of
(Inv. 3) carpeting are needed to cover the floor?

28. The radius of this circle is 15 millimeters. The diameter of
(21, 69) the circle is how many centimeters?

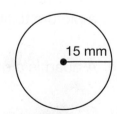
15 mm

*29. a. (Verify) Which of these letters has two lines of symmetry?
(79, 81)

V W X Y Z

b. (Verify) Which two letters have rotational symmetry?

c. Multiple Choice The angle formed by the letter V measures about how many degrees?

   A 45°   **B** 90°   **C** 135°   **D** 180°

*30. Rihanne and Kendra sat across the table from each other in the café.
(73) When Rihanne was finished looking at the one-page menu, she moved it over to Kendra's side of the table so Kendra could read it. Which two transformations did Rihanne use to move the menu?

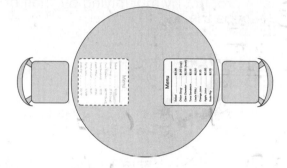

Real-World Connection

A long mountain trail has an upward elevation of 4780 feet.

a. If you were to hike the trail five hours each day for four days, how many feet would be the average elevation gain each day?

b. What would be the average elevation gain for each hour of hiking?

• Two-Step Problems About a Fraction of a Group

Power Up

facts   Power Up H

mental math

Find each product by multiplying by "half of 10" in **a–c.**

a. Number Sense: 5×46

b. Number Sense: 5×62

c. Number Sense: 5×240

d. Money: The price of the blouse is $24.87. Sales tax is $1.95. What is the total cost?

e. Measurement: The large glass of water weighed half a kilogram. How many grams is half a kilogram?

f. Estimation: The package of 10 pencils costs $1.98. Round that price to the nearest dollar and then divide by 10 to estimate the cost per pencil.

g. Calculation: $\sqrt{4}$, $\times 7$, $+ 1$, $+ 10$, $\sqrt{}$, $- 4$

h. Roman Numerals: Write 15 in Roman numerals.

problem solving

Choose an appropriate problem-solving strategy to solve this problem. On February 4, Edgar remembered that his two library books were due on January 28. The fine for late books is 15¢ per book per day. If he returns the books on February 4, what will be the total fine?

New Concept

The word problems in this lesson are two-step problems involving fractions of a group. First we divide to find the number in one part. Then we multiply to find the number in more than one part.

Example 1

Thinking Skill

Verify

What are the two steps needed to find the number of campers who wore green jackets?

There were 30 campers in the state park. Two thirds of them wore green jackets. How many campers wore green jackets?

The word *thirds* tells us there were 3 equal groups. First we find the number of campers in each group. Since there were 30 campers altogether, we divide 30 by 3.

$$\begin{array}{r} 10 \\ 3\overline{)30} \end{array}$$

There were 10 campers in each group. We draw this diagram:

30 campers

$\frac{2}{3}$ wore green jackets.
| 10 campers |
| 10 campers |

$\frac{1}{3}$ did not wear green jackets.
| 10 campers |

Two thirds wore green jackets. In two groups there were 2×10 campers, or **20 campers** who wore green jackets. We also see that one group did not wear green jackets, so 10 campers did not wear green jackets.

Example 2

The force of gravity on Mars is about $\frac{2}{5}$ the force of gravity on Earth. A rock brought back to Earth from Mars weighs 50 pounds. How much did the rock weigh on Mars?

The mass of the rock is the same on Earth as it was on Mars because it is the same amount of rock. However, Earth is more massive than Mars, so the force of gravity is greater on Earth. The rock on Mars weighed only $\frac{2}{5}$ of its weight on Earth. To find $\frac{2}{5}$ of 50 pounds, we first find $\frac{1}{5}$ of 50 pounds by dividing 50 pounds by 5.

$$50 \text{ pounds} \div 5 = 10 \text{ pounds}$$

weight of the rock on Mars
| 10 pounds |
| 10 pounds |
| 10 pounds |
| 10 pounds |
| 10 pounds |

Each fifth is 10 pounds, so $\frac{2}{5}$ is 20 pounds. We find that the rock that weighs 50 pounds on Earth weighed only **20 pounds** on Mars.

Discuss Why did the weight of the rock change when it was brought to Earth? How does the mass of the rock on Mars compare to the mass of the rock on Earth?

Represent Diagram each problem. Then answer the question.

a. Three fourths of the 24 checkers were still on the board. How many checkers were still on the board?

b. Two fifths of 30 students studied more than one hour for a test. How many students studied for more than one hour?

c. The force of gravity on Mercury is about $\frac{1}{3}$ the force of gravity on Earth. How much less would a tire weigh on Mercury if it weighs 42 lb on Earth? Would the mass be the same? Why or why not?

d. Explain the difference between weight and mass.

Written Practice *Distributed and Integrated*

* 1. **Interpret** Use this tally sheet to answer parts **a–c.**
(Inv. 7)

Results of Class Election

Candidate	Tally
Irma	卌 II
Hamish	卌 I
Thanh	卌 III
Marisol	卌 卌 II

a. Who was second in the election?

b. Who received twice as many votes as Hamish?

c. Altogether, how many votes were cast?

2. Write these amounts in order from greatest to least:
(Inv. 4)

$1.45 $2.03 $0.99 $1.48

3. **Formulate** The Osage River in Kansas is 500 miles long. The Kentucky River is 259 miles long. How many miles longer is the Osage River? Write and solve an equation.
(25, 41)

*4. Represent Two fifths of the 20 balloons were yellow. How many
(95) balloons were yellow? Draw a picture to illustrate the problem.

*5. Tim is 5 years younger than DeMario. DeMario is 2 years older
(94) than Lucinda. Lucinda is 11 years old. How old is Tim?
How did you find your answer?

6. Name the shaded part of this group
(Inv. 4, 74)
    a. as a fraction.

    b. as a decimal number.

7. The fraction $\frac{1}{10}$ equals 10%. What percent of the group in problem **6** is
(Inv. 5) shaded?

*8. Estimate the product of 88 and 59. Then find the exact product.
(93)

9. Sue's birthday is May 2. Her birthday will be on what day of
(54) the week in the year 2045?

MAY 2045						
S	M	T	W	T	F	S
	1	2	3	4	5	6
7	8	9	10	11	12	13
14	15	16	17	18	19	20
21	22	23	24	25	26	27
28	29	30	31			

*10. Point *W* represents what number on this number line?
(94)

    600   700

11. $32.63 + $42 + $7.56
(43, 51)

12. $86.45 − ($74.50 + $5)
(43, 45)

13. 83 × 40
(67)

14. 1000 × 53
(85)

15. $9^2 - \sqrt{81}$
(Inv. 3, 62)

*16.   32
(90)   × 16

*17.   67
(90)   × 32

18. $8.95
(58)   ×   4

19. 3)625
(80)

20. 4)714
(53, 76)

21. 6)1385
(80)

22. $\frac{900}{5}$
(80)

23. 3748 ÷ 9
(76)

24. 8*m* = $28.56
(41, 76)

*25. **(Represent)** This circle shows that $\frac{2}{2}$ equals 1. Draw a circle
(89) that shows that $\frac{3}{3}$ equals 1.

26. Find the perimeter and area of this rectangle.
(Inv. 2,
Inv. 3)

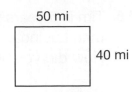

50 mi

40 mi

*27. a. Draw a quadrilateral that is congruent to the quadrilateral
(66, 79) at right. Then write the name for this type of quadrilateral.

b. Draw the line of symmetry on the figure you created.

*28. Compare: 0.05 ◯ 0.050
(91)

*29. **(Explain)** Kelly ran and jumped 9 ft 6 in. How many inches did
(Inv. 2,
94) Kelly jump?

*30. The table shows the relationship between the number of hours Aidan
(Inv. 8) works and the amount of money he earns.

Number of Hours Worked	Income Earned (in dollars)
1	19
2	38
3	57
4	76
5	95

a. **(Generalize)** Write a word sentence that describes the
relationship of the data.

b. **(Predict)** Aidan works 40 hours each week. What is a reasonable
estimate of the amount of income he earns each week? Explain
your answer.

• Average

facts   Power Up H

mental math   Find half of a product in **a–c.**

    a. Number Sense: half of 100×12

    b. Number Sense: half of 100×24

    c. Number Sense: half of 100×48

    d. Money: The salad cost $4.89. Ramona paid for it with a $10 bill. How much change should she receive?

    e. Geometry: The angles of the triangle measured 47°, 43°, and 90°. What is the sum of the angle measures?

    f. Estimation: In 10 minutes, Tevin counted 25 cars that drove through the intersection. About how many cars might Tevin expect to count in 20 minutes?

    g. Calculation: $16 \div 2$, $- 6$, $\times 2$, $\sqrt{}$

    h. Roman Numerals: Write XXXIII in our number system.

problem solving   Choose an appropriate problem-solving strategy to solve this problem. There are three light switches that each control a row of lights in the classroom—a row in front, a row in the middle, and a row in back. Make a tree diagram to find the different ways the rows of lights can be turned on or off. Use the tree diagram to count the total number of combinations.

New Concept

Math Language

An **average** is a way to describe a set of data using one number.

Here we show three stacks of coins:

     8   3   4

There are 15 coins in all. If we rearrange the coins to have an equal number in each stack, we get 5 coins in each stack.

5   5   5

We say that the *average* number of coins in each stack is 5. Finding an average is a two-step process. First we find how many there are altogether. Then we find how many there would be in each group if the groups were equal.

Example

Four vans carried the team to the soccer field. There were 5 players in the first van, 4 players in the second van, 3 players in the third van, and 8 players in the fourth van. What was the average number of players per van?

The average is the number of players there would be in each van if each van carried the same number of players. Imagine starting over and reloading the vans equally. First we need to find the total number of players. We find the total by adding the number of players in each van.

$$
\begin{array}{r}
5 \text{ players} \\
4 \text{ players} \\
3 \text{ players} \\
+\ 8 \text{ players} \\
\hline
20 \text{ players}
\end{array}
$$

Since there were four vans, we divide the 20 players into four equal groups.

$$\frac{20 \text{ players}}{4 \text{ vans}} = 5 \text{ players in each van}$$

If the vans had been loaded equally, there would have been 5 players in each van. Even though the vans were not loaded equally, the average number of players per van was **5 players.**

Justify Explain why the answer is reasonable.

Lesson Practice

a. In three classrooms there were 24, 26, and 28 children. What was the average number of children per classroom?

b. **Analyze** There were two stacks of books on the shelf: one with 17 books and the other with 11 books. Allison moved some books from the taller stack to the shorter stack so that the numbers of books in the two stacks were equal. When she finished, how many books were in each stack?

c. Spencer's scores on his first three games were 85, 85, and 100. What was the average of his first three game scores?

Written Practice
Distributed and Integrated

*1. **Analyze** Freddie is 2 years older than Francesca. Francesca is twice
(94) as old as Chloe. Chloe is 6 years old. How old is Freddie?

*2. **Analyze** What is the total number of days in the first three months of
(54) a leap year?

*3. It costs $1.52 to mail the package. Nate put three 37¢ stamps on
(94) the package. How much more postage does Nate need to mail the package?

*4. Thirty-two desks were arranged as equally as possible in 6 rows.
(88)
   a. How many rows had exactly 5 desks?

   b. How many rows had 6 desks?

*5. **Represent** Two thirds of the 21 riders rode their horses bareback. How
(95) many riders rode bareback? Draw a picture to illustrate the problem.

*6. a. What decimal number names the shaded part of the large
(Inv. 4,
Inv. 5) square at right?

   b. What decimal number names the part that is not shaded?

   c. What percent of the square is shaded?

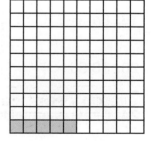

*7. **Explain** Near closing time, 31 children and adults are waiting in
(88) line to board a ride at an amusement park. Eight people board the ride at one time. How many people will be on the last ride of the day? Explain your answer.

8. Round 3874 to the nearest thousand.
(54)

9. (Estimate) Alicia opened a liter of milk and poured half of it into a
(40, pitcher. About how many milliliters of milk did she pour into the pitcher?
Inv. 5) What percent of the milk was still in the container?

10. The sun was up when Mark started working. It was dark when he
(27) stopped working later in the day. How much time had gone by?

Started   Stopped

* 11. For five days Pilar recorded the high temperature. The temperatures
(96) were 79°F, 82°F, 84°F, 81°F, and 74°F. What was the average high
temperature for those five days?

12. (Explain) Leena drove 368 miles in 8 hours. If she drove the same
(60) number of miles each hour, how far did she drive each hour? Explain
how you found your answer.

13.   496,325
(51) +   3,680

14. $36.00
(52) − $30.78

15. $12.45
(22) $ 1.30
           $ 2.00
           $ 0.25
           $ 0.04
           $ 0.32
        + $ 1.29

* 16.   26
(90) × 24

* 17.   25
(90) × 25

18. 8m = $16.40
(41, 80)

19. 60 × 300
(86)

20. $8.56 × 7
(58)

21. 7)845
(80)

22. 9)1000
(76)

23. $\frac{432}{6}$
(65)

* 24. (Represent) Draw and shade a circle that shows that $\frac{4}{4}$ equals 1.
(89)

25. The wall was 8 feet high and 12 feet wide. How many square feet of
(Inv. 3) wallpaper were needed to cover the wall?

26. **Analyze** Below are Tene's scores on the first seven games. Refer to
(94, 96) the scores below to answer parts **a–c.**

$$85, 85, 100, 90, 80, 100, 85$$

   a. Rearrange the scores so that the scores are in order from lowest to highest.

   b. In your answer to part **a,** which score is the middle score in the list?

   c. In the list of game scores, which score occurs most frequently?

*27. **Estimate** What is a reasonable estimate of the number in each
(59, 65) group when 912 objects are separated into 3 equal groups? Explain why your estimate is reasonable.

*28. According to many health experts, a person should drink 64 ounces
(52) of water each day. If Shankeedra's glass holds 8 ounces of water, how many glasses of water should she drink in one day?

*29. Arthur told his classmates that his age in years is a single-digit odd
(10) number greater than one. He also told his classmates that his age is not a prime number. How old is Arthur?

*30. If $y = 3x - 1$, what is y when x is 2?
(94)

Early Finishers
Real-World Connection

Mylah decided she wanted to grow three peanut plants for her science class. After five months, one of her plants is 1 ft 6 in. tall. The second plant is 1 ft 2 in. tall, and the third is 10 inches tall.

   a. Convert the heights of the first two peanut plants to inches, and then find the average height of all of Mylah's plants (in inches).

   b. Convert the average to feet and inches.

• Mean, Median, Range, and Mode

facts   Power Up H

mental math   Fifty is half of 100. Find each product by multiplying by half of 100 in **a–d.**

    a. Number Sense: 50×16

    b. Number Sense: 50×44

    c. Number Sense: 50×26

    d. Number Sense: 50×68

    e. Money: The groceries cost $32.48 and the magazine cost $4.99. What was the total cost?

    f. Estimation: Each box is 30.5 cm tall. Estimate the height (using cm) of a stack of 6 boxes.

    g. Calculation: $200 \div 2, \div 2, \div 2$

    h. Roman Numerals: Write 25 in Roman numerals.

problem solving   Choose an appropriate problem-solving strategy to solve this problem. There are 365 days in a common year, which is about 52 weeks. However, since 52 weeks is exactly 364 days, a year does not start on the same day of the week as the start of the preceding year. If a common year starts on a Tuesday, on what day of the week will the following year begin?

New Concept

In Lesson 96 we practiced finding an average. To find the average of a set of numbers, we added the numbers and then divided by the number of numbers. Another name for the average is the **mean.**

Example 1

Find the mean of Ian's seven game scores.

80, 85, 85, 10, 90, 90, 85

We add the scores and divide by the number of scores. The sum of the scores is 525. We divide the sum by 7.

$$525 \div 7 = 75$$

The mean, or average, of the seven scores is **75.** This means that Ian's seven game scores are equivalent to seven scores of 75. This might seem low since six of Ian's scores were higher than 75. However, his one very low score of 10 lowered his average.

The **median** of a set of numbers is the middle number when the numbers are arranged in order of size. When there is an even set of numbers, the *median* is the average of the two middle numbers.

Example 2

Find the median of Ian's seven game scores.

80, 85, 85, 10, 90, 90, 85

The median score is the middle score. To find the median score, we arrange the scores in order. We begin with the lowest score.

10, 80, 85, 85, 85, 90, 90

3 scores   middle   3 scores

We see that the median score is **85.**

Discuss Explain how to find the median of the following set of numbers.

5, 4, 3, 8, 7, 7

Notice that the low score of 10 does not affect the median. A score that is far from the other scores is called an **outlier.** *Outliers* sometimes affect the mean while having little or no effect on the median. Below we have placed these scores on a line plot. We see that most of the scores are close together.

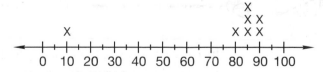

The outlier is far away from the other scores.

The **range** of a set of numbers is the difference between the largest and the smallest numbers in a list. To calculate the *range* of a list, we subtract the smallest number from the largest number.

Example 3

Find the range of Ian's seven game scores.

$$80, 85, 85, 10, 90, 90, 85$$

The scores vary from a low of 10 to a high of 90. The range is the difference of the high and low scores. We subtract 10 from 90 and find that the range is **80.**

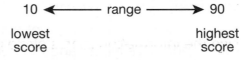

| | lowest
score | | highest
score |

10 ←————— range ————→ 90
    lowest   highest
    score   score

The **mode** of a set of numbers is the number that occurs most often.

Example 4

Find the mode of Ian's seven game scores.

$$80, 85, 85, 10, 90, 90, 85$$

We see that the score of 85 appears three times. No other score appears more than twice. This means the mode is **85.**

Discuss What is the mode of the following set of numbers?

$$5, 5, 3, 6, 8, 7, 7$$

Lesson Practice

a. Analyze Find the mean, median, mode, and range of Janell's game points shown below. Is there an outlier in this set of points?

$$50, 80, 90, 85, 90, 95, 90, 100$$

b. Find the mean, median, mode, and range of this set of numbers:

$$31, 28, 31, 30, 25$$

c. Explain Find the median of the test scores shown below. Explain how you found your answer.

$$75, 80, 80, 90, 95, 100$$

d. Every X on this line plot stands for the age of a child attending a party. How many children attended the party? What is the mode of the ages?

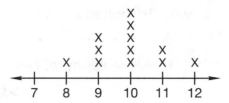

*1. **Interpret** Use the information in this circle graph to answer parts **a–d.**
(Inv. 6)

Activities of 100 Children at the Park

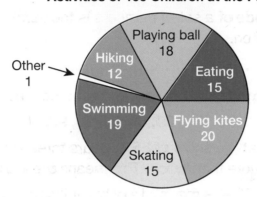

a. Altogether, how many children were at the park?

b. How many children were *not* swimming?

c. How many children were either hiking or skating?

d. How many more children were flying kites than were swimming?

*2. **Represent** Three fourths of the one thousand gold coins were
(95) special gold coins called doubloons. How many doubloons were there? Draw a picture to illustrate the problem.

*3. What percent of the gold coins in problem **2** was doubloons?
(Inv. 5, 95)

4. Write each mixed number as a decimal:
(84)

a. $3\frac{5}{10}$ **b.** $14\frac{21}{1000}$ **c.** $9\frac{4}{100}$

* 5. Estimate the product of 39 and 406. Then find the exact
(93) product.

* 6. If $y = 4x - 2$, what is y when x is 4?
(94)

* 7. Write these fractions in order from least to greatest:
(Inv. 9)

$$\frac{3}{4} \qquad \frac{1}{2} \qquad \frac{5}{8}$$

8. Compare: 2 thousand $\bigcirc$ 24 hundred
(33)

Refer to the rectangle at right to answer problems **9** and **10**.

9. What is the perimeter of the rectangle
(Inv. 2,
  69)   **a.** in millimeters?

   b. in centimeters?

30 mm
10 mm

10. What is the area of the rectangle
(Inv. 3,
  86)   **a.** in square millimeters?

   b. in square centimeters?

11. Santos figured the trip would take seven and a half hours. He left
(27) at 7 a.m. At what time does he think he will arrive?

* 12. (**Analyze**) What is the average (mean) number of days per month in the
(96) first three months of a common year?

13. 25×40 **14.** $98¢ \times 7$
(67)   (48)

15. $\sqrt{36} \times \sqrt{4}$ **16.** $\dfrac{3^3}{3}$
(Inv. 3)   (62)

17. 36
(90) $\times\, 34$

*18. 35
(90) $\times\, 35$

19. 4
(2) 2
1
3
4
7
2
2
3
4
$+\, x$
―――
42

20. $8m = \$70.00$
(41, 76)

21. $6\overline{)1234}$
(80)

22. $800 \div 7$
(65)

23. $487 \div 3$
(65)

24. $\$2.74 + \$0.27 + \$6 + 49¢$
(43)

25. $9.487 - (3.7 + 2.36)$
(45, 50)

*26. (Represent) Draw and shade circles to show that $2\frac{1}{3}$ equals $\frac{7}{3}$.
(89)

*27. (Analyze) Listed below are the number of points Amon scored in his
(97) last nine basketball games, which range from 6 to 10. Refer to these
scores to answer parts **a–e.**

$$8, 7, 7, 8, 6, 10, 9, 10, 7$$

a. What is the mode of the scores?

b. What is the median of the scores?

c. What is the range of the scores?

d. What is the mean of the scores?

e. Are there any outliers?

28. Each school day, Brent's second class begins at 9:00 a.m. What
(81) kind of angle is formed by the minute hand and the hour hand of a
clock at that time?

*29. (Explain) Thirty-one students are entering a classroom. The desks
(58) in the classroom are arranged in rows with 7 desks in each row. If the
students fill the first row of desks, then fill the second row of desks,
and so on, how many full rows of students will there be? How many
students will sit in a row that is not full? Explain your answer.

*30. Melvin was reading a book. When he finished reading every other page,
(73) Melvin flipped the page. Turning a page is like which transformation?

• Geometric Solids

facts   Power Up H

mental math   We can double one factor of a multiplication and take one half of the other factor to find a product.

$$4 \times 18$$

double $\downarrow$ $\quad$ $\downarrow$ half

$$8 \times 9 = 72$$

Find each product by the "double and half" method in **a–d.**

a. Number Sense: 3×14

b. Number Sense: 4×16

c. Number Sense: 5×22

d. Number Sense: 50×24

e. Money: $\$1.00 - 42¢$

f. Estimation: Choose the more reasonable estimate for the height of a ceiling: 250 cm or 250 m.

g. Calculation: 6^2, $+ 4$, $- 30$, $\times 10$

h. Roman Numerals: Write 25 in Roman numerals.

problem solving   Choose an appropriate problem-solving strategy to solve this problem. To get to the room where he will have his yearly medical checkup, Jerome will walk through three doors—a door into the doctor's office building, a door into the waiting room, and a door into the checkup room. Each door might be either open or closed when Jerome gets to it. List the possible combinations of open and closed doors that Jerome might encounter on his way into the checkup room. Use the abbreviations "O" for *open* and "C" for *closed*.

New Concept

Two-dimensional figures such as triangles, rectangles, and circles are flat shapes that cover an area but do not take up space. They have length and width but not depth. Objects that take up space are things such as cars, basketballs, desks, and houses. People also take up space. Geometric shapes that take up space are called **geometric solids.** Solids have three dimensions. The chart below shows the names of some geometric solids.

Geometric Solids

Shape	Name
	Cube (and rectangular prism)
	Rectangular prism (or rectangular solid)
	Triangular prism
	Pyramid
	Cylinder
	Sphere
	Cone

Example 1

Name each shape:

a.

b.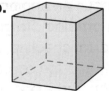

c.

We compare each shape with the chart.

a. sphere   **b. cube**   **c. cone**

Example 2

What is the shape of a soup can?

A soup can has the shape of a **cylinder.**

A flat surface of a solid is called a **face.** Two faces meet at an **edge.** Three or more edges meet at a corner called a *vertex* (plural: *vertices*). The bottom face is called the **base.**

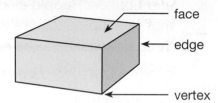

A circular cylinder has one curved surface and two flat circular surfaces. A cone has one curved surface and one flat circular surface. The pointed end of a cone is its **apex.** A sphere has no flat surfaces.

Example 3

a. **How many faces does a box have?**

b. **How many vertices does a box have?**

c. **How many edges does a box have?**

Find a closed, rectangular box in the classroom (a tissue box, for example) to answer the questions above.

a. **6 faces** (top, bottom, left, right, front, back)

b. **8 vertices** (4 around the top, 4 around the bottom)

c. **12 edges** (4 around the top, 4 around the bottom, and 4 running from top to bottom)

Geometric Solids in the Real World

Material needed:
- **Lesson Activity 42**

Looking around us, we see examples of the geometric solids shown in the table of this lesson. With some objects, two or more shapes are combined. For example, in a building we might see a triangular prism and a rectangular prism.

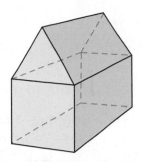

Complete **Lesson Activity 42** by finding and naming an object for each shape. Then draw a picture of each object on the page.

Lesson Practice

In problems **a–d,** name the shape of the object listed.

a. basketball

b. shoe box

c. funnel

d. soda can

e. The figure at right is the same shape as several Egyptian landmarks. What is the shape?

f. The figure in problem **e** has a square base. How many faces does the figure have? How many edges? How many vertices?

Written Practice *Distributed and Integrated*

*1. Use this information to answer parts **a–c.**
(72, 94)

In the Lerma family there are 3 children. Juno is 10 years old. Joaquin is 2 years younger than Jovana. Joaquin is 4 years older than Juno.

   a. How old is Joaquin?

   b. How old is Jovana?

   c. When Joaquin is 16 years old, how old will Jovana be?

*2. D'Andra bought an artichoke and 6 pounds of carrots for $2.76. If the
(94) artichoke cost 84¢, how much did 1 pound of carrots cost? (*Hint:* First find the cost of all the carrots.)

3. Compare. Write >, <, or =.
(33)
    a. 206,353 ◯ 209,124   **b.** 518,060 ◯ 518,006

4. Write these numbers in order from greatest to least:
(33)

        89,611   120,044   102,757   96,720

5. (**Represent**) Write each mixed number as a decimal:
(84)
    a. $5\frac{31}{1000}$ **b.** $16\frac{7}{10}$ **c.** $5\frac{7}{100}$

*6. (**Represent**) Three fifths of the team's 40 points were scored in
(95) the first half. How many points did the team score in the first half?
Draw a picture to illustrate the problem.

*7. One fifth is 20%. What percent is three fifths?
(Inv. 5, 95)

8. (**Represent**) Use words to write 7.68.
(Inv. 4)

9. (**Represent**) Use words to write 76.8.
(Inv. 4)

*10. ✐ (**Explain**) Armondo estimated that the exact product of 78 and 91
(93) was close to 720. Did Armondo make a reasonable estimate? Explain
why or why not.

11. (**Connect**) Name the number of shaded squares below
(Inv. 4)

    a. as a mixed number.

    b. as a decimal.

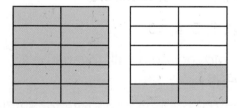

*12. There were 24 people in one line and 16 people in the other line. What
(96) was the average number of people per line?

13. Makayla's school day ends 5 hours 20 minutes after the
(27) time shown on the clock. What time does Makayla's
school day end?

14. Mr. Romano could bake 27 dozen whole wheat muffins in 3 hours.
(60)

    a. How many dozen whole wheat muffins could he bake in 1 hour?

    b. How many dozen whole wheat muffins could he bake in 5 hours?
      (*Hint:* Multiply the answer to part **a** by 5.)

15. 3.65 + 4.2 + 0.625   **16.** $13.70 − $6.85
(50)   (43, 51)

17. 26 × 100   **18.** 9 × 87¢   **19.** 14 × 16
(85)   (48)   (90)

20. 15^2 **21.** $\dfrac{456}{6}$ **22.**   47
(62, 90)   (65)   (67)   × 60

23. 6x = 4248   **24.** 1)$\overline{163}$ **25.** 5)$\overline{\$49.00}$
(80)   (76)   (76, 80)

*26. This table represents the equation y = 2x + 3 and
(94) shows the values of y when x is 2 and when x is 3.
What is y when x is 4?

y = 2x + 3	
x	**y**
2	7
3	9
4	?

27. How many one-foot-square tiles are needed to cover the
(Inv. 3, floor of a room that is 15 feet long and 10 feet wide?
85)

*28. Find the median and mode of this set of numbers:
(97)

                1, 1, 2, 3, 5, 8, 13

*29. What geometric shape is a globe?
(98)

*30. **a.** What is the geometric name for this solid?
(63, 98)

    b. How many faces does this solid have?

    c. Describe the angles.

• Constructing Prisms

Power Up

facts   Power Up J

mental   Find each product by the "double and half" method in **a–c.**
math
    a. Number Sense: 3×18

    b. Number Sense: 15×60

    c. Number Sense: 50×48

    d. Money: Shawntay had $5.00. He spent $1.75 on a birthday card for his brother. How much does he have left?

    e. Fractional Parts: What is $\frac{1}{5}$ of 100?

    f. Estimation: Brittany used $11\frac{3}{4}$ inches of tape to wrap one gift. About how much tape will she need to wrap five more gifts that are the same size as the first?

    g. Calculation: $\sqrt{25}$, $\div 5$, $+ 6$, $\times 2$, $- 11$

    h. Roman Numerals: Write XXVII in our number system.

problem   Choose an appropriate problem-solving strategy to solve this
solving   problem. Danae can walk twice as fast as she can swim. She can run twice as fast as she can walk. She can ride a bike twice as fast as she can run. If Danae can ride her bike a quarter mile in one minute, how long would it take her to swim a quarter mile?

New Concept

In Lesson 98 we named solids by their shapes. In this lesson we will focus our attention on understanding rectangular prisms and triangular prisms.

Consider the shape of a cereal box. The shape is called a *rectangular solid* (or *rectangular prism*). Every panel, or side, of a closed cereal box is a rectangle.

If an empty cereal box or similar container is available, you may refer to it to answer the following questions:

1. A closed cereal box has how many panels?

2. What words could we use to refer to these panels?

3. Without a mirror, what is the largest number of panels that can be seen at one time?

4. Two panels meet at a fold, or seam, in the cardboard. Each fold is an edge. A closed cereal box has how many edges?

5. Three edges meet at each corner of the box. A closed cereal box has how many corners (vertices)?

If we tape an empty cereal box closed and cut it along seven edges, we can "flatten out" the container, as shown below.

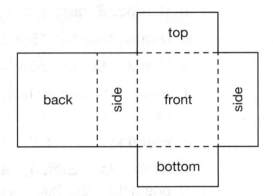

> **Math Language**
>
> A **net** is a 2-dimensional representation of a 3-dimensional geometric figure.

We can see the six rectangles that formed the panels of the closed box. We will use nets like this one to construct the models of solids.

Constructing Prisms

Materials needed:
- **Lesson Activities 43, 44,** and **45**
- scissors
- tape or glue

We can make models of cubes, rectangular prisms, and triangular prisms by cutting, folding, and taping nets of shapes to form 3-dimensional figures. Use **Lesson Activities 43, 44, and 45** to construct two rectangular prisms, two triangular prisms, and two cubes. Then study those figures to answer the questions in the Lesson Practice.

Refer to the cube to answer problems **a–e**.

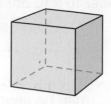

a. What is the shape of each face?

b. Is each face parallel to an opposite face?

c. Is each edge parallel to at least one other edge?

d. Is each edge perpendicular to at least one other edge?

e. What type of angle is formed by every pair of intersecting edges?

Refer to the rectangular prism below to answer problems **f–j.**

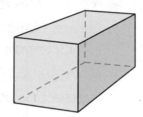

f. What is the shape of each face?

g. Is each face parallel to the opposite face?

h. Is each edge parallel to at least one other edge?

i. Is each edge perpendicular to at least one other edge?

j. What type of angle is formed by every pair of intersecting edges?

Refer to the triangular prism with two faces that are equilateral triangles to answer problems **k–o.**

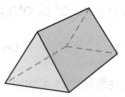

k. What are the shapes of the five faces?

l. Are the triangular faces parallel? Are the rectangular faces parallel?

m. Are the triangular faces congruent? Are the rectangular faces congruent?

n. Do you find pairs of edges that are parallel? That are perpendicular? That intersect but are not perpendicular?

o. What types of angles are formed by the intersecting edges?

Refer to the triangular prism with two faces that are right triangles to answer problems **p–t.**

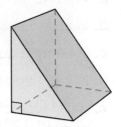

p. What are the shapes of the five faces?

q. Which faces are parallel?

r. Are the triangular faces congruent? Are the rectangular faces congruent?

s. Are there pairs of edges that are parallel? Perpendicular? Intersecting but not perpendicular?

t. What types of angles are formed by the intersecting edges?

Written Practice

Distributed and Integrated

*1. Fifty-three family photographs are being arranged in a photo album. The album has 12 pages altogether, and 6 photographs can be placed on each page.
(88)

   a. How many full pages of photographs will be in the album?

   b. How many photographs will be on the page that is not full?

   c. How many pages in the album will be empty?

2. **Estimate** Abraham Lincoln was born in 1809. How old was he when he issued the Emancipation Proclamation in 1863?
(54)

*3. **Analyze** The parking lot charges $1.25 to park a car for the first hour. It charges 75¢ for each additional hour. How much does it cost to park a car in the lot for 3 hours?
(94)

*4. **(Represent)** Two thirds of the team's 45 points were scored in the
(95) second half. How many points did the team score in the second half?
Draw a picture to illustrate the problem.

*5. Something is wrong with the sign at right. Draw two different
(35) signs that show how to correct the error.

6. **(Analyze)** What is the value of 3 $10 bills, 4 $1 bills, 5 dimes, and
(35) 2 pennies?

7. **(Represent)** Use words to write 6412.5.
(Inv. 4)

8. **(Estimate)** Last year 5139 people attended an outdoor jazz
(59) festival. This year 6902 people attended the festival. Estimate the
total attendance during those years and explain why your estimate
is reasonable.

9. **a.** Cooper opened a 1-gallon bottle of milk and poured out 1 quart.
(40, How many quarts of milk were left in the bottle?
Inv. 5)

b. What percent of the milk was left in the bottle?

10. Look at the coins below. List all of the different amounts you could
(36) make using exactly two coins.

*11. Estimate the product of 39 and 41. Then find the exact product.
(93)

12. Felicia slowly gave the doorknob a quarter turn counterclockwise. How
(75) many degrees did she turn the doorknob?

* 13. Five full buses held 240 students. What was the average number of
(96) students per bus?

14. $68.57
(43, 51) + $36.49
——————

15. $100.00
(52) − $ 5.43
——————

16.
(17)
15
24
36
75
21
8
36
+ 420
——————

17.   12
(87) × 12
————

18. $5.08
(58) ×   7
————

19. 50^2
(62, 86)

20. $\sqrt{144}$
(Inv. 3)

21. $12.08 − (9.61 − 2.4)$
(45, 50)

22. $49 × 51$
(90)

23. $33 × 25$
(90)

24. $\dfrac{848}{8}$
(80)

25. $9w = 6300$
(80)

* 26. **Represent** Draw and shade circles to show that $2\frac{2}{3}$ equals $\frac{8}{3}$.
(89)

* 27. **Represent** Draw a rectangle that is three inches long and one inch
(21, Inv. 3) wide. Then find the perimeter and the area.

* 28. This table represents the equation $y = 3x + 1$ and shows
(94) the values of y when x is 3 and when x is 4. What is y
when x is 5?

$y = 3x + 1$	
x	**y**
3	10
4	13
5	?

* 29. **Classify** Refer to this triangular prism for parts **a** and **b**.
(23, 99)
   a. Describe the angles as acute, right, or obtuse.

   b. Which faces are parallel?

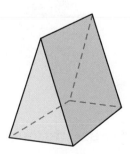

* 30. This pyramid has a square base. How many vertices does
(98) the pyramid have?

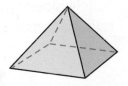

• Constructing Pyramids

facts   Power Up J

mental math   Find each product by the "double and half" method in **a–c**.

    a. Number Sense: 4×14

    b. Number Sense: 25×80

    c. Number Sense: 50×64

    d. Money: Houston paid for a lawn sprinkler that cost $8.16 with a $10 bill. How much change should he receive?

    e. Geometry: What is the diameter of a wheel that has a radius of 14 inches?

    f. Estimation: Estimate 19×41 by rounding each number to the nearest ten before multiplying.

    g. Calculation: $15 - 9$, square the number, $\div\ 4$, $-\ 8$

    h. Roman Numerals: Write 19 in Roman numerals.

problem solving   Franklin's family is moving to a new house, and they have packed their belongings in identical boxes. The picture at right represents the stack of boxes that is inside the moving truck. How many boxes are in the stack?

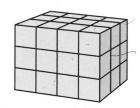

Focus Strategy: Make It Simpler

    (**Understand**) We are shown a picture of identical, stacked boxes. We assume that boxes in the upper layer are supported by boxes in the lower layers. We are asked to find how many boxes are in the stack altogether.

Plan In the picture, we can see three layers of boxes. If we can find how many boxes are in each layer, we can multiply by 3 to find the total number of boxes.

Solve If we look at the top layer of boxes, we see 4 boxes along the front and 3 boxes along the side. Four rows of 3 boxes means there are 4 × 3 boxes = 12 boxes in the top layer. The middle and bottom layers contain the same number of boxes as the top layer. Since there are three layers of boxes, we find that there are 3 × 12 boxes = **36 boxes** in the stack altogether.

Check We know our answer is reasonable because three layers of 12 boxes each is 36 boxes altogether. If we have blocks or unit cubes, we can check our answer by modeling the problem.

New Concept

Math Language

A *plane* is an endless 2-dimensional, flat surface. Lines and plane figures are found on planes.

Recall from Lesson 98 that geometric shapes such as triangles, rectangles, and circles have two dimensions—length and width—but they do not have depth. These kinds of figures occupy area, but they do not take up space. We call shapes such as these plane figures because they are confined to a plane.

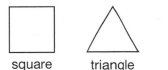

square   triangle   circle

Shapes that take up space, such as cubes, pyramids, and cones, are *geometric solids*. Geometric solids have three dimensions: length, width, and depth. Sometimes we simply call these shapes solids. Solids are not confined to a plane, so to draw them we try to create an optical illusion to suggest their shape.

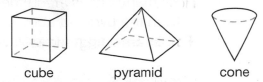

cube   pyramid   cone

In Lesson 99 we studied models of rectangular prisms and triangular prisms. In this lesson we will study models of pyramids.

Activity

Constructing Models of Pyramids

Materials needed:

- **Lesson Activity 46**
- scissors
- glue or tape

Cut out the patterns for the pyramids. The shaded parts of each pattern are tabs to help hold the figures together. Fold the paper along the edges before you glue or tape the seams. You might work with a partner as you construct the models. Refer to the models to answer the questions in the Lesson Practice.

Lesson Practice

Refer to the pyramid with a square base at right to answer problems **a–d.**

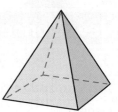

a. How many faces does the pyramid have, and what are their shapes?

b. Does the pyramid have any parallel faces?

c. Does the pyramid have any parallel or perpendicular edges? Explain.

d. In the pyramid above, what types of angles are formed by the intersecting edges?

Refer to the pyramid with the triangular base at right to answer problems **e–h.**

e. How many faces does the pyramid have and what are their shapes?

f. Does the pyramid have any parallel faces?

g. Does the pyramid have any parallel or perpendicular edges?

h. In the pyramid above, what types of angles are formed by intersecting edges?

1. One hundred fifty feet equals how many yards?
(Inv. 2, 71)

2. Tammy gave the clerk $6 to pay for a book. She received 64¢ in change. Tax was 38¢. What was the price of the book?
(83)

3. DaJuan is 2 years older than Rebecca. Rebecca is twice as old as Dillon. DaJuan is 12 years old. How old is Dillon? (*Hint:* First find Rebecca's age.)
(94)

4. Write each decimal as a mixed number:
(84)
    a. 3.295   **b.** 32.9   **c.** 3.09

* 5. a. (**Represent**) Three fourths of the 84 contestants guessed incorrectly. How many contestants guessed incorrectly? Draw a picture to illustrate the problem.
(Inv. 5, 95)

    b. What percent of the contestants guessed incorrectly?

6. These thermometers show the average daily minimum and maximum temperatures in North Little Rock, Arkansas, during the month of January. What is the range of the temperatures?
(18, 97)

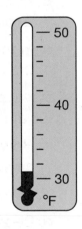 

7. a. What is the diameter of this circle?
(21)

    b. What is the radius of this circle?

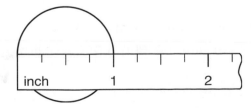

8. **Represent** Use words to write 8.75.
(Inv. 4)

*9. **Estimate** Three students each made a different estimate of the
(93) quotient 2589 ÷ 9. Paulo's estimate was 30, Ka'Dentia's estimate was 300,
and Carter's estimate was 3000. Which student made the best estimate?
Explain your answer.

*10. The first five odd counting numbers are 1, 3, 5, 7, and 9.
(10, 97)

Find the mean and the median of these five numbers.

*11. What geometric shape is a roll of paper towels?
(98)

*12. **a.** **Multiple Choice** Which of these polygons is a parallelogram?
(92)

A   B   C   D

b. Which polygons appear to have at least one obtuse angle?

c. Which polygon does not appear to have any perpendicular sides?

13. $16.25 − ($6 − 50¢)
(43, 45)

14. 5 × 7 × 9   **15.** $7.83 × 6   **16.** 54 × 1000
(62)   (58)   (85)

17.   45   **18.**   32   **19.**   46
(90) × 45   (67) × 40   (90) × 44

20. 6)3625   **21.** 5)3000   **22.** 7n = 987
(80)   (80)   (41, 76)

23. $\dfrac{10^3}{\sqrt{25}}$ **24.** $13.76 ÷ 8   **25.** $\dfrac{234}{4}$
(Inv. 3, 62)   (76)   (68)

*26. **Represent** Draw and shade a circle to show that $\frac{8}{8}$ equals 1.
(56)

27. The perimeter of the square at right is 40 cm. What is the
(Inv. 2, Inv. 3) area of this square? (*Hint:* First find the length of each side.)

*28. **Represent** Draw a triangle that is similar to this isosceles
(66, 79) triangle. Then draw its line of symmetry.

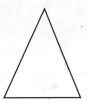

*29. a. Compare: 0.25 $\bigcirc$ 0.250
(91)

   b. Compare: $0.25 $\bigcirc$ 0.25¢

*30. One of these nets could be cut out and folded to form a cube. The
(99) other will not form a cube. Which net will form a cube?

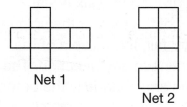

Net 1   Net 2

Real-World
Connection

a. Use a ruler to sketch the front, top, sides, and bottom of a pyramid,
cone, and cube.

b. In your sketches, what do the dashed lines represent?

Focus on

• Probability

Many board games involve an element of **chance.** This means that when we spin a spinner, roll number cubes, or draw a card from a shuffled deck, we cannot know the outcome (result) of the event ahead of time. However, we can often find how *likely* a particular outcome is. The degree of likelihood of an outcome is called its **probability.**

Here we show a spinner. The face is divided into six equal parts called **sectors.** Each sector is $\frac{1}{6}$ of the face of the spinner. Assuming the spinner is balanced and fair, then a spin of the arrow can end up with the arrow pointing in any direction. The letter that names the sector where the arrow lands is the outcome of the spin. For the questions that follow, ignore the possibility that the arrow may stop on a line.

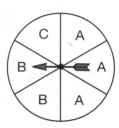

1. If the arrow is spun once, what outcomes are possible?

2. **Explain** On which letter is the arrow most likely to stop and why?

3. **List** Write the possible outcomes of a spin in order from least likely to most likely.

4. Which outcome of a spin is twice as likely as the outcome C?

5. **Predict** If the arrow is spun many times, then about half the outcomes are likely to be which sector?

6. **Multiple Choice** If the arrow is spun many times, then what fraction of the spins are likely to stop in sector C?

   A $\frac{1}{6}$ **B** $\frac{1}{3}$ **C** $\frac{1}{2}$ **D** $\frac{5}{6}$

7. **Multiple Choice** In 60 spins, about how many times should we expect it to stop in sector C?

   A about 6 times   **B** about 10 times
   C about 20 times   **D** about 30 times

The probability of an outcome can be expressed as a number ranging from 0 to 1. An outcome that cannot happen has a probability of 0. An outcome that is **certain** to happen has a probability of 1. An outcome that could happen but is not certain to happen is expressed as a fraction between 0 and 1.

Use the spinner at right to answer problems **8–10**.

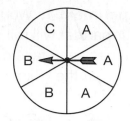

8. **Explain** What is the probability that the arrow will stop in sector D? Why?

9. **Explain** What is the probability that the outcome will be one of the first three letters of the alphabet? Why?

10. What is the probability that the arrow will stop in sector C?

We show a standard dot cube at right.

11. What numbers are represented by the dots on the faces of a dot cube?

12. **Justify** If a dot cube is rolled once, which number is most likely to end up on top? Why?

13. **Multiple Choice** If a dot cube is rolled many times, about how often would we expect to roll a number greater than 3?

    A less than half the time   **B** about half the time

    C more than half the time   **D** none of the time

14. If a dot cube is rolled once, what is the probability of rolling a 7?

15. With one roll of a dot cube, what is the probability of rolling a 1?

16. **Multiple Choice** How would we describe the likelihood of rolling a 6 with one roll of a dot cube?

    A very likely   **B** just as likely to roll a 6 as not to roll a 6

    C unlikely   **D** certain

The **chance** of an event is sometimes expressed as a percent from 0% to 100%. For example, if a meteorologist forecasts that the chance of rain is 20%, then the meteorologist is stating that it might rain, but that it is more likely not to rain. A forecast of 100% chance of rain means that the meteorologist believes it is certain to rain.

17. The weather forecast stated that the chance of rain is 40%. According to the forecast, is it more likely to rain or not to rain?

18. The meteorologist said that the chance of rain is 80%. This means that the chance it will not rain is what percent?

Probability Experiments

Materials needed:

- dot cube
- **Lesson Activity 47**

Experiment 1: Work with a partner for this experiment. You and your partner will roll one dot cube 36 times and tally the number of times each face of the dot cube turns up. You will record the results in the "Experiment 1" table on **Lesson Activity 47.** (A copy of the table is shown below.)

Predict Before starting the experiment, predict the number of times each outcome will occur during the experiment. Write your predictions in the column labeled "Prediction."

36 Rolls of One Dot Cube

Outcome	Prediction	Tally	Total Frequency
1			
2			
3			
4			
5			
6			

Now begin rolling the dot cube. Make a tally mark for each roll in the appropriate box in the "Tally" column. When all groups have finished, report your results to the class. As a class, total the groups' tallies for each outcome, and write these totals in the boxes under "Total Frequency."

19. Make a bar graph using the data from your table.

20. What conclusions can you draw from the results of Experiment 1?

21. Is it easier to compare data using the bar graph or the table?

Experiment 2: In this experiment, you and your group will roll a pair of dot cubes 36 times and tally the outcomes. For each roll, the outcome will be the sum of the two numbers that end up on top. You will record your results in the "Experiment 2" table on **Lesson Activity 47.**

Form groups so that each group can have two number cubes.

Predict Before starting the experiment, predict as a group the number of times each outcome will occur during the experiment. Write your predictions in the column labeled "Prediction."

36 Rolls of Two Dot Cubes

Outcome	Prediction	Tally	Total Frequency
2			
3			
4			
5			
6			
7			
8			
9			
10			
11			
12			

Now begin rolling the dot cubes. Each time you roll a pair of dot cubes, make a tally mark in the appropriate box. When all groups have finished, report your results to the class. As a class, total the groups' tallies for each outcome and record these totals in the "Total Frequency" column.

22. Which outcome(s) occurred most frequently? Why?

23. Which outcome(s) occurred least frequently? Why?

24. What conclusions can you draw from the results of Experiment 2?

25. Model What are all the possible combinations you could roll with a sum of 7 as the result? Explain.

• Tables and Schedules

facts   Power Up J

mental math   Thinking of quarters can make mentally adding and subtracting numbers ending in 25, 50, and 75 easier.

    a. Number Sense: $350 + 175$

    b. Number Sense: $325 - 150$

    c. Number Sense: $175 + 125$

    d. Money: Each ticket costs $10.00 if purchased at the concert hall. A ticket costs $1.95 less if it is purchased in advance. What is the advance price for a ticket?

    e. Time: The year 2011 begins on a Saturday. On what day of the week will the year 2012 begin?

    f. Estimation: Estimate 24×21. Round 24 to 25, round 21 to 20, and then multiply.

    g. Calculation: 10% of 70, $- 5$, $\times 50$, $\sqrt{}$

    h. Roman Numerals: Compare: 29 $\bigcirc$ XXXI

problem solving   Choose an appropriate problem-solving strategy to solve this problem. Congress meets in Washington, D.C., to make laws for the United States. The 535 members of the U.S. Congress are divided into two groups—representatives and senators. There are 2 senators from each of the 50 states. The rest of the people in the U.S. Congress are representatives. How many senators are there? How many representatives are there?

We have studied graphs that present number information in picture form. Another way of presenting number information is in a **table.**

Example 1

Visit www. SaxonMath.com/ Int4Activities for an online activity.

Use the information in this table to answer the questions that follow:

Heights of Major Mountains

Mountain	Feet	Meters
Everest	29,035	8850
McKinley	20,320	6194
Kilimanjaro	19,340	5895
Matterhorn	14,691	4478
Pikes Peak	14,110	4301
Fuji	12,388	3776

a. The Matterhorn is how many meters taller than Pikes Peak?

b. McKinley is how many feet taller than Kilimanjaro?

We compare the heights by subtracting.

a. We use the numbers from the meters column.

$$\begin{array}{r} \text{Matterhorn} \quad 4478 \text{ m} \\ \text{Pikes Peak} \quad -\ 4301 \text{ m} \\ \hline \textbf{177 m} \end{array}$$

b. We use the numbers from the feet column.

$$\begin{array}{r} \text{McKinley} \quad 20{,}320 \text{ ft} \\ \text{Kilimanjaro} \quad -\ 19{,}340 \text{ ft} \\ \hline \textbf{980 ft} \end{array}$$

Estimate About how many miles high is Everest? (A mile is 5280 feet.)

A **schedule** is a list of events organized by the times at which they are planned to occur.

Example 2

Li Ming follows this schedule on school days:

School-Day Schedule	
6:30 a.m.	Wake up, dress, eat breakfast
7:30 a.m.	Leave for school
8:00 a.m.	School starts
12:00 p.m.	Eat lunch
2:45 p.m.	School ends, walk home
3:15 p.m.	Eat snack
3:30 p.m.	Start homework
5:00 p.m.	Play
6:00 p.m.	Eat dinner
7:00 p.m.	Watch TV
8:00 p.m.	Read
8:30 p.m.	Shower
9:00 p.m.	Go to bed

Thinking Skill

Analyze

If Li Ming watched television from 7:00 p.m. to 8:30 p.m., how many half-hour shows could she watch?

If lunch and recess together last 45 minutes, then how many hours does Li Ming spend in class?

School starts at 8:00 a.m. and ends at 2:45 p.m., which is a span of 6 hours 45 minutes. Since 45 minutes of school time is spent on lunch and recess, the time spent in class is **6 hours.**

Example 3

On Saturday morning, Cameron wakes up at 8:00 a.m. His softball game starts at 10:30 a.m. How long after he wakes up does his softball game start?

One clock below shows when Cameron wakes up, and the other shows when his game begins. Starting from when he wakes up, we count forward one hour to 9:00 a.m., two hours to 10:00 a.m., and 30 minutes to 10:30 a.m. We find that Cameron's game starts **2 hours 30 minutes (or $2\frac{1}{2}$ hrs)** after he wakes up.

Analyze If it takes Cameron 25 minutes to drive to the game, what time should he leave his house in order to arrive at the game 15 minutes early? Explain your reasoning.

Make a Table

Material needed:
- thermometer

a. Use a thermometer to measure the temperature outside your classroom for five days. Measure the temperature at the same time each day. Make a table like the one below and record the temperatures in both Celsius and Fahrenheit degrees.

Daily Temperature at _____ o'clock for Week of _____

	Mon	Tue	Wed	Thu	Fri
Celsius					
Fahrenheit					

b. Make a second table like the one below to record the change in temperature from one day to the next. For example, if the temperature Monday was 75°F and Tuesday was 72°F, then the temperature was three degrees lower, which we record as −3°.

	Mon → Tue	Tue → Wed	Wed → Thu	Thu → Fri
Celsius				
Fahrenheit				

Lesson Practice Refer to the table and the schedule in Examples 1 and 2 to answer problems **a–c.**

a. Kilimanjaro is how many meters taller than Fuji?

b. Everest is how many feet taller than the Matterhorn?

c. How much sleep does Li Ming get on a school night if she follows her schedule?

d. Using the thermometers shown, how much did the temperature change between 4 p.m. and 12 a.m.?

---

*1. (**Interpret**) Use the information in the table below to answer parts **a–c.**
(Inv. 6, 101)

Average Yearly Rainfall

City	Rainfall (in inches)
Boston	43
Chicago	36
Denver	16
Houston	48
San Francisco	20

a. Which cities listed in the table average less than 2 feet of rain per year?

b. In one year Houston received 62 inches of rain. This was how much more than its yearly average?

c. Copy and complete the bar graph below to show the information in the rainfall table.

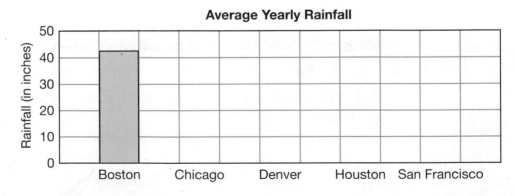

Average Yearly Rainfall

---

*2. **(Represent)** Five sixths of the 288 marchers were out of step. How
(95) many marchers were out of step? Draw a picture to illustrate the
problem.

*3. **(Represent)** Something is wrong with this sign. Draw
(35) two different signs that show how to correct the error.

4. What is the radius of this circle in millimeters?
(21, 69)

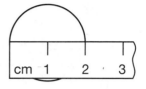

*5. ✏️ **(Conclude)** The chance of rain is 60%. Is it more likely that it will
(Inv. 10) rain or that it will not rain? Explain your answer.

*6. Estimate the product of 88 and 22. Then find the actual product.
(93)

7. Apples were priced at 53¢ per pound. What was the cost of 5 pounds
(49) of apples?

8. **(Represent)** Write the number 3708 in expanded form. Then use words
(16, 33) to write the number.

9. The top of a doorway is about two meters from the floor. Two meters is
(Inv. 2) how many centimeters?

*10. Four pounds of pears cost $1.20. What did 1 pound of pears cost?
(94) What did 6 pounds of pears cost?

11. Mike drove his car 150 miles in 3 hours. What was his average speed in
(60) miles per hour?

12. $46.00
(52)   − $45.56

13. 10,165
(52)   −   856

14. $ 0.63
(43, 51) $ 1.49
         $12.24
         $ 0.38
         $ 0.06
         $ 5.00
       + $ 1.20

*15. 70^2
(62, 86)

16. 71×69
(90)

17. $4\overline{)\$30.00}$
(76, 80)

18. $3\overline{)263}$
(68)

19. $5x = 4080$
(76)

20. $\dfrac{344}{8}$
(65)

21.   37
(67) $\times$ 60

22.   56
(90) $\times$ 42

23. $5.97
(58) $\times$ 8

24. $10.000 - (4.468 - 2.3)$
(45, 50)

*25. Find the mean, median, mode, and range of this set of numbers:
(97)

$$3, 1, 4, 1, 6$$

*26. (Represent) Draw and shade circles to show that 2 equals $\frac{4}{2}$.
(89)

*27. a. (Represent) Draw a square with sides 4 cm long.
(21,
Inv. 3)

b. Find the perimeter and the area of the square you drew.

*28. (Conclude) Which of these nets can be folded to form a pyramid?
(100)

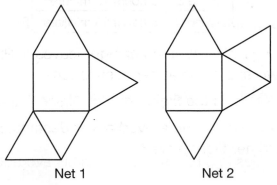

Net 1   Net 2

*29. If $y = 6x - 4$, what is y when
(94)
a. x is 5?   **b.** x is 8?

*30. In this pattern of loose tiles, there are triangles and squares:
<small>(66, 78)</small>

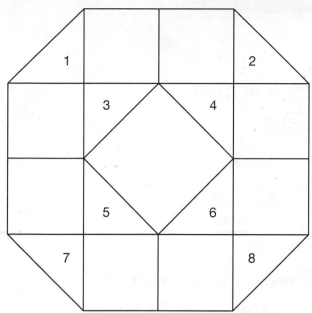

a. What transformation could be performed on triangle 7 to see if it is congruent to triangle 4?

b. What transformation could be performed on triangle 1 to see if it is congruent to triangle 3?

Real-World Connection

Use the table below to answer parts **a–c.**

Airline	Flight Time
Airline A	2 hours 45 minutes
Airline B	3 hours 15 minutes
Airline C	6 hours 35 minutes

a. Maria is taking Airline A, and her flight leaves at 9:00 a.m. What time will she arrive at her destination?

b. How much longer is the flight time for Airline B than Airline A?

c. If Carol took Airline C and arrived at her destination at 10:00 p.m., what time did her flight leave?

- **Tenths and Hundredths on a Number Line**

facts   Power Up A

mental
math

    a. Number Sense: 425 − 175

    b. Number Sense: 4 × 18

    c. Money: Gabriella purchased a sandwich for $3.65 and a beverage for $0.98. What was the total price?

    d. Geometry: How many vertices do 4 hexagons have?

    e. Time: The year 2012 begins on a Sunday. On what day of the week will the year 2013 begin? (Remember that 2012 is a leap year.)

    f. Estimation: Estimate the product of 19 × 31 by rounding one number up and the other number down.

    g. Calculation: 4 × 5, − 5, + 6, ÷ 7

    h. Roman Numerals: Write 24 in Roman numerals.

problem
solving

Choose an appropriate problem-solving strategy to solve this problem. Nalo said, "An inch is less than 10% of a foot." Write a short paragraph explaining why you agree or disagree with Nalo's statement.

We have used decimal numbers to name lengths that include a fraction of a centimeter. For instance, the length of this segment can be written as 23 millimeters or 2.3 centimeters:

Thinking Skill

Generalize

How are rulers and number lines the same? How are they different?

Likewise, on the following number line, the distance between every two whole numbers is divided into ten equal parts. The arrow is pointing to the number three and one tenth, which we can write as a mixed number or as a decimal.

$3\frac{1}{10}$ or 3.1

If the distance between whole numbers on a number line is divided into 100 parts, then points between whole numbers may need to be written with two decimal places. The arrow below is pointing to three and twenty-five hundredths, which can be written as 3.25 or as $3\frac{25}{100}$.

If you inspect a meterstick, you will see that it is divided into 100 centimeters. Each centimeter is $\frac{1}{100}$ of a meter, so a pencil that is 18 cm long is 0.18 m (eighteen hundredths of a meter) long.

Example 1

Santiago is 162 cm tall. What is Santiago's height in meters?

One hundred centimeters equals a meter, so Santiago's height is one meter plus 62 centimeters. Since 62 centimeters is 62 hundredths of a meter, Santiago is **1.62 meters** tall.

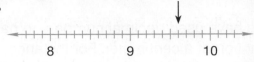

Example 2

Write the decimal number to which each arrow points:

a.

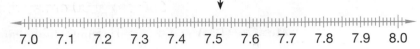

b.

| | 7.0 7.1 7.2 7.3 7.4 7.5 7.6 7.7 7.8 7.9 8.0 |

a. 9.6

b. 7.52

Example 3

a. Round 9.6 to the nearest whole number.

b. Round 7.52 to the nearest tenth.

a. The decimal number 9.6 is between the whole numbers 9 and 10. Halfway from 9 to 10 is 9.5, and 9.6 is greater than 9.5. So 9.6 rounds to **10.**

b. Rounding 7.52 to the nearest tenth is like rounding $7.52 to the nearest ten cents. Just as $7.52 is between $7.50 and $7.60, 7.52 is between 7.5 and 7.6. It is closer to **7.5,** as we can see on the number line in Example 2.

Example 4

Estimate the sum of 4.87 and 3.11 to the nearest whole number.

First we round 4.87 to 5. We round 3.11 to 3. Then we add 5 and 3. The sum is **8.**

Measuring Objects with a Meterstick

Material needed:
- meterstick

a. Using a meterstick, measure the heights and widths of various rectangular objects in the classroom, such as doors, tabletops, desktops, or books. Measure to the nearest centimeter and record each measurement twice: once in centimeters and once in meters.

Here is an example:

| height and width of door | 203 cm (2.03 m) high, 90 cm (0.90 m) wide |

b. Estimate the area of each rectangular object you measured in part **a.** Here is an example:

area of door

200 cm × 90 cm = 18,000 sq. cm

Lesson Practice

a. Mackenzie jumped over a bar that was 167 cm high. How many meters high was the bar?

Write the decimal number and mixed number to which each arrow is pointing:

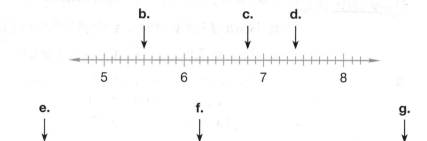

h. Locate 6.8 on the number line and round to the nearest whole number.

i. Round 4.44 to the nearest whole number.

j. Locate 4.4 on the number line and round to the nearest whole number.

k. Estimate the sum of 6.8 and 5.9.

Written Practice   *Distributed and Integrated*

*1. **(Analyze)** All 110 books must be packed in boxes. Each box will hold
(88)   8 books.

   a. How many boxes can be filled?

   b. How many boxes are needed to hold all the books?

*2. **Formulate** What number is five more than the product of six and
(94) seven? Write an expression.

*3. **Explain** Trevor paid $7 for the tape. He received a quarter and
(83) two dimes as change. Tax was 42¢. What was the price of the tape?
Explain how you found your answer.

*4. a. **Represent** Four fifths of the 600 gymnasts did back handsprings.
(70, 95) How many gymnasts did back handsprings? Draw a picture to
illustrate the problem.

b. What percent of the gymnasts did not do back handsprings?

5. **Explain** Mrs. Tyrone is arranging 29 desks into rows. If she starts
(88) by putting 8 desks in each row, how many desks will be in the last row?
Explain how you know.

6. **Analyze** What is the value of two $100 bills, five $10 bills, four $1
(35) bills, 3 dimes, and 1 penny?

7. a. Find the length of this line segment in millimeters.
(69)

b. Find the length of the segment in centimeters. Write the answer as a
decimal number.

```
mm 10    20    30    40
|llllllllll|llllllllll|llllllllll|llllllllll|lll

   _____

|llllllllll|llllllllll|llllllllll|llllllllll|
cm  1     2     3     4
```

8. **Represent** Use words to write 12.67.
(Inv. 4)

*9. a. Round 3834 to the nearest thousand.
(54,
102)

b. Round 38.34 to the nearest whole number.

10. The diameter of a circle is 1 meter. What is the radius of the circle in
(Inv. 2,
21) centimeters?

*11. Find the sum of two hundred eighty-six thousand, five hundred fourteen
(34, 51) and one hundred thirty-seven thousand, two.

12. Seven pairs of beach sandals cost $56. What is the cost of one pair?
(94) What is the cost of ten pairs?

*13. There were 36 children in one line and 24 children in the other line.
(96) What is the average number of children per line?

*14. If the arrow is spun once, what is the probability that it
(Inv. 10) will stop in sector C?

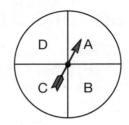

15. $7.486 - (6.47 + 0.5)$ **16.** 40×50
(45, 50)   (86)

17. 41×49 **18.** $2^3 \times 5 \times \sqrt{49}$
(90)   (Inv. 3, 62)

*19.   32   ***20.**   38
(90) $\times\ 17$ (67) $\times\ \ 40$

21. $7 + 4 + 6 + 8 + 5 + 2 + 7 + 3 + k = 47$
(2)

*22. $8\overline{)360}$ ***23.** $4\overline{)810}$ ***24.** $7\overline{)356}$
(65)   (80)   (65)

*25. $6n = \$4.38$ **26.** $7162 \div 9$ **27.** $\dfrac{1414}{2}$
(76)   (76)   (80)

*28. Draw and shade circles to show that 2 equals $\frac{8}{4}$.
(89)

*29. The basketball player was 211 centimeters tall. Write the height of the
(Inv. 2) basketball player in meters.

30. How many square yards of carpeting are needed to cover the floor of a
(Inv. 3, 85) classroom that is 15 yards long and 10 yards wide?

• Fractions Equal to 1 and Fractions Equal to $\frac{1}{2}$

facts　Power Up A

mental math

a. Number Sense: $450 - 175$

b. Number Sense: 50×42

c. Money: Casius gave the clerk $2.00 for lemons that cost $1.62. How much change should he receive?

d. Time: Which date occurs only once every four years?

e. Powers/Roots: $2^3 \div 2$

f. Estimation: Micalynn purchased 4 toothbrushes for $11.56. Round this amount to the nearest dollar and then divide by 4 to estimate the cost per toothbrush.

g. Calculation: $\sqrt{36}$, $\times\, 3$, $+\, 2$, $\div\, 10$, $-\, 1$

h. Roman Numerals: Compare: 19 ◯ XVIII

problem solving

Choose an appropriate problem-solving strategy to solve this problem. At the mall, Dirk saw a display of basketballs that were packaged individually in boxes and stacked. The stack of boxes is shown at right. Dirk was quickly able to figure how many basketballs were in the stack. How many basketballs were in the stack? How might Dirk have figured the number of basketballs without counting each box?

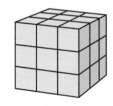

New Concept

Each of the following circles is divided into parts. Together, the parts of each circle make up a whole.

We see that 2 halves is the same as 1 whole. We also see that 3 thirds, 4 fourths, and 5 fifths are ways to say 1 whole. If the numerator (top number) and the denominator (bottom number) of a fraction are the same, the fraction equals 1.

$$1 = \frac{2}{2} \qquad 1 = \frac{3}{3} \qquad 1 = \frac{4}{4} \qquad 1 = \frac{5}{5}$$

Example 1

Which of these fractions equals 1?

$$\frac{1}{6} \qquad \frac{5}{6} \qquad \frac{6}{6} \qquad \frac{7}{6}$$

A fraction equals 1 if its numerator and denominator are equal. The fraction equal to 1 is $\frac{6}{6}$.

Model Use fraction manipulatives to verify that $\frac{6}{6} = 1$.

Example 2

Write a fraction equal to 1 that has a denominator of 7.

A fraction equals 1 if its numerator and denominator are the same. If the denominator is 7, the numerator must also be 7. We write $\frac{7}{7}$.

If the numerator of a fraction is half the denominator, then the fraction equals $\frac{1}{2}$. Notice below that the top number of each fraction illustrated is half of the bottom number of the fraction.

$$\frac{1}{2} \qquad \frac{2}{4} \qquad \frac{3}{6} \qquad \frac{4}{8}$$

If the numerator is less than half the denominator, the fraction is less than $\frac{1}{2}$. If the numerator is greater than half the denominator, the fraction is greater than $\frac{1}{2}$.

Model Use fraction manipulatives to verify that $\frac{5}{10} = \frac{1}{2}$.

Example 3

a. Which fraction below equals $\frac{1}{2}$?

b. Which is less than $\frac{1}{2}$?

c. Which is greater than $\frac{1}{2}$?

$$\frac{3}{7} \qquad \frac{6}{12} \qquad \frac{5}{9}$$

a. Since 6 is half of 12, the fraction equal to $\frac{1}{2}$ is $\frac{6}{12}$.

b. Since 3 is less than half of 7, the fraction less than $\frac{1}{2}$ is $\frac{3}{7}$.

c. Since 5 is greater than half of 9, the fraction greater than $\frac{1}{2}$ is $\frac{5}{9}$.

Example 4

Compare: $\frac{3}{8} \bigcirc \frac{1}{2}$

Since 3 is less than half of 8, we know that $\frac{3}{8}$ is less than $\frac{1}{2}$.

$$\frac{3}{8} < \frac{1}{2}$$

Represent Make a sketch that proves the answer is correct.

Example 5

Round $6\frac{7}{10}$ to the nearest whole number.

Halfway between 6 and 7 is $6\frac{1}{2}$. We know that $6\frac{7}{10}$ is greater than $6\frac{1}{2}$ because $\frac{7}{10}$ is greater than $\frac{5}{10}$, which equals $\frac{1}{2}$.

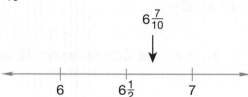

This means $6\frac{7}{10}$ rounds to **7**.

Example 6

Estimate the perimeter and area of this rectangle.

$7\frac{7}{8}$ in.

$4\frac{1}{4}$ in.

First we round each dimension to the nearest whole number of inches. Since $\frac{7}{8}$ is greater than $\frac{1}{2}$, we round $7\frac{7}{8}$ in. up to 8 in. Since $\frac{1}{4}$ is less than $\frac{1}{2}$, we round $4\frac{1}{4}$ in. down to 4 in. Then we use 8 in. and 4 in. to estimate the perimeter and area.

Perimeter: 8 in. + 4 in. + 8 in. + 4 in. = **24 in.**

Area: 8 in. × 4 in. = **32 sq. in.**

Lesson Practice

a. Write a fraction equal to 1 that has a denominator of 6.

b. Multiple Choice Which of these fractions equals 1?

A $\frac{1}{10}$ **B** $\frac{9}{10}$ **C** $\frac{10}{10}$ **D** $\frac{11}{10}$

What fraction name for 1 is shown by each picture?

c.   **d.**

e. Write a fraction equal to $\frac{1}{2}$ with a denominator of 12.

f. Compare: $\frac{9}{20} \bigcirc \frac{1}{2}$

g. **Estimate** Round $5\frac{3}{8}$ to the nearest whole number.

h. Estimate the perimeter and area of a rectangle that is $6\frac{3}{4}$ in. long and $4\frac{3}{8}$ in. wide.

Written Practice   *Distributed and Integrated*

1. **Analyze** Find an even number between 79 and 89 that can be divided by 6 without a remainder.
(64)

2. How many minutes is 3 hours?
(19, 49)

*3. Victor has $8. Dana has $2 less than Victor. How much money do they have altogether?
(94)

*4. **Represent** Write each fraction or mixed number as a decimal number:
(84)

a. $\frac{3}{10}$ **b.** $4\frac{99}{100}$ **c.** $12\frac{1}{1000}$

*5. **Represent** Five eighths of the 40 students wore school colors. How many students wore school colors? Draw a picture to illustrate the problem.
(95)

6. a. What is the diameter of this circle in centimeters?
(21, 69)

    b. What is the radius of this circle in centimeters?

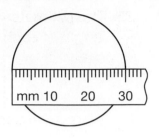

7. The radius of a circle is what percent of the diameter?
(21, Inv. 5)

8. Estimate the product of 49 and 68. Then find the actual product.
(93)

*9. ✎ **Explain** Pavan has filled a pitcher with iced tea for two guests and
(88) himself. The capacity of the pitcher is two quarts. How many 10-ounce
glasses of iced tea can be poured from the pitcher? Explain your answer.

*10. In row 1 there were 6 students, in row 2 there were 4 students, in
(96) row 3 there were 6 students, and in row 4 there were 4 students. What
was the average number of students per row?

*11. Gretchen paid $20 for five identical bottles of fruit juice. She received
(94) $6 in change. What was the price of one bottle of juice?

*12. **Analyze** Find the median, mode, and range of Vonda's game scores.
(97) (Since there is an even number of scores, the median is the average of
the two middle scores.)

100, 80, 90, 85, 100, 90, 100, 100

13. $3.85   **14.**   48   **15.**   16   **16.**   5
(58) $\times$ 7   (90) $\times$ 29   (17)   15   (2)   4

                                                       23   3

17. 60^2 **18.** 59×61 8   7
(62, 86)   (90)   217   2

                                                       20   5

19. $\dfrac{400}{5}$ **20.** $6\overline{)582}$ 6   8
(71)   (65)   + 317   1

21. $9\overline{)\$37.53}$ **22.** $7\overline{)420}$ 4
(76)   (65)   + n

                                                                   45

23. $7.500 - (3.250 - 0.125)$
(43, 45)

*24. **Represent** Draw and shade circles to show that $3\frac{3}{4}$ equals $\frac{15}{4}$.
(89)

25.
(Inv. 2, Inv. 3) The perimeter of this square is 20 inches. What is the length of each side of the square? What is the area of the square?

*26.
(103) Write a fraction equal to 1 with a denominator of 8.

*27.
(Inv. 10) **Explain** If two dot cubes are rolled together, which outcome is more likely: dots totaling 12 or dots totaling 7? Explain your answer.

*28.
(Inv. 2, 102) Songhi measured the paper in her notebook and found that it was 28 cm long. Write the length of her paper in meters.

*29.
(103) **Estimate** Round $12\frac{5}{12}$ to the nearest whole number.

*30.
(23, 98) **a.** **Classify** What is the geometric name for the shape of a cereal box?

b. How many edges does this box have?

c. Describe the angles.

Real-World Connection

Eight students have decided to paint a rectangular mural in the school cafeteria. Five of Mrs. Lowery's students and three of Mr. Rushing's students will be painting equal sections for the mural.

a. Draw a diagram representing how much of the mural each class will paint.

b. Are Mrs. Lowery's or Mr. Rushing's students painting more than half of the mural?

c. Explain your answer for part **b.**

• Changing Improper Fractions to Whole or Mixed Numbers

Power Up

facts   Power Up A

mental math   Think of one cent more or less than quarters in **a–c.**

   a. Number Sense: 425 + 374

   b. Number Sense: 550 − 324

   c. Number Sense: $4.49 + $2.26

   d. Number Sense: 15 × 40

   e. Time: Each section of the test takes 25 minutes. There is a 5-minute break between sections. If the class starts the test at 9:00 a.m., how many sections can the class finish by 10:30 a.m.?

   f. Estimation: Estimate 35 × 25. Round 35 to 40, round 25 down to 20, and then multiply.

   g. Calculation: 2 × 2, square the number, + 4, ÷ 5, − 4

   h. Roman Numerals: Write 34 in Roman numerals.

problem solving   Choose an appropriate problem-solving strategy to solve this problem. Todd rode his bicycle down his 50-foot driveway and counted eight full turns of the front wheel. How many times will the front wheel turn if he rides 100 yards?

New Concept

If the numerator of a fraction is equal to or greater than the denominator, the fraction is an *improper fraction.* All of these fractions are improper fractions:

$$\frac{3}{2} \qquad \frac{5}{4} \qquad \frac{10}{3} \qquad \frac{9}{4} \qquad \frac{5}{5}$$

Model Use fraction manipulatives to show $\frac{3}{2}$ and $\frac{5}{4}$ as mixed numbers.

To write an improper fraction as a whole or mixed number, we divide to find out how many wholes the improper fraction contains. If there is no remainder, we write the improper fraction as a whole number. If there is a remainder, the remainder becomes the numerator in a mixed number.

Example 1

Write $\frac{13}{5}$ as a mixed number. Draw a picture to show that the improper fraction and mixed number are equal.

To find the number of wholes, we divide.

$$\begin{array}{r} 2 \longleftarrow \text{wholes} \\ 5\overline{)13} \\ \underline{10} \\ 3 \longleftarrow \text{remainder of 3} \end{array}$$

This division tells us that $\frac{13}{5}$ equals two wholes with three fifths left over. We write this as **$2\frac{3}{5}$.** We can see that $\frac{13}{5}$ equals $2\frac{3}{5}$ if we draw a picture.

$$\frac{13}{5} \quad = \quad \frac{5}{5} \quad + \quad \frac{5}{5} \quad + \quad \frac{3}{5} \quad = \quad 2\frac{3}{5}$$

Example 2

Write $\frac{10}{3}$ as a mixed number. Then draw a picture to show that the improper fraction and mixed number are equal.

First we divide.

$$\begin{array}{r} 3 \\ 3\overline{)10} \\ \underline{9} \\ 1 \end{array}$$

From the division we see that there are three wholes. One third is left over. We write $3\frac{1}{3}$. Then we draw a picture to show that $\frac{10}{3}$ equals $3\frac{1}{3}$.

$$\frac{10}{3} = 3\frac{1}{3}$$

Formulate Give a real-world example for dividing items into groups of $3\frac{1}{3}$.

Example 3

Write $\frac{12}{4}$ as a whole number. Then draw a picture to show that the improper fraction and whole number are equal.

First we divide.

$$\begin{array}{r} 3 \\ 4\overline{)12} \\ \underline{12} \\ 0 \end{array}$$

We have three wholes and no remainder. Our picture looks like this:

    $\frac{12}{4} = 3$

Discuss Explain how $\frac{4}{4}$ is related to $\frac{12}{4}$.

Lesson Practice

Represent Change each improper fraction to a whole number or to a mixed number. Then draw a picture to show that the improper fraction is equal to the number you wrote.

a. $\frac{7}{2}$ **b.** $\frac{12}{3}$ **c.** $\frac{8}{3}$ **d.** $\frac{15}{5}$

Written Practice   *Distributed and Integrated*

*1. **a.** If the perimeter of a square is 280 feet, how long is each side of the
(Inv. 2)   square?

b. What is the area?

*2. There are 365 days in a common year. How many full weeks are there
(54, 88)   in 365 days?

*3. Nia passed out crayons to 6 of her friends. Each friend received
(88, 94)   3 crayons. There were 2 crayons left for Nia. How many crayons
    did Nia have when she began?

*4. **(Represent)** Three fifths of the 60 trees in the orchard were more than
(95)   10 feet tall. How many trees were more than 10 feet tall? Draw a
picture to illustrate the problem.

5. a. Find the length of this line segment in millimeters.
(69)

b. Find the length of the line segment in centimeters. Write the answer
as a decimal number.

*6. What fraction name for 1 is shown by this circle?
(103)

*7. Round $350,454 to the nearest thousand, to the nearest hundred, and
(20, 54)   to the nearest ten.

*8. Copy this number line. Then make a dot at $\frac{1}{2}$ and label the dot point *A.*
(37, 102)   Make a dot at 1.3 and label the dot point *B.* Make a dot at $1\frac{7}{10}$ and label
the dot point *C.*

```
<-++|++++++++++++|++++++++++++|+++->
    0           1           2
```

*9. **(Represent)** Change the improper fraction $\frac{5}{4}$ to a mixed number. Draw
(104)   a picture to show that the improper fraction and the mixed number are
equal.

* 10. *(Inv. 6)* **Interpret** The bar graph shows the number of students in fourth grade at Sebastian's school. Use the graph to answer the questions that follow.

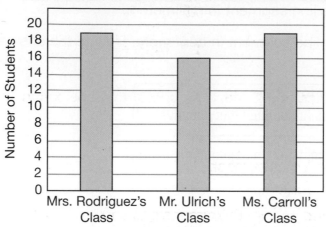

The Number of 4th Graders at Sebastian's School

a. How many fewer students are in Mr. Ulrich's class than in Ms. Carroll's class or in Mrs. Rodriguez's class?

b. Altogether, how many fourth grade students does the bar graph represent?

c. Which measure of the data is greater: the range or the median? Explain your answer.

11. *(49, 67)* The baker used 30 pounds of flour each day to make bread. How many pounds of flour did the baker use in 73 days?

12. *(96)* The chef used 132 pounds of potatoes every 6 days. On average, how many pounds of potatoes were used each day?

13. *(43)* $6.52 + $12 + $1.74 + 26¢

14. *(50)* 3.65 + 2.7 + 0.454 + 2.0

15. *(43, 45)* $80 − ($63.72 + $2)

16. *(52)* 37,614 − 29,148

17. *(61)* $9w = 9 \cdot 26$

* 18. *(62)* 3^4

19. *(85)* 24 × 1000

20. *(48)* 79¢ × 6

21. 50
(86) × 50

22. 51
(90) × 49

23. 47
(90) × 63

24. 4)810
(76)

25. 5)490
(65)

26 6)362
(65, 68)

27. 1435 ÷ √49
(Inv. 3, 80)

*28. How many 8-ounce glasses of milk can be poured from one gallon
(40) of milk?

*29. Round $16\frac{5}{8}$ to the nearest whole number.
(103)

*30. Estimate the area of a window with the dimensions shown.
(Inv. 3)

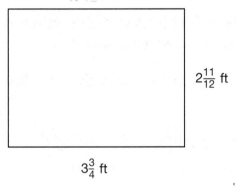

$2\frac{11}{12}$ ft

$3\frac{3}{4}$ ft

Real-World
Connection

Joyce went fishing for crustaceans with her brothers and caught $2\frac{1}{4}$ pounds of crab, $1\frac{1}{4}$ pounds of lobster, and $2\frac{3}{4}$ pounds of shrimp.

a. Write each mixed number as an improper fraction.

b. Use fraction manipulatives or diagrams to show each amount and then find the total number of pounds of crustaceans that Joyce caught.

c. Which crustacean did Joyce catch the most pounds of?

• Dividing by 10

Power Up

facts
Power Up A

mental math
Think of one cent more or less than quarters in **a–c.**

   a. Number Sense: $126 + 375$

   b. Number Sense: $651 - 225$

   c. Number Sense: $\$6.51 + \$2.75$

   d. Money: The atlas cost $16.25. Amol paid for it with a $20 bill. How much change should he receive?

   e. Measurement: Fran drank $1\frac{1}{2}$ quarts of water. How many pints did she drink?

   f. Estimation: Estimate 32×28.

   g. Calculation: $40 \div 4$, $\times 6$, $+ 4$, $\sqrt{}$, $- 8$

   h. Roman Numerals: Compare: XIX $\bigcirc$ 20

problem solving
Choose an appropriate problem-solving strategy to solve this problem. This sequence has an alternating pattern. Copy this sequence on your paper, and continue the sequence to 18. Then describe the pattern in words.

$$0, 5, 3, 8, 6, 11, 9, 14, \ldots$$

New Concept

Thinking Skill

Verify

What are the 4 steps in division?

We have used a four-step procedure to divide by one-digit numbers. We will use the same four-step procedure to divide by two-digit numbers. In this lesson we will learn how to divide by 10.

Divide: $10\overline{)432}$

Ten will not divide into 4 but will divide into 43 four times. In Step 1 we are careful to write the 4 above the 3 in 432.

Step 1: We find $10\overline{)43}$ and write "4."

Step 2: We multiply 4 by 10 and write "40."

Step 3: We subtract 40 from 43 and write "3."

Step 4: We bring down the 2, making 32.

$$\begin{array}{r} 4 \\ 10\overline{)432} \\ \underline{40} \\ 32 \end{array}$$

Repeat:

Step 1: We divide 32 by 10 and write "3."

Step 2: We multiply 3 by 10 and write "30."

Step 3: We subtract 30 from 32 and write "2."

Step 4: There is no number to bring down.

The answer is 43 with a remainder of 2.

$$\begin{array}{r} \mathbf{43\ R\ 2} \\ 10\overline{)432} \\ \underline{40} \\ 32 \\ \underline{30} \\ 2 \end{array}$$

Thinking Skill

Discuss

Why do we place the digit 4 in the tens place of the quotient?

Notice that the remainder is the last digit of the dividend. When dividing by 10, there will be no remainder if the last digit of the whole-number dividend is zero. Otherwise, the remainder will be the last digit of the dividend.

Justify How can we check the answer?

Lesson Practice Divide:

a. $10\overline{)73}$ b. $10\overline{)342}$

c. $10\overline{)243}$ d. $10\overline{)720}$

e. $10\overline{)561}$ f. $10\overline{)380}$

g. **Multiple Choice** Which of these numbers can be divided by 10 without a remainder?

  A 365   **B** 472   **C** 560   **D** 307

Written Practice   *Distributed and Integrated*

1. How many 6¢ erasers can be bought with 2 quarters?
(88)

2. Two quarters are what percent of a dollar?
(Inv. 5)

3. D'Jmon has $8. Parisa has $2 more than D'Jmon. How much money
(94) do they have altogether?

* 4. (Represent) Three fourths of the 20 students in a class participate
(95) in an after-school activity. What number of students participate?
Draw a picture to illustrate and solve the problem.

* 5. (Justify) If one card is drawn from a standard deck of playing cards,
(Inv. 10) is it more likely that the card will be a "number card" or a "face card"?
Explain your answer.

* 6. Write a fraction equal to one that has a denominator of 10.
(103)

7. (Represent) Write 86.743 with words.
(84)

* 8. (Estimate) There are many ways to make an estimate. Describe two
(59) different ways to estimate the difference of 496 subtracted from 605.

* 9. Change each improper fraction to a whole number or a mixed number:
(104)
a. $\frac{9}{5}$ **b.** $\frac{9}{3}$ **c.** $\frac{9}{2}$

* 10. (Estimate) Soon after James Marshall discovered gold at John Sutter's
(94, 105) mill in California on January 24, 1848, the "gold rush" began. If 2400
people came in 10 days, about how many came each day? About how
many people came in 1 week?

11. Find the length of this segment to the nearest tenth of a centimeter.
(69) Write the length as a decimal number.

* 12. A miner bought 6 bags of flour for $4.20 per bag and 8 pounds of salt
(94) for 12¢ per pound. How much money did the miner spend?

* 13. a. Which digit in 86.743 is in the tenths place?
(91, 102)

   b. Is 86.74 closer to 86.7 or 86.8?

* 14. Draw a trapezoid.
(92)

15. $4.867 - (2.8 + 0.56)$
(45, 50)

16. 30^2 **17.** 54×29
(62, 86)   (90)

* 18. $10\overline{)230}$ **19.** $7\overline{)2383}$
(105)   (80)

* 20. $372 \div 10$ **21.** $8c = \$5.76$ **22.**   12
(105)   (41)   (17)   26
                                                                  13
23.   351,426   **24.**   \$50.00   35
(51)   + 449,576   (52)   − \$49.49   110
                                                                   8
25.   \$12.49   **26.**   73   + 15
(48)   ×   8   (90)   × 62

* 27. a. A field is 300 feet long and 200 feet wide. How many
(Inv. 2)   feet of fencing would be needed to go around the field?

   b. ✏️ **Explain** Is this problem about perimeter or area?
   How do you know?

* 28. Which letters in **MATH** have one line of symmetry? Which have two lines
(79)   of symmetry? Which have rotational symmetry?

* 29. Which transformation can make the digit 6 look like the digit 9?
(73)

*30. (Interpret) Use this chart to answer parts **a–c.**
(101)

Mileage Chart

	Atlanta	Boston	Chicago	Kansas City	Los Angeles	New York City	Wash., D.C.
Chicago	674	963		499	2054	802	671
Dallas	795	1748	917	489	1387	1552	1319
Denver	1398	1949	996	600	1059	1771	1616
Los Angeles	2182	2979	2054	1589		2786	2631
New York City	841	206	802	1198	2786		233
St. Louis	541	1141	289	257	1845	948	793

a. The distance from Los Angeles to Boston is how much greater than the distance from Los Angeles to New York City?

b. Heather is planning a trip from Chicago to Dallas to Los Angeles to Chicago. How many miles will her trip be?

c. There are three empty boxes in the chart. What number would go in these boxes?

Real-World Connection

There are 728 students in the auditorium. Ten students can fit in each row. The students are to fill as many rows as possible.

a. Divide 728 by 10.

b. How many rows are filled?

c. How many rows are only partly filled? Why?

LESSON 106

• Evaluating Expressions

facts   Power Up A

mental math   Find each fraction of 24.

     a. Fractional Parts: $\frac{1}{2}$ of 24

     b. Fractional Parts: $\frac{1}{3}$ of 24

     c. Fractional Parts: $\frac{1}{4}$ of 24

     d. Number Sense: 4×18

     e. Money: Stefano has $3.75 in his pocket and $4.51 in his piggy bank. Altogether, how much money does Stefano have?

     f. Estimation: Estimate 62×19.

     g. Calculation: 5^2, $+ 10$, $- 3$, $\div 4$, $\times 2$

     h. Roman Numerals:[1] Write CX in our number system.

problem solving   Choose an appropriate problem-solving strategy to solve this problem. Two cups make a pint. Two pints make a quart. Two quarts make a half gallon, and two half gallons make a gallon. A pint of water weighs about one pound. Find the approximate weight of a cup, a quart, a half gallon, and a gallon of water.

New Concept

Math Language

We can *evaluate* an expression by replacing a letter with a number. Then we perform the operations to simplify the expression.

What is the value of the following expression?

$$n + 7$$

The value of the expression depends on the value of *n*. If we know a value for *n,* then we can **evaluate** the expression by adding 7 to the value of *n.*

---

[1] In Lessons 106–120, the Mental Math section "Roman Numerals" reviews concepts from Appendix Topic B. You may skip these Mental Math problems if you have not covered Appendix Topic B.

If *r* is 5, then what is the value of each of these expressions?

    a. *r* + 3   **b.** *r* − 3   **c.** 3*r*

We are told that the value of *r* is 5. To find the value of each expression, we substitute 5 in place of *r* and perform the calculation.

    a. *r* + 3   **b.** *r* − 3   **c.** 3*r*

     5 + 3 = **8**   5 − 3 = **2**   3 × 5 = **15**

Lesson Practice

a. If *m* equals 12, then what is the value of *m* − 10?

b. Evaluate *a* + *b* when *a* = 9 and *b* = 15.

c. What is the value of *xy* when *x* is 6 and *y* is 7?

d. What is the value of w^2 when *w* is 5?

e. If *A* = *lw*, then what is *A* when *l* is 8 and *w* is 4?

f. Evaluate $\frac{m}{n}$, using *m* = 12 and *n* = 3.

g. Find the value of $\sqrt{t}$ when *t* is 16.

Written Practice   *Distributed and Integrated*

* 1.
(94)
  Use this information to answer parts **a–c.**

    Nara has 6 cats. Each cat eats half of a can of food each day. Cat food costs 47¢ per can.

  a. How many cans of cat food are eaten each day?

  b. How much does Nara spend on cat food per day?

  c. How much does Nara spend on cat food in a week?

* 2.
(63)
  a. Sketch a right triangle. Label the vertices *A*, *B*, and *C*, so that *C* is at the right angle.

  b. Name two segments that are perpendicular.

  c. Name two segments that intersect but are not perpendicular.

  d. Can a triangle have two parallel sides?

* 3. **(Represent)** Four students are planning a race. Draw a tree diagram to
(39) show all of the different ways that Quinton, Katelyn, and Nafuna can finish
the race if Rita wins the race. Then list all the possible combinations.

| Quinton | Katelyn | Nafuna | Rita |

4. If the perimeter of a square classroom is 120 feet, then how long is
(Inv. 3, 86) each side of the classroom? What is the area of the classroom?

* 5. **(Represent)** Math was the favorite class of five sevenths of the
(95) 28 students. Math was the favorite class of how many students?
Draw a picture to illustrate the problem.

* 6. **(Analyze)** Something is wrong with this sign. Draw
(99) two different signs to show how to correct the error.

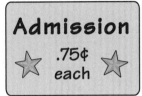

7. If the radius of a circle is $1\frac{1}{2}$ inches, then what is the diameter of the
(21, 39) circle?

8. **(Represent)** Use words to write 523.43.
(Inv. 4)

9. **(Estimate)** Colin used rounding to estimate the product of 61 and 397.
(93) What estimate did Colin make? Explain your answer.

* 10. Change each improper fraction to a whole number or a mixed number:
(104)
    a. $\frac{10}{10}$ **b.** $\frac{10}{5}$ **c.** $\frac{10}{3}$

* 11. LaTonya went to the fair with $20. She paid $6.85 for a necklace and
(94) $4.50 for lunch. Then she bought bottled water for 75¢. How much
money did she have left?

* 12. **(Explain)** Clara bought two dolls priced at $7.40 each. The tax was
(83) 98¢. She paid the clerk with a $20 bill. How much change did she get
back? Explain why your answer is reasonable.

13. The big truck that transported the Ferris wheel could go only 140 miles
(60) in 5 hours. What was the truck's average speed in miles per hour?

*14. Compare: $\dfrac{49}{100}$ ○ $\dfrac{1}{2}$
(103)

*15. a. **Estimate** Round $12.25 to the nearest dollar.
(20, 102)
   b. Round 12.25 to the nearest whole number.

*16. a. Which digit in 36.47 is in the tenths place?
(91, 102)
   b. **Estimate** Is 36.47 closer to 36.4 or to 36.5?

17. 73.48   **18.** $65.00   **19.** 24,375   **20.** $3.68
(50)   5.63   (52)   − $29.87   (52)   − 8,416   (58) ×   9
      + 17.9

21. 89 × 91   **22.** 3)$\overline{3210}$ ***23.** 10)$\overline{4300}$
(90)   (76)   (105)

24. 6)$\overline{\$57.24}$ **25.** 765 ÷ 9   ***26.** 563 ÷ 10
(76)   (65)   (105)

*27. Find the value of n^2 when n is 90.
(106)

*28. Find the value of $\dfrac{m}{\sqrt{m}}$ when m is 36.
(106)

*29. a. **Multiple Choice** The sum of $6\frac{3}{4}$ and $5\frac{3}{5}$ is between which two
(59)   numbers?

   A 5 and 7   **B** 30 and 40   **C** 0 and 2   **D** 11 and 13

   b. Explain your answer for part **a.**

*30. The African bush elephant is the heaviest land mammal on Earth. Even
(77) though it eats only twigs, leaves, fruit, and grass, an African bush
elephant can weigh 7 tons. Seven tons is how many pounds?

• Adding and Subtracting Fractions with Common Denominators

Power Up

facts   Power Up B

mental math   Find each fraction of 30 in **a–c**.

   a. Fractional Parts: $\frac{1}{2}$ of 30

   b. Fractional Parts: $\frac{1}{3}$ of 30

   c. Fractional Parts: $\frac{1}{5}$ of 30

   d. Number Sense: 50×28

   e. Time: The soccer match ended at 1:15 p.m. The match had started $1\frac{1}{2}$ hours earlier. When did the match begin?

   f. Estimation: To estimate 26×19, round 26 down to 25, round 19 up to 20, and then multiply.

   g. Calculation: 5×2, $\times 10$, $\div 2$, $- 1$, $\sqrt{}$

   h. Roman Numerals: Write LXV in our number system. 65

problem solving   Choose an appropriate problem-solving strategy to solve this problem. In parts of the country where "daylight saving time" is observed, we follow the rule "spring forward, fall back." This rule means we turn the clock forward one hour in the spring and back one hour in the fall. Officially, clocks are reset at 2 a.m. on a Sunday. How many hours long are each of those Sundays when the clocks are reset?

New Concept

When adding fractions, it helps to think of the denominators as objects such as apples. Just as 1 apple plus 1 apple equals 2 apples, 1 third plus 1 third equals 2 thirds.

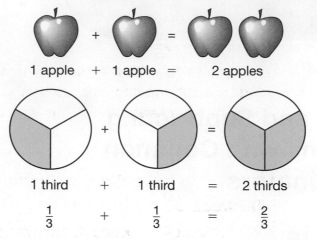

1 apple + 1 apple = 2 apples

1 third + 1 third = 2 thirds

$$\frac{1}{3} + \frac{1}{3} = \frac{2}{3}$$

When we add fractions, we add the numerators (top numbers). We do not add the denominators (bottom numbers).

Example 1

Blake mixed $\frac{3}{5}$ of a pound of cashews with $\frac{1}{5}$ of a pound of pecans. What is the weight in pounds of the cashew and pecan mixture?

We add only the top numbers. Three fifths plus one fifth is four fifths. The weight of the cashew and pecan mixture is $\frac{4}{5}$ **of a pound.**

$$\frac{3}{5} + \frac{1}{5} = \frac{4}{5}$$

Likewise, when we subtract fractions, we subtract only the numerators. The denominator does not change. For example, five sevenths minus two sevenths is three sevenths.

$$\frac{5}{7} - \frac{2}{7} = \frac{3}{7}$$

Example 2

To make a small bow for a present, D'Nietra cut $\frac{1}{5}$ of a yard of ribbon from a length of ribbon that was $\frac{3}{5}$ of a yard long. What is the length of the ribbon that was not used for the bow?

We subtract only the numerators. Three fifths minus one fifth is two fifths. The length of the ribbon not used for the bow is $\frac{2}{5}$ **of a yard.**

$$\frac{3}{5} - \frac{1}{5} = \frac{2}{5}$$

Discuss How can we check the answer?

Recall that a mixed number is a whole number plus a fraction, such as $2\frac{3}{5}$. To add mixed numbers, we add the fraction parts and then the whole-number parts.

Example 3

Add: $2\frac{3}{5} + 3\frac{1}{5}$

It is helpful to write the numbers one above the other. First we add the fractions and get $\frac{4}{5}$. Then we add the whole numbers and get 5. The sum of the mixed numbers is $5\frac{4}{5}$.

$$\begin{array}{r} 2\frac{3}{5} \\ +3\frac{1}{5} \\ \hline 5\frac{4}{5} \end{array}$$

Example 4

Subtract: $5\frac{2}{3} - 1\frac{1}{3}$

We subtract the second number from the first number. To do this, we write the first number above the second number. We subtract the fractions and get $\frac{1}{3}$. Then we subtract the whole numbers and get 4. The difference is $4\frac{1}{3}$.

$$\begin{array}{r} 5\frac{2}{3} \\ -1\frac{1}{3} \\ \hline 4\frac{1}{3} \end{array}$$

Example 5

In the race Martin rode his bike $7\frac{1}{2}$ miles and ran $2\frac{1}{2}$ miles. Altogether, how far did Martin ride his bike and run?

This is a story about combining. We add $7\frac{1}{2}$ miles and $2\frac{1}{2}$ miles. The two half miles combine to make a whole mile. The total distance is **10 miles.**

$$\begin{array}{r} 7\frac{1}{2} \\ +2\frac{1}{2} \\ \hline 9\frac{2}{2} = 10 \end{array}$$

Lesson Practice Find each sum or difference:

a. $\frac{1}{3} + \frac{1}{3}$ b. $\frac{1}{4} + \frac{2}{4}$ c. $\frac{3}{10} + \frac{4}{10}$

d. $\frac{2}{3} - \frac{1}{3}$ e. $\frac{3}{4} - \frac{2}{4}$ f. $\frac{9}{10} - \frac{6}{10}$

g. $2\frac{1}{4} + 4\frac{2}{4}$ h. $5\frac{3}{8} + 1\frac{2}{8}$ i. $8 + 1\frac{2}{5}$

j. $4\frac{3}{5} - 1\frac{1}{5}$ k. $9\frac{3}{4} - 4\frac{2}{4}$ l. $12\frac{8}{9} - 3\frac{3}{9}$

m. How much is three eighths plus four eighths?

n. The troop hiked to the end of the trail and back. If the trail was $3\frac{1}{2}$ miles long, how far did the troop hike?

*1. **Justify** Hayley bought 5 tickets for $2.75 each. She paid for them
(83) with a $20 bill. How much change should she receive? Explain why
your answer is reasonable.

2. If fifty cents is divided equally among 3 friends, there will be some
(88) cents left. How many cents will be left?

3. What is the difference when four hundred nine is subtracted from
(30) nine hundred four?

*4. **Represent** Two fifths of the 45 stamps were from Brazil. How
(95) many stamps were from Brazil? Draw a picture to illustrate the
problem.

*5. a. Find the length of this line segment in millimeters.
(69)
b. Find the length of the segment in centimeters.

*6. a. The pizza was cut into 10 equal slices. The entire sliced
(Inv. 5, pizza shows what fraction name for 1?
103)
b. One slice of the pizza is what percent of the whole
pizza?

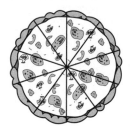

*7. Multiple Choice If a number cube is tossed once, which of these is
(Inv. 10) the most likely outcome?

   A 1   **B** 3
   C a number greater than 1   **D** a number less than 3

8. **Estimate** Round 5167 to the nearest thousand.
(54)

*9. Change the improper fraction $\frac{9}{4}$ to a mixed number.
(104)

* 10. Multiple Choice Which of these fractions is *not* equal to 1?
(103)

A $\frac{12}{12}$ B $\frac{11}{11}$ C $\frac{11}{10}$ D $\frac{10}{10}$

11. In the summer of 1926, there were only 17 stores in the town. Today
(48, 72) there are 8 times as many stores in the town. How many stores are in
the town today?

12. The wagon train took 9 days to make the 243-mile journey. What was
(96) the average number of miles traveled per day?

* 13. ✏️ **Explain** On Saturday Jacinda played outside for $1\frac{1}{2}$ hours and
(107) played board games for $2\frac{1}{2}$ hours. Altogether, how much time did
Jacinda spend playing outside and playing board games? Explain
how you found your answer.

* 14. Estimate Round $8\frac{21}{100}$ to the nearest whole number.
(37, 59)

15.   36.31   *** 16.** $\frac{5}{8} + \frac{2}{8}$ **17.**   6
(50) $-\ \ 7.4$ (107)   (2)   5
                                                            4
                                                            3
* 18. $\frac{9}{10} - \frac{2}{10}$ *** 19.** $3\frac{2}{5} + 1\frac{1}{5}$ $+\ n$
(107)   (107)   ——
                                                            25

20. 27×32 **21.** 62×15 **22.** $7^2 + \sqrt{49}$
(90)   (90)   (Inv. 3, 62)

* 23. $10\overline{)460}$ **24.** $9\overline{)\$27.36}$ **25.** $6w = 2316$
(105)   (76, 80)   (41, 76)

26. $1543 \div 7$ *** 27.** $532 \div 10$ **28.** $\frac{256}{8}$
(80)   (105)   (65)

* 29. a. How many square feet of shingles are needed to cover a rectangular
(Inv. 3, 86)   roof that is 40 feet wide and 60 feet long?

b. Is this problem about area or perimeter? How do you know?

30. Shaun walked $2\frac{1}{5}$ miles on Monday. He walked $3\frac{4}{5}$ miles on Wednesday.
(107) How many more miles did Shaun walk on Wednesday than on Monday?

- ## Formulas
- ## Distributive Property

facts   Power Up B

mental math   Find each fraction of 36 in **a–c.**

   a. Fractional Parts: $\frac{1}{2}$ of 36

   b. Fractional Parts: $\frac{1}{3}$ of 36

   c. Fractional Parts: $\frac{1}{4}$ of 36

   d. Number Sense: $83 - 68$

   e. Geometry: What is the perimeter of a hexagon with sides that are each 5 cm long?

   f. Estimation: Camille is cutting lengths of yarn that are each $7\frac{3}{4}$ inches long. If she must cut 6 pieces of yarn, about how many inches of yarn will she need?

   g. Calculation: $10 \div 2, \times 8, - 4, \div 6$

   h. Roman Numerals: Write CL in our number system.

problem solving   Choose an appropriate problem-solving strategy to solve this problem. In this sequence, each term is the sum of the two preceding terms. Copy this sequence and find the next four terms.

$$1, 1, 2, 3, 5, 8, \underline{\hspace{1em}}, \underline{\hspace{1em}}, \underline{\hspace{1em}}, \underline{\hspace{1em}}, \ldots$$

Formulas   Recall that we find the area of a rectangle by multiplying its length by its width.

$$Area = length \times width$$

This expression is a *formula* for finding the area of any rectangle. Usually formulas are written so that a letter represents each measure.

Below we list several common formulas. In these formulas, *P* stands for perimeter, and *s* represents the side length of a square.

Some Common Formulas

Area of a rectangle	$A = lw$
Perimeter of a rectangle	$P = 2(l + w)$ $P = 2l + 2w$
Area of a square	$A = s^2$
Perimeter of a square	$P = 4s$

Some figures are combinations of rectangles. In Example 1, we see that the floor area of the house can be found by dividing the figure into rectangles and then adding the areas of the rectangles.

Example 1

The diagram shows the blueprint of a one-story house.

   a. What is the perimeter of the house?

   b. What is the floor area of the house?

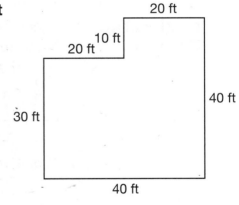

   a. The perimeter of the house is the distance around the house. We add the lengths of the six sides.

$$30 + 40 + 40 + 20 + 10 + 20 = 160$$

Adding the lengths of the sides, we find that the perimeter of the house is **160 ft.**

   b. To find the floor area, we first divide the figure into two rectangles. We show one way to do this on the next page.

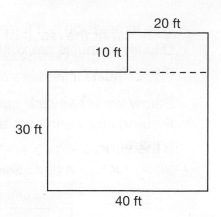

We have divided the figure with dashes, and we have labeled the length and width of both rectangles. Now we find the area of each rectangle.

$$
\begin{array}{r}
\text{Small rectangle} = 200 \text{ sq. ft} \\
+ \text{ Large rectangle} = 1200 \text{ sq. ft} \\
\hline
\text{Total Area of Figure} = 1400 \text{ sq. ft}
\end{array}
$$

Adding the areas of the two rectangles, we find that the total floor area is **1400 sq. ft.**

Distributive Property

There are two formulas for the perimeter of a rectangle. One of the formulas is

$$P = 2(l + w)$$

This formula tells us to add the length and width of a rectangle and then multiply by 2. Applying this formula to the rectangle below, we add 8 cm to 5 cm and get 13 cm. Then we double 13 cm and get 26 cm.

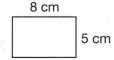

The other formula for the perimeter of a rectangle is

$$P = 2l + 2w$$

This formula tells us to double the length, double the width, and then add the results. Applying this formula to the same rectangle, we double 8 cm and get 16 cm. Then we double 5 cm and get 10 cm. Then we add 16 cm to 10 cm and get 26 cm.

We see that the result of our calculations is the same using either formula for the perimeter of a rectangle. The equality of these two formulas illustrates an important property of mathematics called the **Distributive Property.**

$$2(l + w) = 2l + 2w$$

In the expression $2(l + w)$, both l and w are multiplied by 2. In other words, the multiplication by 2 is distributed over both l and w.

$$2(l + w)$$

When we multiply 2 by l, the product is $2l$.

When we multiply 2 by w, the product is $2w$.

Example 2

Use the Distributive Property to multiply:

$$4(20 + 3)$$

This problem is the same as 4×23, except that 23 is written as $20 + 3$. We are used to adding 20 and 3 before multiplying, but the Distributive Property allows us to multiply first and then add the products.

$$4(20 + 3) = 80 + 12 = 92$$

Thinking Skill

Evaluate

Why is 4×23 the same as $4(20 + 3)$?

Lesson Practice

The figure below shows the boundary of a garden. Refer to the figure to solve problems **a** and **b**.

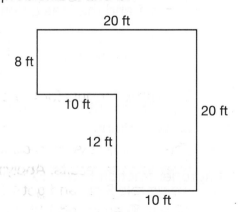

20 ft

8 ft

10 ft

20 ft

12 ft

10 ft

a. How many feet of wire fence are needed to enclose the garden along its boundary?

b. What is the area of the garden?

c. Use the Distributive Property to multiply:

$$6(10 + 6)$$

d. Use the formula $P = 2(l + w)$ to find the perimeter of a rectangle that is 15 cm long and 10 cm wide.

e. Use the formula $A = s^2$ to find the area of a square with sides 20 feet long.

Written Practice
Distributed and Integrated

*1. **(Analyze)** Cody bought 8 pounds of oranges. He gave the storekeeper a
(94) $5 bill and received $1.96 in change. What did 1 pound of oranges cost? What is the first step in solving this problem?

2. After baking a dozen raisin muffins, Ethan ate two muffins for a snack.
(94) Then he placed half of the remaining muffins in the freezer. How many muffins did Ethan place in the freezer?

3. What number is six less than the product of five and four?
(94)

4. Two thirds of the 12 guitar strings were out of tune. How many guitar
(95) strings were out of tune? Draw a picture to illustrate the problem.

*5. What is the probability that a rolled dot cube will stop with exactly
(Inv. 10) two dots on top?

*6. Write a fraction equal to 1 and that has a denominator of 5.
(103)

7. **(Represent)** Use words to write $397\frac{3}{4}$.
(35)

8. Estimate the sum of 4178 and 6899 by rounding both numbers to the
(59) nearest thousand before adding.

*9. Change each improper fraction to a whole number or a mixed number:
(104)
  a. $\frac{7}{3}$ **b.** $\frac{8}{4}$ **c.** $\frac{9}{5}$

*10. The hiking club went on hikes of 8 miles, 15 miles, 11 miles, and
(96) 18 miles. What was the average length of the club's hikes?

* 11. For the first 3 hours, the hikers hiked at 3 miles per hour. For the next
(57, 94) 2 hours, they hiked at 4 miles per hour. If the total trip was 25 miles, how far did they still have to go?

12. What percent of a quart is a pint?
(40, Inv. 5)

13. 41.6 + 13.17 + 9.2
(50)

14. $h + 8.7 = 26.47$
(50)

* 15. $6\frac{3}{8} + 4\frac{2}{8}$
(107)

* 16. $4\frac{7}{10} - 1\frac{6}{10}$
(107)

* 17. We may write 48 as 40 + 8. Use the Distributive Property to find 5(40 + 8).
(108)

* 18. (Analyze) Two fifths of the students rode the bus, and one fifth
(107) traveled by car. What fraction of the students either rode the bus or traveled by car?

19. $\$0.48 \times 5$
(48)

20. 80^2
(62, 86)

21. $\sqrt{25} \times \sqrt{25}$
(Inv. 3)

22. $4d = \$6.36$
(41, 76)

* 23. $10\overline{)520}$
(105)

24. $\frac{175}{5}$
(65)

* 25. What is the perimeter and area of this square?
(Inv. 2, Inv. 3)

10 in.

* 26. If a 3 in. by 4 in. rectangle is cut from the square in problem **25,** then
(Inv. 3, 108) what is the perimeter and area of the remaining figure?

* 27. The tabletop was 76 cm above the floor. The tabletop was how many
(69, 102) meters above the floor?

*28.  **Interpret** Use the line graph to answer parts **a–c**.
(Inv. 6, 97)

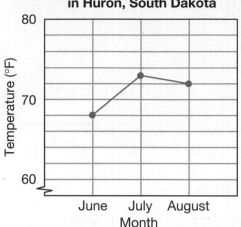

**Average Summer Temperatures
in Huron, South Dakota**

a. Write the names of the months in order from warmest to coolest.

b. How many degrees warmer is the average temperature during July than the average temperature during June?

c. Write a sentence that explains how the mean temperature compares to the median temperature.

*29. There were $3\frac{4}{5}$ potpies in the chef's kitchen. Then the chef removed $1\frac{3}{5}$
(107) of the potpies. How many potpies remained in the chef's kitchen?

*30. Multiple Choice The mixed numbers $5\frac{3}{8}$ and $7\frac{4}{5}$ do not have common
(103) denominators, but we know their sum is between which two numbers?

A 14 and 16   **B** 12 and 14

C 10 and 12   **D** 5 and 8

Early Finishers

Real-World Connection

Cardinal Elementary is preparing the stage for a school play. The stage will be covered with hay. The rectangular stage has a length of 12 feet and a width of 14 feet.

a. How much area must be covered with hay?

b. The perimeter of the stage will be outlined with grass. Use the formula 2(*l* + *w*) to find the number of feet the grass will cover.

LESSON
109

• Equivalent Fractions

facts   Power Up B

mental math   Find each fraction of 40 in **a–c.**

   a. Fractional Parts: $\frac{1}{2}$ of 40

   b. Fractional Parts: $\frac{1}{4}$ of 40

   c. Fractional Parts: $\frac{1}{10}$ of 40

   d. Money: S'Vanna gave the clerk a $10 bill for a half gallon of milk that cost $1.95. How much change should she receive?

   e. Time: Nia was born on a Monday in April 2000. On what day of the week was her first birthday?

   f. Estimation: Estimate the area of the rectangle shown at right.

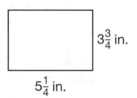

$3\frac{3}{4}$ in.

$5\frac{1}{4}$ in.

   g. Calculation: $\sqrt{64}$, − 3, × 7, − 3, ÷ 8

   h. Roman Numerals: Write XL in our number system.

problem solving   Choose an appropriate problem-solving strategy to solve this problem. There are four parking spaces (1, 2, 3, and 4) in the row nearest to the entrance of the building. Suppose only two of the four parking spaces are filled. What are the combinations of two parking spaces that could have cars in them?

New Concept

Math Language

Equivalent is another word for equal. For example, $\frac{1}{2}$ and $\frac{2}{4}$ are equivalent fractions, as well as equal fractions.

Equal portions of each circle below have been shaded. We see that different fractions are used to name the shaded portions.

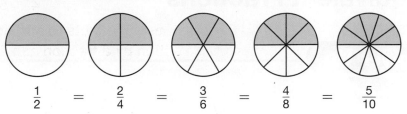

$$\frac{1}{2} \quad = \quad \frac{2}{4} \quad = \quad \frac{3}{6} \quad = \quad \frac{4}{8} \quad = \quad \frac{5}{10}$$

These fractions all name the same amount. Different fractions that name the same amount are called **equivalent fractions**.

Example 1

The rectangle on the left has three equal parts. We see that two parts are shaded, so two thirds of the figure is shaded.

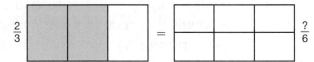

The rectangle on the right has six equal parts. How many parts must be shaded so that the same fraction of this rectangle is shaded?

We see that **four parts** out of six must be shaded. This means two thirds is the same as four sixths.

Thinking Skill

Conclude

Would we use a translation, a reflection, or a rotation to decide if the shaded areas of the rectangles are congruent?

$$\frac{2}{3} \text{ and } \frac{4}{6} \text{ are equivalent fractions.}$$

Example 2

What equivalent fractions are shown at right?

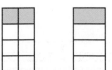

An equal portion of each rectangle is shaded. The rectangles shown are equal.

$$\frac{2}{8} = \frac{1}{4}$$

Verify

What property states that we can multiply any number by 1 and the answer is that number?

We remember that when we multiply a number by 1, the answer equals the number we multiplied.

$$2 \times 1 = 2 \qquad 2000 \times 1 = 2000 \qquad \frac{1}{2} \times 1 = \frac{1}{2}$$

We also remember that there are many ways to write "1."

$$1 = \frac{2}{2} = \frac{3}{3} = \frac{4}{4} = \frac{5}{5} = \frac{6}{6} = \cdots$$

We can use these two facts to find equivalent fractions. If we multiply a fraction by a fraction name for 1, the product is an equivalent fraction.

$$\frac{1}{2} \times \mathbf{1}\,\frac{2}{2} = \frac{2}{4} \qquad \begin{array}{l}(1 \times 2 = 2) \\ (2 \times 2 = 4)\end{array}$$

By multiplying $\frac{1}{2}$ by $\frac{2}{2}$, which is a fraction name for 1, we find that $\frac{1}{2}$ equals $\frac{2}{4}$. Notice that we multiply numerator by numerator and denominator by denominator. We can find other fractions equal to $\frac{1}{2}$ by multiplying by other fraction names for 1:

$$\frac{1}{2} \times \mathbf{1}\,\frac{3}{3} = \frac{3}{6} \qquad \frac{1}{2} \times \mathbf{1}\,\frac{4}{4} = \frac{4}{8} \qquad \frac{1}{2} \times \mathbf{1}\,\frac{5}{5} = \frac{5}{10}$$

Example 3

Find four fractions equal to $\frac{1}{3}$ by multiplying $\frac{1}{3}$ by $\frac{2}{2}, \frac{3}{3}, \frac{4}{4},$ and $\frac{5}{5}$.

$$\frac{1}{3} \times \frac{2}{2} = \frac{\mathbf{2}}{\mathbf{6}} \qquad\qquad \frac{1}{3} \times \frac{3}{3} = \frac{\mathbf{3}}{\mathbf{9}}$$

$$\frac{1}{3} \times \frac{4}{4} = \frac{\mathbf{4}}{\mathbf{12}} \qquad\qquad \frac{1}{3} \times \frac{5}{5} = \frac{\mathbf{5}}{\mathbf{15}}$$

Each of our answers is a fraction equal to $\frac{1}{3}$.

Lesson Practice   Name the equivalent fractions shown:

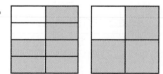

a.

b.

Draw pictures to show that the following pairs of fractions are equivalent:

c. $\dfrac{2}{4} = \dfrac{1}{2}$ **d.** $\dfrac{4}{6} = \dfrac{2}{3}$ **e.** $\dfrac{2}{8} = \dfrac{1}{4}$

Find four equivalent fractions for each fraction below. To do this, multiply each fraction by $\dfrac{2}{2}$, $\dfrac{3}{3}$, $\dfrac{4}{4}$, and $\dfrac{5}{5}$.

f. $\dfrac{1}{4}$ **g.** $\dfrac{5}{6}$ **h.** $\dfrac{2}{5}$ **i.** $\dfrac{1}{10}$

Written Practice

Distributed and Integrated

1. **Interpret** The pictograph shows the number of motor vehicles that
(Inv. 6) were driven past Sylvia's home during 1 hour. Use the pictograph to answer the questions that follow.

Type of Vehicle	Number of Vehicles
Cars	⬭⬭⬭⬭⬭⬭
Trucks	⬭⬭
Mopeds	◖
Motorcycles	⬭◖

Key: ⬭ = 4 vehicles

a. What kind of vehicle was driven past Sylvia's home two times?

b. Write a word sentence that compares the number of trucks to the number of cars.

c. Suppose ten bicyclists rode past Sylvia's house. In the pictograph, how many symbols would be needed to show the number of bicycles? Explain your answer.

*2. What number is six less than the sum of seven and eight? Write an
(94) expression.

*3. Nell read three tenths of 180 pages in one day. How many pages did
(95) she read in one day?

4. The thermometer shows the temperature of a warm
(18) October day in Buffalo, New York. What temperature does
the thermometer show?

5. A circular disc, divided into 8 equal pieces, represents what fraction
(103) name for 1?

6. a. What is the diameter of this dime?
(21, 69)
  b. What is the radius of the dime?

  c. What is the diameter of the dime in centimeters?

7. There are 11 players on a football team, so when two teams play, there
(32) are 22 players on the field at one time. Across the county on a Friday
night in October, many games are played. The table shows the number
of players on the field for a given number of games. How many players
are on the field in 5 games? 10 games?

Number of games	1	2	3	4	5
Number of players	22	44	66	88	?

8. Rick left home in the afternoon at the time shown on the
(19) clock and arrived at a friend's house 15 minutes later. At
what time did Rick arrive at his friend's house?

*9. (**Represent**) Change the improper fraction $\frac{5}{2}$ to a mixed number. Draw
(104) a picture that shows that the improper fraction and the mixed number
are equal.

*10. Use the information below to answer parts **a** and **b.**
(94, 96)

> *Chico did 12 push-ups on the first day. On each of the next four days, he did two more push-ups than he did the day before.*

    a. Altogether, Chico did how many push-ups in five days?

    b. What was the average number of push-ups Chico did per day?

*11. The dashes in this polygon divide the figure into
(Inv. 3, 79) two rectangles.

    a. What is the area of rectangle *A*?

    b. What is the area of rectangle *B*?

    c. What is the area of the whole polygon?

    d. Do the dashes show a line of symmetry for the figure?

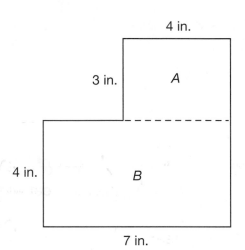

*12. (Analyze) There were red checkers and black checkers on the
(94) checkerboard. There were 8 more red checkers than black checkers. Altogether, there were 20 checkers. How many checkers were red, and how many were black? Guess and check to solve.

*13. Find three fractions equivalent to $\frac{2}{3}$ by multiplying $\frac{2}{3}$ by $\frac{2}{2}$, $\frac{3}{3}$, and $\frac{10}{10}$.
(109)

*14. Since 63 equals 60 + 3, we may find 5 × 63 by finding 5(60 + 3).
(108) Use the Distributive Property to find 5(60 + 3).

*15. Find *ac* when *a* is 18 and *c* is 22.
(106)

16. To open the window, Natalie slides the rectangular pane
(73) of glass on the right to the position of the pane on the left. Which transformation describes the movement of the pane of glass?

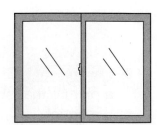

17. Find the median, mode, and range of this set of scores:
(97)

        100, 100, 95, 90, 90, 80, 80, 80, 60

*18. **Multiple Choice** If a quadrilateral has two pairs of parallel sides, then
(92)   the quadrilateral is certain to be a _____ .

  A rectangle   **B** parallelogram

  C trapezoid   **D** square

19. $v + 8.5 = 24.34$ **20.** $26.4 - 15.18$
(50)   (91)

21. $4 \times 3 \times 2 \times 1$ **22.** 26×30
(62)   (67)

23. $8\overline{)\$16.48}$ ***24.** $10n = 250$
(76, 80)   (41, 105)

*25. $\dfrac{5}{12} + \dfrac{6}{12}$ ***26.** $\dfrac{8}{12} - \dfrac{3}{12}$
(107)   (107)

27. How many square feet of paper are needed to cover a bulletin board
(Inv. 3)   that is 3 feet tall and 6 feet wide?

*28. The bread recipe calls for $7\frac{1}{2}$ cups of flour to make 2 loaves of bread.
(107)   The baker wants to make 4 loaves of bread. How many cups of flour
   does the baker need?

*29. The backpackers camped in a tent. Refer to the figure at right to
(98)   answer parts **a–c.**

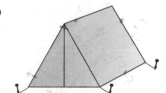

  a. The tent has the shape of what geometric solid?

  b. Including the bottom, how many faces does it have?

  c. How many edges does it have?

*30. The flag of the United States has thirteen stripes. Six of the stripes are
(11, 74)   white, and the rest of the stripes are red.

  a. How many red stripes are on the flag?

  b. What fraction of the stripes on the flag are white?

  c. What fraction of the stripes on the flag are red?

• Dividing by Multiples of 10

facts   Power Up B

mental math

Find each fraction of 100 in **a–c.**

   a. Fractional Parts: $\frac{1}{2}$ of 100

   b. Fractional Parts: $\frac{1}{4}$ of 100

   c. Fractional Parts: $\frac{1}{10}$ of 100

   d. Number Sense: 5×46

   e. Money: Doug purchased socks for $4.37 and a hairbrush for $2.98. How much did he spend?

   f. Estimation: Estimate the area of the rectangle shown at right.

   g. Calculation: 12×3, $\sqrt{}$, $\div 2$, $\div 3$

   h. Roman Numerals: Write MCX in our number system.

$2\frac{3}{4}$ in.

$5\frac{3}{4}$ in.

problem solving

Choose an appropriate problem-solving strategy to solve this problem. Using at least one of each coin from a penny through a half-dollar, which nine coins would be needed to make exactly 99¢?

In this lesson we will begin dividing by multiples of 10. Multiples of 10 are the numbers 10, 20, 30, 40, 50, 60, and so on. To help us divide by a two-digit number, we may think of dividing by the first digit only.

To help us divide this: $20\overline{)72}$

we may think this: $2\overline{)7}$

We use the easier division to estimate the answer to the more difficult division. Since there are three 2s in 7, we estimate that there are also three 20s in 72. Since we are dividing 72 by 20, we write the 3 above the 2 in 72.

$$\begin{array}{r} 3 \\ 20\overline{)72} \end{array}$$

This is correct.
The 3 above the 2 means there are three 20s in 72.

$$\begin{array}{r} 3 \\ 20\overline{)72} \end{array}$$

This is not correct!
Do not write the 3 above the 7. This would mean there are three 20s in 7, which is not true.

It is important to place the digits in the answer correctly.

Now we complete the multiplication and subtraction steps to find the remainder.

$$\begin{array}{r} 3\,R\,12 \\ 20\overline{)72} \\ \underline{60} \\ 12 \end{array}$$ ← We write the answer this way.

Example

Thinking Skill

Discuss

Why do we write the digit 4 in the ones place of the quotient?

Divide: $30\overline{)127}$

To help us divide, we mentally block out the last digit of each number. So we think "$3\overline{)12}$." Since there are four 3s in 12, we estimate that there are also four 30s in 127. We write "4" above the 7 of 127. Next we multiply 4 by 30 and write "120." Then we subtract 120 from 127 and write "7" as the remainder.

$$\begin{array}{r} 4\,R\,7 \\ 30\overline{)127} \\ \underline{120} \\ 7 \end{array}$$

Justify Explain how you can check the answer using a calculator.

Lesson Practice

Divide:

a. $30\overline{)72}$ **b.** $20\overline{)87}$ **c.** $40\overline{)95}$

d. $20\overline{)127}$ **e.** $40\overline{)127}$ **f.** $30\overline{)217}$

Written Practice

Distributed and Integrated

*1. **(Analyze)** Eighty students were divided among three classrooms as equally as possible. Write three numbers to show how many students were in each of the three classrooms.
(88)

*2. **Formulate** When the sum of three and four is subtracted from the
(94) product of three and four, what is the difference? Write an equation.

3. **Explain** Inma is twice as old as her sister and three years younger
(94) than her brother. Inma's sister is six years old. How old is Inma's
brother? What is the first step?

*4. Four ninths of 513 fans cheered when the touchdown was scored. How
(95) many fans cheered?

5. This sign has an error. Draw two different signs that show
(35) how to correct the error.

Cash for cans

.85¢
per
pound

*6. **Connect** These circles show fractions equivalent to $\frac{1}{2}$.
(109) Name the fractions shown.

*7. **Predict** The chance of winning the jackpot is 1%. Which is more
(Inv. 10) likely, winning or not winning?

*8. **Explain** In a sporting goods store, an aluminum baseball bat sells
(20, 22) for $38.49, a baseball sells for $4.99, and a baseball glove sells for
$24.95. What is a reasonable estimate of the cost to purchase a bat, a
glove, and two baseballs? Explain why your estimate is reasonable.

*9. Change the improper fraction $\frac{5}{2}$ to a mixed number.
(104)

10. Paul ran 7 miles in 42 minutes. What was the average number of minutes
(60, 96) it took Paul to run one mile?

*11. Kia bought 3 scarves priced at $2.75 each. Tax was 58¢. She paid with a
(83) $10 bill. How much change should Kia receive?

12. **Analyze** Two tickets for the play cost $26. At that rate, how much
(94) would twenty tickets cost?

*13. Hikaru is $49\frac{1}{2}$ inches tall. Dawn is $47\frac{1}{2}$ inches tall. Hikaru is how many
(107) inches taller than Dawn?

14. $7.43 + 6.25 + 12.7$
(50)

15. $q + 7.5 = 14.36$
(50)

16. 90×8000
(86)

17. $8 \times 73¢$
(48)

18. $7 \times 6 \times 5 \times 0$
(62)

19. 15^2
(Inv. 3,
62)

20. 60×5^2
(62, 67)

21. $\sqrt{49} \times \sqrt{49}$
(Inv. 3)

*22. $5\frac{1}{3} + 3\frac{1}{3}$
(107)

*23. $4\frac{4}{5} - 3\frac{3}{5}$
(107)

*24. $\dfrac{1240}{10}$
(105)

*25. $60\overline{)240}$
(110)

26. This square has a perimeter of 8 cm. Find the length of
(Inv. 2,
Inv. 3) each side. Then find the area of the square.

*27. Refer to the bus schedule below to answer parts **a–c.**
(27, 101)

Route 346

Terminal	6:43 a.m	7:25 a.m.	3:45 p.m.
5th & Western	6:50 a.m.	7:32 a.m.	3:50 p.m.
5th & Cypress	6:54 a.m.	7:36 a.m.	3:55 p.m.
Cypress & Hill	7:01 a.m.	7:43 a.m.	4:03 p.m.
Hill & Lincoln	7:08 a.m.	7:50 a.m.	4:12 p.m.
Lincoln & 5th	7:16 a.m.	7:58 a.m.	4:20 p.m.

a. Ella catches the 6:50 a.m. bus at 5th and Western. When can she expect to arrive at Hill and Lincoln?

b. If the bus runs on schedule, how many minutes is her ride?

c. If Ella misses the 6:50 a.m. bus, then when can she catch the next Route 346 bus at that corner?

28. **Predict** When Xena says a number, Yihana doubles the number and
(94) adds 3. Xena and Yihana record their numbers in a table.

X	1	2	5	7
Y	5	7	13	17

What number does Yihana record in the table if Xena says 11?

*29. Workers are replacing a section of broken sidewalk. Before pouring the
(Inv. 3, 108) concrete, the workers build a frame along the perimeter.

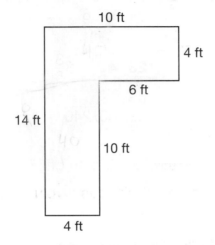

a. What is the perimeter of the replaced sidewalk?

b. What is the area of the replaced sidewalk?

*30. ✎ **Represent** A variety of morning times and temperatures are shown
(Inv. 6) in the table below.

Morning Temperatures

Time	Temperature (°F)
12:00 a.m.	51
2:00 a.m.	48
4:00 a.m.	49
6:00 a.m.	50
8:00 a.m.	56
10:00 a.m.	62

Display the data in a line graph. Then write one statement that describes
the data.

Focus on
• Volume

Shapes such as cubes, pyramids, and cones take up space. The amount of space a shape occupies is called its **volume.** We measure volume with **cubic units** like cubic centimeters, cubic inches, cubic feet, and cubic meters.

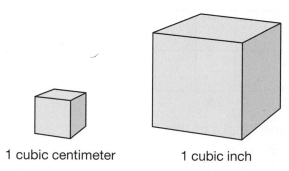

1 cubic centimeter   1 cubic inch

The model of the cube we constructed in Lesson 99 has a volume of one cubic inch.

Here is a model of a rectangular solid built with cubes that each have a volume of 1 cubic centimeter. To find the volume of the rectangular solid, we can count the number of cubic centimeters used to build it.

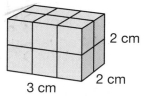

One way to count the small cubes is to count the cubes in one layer and then multiply that number by the number of layers. There are six cubes on the top layer, and there are two layers. The volume of the rectangular solid is 12 cubic centimeters.

Count cubes to find the volume of each rectangular solid below. Notice the units used in each figure.

1.
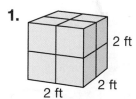

2.
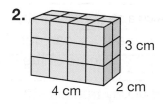

3.
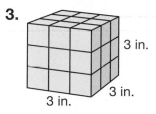

4.
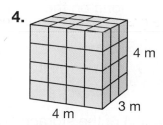

Another way to calculate the volume of a rectangular solid is to multiply the length, the width, and the height (depth) of the solid. The product of the three measures is the volume of the rectangular solid in cubic units. Use this multiplication method to find the volume of each rectangular solid in problems **1–4.**

Recall that 3 feet equals 1 yard and that 9 square feet make up 1 square yard. Use this information to help you solve problem **5.**

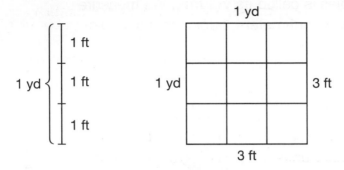

5. **Analyze** The length, width, and height of this cube are each 1 yard, so the volume of the cube is 1 cubic yard. What is the volume of the cube in cubic feet?

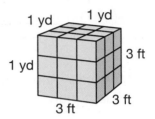

6. One foot equals 12 inches. One square foot equals 144 square inches. The volume of this figure is 1 cubic foot. What is its volume in cubic inches?

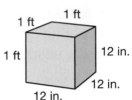

7. **Analyze** One meter equals 100 centimeters. One square meter equals 10,000 square centimeters. A shape with a volume of 1 cubic meter has a volume of how many cubic centimeters?

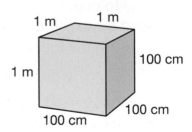

Items that we see on store shelves are usually shipped to stores in trucks. The amount of merchandise a truck can carry depends upon the capacity of the truck's trailer and the volume of the items being shipped.

Suppose the storage area of a delivery truck is shaped like a box that is 5 feet wide, 6 feet high, and 20 feet long on the inside.

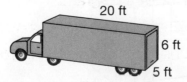

8. What is the volume (capacity) of the storage area in cubic feet?

Now suppose the truck is to be loaded with boxes with the dimensions shown at right. The first boxes are stacked against the back wall (which is 5 feet wide and 6 feet high).

3 ft

$2\frac{1}{2}$ ft   2 ft

9. **Represent** How many of these boxes can be stacked against the back wall? Draw a diagram.

10. **Explain** If same-size boxes continue to be stacked in the truck in the same manner, then how many boxes will fit in the truck? Explain your answer.

Activity 1

Estimating Volume

As a class, calculate the volume of your classroom twice, once in metric units and once in customary units. First estimate the volume in cubic meters by finding the number of boxes, one meter on each edge, that could be packed into the room. (Assume all cabinets and other furniture pieces are moved out of the room.)

11. **Estimate** What needs to be measured before the calculation can be performed? What units should be used? Record the room's dimensions to the nearest meter.

12. Use the dimensions of the room to estimate the volume of your classroom in cubic meters.

Perform a second calculation for the volume of the classroom, this time in cubic feet.

13. **Estimate** Record the length, width, and height of the room in feet. (Round to the nearest foot.)

14. Use the dimensions of the room to estimate the volume of your classroom in cubic feet.

A classroom with 30 desks may seem full. However, many more than 30 desks can fit into most classrooms. Suppose student desks were shipped in boxes 3 feet long, 2 feet wide, and 3 feet tall.

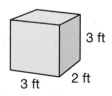

3 ft

3 ft   2 ft

15. **Represent** How many boxes of this size could be stacked against one wall of your classroom? Draw a diagram.

16. **Estimate** How many such stacks could fit in the classroom?

17. **Estimate** Altogether, how many boxed desks could fit in your classroom?

Activity 2

Estimating Perimeter, Area, and Volume

Material needed:
- **Lesson Activity 48**

Choose a rectangular room at school or at home and complete the tasks described on **Lesson Activity 48.**

Investigate Further

a. In a group, use the 1-inch paper cube manipulatives from Lesson 99 and tape or glue to model unusual shapes. Write the volume in pencil on the bottom of your shape. Ask other students to estimate the volume of your three-dimensional shape and compare your estimates.

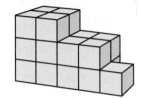

Option:

Work together as a class to tape the 1-inch paper cubes into one large structure. Display the figure and ask classroom guests to estimate the volume.

b. The rectangle has a length of 3 units and a width of 1 unit.

This table shows the values for *l* when *w* = 1, 2, 3, and 4.

3 units (*l*)

1 unit (*w*)

w	l
1	3
2	6
3	9
4	12

- Write an equation to show the relationship between the two sets of data.

- Use your equation to determine the length when the width is 8 units.

c. Get an empty container from your teacher. Estimate the number of cups of water your container holds. Using cups, determine exactly how many cups of water your container holds. How close was your estimate to the actual number of cups of water your container holds?

d. Get an empty container from your teacher. Estimate the number of milliliters your container holds. Using milliliters, determine exactly how many milliliters of water your container holds. How close was your estimate to the actual milliliters of water your container holds?

- **Estimating Perimeter, Area, and Volume**

facts	Power Up C
mental math	Find each fraction of 60 in **a–c**.

    a. Fractional Parts: $\frac{1}{3}$ of 60

    b. Fractional Parts: $\frac{2}{3}$ of 60

    c. Fractional Parts: $\frac{3}{3}$ of 60

    d. Number Sense: 50×46

    e. Probability: With one roll of a dot cube, what is the probability of rolling a 4?

    f. Estimation: Estimate 49×21.

    g. Calculation: $\frac{1}{3}$ of 90, $+\ 50$, $+\ 1$, $\sqrt{\ }$, $\sqrt{\ }$, $-\ 2$

    h. Roman Numerals: Compare XLVI $\bigcirc$ 45

problem solving

Choose an appropriate problem-solving strategy to solve this problem. Marco paid a dollar for an item that cost 54¢. He received four coins in change. What four coins did he receive?

To estimate the areas of shapes, we can use a grid. On the following page, we show a triangle drawn on 1-inch grid paper. We will describe two strategies that can be used to estimate the area of the triangle.

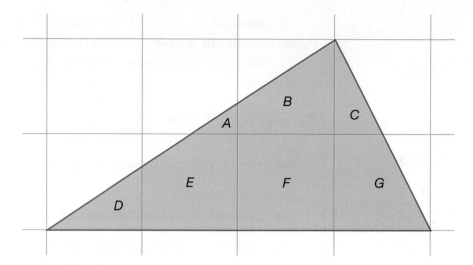

First strategy:

Look within the outline of the figure. Count all the whole squares. Then estimate the number of whole squares that could be formed with the remaining partial squares.

Using this strategy, we count *F* as a whole square. *C* and *G* could fit together like puzzle pieces to make another square. *D* and *B* could make a third square. *A* and *E* could make a fourth square. We estimate that the area of the triangle is about 4 square inches.

Second strategy:

Look within the outline of the figure. Count all the whole squares as in the first strategy. Then count all the squares that seem to have at least half their area within the outline of the figure. Do not count the squares that have less than half their area within the figure.

Using this strategy, we again count *F* as a whole square. Then we count *E, B,* and *G* because at least half the area of each square is within the outline of the triangle. We do not count *A, C,* or *D.* Using this strategy, we again estimate the area of the triangle to be about 4 square inches.

Both strategies help us estimate areas. An estimate is an **approximation.** Estimates may differ slightly from person to person. The goal is to make each estimate carefully.

We can also estimate the perimeter of the triangle.

We see that the base of the triangle is 4 units. The other two sides are a little more than 3 units and a little more than 2 units. So the perimeter is a little more than 9 units, or perhaps 10 units.

Activity 1

Estimating Perimeter and Area

Materials needed:

- **Lesson Activities 20** and **21**

1. Outline your hand on **Lesson Activity 21** (1-inch grid). Then estimate the area of your handprint.

2. Outline your hand again, this time on **Lesson Activity 20** (1-cm grid). Then estimate the perimeter and area of your handprint.

One way to estimate the volume of a container is to first fill the container with unit cubes and then count the number of cubes in the container.

Activity 2

Estimating Volume

Material needed:

- **Lesson Activity 45** or unit cubes

Select a box about the size of a tissue box and fit as many unit cubes in it as you can. Estimate the volume of the box by counting the number of cubes.

Lesson Practice Estimate the perimeter and area of each figure on these grids. Each small square represents one square centimeter in problem **a.** Each small square represents one square inch in problem **b.**

a.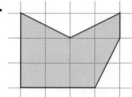

b.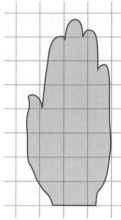

c. **Estimate** On the floor of the classroom, mark off 1 square foot, 1 square yard, and 1 square meter. Estimate the number of each kind of square it would take to cover the whole floor.

Written Practice *Distributed and Integrated*

---

*1. **a.** Three hundred seconds is how many minutes? (There are
(52, 110) 60 seconds in each minute.)

b. Sixty minutes is how many seconds?

*2. **Explain** Trevor, Ann, and Lee were playing marbles. Ann had twice
(94) as many marbles as Trevor had, and Lee had 5 more marbles than Ann had. Trevor had 9 marbles. How many marbles did Lee have? What is the first step?

3. On each of 5 bookshelves there are 44 books. How many books are on
(49) all 5 bookshelves?

*4. **a.** Nine tenths of the 30 students turned in their homework. How many
(Inv. 5, students turned in their homework?
95)

b. What percent of the students did not turn in their homework?

5.
(37, 102) For parts **a–c,** refer to this number line:

a. The number for point *A* is what fraction?

b. The number for point *B* is what decimal number?

c. The number for point *C* is what fraction?

6.
(103) What fraction name for 1 has a denominator of 3?

*7.
(109) What equivalent fractions are shown?

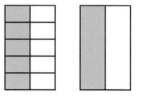

*8.
(109) (**Represent**) Draw a picture to show that $\frac{6}{8}$ and $\frac{3}{4}$ are equivalent fractions.

9.
(96) Below is a golf scorecard for 9 holes of miniature golf. What was Michelle's average score per hole?

Putt 'N' Putt

Player	1	2	3	4	5	6	7	8	9	Total
Michelle	6	7	5	2	4	1	3	5	3	36
Mary	5	4	4	3	4	3	2	5	3	33

10.
(27) It was 11:00 a.m., and Sarah had to clean the laboratory by 4:20 p.m. How much time did she have to clean the lab?

*11.
(63) Draw a quadrilateral that has two sides that are parallel, a third side that is perpendicular to the parallel sides, and a fourth side that is not perpendicular to the parallel sides. What type of quadrilateral did you draw?

12.
(55) The factors of 10 are 1, 2, 5, 10. The factors of 15 are 1, 3, 5, 15. Which number is the largest factor of both 10 and 15?

13.
(55) List the factors of 8. List the factors of 12. Which number is the largest factor of both 8 and 12?

14. $4.3 + 12.6 + 3.75$
(50)

15. $364.1 - 16.41$
(91)

*16. $\dfrac{5}{8} + \dfrac{2}{8}$
(107)

*17. $\dfrac{3}{5} + \dfrac{1}{5}$
(107)

*18. $1\dfrac{9}{10} - 1\dfrac{2}{10}$
(107)

19. 60×800
(86)

20. 73×48
(90)

21. $9 \times 78¢$
(48)

22. 10^3
(62, 86)

23. $4x = 3500$
(41, 76)

24. $\dfrac{4824}{8}$
(80)

*25. $60\overline{)540}$
(110)

*26. $10\overline{)463}$
(105)

*27. Estimate the perimeter and area of this figure. Each small
(111) square represents one square inch.

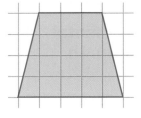

*28. **Represent** Draw a rectangle that is 4 cm long and 1 cm wide. Then
(21,
Inv. 5) shade 25% of it.

29. Multiple Choice Which of the following is a cylinder?
(98)

A   **B**    **C**    **D**

*30. **Justify** What is the volume of this rectangular solid?
(Inv. 11) Explain why your answer is reasonable.

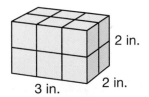

2 in.

2 in.

3 in.

*Real-World
Connection*

a. Choose a box in your classroom, and estimate its perimeter, area, and volume. Then find the actual perimeter, area, and volume.

b. Explain how you found the perimeter, area, and volume of the box.

• Reducing Fractions

facts

Power Up G

mental math

Find each fraction of 60 in **a–c.**

    a. Fractional Parts: $\frac{1}{4}$ of 60

    b. Fractional Parts: $\frac{2}{4}$ of 60

    c. Fractional Parts: $\frac{3}{4}$ of 60

    d. Number Sense: 30×12

    e. Money: Taima had $10.00. Then she spent $5.63 on a journal. How much money does she have left?

    f. Estimation: Eight bottles of laundry detergent cost $40.32. Round that amount to the nearest dollar and then divide by 8 to estimate the cost per bottle.

    g. Calculation: $\frac{1}{2}$ of 24, $\div$ 6, square the number, + 8, $\times$ 2

    h. Roman Numerals: Write MMCL in our number system.

problem solving

Choose an appropriate problem-solving strategy to solve this problem. Find the next five terms in this sequence. Then describe the sequence in words.

$$\frac{1}{2}, \frac{2}{4}, \frac{3}{6}, \frac{4}{8}, \underline{\quad}, \underline{\quad}, \underline{\quad}, \underline{\quad}, \underline{\quad}, \dots$$

New Concept

Recall from Investigation 9 that when we *reduce* a fraction, we find an equivalent fraction written with smaller numbers. The picture below shows $\frac{4}{6}$ reduced to $\frac{2}{3}$.

Visit www.
SaxonMath.com/
Int4Activities
for a calculator
activity.

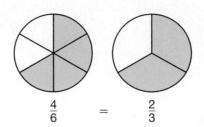

$$\frac{4}{6} \quad = \quad \frac{2}{3}$$

Not all fractions can be reduced. Only a fraction whose numerator and denominator can be divided by the same number can be reduced. Since both the numerator and denominator of $\frac{4}{6}$ can be divided by 2, we can reduce the fraction $\frac{4}{6}$.

To reduce a fraction, we will use a fraction that is equal to 1. To reduce $\frac{4}{6}$, we will use the fraction $\frac{2}{2}$. We divide both 4 and 6 by 2, as shown below.

$$\frac{4}{6} \div \frac{2}{2} = \frac{4 \div 2}{6 \div 2} = \frac{2}{3}$$

Example

Thinking Skill

Discuss

How do we know that both 6 and 8 are divisible by 2?

Write the reduced form of each fraction:

a. $\dfrac{6}{8}$ 　　　b. $\dfrac{3}{6}$ 　　　c. $\dfrac{6}{7}$

a. The numerator and denominator are 6 and 8. These numbers can be divided by 2. That means we can reduce the fraction by dividing 6 and 8 by 2.

$$\frac{6}{8} \div \frac{2}{2} = \frac{6 \div 2}{8 \div 2} = \frac{3}{4}$$

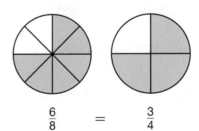

$$\frac{6}{8} \quad = \quad \frac{3}{4}$$

b. The numerator and denominator are 3 and 6. These numbers can be divided by 3, so we reduce $\frac{3}{6}$ by dividing both 3 and 6 by 3.

$$\frac{3}{6} \div \frac{3}{3} = \frac{3 \div 3}{6 \div 3} = \frac{1}{2}$$

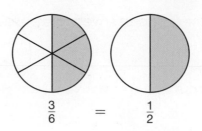

$$\frac{3}{6} \quad = \quad \frac{1}{2}$$

c. The numerator is 6 and the denominator is 7. The only number that divides 6 and 7 is 1. Dividing the terms of a fraction by 1 does not reduce the fraction.

$$\frac{6}{7} \div \frac{1}{1} = \frac{6 \div 1}{7 \div 1} = \frac{6}{7}$$

The fraction $\frac{6}{7}$ cannot be reduced.

Justify Which number, 6 or 7, is prime? Explain why.

Lesson Practice Write the reduced form of each fraction:

a. $\frac{2}{4}$ **b.** $\frac{2}{6}$ **c.** $\frac{3}{9}$ **d.** $\frac{3}{8}$

e. $\frac{2}{10}$ **f.** $\frac{4}{10}$ **g.** $\frac{9}{12}$ **h.** $\frac{9}{10}$

Written Practice   *Distributed and Integrated*

* 1. Use the following information to answer parts **a** and **b**:
(94)

One fence board costs 90¢. It takes 10 boards to build 5 feet of fence.

a. How many boards are needed to build 50 feet of fence?

b. How much will the boards cost altogether?

2. Find the perimeter and area of this rectangle:
(Inv. 2, Inv. 3)

3 cm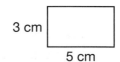

5 cm

3. a. Find the length of this line segment in millimeters.
(69)

b. Find the length of the segment in centimeters.

mm 10   20   30   40   50

cm 1   2   3   4   5

*4. Five ninths of the 36 horses were gray. How many of the horses were
(95) gray?

*5. Change each improper fraction to a whole number or a mixed number:
(104)
a. $\dfrac{15}{2}$ **b.** $\dfrac{15}{3}$ **c.** $\dfrac{15}{4}$

*6. Angelina's mom is more than 32 years old but less than 40 years
(55) old, and her age in years is a prime number. How old is Angelina's
mom?

*7. a. What equivalent fractions are shown in the pictures at
(Inv. 5, right?
109)

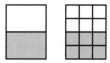

b. What percent of each large rectangle is shaded?

*8. A regular polygon has all sides the same length and all angles the
(79, 92) same measure.

a. Draw a regular quadrilateral. Show all the lines of symmetry.

b. A regular quadrilateral has how many lines of symmetry?

c. Does a regular quadrilateral have rotational symmetry?

*9. Write the reduced form of each fraction:
(112)
a. $\dfrac{3}{6}$ **b.** $\dfrac{4}{6}$ **c.** $\dfrac{6}{12}$

10. In three tries, Rodney bounced the soccer ball on his foot 23 times,
(96) 36 times, and 34 times. What was the average number of bounces in
each try?

11. T-shirts were priced at $5 each. Yoshi had $27 and bought 5 T-shirts.
(83) Tax was $1.50. How much money did he have left?

*12. $3\dfrac{3}{9} + 4\dfrac{4}{9}$ ***13.** $\dfrac{1}{7} + \dfrac{2}{7} + \dfrac{3}{7}$ **14.**
(107)   (107)   (50)

$$\begin{array}{r} 37.2 \\ 135.7 \\ 10.62 \\ 2.47 \\ + \ 14.0 \end{array}$$

*15. $\dfrac{11}{12} - \dfrac{10}{12}$ ***16.** $\dfrac{8}{10} - \dfrac{5}{10}$
(107)   (107)

17. 48
(90) × 36

18. 72
(90) × 58

19. $4.08
(58) × 7

20. 25.42 + 24.8
(50)

21. 36.2 − 4.27
(50)

*22. 90 ÷ 20
(110)

23. $\frac{5}{8} - \frac{5}{8}$
(107)

24. 7)2549
(76)

*25. $19.40 ÷ 10
(105)

26. What number is halfway between 400,000 and 500,000?
(Inv. 1)

27. (**Predict**) What is the probability that a tossed coin will land heads up?
(Inv. 10)

*28. **a.** What is the geometric name for the shape of this box?
(98,
Inv. 11)

b. What is the volume of the box?

c. True or False: All of the opposite faces of the box are parallel.

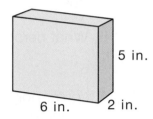

5 in.

6 in.   2 in.

29. Mallory opened her notebook and turned a page from the right side to the
(73) left. Turning the page is like which geometric transformation?

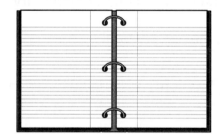

*30. ✏️ (**Explain**) Estimate the perimeter and area of this shoe
(111) print. Each small square represents one square inch.
Describe the method you used.

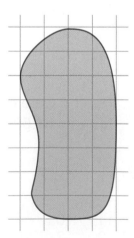

• Multiplying a Three-Digit Number by a Two-Digit Number

facts   Power Up I

mental math   An odd number can be written as an even number plus 1. For example, 9 is 8 + 1. So half of 9 is half of 8 plus half of 1, which is $4 + \frac{1}{2}$, or $4\frac{1}{2}$. Use this strategy to find half of each odd number in **a–d.**

    a. Fractional Parts: 7

    b. Fractional Parts: 11

    c. Fractional Parts: 21

    d. Fractional Parts: 33

    e. Probability: If the chance of rain is 30%, what is the chance that it will not rain?

    f. Estimation: Uzuri's mother filled the car with gasoline, which cost $33.43. Then her mother bought snacks for $4.48. Estimate the total cost.

    g. Calculation: $\frac{1}{2}$ of 100, $- 1$, $\sqrt{}$, $+ 2$, $\sqrt{}$, $+ 1$, $\sqrt{}$

    h. Roman Numerals: Compare MD $\bigcirc$ 2000

problem solving   Choose an appropriate problem-solving strategy to solve this problem. The numbers 1, 8, and 27 begin the sequence below. (Notice that $1 = 1^3$, $8 = 2^3$, and $27 = 3^3$.) Find the next three numbers in the sequence.

$$1, 8, 27, \text{\_\_\_}, \text{\_\_\_}, \text{\_\_\_}, \ldots$$

We have learned to multiply a two-digit number by another two-digit number. In this lesson we will learn to multiply a three-digit number by a two-digit number.

Example 1

A bakery is open 364 days each year. On each of those days, the bakery owner bakes 24 loaves of bread. How many loaves of bread does the owner bake each year?

Thinking Skill

Justify

Why are there two partial products?

We write the three-digit number above the two-digit number so that the last digits in each number are lined up. We multiply 364 by 4. Next we multiply 364 by 2. Since this 2 is actually 20, we write the last digit of this product in the tens place, which is under the 2 in 24. Then we add and find that the owner bakes **8736 loaves of bread** each year.

$$
\begin{array}{r}
1 \\
2\,1 \\
364 \\
\times\quad 24 \\
\hline
1456 \\
+728 \\
\hline
8736
\end{array}
$$

Example 2

During summer vacation, a school principal ordered 38 paperback dictionaries for the school bookstore. The cost of each dictionary was $4.07. What was the total cost of the dictionaries?

Thinking Skill

Generalize

When one factor of a multiplication problem is dollars and cents, how many decimal places will be in the product? Name the places.

We will ignore the dollar sign and decimal point until we are finished multiplying. First we multiply 407 by 8. Then we multiply 407 by 3 (which is actually 30), remembering to shift the digits of the product one place to the left. We add and find that the product is 15466. Now we write the dollar sign and insert the decimal point two places from the right. We find that the total cost of the dictionaries was **$154.66.**

$$
\begin{array}{r}
2 \\
5 \\
\$4.07 \\
\times\quad 38 \\
\hline
32\,56 \\
+\,122\,1 \\
\hline
\$154.66
\end{array}
$$

Lesson Practice Multiply:

a. 235×24 **b.** 14×430 **c.** $\$1.25 \times 24$

d. $\begin{array}{r} 406 \\ \times\ 32 \\ \hline \end{array}$ **e.** $\begin{array}{r} \$6.20 \\ \times\quad 31 \\ \hline \end{array}$ **f.** $\begin{array}{r} 562 \\ \times\ 47 \\ \hline \end{array}$

1. Carrie drove to visit her cousin who lives 3000 miles away. If Carrie
(11, 52) drove 638 miles the first day, 456 miles the second day, and 589 miles the third day, how much farther does she need to drive to get to her cousin's house?

2. Find the perimeter and area of this square:
(Inv. 2, Inv. 3)

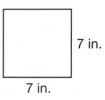

7 in.

7 in.

3. If the perimeter of a square is 2 meters, then each side is how many
(Inv. 2) centimeters long?

* 4. The figure below shows the shape and dimensions of a room.
(Inv. 3, 108)

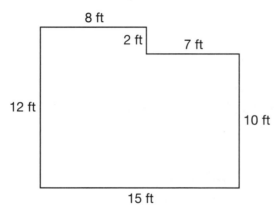

8 ft

2 ft   7 ft

12 ft

10 ft

15 ft

a. How many feet of molding are needed to go around the perimeter of the room?

b. How many 1-foot square floor tiles are needed to cover the floor?

5. (**Estimate**) Round 6843 to the nearest thousand.
(54)

* 6. Write the reduced form of each fraction:
(112)

a. $\frac{4}{5}$
b. $\frac{5}{10}$
c. $\frac{4}{10}$

7. (**Represent**) Write 374.251 using words.
(84)

* 8. **(Represent)** Draw a picture to show that $\frac{1}{2}$ and $\frac{4}{8}$ are equivalent
(109) fractions.

* 9. **(Connect)** Write three fractions equivalent to $\frac{1}{4}$.
(109)

10. The concession stand at an elementary school basketball tournament
(96) earned a profit of $750 during a 3-day tournament. What is the average
profit earned during each day of the tournament?

* 11. **(Estimate)** The explorer Zebulon Pike estimated that the mountain's
(12, 51) height was eight thousand, seven hundred forty-two feet. His estimate
was five thousand, three hundred sixty-eight feet less than the actual
height. Today we call this mountain Pikes Peak. What is the height of
Pikes Peak?

12. $6\overline{)4837}$ **13.** $\dfrac{1372}{\sqrt{16}}$ *** 14.** $40\overline{)960}$ *** 15.** $20\overline{)1360}$
(80)   (Inv. 3, 76)   (110)   (110)

16. $30.07 - 3.7$ **17.** $46.0 - 12.46$ **18.** $\begin{array}{r} 37.15 \\ 6.84 \\ 1.29 \\ 29.1 \\ + \ 3.6 \\ \hline \end{array}$
(50)   (91)   (50)

* 19. $\begin{array}{r} \$3.20 \\ \times \quad 46 \\ \hline \end{array}$ *** 20.** $\begin{array}{r} 307 \\ \times \quad 25 \\ \hline \end{array}$
(113)   (113)

* 21. $\dfrac{8}{15} + \dfrac{6}{15}$ *** 22.** $4\dfrac{4}{5} - 1\dfrac{3}{5}$
(107)   (107)

* 23. Estimate the perimeter and area of this triangle. Each
(111) small square represents one square centimeter.

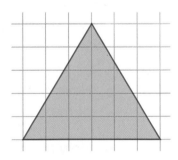

24. **(Conclude)** Write the next three numbers in this counting sequence:
(3)

$$\dots, 10{,}000, 20{,}000, 30{,}000, \dots$$

*25. **a. Multiple Choice** Which of these triangles appears to be an
(63, 78)   equilateral triangle?

A   **B**   **C**   **D**

b. Describe the angles in triangle **B.**

c. Describe the segments in triangle **B.**

26. **Multiple Choice** To remove the lid from the pickle jar, J'Rhonda
(75)   turned the lid counterclockwise two full turns. J'Rhonda turned the lid
about how many degrees?

   A 360°   **B** 180°   **C** 720°   **D** 90°

*27. **a.** Which of the letters below has no lines of symmetry?
(79)

M I C K E Y

b. Which letter has rotational symmetry?

*28. Triangles *ABC* and *DEF* are congruent. Which
(73)   transformations would move △*ABC* to the position
of △*DEF*?

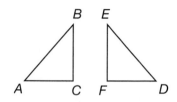

*29. If each side of an equilateral triangle is $2\frac{1}{4}$ inches long, what is the
(Inv. 2,   perimeter of the triangle?
107)

*30. What is the volume of this stack of cubes?
(Inv. 11)

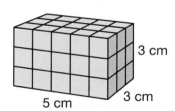

3 cm

5 cm   3 cm

• Simplifying Fraction Answers

facts   Power Up H

mental math

    a. Percent: 25% of 24

    b. Percent: 50% of 24

    c. Percent: 75% of 24

    d. Number Sense: 20×250

    e. Measurement: The half-gallon container is half full. How many quarts of liquid are in the container?

    f. Estimation: Each square folding table is 122 cm on each side. Estimate the total length of 4 folding tables if they are lined up in a row.

    g. Calculation: $6^2 - 6, + 20, \div 2, - 1, \div 2$

    h. Roman Numerals: Write MDX in our number system.

problem solving

Choose an appropriate problem-solving strategy to solve this problem. Nala solved a division problem and then erased some of the digits from the problem. She gave it to Eduardo as a problem-solving exercise. Find the missing digits for Eduardo.

$$
\begin{array}{r}
8\ \_ \\
\_\,)\overline{\_\ \_\ 7} \\
2\ 4 \\
\overline{} \\
2\ \_ \\
\overline{} \\
0
\end{array}
$$

We often write answers to math problems in the simplest form possible. If an answer contains a fraction, there are two procedures that we usually follow.

1. We write improper fractions as mixed numbers (or whole numbers).

2. We reduce fractions when possible.

Example 1

Thinking Skill

Justify

Explain why $\frac{4}{3} = 1\frac{1}{3}$.

Add: $\dfrac{2}{3} + \dfrac{2}{3}$

We add the fractions and get the sum $\frac{4}{3}$. Notice that $\frac{4}{3}$ is an improper fraction. We take the extra step of changing $\frac{4}{3}$ to the mixed number $\mathbf{1\frac{1}{3}}$.

$$\frac{2}{3} + \frac{2}{3} = \frac{4}{3}$$

$$\frac{4}{3} = 1\frac{1}{3}$$

Example 2

Subtract: $\dfrac{3}{4} - \dfrac{1}{4}$

We subtract and get the difference $\frac{2}{4}$. Notice that $\frac{2}{4}$ can be reduced. We take the extra step of reducing $\frac{2}{4}$ to $\frac{1}{2}$.

$$\frac{3}{4} - \frac{1}{4} = \frac{2}{4}$$

$$\frac{2}{4} = \frac{1}{2}$$

Example 3

Nicholas exercises each day by walking. The route he walks each morning is $3\frac{1}{3}$ miles long, and the route he walks each evening is $4\frac{2}{3}$ miles long. Altogether, how many miles does Nicholas walk each day?

We add the mixed numbers and get the sum $7\frac{3}{3}$. Notice that $\frac{3}{3}$ is an improper fraction equal to 1. So $7\frac{3}{3} = 7 + 1$, which is 8. Nicholas walks **8 miles** altogether.

$$3\frac{1}{3} + 4\frac{2}{3} = 7\frac{3}{3}$$

$$7\frac{3}{3} = 8$$

Example 4

Add: $5\dfrac{3}{5} + 6\dfrac{4}{5}$

We add the mixed numbers and get $11\frac{7}{5}$. Notice that $\frac{7}{5}$ is an improper fraction that can be changed to $1\frac{2}{5}$. So $11\frac{7}{5}$ equals $11 + 1\frac{2}{5}$, which is $\mathbf{12\frac{2}{5}}$.

$$5\frac{3}{5} + 6\frac{4}{5} = 11\frac{7}{5}$$

$$11\frac{7}{5} = 12\frac{2}{5}$$

Example 5

A piece of fabric $1\frac{3}{8}$ yards in length was cut from a bolt of fabric that measured $6\frac{5}{8}$ yards long. How long is the piece of fabric left on the bolt?

Thinking Skills

Represent

Draw a picture to show that $\frac{2}{8} = \frac{1}{4}$.

We subtract and get $5\frac{2}{8}$. Notice that $\frac{2}{8}$ can be reduced, so we reduce $\frac{2}{8}$ to $\frac{1}{4}$ and get $5\frac{1}{4}$. The length of the fabric is **$5\frac{1}{4}$ yards.**

$$6\frac{5}{8} - 1\frac{3}{8} = 5\frac{2}{8}$$

$$5\frac{2}{8} = 5\frac{1}{4}$$

Lesson Practice Simplify the answer to each sum or difference:

a. $\frac{4}{5} + \frac{4}{5}$

b. $\frac{5}{6} - \frac{1}{6}$

c. $3\frac{2}{3} + 1\frac{2}{3}$

d. $5\frac{1}{4} + 6\frac{3}{4}$

e. $7\frac{7}{8} - 1\frac{1}{8}$

f. $5\frac{3}{5} + 1\frac{3}{5}$

Written Practice *Distributed and Integrated*

*1. **Justify** Tessa made 70 photocopies. If she paid 6¢ per copy
(83) and the total tax was 25¢, how much change should she have gotten back from a $5 bill? Is your answer reasonable? Why or why not?

2. a. What is the area of this square?
(Inv. 2, Inv. 3)
  b. What is the perimeter of the square?

6 cm

*3. Use the information below to answer parts **a** and **b.**
(94, 96)
  Walker has $9. Dembe has twice as much money as Walker. Chris has $6 more than Dembe.

  a. How much money does Chris have?

  b. What is the average amount of money each boy has?

4. Use this table to answer the questions that follow:
(32)

Number of Bagels	12	24	36	48	60
Number of Dozens	1	2	3	4	5

  a. **Generalize** Write a rule that describes the relationship of the data.

  b. **Predict** How many bagels is 12 dozen bagels?

5. **Analyze** There are 40 quarters in a roll of quarters. What is the value
(94) of 2 rolls of quarters?

6. **Estimate** Lucio estimated that the exact quotient of 1754 divided
(76) by 9 was close to 20. Did Lucio make a reasonable estimate? Explain
why or why not.

*7. Write the reduced form of each fraction:
(112)
    a. $\frac{2}{12}$ **b.** $\frac{6}{8}$ **c.** $\frac{3}{9}$

*8. **Analyze** Find a fraction equal to $\frac{1}{3}$ by multiplying $\frac{1}{3}$ by $\frac{2}{2}$. Write that
(107, 109) fraction, and then add it to $\frac{3}{6}$. What is the sum?

*9. **Conclude** The three runners wore black, red, and green T-shirts. The
(72) runner wearing green finished one place ahead of the runner wearing
black, and the runner wearing red was not last. Who finished first?
Draw a diagram to solve this problem.

*10. If an event cannot happen, its probability is 0. If an event is certain to
(Inv. 10) happen, its probability is 1. What is the probability of rolling a 7 with
one roll of a standard number cube?

11. Dresses were on sale for 50% off. If the regular price of the dress
(Inv. 5, 70) was $40, then what was the sale price?

12. $4.62 + 16.7 + 9.8$ **13.** $14.62 - (6.3 - 2.37)$
(50)   (45, 91)

*14. $\frac{3}{5} + \frac{4}{5}$ ***15.** $16 + 3\frac{3}{4}$ ***16.** $1\frac{2}{3} + 3\frac{1}{3}$
(114)   (107)   (114)

*17. $\frac{2}{5} + \frac{3}{5}$ ***18.** $7\frac{4}{5} + 7\frac{1}{5}$ ***19.** $6\frac{2}{3} + 3\frac{2}{3}$
(114)   (114)   (114)

*20. 372×39 ***21.** 47×142 ***22.** $360 \times \sqrt{36}$
(113)   (113)   (Inv. 3, 58)

*23. Estimate the area of this circle. Each small square
(111) represents one square centimeter.

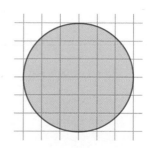

24. $8y = 4832$
(41, 80)

25. $\dfrac{2840}{2^3}$
(62, 76)

*26. $30\overline{)963}$
(110)

*27. (Represent) Which arrow could be pointing to 427,063?
(Inv. 1)

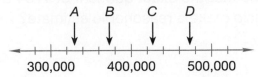

        A   B   C   D

300,000   400,000   500,000

*28. If the length of each side of a square is $1\frac{1}{4}$ inches, then what is the
(Inv. 2, 114) perimeter of the square?

29. What is the geometric shape of a volleyball?
(98)

*30. Use the Distributive Property to multiply:
(108)

$$5(20 + 6)$$

Early Finishers

Real-World Connection

Lun Lun is a giant panda at the Atlanta Zoo. Lun Lun eats about 210 pounds of bamboo a week.

a. If he eats $\frac{1}{7}$ of the bamboo on Monday and $\frac{2}{7}$ on Tuesday, what fractional part of his weekly serving did Lun Lun eat?

b. If Lun Lun eats $\frac{3}{7}$ of his bamboo Wednesday through Saturday, how much bamboo will he have left on Sunday? Write your answer as a fraction.

LESSON
115

• Renaming Fractions

Power Up

facts　　　　Power Up H

**mental
math**

    a. Percent: 25% of 36

    b. Percent: 75% of 36

    c. Percent: 100% of 36

    d. Percent: Three of the 30 students are left-handed. What percent of the students are left-handed?

    e. Measurement: A'Narra hit the softball 116 feet. Then the ball rolled 29 feet. How many feet did the softball travel?

    f. Estimation: Estimate 16 × 49. First round 49 to the nearest ten; then use the "double and half" method.

    g. Calculation: 3 × 20, + 40, $\sqrt{}$, − 7, square the number

    h. Roman Numerals: Compare: 65 ◯ LXV

**problem
solving**

Choose an appropriate problem-solving strategy to solve this problem. Find the next three terms of this sequence. Then describe the sequence in words.

$$\ldots, \$1000.00, \$100.00, \$10.00, \underline{}, \underline{}, \underline{}, \ldots$$

New Concept

Remember that when we multiply a fraction by a fraction name for 1, the result is an equivalent fraction. For example, if we multiply $\frac{1}{2}$ by $\frac{2}{2}$, we get $\frac{2}{4}$. The fractions $\frac{1}{2}$ and $\frac{2}{4}$ are equivalent fractions because they have the same value.

$$\frac{1}{2} \times \mathbf{1}\frac{2}{2} = \frac{2}{4}$$

Sometimes we must choose a particular multiplier that is equal to 1.

Example 1

Thinking Skill

Discuss

How can we check the answer?

Find the equivalent fraction for $\frac{1}{4}$ whose denominator is 12.

To change 4 to 12, we must multiply by 3. So we multiply $\frac{1}{4}$ by $\frac{3}{3}$.

$$\frac{1}{4} \times \frac{3}{3} = \frac{3}{12}$$

The fraction $\frac{1}{4}$ is equivalent to $\frac{3}{12}$.

Example 2

Thinking Skill

Verify

How can we check the answer?

Complete the equivalent fraction: $\frac{2}{3} = \frac{?}{15}$

The denominator changed from 3 to 15. Since the denominator was multiplied by 5, the correct multiplier is $\frac{5}{5}$.

$$\frac{2}{3} \times \frac{5}{5} = \frac{10}{15}$$

Thus, the missing numerator of the equivalent fraction is **10**.

Lesson Practice   Complete each equivalent fraction:

a. $\frac{1}{4} = \frac{?}{12}$ **b.** $\frac{2}{3} = \frac{?}{12}$ **c.** $\frac{5}{6} = \frac{?}{12}$

d. $\frac{3}{5} = \frac{?}{10}$ **e.** $\frac{2}{3} = \frac{?}{9}$ **f.** $\frac{3}{4} = \frac{?}{8}$

Written Practice   *Distributed and Integrated*

1. If a can of soup costs $1.50 and serves 3 people, how much would it cost to serve soup to 12 people?
(94)

*2. The polygon at right is divided into two rectangles.
(Inv. 3, 108)

    a. What is the perimeter of the figure?

    b. What is the area of the figure?

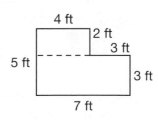

3. What number is eight less than the product of nine and ten? Write an expression.
(94)

4. Sanjay needs to learn 306 new words for the regional spelling bee.
(95) He has already memorized $\frac{2}{3}$ of the new words. How many words
does Sanjay still need to memorize? Draw a picture to illustrate the
problem.

*5. a. Find the length of this line segment in centimeters.
(69)

b. Find the length of the segment in millimeters.

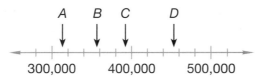

6. (**Represent**) Use words to write 356,420.
(33)

*7. (**Represent**) Which arrow could be pointing to 356,420?
(Inv. 1)

A   B C   D

300,000   400,000   500,000

*8. Complete each equivalent fraction:
(115)

a. $\frac{1}{2} = \frac{?}{6}$ **b.** $\frac{1}{3} = \frac{?}{6}$ **c.** $\frac{2}{3} = \frac{?}{6}$

*9. Write the reduced form of each fraction:
(112)

a. $\frac{2}{6}$ **b.** $\frac{6}{9}$ **c.** $\frac{9}{16}$

*10. a. There were 40 workers on the job. Of those workers, 10 had worked
(Inv. 5, overtime. What fraction of the workers had worked overtime?
112) (Remember to reduce the fraction.)

b. What percent of the workers had worked overtime?

11. How many different three-digit numbers can you write using the digits
(3) 6, 3, and 2? Each digit may be used only once in every number you
write.

12. (**Conclude**) Jamar received $10 for his tenth birthday. Each year after
(3, 94) that, he received $1 more than he did on his previous birthday. He
saved all his birthday money. In all, how much birthday money did
Jamar have on his fifteenth birthday?

*13. **(Analyze)** Every morning Marta walks $2\frac{1}{2}$ miles. How many miles does
(114) Marta walk in two mornings?

14. $9.36 - (4.37 - 3.8)$
(45, 50)

15. $24.32 - (8.61 + 12.5)$
(45, 50)

*16. $5\frac{5}{8} + 3\frac{3}{8}$
(114)

*17. $6\frac{3}{10} + 1\frac{2}{10}$
(114)

*18. $8\frac{2}{3} - 5\frac{1}{3}$
(107)

*19. $4\frac{3}{4} - 2\frac{1}{4}$
(114)

*20. 125×16
(113)

*21. $12 \times \$1.50$
(113)

22. $6m = 3642$
(80)

23. $\$125 \div 5$
(65, 76)

*24. $40\overline{)645}$
(110)

25. $3m = 6^2$
(61, 62)

26. **(Evaluate)** If n is 16, then what does $3n$ equal?
(106)

27. In three classrooms there were 18, 21, and 21 students. What was the
(96) average number of students per classroom?

28. Dion's temperature is 99.8°F. Normal body temperature is about
(31, 43) 98.6°F. Dion's temperature is how many degrees above normal body
temperature?

*29. Estimate the perimeter and area of this piece of land. Each
(111) small square represents one square mile.

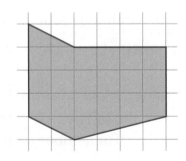

*30. **(Predict)** If the arrow is spun, what is the probability that
(Inv. 10) it will stop on a number greater than 5?

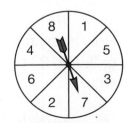

• Common Denominators

facts   Power Up H

mental math

    a. Percent: 10% of 60

    b. Percent: 20% of 60

    c. Percent: 30% of 60

    d. Fractional Parts: $\frac{1}{2}$ of 27

    e. Probability: Use one of the words *certain, likely, unlikely,* or *impossible* to describe the likelihood of this situation: *Joel will roll a number greater than 0 with a standard dot cube.*

    f. Estimation: Estimate 14 × 41. First round 41 to the nearest ten; then use the "double and half" method.

    g. Calculation: 11 × 3, + 3, ÷ 9, − 4 × 1

    h. Roman Numerals: Write CM in our number system.

problem solving

Choose an appropriate problem-solving strategy to solve this problem. Kamaria keeps DVDs in a box that is 15 inches long, $7\frac{3}{4}$ inches wide, and $5\frac{1}{4}$ inches tall. The DVDs are $7\frac{1}{2}$ inches long, $5\frac{1}{4}$ inches wide, and $\frac{1}{2}$ inch thick. What is the greatest number of DVDs she can fit into the box?

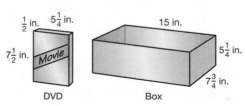

New Concept

Two or more fractions have **common denominators** if their denominators are equal.

$$\frac{3}{8} \qquad \frac{5}{8} \qquad\qquad \frac{3}{8} \qquad \frac{5}{9}$$

These two fractions have common denominators.

These two fractions do *not* have common denominators.

In this lesson we will use common denominators to rename fractions whose denominators are not equal.

Example 1

Math Language

One way to find a *common denominator* is to multiply the denominators.

$3 \times 4 = 12$

When we multiply two numbers, each number is a factor of the product.

Rename $\frac{2}{3}$ and $\frac{3}{4}$ so that they have a common denominator of 12.

To rename a fraction, we multiply it by a fraction name for 1. To change the denominator of $\frac{2}{3}$ to 12, we multiply $\frac{2}{3}$ by $\frac{4}{4}$. To change the denominator of $\frac{3}{4}$ to 12, we multiply $\frac{3}{4}$ by $\frac{3}{3}$.

$$\frac{2}{3} \times \frac{4}{4} = \frac{8}{12} \qquad\qquad \frac{3}{4} \times \frac{3}{3} = \frac{9}{12}$$

$$\frac{2}{3} = \frac{8}{12} \qquad\qquad \frac{3}{4} = \frac{9}{12}$$

Example 2

Rename $\frac{1}{2}$ and $\frac{1}{3}$ so that they have a common denominator.

This time we need to find a common denominator before we can rename the fractions. The denominators are 2 and 3. The product of 2 and 3 is 6, so 6 is a common denominator.

To get denominators of 6, we multiply $\frac{1}{2}$ by $\frac{3}{3}$, and we multiply $\frac{1}{3}$ by $\frac{2}{2}$.

$$\frac{1}{2} \times \frac{3}{3} = \frac{3}{6} \qquad\qquad \frac{1}{3} \times \frac{2}{2} = \frac{2}{6}$$

$$\frac{1}{2} = \frac{3}{6} \qquad\qquad \frac{1}{3} = \frac{2}{6}$$

In Examples 1 and 2, we found a common denominator of two fractions by multiplying the denominators. This method works for any two fractions. However, this method often produces a denominator larger than necessary. For example, a common denominator for $\frac{1}{2}$ and $\frac{3}{8}$ is 16, but a lower common denominator is 8. We usually look for the **least common denominator** when we want to rename fractions with common denominators.

Example 3

Write $\frac{1}{3}$ and $\frac{1}{6}$ with common denominators.

A common denominator is the product of 3 and 6, which is 18. However, the least common denominator is 6 because $\frac{1}{3}$ can be renamed as sixths.

$$\frac{1}{3} \cdot \frac{2}{2} = \frac{2}{6}$$

The fractions are $\frac{2}{6}$ and $\frac{1}{6}$.

Lesson Practice

a. Rename $\frac{1}{2}$ and $\frac{1}{5}$ so that they have a common denominator of 10.

b. Rename $\frac{1}{2}$ and $\frac{5}{6}$ so that they have a common denominator of 12.

Rename each pair of fractions using their least common denominator:

c. $\frac{1}{2}$ and $\frac{2}{3}$

d. $\frac{1}{3}$ and $\frac{1}{4}$

e. $\frac{1}{2}$ and $\frac{3}{5}$

f. $\frac{2}{3}$ and $\frac{2}{5}$

Written Practice   *Distributed and Integrated*

1. Evan found 24 seashells. If he gave one fourth of them to his brother, how many did he keep?
(95)

2. Rectangular Park is 2 miles long and 1 mile wide. Gordon ran around the park twice. How many miles did he run?
(Inv. 2)

2 mi

1 mi

*3. If 2 oranges cost 42¢, how much would 8 oranges cost?
(94)

4. a. **Represent** Three fourths of the 64 baseball cards showed rookie
_(Inv. 5, 95) players. How many of the baseball cards showed rookie players?
Draw a picture to illustrate the problem.

b. What percent of the baseball cards showed rookie players?

5. Write these numbers in order from greatest to least:
_(Inv. 9)

$$7.2 \quad 7\frac{7}{10} \quad 7\frac{3}{10} \quad 7.5$$

*6. **Multiple Choice** Which of these fractions is *not* equivalent to $\frac{1}{2}$?
_(103, 109)
A $\frac{3}{6}$ **B** $\frac{5}{10}$ **C** $\frac{10}{21}$ **D** $\frac{50}{100}$

*7. Complete each equivalent fraction:
₍₁₁₅₎
a. $\frac{1}{2} = \frac{?}{12}$ **b.** $\frac{1}{3} = \frac{?}{12}$ **c.** $\frac{1}{4} = \frac{?}{12}$

*8. Write the reduced form of each fraction:
₍₁₁₂₎
a. $\frac{5}{10}$ **b.** $\frac{8}{15}$ **c.** $\frac{6}{12}$

9. **Analyze** Darlene paid 42¢ for 6 clips and 64¢ for 8 erasers. What was
₍₉₄₎ the cost of each clip and each eraser? What would be the total cost of
10 clips and 20 erasers?

10. **Conclude** There were 14 volunteers the first year, 16 volunteers
_(3, 72) the second year, and 18 volunteers the third year. If the number of
volunteers continued to increase by 2 each year, how many volunteers
would there be in the tenth year? Explain how you know.

*11. a. Rename $\frac{1}{4}$ and $\frac{2}{3}$ by multiplying the denominators.
₍₁₁₆₎

b. Rename $\frac{1}{3}$ and $\frac{3}{4}$ using their least common denominator.

12. **Predict** A standard dot cube is rolled. What is the probability that
_(Inv. 10) the number of dots rolled will be less than seven?

13. $47.14 - (3.63 + 36.3)$ **14.** $50.1 + (6.4 - 1.46)$
_(45, 50) _(45, 50)

*15. $\frac{3}{4} + \frac{3}{4} + \frac{3}{4}$ ***16.** $4\frac{1}{6} + 1\frac{1}{6}$ ***17.** $5\frac{3}{5} + 1\frac{2}{5}$
₍₁₁₄₎ ₍₁₁₄₎ ₍₁₁₄₎

*18. $\frac{5}{6} + \frac{1}{6}$
_(114)_

*19. $12\frac{3}{4} - 3\frac{1}{4}$
_(114)_

*20. $6\frac{1}{5} - 1\frac{1}{5}$
_(114)_

*21. 340×15
_(113)_

*22. 26×307
_(113)_

*23. 70×250
_(113)_

24. $\frac{3550}{5}$
_(80)_

*25. $432 \div 30$
_(110)_

26. $9)\overline{5784}$
_(76)_

*27. Karen is planning a trip to Los Angeles from Chicago for her vacation.
_(19, 101)_ She finds the following two round-trip flight schedules. Use the information below to answer parts **a–c.**

Passengers: 1			Price: $246.00	
Flight number	Departure city	Date Time	Arrival city	Date Time
12A	ORD Chicago	7/21 06:11 p.m.	LAX Los Angeles	7/21 08:21 p.m.
46	LAX Los Angeles	7/28 06:39 p.m.	ORD Chicago	7/29 12:29 a.m.

Passengers: 1			Price: $412.00	
Flight number	Departure city	Date Time	Arrival city	Date Time
24	ORD Chicago	7/21 08:17 a.m.	LAX Los Angeles	7/21 10:28 a.m.
142	LAX Los Angeles	7/28 03:28 p.m.	ORD Chicago	7/28 09:18 p.m.

a. If Karen wants to arrive in Los Angeles in the morning, how much will she pay for airfare?

b. If Karen chooses the more economical round-trip, when is her return flight scheduled to land?

c. Multiple Choice There is a 2-hour time difference between Chicago and Los Angeles. About how long does a flight between those cities last?

A 2 hours **B** 4 hours **C** 6 hours **D** 8 hours

For problems **28** and **29,** refer to the pentagon at right.

*28. Estimate the area of the pentagon. Each small square
(111) represents one square inch.

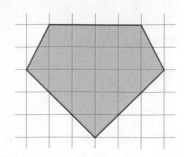

*29. a. Does the pentagon have reflective symmetry?
(79)

    b. Does the pentagon have rotational symmetry?

*30. Refer to the figure to answer parts **a** and **b.**
(73, 108)

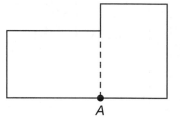

    a. The hexagon is formed by two joined rectangles. Which
transformation would move one rectangle to the position
of the other rectangle?

    b. If each rectangle is 5 inches by 7 inches, then what is the
area of the hexagon?

*Real-World
Connection*

A science fair was being held at Emmy's school. She wanted to design
an experiment that tested giving bean plants liquids other than water.
Emmy decided to test giving vinegar to a plant. Emmy had $\frac{9}{15}$ oz of
vinegar. She gave the plant $\frac{2}{5}$ oz of vinegar. How much vinegar does
Emmy have left after her experiment? Simplify your answer.

• Rounding Whole Numbers Through Hundred Millions

Power Up

facts   Power Up J

mental math

a. Percent: 10% of 70

b. Percent: 20% of 70

c. Percent: 30% of 70

d. Percent: 40% of 70

e. Percent: 60% of 70

f. Estimation: Choose the more reasonable estimate for the length of a playground seesaw: 2.7 meters or 2.7 feet.

g. Calculation: $100 \times 5, - 400, \div 4, \sqrt{}$

h. Roman Numerals: Compare CXC $\bigcirc$ 120

problem solving

Choose an appropriate problem-solving strategy to solve this problem. Write the next four fractions in this sequence. Then describe the sequence in words.

$$\frac{1}{4}, \frac{2}{8}, \frac{3}{12}, \underline{\quad}, \underline{\quad}, \underline{\quad}, \underline{\quad}, \dots$$

New Concept

We have rounded whole numbers to the nearest hundred and to the nearest thousand. In this lesson we will practice rounding numbers to the nearest ten thousand, the nearest hundred thousand, and so on through the nearest hundred million.

Recall the locations of the whole-number place values through hundred trillions:

Visit www. SaxonMath.com/ Int4Activities for an online activity.

Whole-Number Place Values

hundred trillions | ten trillions | trillions | hundred billions | ten billions | billions | hundred millions | ten millions | millions | hundred thousands | ten thousands | thousands | hundreds | tens | ones | decimal point

— — — , — — — , — — — , — — — , — — — .

After rounding to the nearest ten thousand, each place to the right of the ten-thousands place will be zero.

Analyze How is the value of each place related to the value of the place to its right?

Example 1

Round 38,274 to the nearest ten thousand.

Counting by ten thousands, we say "ten thousand, twenty thousand, thirty thousand, forty thousand," and so on. We know that 38,274 is between 30,000 and 40,000. Halfway between is 35,000. Since 38,274 is greater than 35,000, we round up to **40,000.**

After rounding to the nearest hundred thousand, each place to the right of the hundred-thousands place will be zero.

Example 2

Round 47,681 to the nearest thousand.

Counting by thousands, 47,681 is between 47,000 and 48,000. Halfway between is 47,500. Since 47,681 is greater than 47,500, we round up to **48,000.**

Example 3

Round 427,063 to the nearest hundred thousand.

Counting by hundred thousands, we say "one hundred thousand, two hundred thousand, three hundred thousand, four hundred thousand," and so on. We know that 427,063 is between 400,000 and 500,000. Halfway between is 450,000. Since 427,063 is less than halfway between 400,000 and 500,000, we round down to **400,000.**

Example 4

Round 12,876,250 to the nearest million.

The number begins with "twelve million." Counting by millions from 12 million, we say "twelve million, thirteen million," and so on. We know that 12,876,250 is between 12 million and 13 million. Since 12,876,250 is more than halfway to 13 million, we round up to **13,000,000.**

Lesson Practice   **Estimate** Round each number to the nearest ten thousand:

a. 19,362   **b.** 31,289

Estimate Round each number to the nearest hundred thousand:

c. 868,367   **d.** 517,867

e. Round 2,156,324 to the nearest million.

f. Round 28,376,000 to the nearest ten million.

g. Round 412,500,000 to the nearest hundred million.

Written Practice   *Distributed and Integrated*

1. **Explain** Forty-five students are separated into four groups.
(88)   The number of students in each group is as equal as possible. How many students are in the largest group? Explain your reasoning.

2. **a.** What is the area of this rectangle?
(Inv. 2, Inv. 3)   **b.** What is the perimeter of this rectangle?

12 cm

8 cm

*3. **Represent** Iggy answered $\frac{5}{6}$ of the 90 questions correctly.
(95)   How many questions did Iggy answer correctly? Draw a picture to illustrate the problem.

4. Name the shape of each object:
(98)   **a.** roll of paper towels   **b.** baseball

* 5. Write the reduced form of each fraction:
_(112)_

  a. $\dfrac{3}{6}$ **b.** $\dfrac{5}{15}$ **c.** $\dfrac{8}{12}$

* 6. Rename $\dfrac{3}{4}$ and $\dfrac{5}{6}$ using their least common denominator.
_(116)_

7. Which digit is in the ten-millions place in 328,496,175?
_(33)_

8. (Analyze) Draw a picture to help you solve this problem:
_(25)_

 The town of Winder is between Atlanta and Athens. It is 73 miles from Athens to Atlanta. It is 23 miles from Winder to Athens. How many miles is it from Winder to Atlanta?

9. Caleb volunteers after school as a tutor. Each afternoon he begins a tutoring session at the time shown on the clock and finishes three quarters of an hour later. What time does each tutoring session end?
_(27)_

10. These thermometers show the average daily minimum and maximum temperatures in Helena, Montana, during the month of July. What are those temperatures?
_(18)_

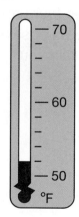 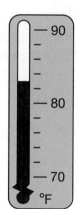

11. 4.36 + 12.7 + 10.72
_(50)_

12. 8.54 − (4.2 − 2.17)
_(45, 91)_

* 13. $\dfrac{5}{9} + \dfrac{5}{9}$
_(114)_

* 14. $3\dfrac{2}{3} + 1\dfrac{2}{3}$
_(114)_

15. $4\dfrac{5}{8} + 1$
_(107)_

* 16. $7\dfrac{2}{3} + 1\dfrac{2}{3}$
_(114)_

* 17. $4\dfrac{4}{9} + 1\dfrac{1}{9}$
_(107)_

* 18. $\dfrac{11}{12} + \dfrac{1}{12}$
_(114)_

* 19. 570 × 64
_(113)_

* 20. 382 × 31
_(113)_

21. 54 × 18
_(90)_

22. $\frac{3731}{7}$
(76)

23. $9\overline{)5432}$
(80)

*24. $60\overline{)548}$
(110)

25. **Predict** The first five square numbers are 1, 4, 9, 16, and 25.
(Inv. 3)

What is the eighth term of this sequence? Write an equation to support your answer.

*26. **Estimate** In the year 2000, the population of Texas was 20,851,820. Round that number to the nearest million.
(117)

*27. a. Multiple Choice Hasana built a square frame using pieces of wood, but when he leaned against it, the frame shifted to this shape at right. What word does *not* name this shape?
(92)

   A quadrilateral   **B** parallelogram

   C rhombus   **D** trapezoid

b. Describe the angles.

c. Describe the sides.

28. If the perimeter of a square is 6 centimeters, then each side is how many millimeters long?
(Inv. 2, 69)

*29. a. This cube is made up of how many smaller cubes?
(98)

b. A cube has how many more vertices than this pyramid?

*30.  **Interpret** The graph shows the approximate elevations of four
(Inv. 6) cities in the United States.

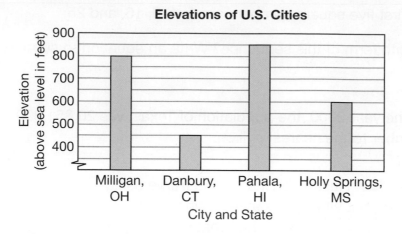

Elevations of U.S. Cities

Use the graph to answer parts **a** and **b**.

a. Which cities have an elevation difference of 250 feet?

b. Which city is nearest sea level? Explain your answer.

Early Finishers

Real-World Connection

Earth is the third planet from the sun in our solar system. The average distance from Earth to the sun is 92,750,000 miles. Mars is the fourth planet from the sun in our solar system. The average distance from Mars to the sun is 141,650,000 miles.

a. Round each distance to the nearest hundred thousand miles.

b. Round each distance to the nearest million miles.

• Dividing by Two-Digit Numbers

facts	Power Up I
mental math	**a. Percent:** 50% of 34
	b. Percent: 50% of 25
	c. Percent: 100% of 25
	d. Number Sense: 5×66
	e. Money: Toby gave the clerk a $10 bill to purchase batting gloves that cost $9.13. How much change should he receive?
	f. Estimation: Stan purchased 2 books priced at $8.95 each and another book that cost $13.88. Estimate the total cost of the books.
	g. Calculation: $5 \times 6, - 6, - 4, \div 5, \div 4$
	h. Roman Numerals: Write XCI in our number system.

problem solving

Choose an appropriate problem-solving strategy to solve this problem. In this Venn diagram, the outer circle stands for multiples of 5. The inner circle stands for multiples of 10. The inner circle is completely contained by the outer circle because every multiple of 10 is also a multiple of 5. Copy this Venn diagram on your paper, and place the numbers 15, 20, 45, 70, and 63.

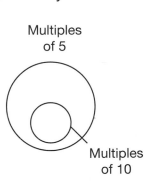

Multiples of 5

Multiples of 10

We have divided by two-digit numbers that are multiples of 10. In this lesson we will begin dividing by other two-digit numbers. Sometimes, when dividing by two-digit numbers, we might accidentally choose an "answer" that is too large. If this happens, we start over and try a smaller number.

Example 1

Thinking Skill

Verify

What are the 4 steps in division?

Divide: $31\overline{)95}$

Step 1: To help us divide $31\overline{)95}$, we may think "$3\overline{)9}$." We write "3" above the 5 in 95.

$$\begin{array}{r} 3\text{ R} \\ 31\overline{)95} \\ \underline{93} \\ 2 \end{array}$$

Step 2: We multiply 3 by 31 and write "93."

Step 3: We subtract 93 from 95 and write "2."

Step 4: There are no digits to bring down. The answer is **3 R 2.**

Example 2

Divide: $43\overline{)246}$

Step 1: To help us divide $43\overline{)246}$, we may think "$4\overline{)24}$." We write "6" above the 6 in 246.

$$\begin{array}{r} 6 \\ 43\overline{)246} \\ \underline{258} \end{array} \leftarrow \text{too large}$$

Step 2: We multiply 6 by 43 and write "258." We see that 258 is greater than 246, so 6 is too large for our answer.

Start Over:

Step 1: This time we try 5 as our answer.

Step 2: We multiply 5 by 43 and write "215."

$$\begin{array}{r} 5\text{ R }31 \\ 43\overline{)246} \\ \underline{215} \\ 31 \end{array}$$

Step 3: We subtract 215 from 246 and write "31."

Step 4: There are no digits to bring down. The answer is **5 R 31.**

Justify How can we check the answer?

Example 3

Four hundred eighty-seven students will be assigned to classrooms so that the average number of students in each room is 21. How many classrooms of students will there be?

We divide 487 by 21. We follow the four steps: divide, multiply, subtract, and bring down.

Thinking Skill

Discuss

Why do we write the digit 2 in the tens place of the quotient?

Step 1: We break the problem into a smaller division problem. We think "21)48" and write "2" above the 8 in 487.

$$\begin{array}{r} 2 \\ 21\overline{)487} \\ \underline{42} \\ 67 \end{array}$$

Step 2: We multiply 2 by 21 and write "42."

Step 3: We subtract 42 from 48 and write "6."

Step 4: We bring down the 7, making 67.

Repeat:

Step 1: We divide 67 by 21 and write "3" above the division box.

Step 2: We multiply 3 by 21 and write "63."

Step 3: We subtract 63 from 67 and write "4."

Step 4: There are no digits to bring down. The answer is 23 R 4.

$$\begin{array}{r} 23\ R\ 4 \\ 21\overline{)487} \\ \underline{42} \\ 67 \\ \underline{63} \\ 4 \end{array}$$

The quotient 23 R 4 means that 487 students will fill **23 classrooms** with 21 students and there will be 4 extra students. Four students are not enough for another classroom, so some classrooms will have more than 21 students.

Lesson Practice   Divide:

a. 32)128   **b.** 21)90   **c.** 25)68

d. 42)250   **e.** 41)880   **f.** 11)555

Written Practice   *Distributed and Integrated*

*1. **Interpret** Use the information in the graph
(Inv. 6) to answer parts **a–c.**

a. On which day was the temperature the highest?

b. What was the high temperature on Tuesday?

c. From Monday to Wednesday, the high temperature went up how many degrees?

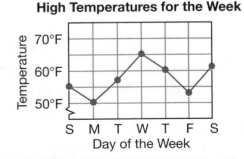

High Temperatures for the Week

2. a. What is the perimeter of this rectangle?
(Inv. 2, Inv. 3)

b. What is the area of the rectangle?

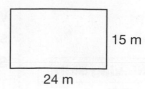

15 m

24 m

3. (Analyze) The first five square numbers are 1, 4, 9, 16, and 25, and their
(96) average is 11. What is the average of the next five square numbers?

4. What percent of the months of the year begin with the letter J?
(Inv. 5, 54)

5. There are 52 cards in a deck. Four of the cards are aces. What is the
(Inv. 10, 112) probability of drawing an ace from a full deck of cards?

6. (Classify) Name each shape:
(98)

a.

b.

c.

* 7. Write the reduced form of each fraction:
(112)

a. $\frac{6}{8}$

b. $\frac{4}{9}$

c. $\frac{4}{16}$

* 8. Rename $\frac{2}{3}$ and $\frac{3}{4}$ using their least common denominators.
(116)

* 9. (Represent) Use words to write the number 27386415.
(34)

10. (Represent) Point *W* stands for what number on this number line?
(94)

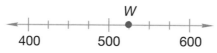

W

400   500   600

* 11. (Represent) Draw two parallel segments that are one inch long and
(23, 92) one inch apart. Then make a quadrilateral by drawing two more parallel
segments. What type of quadrilateral did you draw?

* 12. $4\frac{4}{5} + 3\frac{3}{5}$
(114)

* 13. $5\frac{1}{6} + 1\frac{2}{6}$
(114)

* 14. $7\frac{3}{4} + \frac{1}{4}$
(114)

* 15. $13\overline{)50}$
(118)

* 16. $72\overline{)297}$
(118)

17. $5\frac{3}{8} + 5\frac{1}{8}$
(114)

18. $4\frac{1}{6} + 2\frac{1}{6}$
(114)

19. 720×36
(113)

20. 147×54
(113)

21. $8\overline{)5766}$
(80)

*22. $21\overline{)441}$
(118)

23. $4.75 + 16.14 + 10.9$
(50)

24. $18.4 - (4.32 - 2.6)$
(45, 91)

*25. (Estimate) In the year 2000, the population of the state of New York
(117) was 18,976,457. Round that number to the nearest million.

*26. (Estimate) Round 297,576,320 to the nearest hundred million.
(117)

*27. In Jahzara's first nine games she earned these scores:
(97)

$$90, 95, 80, 85, 100, 95, 75, 95, 90$$

Use this information to answer parts **a** and **b**.

　a. What is the median and range of Jahzara's scores?

　b. What is the mode of Jahzara's scores?

28. Write these numbers in order from least to greatest:
(Inv. 9)

$$5\frac{11}{100} \qquad 5.67 \qquad 5.02 \qquad 5\frac{83}{100}$$

29. Yasmine wanted to divide 57 buttons into 13 groups. How many groups
(118) will Yasmine have? Will there be any buttons left over?

30. Rename $\frac{2}{3}$ and $\frac{3}{5}$ so that they have a common denominator of 15.
(116)

LESSON 119

• Adding and Subtracting Fractions with Different Denominators

Power Up

facts

Power Up J

mental math

a. Percent: 50% of 90

b. Percent: 10% of 90

c. Percent: 90% of 90

d. Number Sense: 5×84

e. Probability: Use one of the words *certain, likely, unlikely,* or *impossible* to describe the likelihood that Hannah can flip a coin 100 times and get heads every time.

f. Estimation: Estimate 48×34. Increase 48 by 2 and decrease 34 by 2; then use the "double and half" method.

g. Calculation: 50% of 10, $+ 7, - 8, \div 2, \div 2$

h. Roman Numerals: Compare: XCIV $\bigcirc$ 110

problem solving

Choose an appropriate problem-solving strategy to solve this problem. Kathy has a two-digit combination lock for her bicycle. She can choose any combination to set from 00 to 99. Kathy wants to set a combination in which the second digit is greater than the first digit, such as 05 or 47 but not 42. How many possibilities can Kathy choose from? Explain how you found your answer.

New Concept

In order to add or subtract fractions that have different denominators, we must first rename the fractions so that they have common denominators. Recall that we rename a fraction by multiplying it by a fraction name for 1.

Example 1

Discuss

Why can we use 8 as the common denominator?

A recipe calls for $\frac{1}{4}$ of a cup of whole milk and $\frac{3}{8}$ of a cup of skim milk. What amount of milk does the recipe call for altogether?

The denominators are different. Notice that a common denominator is 8. We rename $\frac{1}{4}$ by multiplying it by $\frac{2}{2}$. The result is $\frac{2}{8}$. Now we can add.

Rename.

$$\frac{1}{4} \times \frac{2}{2} = \frac{2}{8}$$
$$+ \frac{3}{8} \qquad = \frac{3}{8}$$
$$\overline{\qquad \frac{5}{8}}$$

Add.

Altogether, the recipe calls for $\frac{5}{8}$ **cup of milk.**

Example 2

Chuck looked at the clock and saw that the lunch bell would ring in $\frac{5}{6}$ of an hour. Chuck looked at the clock again $\frac{1}{2}$ hour later. At that time, what fraction of an hour remained until the lunch bell rang?

At first, $\frac{5}{6}$ of an hour remained. Then $\frac{1}{2}$ hour went by. If we subtract $\frac{1}{2}$ from $\frac{5}{6}$, we can find what fraction of an hour remains. The denominators are different, but we can rename $\frac{1}{2}$ as a fraction whose denominator is 6. Then we subtract and reduce the answer.

Rename.

$$\frac{5}{6} \qquad = \frac{5}{6}$$
$$- \frac{1}{2} \times \frac{3}{3} = \frac{3}{6}$$
$$\overline{\qquad \frac{2}{6} = \frac{1}{3}}$$

Subtract.

Reduce.

We find that $\frac{1}{3}$ **hour** remained until lunch.

Lesson Practice

Find each sum or difference. Reduce when possible.

a. $\frac{1}{2} + \frac{2}{6}$

b. $\frac{1}{3} + \frac{1}{9}$

c. $\frac{1}{8} + \frac{1}{2}$

d. $\frac{3}{8} - \frac{1}{4}$

e. $\frac{2}{3} - \frac{2}{9}$

f. $\frac{7}{8} - \frac{1}{2}$

1. Zuna used 1-foot-square floor tiles to cover the floor of a room
(Inv. 3, 90) 15 feet long and 12 feet wide. How many floor tiles did she use?

2. a. What is the perimeter of this triangle?
(Inv. 2, 78)
b. Is this triangle equilateral, isosceles, or scalene?

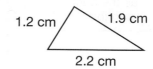
1.2 cm   1.9 cm
2.2 cm

*3. (**Represent**) Elsa found that $\frac{3}{8}$ of the 32 pencils in the room had no
(95) erasers. How many pencils had no erasers? Draw a picture to illustrate
the problem.

4. a. Seventy-two pencils is how many dozen pencils?
(41, Inv. 5)
b. How many pencils is 50% of one dozen pencils?

*5. (**Estimate**) Using rounding or compatible numbers, which numbers
(42, 49) would you choose to estimate the exact product of 75 × 75? Explain
your reasoning.

6. This cube is constructed of smaller cubes that are each
(Inv. 11) one cubic centimeter in volume. What is the volume of the
larger cube?

7. Fausta bought 2 DVDs priced at $21.95 each and 2 CDs priced at
(83) $14.99 each. The tax was $4.62. What was the total cost of the items?
Explain how you found your answer.

8. T'Ron drove 285 miles in 5 hours. What was his average speed in
(96) miles per hour?

9. Multiple Choice Which of these fractions is *not* equivalent to $\frac{1}{2}$?
(103, 109)
   A $\frac{4}{8}$ **B** $\frac{11}{22}$ **C** $\frac{15}{30}$ **D** $\frac{12}{25}$

*10. Write the reduced form of each fraction:
(112)
   a. $\frac{8}{10}$ **b.** $\frac{6}{15}$ **c.** $\frac{8}{16}$

*11. **Represent** Use words to write the number 123415720.
(33)

12. $8.3 + 4.72 + 0.6 + 12.1$
(50)

13. $17.42 - (6.7 - 1.23)$
(45, 91)

*14. $3\dfrac{3}{8} + 3\dfrac{3}{8}$
(114)

*15. $\dfrac{1}{4} + \dfrac{1}{8}$
(119)

*16. $\dfrac{1}{2} + \dfrac{1}{6}$
(119)

*17. $5\dfrac{5}{6} - 1\dfrac{1}{6}$
(114)

*18. $\dfrac{1}{4} - \dfrac{1}{8}$
(119)

*19. $\dfrac{1}{2} - \dfrac{1}{6}$
(119)

*20. 87×16
(90)

*21. 49×340
(86, 113)

*22. 504×30
(86, 113)

23. $\$35.40 \div 6$
(71, 80)

24. $\dfrac{5784}{4}$
(76)

25. $7\overline{)2385}$
(80)

26. $30\overline{)450}$
(110)

*27. $32\overline{)450}$
(118)

*28. $15\overline{)450}$
(118)

*29. **Predict** What is the probability of drawing a heart from a full deck of
(Inv. 10, 112) cards? (*Hint:* There are 13 hearts in a deck.)

*30. **Represent** Draw a rectangle that is 5 cm long and 2 cm wide, and
(21, Inv. 5) divide the rectangle into square centimeters. Then shade 30% of the
rectangle.

Real-World Connection

Vic wants to make a CD for his party. He bought a blank CD that holds 4 hours of music. One half of the space on Vic's CD is rock music, $\dfrac{1}{4}$ is hip-hop music, and $\dfrac{1}{8}$ is jazz. He wants to add a few country songs to the CD in the remaining space. The method Vic used to calculate the amount of space he has left to add country songs is shown below:

$\dfrac{1}{2} + \dfrac{1}{4} + \dfrac{1}{8} = \dfrac{2}{4} + \dfrac{1}{4} + \dfrac{1}{8} = \dfrac{3}{4} + \dfrac{1}{8} = \dfrac{6}{8} + \dfrac{1}{8} = \dfrac{7}{8}$ of music recorded.

4 hours $- \dfrac{7}{8} = \dfrac{32}{8} - \dfrac{7}{8} = \dfrac{25}{8} = 3\dfrac{1}{8}$ hours left.

Is Vic's calculation correct? If not, where did he go wrong and what is the correct answer?

Adding and Subtracting Mixed Numbers with Different Denominators

facts   Power Up J

mental math

   a. Percent: 75% of 60

   b. Percent: 70% of 60

   c. Percent: 90% of 60

   d. Number Sense: 20×23

   e. Measurement: A cubit is about 18 inches. About how many feet is two cubits?

   f. Estimation: If Ricardo has $12, does he have enough money to buy 4 maps that cost $2.87 each?

   g. Calculation: $\frac{1}{2}$ of 44, $- 12$, $- 6$, $\times 6$

   h. Roman Numerals: Write MCM in our number system.

problem solving

Choose an appropriate problem-solving strategy to solve this problem. Find the next eight numbers in this sequence. Then describe the sequence in words.

$$\frac{1}{8}, \frac{1}{4}, \frac{3}{8}, \frac{1}{2}, \frac{5}{8}, \frac{3}{4}, \frac{7}{8}, 1, \underline{\quad}, \underline{\quad}, \underline{\quad}, \underline{\quad},$$
$$\underline{\quad}, \underline{\quad}, \underline{\quad}, \underline{\quad}, \ldots$$

To add or subtract mixed numbers, we first make sure the fractions have common denominators.

Example 1

Add: $4\frac{1}{6} + 2\frac{1}{2}$

Thinking Skill

Connect

What are the steps for adding and subtracting fractions and mixed numbers that have different denominators?

The denominators of the fractions are not the same. We can rename $\frac{1}{2}$ so that it has a denominator of 6 by multiplying $\frac{1}{2}$ by $\frac{3}{3}$. Then we add, remembering to reduce the fraction part of our answer.

$$4\frac{1}{6} = 4\frac{1}{6}$$
$$+ 2\frac{1}{2} = 2\frac{3}{6}$$
$$\overline{\qquad\qquad}$$
$$6\frac{4}{6} = 6\frac{2}{3}$$

Example 2

A bicycle trail in a state park is $5\frac{3}{4}$ miles long. The trail is flat for $3\frac{1}{2}$ miles. How many miles of the trail are not flat? Draw a number line and use numbers to show the subtraction.

We first rewrite the problem so that the fractions have common denominators. We can rename $\frac{1}{2}$ so that it has a denominator of 4 by multiplying $\frac{1}{2}$ by $\frac{2}{2}$. Then we subtract.

$$5\frac{3}{4} = 5\frac{3}{4}$$
$$- 3\frac{1}{2} \times \frac{2}{2} = 3\frac{2}{4}$$
$$\overline{\qquad\qquad}$$
$$2\frac{1}{4}$$

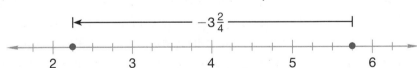

We find that **$2\frac{1}{4}$ miles** are not flat.

Lesson Practice

Add. Reduce when possible.

a. $3\frac{1}{2} + 1\frac{1}{4}$ 　　　　　　　　**b.** $4\frac{3}{4} + 1\frac{1}{8}$

c. $4\frac{1}{5} + 1\frac{3}{10}$ 　　　　　　　**d.** $6\frac{1}{6} + 1\frac{1}{3}$

Subtract. Reduce when possible.

e. $3\frac{7}{8} - 1\frac{1}{4}$ 　　　　　　　　**f.** $2\frac{3}{5} - 2\frac{1}{10}$

g. $6\frac{7}{12} - 1\frac{1}{6}$ 　　　　　　　**h.** $4\frac{3}{4} - 1\frac{1}{2}$

1. The Lorenzos drank 11 gallons of milk each month. How many quarts
(40) of milk did they drink each month?

2. Sixty people are in the marching band. If one fourth of them play trumpet,
(95) how many do not play trumpet? Draw a picture to illustrate the problem.

3. a. What is the area of this square?
(Inv. 2,
Inv. 3)
    b. What is the perimeter of the square?

10 mm

*4. a. (Analyze) Esteban is 8 inches taller than Trevin. Trevin is 5 inches taller
(94, 96)   than Chelsea. Estaban is 61 inches tall. How many inches tall is Chelsea?

    b. What is the average height of the three children?

5. Which line segments in figure *ABCD* appear to be parallel?
(23)

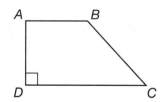

6. (Explain) Mayville is between Altoona and Watson. It is 47 miles from
(25) Mayville to Altoona. It is 24 miles from Mayville to Watson. How far is it
from Altoona to Watson? Explain why your answer is reasonable.

*7. (Predict) If the arrow is spun, what is the probability that it
(Inv. 10) will stop on a number greater than 4?

*8. (Estimate) The asking price for the new house was $298,900. Round
(117) that amount of money to the nearest hundred thousand dollars.

*9. **(Classify)** Name each of the shapes below. Then list the number of
_(98)_ vertices, edges, and faces that each shape has.

a.

b.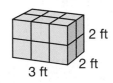

*10. Write the reduced form of each fraction:
_(112)_

a. $\frac{9}{15}$
b. $\frac{10}{12}$
c. $\frac{12}{16}$

11. **(Represent)** Use digits to write one hundred nineteen million, two
_(34)_ hundred forty-seven thousand, nine hundred eighty-four.

12. $14.94 - (8.6 - 4.7)$
_(45, 50)_

13. $6.8 - (1.37 + 2.2)$
_(45, 91)_

*14. $3\frac{2}{5} + 1\frac{4}{5}$
_(114)_

*15. $\frac{5}{8} + \frac{1}{4}$
_(119)_

*16. $1\frac{1}{3} + 1\frac{1}{6}$
_(120)_

*17. $5\frac{9}{10} - 1\frac{1}{5}$
_(120)_

*18. $\frac{5}{8} - \frac{1}{4}$
_(119)_

*19. $\frac{1}{3} - \frac{1}{6}$
_(119)_

*20. 38×217
_(113)_

*21. 173×60
_(113)_

*22. 90×500
_(86)_

23. $7\overline{)2942}$
_(80)_

24. $10\overline{)453}$
_(105)_

*25. $11\overline{)453}$
_(118)_

*26. Evaluate $m + n$ when m is $3\frac{2}{5}$ and n is $2\frac{1}{10}$.
_(106, 120)_

27. What is the volume of this rectangular solid?
(Inv. 11)

2 ft

2 ft

3 ft

*28. **(Connect)** Segment AC is $3\frac{1}{2}$ inches long. Segment AB is $1\frac{1}{2}$ inches
_(114)_ long. How long is segment BC?

A   B   C

*29. **(Estimate)** Fewer people live in Wyoming than in any other state.
_(117)_ According to the 2000 U.S. census, 493,782 people lived in
Wyoming. Round this number of people to the nearest hundred
thousand.

30. One half of a dollar plus $\frac{1}{4}$ of a dollar totals what percent of a dollar?
(36, Inv. 5)

Focus on

• Solving Balanced Equations

An *equation* states that two quantities are equal. One model for an equation is a balanced scale. The scale below is balanced because the combined weight on one side of the scale equals the combined weight on the other side. The weight of each block is given by its number. We do not know the weight of the block labeled *N*. Below the scale we have written an equation for the illustration.

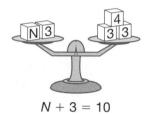

$$N + 3 = 10$$

We can find the weight *N* by removing a weight of 3 from each side of the scale. Then *N* is alone on one side of the scale, and the weight on the other side of the scale must equal *N*.

Remove 3 from each side of the scale:

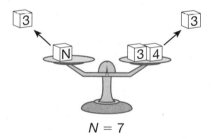

$$N = 7$$

Another balanced scale is shown below. We see that two blocks of weight *X* balances four blocks of weight 3.

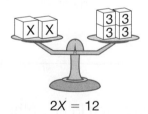

$$2X = 12$$

We can find the weight *X* by removing half of the weight from each side of the scale. Now one block of weight *X* balances two blocks of weight 3.

Remove half the weight from each side of the scale:

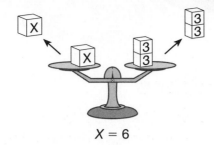

$$X = 6$$

Solving Equations

Material needed:

- **Lesson Activity 49**

As a class, work problems **1–8** on **Lesson Activity 49.** Write an equation for each illustration, and discuss how to get the lettered block alone on one side of the scale while keeping the scale balanced.

Investigate Further

a. Create an equation for the class to solve using the model of a balanced scale and an unknown weight.

b. Copy the table below for the equation $y = \frac{x + 1}{2}$ and find the missing values for y.

x	1	5	7	11	
y	1	3			

c. Choose a different odd number for x to complete the table, and then find y.

• Roman Numerals Through 39

New Concept

Roman numerals were used by the ancient Romans to write numbers. Today Roman numerals are still used to number such things as book chapters, movie sequels, and Super Bowl games. We might also find Roman numerals on clocks and buildings.

Some examples of Roman numerals are as follows:

I   which stands for 1

V   which stands for 5

X   which stands for 10

The Roman numeral system does not use place value. Instead, the values of the numerals are added or subtracted, depending on their position. For example:

II   means   1 plus 1, which is 2   (II does not mean "11")

Below we list the Roman numerals for the numbers 1 through 20. Study the patterns.

1 = I	11 = XI
2 = II	12 = XII
3 = III	13 = XIII
4 = IV	14 = XIV
5 = V	15 = XV
6 = VI	16 = XVI
7 = VII	17 = XVII
8 = VIII	18 = XVIII
9 = IX	19 = XIX
10 = X	20 = XX

The multiples of 5 are 5, 10, 15, 20, and so on. The numbers that are one less than these (4, 9, 14, 19, ...) have Roman numerals that involve subtraction.

$$4 = IV \quad \text{("one less than five")}$$

$$9 = IX \quad \text{("one less than ten")}$$

$$14 = XIV \quad \text{(ten plus "one less than five")}$$

$$19 = XIX \quad \text{(ten plus "one less than ten")}$$

In each case where a smaller Roman numeral (I) precedes a larger Roman numeral (V or X), we subtract the smaller number from the larger number.

Example

a. Write XXVII in our number system.[1]

b. Write 34 in Roman numerals.

a. We can break up the Roman numeral and see that it equals 2 tens plus 1 five plus 2 ones.

$$XX \quad V \quad II$$

$$20 + 5 + 2 = \mathbf{27}$$

b. We think of 34 as "30 plus 4."

$$30 + 4$$

$$XXX \quad IV$$

The Roman numeral for 34 is **XXXIV.**

Lesson Practice

Write the Roman numerals for 1 to 39 in order.

---

[1] The modern world has adopted the Hindu-Arabic number system with the digits 0, 1, 2, 3, 4, 5, 6, 7, 8, 9, and base-ten place value. For simplicity, we refer to the Hindu-Arabic system as "our number system."

• Roman Numerals Through Thousands

We have practiced using these Roman numerals:

I   V   X

With these numerals we can write counting numbers up to XXXIX (39). To write larger numbers, we must use the Roman numerals L (50), C (100), D (500), and M (1000). The table below shows the different Roman numeral "digits" we have learned, as well as their respective values.

Numeral	Value
I	1
V	5
X	10
L	50
C	100
D	500
M	1000

Example

Write each Roman numeral in our number system:

    a. LXX   **b. DCCL**   **c. XLIV**   **d. MMI**

a. LXX is 50 + 10 + 10, which is **70.**

b. DCCL is 500 + 100 + 100 + 50, which is **750.**

c. XLIV is "10 less than 50" plus "1 less than 5"; that is, 40 + 4 = **44.**

d. MMI is 1000 + 1000 + 1, which is **2001.**

Lesson Practice   Write each Roman numeral in our number system:

     a. CCCLXII   **b.** CCLXXXV   **c.** CD

     d. XLVII   **e.** MMMCCLVI   **f.** MCMXCIX

A

acute angle
(23)

An angle whose measure is more than 0° and less than 90°.

acute angle   not **acute angles**

*An **acute angle** is smaller than both a right angle and an obtuse angle.*

ángulo agudo

Ángulo que mide más de 0° y menos de 90°.

*Un **ángulo agudo** es menor que un ángulo recto y que un ángulo obtuso.*

---

acute triangle
(78)

A triangle whose largest angle measures less than 90°.

acute triangle   not **acute triangles**

triángulo acutángulo

Triángulo cuyo ángulo mayor es menor que 90°.

---

addend
(1)

Any one of the numbers in an addition problem.

$2 + 3 = 5$ The **addends** in this problem are 2 and 3.

sumando

Cualquiera de los números en un problema de suma.

$2 + 3 = 5$ Los **sumandos** en este problema son el 2 y el 3.

---

addition
(1)

An operation that combines two or more numbers to find a total number.

$7 + 6 = 13$ We use **addition** to combine 7 and 6.

suma

Una operación que combina dos o mas números para encontrar un número total.

$7 + 6 = 13$ Usamos la **suma** para combinar el 7 y el 6.

---

a.m.
(19)

The period of time from midnight to just before noon.

*I get up at 7 **a.m.,** which is 7 o'clock in the morning.*

a.m.

Período de tiempo desde la medianoche hasta justo antes del mediodía.

*Me levanto a las 7 **a.m.,** lo cual es las 7 en punto de la mañana.*

---

angle
(23)

The opening that is formed when two lines, line segments, or rays intersect.

*These line segments form an **angle.***

ángulo

Abertura que se forma cuando se intersecan dos rectas, segmentos de recta o rayos.

*Estos segmentos de recta forman un **ángulo.***

---

apex (98)	The vertex (pointed end) of a cone.
ápice	El vértice (punta) de un cono.

approximation (111)	*See* **estimate.**
aproximación	*Ver* **estimar.**

area (Inv. 3)	The number of square units needed to cover a surface.

5 in.

2 in.

*The **area** of this rectangle is 10 square inches.*

área	El número de unidades cuadradas que se necesita para cubrir una superficie.
	*El **área** de este rectángulo es de 10 pulgadas cuadradas.*

array (Inv. 3)	A rectangular arrangement of numbers or symbols in columns and rows.

X X X
X X X   *This is a 3-by-4 **array** of Xs.*
X X X   *It has 3 columns and 4 rows.*
X X X

matriz	Un arreglo rectangular de números o símbolos en columnas y filas.
	*Esta es una **matriz** de Xs de 3 por 4. Tiene 3 columnas y 4 filas.*

Associative Property of Addition (45)	The grouping of addends does not affect their sum. In symbolic form, $a + (b + c) = (a + b) + c$. Unlike addition, subtraction is not associative.

$$(8 + 4) + 2 = 8 + (4 + 2) \qquad (8 - 4) - 2 \neq 8 - (4 - 2)$$

*Addition is **associative**.*   *Subtraction is not **associative**.*

propiedad asociativa de la suma	La agrupación de los sumandos no altera la suma. En forma simbólica, $a + (b + c) = (a + b) + c$. A diferencia de la suma, la resta no es asociativa.

$$(8 + 4) + 2 = 8 + (4 + 2) \qquad\qquad (8 - 4) - 2 \neq 8 - (4 - 2)$$

*La suma es **asociativa**.*   *La resta no es **asociativa**.*

Associative Property of Multiplication (45)	The grouping of factors does not affect their product. In symbolic form, $a \times (b \times c) = (a \times b) \times c$. Unlike multiplication, division is not associative.

$$(8 \times 4) \times 2 = 8 \times (4 \times 2) \qquad (8 \div 4) \div 2 \neq 8 \div (4 \div 2)$$

*Multiplication is **associative**.*   *Division is not **associative**.*

propiedad asociativa de la multiplicación	La agrupación de los factores no altera el producto. En forma simbólica, $a \times (b \times c) = (a \times b) \times c$. A diferencia de la multiplicación, la división no es asociativa.

$$(8 \times 4) \times 2 = 8 \times (4 \times 2) \qquad\qquad (8 \div 4) \div 2 \neq 8 \div (4 \div 2)$$

*La multiplicación es **asociativa**.*   *La división no es **asociativa**.*

| **average** | The number found when the sum of two or more numbers is divided by the number of addends in the sum; also called *mean*. |

(96)

To find the **average** of the numbers 5, 6, and 10, first add.

$$5 + 6 + 10 = 21$$

Then, since there were three addends, divide the sum by 3.

$$21 \div 3 = 7$$

The **average** of 5, 6, and 10 is 7.

promedio Número que se obtiene al dividir la suma de dos o más números por la cantidad de sumandos; también se le llama *media*.

Para calcular el **promedio** de los números 5, 6 y 10, primero se suman.

$$5 + 6 + 10 = 21$$

Como hay tres sumandos, se divide la suma entre 3.

$$21 \div 3 = 7$$

El **promedio** de 5, 6 y 10 es 7.

B

bar graph

(Inv. 6)

A graph that uses rectangles (bars) to show numbers or measurements.

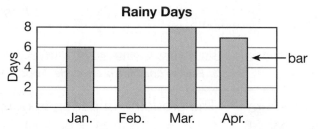

This **bar graph** shows how many rainy days there were in each of these four months.

gráfica de barras Una gráfica que utiliza rectángulos (barras) para mostrar números o medidas.

Esta **gráfica de barras** muestra cuántos días lluviosos hubo en cada uno de estos cuatro meses.

base

(62, 98)

1. The lower number in an exponential expression.

$$base \longrightarrow 5^3 \longleftarrow exponent$$

5^3 means $5 \times 5 \times 5$, and its value is 125.

2. A designated side or face of a geometric figure.

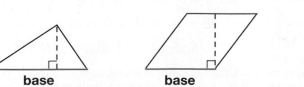

base **1.** El número inferior en una expresión exponencial.

$$base \longrightarrow 5^3 \longleftarrow exponente$$

5^3 significa $5 \times 5 \times 5$, y su valor es 125.

2. Lado (o cara) determinado de una figura geométrica.

base-ten system *(Inv. 4)*	A place-value system in which each place value is 10 times larger than the place value to its right.
	*The decimal system is a **base-ten system.***
sistema base diez	Un sistema de valor posicional en el cual cada valor posicional es 10 veces mayor que el valor posicional que está a su derecha.
	*El sistema decimal es un **sistema base diez.***
bias *(Inv. 7)*	Favoring one choice over another in a survey.
	"Which do you prefer with lunch: cool, sweet lemonade or milk that has been out of the refrigerator for an hour?"
	*Words like "cool" and "sweet" **bias** this survey question to favor the choice of lemonade.*
sesgo	Dar preferencia a una opción más que a otras en una encuesta.
	*"¿Qué prefieres tomar en tu almuerzo: una limonada dulce y fresca o leche que ha estado una hora fuera del refrigerador?" Palabras como "dulce" y "fresca" introducen **sesgo** en esta pregunta de encuesta para favorecer a la opción de limonada.*
borrowing *(15)*	See **regrouping.**
tomar prestado	*Ver **reagrupar.***

C

calendar *(54)*	A chart that shows the days of the week and their dates.

SEPTEMBER 2007

S	M	T	W	T	F	S
						1
2	3	4	5	6	7	8
9	10	11	12	13	14	15
16	17	18	19	20	21	22
23	24	25	26	27	28	29
30						

calendar

calendario	Una tabla que muestra los días de la semana y sus fechas.
capacity *(40)*	The amount of liquid a container can hold.
	*Cups, gallons, and liters are units of **capacity.***
capacidad	Cantidad de líquido que puede contener un recipiente.
	*Tazas, galones y litros son medidas de **capacidad.***
cardinal numbers *(5)*	The counting numbers 1, 2, 3, 4, ...
números cardinales	Los números de conteo 1, 2, 3, 4, ...

Celsius
(18)

A scale used on some thermometers to measure temperature.

*On the **Celsius** scale, water freezes at 0°C and boils at 100°C.*

Celsius

Escala que se usa en algunos termómetros para medir la temperatura.

*En la escala **Celsius**, el agua se congela a 0°C y hierve a 100°C.*

---

center
(21)

The point inside a circle from which all points on the circle are equally distant.

*The **center** of circle A is 2 inches from every point on the circle.*

centro

Punto interior de un círculo o esfera, que equidista de cualquier punto del círculo o de la esfera.

*El **centro** del círculo A está a 2 pulgadas de cualquier punto del círculo.*

---

centimeter
(Inv. 2)

One hundredth of a meter.

*The width of your little finger is about one **centimeter**.*

centímetro

Una centésima de un metro.

*El ancho de tu dedo meñique mide aproximadamente un **centímetro**.*

---

century
(54)

A period of one hundred years.

*The years 2001–2100 make up one **century**.*

siglo

Un período de cien años.

*Los años 2001–2100 forman un **siglo**.*

---

certain
(Inv. 10)

We say that an event is **certain** when the event's probability is 1. This means the event will definitely occur.

seguro

Decimos que un suceso es **seguro** cuando la probabilidad del suceso es 1. Esto significa que el suceso ocurrirá definitivamente.

---

chance
(Inv. 10)

A way of expressing the likelihood of an event; the probability of an event expressed as a percent.

*The **chance** of rain is 20%. It is not likely to rain.*

*There is a 90% **chance** of snow. It is likely to snow.*

posibilidad

Modo de expresar la probabilidad de ocurrencia de un suceso; la probabilidad de un suceso expresada como porcentaje.

*La **posibilidad** de lluvia es del 20%. Es poco probable que llueva.*

*Hay un 90% de **posibilidad** de nieve. Es muy probable que nieve.*

chronological order *(54)*	The order of dates or times when listed from earliest to latest. *1951, 1962, 1969, 1973, 1981, 2001* *These years are listed in **chronological order.** They are listed from earliest to latest.*
orden cronológico	El orden de fechas o tiempos cuando se enlistan del más temprano al más tardío. *1952, 1962, 1969, 1973, 1981, 2001* *Estos años están listados en **orden cronológico.** Están listados del más temprano al más tardío.*

circle *(21)*	A closed, curved shape in which all points on the shape are the same distance from its center. 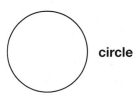 circle
círculo	Una forma cerrada curva en la cual todos los puntos en la figura están a la misma distancia de su centro.

circle graph *(Inv. 6)*	A graph made of a circle divided into sectors. Also called *pie chart* or *pie graph.* **Shoe Colors of Students** 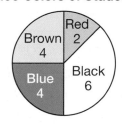 *This **circle graph** displays data on students' shoe color.*
gráfica circular	Una gráfica que consiste de un círculo dividido en sectores. *Esta **gráfica circular** representa los datos de los colores de los zapatos de los estudiantes.*

circumference *(21)*	The distance around a circle; the perimeter of a circle. 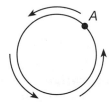 *If the distance from point A around to point A is 3 inches, then the **circumference** of the circle is 3 inches.*
circunferencia	La distancia alrededor de un círculo; el perímetro de un círculo. *Si la distancia desde el punto A alrededor del círculo hasta el punto A es 3 pulgadas, entonces la **circunferencia** o perímetro del círculo mide 3 pulgadas.*

clockwise (75)	The same direction as the movement of a clock's hands.

clockwise turn   counterclockwise turn

en el sentido de las **manecillas del reloj**	La misma dirección que el movimiento de las manecillas de un reloj.

combinations (36)	One or more parts selected from a set that are placed in groups in which order is not important. **Combinations** *of the letters A, B, C, D, and E are AB, BC, CD, DE, AC, BD, CE, BE, and AE.*
combinaciones	Una o mas partes seleccionadas de un conjunto que son colocadas en grupos donde el orden no es importante.

common **denominators** (116)	Denominators that are the same. *The fractions $\frac{2}{5}$ and $\frac{3}{5}$ have* **common denominators.**
denominadores comunes	Denominadores que son iguales. *Las fracciones $\frac{2}{5}$ y $\frac{3}{5}$ tienen* **denominadores comunes.**

common year (54)	A year with 365 days; not a leap year. *The year 2000 is a leap year, but 2001 is a* **common year.** *In a* **common year** *February has 28 days. In a leap year it has 29 days.*
año común	Un año con 365 días; no un año bisiesto. *El año 2000 es un año bisiesto, pero 2001 es un* **año común.** *En un* **año común** *febrero tiene 28 días. En un año bisiesto tiene 29 días.*

Commutative **Property of** **Addition** (1)	Changing the order of addends does not change their sum. In symbolic form, $a + b = b + a$. Unlike addition, subtraction is not commutative. $8 + 2 = 2 + 8 \qquad\qquad 8 - 2 \neq 2 - 8$ *Addition is* **commutative.** *Subtraction is not* **commutative.**
propiedad conmutativa **de la suma**	El orden de los sumandos no altera la suma. En forma simbólica, $a + b = b + a$. A diferencia de la suma, la resta no es conmutativa. $8 + 2 = 2 + 8 \qquad\qquad 8 - 2 \neq 2 - 8$ *La suma es* **conmutativa.** *La resta no es* **conmutativa.**

Commutative Property of Multiplication *(28)*	Changing the order of factors does not change their product. In symbolic form, $a \times b = b \times a$. Unlike multiplication, division is not commutative.

$$8 \times 2 = 2 \times 8 \qquad\qquad 8 \div 2 \neq 2 \div 8$$

*Multiplication is **commutative**.   Division is not **commutative**.*

propiedad conmutativa de la multiplicación	El orden de los factores no altera el producto. En forma simbólica, $a \times b = b \times a$. A diferencia de la multiplicación, la división no es conmutativa.

$$8 \times 2 = 2 \times 8 \qquad\qquad 8 \div 2 \neq 2 \div 8$$

*La multiplicación es **conmutativa**.   La división no es **conmutativa**.*

---

comparison symbol *(Inv. 1)*	A mathematical symbol used to compare numbers. ***Comparison symbols** include the equal sign (=) and the "greater than/less than" symbols (> or <).*
símbolo de comparación	Un símbolo matemático que se usa para comparar números. *Los símbolos de comparación incluyen el signo de igualdad (=) y los símbolos de "mayor que/menor que" (> ó <).*

---

compass *(21)*	A tool used to draw circles and arcs.

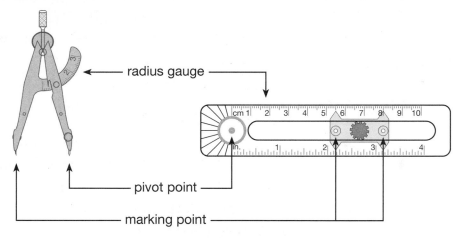

two types of **compasses**

compás	Instrumento para dibujar círculos y arcos.

---

compatible numbers *(22)*	Numbers that are close in value to the actual numbers and are easy to add, subtract, multiply, or divide.
números compatibles	Números que tienen un valor cercano a los números reales y que son fáciles de sumar, restar, multiplicar, o dividir.

composite numbers *(55)*	A counting number greater than 1 that is divisible by a number other than itself and 1. Every composite number has three or more factors. Every composite number can be expressed as a product of two or more prime numbers.

*9 is divisible by 1, 3, and 9. It is **composite.***

*11 is divisible by 1 and 11. It is not **composite.***

números compuestos — Un número de conteo mayor que 1, divisible entre algún otro número distinto de sí mismo y de 1. Cada número compuesto tiene tres o más factores. Cada número de conteo puede ser expresado como el producto de dos o más números primos.

*9 es divisible entre 1, 3 y 9. Es **compuesto.***

*11 es divisible entre 1 y 11. No es **compuesto.***

---

cone *(98)* A three-dimensional solid with one curved surface and one flat, circular surface. The pointed end of a cone is its apex.

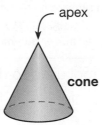

apex

cone

cono — Un sólido tridimensional con una superficie curva y una superficie plana y circular. El extremo puntiagudo de un cono es su ápice.

---

congruent *(56)* Having the same size and shape.

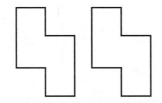

*These polygons are **congruent.** They have the same size and shape.*

congruentes — Que tienen igual tamaño y forma.

*Estos polígonos son **congruentes.** Tienen igual tamaño y forma.*

coordinate(s)
(Inv. 8)

1. A number used to locate a point on a number line.

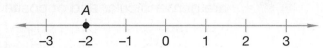

*The **coordinate** of point A is −2.*

2. A pair of numbers used to locate a point on a coordinate plane.

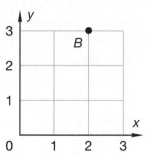

*The **coordinates** of point B are (2, 3). The x-coordinate is listed first, and the y-coordinate is listed second.*

coordenada(s)

1. Número que se utiliza para ubicar un punto sobre una recta numérica.

*La **coordenada** del punto A es −2.*

2. Par ordenado de números que se utiliza para ubicar un punto sobre un plano coordenado.

*Las **coordenadas** del punto B son (2, 3). La coordenada x se escribe primero, seguida de la coordenada y.*

---

counter-clockwise
(75)

The direction opposite of the movement of a clock's hands.

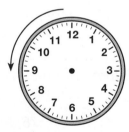 

counterclockwise turn   clockwise turn

en sentido contrario a las manecillas del reloj

La dirección opuesta al movimiento de las manecillas de un reloj.

---

counting numbers
(3)

The numbers used to count; the numbers in this sequence: 1, 2, 3, 4, 5, 6, 7, 8, 9, ...

*The numbers 12 and 37 are **counting numbers,** but 0.98 and $\frac{1}{2}$ are not.*

números de conteo

Números que se utilizan para contar; los números en esta secuencia: 1, 2, 3, 4, 5, 6, 7, 8, 9, ...

*Los números 12 y 37 son **números de conteo,** pero 0.98 y $\frac{1}{2}$ no son **números de conteo.***

cube *(98)*	A three-dimensional solid with six square faces. Adjacent faces are perpendicular and opposite faces are parallel. **cube**
cubo	Un sólido tridimensional con seis caras cuadradas. Las caras adyacentes son perpendiculares y las caras opuestas son paralelas.

cubic unit *(Inv. 11)*	A cube with edges of designated length. Cubic units are used to measure volume. *The shaded part is 1 **cubic unit.** The volume of the large cube is 8 **cubic units.***
unidad cúbica	Un cubo con aristas de una longitud designada. Las unidades cúbicas se usan para medir volumen. *La parte sombreada tiene 1 **unidad cúbica.** El volumen del cubo mayor es de 8 **unidades cúbicas.***

cylinder *(98)*	A three-dimensional solid with two circular bases that are opposite and parallel to each other. **cylinder**
cilindro	Un sólido tridimensional con dos bases circulares que son opuestas y paralelas entre sí.

D

data *(Inv. 7)*	(Singular: *datum*) Information gathered from observations or calculations. *82, 76, 95, 86, 98, 97, 93* *These **data** are average daily temperatures for one week in Utah.*
datos	Información reunida de observaciones o cálculos. *Estos **datos** son el promedio diario de las temperaturas de una semana en Utah.*

decade *(54)*	A period of ten years. *The years 2001–2010 make up one **decade.***
década	Un periodo de diez años. *Los años 2001–2010 forman una **década.***

decagon *(63)*	A polygon with ten sides.

decagon

decágono	Un polígono de diez lados.

---

decimal number *(Inv. 4)*	A numeral that contains a decimal point. *23.94 is a **decimal number** because it contains a decimal point.*
número decimal	Número que contiene un punto decimal. *23.94 es un **número decimal**, porque tiene punto decimal.*

---

decimal place(s) *(Inv. 4)*	Places to the right of a decimal point. *5.47 has two **decimal places.*** *6.3 has one **decimal place.*** *8 has no **decimal places.***
cifras decimales	Lugares ubicados a la derecha del punto decimal. *5.47 tiene dos **cifras decimales.*** *6.3 tiene una **cifra decimal.*** *8 no tiene **cifras decimales.***

---

decimal point *(22)*	A symbol used to separate the ones place from the tenths place in decimal numbers (or dollars from cents in money).

34.15

↑

decimal point

punto decimal	Un símbolo que se usa para separar el lugar de las unidades del lugar de las décimas en números decimales (o los dólares de los centavos en dinero).

degree (°)
(18, 75)

1. A unit for measuring temperature.

Water boils.

*There are 100 **degrees** (100°) between the freezing and boiling points of water on the Celsius scale.*

Water freezes.

2. A unit for measuring angles.

90°

*There are 90 **degrees** (90°) in a right angle.*

grado (°)

1. Unidad para medir temperatura.

*Hay 100 **grados** de diferencia entre los puntos de ebullición y congelación del agua en la escala Celsius, o escala centígrada.*

2. Unidad para medir ángulos.

*Un ángulo recto mide 90 **grados** (90°).*

---

denominator
(22)

The bottom number of a fraction; the number that tells how many parts are in a whole.

$\frac{1}{4}$

*The **denominator** of the fraction is 4. There are 4 parts in the whole circle.*

denominador

El número inferior de una fracción; el número que indica cuántas partes hay en un entero.

*El **denominador** de la fracción es 4. Hay 4 partes en el círculo completo.*

---

diameter
(21)

The distance across a circle through its center.

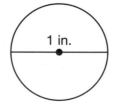

1 in.

*The **diameter** of this circle is 1 inch.*

diámetro

Distancia que atravieza un círculo a través de su centro.

*El **diámetro** de este círculo mide 1 pulgada.*

difference *(6)*	The result of subtraction. $12 - 8 = 4$ The **difference** in this problem is 4.
diferencia	Resultado de una resta. $12 - 8 = 4$ La **diferencia** en este problema es 4.
digit *(3)*	Any of the symbols used to write numbers: 0, 1, 2, 3, 4, 5, 6, 7, 8, 9. *The last **digit** in the number 2587 is 7.*
dígito	Cualquiera de los símbolos que se utilizan para escribir números: 0, 1, 2, 3, 4, 5, 6, 7, 8, 9. *El último **dígito** del número 2587 es 7.*
digital form *(19)*	When referring to clock time, digital form is a way to write time that uses a colon and a.m. or p.m. *11:30 a.m. is **digital form.***
forma digital	Cuando nos referimos al tiempo marcado por un reloj, la forma digital es una manera de escribir tiempo que usa dos puntos y a.m. o p.m. *11:30 a.m. está en **forma digital.***
Distributive Property *(108)*	A number times the sum of two addends is equal to the sum of that same number times each individual addend. $$a \times (b + c) = (a \times b) + (a \times c)$$ $$8 \times (2 + 3) = (8 \times 2) + (8 \times 3)$$ $$8 \times 5 = 16 + 24$$ $$40 = 40$$ *Multiplication is **distributive** over addition.*
propiedad distributiva	Un número multiplicado por la suma de dos sumandos es igual a la suma de los productos de ese número por cada uno de los sumandos. $$a \times (b + c) = (a \times b) + (a \times c)$$ $$8 \times (2 + 3) = (8 \times 2) + (8 \times 3)$$ $$8 \times 5 = 16 + 24$$ $$40 = 40$$ *La multiplicación es **distributiva** con respecto a la suma.*
dividend *(65)*	A number that is divided. $12 \div 3 = 4$ $3\overline{)12}$ $\dfrac{12}{3} = 4$ *The **dividend** is 12 in each of these problems.*
dividendo	Número que se divide. $12 \div 3 = 4$ $3\overline{)12}$ $\dfrac{12}{3} = 4$ *El **dividendo** es 12 en cada una de estas operaciones.*

divisible
(55)

Able to be divided by a whole number without a remainder.

$$\frac{5}{4)\overline{20}}$$ *The number 20 is **divisible** by 4, since 20 ÷ 4 has no remainder.*

$$\frac{6\ R\ 2}{3)\overline{20}}$$ *The number 20 is not **divisible** by 3, since 20 ÷ 3 has a remainder.*

divisible   Número que se puede dividir exactamente por un entero, es decir, sin residuo.

$$\frac{5}{4)\overline{20}}$$ *El número 20 es **divisible** entre 4, ya que 20 ÷ 4 no tiene residuo.*

$$\frac{6\ R\ 2}{3)\overline{20}}$$ *El número 20 no es **divisible** entre 3, ya que 20 ÷ 3 tiene residuo.*

division
(46)

An operation that separates a number into a given number of equal parts or into a number of parts of a given size.

$21 ÷ 3 = 7$ *We use **division** to separate 21 into 3 groups of 7.*

división   Una operación que separa un número en un número dado de partes iguales o en un número de partes de una medida dada.

Usamos la división para separar 21 en 3 grupos de 7.

divisor
(65)

A number by which another number is divided.

$12 ÷ 3 = 4$ $3)\overline{12}$ with quotient 4 $\dfrac{12}{3} = 4$ *The **divisor** is 3 in each of these problems.*

divisor   Número que divide a otro en una división.

$12 ÷ 3 = 4$ $3)\overline{12}$ with quotient 4 $\dfrac{12}{3} = 4$ *El **divisor** es 3 en cada una de estas operaciones.*

dozen
(49)

A group of twelve.

*The carton holds a **dozen** eggs.*

The carton holds 12 eggs.

docena   Un grupo de doce.

*El cartón contiene una **docena** de huevos.*

El cartón contiene 12 huevos.

E

edge
(98)

A line segment formed where two faces of a solid intersect.

*The arrow is pointing to one **edge** of this cube. A cube has 12 **edges**.*

arista   Segmento de recta formado donde se intersecan dos caras de un sólido.

*La flecha apunta hacia una **arista** de este cubo. Un cubo tiene 12 **aristas**.*

elapsed time (19)	The difference between a starting time and an ending time. *The race started at 6:30 p.m. and finished at 9:12 p.m. The* ***elapsed time*** *of the race was 2 hours 42 minutes.*
tiempo transcurrido	La diferencia entre el tiempo de comienzo y tiempo final. *La carrera comenzó a las 6:30 p.m. y terminó a las 9:12 p.m . El* ***tiempo transcurrido*** *de la carrera fue de 2 horas 42 minutos.*

endpoint(s) (23)	The point(s) at which a line segment ends. A ●────────────────● B *Points A and B are the* ***endpoints*** *of line segment AB.*
punto(s) extremo(s)	Punto(s) donde termina un segmento de recta. *Los puntos A y B son los* ***puntos extremos*** *del segmento AB.*

equals (Inv. 1)	Has the same value as. *12 inches* ***equals*** *1 foot.*
es igual a	Con el mismo valor. *12 pulgadas* ***es igual a*** *1 pie.*

equation (2)	A number sentence that uses an equal sign (=) to show that two quantities are equal. $x = 3$ $3 + 7 = 10$ $4 + 1$ $x < 7$ **equations** not **equations**
ecuación	Enunciado que usa el símbolo de igualdad (=) para indicar que dos cantidades son iguales. $x = 3$ $3 + 7 = 10$ $4 + 1$ $x < 7$ son **ecuaciones** no son **ecuaciones**

equiangular (78)	A figure with angles of the same measurement. *An equilateral triangle is also* ***equiangular*** *because its angles each measure 60°.*
equiangular	Una figura con ángulos de la misma medida. *Un triángulo equilátero es también* ***equiangular*** *porque sus tres ángulos miden 60°.*

equilateral triangle (21)	A triangle in which all sides are the same length and all angles are the same measure. *This is an* ***equilateral triangle.*** *All of its sides are the same length.* *All of its angles are the same measure.*
triángulo equilátero	Triángulo que tiene todos sus lados de la misma longitud. *Éste es un* ***triángulo equilátero.*** *Sus tres lados tienen la misma longitud. Todos sus ángulos miden los mismo.*

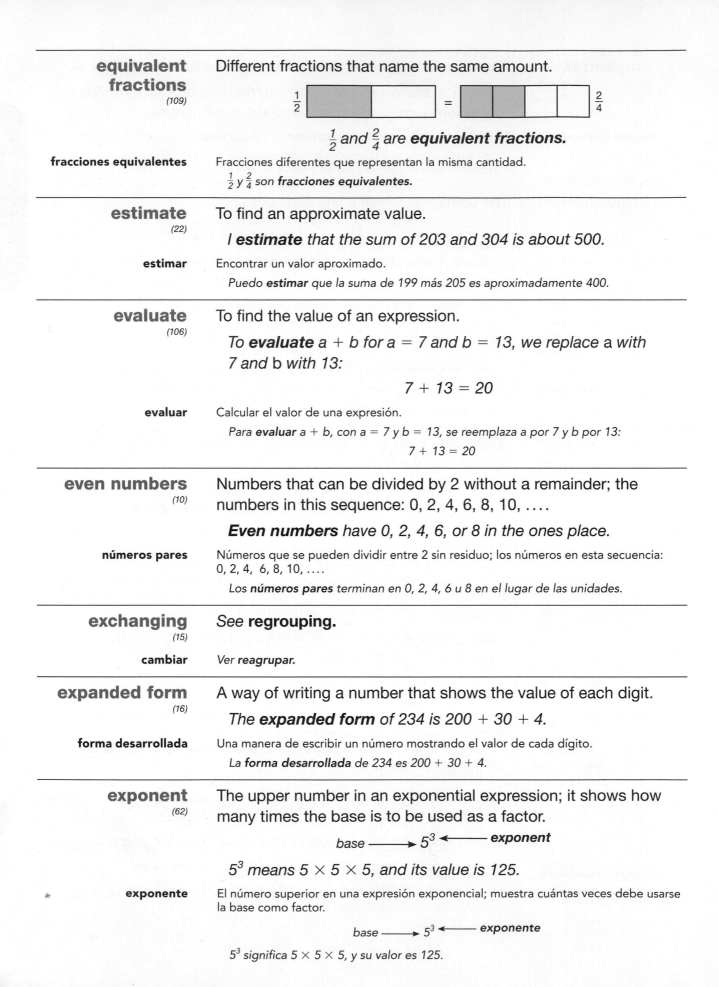

equivalent fractions (109)	Different fractions that name the same amount.
	$\frac{1}{2}$ and $\frac{2}{4}$ are **equivalent fractions.**
fracciones equivalentes	Fracciones diferentes que representan la misma cantidad.
	$\frac{1}{2}$ y $\frac{2}{4}$ son **fracciones equivalentes.**

estimate (22)	To find an approximate value.
	*I **estimate** that the sum of 203 and 304 is about 500.*
estimar	Encontrar un valor aproximado.
	*Puedo **estimar** que la suma de 199 más 205 es aproximadamente 400.*

evaluate (106)	To find the value of an expression.
	*To **evaluate** a + b for a = 7 and b = 13, we replace a with 7 and b with 13:*
	$7 + 13 = 20$
evaluar	Calcular el valor de una expresión.
	*Para **evaluar** a + b, con a = 7 y b = 13, se reemplaza a por 7 y b por 13:*
	$7 + 13 = 20$

even numbers (10)	Numbers that can be divided by 2 without a remainder; the numbers in this sequence: 0, 2, 4, 6, 8, 10, ...
	***Even numbers** have 0, 2, 4, 6, or 8 in the ones place.*
números pares	Números que se pueden dividir entre 2 sin residuo; los números en esta secuencia: 0, 2, 4, 6, 8, 10, ...
	*Los **números pares** terminan en 0, 2, 4, 6 u 8 en el lugar de las unidades.*

| **exchanging** (15) | *See **regrouping.*** |
| **cambiar** | *Ver **reagrupar.*** |

expanded form (16)	A way of writing a number that shows the value of each digit.
	*The **expanded form** of 234 is 200 + 30 + 4.*
forma desarrollada	Una manera de escribir un número mostrando el valor de cada dígito.
	*La **forma desarrollada** de 234 es 200 + 30 + 4.*

exponent (62)	The upper number in an exponential expression; it shows how many times the base is to be used as a factor.
	base $\longrightarrow 5^3 \longleftarrow$ **exponent**
	5^3 means $5 \times 5 \times 5$, and its value is 125.
exponente	El número superior en una expresión exponencial; muestra cuántas veces debe usarse la base como factor.
	base $\longrightarrow 5^3 \longleftarrow$ **exponente**
	5^3 significa $5 \times 5 \times 5$, y su valor es 125.

exponential expression *(62)*	An expression that indicates that the base is to be used as a factor the number of times shown by the exponent.
	$$4^3 = 4 \times 4 \times 4 = 64$$
	*The **exponential expression** 4^3 uses 4 as a factor 3 times. Its value is 64.*
expresión exponencial	Expresión que indica que la base debe usarse como factor el número de veces que indica el exponente.
	$$4^3 = 4 \times 4 \times 4 = 64$$
	*La **expresión exponencial** 4^3 se calcula usando 3 veces el 4 como factor. Su valor es 64.*
expression *(6)*	A number, a letter, or a combination of both. Expressions do not include comparison symbols, such as an equal sign.
	*3n is an **expression** that can also be written as $3 \times n$.*
expresión	Un número, una letra o una combinación de los dos.
	*Las **expresiones** no incluyen símbolos de comparación, como el signo de igual. 3n es una **expresión** que también puede ser escrita como $3 \times n$.*

F

face *(98)*	A flat surface of a geometric solid.
	*The arrow is pointing to one **face** of the cube. A cube has six **faces.***
cara	Superficie plana de un cuerpo geométrico.
	*La flecha apunta a una **cara** del cubo. Un cubo tiene seis **caras.***
fact family *(6)*	A group of three numbers related by addition and subtraction or by multiplication and division.
	*The numbers 3, 4, and 7 are a **fact family.** They make these four facts:*
	$$3 + 4 = 7 \qquad 4 + 3 = 7 \qquad 7 - 3 = 4 \qquad 7 - 4 = 3$$
familia de operaciones	Grupo de tres números relacionados por sumas y restas o por multiplicaciones y divisiones.
	*Los números 3, 4 y 7 forman una **familia de operaciones.** Con ellos se pueden formar estas cuatro operaciones:*
	$$3 + 4 = 7 \qquad 4 + 3 = 7 \qquad 7 - 3 = 4 \qquad 7 - 4 = 3$$
factor *(28)*	Any one of the numbers multiplied in a multiplication problem.
	$$2 \times 3 = 6 \qquad \text{The **factors** in this problem are 2 and 3.}$$
factor	Cualquier número que se multiplica en un problema de multiplicación.
	$$2 \times 3 = 6 \qquad \text{Los **factores** en este problema son 2 y 3.}$$

Fahrenheit *(18)*	A scale used on some thermometers to measure temperature. *On the **Fahrenheit** scale, water freezes at 32°F and boils at 212°F.*
Fahrenheit	Escala que se usa en algunos termómetros para medir la temperatura. *En la **escala Fahrenheit**, el agua se congela a 32°F y hierve a 212°F.*

fluid ounce *(40)*	A unit of liquid measurement in the customary system. *There are 8 **fluid ounces** in a cup, 16 **fluid ounces** in a pint, and 32 **fluid ounces** in a quart.*
onza líquida (oz. liq.)	Una unidad de medida para líquidos en el sistema usual. *Hay 8 **onzas líquidas** en una taza, 16 **onzas líquidas** en una pinta y 32 **onzas líquidas** en un cuarto.*

formula *(1)*	An expression or equation that describes a method for solving a certain type of problem. We often write formulas with letters that stand for complete words. *A **formula** for the perimeter of a rectangle is $P = 2l + 2w$, where P stands for "perimeter," l stands for "length," and w stands for "width."*
fórmula	Una expresión o ecuación que describe un método para resolver cierto tipo de problemas. Frecuentemente escribimos **fórmulas** con letras que representan palabras completas. *Una **fórmula** para el perímetro del rectángulo es $P = 2l + 2w$, donde P representa "perímetro", l representa "longitud" y w representa "ancho".*

fraction *(22)*	A number that names part of a whole. $\frac{1}{4}$ *of the circle is shaded.* $\frac{1}{4}$ *is a **fraction.***
fracción	Número que representa una parte de un entero. $\frac{1}{4}$ *del círculo está sombreado.* $\frac{1}{4}$ *es una **fracción.***

full turn *(75)*	A turn measuring 360°.
giro completo	Giro que mide 360°.

G

geometric solid *(98)*	A shape that takes up space.

geometric solids: cube, cylinder

not geometric solids: circle, rectangle, hexagon

sólido geométrico	Una figura que ocupa espacio.

geometry
(73)

A major branch of mathematics that deals with shapes, sizes, and other properties of figures.

*Some of the figures we study in **geometry** are angles, circles, and polygons.*

geometría

Rama importante de las matemáticas, que trata de las formas, tamaños y otras propiedades de las figuras.

*Algunas de las figuras que se estudian en **geometría** son los ángulos, círculos y polígonos.*

---

graph
(Inv. 6)

A diagram that shows data in an organized way. *See also* **bar graph, circle graph, line graph,** *and* **pictograph.**

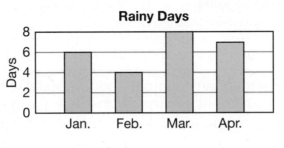

bar **graph**

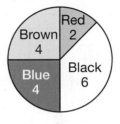

circle **graph**

gráfica

Diagrama que muestra datos de una forma organizada. *Ver también* **gráfica de barras, gráfica circular, gráfica lineal,** y **pictograma.**

---

greater than
(Inv. 1)

Having a larger value than.

$5 > 3$ Five is **greater than** three.

mayor que

Que tiene un valor mayor que.

$5 > 3$ Cinco es **mayor que** tres.

H

---

half
(22)

One of two equal parts that together equal a whole.

mitad

Una de dos partes iguales que juntas forman un entero.

---

half turn
(75)

A turn measuring 180°.

medio giro

Un giro que mide 180°.

---

hexagon
(63)

A polygon with six sides.

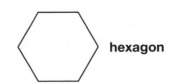

hexagon

hexágono

Un polígono con seis lados.

horizontal *(23)*	Side to side; perpendicular to vertical.

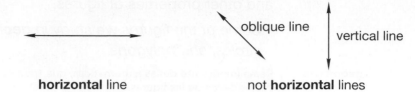

horizontal line   not **horizontal** lines

horizontal	Lado a lado; perpendicular a la vertical.

---

hundredth(s) *(Inv. 4)*	One of one hundred parts. *The decimal form of one **hundredth** is 0.01.*
centésima(s)	Una de cien partes. *La forma decimal de una **centésima** es 0.01.*

I

Identity Property of Addition *(1)*	The sum of any number and 0 is equal to the initial number. In symbolic form, $a + 0 = a$. The number 0 is referred to as the *additive identity.* *The **Identity Property of Addition** is shown by this statement:* <div align="center">$13 + 0 = 13$</div>
propiedad de identidad de la suma	La suma de cualquier número más 0 es igual al número inicial. En forma simbólica, $a + 0 = a$. El número 0 se conoce como *identidad aditiva.* *La **propiedad de identidad de la suma** se muestra en el siguiente enunciado:* <div align="center">$13 + 0 = 13$</div>

Identity Property of Multiplication *(28)*	The product of any number and 1 is equal to the initial number. In symbolic form, $a \times 1 = a$. The number 1 is referred to as the *multiplicative identity.* *The **Identity Property of Multiplication** is shown by this statement:* <div align="center">$94 \times 1 = 94$</div>
propiedad de identidad de la multiplicación	El producto de cualquier número por 1 es igual al número inicial. En forma simbólica, $a \times 1 = a$. El número 1 se conoce como *identidad multiplicativa.* *La **propiedad de identidad de la multiplicación** se muestra en el siguiente enunciado:* <div align="center">$94 \times 1 = 94$</div>

improper fraction *(89)*	A fraction with a numerator greater than or equal to the denominator. $\dfrac{4}{3}$ $\dfrac{2}{2}$ *These fractions are **improper fractions.***
fracción impropia	Fracción con el numerador igual o mayor que el denominador. $\dfrac{4}{3}$ $\dfrac{2}{2}$ *Estas fracciones son **fracciones impropias.***

intersect
(23)

To share a common point or points.

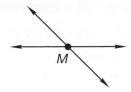

*These two lines **intersect.**
They share the common point M.*

intersecar

Compartir uno o varios puntos en común.

*Estas dos rectas se **intersecan.***

Tienen el punto común M.

---

intersecting lines
(23)

Lines that cross.

intersecting lines

líneas que se cruzan o intersecan

Líneas que se cruzan.

---

inverse operation(s)
(24)

An operation that undoes another.

*Subtraction is the **inverse operation** of addition.*

operaciones inversas

Una operación que cancela a otra.

*La resta es la **operación inversa** de la suma.*

---

isosceles triangle
(78)

A triangle with at least two sides of equal length and two angles of equal measure.

*Two of the sides of
this **isosceles triangle**
have equal lengths.
Two of the angles have
equal measures.*

triángulo isósceles

Triángulo que tiene por lo menos dos lados de igual longitud y dos lados de igual medida.

*Dos de los lados de este **triángulo isósceles** tienen igual longitud.*

Dos de los ángulos tienen medidas iguales.

K

key
(Inv. 6)

See **legend.**

clave

Ver **rótulo.**

---

kilometer
(Inv. 2)

A metric unit of length equal to 1000 meters.

*One **kilometer** is approximately 0.62 mile.*

kilómetro

Una unidad métrica de longitud igual a 1000 metros.

*Un **kilómetro** es aproximadamente 0.62 milla.*

L

leap year *(54)*	A year with 366 days; not a common year. *In a **leap year**, February has 29 days.*
año bisiesto	Un año con 366 dias; no un año común. *En un **año bisiesto** febrero tiene 29 días.*

least common denominator (LCD) *(116)*	The least common multiple of the denominators of two or more fractions. *The **least common denominator** of $\frac{5}{6}$ and $\frac{3}{8}$ is the least common multiple of 6 and 8, which is 24.*
mínimo común denominador (mcd)	El mínimo común múltiplo de los denominadores de dos o más fracciones. *El **mínimo común denominador** de $\frac{5}{6}$ y $\frac{3}{8}$ es el mínimo común múltiplo de 6 y 8, que es 24.*

legend *(Inv. 6)*	A notation on a map, graph, or diagram that describes the meaning of the symbols and/or the scale used.

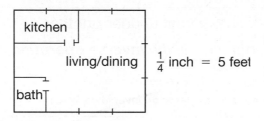

*The **legend** of this scale drawing shows that $\frac{1}{4}$ inch represents 5 feet.*

rótulo	Una anotación en un mapa, gráfica o diagrama que describe el significado de los símbolos y/o la escala usada. *El **rótulo** en el dibujo de esta escala muestra que $\frac{1}{4}$ de pulgada representa 5 pies.*

less than *(Inv. 1)*	Having a smaller value than. $3 < 5$ *Three is **less than** five.*
menor que	Con un valor menor que. $3 < 5$ *Tres es **menor que** cinco.*

line *(Inv. 1)*	A straight collection of points extending in opposite directions without end.

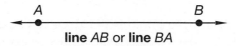

line *AB* or **line** *BA*

recta	Un grupo de puntos en línea recta que se extienden sin fin en direcciones opuestas.

line graph *(Inv. 6)*	A graph that connects points to show how information changes over time. 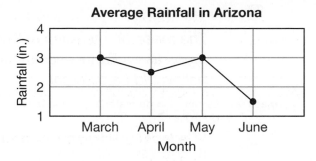 *This **line graph** shows the average rainfall in Arizona over four months.*
gráfica lineal	Una gráfica que conecta puntos para mostrar como la información cambia con el tiempo. *Esta **gráfica lineal** muestra el promedio de lluvias en Arizona en un periodo de cuatro meses.*
line of symmetry *(79)*	A line that divides a figure into two halves that are mirror images of each other. *See also* **symmetry.** 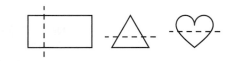 **lines of symmetry** not **lines of symmetry**
eje de simetría	Una línea que divide una figura en dos mitades que son imágenes especulares una de otra. *Ver también* **simetría.**
line segment *(Inv. 1)*	A part of a line with two distinct endpoints. 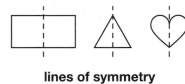 $\overline{AB}$ *is a **line segment.***
segmento de recta	Una parte de una línea con dos extremos específicos. $\overline{AB}$ *es un **segmento de recta.***
liter *(40)*	A metric unit of capacity or volume. *A **liter** is a little more than a quart.*
litro	Una unidad métrica de capacidad o volumen. *Un **litro** es un poco más que un cuarto.*
lowest terms *(Inv. 9)*	A fraction is in *lowest terms* if it cannot be reduced. *In **lowest terms,** the fraction $\frac{8}{20}$ is $\frac{2}{5}$.*
mínima expresión	Una fracción está en su mínima expresión si no se puede reducir. *En su **mínima expresión** la fracción $\frac{8}{20}$ es $\frac{2}{5}$.*

mass
(77)

The amount of matter an object contains. A kilogram is a metric unit of mass.

*The **mass** of a bowling ball would be the same on the moon as on Earth, even though the weight of the bowling ball would be different.*

masa

La cantidad de materia que contiene un objeto. Un kilogramo es una unidad métrica de masa.

*La **masa** de una bola de boliche es la misma en la Luna que en la Tierra. Aunque el peso de la bola de boliche es diferente.*

---

mean
(97)

*See **average.***

media

*Ver **promedio.***

---

median
(97)

The middle number (or the average of the two central numbers) of a list of data when the numbers are arranged in order from the least to the greatest.

1, 1, 2, 4, 5, 7, 9, 15, 24, 36, 44

*In this list of data, 7 is the **median.***

mediana

Número que está en medio (o el promedio de los dos números centrales) en una lista de datos, cuando los números se ordenan de menor a mayor.

1, 1, 2, 4, 5, 7, 9, 15, 24, 36, 44

*En esta lista de datos, 7 es la **mediana.***

---

meter
(Inv. 2)

The basic unit of length in the metric system.

*A **meter** is equal to 100 centimeters, and it is slightly longer than 1 yard.*

*Many classrooms are about 10 **meters** long and 10 **meters** wide.*

metro

La unidad básica de longitud en el sistema métrico

*Un **metro** es igual a 100 centímetros y es un poco más largo que una yarda.*

*Muchos salones de clase son de alrededor de 10 **metros** de largo y 10 **metros** de ancho.*

---

metric system
(Inv. 2)

An international system of measurement in which units are related by a power of ten. Also called the *International System.*

*Centimeters and kilograms are units in the **metric system.***

sistema métrico

Un sistema internacional de medidas en donde las unidades se relacionan con una potencia de diez. También llamado el *Sistema internacional.*

*Los centímetros y los kilogramos son unidades del **sistema métrico.***

---

midnight
(19)

12:00 a.m.

***Midnight** is one hour after 11 p.m.*

medianoche

12:00 a.m.

*La **medianoche** es una hora después de las 11 p.m.*

mill *(91)*	An amount of money equal to one thousandth of a dollar (one tenth of a penny). *The gasoline price of $3.199 per gallon equals $3.19 plus 9 **mills**.*
mil (milésima parte de un dólar)	Una cantidad de dinero igual a una milésima de un dólar (una décima de una moneda de un centavo). *El precio de la gasolina es de $3.199 por galón igual a $3.19 más 9 **milésimas** de dólar.*
millimeter *(Inv. 2)*	A metric unit of length. *There are 1000 **millimeters** in 1 meter and 10 **millimeters** in 1 centimeter.*
milímetro	Una unidad métrica de longitud *Hay 1000 **milímetros** en 1 metro y 10 **milímetros** en 1 centímetro.*
mixed number *(35)*	A number expressed as a whole number plus a fraction. *The **mixed number** $5\frac{3}{4}$ means "five and three fourths."*
número mixto	Un número expresado como un número entero más una fracción. *El **número mixto** $5\frac{3}{4}$ significa "cinco y tres cuartos."*
mode *(97)*	The number or numbers that appear most often in a list of data. *5, 12, 32, 5, 16, 5, 7, 12* *In this list of data, the number 5 is the **mode**.*
moda	Número o números que aparecen con más frecuencia en una lista de datos. *5, 12, 32, 5, 16, 5, 7, 12* *En esta lista de datos, el número 5 es la **moda**.*
multiple *(20)*	A product of a counting number and another number. *The **multiples** of 3 include 3, 6, 9, and 12.*
múltiplo	Producto de un número de conteo y otro número. *Los **múltiplos** de 3 incluyen 3, 6, 9 y 12.*
multiplication *(27)*	An operation that uses a number as an addend a specified number of times. *7 × 3 = 21* *We can use **multiplication** to* *7 + 7 + 7 = 21* *use 7 as an addend 3 times.*
multiplicación	Una operación que usa un número como sumando un número específico de veces. *7 × 3 = 21* *Podemos usar la **multiplicación** para usar* *7 + 7 + 7 = 21* *el 7 como sumando 3 veces.*

multiplication table *(28)*	A table used to find the product of two numbers. The product of two numbers is found at the intersection of the row and the column for the two numbers.
tabla de multiplicación	Una tabla que se usa para encontrar el producto de dos números. El producto de dos números se encuentra en la intersección de la fila y la columna para los dos números.

N

negative numbers *(Inv. 1)*	Numbers less than zero. −15 and −2.86 are **negative numbers.** 19 and 0.74 are not **negative numbers.**
números negativos	Los números menores que cero. −15 y −2.86 son **números negativos.** 19 y 0.74 no son **números negativos.**

net *(99)*	An arrangement of edge-joined polygons that can be folded to become the faces of the geometric solid.

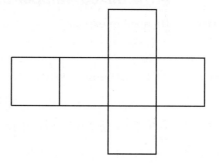

red	Un arreglo de polígonos unidos por el borde que pueden ser doblados para convertirse en las caras de un sólido geométrico.

noon *(19)*	12:00 p.m. **Noon** is one hour after 11 a.m.
mediodía	12:00 p.m. **Mediodía** es una hora después de las 11 a.m.

number line *(Inv. 1)*	A line for representing and graphing numbers. Each point on the line corresponds to a number.

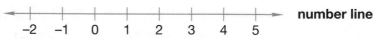

recta numérica	Recta para representar y graficar números. Cada punto de la recta corresponde a un número.

number sentence *(1)*	A complete sentence that uses numbers and symbols instead of words. *See also* **equation.** The **number sentence** *4 + 5 = 9 means "four plus five equals nine."*
enunciado numérico	Un enunciado completo que usa números y símbolos en lugar de palabras. *Ver también* **ecuación.** *El **enunciado numérico** 4 + 5 = 9 significa "cuatro más cinco es igual a nueve".*

numeral *(Appendix A)*	A symbol or group of symbols that represents a number. *4, 72, and $\frac{1}{2}$ are examples of **numerals.** "Four," "seventy-two," and "one half" are words that name numbers but are not **numerals.***
numeral	Símbolo, o grupo de símbolos numéricos, que representa un número. *4, 72 y $\frac{1}{2}$ son ejemplos de **numerales.** "Cuatro", "setenta y dos" y "un medio" son palabras que identifican números, pero no son **numerales.***

numerator *(22)*	The top number of a fraction; the number that tells how many parts of a whole are counted. $\frac{1}{4}$ *The **numerator** of the fraction is 1. One part of the whole circle is shaded.*
numerador	El término superior de una fracción. El número que nos dice cuantas partes de un entero se cuentan. *El **numerador** de la fracción es 1.* *Una parte del círculo completo esta sombreada.*

O

oblique *(23)*	Slanted or sloping; not horizontal or vertical. 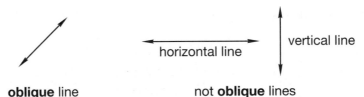 **oblique** line not **oblique** lines
oblicuo	Sesgado o inclinado; no horizontal o vertical.

obtuse angle *(23)*	An angle whose measure is more than 90° and less than 180°.

obtuse angle

not **obtuse angles** (right angle, acute angle)

*An **obtuse angle** is larger than both a right angle and an acute angle.*

ángulo obtuso	Ángulo que mide más de 90° y menos de 180°. *Un **ángulo obtuso** es más grande que un ángulo recto y que un ángulo agudo.*

obtuse triangle *(78)*	A triangle whose largest angle measures more than 90° and less than 180°.

obtuse triangle

not **obtuse triangles** (acute triangle, right triangle)

triángulo obtusángulo	Triángulo cuyo ángulo mayor mide más que 90° y menos que 180°.

octagon *(63)*	A polygon with eight sides.

octagon

octágono	Un polígono con ocho lados.

odd numbers *(10)*	Numbers that have a remainder of 1 when divided by 2; the numbers in this sequence: 1, 3, 5, 7, 9, 11, ... ***Odd numbers** have 1, 3, 5, 7, or 9 in the ones place.*
números impares	Números que cuando se dividen entre 2 tienen residuo de 1; los números en esta secuencia: 1, 3, 5, 7, 9, 11.... *Los **números impares** tienen 1, 3, 5, 7 ó 9 en el lugar de las unidades.*

order of operations *(45)*	The set of rules for the order in which to solve math problems. *Following the **order of operations**, we multiply and divide within an expression before we add and subtract.*
orden de operaciones	El conjunto de reglas del orden para resolver problemas matemáticos. *Siguiendo el **orden de operaciones** multiplicamos y dividimos dentro de la expresión antes de sumar y restar.*

ordinal numbers *(5)*	Numbers that describe position or order. *"First," "second," and "third" are **ordinal numbers.***
números ordinales	Números que describen posición u orden. *"Primero", "segundo" y "tercero" son **números ordinales.***

orientation
(73)

Position of a figure.

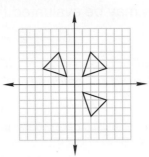

*The illustration shows the same triangle in three different **orientations.***

orientación

Posición de una figura.

*La ilustración muestra el mismo triángulo en tres **orientaciones** diferentes.*

ounce
(77)

A unit of weight in the customary system. Also a measure of capacity. *See also **fluid ounce.***

*Sixteen **ounces** equals a pound. Sixteen **fluid ounces** equals a pint.*

onza

Una unidad de peso en el sistema usual. También es una medida de capacidad. *Ver también **onza líquida.***

*Dieciseis **onzas** es igual a una libra. Dieciseis **onzas líquidas** es igual a una pinta.*

outlier
(97)

A number in a list of data that is distant from the other numbers in a list of data.

1, 5, 4, 3, 6, 28, 7, 2

*In the data, the number 28 is an **outlier** because it is distant from the other numbers in the list.*

valor lejano

Un número en una lista de datos que es distante de los demás números en la lista.

*En los datos el número 28 es un **valor extremo,** porque su valor es mayor que el de los demás números de la lista.*

P

parallel lines
(23)

Lines that stay the same distance apart; lines that do not cross.

 parallel lines

rectas paralelas

Rectas que permanecen separadas a la misma distancia y que nunca se cruzan.

parallelogram
(92)

A quadrilateral that has two pairs of parallel sides.

parallelograms   not a **parallelogram**

paralelogramo

Cuadrilátero que tiene dos pares de lados paralelos.

parentheses (45)	A pair of symbols used to separate parts of an expression so that those parts may be evaluated first: ( ). *15 − (12 − 4)* *In the expression 15 − (12 − 4), the **parentheses** indicate that 12 − 4 should be calculated before subtracting the result from 15.*
paréntesis	Un par de símbolos que se usan para separar partes de una expresión para que esas partes puedan ser evaluadas primero. *15 − (12 − 4)* *En la expresión 15 − (12 − 4) el **paréntesis** indica que 12 − 4 debe ser calculado antes de restar el resultado de 15.*
pentagon (63)	A polygon with five sides. 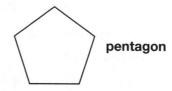 **pentagon**
pentágono	Un polígono con cinco lados.
per (57)	A term that means "in each." *A car traveling 50 miles **per** hour (50 mph) is traveling 50 miles in each hour.*
por cada	Un término que significa "en cada". *Un carro viajando 50 millas por hora (50 mph) está viajando 50 millas **por cada** hora.*
percent (Inv. 5)	A fraction whose denominator of 100 is expressed as a percent sign (%). <div align="center">$\frac{99}{100} = 99\% = 99\ \textbf{\textit{percent}}$</div>
porcentaje	Fracción cuyo denominador de 100 se expresa con un signo (%), que se lee por ciento.
perfect square (Inv. 3)	*See* **square number.**
cuadrado perfecto	Ver **número al cuadrado.**
perimeter (Inv. 2)	The distance around a closed, flat shape. 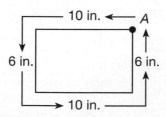 *The **perimeter** of this rectangle (from point A around to point A) is 32 inches.*
perímetro	Distancia alrededor de una figura cerrada y plana. *El **perímetro** de este rectángulo (desde el punto A alrededor del rectángulo hasta el punto A) es 32 pulgadas.*

perpendicular lines
(23)

Two lines that intersect at right angles.

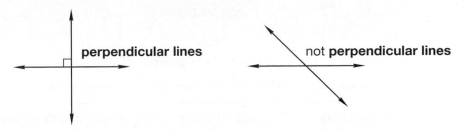

perpendicular lines   not **perpendicular lines**

rectas perpendiculares

Dos rectas que intersecan en ángulos rectos.

---

pictograph
(Inv. 6)

A graph that uses symbols to represent data.

Stars We Saw	
Tom	☆ ☆ ☆ ☆ ☆
Bob	☆ ☆
Sue	☆ ☆ ☆ ☆
Ming	☆ ☆ ☆ ☆ ☆
Juan	☆ ☆ ☆ ☆ ☆ ☆

*This is a **pictograph**. It shows how many stars each person saw.*

pictograma

Gráfica que utiliza símbolos para representar datos.

*Éste es un **pictograma**. Muestra el número de estrellas que vio cada persona.*

---

pie graph
(Inv. 6)

See **circle graph.**

gráfica circular

Ver **gráfica circular.**

---

place value
(4)

The value of a digit based on its position within a number.

341
23
+ 7
371

Place value** tells us that 4 in 341 is worth "4 tens." In addition problems we align digits with the same **place value.

valor posicional

Valor de un dígito de acuerdo al lugar que ocupa en el número.

341
23
+ 7
371

*El **valor posicional** indica que el 4 en 341 vale "cuatro decenas". En los problemas de suma y resta, se alinean los dígitos que tienen el mismo **valor posicional**.*

---

p.m.
(19)

The period of time from noon to just before midnight.

*I go to bed at 9 **p.m.**, which is 9 o'clock at night.*

p.m.

Período de tiempo desde el mediodía hasta justo la medianoche.

*Me voy a dormir a las 9 **p.m.** lo cual es las 9 de la noche.*

---

point
(23)

An exact position.

•A   *This dot represents **point** A.*

punto

Una posición exacta.

*Esta marca representa el **punto** A.*

polygon *(63)*	A closed, flat shape with straight sides.

polygons   not **polygons**

polígono	Figura cerrada y plana que tiene lados rectos.

---

population *(Inv. 7)*	A group of people about whom information is gathered during a survey. *A soft drink company wanted to know the favorite beverage of people in Indiana. The **population** they gathered information about was the people of Indiana.*
población	Un grupo de gente de la cual se obtiene información durante una encuesta. *Una compañía de sodas quería saber cuál es la bebida favorita de la gente en Indiana. La **población** de la cual recolectareon información fue la gente de Indiana.*

---

positive numbers *(Inv. 1)*	Numbers greater than zero. *0.25 and 157 are **positive numbers.*** *−40 and 0 are not **positive numbers.***
números positivos	Números mayores que cero. *0.25 y 157 son **números positivos.*** *−40 y 0 no son **números positivos.***

---

pound *(77)*	A customary measurement of weight. *One **pound** is 16 ounces.*
libra	Una medida usual de peso. *Una **libra** es igual a 16 onzas.*

---

prime number *(55)*	A counting number greater than 1 whose only two factors are the number 1 and itself. *7 is a **prime number.** Its only factors are 1 and 7.* *10 is not a **prime number.** Its factors are 1, 2, 5, and 10.*
número primo	Número natural mayor que 1, cuyos dos únicos factores son el 1 y el propio número. *7 es un **número primo.** Sus únicos factores son 1 y 7.* *10 no es un **número primo.** Sus factores son 1, 2, 5 y 10.*

probability
(Inv. 10)

A way of describing the likelihood of an event; the ratio of favorable outcomes to all possible outcomes.

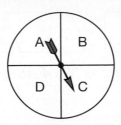

*The **probability** of the spinner landing on C is $\frac{1}{4}$.*

probabilidad

Manera de describir la ocurrencia de un suceso; la razón de resultados favorables a todos los resultados posibles.

*La **probabilidad** de obtener 3 al lanzar un cubo estándar de números es $\frac{1}{6}$.*

---

product
(28)

The result of multiplication.

$5 \times 3 = 15$ The **product** of 5 and 3 is 15.

producto

Resultado de una multiplicación.

$5 \times 3 = 15$ El **producto** de 5 por 3 es 15.

---

proper fraction
(89)

A fraction whose denominator is greater than its numerator.

$\frac{3}{4}$ is a **proper fraction.**

$\frac{4}{3}$ is not a **proper fraction.**

fracción propia

Una fracción cuyo denominador es mayor que el numerador.

$\frac{3}{4}$ es una **fracción propia.**

$\frac{4}{3}$ no es una **fracción propia.**

Property of Zero for Multiplication
(28)

Zero times any number is zero. In symbolic form, $0 \times a = 0$.

The **Property of Zero for Multiplication** tells us that $89 \times 0 = 0$.

propiedad del cero en la multiplicación

Cero multiplicado por cualquier número es cero. En forma simbólica, $0 \times a = 0$.

*La **propiedad del cero en la multiplicación** dice que $89 \times 0 = 0$.*

---

pyramid
(98)

A three-dimensional solid with a polygon as its base and triangular faces that meet at a vertex.

pyramid

pirámide

Figura geométrica de tres dimensiones, con un polígono en su base y caras triangulares que se encuentran en un vértice.

quadrilateral
(63)

Any four-sided polygon.

Each of these polygons has 4 sides. They are all **quadrilaterals.**

cuadrilátero

Cualquier polígono de cuatro lados.

Cada uno de estos polígonos tiene 4 lados. Todos son **cuadriláteros.**

---

quarter
(22)

A term that means one-fourth.

cuarto

Un término que significa un cuarto.

---

quarter turn
(75)

A turn measuring 90°.

cuarto de giro

Un giro que mide 90°.

---

quotient
(65)

The result of division.

$$12 \div 3 = 4 \qquad 3\overline{)12}^{\,4} \qquad \frac{12}{3} = 4$$

The **quotient** *is 4 in each of these problems.*

cociente

Resultado de una división.

El **cociente** *es 4 en cada una de estas operaciones.*

---

radius
(21)

(Plural: *radii*) The distance from the center of a circle to a point on the circle.

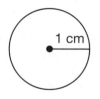

1 cm

The **radius** *of this circle is 1 centimeter.*

radio

Distancia desde el centro de un círculo hasta un punto del círculo.

El **radio** *de este círculo mide 1 centímetro.*

---

range
(97)

The difference between the largest number and smallest number in a list.

5, 17, 12, 34, 28, 13

To calculate the **range** *of this list, we subtract the smallest number from the largest number. The* **range** *of this list is 29.*

intervalo

Diferencia entre el número mayor y el número menor de una lista.

5, 17, 12, 34, 28, 13

Para calcular el **intervalo** *de esta lista, se resta el número menor del número mayor. El* **intervalo** *de esta lista es 29.*

rate *(57)*	A measure of how far or how many are in one time group. *The leaky faucet wasted water at the **rate** of 1 liter per day.*
tasa	Una medida de cuánto hay en un grupo por unidad de tiempo. *La llave de agua con fuga desperdiciaba agua a una **tasa** de 1 litro al día.*

ray *(23)*	A part of a line that begins at a point and continues without end in one direction.

$$A \bullet \longrightarrow B \bullet \longrightarrow$$

ray AB $(\overrightarrow{AB})$

rayo	Parte de una recta que empieza en un punto y continúa indefinidamente en una dirección.

rectangle *(92)*	A quadrilateral that has four right angles.

rectangles   not **rectangles**

rectángulo	Cuadrilátero que tiene cuatro ángulos rectos.

rectangular prism *(98)*	A geometric solid with 6 rectangular faces.

rectangular prism

prisma rectangular	Un sólido geométrico con 6 caras rectangulares.

reduce *(Inv. 9)*	To rewrite a fraction in lowest terms. *If we **reduce** the fraction $\frac{9}{12}$, we get $\frac{3}{4}$.*
reducir	Escribir una fracción a su mínima expresión. *Si reducimos $\frac{9}{12}$, obtenemos $\frac{3}{4}$.*

reflection *(73)*	Flipping a figure to produce a mirror image.

reflection

figure   **image**

reflexión	Voltear una figura para obtener una imagen como si fuera reflejada en un espejo.

reflective symmetry
(79)

A figure has reflective symmetry if it can be divided into two halves that are mirror images of each other. *See also* **line of symmetry.**

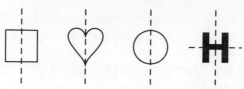

These figures have **reflective symmetry.**

These figures do not have **reflective symmetry.**

simetría de reflexión

Una figura tiene simetría de reflexión si puede ser dividida en dos mitades una de las cuales es la imagen espejo de la otra. *Ver también* **línea de simetría.**

---

regrouping
(15)

To rearrange quantities in place values of numbers during calculations.

$$214 \longrightarrow \overset{1\ 10\ 14}{\cancel{2}\cancel{1}\cancel{4}}$$
$$- 39 \qquad\quad - 39$$
$$\overline{\qquad\quad 175}$$

*Subtraction of 39 from 214 requires **regrouping.***

reagrupar

Reordenar cantidades según los valores poscionales de números al hacer cálculos.

*La resta de 39 de 214 requiere **reagrupación.***

---

regular polygon
(63)

A polygon in which all sides have equal lengths and all angles have equal measures.

regular polygons   not **regular polygons**

polígono regular

Polígono en el cual todos los lados tienen la misma longitud y todos los ángulos tienen la misma medida.

---

remainder
(53)

An amount that is left after division.

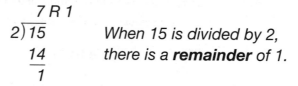

*When 15 is divided by 2, there is a **remainder** of 1.*

residuo

Cantidad que queda después de dividir.

$$\begin{array}{r} 7\,R\,1 \\ 2\overline{)15} \\ 14 \\ \hline 1 \end{array}$$

*Cuando se divide 15 entre 2, queda **residuo** 1.*

rhombus *(92)*	A parallelogram with all four sides of equal length.

rhombuses   not **rhombuses**

rombo	Paralelogramo con sus cuatro lados de igual longitud.

right angle *(23)*	An angle that forms a square corner and measures 90°. It is often marked with a small square.

obtuse angle   acute angle

right angle   not **right angles**

*A **right angle** is larger than an acute angle and smaller than an obtuse angle.*

ángulo recto	Ángulo que forma una esquina cuadrada y mide 90°. Se indica con frecuencia con un pequeño cuadrado. *Un **ángulo recto** es mayor que un ángulo agudo y más pequeño que un ángulo obtuso.*

right triangle *(78)*	A triangle whose largest angle measures 90°.

acute triangle   obtuse triangle

right triangle   not **right triangles**

triángulo rectángulo	Triángulo cuyo ángulo mayor mide 90°.

Roman numerals *(Appendix A)*	Symbols used by the ancient Romans to write numbers. *The **Roman numeral** for 3 is III.* *The **Roman numeral** for 13 is XIII.*

números romanos	Símbolos usados por los antiguos romanos para escribir números. *El **número romano** para el 3 es III.* *El **número romano** para el 13 es XIII.*

rotation *(73)*	Turning a figure about a specified point called the *center of* rotation.

rotation

figure   image

rotación	Giro de una figura alrededor de un punto específico llamado centro de rotación.

rotational symmetry *(79)*	A figure has rotational symmetry if it can be rotated less than a full turn and appear in its original orientation.

	These figures have **rotational symmetry**. These figures do not have **rotational symmetry**.
simetría de rotación	Una figura tiene simetría de rotación si puede ser rotada menos que un giro completo y aparecer en su orientación original.

round *(20)*	To express a calculation or measure to a specific degree of accuracy. *To the nearest hundred dollars, $294 **rounds** to $300.*
redondear	Expresar un cálculo o medida hasta cierto grado de precisión. *A la centena de dólares más cercana, $294 se **redondea** a $300.*

S

sales tax *(83)*	The tax charged on the sale of an item and based upon the item's purchase price. *If the **sales-tax** rate is 8%, the **sales tax** on a $5.00 item will be $5.00 × 8% = $0.40.*
impuesto sobre la venta	Impuesto que se carga al vender un objeto y que se calcula como un porcentaje del precio del objeto. *Si la tasa de impuesto es 8%, el **impuesto sobre la venta** de un objeto que cuesta $5.00 es: $5.00 × 8% = $0.40.*

sample *(Inv. 7)*	A part of a population used to conduct a survey. *Mya wanted to know the favorite television show of the fourth-grade students at her school. She asked only the students in Room 3 her survey question. In her survey, the population was the fourth-grade students at the school, and the **sample** was the students in Room 3.*
muestra	Una parte de una población que se usa para realizar una encuesta. *Mya quería saber cuál es el programa favorito de los estudiantes de cuarto grado de su escuela. Ella hizo la pregunta de su encuesta a sólo el Salón 3. En su encuesta, la población era los estudiantes del cuarto grado de su escuela, y su **muestra** fue los estudiantes del Salón 3.*

scale *(18)*	A type of number line used for measuring.

cm	1	2	3	4	5	6	7

*The distance between each mark on this ruler's **scale** is 1 centimeter.*

escala	Un tipo de recta numérica que se usa para medir. *La distancia entre cada marca en la **escala** de esta regla es 1 centímetro.*

scalene triangle	A triangle with three sides of different lengths.

(78)

All three sides of this **scalene triangle** have different lengths.

triángulo escaleno

Triángulo con todos sus lados de diferente longitud.

*Los tres lados de este **triángulo escaleno** tienen diferente longitud.*

---

schedule

(101)

A list of events organized by the times at which they are planned to occur.

Sarah's Class Schedule

Time	Class
8:15 a.m.	Homeroom
9:00 a.m.	Science
10:15 a.m.	Reading
11:30 a.m.	Lunch and recess
12:15 p.m.	Math
1:30 p.m.	English
2:45 p.m.	Art and music
3:30 p.m.	End of school

calendario, horario

Una lista de sucesos organizados según la hora cuando están planeados.

---

sector

(Inv. 10)

A region bordered by part of a circle and two radii.

*This circle is divided into 3 **sectors**. One **sector** of the circle is shaded.*

sector

Región de un círculo limitada por un arco y dos radios.

*Este círculo esta dividido en 3 **sectores**. Un **sector** del círculo está sombreado.*

---

segment

(Inv. 1)

See **line segment.**

segmento

Ver **segmento de recta.**

---

sequence

(3)

A list of numbers arranged according to a certain rule.

*The numbers 5, 10, 15, 20, ... form a **sequence**. The rule is "count up by fives."*

secuencia

Lista de números ordenados de acuerdo a una regla.

*Los números 5, 10, 15, 20, ... forman una **secuencia**. La regla es "contar hacia adelante de cinco en cinco".*

side *(63)*	A line segment that is part of a polygon. 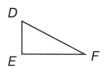 *The arrow is pointing to one side.* *This pentagon has 5 **sides.***
lado	Segmento de recta que forma parte de un polígono. *La flecha apunta hacia un lado. Este pentágono tiene 5 **lados.***

similar *(66)*	Having the same shape but not necessarily the same size. Dimensions of similar figures are proportional. 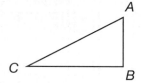 *△ABC and △DEF are **similar.** They have the same shape,* *but not the same size.*
semejante	Que tiene la misma forma, pero no necesariamente el mismo tamaño. Las dimensiones de figuras semejantes son proporcionales. *△ABC y △DEF son **semejantes.** Tienen la misma forma, pero diferente tamaño.*

solid *(98)*	*See **geometric solid.***
sólido	*Ver **sólido geométrico.***

sphere *(98)*	A round geometric solid having every point on its surface at an equal distance from its center. **sphere**
esfera	Un sólido geométrico redondo que tiene cada punto de su superficie a la misma distancia de su centro.

square *(92, Inv. 3)*	**1.** A rectangle with all four sides of equal length. 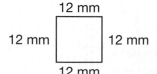 *All four sides of this **square*** *are 12 millimeters long.* **2.** The product of a number and itself. *The **square** of 4 is 16.*
cuadrado	**1.** Un rectángulo con sus cuatro lados de igual longitud. *Los cuatro lados de este **cuadrado** miden 12 milímetros.* **2.** El producto de un número por sí mismo. *El **cuadrado** de 4 es 16.*

square centimeter *(Inv. 3)*	A measure of area equal to that of a square with sides of 1 centimeter long.

$$1\text{ cm }\square\quad\textbf{square centimeter}$$
$$1\text{ cm}$$

centímetro cuadrado	Medida de un área igual a la de un cuadrado con lados de 1 centímetro.

square inch *(Inv. 3)*	A measure of area equal to that of a square with 1-inch sides.

$$1\text{ in. }\square\quad\textbf{square inch}$$
$$1\text{ in.}$$

pulgada cuadrada	Medida de un área igual a la de un cuadrado con lados de 1 pulgada.

square number *(Inv. 3)*	The product when a whole number is multiplied by itself. *The number 9 is a **square number** because $9 = 3^2$.*
número al cuadrado	El producto de un número entero multiplicado por sí mismo. *El número 9 es un **número al cuadrado** porque $9 = 3^2$.*

square root *(Inv. 3)*	One of two equal factors of a number. The symbol for the principal, or positive, ***square root*** of a number is $\sqrt{}$. *A **square root** of 49 is 7 because $7 \times 7 = 49$.*
raíz cuadrada	Uno de dos factores iguales de un número. El símbolo de la raíz cuadrada de un número es $\sqrt{}$, y se le llama *radical*. *La **raíz cuadrada** de 49 es 7, porque $7 \times 7 = 49$.*

square unit *(Inv. 3)*	An area equal to the area of a square with sides of designated length. *The shaded part is 1 **square unit.** The area of the large rectangle is 8 **square units.***
unidad cuadrada	Un área igual al área de un cuadrado con lados de una longitud designada. *La parte sombreda es 1 **unidad cuadrada.** El área del rectángulo grande es de 8 **unidades cuadradas.***

straight angle *(81)*	An angle that measures 180° and thus forms a straight line.

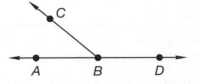

*Angle ABD is a **straight angle.** Angles ABC and CBD are not **straight angles.***

ángulo llano	Ángulo que mide 180° y cuyos lados forman una línea recta. *El ángulo ABD es un **ángulo llano.** Los ángulos ABC y CBD no son **ángulos llanos.***

subtraction (6)	The arithmetic operation that reduces a number by an amount determined by another number
	$15 - 12 = 3$ *We use **subtraction** to take 12 away from 15.*
resta	La operación aritmética que reduce un número por cierta cantidad determinada por otro número.
	$15 - 12 = 3$ *Utilizamos la **resta** para quitar 12 de 15.*

sum (1)	The result of addition.
	$2 + 3 = 5$ *The **sum** of 2 and 3 is 5.*
suma	Resultado de una suma.
	$2 + 3 = 5$ *La **suma** de 2 más 3 es 5.*

survey (Inv. 7)	A method of collecting data about a particular population.
	*Mia conducted a **survey** by asking each of her classmates the name of his or her favorite television show.*
encuesta	Método de reunir información acerca de una población en particular.
	*Mia hizo una **encuesta** entre sus compañeros para averiguar cuál era su programa favorito de televisión.*

symmetry (79)

Correspondence in size and shape on either side of a dividing line. This type of symmetry is known as *reflective symmetry. See also* **line of symmetry.**

These figures have **reflective symmetry.**   These figures do not have **reflective symmetry.**

simetría

Correspondencia en tamaño y forma a cada lado de una línea divisoria. Este tipo de simetría es conocida como *simetría de reflexión. Ver también* **línea de simetría.**

T

table (101)

A way of organizing data in columns and rows.

Our Group Scores

Name	Grade
Group 1	98
Group 2	72
Group 3	85
Group 4	96

*This **table** shows the scores of four groups.*

tabla

Una manera de organizar datos en columnas y filas.

*Esta **tabla** muestra las calificaciones de cuatro grupos.*

tally mark *(Inv. 7)*	A small mark used to help keep track of a count. |||| *I used **tally marks** to count cars.* *I counted five cars.*
marca de conteo	Una pequeña marca que se usa para llevar la cuenta. *Usé **marcas de conteo** para contar carros. Yo conté cinco carros.*

tenth *(Inv. 4)*	One out of ten parts, or $\frac{1}{10}$. *The decimal form of one **tenth** is 0.1.*
décimo(a)	Una de diez partes ó $\frac{1}{10}$. *La forma decimal de un **décimo** es 0.1.*

tessellation *(82)*	The repeated use of shapes to fill a flat surface without gaps or overlaps.

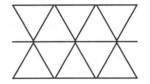 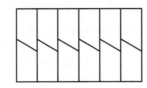 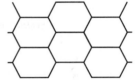

tessellations

mosaico	El uso repetido de figuras para llenar una superficie plana sin crear huecos o traslapes.

thousandth *(84)*	One out of 1000 parts. *One **thousandth** in decimal form is 0.001.*
milésimo(a)	Una de mil partes. *Una **milésima** en forma decimal es 0.001.*

tick mark *(Inv. 1)*	A mark dividing a number line into smaller portions.
marca de un punto	Una marca que divide a una recta numérica en partes más pequeñas.

ton *(77)*	A customary measurement of weight.
tonelada	Una medida usual de peso.

transformation *(73)*	Changing a figure's position through rotation, reflection, or translation.

Transformations

Movement	Name
Flip	Reflection
Slide	Translation
Turn	Rotation

transformación	Cambio en la posición de una figura por medio de una rotación, reflexión o traslación.

translation
(73)

Sliding a figure from one position to another without turning or flipping the figure.

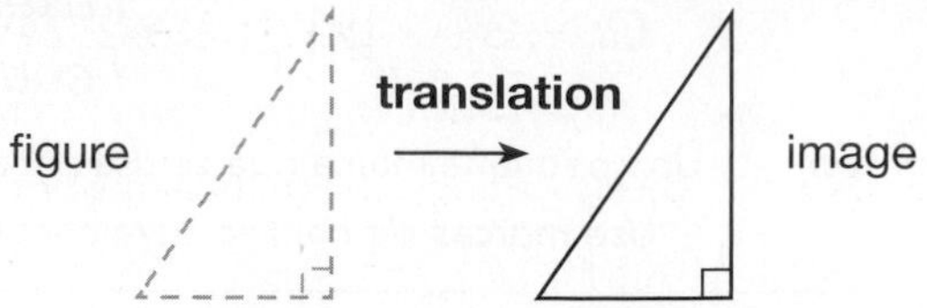

figure →translation→ image

traslación — Deslizamiento de una figura de una posición a otra, sin rotar ni voltear la figura.

trapezoid
(92)

A quadrilateral with exactly one pair of parallel sides.

trapezoids   not **trapezoids**

trapecio — Cuadrilátero que tiene exactamente un par de lados paralelos.

tree diagram
(82)

A way to use branches to organize the choices of a combination problem.

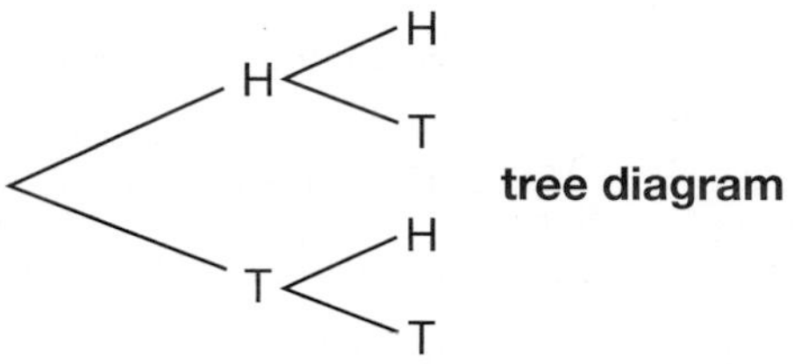

H
H< T
H
T< T

tree diagram

diagrama de árbol — Una manera de usar ramas para organizar los opciones de un problema de comparación.

triangle
(63)

A polygon with three sides and three angles.

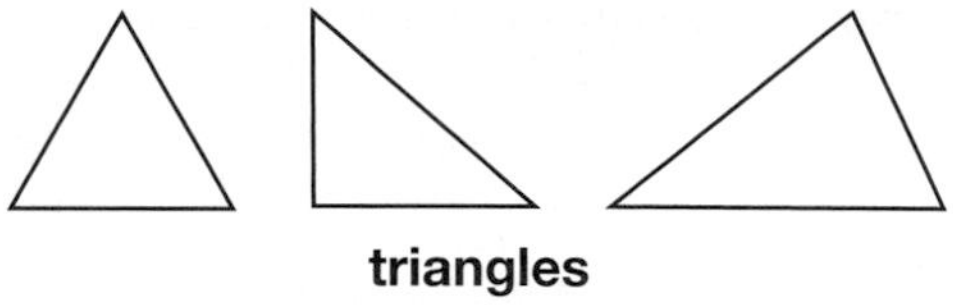

triangles

triángulo — Un polígono con tres lados y tres ángulos.

triangular prism
(98)

A geometric solid with 3 rectangular faces and 2 triangular bases.

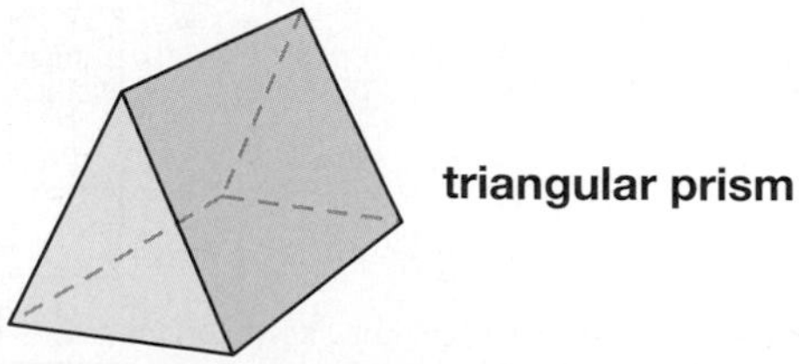

triangular prism

prisma triangular — Un sólido geométrico con 3 caras rectangulares y 2 bases triangulares.

unit *(Inv. 2)*	Any standard object or quantity used for measurement. *Grams, pounds, liters, gallons, inches, and meters are all **units.***
unidad	Cualquier objeto o cantidad estándar que se usa para medir. *Gramos, libras, galones, pulgadas y metros son **unidades.***
U.S. Customary System *(Inv. 2)*	A system of measurement used almost exclusively in the United States. *Pounds, quarts, and feet are units in the **U.S. Customary System.***
Sistema usual de EE.UU.	Unidades de medida que se usan exclusivamente en EE.UU. *Libras, cuartos y pies son unidades del **Sistema usual de EE.UU.***

vertex *(23)*	(Plural: *vertices*) A point of an angle, polygon, or solid where two or more lines, rays, or segments meet.

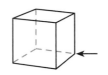

*The arrow is pointing to one **vertex** of this cube. A cube has eight **vertices.***

vértice	Punto de un ángulo, polígono o sólido, donde se unen dos o más rectas, semirrectas o segmentos de recta. *La flecha apunta hacia un **vértice** de este cubo. Un cubo tiene ocho **vértices.***
vertical *(23)*	Upright; perpendicular to horizontal.

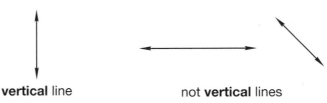

vertical line   not **vertical** lines

vertical	Hacia arriba; perpendicular a la horizontal.
volume *(Inv. 11)*	The amount of space a solid shape occupies. Volume is measured in cubic units.

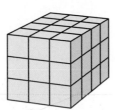

*This rectangular prism is 3 units wide, 3 units high, and 4 units deep. Its **volume** is $3 \cdot 3 \cdot 4 = 36$ cubic units.*

volumen	La cantidad de espacio ocupado por una figura sólida. El volumen se mide en unidades cúbicas. *Este prisma rectangular tiene 3 unidades de ancho, 3 unidades de altura y 4 unidades de profundidad. Su **volumen** es $3 \cdot 3 \cdot 4 = 36$ unidades cúbicas.*

W

weight
(77)

The measure of the force of gravity on an object. Units of weight in the customary system include ounces, pounds, and tons.

*The **weight** of a bowling ball would be less on the moon than on Earth because the force of gravity is weaker on the moon.*

peso

La medida de la fuerza de gravedad sobre un objeto. Las unidades de peso en el sistema usual incluyen onzas, libras y toneladas.

*El **peso** de una bola de boliche es menor en la Luna que en la Tierra porque la fuerza de gravedad es menor en la Luna.*

whole numbers
(7)

All the numbers in this sequence: 0, 1, 2, 3, 4, 5, 6, 7, 8, 9, ...

*The number 35 is a **whole number,** but $35\frac{1}{2}$ and 3.2 are not. **Whole numbers** are the counting numbers and zero.*

números enteros

Todos los números en esta secuencia: 0, 1, 2, 3, 4, 5, 6, 7, 8, 9 ....

*El número 35 es un **número entero** pero $35\frac{1}{2}$ y 3.2 no lo son.*

*Los **números enteros** son los números de conteo y el cero.*

Y

yard
(Inv. 2)

A customary measurement of length.

yarda

Una medida usual de longitud.

Symbols

Symbol	Meaning	Example
$\triangle$	Triangle	$\triangle ABC$
$\angle$	Angle	$\angle ABC$
$\rightarrow$	Ray	$\overrightarrow{AB}$
$\leftrightarrow$	Line	$\overleftrightarrow{AB}$
$-$	Line segment	$\overline{AB}$
$\perp$	Perpendicular to	$AB \perp BC$
$\parallel$	Parallel to	$AB \parallel BC$
$<$	Less than	$2 < 3$
$>$	Greater than	$3 > 2$
$=$	Equal to	$2 = 2$
°F	Degrees Fahrenheit	100°F
°C	Degrees Celsius	32°C
$\llcorner$	Right angle (90° angle)	
...	And so on	1, 2, 3, ...
$\times$	Multiply	9×3
$\cdot$	Multiply	$3 \cdot 3 = 9$
$\div$	Divide	$9 \div 3$
$+$	Add	$9 + 3$
$-$	Subtract	$9 - 3$
$\overline{)}$	Divided into	$3\overline{)9}$
R or r	Remainder	3 R 2
%	Percent	50%
x^2	"x" squared (times itself)	$3^2 = 3 \times 3 = 9$
x^3	"x" cubed	$3^3 = 3 \times 3 \times 3 = 27$
$\sqrt{}$	Square root	$\sqrt{9} = 3$ because $3 \times 3 = 9$.

Abbreviations

Abbreviation	Meaning
ft	Foot
in.	Inch
yd	Yard
mi	Mile
m	Meter
cm	Centimeter
mm	Millimeter
km	Kilometer
L	Liter
ml or mL	Milliliter
lb	Pound
oz	Ounce
kg	Kilogram
g	Gram
mg	Milligram
qt	Quart
pt	Pint
c	Cup
gal	Gallon

Formulas

Purpose	Formula
Perimeter of a rectangle	$P = 2l + 2w$
Perimeter of a square	$P = 4s$
Area of a square	$A = s^2$
Area of a rectangle	$A = l \cdot w$
Volume of a cube	$V = s^3$
Volume of a rectangular prism	$V = l \cdot w \cdot h$

Símbolos/Signos

Símbolo/Signo	Significa	Ejemplo
△	Triángulo	$\triangle ABC$
∠	Ángulo	$\angle ABC$
→	Rayo	$\overrightarrow{AB}$
↔	Recta	$\overleftrightarrow{AB}$
—	Segmento de recta	$\overline{AB}$
⊥	Perpendicular a	$AB \perp BC$
||	Paralelo a	$AB \parallel BC$
<	Menor que	$2 < 3$
>	Mayor que	$3 > 2$
=	Igual a	$2 = 2$
°F	Grados Fahrenheit	100°F
°C	Grados Celsius	32°C
∟	Ángulo recto (ángulo de 90°)	⌐
…	Y más, etcétera	1, 2, 3, …
×	Multiplica	9×3
·	Multiplica	$3 \cdot 3 = 9$
÷	Divide	$9 \div 3$
+	Suma	$9 + 3$
−	Resta	$9 - 3$
$\sqrt{}$	Dividido entre	$3\overline{)9}$
R or r	Residuo	3 R 2
%	Por ciento, porcentaje	50%
x^2	"x" al cuadrado (por sí mismo)	$3^2 = 3 \times 3 = 9$
x^3	"x" al cubo	$3^3 = 3 \times 3 \times 3 = 27$
$\sqrt{}$	Raíz cuadrada	$\sqrt{9} = 3$ por que $3 \times 3 = 9$.

Abreviaturas

Abreviatura	Significa
pie	pie
pulg	pulgada
yd	yarda
mi	milla
m	metro
cm	centímetro
mm	milímetro
km	kilómetro
L	litro
mL	mililitro
lb	libra
oz	onza
kg	kilogramo
g	gramo
mg	miligramo
ct	cuarto
pt	pinta
tz	taza
gal	galón

Fórmulas

Propósito	Fórmula
Perímetro	$P = 2L + 2a$
Perímetro de un cuadrado	$P = 4l$
Área de un cuadrado	$A = l^2$
Área de un rectángulo	$A = L \cdot a$
Volumen de un cubo	$V = l^3$
Volumen de un prisma rectangular	$V = L \cdot a \cdot h$

Angles, *continued*
in clocks, 520
comparing, 142–143
letters to represent, 143
measuring, 520
in polygons, 586
in triangles, 143, 496–497

Apexes of cones, 620

Approximation, 705. *See also* **Estimating**

Area, 186–188
estimating, 702
as a model for multiplication, 186
of rectangles, 680–682
of squares, 401, 681
of triangles and other shapes, estimating, 704–706

Arithmetic, estimating answers by rounding numbers, 377–379, 592. *See also* **Estimating**; **Rounding**

Arrays
and finding factors, 353–354
to model multiplication, 185

Associative Property
of Addition, 8, 288–289
of Multiplication, 289, 400

Average, 607–608. *See also* **Mean**

B

Balanced equations. *See* **Equations**

Bar graphs, 388, 390

Bases (powers), 401

Bases of geometric solids, 620

Base-ten system, 25, 256

Bias, 451

Billions (place value), 736

Borrowing, in subtraction, 88–91, 179–181

Brackets. *See* **Parentheses**

C

C. *See* **Roman numerals**

°C (Celsius), 105–106

c (cup), 250–252

Calendars, 345

Capacity of containers, 250–252, 706. *See also* individual units of measurement

Cardinal numbers, 30. *See also* **Counting numbers**; **Whole numbers**

Carrying. *See* Regrouping

Celsius (°C), 105–106

Center, of a circle, 129

Centimeter (cm), 123, 440–442, 649

Centimeter scales and rulers, 123, 441. *See also* **Rulers**

Central tendency, measures of. *See* **Mean**; **Median**; **Mode**

Centuries and century years, 345

Certainty, 636. *See also* **Probability**

Chance, 636, 637. *See also* **Probability**

Chronological order, 346

Circle graph, 389, 391–392

Circles, 128–130
center of, 129
drawing fractions with, 159

Circumference, 129

Clocks, 110–113. *See also* **Time**
angles in, 520

Clockwise turns, 478–480

cm (centimeter), 123, 440–442, 649

Combinations, 227

Commas, writing numbers with, 206–208, 212–215

Common denominators, 730–731

Common years, 345. *See also* **Years**

Commutative Property
of Addition, 8–9, 12–13
of Multiplication, 171

Comparing numbers with comparison symbols, 64–65

Compasses, to draw circles, 129

Compatible numbers, 136–137
division and, 378

Composite numbers, 354–355

Cones, 619–620

Congruent figures, 361, 425–426, 466–467
triangles, 425

Containers, volume of, 250–252. *See also* individual units of measurement
estimating, 706

Continuous data, 388. *See also* **Data**

Coordinates and coordinate planes, 517

Counterclockwise turns, 478–480

Counting numbers, 19. *See also* **Cardinal numbers**; **Whole numbers**

Cubed numbers, 401

Cubes, 619

Cubic units, 699–700

Cup (c), 250–252

Cylinders, 619–620

D

D. *See* **Roman numerals**

Dashes. *See* **Hyphens**, in written numbers

Data. *See also* **Relationships**, analyzing and graphing
continuous, 388
displaying on graphs, 387–393
and surveys, 451–454

Dates, 31–32

F

°F (Fahrenheit), 105–106

Faces of solids, 620

Fact families
addition and subtraction, 37, 148–149
multiplication and division, 303

Factors, 265, 295–296, 353. *See also* **Multiples**
of 0, 1, 2, and 5, 176
of 6, 7, and 9, 354
arrays and, 353–354
as bases in powers, 401
missing, 265–266, 296–298
multiplication, 171
of three or more factors, 400

Fahrenheit (°F), 105–106

Figures. *See also* **Planes and plane figures**;
Polygons; **Shapes**; specific figures
congruent, 361, 425–426, 466–467
similar, 425–426

fl oz (fluid ounce), 250–252

Flips, 467–468

Fluid ounce (fl oz), 250–252

Formulas. *See also* **Equations; Expressions**
addition, 9–10, 69
area of rectangles and squares, 680–682
larger–smaller–difference problems, 193–195
perimeter of rectangles and squares, 124, 681–683
subtraction, 152–155, 193–195
volume of rectangular solids, 700

Fourth ($\frac{1}{4}$), 259, 574, 655–656

Fractions, 260, 446. *See also* **Denominators; Mixed
numbers; Numerators**; specific types of fractions
$\frac{1}{2}$, 259, 574, 655–656
$\frac{1}{4}$, 228, 259, 324, 574–575
1, dividing by, 711–712
1, equal to, 654–655
adding
with common denominators, 675–677
with different denominators, 746–747, 750–751
circles, drawing with, 159
common denominators, 730–731
comparing, 135, 360–361, 656
decimal numbers and, 260–261, 575–577
of dollars, 228–230. *See also* **Fractions: money**
drawing with circles, 159
manipulatives, 574–577
mixed numbers and, 219, 564
of money, 135, 228–230, 256
multiplying by 1, 689, 725–726
naming, 134–137
on a number line, 234–235
and percents, 322. *See also* **Percents**
pictures of, 158–159, 360–361
reducing, 575, 710–712
remaining, 395
renaming, 725–726, 730, 746–747
of sets, 474

simplifying answers, 720–722
subtracting
with common denominators, 675–677
with different denominators, 746–747, 750–751
and the thousandths place, 539–540
of unit squares, 258–259
word problems, 446–448, 602–603

Full turns, 478. *See also* **Turns**

G

g (gram), 491–492

Gallon (gal), 250–252

Geometric solids, 619–620, 631. *See also* specific
solids

Geometry, 466

Gram (g), 491–492

Graphs, 387–392
and points on coordinate planes, 517
relationships and, 515–517

Greater than (>), 64–65

Grid paper, to estimate area of shapes, 704–706

Grouping, of even and odd numbers, 56–57

H

Half ($\frac{1}{2}$), 228, 259, 324, 574–575

Half turns, 478. *See also* **Turns**

Half-lines, 141–144

Hexagons, 406
in tessellations, 526

Hours, 110–113. *See also* **Time**

"How many fewer/more" problems, 193–195

Hundred billions (place value), 735–737

Hundred millions (place value), 212–215
rounding to, 735–737

Hundred thousands (place value), 206–208
rounding to, 735–737

Hundred trillions (place value), 735–737

Hundreds (place value), 25–26, 78, 206–208, 579
rounding numbers to, 271–272, 347, 735–737
and rounding to thousands, 347

Hundredths (place value), 256–259, 261, 318, 579,
649–650

Hyphens, in written numbers, 40

I

I. *See* **Roman numerals**

Identity element, in addition, 8

Identity Property
of Addition, 8
of Multiplication, 171

Improper fractions, 564
changing to whole and mixed numbers, 660–662

in (inch), 122

"In each" problems, 365–366

Inch (in), 122

Inch scales and rulers, 122, 244–246. See also Rulers

Intersecting lines and segments, 142

Inverse operations, 148–149
  multiplication/division, 296–298

Isosceles triangles, 497
  lines of symmetry, 502

K

Kilogram (kg), 491–492

Kilometer (km), 123

L

L. See Roman numerals

L (liter), 251–252

"Larger − smaller = difference" problems, 264–265

Larger–smaller–difference formula, 193–195

"Later–earlier–difference" problems, 346

lb (pound), 490

Leap years, 345

Least common denominator (LCD), 731. See also Denominators

Length, units of, 122–123

Less than (<), 64–65

Letters
  lines of symmetry in, 503
  to represent angles, 143
  to represent numbers, 10–13, 68–69, 73, 84–85, 95–96, 124, 148–149, 266, 296, 333, 383–384, 396, 671–672, 680–683, 745–755. See also Numbers: missing
  rotational symmetry of, 504

Line graphs, 388–389, 391

Line segments, 60, 141–144. See also Lines
  naming, 290
  in polygons, 405

Lines, 60, 141–144
  intersection of, 142
  naming, 289
  parallel and perpendicular, 141–142

Lines of symmetry, 502–503

Liter (L), 251–252

Long division, 412–413, 418–419, 435–436, 485, 510, 666–667, 742–743. See also Division

M

M. See Roman numerals

m (meter), 122–123

Mass, 490–492

Mean, 612–613. See also Average

Measures of central tendency. See Mean; Median; Mode

Measuring
  on an inch scale, 244–246
  on a centimeter scale, 441
  on a millimeter scale, 441–442
  scales, 104

Median, 613

Memory group (multiplication), 238–239

Meter (m), 122–123

Metersticks, 649

Metric system, 122, 251
  decimal numbers, writing numbers as, 441–442
  mass, units of, 491–492

mi (mile), 122

Middle, 613

Midnight, 111

Mile (mi), 122

Millimeter (mm) and millimeter scale, 123, 440–442. See also Rulers

Millions (place value), 212–215
  rounding to, 735–737

Mills, 579

Minutes, 110–113. See also Time

Mirror images, 502–503

Missing numbers, 12–13, 20, 72–73, 84–85, 95–96, 154, 265–266, 296–298. See also Letters, to represent numbers; individual operations

Mixed numbers. See also Fractions
  adding, 676–677, 750–751
  improper fractions and, 219, 564
  changing to, 660–662
  money, 220–221
  on a number line, 234–235
  rounding, 656–657
  subtracting, 750–751

mm (millimeter), 123, 440–442

Mode, 614

Money, 220–221
  ¢ and $ (cent and dollar signs), 220
  adding, 46–47, 135–137, 277
  decimal numbers and, 257
  dividing, 486
  fractions of, 135, 228–230, 256
  mixed numbers and, 220–221
  multiplying, 372, 716
  place value and, 24–25, 579–580
  regrouping when adding, 136
  rounding, 118–119
  sales tax, 532–534
  subtracting, 180, 277

Months, 345
  ordinal numbers and, 31

P

Parallel lines, 141

Parallelograms, 585. *See also* **Rectangles**; **Squares**

Parentheses, 288–289. *See also* **Order of operations**

Partial products, 553, 569

"Part–part–whole" problems, 69

Patterns, 19

PEMDAS, 289. *See also* **Order of operations**

Pencil–and–paper method for division, 412–413, 418–419, 435–436, 485, 510, 666–667, 742–743

Pentagons, 406

Per ("in each"), 365. *See also* **Rate problems**

Percents, 322–324
  estimating, 323
  remaining from a whole, 323

Perfect squares. *See* **Square numbers**

Perimeter, 124, 128
  estimating, 702, 704–706
  of rectangles and squares, 124, 126, 681, 681–683

Perpendicular lines, 142

Pictographs, 387, 390

Pictures, of fractions, 158–159, 360–361

Pie graphs, 389, 391–392

Pint (pt), 250–252

Place value, 24–26, 206–208, 212–215. *See also*
  specific places
  0 and, 25
  addition and, 46–47, 78–79, 277, 318–319, 327
  base-ten system, 256
  commas and, 206–208, 212–215
  decimal numbers and, 579–580
  money and, 24–25, 579–580
  multiplication and, 270, 283, 308–309, 371–372
  regrouping
    when adding, 50–52, 78–79, 100–101, 136
    when subtracting, 88–91, 179–181, 264–266
  rounding, 735–737
  subtraction and, 83–84, 180, 264, 277, 318–319, 332
  writing numbers, 40–41

Planes and **plane figures,** 631

p.m. (hours after noon), 111–113

Points, 141

Points (coordinates), 517

Polygons, 405–407. *See also* **Figures**; **Shapes**;
  specific shapes
  angles in, 586
  lines of symmetry, 502–503

Populations (surveys), 451–452

Position of numbers. *See* **Ordinal numbers**

Positive numbers, 62–63

Pound (lb), 490

Powers. *See* **Exponents**

Prime numbers, 354–355

Prisms, 619. *See also* specific prisms and other solids

Probability, 636–639

Problems. *See* **Word problems**

Problem–solving
  process, 1–4, 10, 194. *See also* **Word problems**
  strategies, 4–6
  writing and, 6

Product (multiplication), 171, 265, 295–296. *See also* **Multiplication**
  partial, 553, 569

Proper fractions, 564

Property of Zero for Multiplication, 171

pt (pint), 250–252

Pyramids, 631

Q

qt (quart), 250–252

Quadrilaterals, 406–407, 584. *See also* **Rectangles**; **Squares**
  classifying, 584–586
  in tessellations, 526. *See also* **Tessellations**

Quart (qt), 250–252

Quarter ($\frac{1}{4}$), 259, 574, 655–656

Quarter turns, 478. *See also* **Turns**

Quotients, 417–418

R

R. *See* **Remainder**

Radius, 129

Range, 614

Rate problems, 365–366
  with a given total, 383–384

Rays, 141–144

Rectangles, 128–130, 189, 585
  area of, 680–682
  drawing fractions with, 158–159
  lines of symmetry in, 502
  perimeter of, 124, 681–683

Rectangular prisms, 619, 624–625

Reducing fractions, 575, 710–712

Reflections, 467–468

Reflective symmetry, 502–503

Regrouping
  in addition, 50–52, 78–79, 100–101, 136
  money, 136
  in multiplication, 308–309
  place value, 50–52, 78–79, 88–91, 100–101, 136, 179–181, 264–266
  in subtraction, 88–91, 179–181, 264–266
  three-digit numbers, 179–181

Regular polygons, 406. *See also* **Polygons**

Relationships, analyzing and graphing, 514–518

INDEX